MOON

H A

D0707014

THAILAND

SUZANNE NAM

Contents

Discover Thailand

Thailand is more than just beaches, Buddhism, protests, and go-go bars. Though smaller than Texas, the country offers an astounding variety of sights, sounds, and experiences. Ride atop an elephant in the Mae Sa Valley, swim with whale sharks off the Andaman coast, and get a glimpse of spiritual greatness at the many Buddhist temples scattered across the country. And at the end of each day — whether it has been relaxing or exhausting — you'll have the chance to rest your head at one of the world's top-rated luxury hotels or keep it old-school in a $15-per-night coldwater guesthouse.

Bangkok, the country's metropolis, is a mix of modern buildings, Chinese-style shophouses, simple one-story huts, and grand Buddhist temples. The economy is still moving at light speed, and in the background small swaths of rainforest peek out of the empty spaces between apartment complexes and shopping malls. Monks in orange robes walk calmly through crowds of people in office attire rushing to work. And every block of the city is lined with street stalls selling spicy papaya salads, vegetable curries, and Thai iced tea, served, curiously, in plastic bags.

Outside the city, the pace slows and the stunning physical landscape unfolds. Sleepy fishing villages offer relaxation in quaint bungalows surrounded by crystal-clear azure waters and soft white-sand beaches, with

paddy fields, lush green rainforest, and mountain ranges never far away. Hiking and water sports are abundant along the southern peninsula. Some of the best diving in the world awaits on the islands offshore, and the hundreds of temple and palace ruins to the north span more than 1,000 years of history.

Getting around can seem overwhelming because of a decidedly foreign language, the indecipherable Thai script, and surprising customs. But this is one of the friendliest countries you'll ever visit. While you may not always get what you want, people will treat you with kindness, whether you are in a big city or in the middle of nowhere.

However much time you spend in Thailand, it won't take long for its relaxed *sabai* attitude to infuse you. Even if you only have a few days, you will be able to get a good sense of this country and its people's spirit. Longer than that, and you may find yourself thinking about how easy it would be to spend months or years here – maybe even a lifetime.

Planning Your Trip

▶ WHERE TO GO

Bangkok

The sprawling capital city has a multitude of sights to offer. The Grand Palace and Wat Phra Kaew in Ko Rattanakosin are not to be missed, while the trendy mega shopping malls in and around Siam Square are the best for shopping excursions. Inexpensive street stalls selling everything from grilled bananas to pad thai and world-class restaurants offering up the latest fusion foods will satisfy the most discerning foodie.

The Eastern Seaboard

The eastern seaboard provinces offer a strange mix of crowded party beaches, industrial zones, sleepy fishing villages, and vast stretches of pristine coastline. Pattaya has a sordid past and a party reputation, but

Bangkok's Grand Palace

IF YOU HAVE . . .

- **ONE WEEK:** Visit Bangkok and the Andaman Coast.
- **TWO WEEKS:** Add Chiang Mai and Northern Thailand.
- **THREE WEEKS:** Add Isan's Khmer ruins.
- **ONE MONTH:** Add Central Thailand's historic ruins.

Reclining Buddha at Wat Pho, Bangkok

it's trying to clean up its act and is somewhat family-friendly now. Travel a little farther south and you'll find rare French-influenced architecture, quiet mango groves, and some of the least-crowded beaches in the country in Chanthaburi Province. Trat, the southernmost province, boasts 52 offshore islands, including Ko Chang, as well as an expansive marine national park.

The Upper Southern Gulf

This thin strip of land offers a plethora of outdoor activities. Visit Hua Hin and neighboring beaches if you want to see where Bangkok

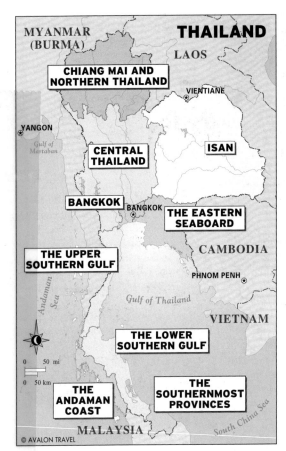

MYANMAR (BURMA)

THAILAND

LAOS

CHIANG MAI AND NORTHERN THAILAND

VIENTIANE

YANGON

Gulf of Martaban

CENTRAL THAILAND

ISAN

BANGKOK

Bangkok

THE EASTERN SEABOARD

CAMBODIA

THE UPPER SOUTHERN GULF

PHNOM PENH

Andaman Sea

Gulf of Thailand

VIETNAM

THE LOWER SOUTHERN GULF

0   50 mi

0   50 km

THE ANDAMAN COAST

THE SOUTHERNMOST PROVINCES

South China Sea

MALAYSIA

© AVALON TRAVEL

to explore. Phuket, the country's largest island and biggest tourist destination, boasts some of the best beaches in the world. The rest of the region is still supported by agriculture and a thriving fishing industry, and it remains relatively undeveloped.

The Lower Southern Gulf

Coconut groves, rubber plantations, and forested mountains characterize Thailand's lower southern gulf. Once a bustling entrepôt, this region is still a significant commercial center for southern Thailand. Popular island destinations—Ko Samui, Ko Pha-Ngan, and Ko Tao—provide everything from luxury resorts to coconut-thatched beach bungalows. The largest province, Nakhon Si Thammarat, offers a tutorial of the region's cultural history. The remains of the ancient walled city of Ligor, Buddhist

residents spend their weekends. Khao Sam Roi Yot National Park boasts ethereal peaks and amazing views of the gulf. Visit the small, less-visited city of Petchaburi to see some amazing Buddhist *wats*.

The Andaman Coast

The peninsula's west coast is undoubtedly the most beautiful region in the country, with postcard-perfect islands and lush rainforests and mountain ranges. The warm, clear waters offer excellent opportunities to snorkel and scuba dive, with stunning limestone rock formations, waterfalls, and caves

islands along the Andaman Coast

Ayutthaya Historical Park

Kingdom, and the ancient temples of Lopburi chart the history of civilizations that have populated current-day Thailand since the 6th century. In Kanchanaburi Province, the terrain becomes more rugged and mountainous, with caves, waterfalls, and wildlife sanctuaries that offer opportunities for outdoor activities.

Chiang Mai and Northern Thailand

With its cooler climate, diversity of ethnic groups, and proximity to Laos, Burma, and China, northern Thailand has a different feel from the rest of the country. From the 13th to the 16th centuries, the city of Chiang Mai was the heart of the Lanna Kingdom. Today's Chiang Mai, though a large, sprawling modern city, at its heart is a charming historic old city filled with crumbling walls, ancient temples, and plenty of charming places to eat and sleep. The broader region is primarily rural, with paddy fields punctuated by forests and mountain ranges.

temples, Hindu shrines, and Muslim mosques are all easily accessible here.

Central Thailand

There are more than a millennium's worth of artifacts to explore in this quiet rural region. The crumbling ruins of the former capital Sukhothai, the ruins of the Ayutthaya

Isan

The country's largest and poorest region is also

ruins of Wat Prasat Phanom Rung in Buriram, Isan

one of the most interesting and rewarding to visit. The mostly agricultural area is home to scores of amazing ruins from the Khmer Empire. Phanom Rung and Phimai are among the two best Khmer ruins in the country. The people of Isan, once more aligned with neighboring Laos than Siam, retain a distinctly Thai culture. Many would argue that the region's spicy cuisine is the best in the country—reason enough to visit the area.

The Southernmost Provinces

The provinces of Yala, Pattani, and Narathiwat are historically part of a Malay region with Malay traditions and even a separate language (Yawi). Against a backdrop of charming little seaside towns, the predominance of Buddhism gives way to Islam, and the relations among Southeast Asia's religions and ethnic groups becomes much more complex. Home to a separatist movement, the region has seen virtually unabated violence since 2004. While tourists have not been specifically targeted, bombings in markets, teashops, and hotels have made it increasingly dangerous to visit.

▶ WHEN TO GO

Thailand's best weather is in the cool season, from November to February. This is when temperatures drop into the 20s Celsius and the humidity becomes far less oppressive. This is the most popular time to visit; you'll see plenty of other travelers and peak pricing, especially around Christmas or New Year's. Although people visit Thailand year-round, the low season is generally July to October, when most of the country is subject to monsoon rains. Don't write off this season completely, as it doesn't rain all day or even every day. If you don't mind a few rainy days, you'll pay significantly less for accommodations, and most destinations will be far less crowded. The hot season (March–May) means higher temperatures and lots of humidity. If you don't mind the heat, there are fewer visitors and lower prices.

▶ BEFORE YOU GO

Passports and Visas

Visitors from most countries do not need to apply for a visa before arriving in Thailand and are granted a 30-day visa on arrival. Make sure you have a valid passport with at least six months validity before it expires.

Transportation

You'll most likely be arriving at Suvarnabhumi International Airport, just outside of Bangkok. From there you can catch a flight to anywhere else in the country. Low-cost carriers, such as Air Asia, offer frequent flights and amazing deals on flights within Thailand, but if you're planning on anything more than a cursory exploration of northern and northeastern Thailand, you should rent a car. Public transportation is easy and inexpensive if you are traveling from one urban area to another, but heading to farther-flung parts of the country by bus or train requires patience and can be unmanageable unless you have some skill with the Thai language.

Explore Thailand

▶ THE BEST OF THAILAND

Thailand is only twice the size of Wyoming, so it is possible to see the country's most remarkable cultural and natural destinations in a two-week period, provided you plan well. This itinerary will take you from the bustling streets of Bangkok to Chiang Mai in the north, where you'll spend a few days hiking in the mountains, to Isan in the northeast to see some of the best Khmer ruins, and then finally down to the Andaman Coast, where you'll get to tour waterfalls, snorkel, dive, and enjoy some quiet time on the beach. You'll get from region to region by air and travel through Chiang Mai and Isan by rental car. With a few extra days, you can forgo air travel and easily drive for most of the journey.

Day 1

Plan to spend your first day in Bangkok,

Siam Square is one of Bangkok's main shopping areas.

shaking off jet lag and enjoying some of the more relaxing diversions in the Old City. Head to The Grand Palace and adjacent Wat Pho to see a bit of the Chakri Dynasty's glory up close. After touring these two sights, linger in the Old City area for an invigorating Thai massage at Wat Pho's Thai Massage School. Next, head to one of the nearby restaurants on the river. If you're a beer fan, treat yourself to an ice-cold Singha or Chang while you watch the sunset. If you have some energy left after dinner, take a walk around Phra Athit Road to enjoy some casual live music and the local college bar scene.

Day 2

Take a river ferry to the Old City and spend a few hours at The National Museum, then walk over to Wat Phra Kaew to view one of the country's most important Buddhist figures, the Emerald Buddha. Hop in a taxi and head for Siam Square to do a little shopping and some people-watching. When you've had your fill of both, head back to your hotel for a bit of rest, then to Chinatown for dinner at one of the hundreds of street-side stalls.

Day 3

In the morning, head for the airport (make sure to check whether you're leaving from the old Don Muang or the new Suvarnabhumi Airport) and take a short flight to Chiang Mai. Plan on spending a couple of days exploring the largest city in the north, mostly on foot. After you check into your hotel, spend the day exploring all of the city's *wats* and arrange a trip to the mountains with

The Grand Palace at twilight, Bangkok

your hotel or one of the many tour agencies in the city.

Day 4

Spend the early part of the day learning how to make some of your favorite Thai dishes at one of the city's many cooking schools. After you've enjoyed your creations, make your way by taxi to look at local products on the Handicraft Highway.

Day 5

Pick up a rental car in the city or at the airport, and head for Doi Suthep to view the temple on the side of the mountain and get a bird's-eye view of the area. Then head for Route 1096 and begin the Mae Sa Loop. The scenery is among the best in the region, so make sure to bring your camera. Stop first at the Queen Sirikit Botanic Garden and enjoy some fresh air and beautiful flora. Spend the night in the Mae Sa Valley.

Day 6

Set out early to catch an elephant show at the Mae Sa Elephant Camp, and if you're feeling brave, climb atop one for the ride of a lifetime. Afterward, continue along the Mae Sa Loop to the Mae Sa Valley Crafts Village if you want to do some more shopping; otherwise return to Chiang Mai for dinner by the river. Spend the night in Chiang Mai.

Day 7

Head out on a one-day tour of some surrounding hill-tribe villages. Some tours visit three villages in one day. Possibilities include the Karen, Lisu, and Akha villages. When you return to Chiang Mai, you'll probably be tired and a little muddy from

sunset over Chiang Mai's Wat Chedi Luang

BEST BEACHES

Thailand beaches offer something for everyone, whether you're looking for a quiet place to relax under a palm tree or a chance to lie out all day and party all night.

BEST BEACHES FOR FAMILIES

- **Hua Hin Beach:** An easy drive from Bangkok, this long, flat beach in the upper southern gulf region attracts plenty of vacationing families. Reasonably priced accommodations are available within walking distance from the beach, and there are enough activities to keep everyone entertained – without the feeling that you're going to be dodging Jet Skis or parasails every minute.

- **Surin Beach:** The small, curved beach on northwest Phuket, on the Andaman Sea, is surrounded by pine trees and hotels, with none of the party scene of the island's southern beaches.

PRETTIEST BEACHES

- **West Rai Le:** Surrounded by limestone cliffs, this small stretch of beach in Krabi on the Andaman coast has some of the best scenery in the country. Kayak rental on the beach, plenty of rock-climbing routes, and easy day trips to snorkeling spots make West Rai Le a great choice if you're looking for some adventure too.

- **Ton Sai Bay:** Crystal-clear blue waters surrounded by limestone mountains characterize this bay on Ko Phi Phi, one of Thailand's most popular small islands. The breathtaking scenery and inexpensive bungalows make Ton Sai Bay a popular spot.

BEST PARTY BEACHES

- **Patong Beach:** It's not just the long, wide beach, soft sand, and warm water that make Patong a great choice; it also has the most vibrant nightlife scene on the island of Phuket. Scores of bars and discos are usually filled with visitors and locals till all hours of the night.

- **Pattaya Beach:** Seedy and strange, Pattaya Beach on the eastern seaboard is nonetheless the place to go if you're looking to dance and drink all night, then sleep it off on a beach chair.

Hua Hin Beach

Panyi Island in the Phang Nga Bay

the hiking. Take a short break and head out to the Night Market for a quick, easy dinner.

Day 8

After breakfast, go to the airport to catch your flight to Phuket. Right now Thai Airways has one direct flight per day, but you may end up switching planes in Bangkok. After you arrive in Phuket, grab a taxi to your hotel on one of the island's many beaches, drop off your stuff, and take a refreshing swim in the Indian Ocean. Back at your hotel, arrange a snorkeling or scuba diving tour (if you're already scuba certified) of Ko Phi Phi and the surrounding islands for the next day. Then head to Patong Beach for a seafood meal on the water and experience a little nightlife. You could also head to Surin Beach for a quieter evening.

Day 9

Wake up early to make sure you don't miss your ride to the pier for the tour of Ko Phi Phi and the surrounding islands; most tours start their pickups at 7 A.M. After you've arrived at the boat, hang on for some island-hopping. Spend the day snorkeling or diving around some of Phang Nga Bay's most beautiful islands. Don't worry about lunch; it's always included in these day tours. When you get back to your hotel, relax for a while by the water before getting ready for dinner.

Day 10

Spend the day lounging and relaxing on the beach. Arrange a ride into Phuket Town for dinner; stop at Raya Thai if you can get a table.

Day 11

If you're feeling like you've already seen enough, spend another day on the beach. If you've had enough beach time, head to Rawai Beach to walk through the small fishing village. You won't be able to do any swimming or sunbathing there, so don't worry about packing a towel. During the evening, ditch the flip-flops and bathing suit for something a little more formal and have dinner at one of Kata Beach's fancier restaurants.

Days 12-13

Drive or take a taxi to Sirinat National Park in the northern part of the island to spend the morning swimming and relaxing on the quiet beach. Then drive east to the Khao Phra Thaeo Wildlife Sanctuary to pay a visit to the gibbons at the Gibbon Rehabilitation Project (make sure to call in advance). For your final night in Phuket, head back to Patong Beach or Kata Beach.

Wake up early and have one last walk or swim on the beach before packing up and heading to the airport.

▶ BEST OF BANGKOK: THE LIFE OF THE CITY

Thailand's largest city is not only home to some interesting tourist sights, it's also home to millions of people living everyday lives most visitors don't get a chance to see. This four-day strategy includes some of the city's best sights but also gets you into some less-visited neighborhoods to experience the life of the city. For most of this itinerary you can get around by using the river ferry system; otherwise you can take a taxi.

Day 1

Have a quick breakfast in your hotel, then head straight to the Central pier. Grab a ferry on the Chao Phraya headed north and get off at Chang pier. Wander the surrounding streets for a bit before entering The Grand Palace compound. Take your time looking at the different buildings, and spend some quiet time at Wat Phra Kaew, home to the Emerald Buddha. By noon, it will be getting pretty hot outside, so walk over to Phra Athit Road, or take the ferry two stops north to Phra Athit and pop into one of the local restaurants that line the road for something to eat.

After lunch, you might want to grab an iced coffee or iced tea at one of the cafés. A good choice for comfortable seats and air-conditioning is Coffee & More in Ban Phra Athit. Once you've cooled off and refreshed, hail a taxi or a *tuk tuk* to the Vimanmek Teak Mansion. After taking the mandatory

tour, spend some time walking the grounds and poke your head into the Royal Elephant Museum for a few minutes. Afterward, go back to your hotel for some much-needed rest and maybe even a quick swim in the pool before getting ready for dinner.

Plan on dining at one of the restaurants along the riverside. Make your way to the river and take the ferry to get there; the view of the buildings and temples at sunset is lovely. A great choice for dinner is Arun Residence, with a view of Wat Arun. If you don't feel

Wat Arun

Bangkok boasts some of the best street food in the world.

Yaowarat, Bangkok's Chinatown, is filled with neon and traffic.

like calling it a night just yet, head over to the Khao San Road neighborhood to have a drink and witness the spectacle of Thailand's infamous backpacker ghetto.

Day 2

Start by taking a ferry to Chang pier. When you get off the boat, head to The National Museum. If it's Wednesday or Thursday, get there before 9:30 A.M. so you can take the free English-language tour. After a couple of hours, make your way to Wat Pho, either on foot or by *tuk tuk.* After spending some time meditating with the giant reclining Buddha, walk over to the Tha Tian pier and take a cross-river ferry to Wat Arun. Depending on the time and your appetite, have lunch before or after visiting the temple. If you're looking for something more formal, try the Patravadi Theatre or Supatra River House. Otherwise, the streets surrounding the temple are full of food vendors.

After you've finished touring Wat Arun and eaten lunch, head back to your hotel to relax for a couple of hours. In the late afternoon, take the Skytrain to Siam Square for a little shopping. If you can bear another museum,

head over to the Jim Thompson House and Museum, one stop away at National Stadium. Afterward, take the Skytrain to Thong Lor and have dinner at the outdoor market. Finish the evening with a drink and some live music. Brown Sugar, Ad Makers, and Saxophone are all great choices.

Day 3

Start the day by touring more sights in the Old City. Once the *wats* have closed up and the sun's starting to set, head for Phayap pier, just a few stops north of the Old City (make sure to set out before the boats stop running, around 7 P.M.). When you get off the boat, head straight down the street to the large intersection, where you'll enter Si Yan, one of the best food neighborhoods in the city. Wander around and select from the dozens of vendors selling everything from *tom yam kung* to *namtok mu* for your dinner.

Day 4

Take the river ferry to Surawongse pier in Chinatown. When you get off the boat, look for one of the vendors selling *jok,* a rice porridge traditionally eaten for breakfast. Make

FIVE STARS AT THREE-STAR PRICES

Few places in the world will offer you more for your money. While those on a tight budget will appreciate the plentiful US$20 guesthouses and casual meals for US$1, those looking to splash out a little will find a little bit goes a long way. If you're traveling off-peak, you'll be able to book rooms in five-star resorts for just over US$100. Even during peak season, you'll be paying a fraction of what you would back home for luxury accommodations and excellent meals.

ACCOMMODATIONS

- **Aleenta, Pranburi:** The resort in the upper southern gulf region is small and laid-back, the guest rooms spacious and modern, and the staff friendly and accommodating. Those looking for peace, quiet, and luxury will enjoy this reasonably priced resort on a peaceful beach.

- **Twin Palms, Phuket:** This trendy, modern resort on Surin Beach, one of Phuket's most relaxed beaches, caters to the business-class crowd, and while the rates aren't necessarily cheap, you get top-range accommodations for mid-range prices.

- **Railei Beach Club, Krabi:** Rent your own house just steps from the beach. Grounds are quiet and lush, and most of the houses come with their own kitchens. If you don't want to cook yourself, staff will gladly put together a personalized meal for you.

- **Kirimaya Resort, Khao Yai National Park:** If camping in the national park isn't your thing, stay at this posh resort just outside. Guest rooms are lush and modern, and the views of the surrounding mountains are spectacular. If you really want to splurge, opt for one of the tent villas.

RESTAURANTS

- **Blue Elephant, Bangkok:** A beautifully restored building, excellent Thai food, and top-notch staff make this Bangkok favorite the right place to go for a special night out, but it won't break the bank.

- **Zanotti, Bangkok:** One of Thailand's best Italian restaurants has a beautiful dining room and expertly prepared dishes from all over Italy. Many ingredients are imported, so you'll be getting a meal more authentic than you might at home.

- **Silk, Phuket:** The dining room of this one-of-a-kind spot in Surin seems to cater to the see-and-be-seen crowd. Although you'll have to leave the flip-flops in your hotel room to have cocktails or dinner here, the style belies the reasonable prices.

TAILOR-MADE CLOTHING

Hundreds of inexpensive tailors across the country can put together personally fitted dress shirts, suits, and evening gowns for less than the price you would pay off the rack at home. In Bangkok, custom-made suits for men and women can start at 6,000B.

ACTIVITIES

- **Diving:** Get your PADI diving certification for around 12,000B while you're visiting. Choose from one of more than 100 shops on Thailand's beaches and islands.

- **Island Hopping:** Charter a longtail boat for a few hours to take you to some of the Andaman coast or southern gulf's small islands. Pack a picnic lunch, grab a snorkel, and expect to pay under 1,000B per person.

sure to get a side order of crispy crullers to go with it. After you've had your fill, head out along Surawongse Road and enter the large covered market. Wind your way slowly through the tunnel-like market, taking time to look at the objects on sale, from hair clips and pocketbooks to steamed buns and produce.

When you emerge back into the sunshine, get back on the ferry and head for Wat Mahathat. You won't be spending much time inside the temple; instead wander around the Amulet Market, where you'll likely see plenty of monks and laypeople carefully inspecting these venerated objects. Walk toward Thammasat University for a quick *cha yen* at one of the many small cafés in the area.

In the evening, take a taxi to the Khlong Toei Port and wind your way toward the pier, where you'll buy a ticket to Bang Krabue across the river. These aren't the typical large ferry boats—more like a small version of the longtail boats seen plying the river—so climb in carefully. When you get across the river, you'll be in a small neighborhood on stilts, elevated above the Chao Phraya. Walk through to the street and grab a taxi for one of the river restaurants in Phra Pradaeng. You can take a taxi back to Bangkok from the restaurant, but even if it's late, the boat will take you back to Khlong Toei for a few hundred baht. This might be the best part of the trip, as you'll be crossing the river under moonlight.

► THOUSAND-YEAR JOURNEY: TOURING THE TEMPLES

In one week, journey through over 1,000 years of history by wandering through Thailand's most breathtaking temples, from the time the Khmer Empire ruled the region to the present day. Begin in Bangkok, where you'll see the temples most important to the Chakri Dynasty. Continue on to Ayutthaya, where you'll see the ruins of the Ayutthaya Empire; east to Isan, where you'll get to see temple ruins from the Khmer Empire; and end in Chiang Mai.

Day 1

Start your trip in Bangkok, where you'll spend the first day touring Wat Phra Kaew, where the revered Emerald Buddha sits, then to the oldest temple in the city, Wat Pho, populated by hundreds of Buddha statues,

golden ornamental statuettes at the Temple of the Emerald Buddha in Bangkok

including the gigantic Reclining Buddha. When the day is done, make sure to have dinner at Arun Residence, where you'll be able to view the stunning Wat Arun, with its Khmer-style *prang,* from your dining table.

Day 2

Set out early for Ayutthaya Historical Park either by train, car, or taxi. If you're taking the train, pick up a taxi at the train station and arrange to keep it for a few hours as you make your way around the many temple ruins in the small town. Find a spot to eat by the river, preferably at Ban Watcharachai, for a delicious casual lunch. Return to Bangkok in the evening.

Day 3

Rent a car and head out early for the five-hour drive to Isan. Your first stop should be Phimai in Nakhon Ratchasima Province. The temple here, Prasat Phimai, was built by the Khmers in the 11th and 12th centuries, and it marks the beginning of the Khmer highway to Angkor Wat. It demonstrates the importance of the region to the Khmers as well as their amazing engineering prowess. Phanom Rung Historical Park in Buriram Province is your next stop, about an hour's drive from Nakhon Ratchasima. Spend some time in the ruins of the amazing temple complex before heading to one of the neighboring towns, where you'll spend the next couple of nights.

Day 4

In the morning drive to Khao Phra Wihan National Park, where you'll briefly enter Cambodia to see Khao Phra Wihan, a massive Khmer Empire ruins complex. Although it's not as well preserved or restored as Prasat Phimai and Phanom Rung, the sheer size alone makes it worth the visit. Getting to the park, crossing the border, and touring the ruins will probably take you most of the day;

Buddhas in Ayutthaya Historical Park

if you still have time and energy, spend it in the national park itself.

Day 5

Head back to Bangkok in the morning to drop off your car and take a short flight to Chiang Mai. When you arrive, spend the afternoon strolling through the city, stopping on the banks of the Ping River and at the small shops and cafés in the city.

Day 6

Spend today touring the city's *wats.* There are close to 100 within the city walls, but make sure to see Wat Phra Singh and Wat Chiang Man. When you've had your fill of *wats* and the sun is starting to set, head to one of the city's *khan toke* restaurants, where you'll be treated to a traditional Lannathai meal, served in small dishes on an intricately decorated tray.

Day 7

Set out for Doi Suthep to see Wat Phra That Doi Suthep, a temple perched on the side of a mountain complete with golden stupas, graceful *nagas,* and plenty of Buddhist imagery. After you've rung the bells for good luck, take in the view of Chiang Mai from above and head back into town for dinner.

BANGKOK

Exotic, fast-paced, and cosmopolitan, Bangkok is a feast for the senses and a wonder to behold. Home to an estimated 10 million of Thailand's 67 million residents, it is the urban and political center of one of Asia's fastest-growing economies. Although many visitors assume Bangkok is an ancient city, in truth the city is not even 250 years old. Its history and its relevance to the rest of the world are still being made—since 2006, Bangkok has been the site of a coup d'état and two serious civil uprisings, although visitors to the city won't end up in hot spots unless they go out of their way to find them.

The heart of the city begins to beat even before the sun rises, with hundreds of thousands of commuters making their way by car, boat, or train to the country's financial and political center. The pace increases through the day and won't let up come dusk, as going out to dinner is a national pastime: Once evening mealtime rolls around, the streets will again be filled with people from all walks of life navigating their way around and food vendors setting up stands on even the smallest bit of sidewalk. After dinner, city life continues well into the wee hours, in the nightclubs and bars as well as the all-night markets.

Although many visitors see only the modern or well-visited sides of the city, behind the shiny office towers, glitzy malls, backpacker ghettos, and throngs of visitors from around the world is a city full of gilded Buddhist *wats*, bustling markets, quiet communities, and lush bits of rainforest that seem to peek out from every corner. Bangkok also has an intimate

© MING THIEN

HIGHLIGHTS

◖ The Grand Palace: This walled compound filled with glittering buildings and peaceful temples was Bangkok's urban center 200 years ago (page 27).

◖ The National Museum: The best collection of Southeast Asian art in the world is housed on the grounds of a former prince's palace (page 32).

◖ Wat Pho: The oldest and largest temple in Bangkok is also home to the largest Reclining Buddha, a 40-meter-long gilded statue (page 33).

◖ Vimanmek Teak Mansion: Now a museum, the former temporary palace for King Rama V was constructed of blond teakwood and is set on luscious garden grounds (page 38).

◖ Chinatown: Browse the best outdoor covered markets in the city, where vendors sell everything from fragrant herbs and spices to brightly colored beads (page 40).

◖ Wat Arun: This serene, elegant 76-meter-high pagoda sits on the banks of the Chao Phraya River. Called the temple of dawn, it's best viewed from a distance when the sun is rising or setting (page 45).

◖ Siam Square: The city's center of conspicuous consumption is a jumble of malls, markets, and little shops (page 60).

◖ Chatuchak Weekend Market: A massive outdoor weekend market filled with thousands of vendors, Chatuchak is the best place for souvenirs (page 65).

◖ Narai Phand: Head downtown to get all your souvenirs and gifts. This is a great place for one-stop shopping (page 66).

◖ Support Foundation: On the Grand Palace grounds, the Support Foundation store has some of the nicest Thai handicrafts you'll find in one place (page 67).

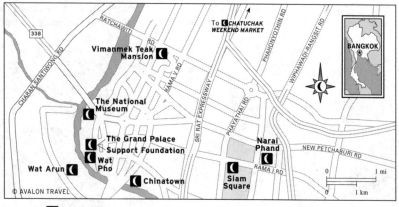

LOOK FOR ◖ TO FIND RECOMMENDED SIGHTS, ACTIVITIES, DINING, AND LODGING.

connection to the water around it. The meandering Chao Phraya River flanks the city's west side, and a series of canals, called *khlong* in Thai, crisscross the city. Although many of them have been paved over since the capital was relocated here from Ayutthaya in 1762, much of the city can still be traversed by boat via a canal system that even in its diminished state dwarfs Venice's.

This truly is an international city, albeit with a decidedly Thai flavor—one of Bangkok's many charms is its ability to be so many things to so many people. If you venture just a couple of steps off the beaten path, you may find yourself in a neighborhood where not a word of English is spoken one minute, and the next you'll be eating at five-star restaurants and partying with an international crowd. The streets seem to flow seamlessly between glistening skyscrapers, posh mega shopping malls, shophouses, and wooden shacks. Bangkok can be overwhelming, with its confused identity, everpresent traffic, and incomprehensible writing system, but once you get your bearings, you'll find its charms hard to resist.

PLANNING YOUR TIME

From Dusit and Bang Lamphu, known as the Old City, to the palaces and *wats* in every corner of Bangkok and the modern international downtown area, it would take a month to see everything the capital city has to offer. But if you're really in a rush, you can check off most of the city's absolute must-see sights in two days—**Wat Pho, The Grand Palace, The National Museum,** trying a bowl of *guay teow* noodle soup and some spicy papaya salad, and even a sunset cruise on the **Chao Phraya River.** If you want to do things at a more relaxed pace and see what life is like for the people who live in Bangkok, plan on at least three days, especially if one of those is spent shaking off jet lag.

Most of the city's important cultural sites are in the Old City, specifically in the **Ko Rattanakosin** and adjacent **Bang Lamphu** areas, but that doesn't mean you should attempt to tackle all of them in one day. The temples

and the palace are stunning, and the museum has an extensive collection of Southeast Asian art, but after six hours on your feet in sweltering heat, you may find it difficult to discern the subtle differences between a Sukhothai period sculpture and one from the Ayutthaya period. Better to try to see those sights early in the day, when you're freshest and the sun and heat don't feel life-threatening. At least one of your afternoons should be spent exploring the city's shopping districts, for no other reason than the fascinating people-watching. Evenings, when it's cooler again, venture out for dinner and a bit of exploration in one of Bangkok's older neighborhoods, or take in one of the city's cultural shows or even a few rounds of Thai boxing. If you have an extra day, make sure to venture beyond the city limits, either just over the river to Thonburi to see the less international version of Bangkok or even to Ayutthaya to explore the temple ruins.

If you're staying in any of the popular tourist areas, you'll find enough people who speak English that you'll be able to get around and find whatever you're looking for. Street signs, addresses, and shop names will all have English as well as Thai script. Still, be prepared for some communications problems—taxi drivers, *tuk tuk* drivers, and clerks at local shops may speak only Thai, so it helps to have someone at your hotel write down what you need to buy or where you need to go in Thai script. In fact, it's a good idea to have someone write down your hotel's name and address too, so you can use it when you need to get back.

Bangkok is best visited during the cool season, preferably in December or early January, when the temperature drops into the 20s Celsius and walking even the most crowded city streets, with the light scent of jasmine in the air, feels like a fleeting glimpse of an exotic dream life. Everyone wants to come to Bangkok during this time of year, so you'll be paying higher prices for your accommodations and dealing with bigger crowds.

Monsoon season in Bangkok is not as bad as it sounds. While it can rain, even torrentially, nearly every day, especially during June and

July, the downpours will generally pass quickly, and the temperature is at least a little cooler than during the hot season.

During hot season, from February to May, temperatures can reach 38°C in Bangkok, and the tropical humid air can feel even more uncomfortable when it's amplified by all the concrete. There's a reason for the expression "Bangkok blanket." Year-round, you should make sure your accommodations have air-conditioning, but if you're here during the hot season, it will be unbearable without it. April 13–15 the whole country celebrates **Songkran,** or Buddhist New Year, and while raucous water fights that last for days may seem totally out of place in a city as sophisticated as Bangkok, at least the dousing has the effect of cooling everyone down a bit. If you visit during this time of year, don't worry about finding a place to stay; many people avoid the city during Songkran.

Organized Tours

Armed with a good map, a few words of Thai, patience, and a sense of humor, you will find Bangkok an easy city to see on your own. If you don't have the time (or the patience), are traveling with a large group, or are physically unable to tolerate the heat and the walking involved, there are scores of agencies offering tours of the city's most popular sights. Many of these tours involve driver service to shuttle you from one place to another without too much substantive information provided, but even this can be worth the relatively little money you'll spend. These types of tours can be found at any travel agency in the city (there are hundreds) or by arrangement with your hotel.

One thing to watch out for—some tour guides (and even taxi drivers and *tuk tuk* drivers) get kickbacks from shops and restaurants when they bring people in. This is especially true of gem stores, so if your guide suggests taking you to a particular place, be wary.

Although you'll pay more, you won't need to worry so much about scams if you're using one of the larger, more established tour companies, such as **Thai Airways' Royal Orchid Holidays** (tel. 02/288-7000, www.thaiair.com), **Diethelm**

Travel Asia (Kian Gwan Bldg., 140 Wireless Rd., tel. 02/660-7000, www.diethelmtravel. com), **Exotissimo** (Zueling House, 6th Fl., 1-7 Silom Rd., tel. 02/636-0360, www.exotissimo.com), or **Viator** (www.viator.com). Tours are typically 800–2,500B per person for a day tour. These companies tend to focus on typical tourist destinations, and there is usually a lot of hand-holding involved, which is great for those who are intimidated by the thought of having to get around Bangkok on their own. The **Association of Thai Travel Agents** (10th Fl., 33/42 Surawongse Rd., tel. 02/237-6046, www.atta.or.th) also organizes half-day and full-day tours of sights such as the Grand Palace and the Damnoen Saduak Floating Market. If their tours are not available, they can also recommend a qualified travel agent in your area in Bangkok.

If you are looking for something more informational or more adventurous, there are some great agencies offering off-the-beaten-track tours. **Smiling Albino** (tel. 02/718-9561, U.S. toll-free tel. 877/842-4929, www.smilingalbino. com) offers active, personalized programs that can include everything from bicycling to nightlife tours. The company's ethos is about having fun and interacting with the community around you, and they also arrange homestays and multiday trips. **Grasshopper Adventures** (tel. 08/7929-5208, www.grasshopperadventures. com) does half-day bicycle tours of Bangkok, leaving from the Khao San Road area and staying in the old part of the city. These tours include bicycle rental and do not require a very high level of physical fitness to enjoy them. **Spiceroads** (14/1 Soi Promsi 2, Sukhumvit Soi 39, tel. 02/712-5305, www.spiceroads.com) offers full-day bike tours out into the surrounding areas of Bangkok, including one that will take you across the river to Prapadaeng and one that goes to a floating market.

ORIENTATION

Bangkok's most important historic sites are located within easy distance of each other in the oldest part of the city. Visitors to the city should make this one of their first stops, as it's here

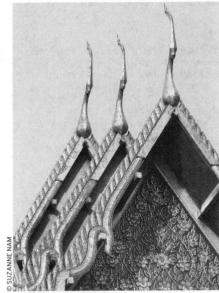

chofas rising to the sky

that you'll find the stunning **Grand Palace** and **Wat Pho** as well as some important museums and idyllic green spaces. **Ko Rattanakosin,** enveloped by a curve in the Chao Phraya River, overflows into **Bang Lamphu** to the north, which also houses some of the country's most important cultural destinations, lots of cheap places to eat and sleep, some charming unpretentious restaurants, and an increasing number of high-end boutique inns.

Farther north is **Dusit,** flanked by the **Chao Phraya** to the west. With fewer tall buildings and many residential neighborhoods, Dusit feels like what the rest of the city would have looked like had it not been for the amazing economic boom over the past few decades—less international and less convenient, certainly, but much more Thai than modern Bangkok.

To the east of Ko Rattanakosin is **Charoen Krung Road,** running southeast, the major avenue through bustling **Chinatown,** lined with shops and markets of all kinds. It ends just near **Hua Lamphong,** the city's main railroad station.

To the east of Hua Lamphong, modern Bangkok begins. Southeast of Hua Lamphong is the **Silom** area, one of the city's main business districts, with tall office buildings, gridlocked rush-hour traffic, and international hangouts, but also some of the nicest green space in the city and plenty of charming noodle shops catering to local office workers.

To the northeast is **Siam Square** (in the Ploenchit and Lower Sukhumvit area), where you can buy anything from a Ferrari to inexpensive locally designed fashions, and then, farther east along Sukhumvit Road, is **Upper Sukhumvit.** On the other side of the Chao Phraya is the quieter, more residential **Thonburi.**

RCA is a little bit out of the city, northeast, and not connected by any other neighborhoods of interest to visitors.

HISTORY

The rise of Bangkok as the country's capital is intertwined with the reign of the Chakri Dynasty, who still rule the hearts of the people of Thailand, if not the country itself. It was King Rama I who founded Bangkok, and King Rama IX who has helped shape the city into what it is today.

Once just a small trading port, Bangkok's rise began after Ayutthaya was sacked by Burmese forces in 1767 and a general named Phraya Taksin finally managed to drive out the invaders. With Ayutthaya in ruins and no assurances that the Burmese wouldn't regroup and come back, Taksin headed south to the flat Chao Phraya delta and set up a new capital on the western banks of the river in what is now known as Thonburi.

Just 15 years later King Rama I, the first ruler of the current Chakri Dynasty, seized power and moved his palace across the river to what is now modern-day Bangkok and bestowed on the city its royal name—Krung Thep Mahanakhon Amon Rattanakosin Mahinthara Ayutthaya Mahadilok Phop Noppharat Ratchathani Burirom Udomratchaniwet Mahasathan Amon Piman Awatan Sathit Sakkathattiya Witsanu Kamprasit, meaning "city of angels, the great

KHLONG TOEI SLUMS

With all the sports cars and expensive shopping malls, it's easy to forget that development has not hit everyone in Thailand equally. Relatively speaking, Bangkok is far more affluent than the countryside, but there are still many people living in poverty here, in conditions that are shocking compared to the luxury surrounding them.

Even in the many affluent neighborhoods filled with high-rise condominiums, there are shantytowns that sprout up on small plots of undeveloped land, under highways, or along railroad tracks. Most are populated by immigrants from the north and northeast of Thailand. Right between Ploenchit and Sukhumvit, running parallel to Sukhumvit Soi 1, is a small slum where people live right along the railroad tracks. The Khlong Toei slums, extending from the edge of Rama IV road on land owned by the Port Authority, are home to tens of thousands of people. Some estimates put the number at 80,000, some at over 100,000. Inside the narrow "streets" are mostly shack homes precariously built, roofed in galvanized steel; residents have limited access to running water and electricity, but otherwise Khlong Toei is something of a large village. There are parents and children, even grandparents. There are food vendors offering noodles, people selling small necessities from their homes; there are even schools.

While perhaps not living in quite the dangerous, crime-filled, lawless communities often associated with the word *slum*, residents of the slums of Bangkok live a precarious life marginalized by society and constantly on the edge. The vast majority are illegal squatters who've taken forsaken land and built up their own small communities. In Bangkok it's not unheard-of to see a slum one day and return the next to find bulldozers and armed guards where homes once stood. The residents of Khlong Toei, which has been around for more than 50 years, have fought long and hard battles with the Port Authority over their right to stay, sometimes prevailing and sometimes being forced out.

Children in the slums are more likely to be raised by a single parent, less likely to go to school, and also more likely to be HIV-positive than the average child in Bangkok.

A handful of nongovernmental organizations such as **Mercy Centre** (www.mercycentre.org) and the **Duang Prateep Foundation** (http://en.dpf.or.th) have been fighting for decades alongside residents to protect these communities, provide grassroots organizing assistance, give children access to education, and provide health care. Duang Prateep Foundation was established by Prateep Ungsongtham Hata, who was born in the Khlong Toei slums. With limited access to school, she took a job as a factory worker and dock worker at age 12 in order to fund her education. At just 16 years old, while still a student herself, she opened her own informal school in the slums and, after earning a degree in education and creating the foundation to better the lives of people in the slums, became the first Asian to be awarded a John D. Rockefeller Youth Award for Outstanding Contribution to Mankind.

Father Joseph H. Maier, an ordained Catholic priest from Washington state, came to Thailand in the 1960s to set up congregations, but by 1973, after setting up a parish in Khlong Toei and becoming a resident himself, realized what the community really needed was kindergartens. His Mercy Centre began as just one small school and now has 30 preschools located in slum communities in Bangkok with 4,000 children ages 3-6 attending every year. Mercy Centre also has an orphanage that cares for 200 children, around 25 percent of whom are HIV-positive.

Both organizations have ad hoc, but fairly well-organized, volunteer programs, but if you're in town for just a few days and happen to be in the neighborhood, you can call to arrange a visit to one of the schools. The Mercy Centre has a weekly Mass in Khlong Toei.

city, the eternal jewel city, the impregnable city of the god Indra, the grand capital of the world endowed with nine precious gems, the happy city, abounding in an enormous Royal Palace that resembles the heavenly abode where reigns the reincarnated god, a city given by Indra and built by Vishnukamwhich." Fortunately, the name has been unofficially shortened to Krung Thep in Thai and Bangkok for the rest of the world.

King Rama I set about a series of ambitious public works projects to bring the new capital on par with the now-destroyed Ayutthaya, including construction of the Grand Palace and the Temple of the Emerald Buddha, Wat Phra Kaew on Ko Rattanakosin. It is this part of the city, surrounded by the meandering Chao Phraya on three sides, and thus called *ko,* meaning island, that has always been Bangkok's historic and cultural heart.

It was not until the reign of King Mongkut (Rama IV), starting in 1851, that Bangkok began to modernize. Under Rama IV several of the city's most important avenues, including Charoen Krung in Chinatown, were built, laying the foundation for what would later become modern Bangkok.

Mongkut's son, King Chulalongkorn (Rama V), continued the development started by his father, building the first permanent bridge connecting Thonburi to Bangkok and covering over some of the city's canals to create more buildable land.

Following World War II, Bangkok underwent a massive urban transformation, largely fueled by rapid industrialization of the country and an influx of migrants from rural areas. City planning during this period was virtually nonexistent, allowing Bangkok to start to assume the confused, uncoordinated nature that characterizes it to this day. During the 1980s and 1990s, the booming development in Thailand and the rest of the region meant unchecked growth at an ever faster speed, and it was during this time that Bangkok was known as the world's worst city for traffic. After the Asian economic crisis in 1997, brought on by the devaluation of the Thai baht by policy makers in Bangkok and which quickly caused shockwaves throughout the region and then the world, development in Bangkok slowed again. Projects were abandoned, and half-built high-rises loomed in the sky like skeletons. After more than a decade of slow and steady recovery, Bangkok has largely emerged from the crisis, although a handful of remaining ghost buildings still mar the skyline. In recent years, the city has seen another development boom, with gigantic shopping malls popping up in the center of the city and luxury condominium developments all over the place.

While Bangkok boasts tall buildings and lots of world-class shopping, the majority of the city's residents still get by on only a few hundred baht per day and live in small shack developments, many of which are located along waterways that have been in operation for 200 years.

Sights

THE OLD CITY–BANG LAMPHU AND KO RATTANAKOSIN
บางลำภู และ เกาะรัตนโกสินทร์

With their maze of little streets, Chinese-style shophouses, and street hawkers selling everything from *kluai ping* (grilled bananas in palm-sugar syrup) to pad thai to made to order on the sidewalk, Ko Rattanakosin and Bang Lamphu are the heart of historic Bangkok. To the west is the impressive Chao Phraya River, and taking one of the commuter ferry boats is probably the best strategy for seeing this area, as even here traffic can slow to a halt during rush hour.

◖ The Grand Palace
พระบรมมหาราชวัง

Ko Rattanakosin is dominated by the sparkling, gilded Grand Palace compound (Na

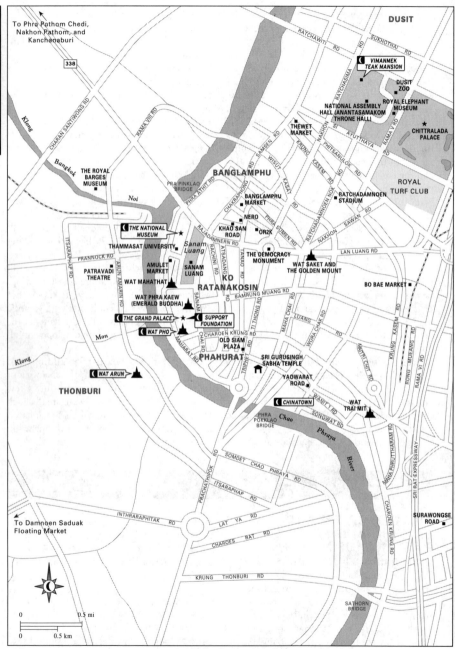

To Phra Pathom Chedi,
Nakhon Pathom, and
Kanchanaburi

`338`

DUSIT

VIMANMEK
TEAK MANSION

DUSIT
ZOO

ROYAL ELEPHANT
MUSEUM

NATIONAL ASSEMBLY
HALL (ANANTASAMAKOM
THRONE HALL)

CHITTRALADA
PALACE

THEWET
MARKET

ROYAL
TURF CLUB

THE ROYAL
BARGES
MUSEUM

BANGLAMPHU

BANGLAMPHU
MARKET

RATCHADAMNOEN
STADIUM

PRA PINKLAO
BRIDGE

NERO

KHAO SAN
ROAD

OR2K

THE NATIONAL
MUSEUM

THAMMASAT UNIVERSITY

Sanam
Luang

THE DEMOCRACY
MONUMENT

WAT SAKET AND
THE GOLDEN MOUNT

BO BAE MARKET

PRANNOCK RD.

PATRAVADI
THEATRE

AMULET
MARKET

SANAM
LUANG

WAT MAHATHAT

KO
RATANAKOSIN

WAT PHRA KAEW
(EMERALD BUDDHA)

THE GRAND PALACE

SUPPORT
FOUNDATION

WAT PHO

Mon

OLD SIAM
PLAZA

PHAHURAT

SRI GURUSINGH
SABHA TEMPLE

Klong

WAT ARUN

THONBURI

YAOWARAT
ROAD

CHINATOWN

WAT
TRAI MIT

PHRA
POKKLAO
BRIDGE

Chao

Phraya

River

To Damnoen Saduak
Floating Market

SURAWONGSE
ROAD

SATHORN
BRIDGE

0   0.5 mi

0   0.5 km

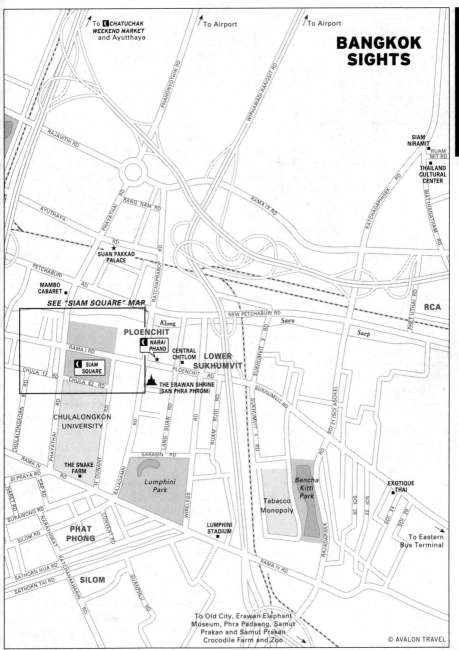

To **CHATUCHAK WEEKEND MARKET** and Ayutthaya

To Airport

To Airport

BANGKOK SIGHTS

SIAM NIRAMIT
RUAM MIT RD
THAILAND CULTURAL CENTER

RAJAVITHI RD

PHAHONYOTHIN RD

WIPHAWADI-RANGSIT RD

RATCHADAPHISEK RD

WATTHANATHAM RD

AYUTHAYA

RANG NAM RD

PHAYATHAI

RD

RAMA IX RD

RD

PETCHABURI

RD

SUAN PAKKAD PALACE

RATCHAPRAROP

PHET UTHAI RD

RCA

MAMBO CABARET

SEE "SIAM SQUARE" MAP

NEW PETCHABURI RD

Saen

Saep

Klong

PLOENCHIT

NARAI PHAND

CENTRAL CHITLOM

LOWER SUKHUMVIT

RAMA I RD

SIAM SQUARE

PLOENCHIT RD

SUKHUMVIT 3

SUKHUMVIT RD

SUKHUMVIT 4

SOI 21 (SOI ASOKE)

CHULA 12 RD

CHULA 62 RD

CHULALONGKORN

THE ERAWAN SHRINE (SAN PHRA PHROM)

CHULALONGKON UNIVERSITY

LANG SUAN RD

RUAM RUDI RD

RD

RD

RAJADAMRI

PHAYATHAI

SARASIN RD

RAMA IV

THE SNAKE FARM

H DUNANT

Lumphini Park

WIRELESS

Bencha Kitti Park

EXOTIQUE THAI

SI PRAYA RD

TAP RD

CONVENT RD

LUMPHINI STADIUM

Tabacco Monopoly

SOI 20

SOI 22

SOI 24

SOI 26

To Eastern Bus Terminal

SURAWONG RD

NARATHIWAT

RAJADAPISEK

SILOM RD

PHAT PHONG

SUANPLU RD

RAMA IV RD

SATHORN NUA RD

RATCHAKHARIN

SILOM

SATHORN TAI RD

To Old City, Erawan Elephant Museum, Phra Padaeng, Samut Prakan and Samut Prakan Crocodile Farm and Zoo

© AVALON TRAVEL

Phra Lan Rd., pier: Chang pier, tel. 02/224-3328, 9 A.M.–4 P.M. daily, 250B), surrounded by fortified whitewashed walls on all sides. Although the palace is only open for visitors during the day, try to pass by once the sun has gone down, when all of the buildings are lit up and the steep carved wooden roofs with *chofas* rising up from the sides and exotic gilded pagodas are that much more breathtaking and beautiful.

Begun in 1782 when King Rama I moved the capital across the river from Thonburi, the buildings' architecture, with their golden pagodas and red-and-green tiled roofs, reflects the layout of Ayutthaya period palaces. When the palace was built, it was meant not only to serve as a home for the king and his family but as the center of all government activity in Thailand. More like a small city than a palace, it currently comprises more than 100 buildings, including Wat Phra Kaew and the former royal residence. Although not all buildings are open to the public, you can tour Wat Phra Kaew and many major palace buildings.

As you enter the compound's white-walled perimeter from Na Phra Lan Road, it's easy to imagine a time when elephants were the main source of land transport and Bangkok was not the bustling metropolis that it is today. Once inside, you'll find Wat Phra Kaew on the left, and in the center of the compound, the Phra Maha Monthain buildings, which were built by Rama I as his personal residence and for coronations. Although the royal family moved their residence to Chittralada Palace in Dusit at the beginning of the 20th century, the interiors of these buildings are closed, but the ornate exterior architecture is worth looking at nonetheless.

To the left of the Phra Maha Monthain group of buildings is the Chakri Maha Prasat building. A mix of Thai and European architecture (it was designed by British architects in the neo–French Renaissance style but has a traditional Thai roof), this building is the most modern on the compound, built in the late 19th century by King Rama V. Within it is the grand audience hall, where the king

still occasionally receives visitors, and the European-style Throne Room. These buildings are not open for public viewing.

To the left is a group of buildings called the Dusit Maha Prasat, which includes the Throne Hall. On this cross-shaped building, the simple white stone walls give way to impressive multi-tiered gilded roofs with a pagoda rising up from the center. This building is open to the public.

To the right of the Phra Maha Monthain buildings in the middle of the compound are the Borophiman Mansion and Siwalai Garden buildings. This area was originally used as a garden, but during the reigns of Rama III and Rama IV, the old gardens were replaced with temples, pavilions, and the strangely out-of-place Borophiman Mansion. Rama V had the European-style mansion (it's the only building on the compound without a Thai-style roof) commissioned as a gift to his son Prince Maha Vajirunahis. Today, it's used to house visiting royalty and heads of state.

Your admission ticket for the Grand Palace will also get you into Wat Phra Kaew and Vimanmek Mansion, as long as you go within seven days. Visitors will be denied entry to the Grand Palace and Wat Phra Kaew if they are wearing tank tops, shorts, flip-flops, or are otherwise immodestly dressed. Just inside the compound is a small building where you can borrow appropriate clothing so long as you leave your ID in exchange.

Wat Phra Kaew
วัดพระแก้ว

Within the palace compound is the Temple of the Emerald Buddha, Wat Phra Kaew, the most sacred Buddhist sight in the country. Unlike most *wats,* there are no resident monks here. The main purpose of the temple is to house a sacred artifact—the **Emerald Buddha.** Made of either jade or green jasper ("emerald" refers to its color, not the material), the Buddha figure sits on a grand golden throne under a golden canopy. The throne, more than three meters high, with golden tiles and surrounded by carved images depicting the life of the Buddha, is a sight to behold. Atop it sits

HOW'S THE WEATHER? ASK THE BUDDHA

Buddha images are often believed to have special powers in Thailand. People keep them in their homes, wear them around their necks, and even place them in their cars. Since its discovery, the Emerald Buddha has always been regarded as having extra special powers and has been particularly significant for Chakri Dynasty kings. The phrase "eternal jewel city" in Bangkok's full name, given by Rama I, is even a reference to the figure.

In previous generations, the "eternal jewel" was taken from its home in Wat Phra Kaew to be used in ceremonies and to ward off plagues and epidemics. In 1820 it was even paraded through the city by road and canal in an effort to end a particularly bad outbreak of cholera.

These days the Buddha stays put, and any outbreaks of disease are treated with modern medicines, but the Buddha still plays a role in some ceremonies.

Three times a year, amid great fanfare, the king of Thailand climbs up to the Emerald Buddha on its pedestal and changes the gold headdress on top of the image. As the king worships nearby, an attendant then removes the figure's current outfit, also made of gold, and puts on another.

For the hot season, starting in March or April, depending on the lunar calendar, the Buddha wears a stepped, pointed crown; a sash; and numerous other bands and bracelets on his arms and legs. For the rainy season, starting in August, the Buddha wears a pointed crown as well, with sapphires and enameling, but instead of the golden bands he wears a full gold-and-ruby robe draped over one shoulder. For the cool season, starting in November, he wears a gold mesh shawl draped over his body. It was Rama I who started the tradition and had the hot and rainy season outfits made for the Emerald Buddha. Rama III had the cool season outfit made later.

---

the barely 50-centimeter-tall Buddha, draped in clothing made of gold.

The provenance of the image is debated, with the prevailing legend asserting that the Emerald Buddha was made in India at some point before the end of the first millennium A.D. Religious lore is difficult to dispute, but most art historians say it was probably made sometime around the 15th century in northern Thailand.

Considering historical writings referring to the Buddha image, most agree that it was at least discovered around the 15th century. There are various tales of how it was found, the most prominent being that lightning struck a pagoda in Chiang Rai and the Emerald Buddha was found inside (you can visit this *wat,* also called Wat Phra Kaew, if you head up north). When found, it was covered in white stucco, certainly less impressive than it is today. Its beauty wasn't revealed until the abbot who discovered it noticed that some of the stucco on the Buddha's nose was flaking off.

After its discovery more than 500 years ago, the Buddha began a complicated journey that took it from Chiang Mai to Luang Phrabang, then the capital of Lan Xang, the Lao Kingdom, in 1552. It remained in Laos until 1779, when General Chao Phraya Chakri, who later became King Rama I, took it as a spoil of war in a battle in Vientiane. Five years later, after Rama I had taken power, moved the capital to Bangkok, and completed Wat Phra Kaew, he brought the Emerald Buddha to its current home.

The interior walls of the *wat* are covered in murals depicting the life of the Buddha (the Ramakien, the Thai version of the Ramayana) and worth more than a casual look.

Sanam Luang
สนามหลวง

Just adjacent to the palace compound is the 12-hectare Sanam Luang. Once a field used for royal ceremonies and events, Sanam Luang is now a wide-open public space used for anything from political demonstrations to live music events.

Amulet Market
ตลาดพระเครื่อง

Just adjacent to Thammasat University and Wat Mahathat is this legendary Bangkok market (between Maharat Rd. and the river, 9 A.M.–5 P.M. daily), where you're more likely to see throngs of orange-clad monks shopping for devotional items than women getting the day's groceries. The market is a series of proper shops and small stalls that spill out onto the street. You'll find Buddhist amulets—small figures of the Buddha or a particular revered monk usually made by a specific temple, as well as the casings and other items necessary to wear the amulets. The shops and stalls also carry Buddha images.

Thammasat University
มหาวิทยาลัยธรรมศาสตร

Just north of the market, the Thammasat University campus (2 Phrachan Rd.) begins. Thammasat is the second-oldest university in the country, and its campus is surrounded by cafés and shops catering to the students.

It was at Thammasat University, and in Sanam Luang, that students gathered in October 1976 to protest the return of military dictator Field Marshal Thanom Kittikachorn after three years in exile. The university was overtaken by the military and police, resulting in the brutal deaths of at least 46 college students (eyewitness accounts put that figure substantially higher) and the wounding of hundreds more.

If you're looking for a place to grab a cup of *cha yen* or *kafae yen* (iced tea or iced coffee) and spend a few baht on the latest trends being worn by the cool kids, Phrachan Road, just adjacent to the campus, is a vibrant, inexpensive place to take a coffee break and do a little shopping and some people-watching.

(The National Museum
พิพิธภัณฑสถานแห่งชาติ

Just south of the National Gallery and north of Thammasat University is the National Museum (Na Phrathat Rd., pier: Chang pier, tel. 02/224-1333, www.thailandmuseum.com or www.museumvolunteersbkk.net/html/museum.html, 9 A.M.–4 P.M. Wed.–Sun., 200B), housing the largest collection of Buddhist art in Southeast Asia. Murals and sculptures provide the backdrop to learn about the Buddhist, Hindu, Vedic, and animist traditions that combine to form Thai Buddhism. Royal collections of palanquins, howdahs, musical instruments, sculptures, masks and puppets, mother-of-pearl inlay, murals, lacquerware, pottery, jewelry, weapons, chariots, and textiles reveal the history of Thai royal diplomacy, ancient court life, and the evolution of Thai arts. The museum has one of the best collections of Southeast Asian art in the world, from prehistory to the modern period, and it is a vast, fantastic, but antiquated museum.

The grounds were originally part of a Wang Na, translated as "front palace," and were the residence of the deputy to Rama I and his court. The Wang Na would have extended south into the Thammasat University grounds to house the Royal Guard and west into the Colleges of Dramatic and Fine Arts grounds to house the large number of wives and children common to monarchs before the 20th century. Sanam Luang, just across the street, was also once part of the palace grounds. In fact, museum pieces are still brought out to the field for special occasions, such as during Songkran, when the famous Phra Buddha Sihing image is paraded for the public to make merit by sprinkling it with lustral water; when an important member of the royal family dies, the 200-year-old royal funeral chariots are rolled out from their specially made hangar on the northeast edge of the grounds.

Rama V transformed the complex into a museum to house his collection of art and artifacts, and later Rama VII expanded the collection and the grounds dedicated to it. Today, it comprises one main building and more than 10 surrounding structures and pavilions.

The best way to see the museum is to visit on a Wednesday or Thursday at 9:30 A.M. to take the two-hour docent-led tour in English, which provides a primer on Southeast Asian arts, Buddhism, Hinduism, royal history, architecture, and general *wat* etiquette as well as instruction on how to navigate the mazelike design of the museum (for a schedule of tours in other languages, check www.museumvolunteersbkk.net/html/museum.html). These tours only scratch the surface of the museum's collection, so those who want a comprehensive look at the collection will need a couple of days.

Touring the National Museum's extensive collection can be daunting. Signage is limited, the layout is confusing, and the unair-conditioned galleries are stuffy. Don't rush through, though, as there is much to learn with a little guidance. Pick up a map when you pay the 200-baht fee at the ticket window, and check large bags and backpacks in the secure lockers. Water bottles are allowed in galleries and are available at the café connected to the Museum Shop. Photography is only permitted on the grounds, not inside any of the buildings. Keep in mind that very little of the museum is air-conditioned, it can get very hot by midday, and for some of the rooms you'll be required to take your shoes off to enter.

◖ Wat Pho
วัดโพธิ์

Just to the south of the Grand Palace compound and just a block from the river is Wat Pho (Maharat Rd., pier: Tha Tian pier, tel. 02/222-0933, 8 A.M.–5 P.M. daily, 30B), the oldest and largest temple in Bangkok. Originally built during the Ayutthaya period in the 16th century, before Bangkok was the capital of Siam, the temple was renovated and expanded during the reign of Rama I and now houses the striking 40-meter gilded **Reclining Buddha.**

Wat Pho is perhaps the most popular tourist attraction in all of Thailand, and when the temple grounds are filled with people from all over the world jockeying for the best spot to snap photos, it can be tough to enjoy the serene, elegant beauty of the hundreds of Buddha images and majesty of the four grand pagodas

© SUZANNE NAM

Reclining Buddha at Wat Pho

NATIONAL MUSEUM SIGHTS

If you don't want to take a full tour of the museum, these galleries and exhibits are worth visiting on their own.

BUDDHAISAWAN CHAPEL

The chapel is adorned with murals dating to the 1790s that serve as a biography of the Buddha. Cast in bronze and plated with gold, the Buddha image in the chapel is the famous and revered Phra Buddha Sihing, said to have miraculously floated to the surface after the boat bringing it to Thailand from Sri Lanka was shipwrecked.

ROYAL FUNERAL CHARIOTS

These ornate chariots were renovated and used for the funeral of Princess Galyani Vadhana, King Bhumibol Adulyadej's older sister, in November 2008. Everything here is displayed with placards and video footage.

THE RED HOUSE

Built on the Grand Palace grounds for Rama I's sister in the 1790s, the Red House was moved to Thonburi on the west side of the Chao Phraya River in the 1820s for use by her daughter. The daughter eventually married Rama II and became Queen Suriyendra. When Queen Suriyendra's son Mongkut became King Rama IV (the King portrayed in *The King and I*) and her son Prince Chutamani (later King Pinklao) the deputy king, the house was moved to its present location at the Wang Na. These many moves were possible because it is constructed without the use of nails and is made of teak, which naturally resists cracking, insects, and decay.

THE PALACE

Enter the palace through Room 5 on your map; if it is closed, walk through Throne Hall to the back, past the throne. The two lovely courtyards separate the three wings containing 14 rooms. Even if you're short on time, give yourself at least a few minutes to walk through the palace.

NORTH AND SOUTH WINGS (SCULPTURAL ART)

These wings feature the famous collection of Buddhist art, but signage is unreliable, and there are many stairs to climb. This self-led walking tour will help you pick out a few key treasures in each time period:

Room S1: Asia Art

As you enter this room, note the wall map showing the trade routes that centered on Thailand. International trade led to the acceptance and incorporation of other cultural, religious, and artistic traditions. The collection of Buddha images allows for a side-by-side comparison of the way different cultures portrayed the Buddha.

Room S6: Ban Chiang

Upstairs, this air-conditioned room has excellent informative signs about the prehistoric culture of Ban Chiang and its preserved pottery.

Room S7: Dvaravati Art

The river-dwelling Mon people predated the Thai culture's ascendency of central Thailand and created Indian-influenced Theravada Buddhist art during the 6th-11th centuries. The Mon were known for their stone sculptures and terra-cotta work. En route to Room S8, find *Buddha on Panasbati*, a relief of the Buddha seated on a composite of the vehicles of the Hindu gods: Brahma's goose, Vishnu's eagle, and Shiva's bull.

Room S8: Java Art (Indonesian Art)

All sculptures in this room are gifts from Java, made there in 9th-12th centuries. Outstanding is the chubby, charming Hindu god Ganesha, son of Shiva, the remover of obstacles and god of knowledge and new beginnings.

Room S9: Srivijaya Art
Srivijaya was a powerful maritime kingdom, incorporating, largely through marriage ties, Java, Sumatra, Malaysia, and Chaiya of Thailand, from the eighth to the 11th centuries. The predominant religion was Mahayana Buddhism. The Padmapani, the bodhisattva of mercy, on the plinth in the center of the room wearing princely attire, is one of the museum's treasures.

Room S4: Ancient Hindu Sculpture
Descend the stairs beneath Ganesha to the Hindu Sculpture room and find, centered on the landing, one of the most artistically significant sculptures found in Thailand: Vishnu. In Thailand, Vishnu is the most revered of the Hindu Trinity.

Room S3: Lopburi Art
Exit to Khmer and Khmer-influenced art of the Lopburi Period (11th–14th centuries). The lintel facing you as you enter tells the creation myth taken from the Mahabharata.

Room N4: Large Buddha Images
In N4 of the North Wing you are greeted by a colossal 3.7-meter Buddha image in teaching gesture from the Dvaravati period, seated as if on a throne. Also, find the two large Buddha heads from the Ayutthaya period and the oldest Ganesha statue in the museum against the wall.

Room N5: Lan Na Art
Contrary to your map, Lan Na Art is on the lower floor only (N5). The kingdom's longevity of rule (1296–1939) and mostly peaceful relations with its neighbors allowed art to flourish, combine many styles, and produce what is considered by some as the most refined bronzes of all.

Rooms N7 and N8: Sukhothai Art
Upstairs, statues of the Hindu gods greet you. Shiva can be identified by the moon in his hair, his third eye, a snake on his shoulder, and a trident in his hands. Vishnu holds a chakra or disc. The female god has been identified as Uma, a gentle consort of Shiva.

Before entering N8, see the sign for correct, but misspelled, information about the very important Sukhothai Kingdom. The walking Buddha is emblematic of the innovative art of this period. See the Red Lacquer Buddha in the case to the left.

Rooms N9 and N10: Ayutthaya Art
Beginning in N8 behind the dividers, find the art from the Ayutthaya Kingdom, founded in 1350 and one of the greatest powers of Southeast Asia until it was destroyed by the Burmese in 1767. Few of the elaborate, bejeweled pieces survived, but Buddha images in full regalia were typical of the time. Find excellent examples of lacquer chests with compositions prized for the balance of color, contained energy, and dynamism of design. On the back wall, a carved cabinet showing lost Ayutthayan buildings is a museum standout.

Rooms N1 and N2: Rattanakosin Art
The modern, ornate style of art you'll find in these galleries is similar to the architecture of the Grand Palace area. The Buddha images are rendered in royal garb with lavish detail (see the back wall) harking back to the opulence of prefall Ayutthaya. The statue at the center is of Brahma the Hindu creator god and is a replica of the very popular Erawan Shrine. Room N2 will introduce the decorative and theatric art objects also seen in the palace.

*– contributed by Jean Harvey,
National Museum docent*

rising up into the air. Visit Wat Pho early in the morning to avoid the rush.

The main attraction is the Reclining Buddha, housed in its own hall to the right of the main entrance. Made when Rama III renovated Wat Pho, the Buddha lives up to all the hype. With mother-of-pearl eyes the size of beach balls and 7.6-meter feet covered in engravings illustrating the 108 qualities of the Buddha, the statue depicts the Buddha serenely passing from earthly life into nirvana. The ornate hall, which barely seems to contain the statue, is covered from floor to ceiling in intricate carvings.

Throughout the grounds are hundreds of sculptures and statues of the Buddha, many taken from Ayutthaya and Sukhothai in central Thailand. Walk around the cloister toward the back of the compound and you'll see 400 larger-than-life golden Buddha figures quietly surrounding the *ubosot,* or coronation hall. Inside the *ubosot* is yet another Buddha, this time a gold and crystal figure seated on a high gold throne. The hall alone, with its ornate two-story-high mural depicting the Ramakien, is worth seeing even if you've had your fill of Buddha for the day.

The temple grounds contain 99 pagodas of varying sizes, including four large tiled pagodas right behind the Hall of the Reclining Buddha. These tall, stepped *chedi* are covered in intricate, colorful tile work that becomes more stunning the closer you get. The first of the three large pagodas that stand in a row was built by Rama I to house an image of the Buddha brought from Ayutthaya. The second and third were build by Rama III to house the ashes of Rama II and for his own ashes, respectively. The fourth, which stands to the side of the first three, was built by Rama IV. Sometimes called the "blue *chedi*" because of the predominance of that color on the tiling, there is no consensus as to the reason it was built. Whatever its purpose, many say it is the most beautiful of the four.

In addition to Buddhas and pagodas, Wat Pho houses a school for traditional Thai massage and Thai medicine (tel. 02/221-2974, www.watpomassage.com, 8:30 A.M.–5:30 P.M.

daily). While you can enter as a student and enroll in anything from a one-week to a three-year course, you can also enter as a client and enjoy a Thai massage after a day of sightseeing for around 400B.

Wat Saket and the Golden Mount
วัดสระเกศราชวรมหาวิหาร/ภูเขาทอง

A couple of kilometers east of Wat Pho and the Grand Palace, you'll notice a large golden pagoda on top of a large hill. Originally built during the Ayutthaya period before the founding of Bangkok, what is now Wat Saket (Soi Wat Saket between Boriphat Rd. and Lan Luang Rd., 8 A.M.–9 P.M. daily, 10B to enter the *chedi*) was completed by Rama V, and the Golden Mount was added to the top. When you arrive, be prepared for a long climb to the top. As you are ascending the steps to the temple, keep an eye out for the numerous, somewhat incongruous small shrines that have been placed here over the years. When you reach the top, you'll enter Wat Saket, a temple that is home to some Buddha relics, but the main attraction is the panoramic view of the city. To see it, climb another set of steps that lead out onto the *chedi*'s terrace.

Compared to Wat Phra Kaew and Wat Arun on the other side of the river, this *wat* will seem unimpressive. But the climb up the stairs and around the hill is worth it for the view of the city from the top.

Democracy Monument
อนุสาวรีย์ประชาธิปไตย

This large art deco–style monument, with its four imposing angel wings marking the intersection of Ratchadamnoen and Din So Roads, was built in 1932 to commemorate the country's transformation from an absolute monarchy to a constitutional monarchy. Italian designer Corrado Feroci, the "father of modern design in Thailand," was commissioned to build the monument. This strikingly incongruous sight is more of a landmark than a destination of its own.

The area surrounding the monument, which also serves as a rotary, is full of shops, cafés, and restaurants.

Khao San Road
ถนนข้าวสาร

Less than two kilometers north of the Grand Palace, in an otherwise rustic and charming part of Bang Lamphu, is Thailand's infamous backpacker ghetto, centered around Khao San Road. If understanding foreign cultures and enjoying the wonders of other countries are the benefits reaped from world travel, Khao San Road is the price you pay. Originally just a handful of cheap hostel-like accommodations catering to shoestring-budget travelers, the street is now literally jam-packed with bars, nightclubs, and guesthouses.

By day, you'll see visitors from around the world hanging out, drinking beer, and watching Western movies in one of the many guesthouses offering such entertainment. By night the street explodes into what can only be described as a zoo. Hawkers sell everything from

CORRADO FEROCI: THE FATHER OF MODERN ART IN THAILAND

Born in Florence in 1892, Corrado Feroci studied at the Academy of Fine Arts in Florence and then taught there for nearly a decade before he arrived in Bangkok. It wasn't like Italian sculptors were flocking to Thailand in the 1920s, but King Rama VI asked the Italian government to send artists to the country as part of a program to help train local artists in European techniques. With the then Siam emerging on the international scene, it was thought necessary to "modernize" by adopting Western art and architecture.

Feroci arrived in Bangkok in 1923 to take a teaching job at the Royal Fine Arts Department, earning a salary of 800B per month. Originally he was contracted to stay just three years, but soon after his original tenure was up he was commissioned to create a statue of King Rama I.

With that projected completed, Feroci set out to prepare teaching materials and a curriculum to train artists, and in 1937 he opened the Silpakorn School of Fine Arts, a government teaching institution. On visiting the school, Prime Minister H. E. Field Marshal P. Pibulsonggram was so impressed with the program that he requested the Thai government upgrade it to a university of fine arts, and Feroci was installed as a professor and dean of painting and sculpture.

In addition to training countless artists, including national artists Sawat Tantisuk and Fua Haripitak, the Italian was also busy at work on various large-scale monuments and statues in the city. Many of his works, including Democracy Monument and Victory Monument, have a look reminiscent of fascist Italy, and this is no coincidence. Most of his work was done right after Thailand transitioned from an absolute monarchy to a constitutional monarchy, and the powers that be sought to use these works to create a sense of nationalism in a country still building its identity.

Feroci created 18 monuments and sculptures in Thailand; his most notable are:

- 1932: King Rama I Monument at the Memorial Bridge

- 1939: Democracy Monument

- 1941: Victory Monument

- 1942: King Rama VI Monument in Lumphini Park

- 1954: King Taksin Monument in Thonburi

After World War II, Feroci was granted Thai citizenship and changed his name to Silpa Bhirasri. Although he returned to Italy for short periods after he moved to Bangkok, he died in Thailand in 1962, a revered and greatly respected figure. The university he founded, the Silpakorn University of Fine Arts, has expanded to enroll thousands of students per year and continues to use his teaching curriculum. Students are often seen wearing T-shirts with his picture on them. The campus has a small museum dedicated to Silpa (Na Phrathat Rd., pier: Tha Chang, tel. 02/223-6162, 9 a.m.-noon and 1-4 p.m. Mon.-Fri., free).

shots of vodka to pad thai to sneakers; bar workers try to lure passersby into bars with promises of cheap drinks and signs saying "We Don't Check ID"; music from the 100 different clubs and bars spills out onto the street. For people-watching, it is unparalleled, although it relates only marginally to anything having to do with Bangkok or Thailand.

On the flip side, the neighborhood surrounding Khao San Road, particularly Phra Athit Road, which runs parallel to the river, has begun to attract many local artists opening shops and studios as well as great places to eat and drink.

DUSIT
ดุสิต

Unlike the modern Bangkok that rises up to the west of Ko Rattanakosin, Dusit, to the north, has remained largely untouched by rapid urbanization. Get off the Chao Phraya Express Boat at Phayap pier and walk around Nakhon Chai Si in the early morning and you'll find people still doing much of their grocery shopping in stalls that line the main streets and the wet markets hidden around various corners.

Traffic in Dusit is nearly as bad as the rest of the city, but being right on the Chao Phraya means river ferries are a fast, fun, and cheap form of transportation.

Chittralada Palace
พระตำหนักจิตรลดารโหฐาน

The current official home of King Bhumibol Adulyadej and Queen Sirikit (Rama V Rd. between Si Ayutthaya Rd. and Ratchawiti Rd.) was once the summer palace of Rama IV. From the outside, with its high walls and surrounding moat, the palace is quite impressive. Unfortunately, that's about as far as you can get—the palace is not open to visitors.

◖ Vimanmek Teak Mansion
พระที่นั่งวิมานเมฆ

Near Chittralada Palace, Vimanmek Mansion (Ratchawiti Rd., tel. 02/628-6300 to 02/628-6309, www.vimanmek.com, 9:30 A.M.–4 P.M. daily, last entry at 3:15 P.M., 50B), itself a former palace, is open to visitors and definitely worth a

stop, as it is the only chance to see how modern royalty lived. Rama V had the teak structure, originally constructed on Ko Si Chang as a royal resort, moved piece by piece and reconstructed on a plot of verdant leafy land in Dusit in 1901.

"I very much enjoy living here. If I were still at the Grand Palace, I would be finding the heat unbearable and would have to set out on another trip," wrote Rama V of the mansion to his son Prince Boripat Sukumbhandhu, and it's no wonder given the beauty and peacefulness of Vimanmek and the surrounding grounds.

The L-shaped mansion, with its surrounding canals and pavilions, was the king's home for six years. After Rama V, one of the wives of Rama VI lived in Vimanmek for a short while, and later Rama VII had the structure renovated to add electricity. For 50 years, however, the structure was used only as a storage facility. It wasn't until 1982, when Queen Sirikit had Vimanmek restored, that it was transformed into a museum.

These days you can view the royal quarters, lavishly appointed with Thai and imported furnishings from the turn of the 20th century, as well as the bright, airy rooms and surrounding buildings that are filled with old Thai cloths and silks, photographs of the royal family, and even the first Thai-language typewriter.

Royal Elephant Museum
พิพิธภัณฑ์สถานแห่งชาติ ช้างต้น

Next door to Vimanmek, in large stables where elephants were once kept by the king, is the Royal Elephant Museum (on the grounds of the Vimanmek Mansion, tel. 02/282-3336, www.thailandmuseum.com/thaimuseum_eng/changton/main.html, 9 A.M.–4 P.M. daily, free). Exhibits explain why elephants have been important to Thai culture and demonstrate what is considered a perfect elephant (these traits include the animal's toenails, skin color, hair, and tail), and there are displays of such curiosities as preserved white elephant skin and elephant hair.

Thewet Market
ตลาดเทเวศน์

If you ever wondered what food shopping in Thailand was like before the advent of the supermarket, walk through the Thewet Market (intersection of Phadung Krung Kasem Rd. and Samsen Rd.) early one morning to watch shoppers buying their daily groceries. Enter the market either from the Thewet pier if you're coming by boat or from Samsen Road (where you'll find vendors selling flowers and potted plants) if you come by land. Toward the river, the market becomes more of a traditional wet market, with fresh fish and other meat, vegetables, and herbs. The market was recently officially renamed Thewarat Market, but everyone still knows it as Thewet Market.

National Assembly Hall (Anantasamakom Throne Hall)
พระที่นั่งอนันตสมาคม

Built during the reign of Rama V, the white-marble

LONGEST REIGNING MONARCH

On June 9, 2006, the whole country came to a standstill to celebrate the 60th anniversary of His Majesty King Bhumibol Adulyadej's crowning as the king of Thailand. For days before and after, almost every person in the country wore shirts, scarves, or hats in yellow, the color signifying the day of the week the king was born. Emperor Akihito and Empress Michiko of Japan, Prince Albert of Monaco, Britain's Prince Andrew, Crown Prince Jigme Khesar of Bhutan, and others – 25 foreign kings, queens, princes, princesses, sheiks, and sultans in all – traveled to Thailand to join in the celebration of the king's reign, which at 60 years makes him the longest-lasting monarch alive today.

Unsurprisingly, the festivities were fit for a king. In an amazing display, the Royal Barges, 52 elegant wooden boats elaborately carved to resemble mythical creatures and manned by more than 2,000 oarsmen, proceeded in perfect synchronicity along the Chao Phraya for the first time in decades. The king's public address from the balcony of the Anantasamakom Throne Hall was attended by an estimated 1 million Thais, all wearing yellow and shouting "Long Live the King." The adoration of the monarch reached a near feverish pitch at all levels of society.

King Bhumibol Adulyadej was born in Cambridge, Massachusetts, while his father, a prince and the half brother of King Rama VI, was studying public health at Harvard University. Never a likely candidate for the throne, he spent most of his early life studying in Switzerland and learning to play the saxophone. His older brother took the throne at just nine years old, shortly after Thailand became a constitutional monarchy, but when Rama XIII mysteriously died of a gunshot wound to the head in 1946, Bhumibol, just 19 at the time and still in college in Lausanne, became king. He switched his courses from sciences to political science and law, finished his degree, and returned to Thailand to assume his duties as king.

Although there were two kings before him who ruled briefly as constitutional monarchs, it is King Bhumibol who has shaped the role the Thai monarchy plays in a democratic society. With limited political powers, his time on the throne has been largely dedicated to the development of rural Thailand and to improving the lives of the country's poor. He has often traveled throughout the country visiting remote villages and promoting sustainable development projects, work for which he was awarded a United Nations Human Development Lifetime Achievement Award in 2006. In the portraits that adorn the walls of nearly every home and business in Thailand, the king is often pictured dressed normally rather than in full regalia, out in the countryside talking to villagers, pencil in hand and camera around his neck.

It is perhaps for this reason that the king, despite having little political power, has become such an important figure in Thai life. The king has rarely involved himself in political matters, or even offered an opinion on whether one prime minister or another military coup maker was taking the country down the right path, and it is often said that the king is "above politics." During times of political crisis he has, however, played a critical role. In 1973 and 1992 he intervened to end violence during uprisings against military rulers.

National Assembly Hall (Uthongnai Rd., tel. 02/244-1549, 9:30 A.M.–4 P.M. daily, free) was designed in the Italian Renaissance style, complete with frescoes portraying important events during the Chakri Dynasty adorning the inner halls and dome.

Originally intended for use as a royal building, it was here, during the reign of Rama VII, that the country's first parliament convened.

Although it's no longer used on a daily basis, the building, a fascinating blend of Asian and European design influences, is still used for special events. It was from a balcony here that King Bhumibol greeted tens of thousands of well-wishers during the celebration of his 60th anniversary on the throne.

The Dusit Zoo
สวนสัตว์ดุสิต (เขาดิน)

Just to the right of National Assembly Hall is the Dusit Zoo (71 Rama V Rd., tel. 02/281-2000, 9 A.M.–6 P.M. daily, 50B), which houses both indigenous animals such as elephants and barking deer and more exotic animals such as ostriches and kangaroos. In the center of the zoo is a large lake where you can rent paddleboats; aside from the variety of Thai snacks available, it's quite a typical zoo.

◖ CHINATOWN
ไชน่าทาวน์

If you look quickly at one of the merchants scooping rice out of a burlap bag in one of the traditional shophouses that line the streets of Chinatown, you may think you're in the Bangkok of 100 years ago. In between Ko Rattanakosin to the west and central Bangkok to the east, Chinatown is one of the city's oldest neighborhoods. Chinese traders and merchants who had originally settled in the area that Rama I chose for the Grand Palace were relocated just south to Sampheng Lane along the Chao Phraya River.

Referred to by locals as **Yaowarat,** after one of the neighborhood's main roads, Chinatown developed simultaneously with Ko Rattanakosin. From one narrow lane in the 19th century, Chinatown expanded into

© SUZANNE NAM

Yaowarat, Bangkok's Chinatown

a thriving commercial zone and residential neighborhood thanks to continual waves of immigrants from southern China moving into the city. While it has continued to thrive commercially for more than 200 years, it has escaped much of the bulldozer development that the rest of Bangkok has experienced.

The neighborhood is defined by two main roads, Yaowarat and Charoen Krung. Along both roads you'll find scores of gold dealers, seafood restaurants, and Chinese herbalists still selling medicines from old wooden drawers. The side streets between Sampheng Lane and Yaowarat Road are crammed full of fresh food markets, shops, and stalls selling everything from shoes in bulk to jewelry and toys. By midday on any weekday, the streets are literally overflowing with hawkers, tourists, and shoppers out for their dinner groceries. Chinatown is best accessed by subway from Hua Lamphong or by river ferry at the Ratchawongse pier.

If you can make it through all the gem shops and antiques dealers on Charoen Krung to the neighborhood's southwest corner, you'll find the Oriental Hotel. Steeped in literary history and enjoying prime waterfront property on the edge of the Chao Phraya, the Oriental is one of the city's oldest and most beautiful hotels.

Wat Trai Mit
วัดไตรมิตรวิทยารามวรวิหาร

Close to Hua Lamphong at the beginning of Chinatown is Wat Trai Mit (Traimit Rd. near Charoen Krung Rd., tel. 02/623-1227, 8 A.M.–5 P.M. daily, 20B), home to purportedly the largest golden Buddha in the world. More than 3.5 meters high, this Buddha image from the Sukhothai period is estimated to weigh at least five tons. Assertions that the Buddha is pure solid gold are likely untrue (if it were solid gold, it would account for about 3 percent of the world's mined gold). Still, the shiny gold statue is like nothing else you will come across. Like the Emerald Buddha, the true nature of this figure was hidden by plaster, probably to protect it from looting during times of war, until the 1950s when the plaster cracked during a move and the gold was discovered. Wat Trai Mit still has some of the plaster on display. Aside from the golden Buddha, the *wat* was otherwise unremarkable, but it underwent extensive renovations in 2008 to expand the space of the *ubosot* and completely rebuild some of the structures and facade to create stunning white-marble and red-roof structures.

Phahurat
พาหุรัด

At the west tip of Chinatown, at the end of Yaowarat Road, is the city's Indian quarter, where a predominately Sikh population settled in Bangkok after the turn of the 20th century. It's hard to tell exactly where the Chinese influence ends and the Indian influence begins, but once you've hit the center of Phahurat you'll notice many of the merchants are dressed in traditional Sikh attire and the shops are selling Indian sweets instead of the typical Thai fare. **Sri Gurusingh Sabha Temple** (565 Chakraphet Rd., tel. 02/221-

1011, 9 A.M.–5 P.M. daily) is said to be the second-largest Sikh temple outside India.

The city's textile quarter, Phahurat is the place to go for fabrics of any kind, including traditional Thai silk. Phahurat market, an immense, lively covered bazaar hidden behind Phahurat Road, is worth a visit even if you're not in the market for sewing notions, beads, or snacks.

CENTRAL BANGKOK-SILOM AREA
เขตสีลม

If one neighborhood could encompass everything that is Bangkok, it would be Silom. On the one hand, it's the city's modern financial center, with high-rise buildings housing the city's banks and investment companies and men and women in suits and ties going to and fro during rush hour. On the other, the side streets are populated with small mom-and-pop stores, and you can get lost in some of the street markets that open up during lunchtime. Walk just a couple of blocks in from one of the main roads and you'll find tree-lined streets with small houses nestled between the high-rises.

When the sun sets and the stockbrokers go home for the day, the streets along Sala Daeng are lined with food vendors selling roti made fresh before your eyes and filled with sliced bananas and sweetened condensed milk, spicy *som tam,* and ubiquitous *guay teow.* The international crowd pours in to have drinks at one of the many Western-style bars. Phat Phong, which looks almost innocent during the day, becomes a bustling night market surrounded by go-go bars.

Lumphini Park
สวนลุมพินี

On the corner of Rama IV and Ratchadamri Roads lies a 56-hectare oasis surrounded by tall buildings and six-lane traffic arteries. When the park was built in the 1920s on land donated by Rama VI (you'll see a large statue of him designed by Feroci if you enter the park from Rama IV Road), it was located far from the center of the city. Bangkok has literally grown up around Lumphini, but the park has remained a luxuriant green reminder of what the area used to look like.

With well-manicured lawns, shady palm trees, and ample places to picnic or just sit, it is the largest public green space in the city. There is an asphalt running track with kilometer markers, a large artificial lake where paddleboats can be rented, and outdoor exercise equipment.

In the evening and on weekends, the park is packed with runners, walkers, and scores of people doing group aerobics.

The Snake Farm
สวนงู สถานเสวภา

The snake farm is actually a part of the Thai Red Cross, a science facility called the **Queen Saovabha Memorial Institute** (1871 Rama IV Rd., tel. 02/252-0164, 8:30 A.M.–4:30 P.M. Mon.–Fri., 8:30 A.M.–noon Sat.–Sun., 70B) where technicians keep local varieties of poisonous snakes to produce antivenin to treat the thousands of people bitten by poisonous snakes in the country each year. In addition to the work and research going on, the facility offers daily tours and shows (10:30 A.M. and 2 P.M. Mon.–Fri., 10:30 A.M. Sat.–Sun.) where visitors can see some of the deadliest snakes in the region up close, learn snake-handling techniques, and watch snakes being milked to extract venom.

CENTRAL BANGKOK–PLOENCHIT AND WESTERN SUKHUMVIT
เพลินจิต และ สุขุมวิทฝั่งตะวันตก

The area surrounding Siam Square and extending west to the beginning of Sukhumvit Road is the city's affluent urban center. Well served by efficient public transportation, with shiny, swanky shopping malls and foreign embassies and their impressive grounds reminiscent of the colonial era, it's a testament to the economic growth that has occurred here in the past few decades and, to a lesser extent, to Thailand's income and class disparities.

Of course, you're still in Bangkok, so interwoven among all that you'll find great street-food stalls, vibrant outdoor markets, and lots of bargain shopping, attracting people from all walks of life. You'll also find some of the worst traffic along the main road, which is overshadowed by the elevated Skytrain tracks. But once you turn onto the side streets, you'll find many quiet residential neighborhoods.

Orientation

The main artery running east–west is called Rama I Road at National Stadium, then becomes Ploenchit Road before crossing the expressway and curving slightly to the south, where it becomes Sukhumvit Road. It's all the same road, but given the heat and the traffic, it's often wiser to go from one place to the other in the area using the Skytrain rather than by taxi or on foot.

The first Skytrain stop in the neighborhood is National Stadium on the Silom Line, right next to the hectic, bargain-oriented Ma Bun Khrong shopping mall (called MBK for short) and the National Stadium sports arena. From here you can take the Skytrain one stop to Siam Square, where you can visit one of the many posher shopping malls, including Siam Paragon. You might not be able to afford to buy anything here except a fast, excellent meal at the food court in the basement. If you have time, visit Siam Square itself, a cluster of small shops and eateries often packed with hip high school and college-age shoppers buying everything from trendy 100-baht T-shirts to Japanese crepes.

Just east is the Chit Lom neighborhood, on the Sukhumvit Line of the Skytrain, where you'll again be bowled over by the sheer number of shops and malls along perpendicular Ratchadamri Road that make up just one of the city's many shopping districts. Ploenchit, the next stop and the next part of the neighborhood, is mostly a residential and business strip, with a good selection of five-star hotels on the main road and on Witthayu Road (running perpendicular), as well as some embassies, including the U.S. Embassy, one of the largest U.S. embassies in the world.

Just to the east of this neighborhood is the beginning of Sukhumvit Road and the Skytrain stops Nana and Asok. Nana, centered around Soi 3 and 4, is another red-light district, although the surrounding neighborhoods also have their share of five-star hotels and the best selection of Middle Eastern food in the city.

Asok is a major intersection with an interchange between the Skytrain and the city's underground subway line, and it divides Upper and Lower Sukhumvit. The Sukhumvit neighborhoods are home to many of the city's foreign residents, and although they don't offer much in terms of sightseeing, they are full of hotels, bars, and restaurants.

North of the Rama I–Ploenchit–Sukhumvit artery is Petchaburi Road, a major thoroughfare. Once you cross Petchaburi, the city starts to regain the Thai-ness that is sometimes obscured by all the international restaurants and shopping malls in the southern part of the neighborhood. It's here that you'll notice the all-night Pratunam Market and some of the best late-night street food.

The Khlong Saen Saep canal runs below Petchaburi Road and has frequent commuter ferry boats running all the way to the Golden Mount in the Old City.

The Erawan Shrine (San Phra Phrom)
ศาลพระพรหม

Only 50 years old, the Erawan Shrine was built by developers to appease evil spirits after a spate of accidents and deaths of workers building a hotel (it's now the site of the Erawan Hyatt). The four-faced golden Brahma that sits on the corner of Ratchadamri and Ploenchit Roads under a sparkling tiled canopy is now immensely popular, and at any hour of the day the shrine will be full of people lighting incense, making offerings, or even paying some of the resident dancers in full traditional Thai costume to perform for the deity in hopes of generating good luck or having wishes come true.

The area surrounding the shrine is lined with vendors selling flower garlands and other objects to be offered to Brahma.

Brahma is not a Buddhist god b[...] one, although he is worshipped at the [...] Thai Buddhists, a relic of the Khmer influence during the Ayutthaya period and an example of the nonexclusive nature of Buddhism.

In 2006 a mentally ill man vandalized the shrine, breaking the Brahma statue into pieces with a hammer. In a sad and horrifying turn of events, bystanders who had witnessed the vandalism attacked and beat the man to death. The shrine was replaced soon after and continues to draw crowds of worshippers.

Wat Patum Wanaram
วัดปทุมวนาราม

Hidden in between two large shopping malls on Rama I Road is Wat Patum, a small temple compound with an elegant little temple and a white pagoda built 150 years ago when the neighborhood was characterized by paddy fields and the only way to visit Wat Patum was to take a boat on the Saen Saep canal. The temple monks have spent the past few years enduring all-night construction, debris from buildings, and increased traffic thanks to the newly renovated Central World Plaza and adjacent office building, but the *wat* remains a calm and peaceful bit of land, serving as a reminder that even as consumerism grows, the importance of Buddhism to Thai culture remains. The compound itself was recently refurbished, and some of the main buildings are now reopened after a couple of years being closed.

Suan Pakkad Palace Museum
พิพิธภัณฑ์วังสวนผักกาด

In the middle of office buildings and busy traffic along Si Ayuttaya Road is a small brown sign indicating the entrance to Suan Pakkad Palace (352–354 Si Ayutthaya Rd., Skytrain: Phaya Thai, tel. 02/246-1775, www.suanpakkad.com, 9 a.m.–4 p.m. daily, 100B). Once you enter you'll find a collection of eight Thai wooden houses brought there by Prince and Princess Chumbhot of Nagara Svarga in the 1950s and set on lush, green grounds in what was, back then, a cabbage patch. The houses themselves now function as exhibit halls to display an impressive collection of Thai art, musical instruments, furniture, and household items from the family's private collection. There is a collection of pottery from Ban Chiang and even a royal barge, but it's the lacquer pavilion that steals the star-studded show here. Believed to be built sometime in the 17th century, the small structure was constructed of beautifully ornate panels, some depicting the life of the Buddha. Although it fell into disrepair, it was reconstructed by the family and brought to the palace. Strewn across Bangkok are a number of private palaces and royal residences, but few are open to the public, which makes Suan Pakkad Palace that much more special.

Jim Thompson House and Museum
บ้านไทยจิม ทอมป์สัน

Sitting on 0.25 hectares of tropical rainforest in the middle of the city abutting the Maha Nag canal, Jim Thompson House (6 Soi Kasemsan 2, Rama I Rd., tel. 02/216-7368, www.jimthompsonhouse.com, 9 A.M.–5 P.M. daily, 100B), the home of a late American entrepreneur and silk maker, offers a peaceful, idealized view of what life in Bangkok looked like 40 years ago.

The house is actually six traditional Thai teak houses brought by Thompson from other parts of the country and assembled together in Bangkok. Some of the homes used were already more than 100 years old and offer an excellently preserved view of Thai architecture from the period.

The compulsory tour offers visitors a personal history of Jim Thompson and his role in helping to create the commercial Thai silk industry and a chance to view some of the best examples of the richly colored silks Thompson pioneered.

Although Thompson disappeared under mysterious circumstances in Malaysia in 1967, the company he founded, the Thai Silk Company, still exports silks all over the world. There are numerous Jim Thompson shops selling their silk products throughout Bangkok.

In addition to being a businessman, Thompson was also a collector of Southeast Asian art. Today, his home is filled with sculpture, Buddhist devotional art, paintings, porcelain, and other artifacts as well as beautiful examples of woven Thai silk.

Bangkok Art and Culture Center
หอศิลปวัฒนธรรมแห่งกรุงเทพมหานคร

Eleven stories of airy, open space filled with modern and contemporary art encircling an open lobby make the Bangkok Art and Culture Center (939 Rama I Rd., Skytrain: National Stadium or Siam Square, tel. 02/214-6630, www.bacc.or.th, 10 A.M.–9 P.M. Tues.–Sun., free), right in the middle of the city's most popular shopping area, feel like a miniature version of New York City's Guggenheim Museum. Ten years in the making, the center opened in 2008 and is exhibiting more and more local artists. For now the structure itself may be the most spectacular attraction at the center, but if curators' plans to fill it come to fruition, that should change.

ACROSS THE RIVER

Although there is plenty to keep visitors occupied west of the Chao Phraya, once you cross the river, Bangkok begins to feel more like a large Thai town than an international city. Small, predominantly working-class neighborhoods abound, as do mom-and-pop shops and fewer tall buildings. If you want to feel like you've left Bangkok without really leaving, spend a few baht on one of the frequent river ferries to cross over.

Phra Pradaeng
พระประแดง

Just across the river and a couple of kilometers south of the center, Bangkok is a little green bubble of land nearly completely encircled by the Chao Phraya. Visiting Phra Pradaeng really is like seeing what life was like in much of Bangkok 50 years ago. There are no tall buildings, the houses along the river are small wooden shacks on stilts, and it's calm: so calm and different from urban Bangkok that at night the high-rises lining the sky across the river look alien and out of place. It's possible to take a taxi to Phra Pradaeng, but it's best to make your way to the Khlong Toei Port. Once there, you'll have to navigate through a maze of food stalls to get to the port itself (enter to the left of the 7-Eleven on the main road; there will be a small *wat* on your left as you make your way down). At the port, buy a ticket for Bang Krabue (13B) and then climb into a small wooden commuter boat for the 10-minute journey. If you stay in Phra Pradaeng for dinner and the regular boats have stopped running, there is always someone at the pier who will be willing to take you back to Khlong Toei for a few hundred baht.

◖ Wat Arun
วัดอรุณ

Wat Arun (34 Arun Amarin Rd., www.watarun.org, 6 A.M.–10 P.M. daily, 20B), the temple of dawn, is perhaps the most breathtaking Buddhist *wat* in the country. Located on the edge of the Chao Phraya directly across from the Grand Palace, the Khmer-style temple with its intricately decorated pagodas covered in a mosaic of Chinese porcelain rises high into the sky and evokes awe. A monastery existed at the site during the Ayutthaya period, before Bangkok was the capital city, but Rama II and Rama III built the large central pagoda and surrounding pagodas.

Wat Arun is best viewed from across the river or, better yet, just as the sun is going down from

aboard a river boat. The temple compound, almost a tiny city on its own, is full of small alleyways, turtle pools, and Buddha figures. To get there, you can take a cross-river ferry (3B) from the Tha Tian pier right next to Wat Pho.

The Royal Barges Museum
พิพิธภัณฑสถานแหงชาติ เรือพระราชพิธี

As far back as the 13th century, kings in this region have used fleets of wooden barges for ceremonial processions, and King Narai the Great's records are full of references to such events using intricately decorated barges. As done today, the royal barge procession involves wooden boats up to 45 meters long with elaborate carvings and gilded decorations, and scores of rowers in full formal dress singing and chanting as they ply their way through the canals and rivers of Bangkok. As the rowers move through the water in perfect synchronicity, the king sits atop a throne under a colorful canopy. The royal barge procession is rarely seen in Thailand, most recently at the anniversary of the king's 60th year on the throne, but the royal barges are kept at the Royal Barges Museum (Arun Amarin Rd., tel. 02/424-0004, 9 A.M.–5 P.M. daily, closed Dec. 31–Jan. 1 and Apr. 12–14, 30B) across the river from the National Museum. Some of the barges can be viewed, along with exhibits explaining their history and the craftsmanship involved in their manufacture. If you bring your camera, you'll be charged an extra 100B.

Nightlife

Nightlife in Bangkok is as varied as the different neighborhoods you'll be exploring. From the Old City's grungy backpacker bars to the chic international nightclubs in the central business area to quiet riverside bars where you'll be able to enjoy an ice-cold Chang beer while you watch life on the Chao Phraya float by, you will be able to find a location to fit your mood any night of the week. Much of the city's nightlife caters to an international crowd, but if you're looking to

see how local youth like to party, head out to Royal Crown Avenue (called RCA) on Rama IX Road, where thousands of college students will be packed into the thumping-loud nightclubs that line the street. If your feet can bear being stepped on and your eardrums can handle the decibel level, the scores of slick nightclubs and thousands of kids all in one area is quite a scene to behold, especially around 2 A.M. when all the clubs close and the crowds empty out.

Even in RCA, much of the music is international, with a heavy preference for hip-hop. But if you want to hear some Thai pop music, the nightclubs on Sarasin east of Lumphini Park are a good option. Much smaller than RCA, Sarasin is easier to get to and a little less overwhelming if you're not used to the crowds.

Although the city has cleaned up its act a bit in recent years, there are still plenty of places where you'll be able to witness the seediness that gave Bangkok its reputation, including Phat Phong in Silom and Nana on Lower Sukhumvit. These places tend to cater to Western men, although women are welcome too.

What you spend on drinks will depend more on where you go than what you're drinking. The same beer you'll pay 200B for in your hotel bar will cost you as little as 50B if you drink it in one of the little shophouse bars on Phra Athit Road in Bang Lamphu. Nightclubs on Sukhumvit will generally charge admission of between 500B and 700B, which will include a couple of drinks. After that expect to spend around 200B for a beer and 250B and up for a cocktail.

Bangkok's reputation as a party town has been somewhat diminished in recent years with the advent of strict laws governing closing times. In Bangkok, most clubs and bars must close at 1 A.M. RCA, because it's exclusively a nightclub neighborhood, stays open until 2 A.M. Generally these rules are strictly enforced, although there are some exceptions, noted below. The legal age for entering a nightclub or bar is 20. Unless you look very young, you won't be asked for identification at smaller bars, however some of the larger nightclubs, including all of the clubs at RCA, require a government-issued ID (i.e., passport) regardless of how old you look. If you don't have one, you will be turned away.

In Bangkok the distinction between bar, nightclub, and live-music venue is blurry, and most places serving drinks will also sometimes have live music, even if it's just one guy singing and strumming a guitar. Likewise, many places also offer full Thai food menus for dinner if you're looking for a casual place to eat.

Finally, remember that Bangkok is a fast-moving city, and the most popular nightclubs today may be old news next year. Make sure to check whether the place you are going is still open, as clubs and especially bars close or change names frequently.

PHAT PHONG
พัฒนพงษ์

Originally a banana plantation, the two narrow side streets connecting Silom and Surawong Roads are the best-known red-light district in Bangkok. Packed full of massage parlors and go-go bars, with vendors selling pirated DVDs (not just X-rated either—these guys seem to have everything from the latest blockbuster movies to American TV series) and bar workers trying to lure you in for a "show," Phat Phong lives up to its notorious reputation.

The two side streets, Phat Phong I and Phat Phong II, have been owned by the Patpongpanich family since the 1960s. It wasn't until the Vietnam War, when U.S. troops came to Bangkok for R&R, that the family started renting out space to bars and clubs.

There are typical go-go bars that pull in anyone and everyone as well as boys-only clubs to attract gays and establishments with girls dressed in all sorts of strange costumes to attract the Japanese crowd. Despite all the sleaze, the area is very safe. Phat Phong also tries to attract those just looking for overpriced souvenirs. The Phat Phong Night Market, which opens up around sunset right in the middle of the clubs and bars and sells everything from Thai boxing regalia to hand-carved soap, has become so big in recent years it spills out onto Silom and Surawong Roads. It's a great place to window-shop, but prices tend to be inflated, and hard bargaining is a necessity.

THE OLD CITY

Despite seemingly being overrun by Western backpackers on extended vacations, Bang Lamphu and the surrounding area has some fun, vibrant bars featuring decent live music, cheap drinks, and friendly groups of Thai college students (thanks to its location right near

Thammasat University). Khao San Road is literally packed with places to go out, although many of them will be packed with fellow foreigners listening to Western music.

Bars

With a casual, relaxed vibe and outdoor seating, **Bar Bali** (58 Phra Athit Rd., tel. 02/629-0318, 6 P.M.–midnight daily) is the perfect place to have a drink after a long day of sightseeing. Art exhibits in addition to live music give the place a slightly hippie-chic feel, attracting students, young artists, and travelers. Just down the street, **Commé** (100/4–5 Phra Athit Rd., no phone, 6 P.M.–midnight daily), an open-air bar with seats spilling out onto the sidewalk, has walls lined with the work of local art students and boasts a collection of vintage motorcycles in the bar. A blend of artsy and casual, Commé is packed with much of the same crowd as Bar Bali.

Despite its name, **Hippie De Bar** (46 Khao San Rd., tel. 02/639-3508, 11 A.M.–1 A.M. daily) stands out as one of the cooler places to grab a drink on Khao San Road. Filled with kitschy objects and set in a courtyard just off the main strip, the two-story bar attracts a mixed crowd of local young adults and a few curious backpackers looking for a (slightly) quieter bar experience.

From the outside, **Molly Bar** (108 Soi Ram Buttri, tel. 02/629-4074, 2 P.M.–2 A.M. daily) looks just like many of the loud bars on neighboring Khao San Road. Once you step inside you'll see the difference—the clientele is more mixed and the music is mostly live Thai folk music. It's still pretty loud and crowded in there. If it's not too hot out, try to grab one of the few outdoor seats. You'll still be able to hear the music from inside.

Phranakorn Bar & Gallery (58/2 Ratchadamnoen Klang Rd., tel. 02/622-0282, 6 P.M.–1 A.M. daily) has three separate levels dedicated to a bar, an art gallery, and billiards, plus a rooftop from which you can gaze at the Golden Mount while enjoying a light meal. Despite offering everything you might possibly want in an evening under one roof (and above it), the bar is casual and inexpensive and just far enough from Khao San Road that you won't find too many other travelers hanging around.

Nightclubs

Right next to Democracy Monument, **Cafe Democ** (78 Ratchadamnoen Klang Rd., tel. 02/622-2571, 11:30 A.M.–1 A.M. Tues.–Sun., cover 100B) is one of Bangkok's best just-below-the-radar music venues. With local and international DJs spinning Wednesday–Sunday and walls covered in graffiti, the club has an underground feel to it. As is common in this part of town, the vibe is friendly and easygoing. For special events, the cover may be higher than the usual 100B.

999 West (100/5–6 Soi Ram Buttri, tel. 02/282-4459, 11 A.M.–2 A.M. daily), the former home of Susie Pub, one of Khao San Road's most popular and oldest live-music venues, hasn't changed too much since the old days. The music is still loud pop, the beer is still cold, and the place is still packed at night. This bar-nightclub attracts a mixed group of young locals, backpackers, and even expats, and it has a fun, relaxed atmosphere.

Gazebo Khao San (44 Jurapong Rd., www. gazebobkk.com, 7 P.M.–2 A.M. daily) is a big, popular club around the corner from Khao San Road and attracts foreign and Thai club goers looking for inexpensive drinks, loud live music, fun atmosphere, and lots of other people. It's not all crazy and crowded, though, as early in the evening you can hang out and enjoy a local band while smoking a hookah at one of their comfortable lounging tables. By midnight it's usually tough to find a spot quiet enough to carry on a conversation. The rooftop venue can get a little hot, but the solution might just be to wear a little less.

Live Music

If you visit 🅒 **Ad Here the 13th** (13 Samsen Rd., tel. 08/9769-4613, 5 P.M.–midnight daily), don't expect fancy drinks or trendy decor. This blues and jazz club on Samsen Road is really all about the music, which gets played live every

THE SEX INDUSTRY

Although prostitution in Thailand is prohibited, it's impossible not to notice the red-light districts, go-go bars, and sex workers (often referred to as "bar girls") populating many of the nightlife spots in Bangkok. The blind eye that authorities seem to turn to these activities has become something more like a full face mask. There are rarely crackdowns or arrests; neighborhoods such as Phat Phong, Nana, and Soi Cowboy seem to exist solely to cater to prurient interests; and there are no signs it's going anywhere.

Bangkok gained its notorious reputation during the Vietnam War, when the city became an R&R spot for U.S. servicemen on leave. It was during this period that Phat Phong went from a normal commercial neighborhood to one filled with massage parlors and hostess bars. Sex is still big business here, as is evident from the hordes of visitors who flock to these places on a nightly basis.

Dancers working in the go-go bars and strip clubs in Bangkok typically earn a salary of about 6,000B per month (about the same as a low-level civil servant, but less than half of what a secretary earns), which is augmented by tips and whatever else they can earn; the women working in bars earn significantly less. Most emigrated from Isan and other poorer, rural parts of Thailand looking for an opportunity to make more money, and they often support whole families back home from the money they earn.

The problem is not one solely created by foreigners, however. Prostitution existed in Thailand long before any Western influences arrived, and it flourishes in areas where there are no foreigners. Whether this is due to the money it generates, the permissive nature of Buddhism, or other cultural factors is up for debate. But the fact remains that, despite all indications to the contrary, it is illegal in Thailand.

© JOHN BROWN

It's impossible not to notice Bangkok's red light districts.

night by the house band and guest performers. There's barely room for the handful of tables and chairs for patrons, but somehow in-the-know music fans have been managing to squeeze themselves in for years.

CHINATOWN

Accessing the nightlife scene in Chinatown is a bit harder for visitors. Most signs are purely in Thai or Chinese, and waitstaff are not as accustomed to people speaking foreign languages as in other parts of the city. The bars are also far less concentrated in this area than on Sukhumvit or Silom. But if you persist, the options include karaoke bars, all-night snooker, and all sorts of open-air restaurants. Start on Yaowarat Road and work your way west down the road into the heart of it. Take time to venture off the main road to the backstreets, and ask local shopkeepers where you can find a beer or whiskey. You may be surprised when they offer up suggestions. Not a place for clubbing or for the typical bar scene, Yaowarat is more appropriate for nighttime strolling punctuated by the occasional cocktail down a side alley.

Live Music

With its animal-print seats, palm trees, and colonial decor, **Bamboo Bar** (48 Oriental Ave., tel. 02/659-9000, ext. 7690, 11 A.M.–1 A.M. Sun.–Thurs., 11 A.M.–2 A.M. Fri.–Sat.) in the Oriental Hotel may be playing to the romanticized image of the wealthy Western foreigner coming in for a cold drink after a long day in the colonies, but it somehow works as the perfect backdrop to some excellent live jazz. The small bar serves up great martinis too.

CENTRAL BANGKOK–SILOM AREA
Bars

If you just want to have a drink without lots of loud music or too many people around, the **Barbican** (9 Soi Thaniya, Skytrain: Sala Daeng, tel. 02/234-3590, www.greatbritish-pub.com, 11:30 A.M.–1 A.M. daily) is one of the quieter bars in the area, and just far enough away from Phat Phong that you won't have to

try to stealthily avoid touts offering Ping-Pong shows as you make your way into the bar. The Barbican is more like an English pub and serves a full menu of Thai and Western food as well. Here you'll often see young local and expat businesspeople grabbing a drink after work.

Billed as Asia's highest outdoor bar, **Moon Bar** (Banyan Tree Hotel, 21/100 S. Sathorn Rd., tel. 02/679-1200, 5 P.M.–1 A.M. daily) is a chance to enjoy a drink with a panoramic view of the city 61 stories up in the air. Take a seat on one of the comfortable lounge chairs and enjoy a tropical cocktail as you take in Bangkok from the sky.

There are two nightlife spots named Tawan Daeng, both worth visiting but completely different. A little outside of the Silom area, past Rama III Road, is **Tawan Daeng Beer Hall** (462 Narathiwat Rd., tel. 02/678-1114, 4:30 P.M.–1 A.M. daily), a gigantic music and drinking spot that attracts large groups of mostly locals for the inexpensive beer. There's live music on some nights, but the main attraction is just the people-watching. (The other Tawan Daeng is described under *Bars* in the *Central Bangkok—Upper Sukhumvit* section.)

One of those small, special bars that can't quite be explained, tiny **Wong's** (27/3 Soi Sri Bamphen, no phone, open until late daily) is something of a Bangkok institution and attracts a mixed crowd of locals, expats, and visitors for late-night drinking and hanging out. The owner, whose late father opened the bar, has the largest collection of old VHS music videos in the country, and they are always playing in the background of this simple, relaxed bar. Wong's is magically immune to regular closing hours, so many people stop in after other bars have closed. Whether it's due to the mandatory tequila shots you'll have to drink if you mess up a game of Jenga or the late hour, be warned that it's nearly impossible to leave Wong's sober. To get here, ask the taxi driver to take you to Soi Ngam Duphli off of Rama IV Road near Lumphini Park. Soi Sri Bamphen is the first left off the *soi*, and Wong's is in a small shophouse on the left side.

LADYBOYS

Dressed to perfection, with silky, shiny hair down to her shoulders, a miniskirt up to her thighs, and an enchanting smile accentuated with just the right touch of makeup, the sexy, ultrafeminine waitress serving you dinner is getting stares from every guy in the room. On closer inspection, the waitress seems a little taller than the average woman, her hips a little slimmer, her presentation a little more perfected . . . her voice a little deeper. Could it be that the woman everyone is looking at is actually a man? In Bangkok, the answer is an unqualified "yes."

Though no one knows the exact figures, it's safe to say Bangkok is home to thousands of *katoey* or ladyboys – men who either live like women, are in the process of undergoing gender reassignment, or have completed the transformation. *Katoey* take women's names and will always use the feminine particle *ka* instead of *kap* when speaking.

While there are cross-dressers and trans-gendered people all over the world, the extent of the phenomena is unique to Thailand. Homosexuality is generally well tolerated, especially in the big cities, and won't be viewed as out of the ordinary by many people. Open transsexuality, still taboo in many cultures, is

also far more accepted here, and more commonplace in Bangkok than in any other city in the world. Discrimination still exists, but you are likely to see *katoey* working in retail shops, offices, and hotels and restaurants.

Some of the biggest and most prestigious hospitals in Thailand offer a myriad of procedures to transform men into women. As a result, many of the ladyboys in the city are amazingly beautiful.

Despite the widespread practice and general level of acceptance, it would be inaccurate to say that the life of a *katoey* is not filled with challenges. The movie *Beautiful Boxer,* based on the life of *muay Thai* champion Parinya Charoenphol, is a wonderful, heartbreaking, and uplifting story about a young boy in the provinces who was born believing he was meant to be a woman. By chance he turns to kickboxing as a way to earn enough money to become a woman, but discovers that he loves the sport and remains a fighter through his transition. The international award-winning, beautifully shot, and well-produced film chronicles his emotional journey from he to she set against a backdrop of kickboxing rounds and cabaret performances.

Nightclubs

Met Bar (27 S. Sathorn Rd., tel. 02/234-3279, 8 P.M.–2 A.M. daily, no cover), with its sleek, modern interior, comfortable lounging seats, and expensive drinks, is for the rich and beautiful of all ages. The club plays a mix of international music for a mixed international and local crowd. It is for members only, so it never feels like you're in a sardine can, but that doesn't mean you can't get in. Metropolitan Hotel guests and people who've eaten at Cy'an next door are welcome, and the doormen are known to let in others who look the part.

Off crowded Silom is **The Balcony** (86–88 Silom Soi 4, tel. 02/235-5891, www.balcony-pub.com, 5:30 P.M.–1 A.M. daily, no cover), a fun, friendly, sometimes zany nightclub that

can get packed on Friday and Saturday nights. In addition to cheap drinks and a very friendly staff, the club also has events every month, including a Pink Olympics and costume nights. Like most of the nightclubs along Soi 4, The Balcony caters primarily to a gay crowd but is in no way exclusive.

On the same street is **Telephone** (114/11 Silom Soi 4, tel. 02/625-3333, www.telephonepub.com, 6 P.M.–1 A.M. daily), named for the telephones at every table that patrons can use to call other tables. OK, it's a bit of a fabulous gay scene, but even if that's not your thing, it's a fun place to people-watch and dance the night away. The upscale **Sphinx** (100 Silom Soi 4, www.sphinxbangkok.com, 6 P.M.–2 A.M. daily), just down the street, attracts a more refined crowd of locals and foreigners who are more interested in hanging out and sipping drinks than jumping up and down to loud music. The loungey, nicely decorated downstairs invites unwinding but doesn't mean it isn't a fun place. If you're looking for a slightly more energetic evening, head upstairs to Pharaohs, their karaoke club.

CENTRAL BANGKOK–PLOENCHIT AND LOWER SUKHUMVIT
Bars

Tucked into a little side *soi* off of Lang Suan, **Cafe Trio** (Soi Mahatek Luang 3, tel. 08/1988-3762, 6 P.M.–1 A.M. daily) is a relaxed oasis in the sea of loud music and crowded clubs that is Bangkok's nightlife scene. Lovely and dynamic Patti, one of the owners (the name refers to the three sisters that own the bar), is usually busy mixing drinks behind the bar but always has time for a little conversation. Most nights you'll even be able to get a comfortable seat below one of Patti's pastels, which decorate the bar.

If getting glammed up and hitting the bars for a big night out with the city's young and restless is what you're looking for, the **Foreign Correspondents Club of Thailand** (Penthouse, Maneeya Center, 518/3 Ploenchit Rd., tel. 02/652-0580, food service noon–2:30 P.M. and 6–9 P.M. Mon.–Fri., bar until 1 A.M. Mon.–Fri., www.fccthai.com) is not the place for you. Populated with foreign and local journalists drinking beer at the bar, which looks like it was plucked from a 1980s television set, the FCCT is more a place to go for a quiet drink and some good conversation about politics or current events in Southeast Asia. There are also revolving photography exhibits lining the walls and frequent talks; be sure to check the website for the schedule.

Live Music

With multiple floors and live jazz and blues every night, **Brown Sugar** (231/20 Sarasin Rd., tel. 02/250-1826, 6 P.M.–1 A.M. daily, no cover) is a perennial favorite place among Bangkok's urban professionals to enjoy a whiskey and listen to music. Located on the edge of Lumphini Park at the Sarasin junction, there

© JOHN BROWN

children selling garlands in the evening

are also a handful of other clubs and bars on the strip, catering to everything from '70s disco to techno and electronica.

A little less urban professional is **Saxophone** (3/8 Phayathai Rd., Skytrain: Victory Monument, tel. 02/246-5472, www.saxophone-pub.com, 6 P.M.–3 A.M. daily, no cover), with live jazz and blues every night. The place is always packed with people from all walks of life, and there's a chilled-out vibe. Like most bars, Saxophone serves up standard Thai food too.

Nightclubs

With its futuristic-retro design, **Syn Bar** (Nai Lert Park Hotel, 2 Wireless Rd., tel. 02/253-0123, 9 A.M.–1 A.M. daily, no cover) is what the set of *Star Trek* would have looked like if the crew of the Enterprise was made up of supermodels. Set inside the otherwise staid Nai Lert Park Hotel, the bar has a small DJ booth, sitting pods suspended from the ceiling by chains, and carpets that sparkle thanks to embedded lights. Small for a nightclub, on some nights the place can be quiet, while on others it's packed with a chic, young international crowd. Welcome to the future, and a fabulous future it is.

Set in the middle of the embassy district, across the street from the Nai Lert Park Hotel and Syn Bar is **The Pent** (31/1 Wireless Rd., tel. 02/655-3890, www.bkcoolclub.com, 6 P.M.–1 A.M. daily, no cover), a strange mix of Playboy Mansion and Thai-pop music hall. There are multiple rooms and floors, pool tables, bars, and lots of female dancers, although this is not a typical go-go bar. Few Western travelers seem to visit here, although it's conveniently located.

Club Culture (Si Ayuttaya Rd. across from the Siam City Hotel, Skytrain: Phayathai, tel. 02/653-7216, www.club-culture-bkk.com, 9 P.M.–2 A.M. daily, no cover) was opened in 2007 by some of the same people who opened the now closed but much-loved Astra on RCA. Club Culture has plenty of international and local DJs spinning house, funk, and electronica, and it pulls in a diverse, hip crowd who seem to share a passion for music.

Sukhumvit is really the center of nightlife in Bangkok, and it seems as though almost every building houses a bar or nightclub on one floor or another. Many of these establishments cater to a mixed crowd of Thais and resident foreigners. Soi 11 is a favorite street for the younger hipster crowd and the expats. It's a bar, it's a restaurant, it's a bed, all set in a futuristic-looking shiny metal pod on stilts in the middle of Bangkok: Despite the apparent design schizophrenia and identity crisis, **Bed Supper Club** (26 Sukhumvit Soi 11, Skytrain: Nana, tel. 02/651-3537, www.bedsupperclub.com, 8 P.M.–1 A.M. daily, cover 400B), with its nightclub on one side and restaurant-lounge on the other, is one of the most popular nightclubs in the city. The exceptionally good-looking waitstaff serves drinks and meals to patrons sitting on beds. If you're with a group, reserve a bed in advance so you can get down to some trance music, techno, or hip-hop and then chill out and sip your drink horizontally. The club also features often strange but always entertaining performance art most nights of the week.

Just down the street is **Q Bar** (34 Sukhumvit Soi 11, tel. 02/252-3274, www.qbarbangkok.com, 8 P.M.–late daily, cover varies), a big hit among expat men and a slightly older local population, although it also attracts a very mixed crowd. The bar is looking quite tattered compared to the early 2000s, when it was sometimes referred to as one of the coolest bars in Southeast Asia, but resident DJs spinning lots of hip-hop and live-music performances still pack the place nearly every night of the week. The bar also pulls in a crowd of single women whose reason for being there is open to speculation.

CENTRAL BANGKOK– UPPER SUKHUMVIT
Bars

The nightlife scene in Upper Sukhumvit is dominated by Thong Lor (Soi 55) and the surrounding side streets. In recent years the neighborhood has become packed with bars, pubs, restaurants, and nightclubs catering to the young and trendy, many of whom live in the area. In the center of Thong Lor and one of Bangkok's trendiest night-out spots, the hip, romantic **Witch's Tavern** (Soi Thong Lor between Thong Lor 8 and 10, tel. 02/391-9791, www.witch-tavern.com, 11 A.M.–2 A.M. daily) is a combo wine bar, live-music venue, and restaurant housed in a Victorian-style building. There's also a location on Soi Ruam Ruedi in the Lower Sukhumvit area.

WTF (7 Sukhumvit Soi 51, www.wtfbangkok.com, daily 6 P.M.–1 A.M.) stands for "wonderful Thai friendships" (or does it?), but this trendy little bar in Thong Lor could as easily be found in Brooklyn, San Francisco, or Berlin. Despite the off-the-charts hipness factor, the proprietors are friendly and unpretentious, the drinks creative and delicious, and the other patrons typically friendly and laid-back. The bar menu is ambitious but doesn't quite deliver; have dinner at Soul Food Mahanakorn around the corner first instead. The bar is also home to an art gallery and performance space. Check the website for current exhibits and events.

If you are up for a fun, culturally enlightening evening out, the other **Tawan Daeng** (484 Pattanakarn Rd., tel. 02/717-2320, 6 P.M.–2 A.M. daily) features Thai country music, Isan food, and a very local atmosphere. The restaurant-bar-nightclub is in a simple house that looks like it belongs in the countryside, and if the image of Thai cowboys out on the Isan plateau pops into your mind, you're in the right place. *Phleng phuea chiwit* means songs for life, a style of Thai folk music that you'll be able to hear performed live, and you'll also hear *molam* music, sung in the Isan dialect with traditional Thai musical instruments. Once in a while you might even catch the famous Aed Carabao (called the Bob Dylan of Thailand) performing to a generally very friendly and upbeat crowd. There's also dancing and singing, and later in the evening the Mekhong whiskey starts flowing, which usually helps dissolve any language barrier you may face, although no amount of whiskey will prepare most Western men for the massage that awaits them when they head to the toilet (it's totally aboveboard and administered by middle-aged men, but still disconcerting to most who have not experienced it before). You'll need to take a taxi to get here, but you can take the Skytrain to Phra Khanong, then grab a taxi from there. Every taxi driver in Bangkok knows where the place is.

Nightclubs

Demo (Thong Lor Soi 10, tel. 02/711-6970, 8 A.M.–2 A.M. daily), an arty, funky music venue, seems to be reaching for edgy but still feels very mainstream thanks to its location in trendy Thong Lor. Still, the club brings in tons of live music and guest DJs spinning house and techno music. The crowd, unsurprisingly, is mostly hip, affluent young locals and expats, and drinks are a little on the pricey side, although they're good. Like most other clubs in the city, things don't really get going till about midnight. Flip-flops or really casual clothes will keep you from getting in.

Across the leafy parking lot from Muse, **Funky Villa** (Thong Lo Soi 10, just behind Muse, tel. 08/5253-2000, 6 P.M.–2 A.M. daily) has much the same *hi-so* (high society) crowd but a little more of a chilled-out atmosphere. For music, you have a combination of live bands and music, and cocktails and beer are pretty reasonable at around 150B.

RCA
อาร์ซีเอ

About 10 minutes by taxi from Asok is RCA, a 2.5-kilometer entertainment zone that fills up with a mostly college-age crowd Friday and Saturday nights. Royal Crown Avenue—its official name, although no one uses it—is nightclub central, and if you're looking for an evening out, it's a great place to go and wander in and out of the various clubs and bars, most of which do not charge an entrance fee. There's not much else going on here, which is why the establishments are allowed to close at 2 A.M. instead of 1 A.M.

Nightclubs

Clubs come and go frequently, but **Slim Flix** (29/18-21 Soi Soonvijai, Rama IX Rd., tel. 02/203-0377, 8 P.M.–2 A.M. daily, no cover) seems to have stood the test of time. It has been open for a few years, a longer shelf life than most venues in this neighborhood. The club is huge, with a mezzanine overlooking the funky modern lounge furniture, but chances are you won't be able to see any of it anyway. After 11 P.M. the Slim side of the joint is usually packed full of kids dancing to hiphop and R&B. Right next door is **Flix,** just as big and crazy as Slim except the DJs are spinning mostly house music. If you can make your way past the crowds, check out the restrooms here. They've brought in live musicians lest you miss getting your groove on while you wait in line.

Route66 (29/33 Soi Soonvijai, Rama IX Rd., tel. 02/203-0407, www.route66club.com, 9 P.M.–2 A.M. daily, no cover), right down the street, features live performers, from Korean hip-hop artists to Linkin Park. It is another crazy, packed scene on the weekends.

At the far end of the road is **Zeta** (29/67–69 Soi Soonvijai, Rama IX Rd., tel. 02/203-0994, www.zetabangkok.com, 9 P.M.–2 A.M. daily, no cover), a live-music venue with pool tables and dancing. You might notice that almost everyone at Zeta is a woman: It's a lesbian club.

Entertainment and Events

THE ARTS
Performing Arts Centers
Thailand's main performing arts center is the **Thailand Cultural Center** (Ratchadapisek Rd., subway: Thailand Cultural Center, tel. 02/247-0028, 500B and up), a complex with multiple auditoriums and an outdoor amphitheater. The center has opera, classical music, modern dance, and other performances featuring both Thai artists and visiting international performers.

Next to Wat Arun and across the river from the Grand Palace is the **Patravadi Theatre** (69/1 Soi Wat Rakhang, Arun Amarin Rd., tel. 02/412-7287, www.patravaditheatre.com), an intimate open-air theater and center for performing arts offering traditional Thai dance and music performances as well as contemporary dance, music, poetry, and films every night of the week. The Patravadi Theatre also has a restaurant and offers dinner performances most evenings as well as occasional dance and other performance demonstrations.

Sala Chalerm Krung (66 Chalerm Krung Rd., tel. 02/222-0434) is an amazing art deco–style theater that was built in the 1930s as a gift from King Rama VII to the people. The theater now hosts a number of cultural events, including regular performances of stories from the Ramakien with elaborately costumed, masked *khon* dancers. Performance schedules change, but currently there are Friday- and Saturday-evening performances of *Hanuman the Mighty,* the story of a monkey who becomes a warrior. Tickets cost 1,000–1,200B and can be purchased online at www.thaiticketmajor.com. If you can't make it for a performance, you can also drop in to the theater during the day to see an exhibition on Thai theater and performing arts.

A little touristy, the performances at **Siam Niramit** (19 Tiamruammit Rd., subway: Thailand Cultural Center, tel. 02/649-9222, www.siamniramit.com, dinner 5:30 P.M. daily, show 8 P.M. daily, show 1,500B, dinner 290B) nonetheless are an entertaining and easy way to learn some Thai history and have fun at the same time. During this spectacular pageant with amazing sets, special effects, and flying characters, you'll learn a little about prehistoric Thailand, a little about the Lanna Kingdom, a little about Ayutthaya, and even some information about Buddhism.

Film
While the proliferation of bootleg DVDs—of even the newest films that you can't legitimately buy yet—in the city has put a real

BANGKOK FESTIVALS AND EVENTS

Thailand's capital city becomes even more vibrant during these annual festivals and events. Many are scheduled according to the lunar calendar, so dates change from year to year. Make sure to check with the Tourism Authority of Thailand (1600 New Petchaburi Rd., Bangkok, tel. 02/250-5500, www.tourismthailand. org, 8:30 A.M.-4:30 P.M. daily) for specific dates when you are visiting.

JANUARY-FEBRUARY
Chinese New Year: The large Chinese Thai population in Bangkok ensures a vibrant and festive celebration, which includes song and dance exhibitions in Yaowarat. Although everyone seems to be in on the celebration (you'll find moon cakes everywhere), services and business opening hours are generally not disrupted.

FEBRUARY-MARCH
Magha Puja Day: According to Buddhist teachings, this holiday commemorates a day in the life of the Buddha when 1,250 of his disciples gathered spontaneously under a full moon to hear him lay down the principles by which they should spread his teachings. The biggest celebration is at Sanam Luang, where thousands of monks gather to hold an evening processional, meditate, and offer blessings.

APRIL
Songkran: Bangkok goes wild during this traditional new year celebration. For three full days, locals and visitors pour out into the streets to pour water on each other. The ritual was probably originally intended to symbolically wash away sins and bad luck. Nowadays, especially around the Khao San Road, Silom, and Nana areas, people bring out big water guns and buckets of water, so expect to get soaked. If you're visiting during this time, some businesses will be closed.

SEPTEMBER-OCTOBER
Kin Jay: For nine days each year, vegetarian food dominates the city and special vegetarian fare can be found everywhere, from street stalls to high-end restaurants. Even carnivores will enjoy trying their favorite Thai dishes without meat. The festival has roots in Chinese traditions and is most strongly practiced in Yaowarat. Look for the yellow and red signs adorning restaurants and street stalls.

OCTOBER-NOVEMBER
Loi Krathong: One of Thailand's most beautiful celebrations takes place along the Chao Phraya, where thousands of people launch small floats covered in flowers and candles. The floats, or *krathong*, symbolize the letting-go of bad luck and bad feelings, and the holiday is usually celebrated by couples. The best place to watch the festivities is near Phra Athit Pier, where groups line up along the river to release their *krathong*. Don't worry if you didn't bring your own float; there will be vendors selling them near the river.

---

dent in the movie-theater business, there are still theaters catering to those who want to experience a movie in a cinema. In Bangkok, moviegoing is more of an experience than just watching a film. First, in the big theaters you can get VIP tickets for about three times the price of regular seats (around 600B), and instead of watching the movie in a regular chair, you'll find love seats, recliners, blankets, and slippers. Second, no matter what seats you buy, every movie will begin with a film homage to the king. The lights go out, the music starts, and everybody stands to watch a short film about the king's good works in Thailand.

Don't worry about getting tickets too far in advance, as there are often multiple screenings of the same films. If one is sold out, just wait 20 minutes for the next one to start.

Most movie theaters in Thailand show films dubbed in Thai, although many of the larger cinemas in Bangkok offer original-language films or subtitles instead. The website www.movieseer.com has film listings with the language indicated.

There are cinemas in every major mall, but the **IMAX Theatre** (tel. 02/515-5555) on the 5th floor of Siam Paragon gets the award for the swankiest. Across the street are a number of cinemas playing a variety of films from Asian art house to Thai horror to American blockbuster. The **Scala** (Siam Sq. Soi 1, Rama I Rd., tel. 02/251-2861) and the **Lido** (tel. 02/252-6498) next door often play films from other parts of Asia as well as bigger international films.

Cabaret

In a city where cross-dressing and gender reassignment are so common that most people don't even notice it, it's no surprise there are a number of over-the-top entertaining transvestite shows. **Calypso Cabaret** (Asia Hotel, 296 Phayathai Rd., Skytrain: Ratchathewi, tel. 02/653-3960, www.calypsocabaret.com, shows 8:15 P.M. and 9:45 P.M. nightly, 1,000B) is a spectacle of sequins and ostrich feathers, with 50 performers lip-synching, singing, and dancing to music from the West, Japan, and Korea.

Mambo Cabaret (59/28 Rama III Rd., tel. 02/294-7381, shows 7:15 P.M., 8:30 P.M., and 10 P.M. nightly, 1,000B) moved from its central Sukhumvit location to another theater south of the Silom area. The performance is professional and entertaining, with transvestites lip-synching and dancing in colorful costumes to international hits, show tunes, and an occasional pop song.

Sports and Recreation

Bangkok isn't known as a particularly sporting city, but there are some great public parks, running opportunities, yoga centers, and sports competitions either to take part in or observe.

PUBLIC PARKS

Sweltering heat and broken sidewalks don't give rise to lots of outdoor activities; still, there are a few parks in the center of the city where you can get some exercise and enjoy some fresh air. All parks listed here have restroom facilities, snack bars, and small outdoor restaurants serving local food if you get hungry after your workout.

Tobacco Monopoly
โรงงานยาสูบ

Although you can't notice it from the main roads, the Tobacco Monopoly (184 Rama IV Rd., tel. 02/253-0353) takes up a large swath of land from the south side of Lower Sukhumvit to Rama IV. This large park is still partly a tobacco processing center, and at times you'll be able to smell the fragrant leaves, but most people come for the tennis and badminton courts, soccer pitches, and open green space.

The best places to enter the park are at the end of Sukhumvit Soi 4 or on Rama IV near the Khlong Toei subway station. Visitors are welcome to use the facilities, although it may be difficult to communicate with the Thai-speaking staff. The park is also home to a lunch market near the Rama IV entrance.

Bencha Kitti Park
สวนเบญจกิตติ

Facing Ratchadapisek Road is the pristine Bencha Kitti Park, which is so well manicured it almost feels inappropriate to be sweating there. The center of the park is an artificial lake, and most people who visit like to run or cycle around it on the well-maintained path (if you come at midday, there is not a lot of shade surrounding the water, making for a hot and bright workout). Toward the back of the park are small playgrounds for children and a meditation area.

Chatuchak Park

Distracted by the famous massive weekend market next door, most visitors to Bangkok forget that there's also a large outdoor park sharing the same name. Chatuchak Park (Pahayotin Rd., Skytrain: Mo Chit, subway: Chatuchak Park, 5 A.M.–9 P.M. daily) is a pretty green park with a well-maintained path for walkers, runners, or bikers and a couple of artificial lakes where visitors can rent paddle-boats. There are also play areas for children and some exercise stations with bars and equipment for those looking for a workout. On weekends, this park is very popular with families.

RUNNING

Running or jogging through the streets of Bangkok is likely to earn you stares and an occasional nip from one of the city's many stray dogs. You'll also spend a lot of time weaving in and out of the myriad of street-food stalls, motorcycle taxis, and pedestrians. An adventure for sure, but if you're looking to pick up speed, it's difficult in the city.

The public parks are well suited for running, although if you want to go a greater distance (Lumphini Park's loop is only 2.5 kilometers), the **Green Path** that connects Lumphini Park to the Tobacco Monopoly and Bencha Kitti Park offers an opportunity for longer runs. The total distance, with a loop in Lumphini Park and a loop in Bencha Kitti Park, is around 8.5 kilometers; aside from one spot where you'll have to leave Lumphini Park and get out onto Wireless Road to connect to the path, you'll mostly be able to avoid traffic and other obstacles.

Hash House Harriers (www.bangkokhhh.com), the irreverent international running group, has long weekend hashes that generally take you just outside of the city, where you'll be able to both see some countryside and get some exercise. Check the website for schedules, and be prepared to drink some beer afterward.

THAI BOXING

Agile young men square off in a ring, using punches, kicks, elbows, and knees to take each other down as fans and gamblers yell in the stands and soft traditional music plays in the background. This is *muay Thai,* frequently

muay Thai, a sometimes brutal, sometimes elegant sport

© SUZANNE NAM

referred to as Thai boxing, a full-contact martial art that has been practiced in Southeast Asia since at least the 16th century. Although the precise history of the sport is unclear, it is at least known that during King Naresuan's reign, *muay Thai* was used in battles against enemies (the Burmese at that time). It slowly evolved from a skill reserved for soldiers to a sport embraced by all classes, and a couple of hundred years later King Prachao Sua was said to have loved the sport so much he often fought incognito in village contests. Laos, Burma, Cambodia, and Malaysia all have similar forms of kickboxing, but in Thailand it has become a national sport, surrounded by tradition and ceremony. Each match begins with both fighters performing a *wai kru,* a languid, elaborate boxing dance accompanied by musicians playing wind instruments in the background.

While the graceful moves of the fighters and ceremony that starts every match gives the impression that the sport is a peaceful one, make no mistake that what you are watching is a brutal sport. Although overwhelmingly popular, the sport was banned in Thailand in the 1920s and then only allowed again a decade later after a series of rules and regulations intended to protect fighters from death was instituted. Knockouts and blood are not uncommon in the ring, and every year there are accidental deaths during the matches that take place all over the country.

Outside the ring is a whole other bit of action worth watching, especially if the sight of the sport itself is too much to bear. Wagering on the fights is not uncommon. Spectators yell, shout, and place bets with bookies who seem to be in all places at once, amazingly adept at paying attention to the crowd and the match and writing down the bets at breakneck speed on small slips of paper.

Lumphini Stadium (Rama IV Rd., subway: Lumphini, tel. 02/252-8765, fights 6:30 P.M. Tues. and Fri., 5 P.M. and 8:30 P.M. Sat., 500–1,500B) and **Ratchadamnoen Stadium** (Ratchadamnoen Nok Ave., tel. 02/281-4205, fights 6:30 P.M. Sun.–Mon. and Wed.–Thurs., 500–1,500B) are both regarded as among the best in the country. If you want to go, the boxing stadium seems to be the one place in Bangkok where locals and foreigners are strictly segregated, and you'll end up paying about four times as much for your ticket as someone from Thailand. Between both stadiums, there are fights every night of the week.

AEROBICS

Just after 6 P.M. every night there are free outdoor aerobics sessions at many of the city's public parks including **Lumphini Park.** It is a bit bizarre to see sometimes hundreds of people dressed in anything from spandex to business suits gathered en masse to dance in synch (or as near as possible) to loud, tinny pop music, but the lessons are free and you don't need to sign up. Just join the group and start moving.

THAI MASSAGE AND SPAS

Thai massage, the vigorous, energizing massage where the therapist uses his or her hands, legs, knees, and feet to push and pull your body, has been described as doing yoga without

using your own energy. Unless you have a back or sports injury or are squeamish about massages in general, it's an experience you should try while visiting Thailand. When you arrive for your massage, you'll be given a set of fresh, loose pajamas to change into; the massage will usually take place on a mat on the floor. There are probably hundreds of small shops in the city offering the service for as little as 300B for a 90-minute session.

Bangkok is also full of high-end full-service spas offering Thai massage, oil massage, facials, and even acupuncture or Botox treatments at some. By Thai standards, prices at these spas are quite expensive, but if you're coming from the United States, you'll find that the price of a one-hour massage at home will get you a full day of pampering. All of the luxury hotels in the city have spa services; here are some stand-alone spas to try. Make sure to make an appointment in advance unless otherwise noted.

Being Spa (88 Sukhumvit Soi 51, Skytrain: Thong Lor, tel. 02/662-6171, www.beingspa.com, 10 A.M.–10 P.M. daily, 1-hour massage 1,400B) is located in an old Thai wooden house with pretty gardens. In addition to massage treatments, the spa offers deep-cleansing facials, body scrubs, and detox wraps. Although the address is Soi 51, the spa is actually off the *soi* (to the left if you are coming from Sukhumvit Road) and can be a little tricky to find; the spa can arrange pick up from the Skytrain station.

Bliss Spa (1747/9 Chan Rd., near Sathorn Rd. and Narathiwat Rd., tel. 02/287-3439, www.blissthai.com, 10 A.M.–8:30 P.M., 1-hour massage 1,000B) is a relaxed, pampering-focused spa that would seem as appropriate in Southern California as it does in Bangkok's Sathorn neighborhood. The spa offers facials, body scrubs, and oil massages and also has a little café on the premises selling coffee, smoothies, salads, and sandwiches.

Coran Spa (27/1–2 Sukhumvit Soi 13, Skytrain: Nana, tel. 02/651-1588, www.coran-bangkok.com, 11 A.M.–10 P.M. daily, 1-hour massage 1,200B), on a green expanse of gated grounds just a few minutes' walk from busy Sukhumvit Road, is a beautiful boutique spa. The facility is spotless, modern, and airy but not sterile. There's also a small organic outdoor café open until 6 P.M. daily with free Wi-Fi. Next door is a traditional massage training center run by the same folks, so you can expect not only pampering but professional treatments. Expect to pay around 5,000B for four hours of treatments. The spa will arrange a driver to pick you up at any nearby address.

Due to its convenient location, reasonable prices, and professional staff, **Divana Spa** (7 Sukhumvit Soi 25, Skytrain: Asok, tel. 02/661-6784, www.divanaspa.com, 11 A.M.– 11 P.M. daily, last appt. 9 P.M., 100-minute massage 1,450B) has been a favorite of locals and expats since it opened in 2002. Despite being just a few minutes from Asok, the spa is tucked away on a quiet side street, and the ambience is relaxing and luxuriant. Expect most of the regular treatments here, but if you're new to Thai massage, try the "East West Allure" treatment, a hybrid of Thai massage and oil massage.

Perhaps the best-value spa in Bangkok is **Health Land** (120 N. Sathorn Rd., tel. 02/637-8883, and 96/1 Sukhumvit Soi 63, tel. 02/392-2233, www.healthlandspa.com, 9 A.M.–11 P.M. daily, 2-hour Thai massage 450B), with four locations in the greater Bangkok area and one in Pattaya. The spas are located in large stand-alone structures and although not luxurious are nicely decorated, clean, and professional. Health Land has been around for many years, and what makes it continue to do so well despite all the competition is the professionalism of the staff and the amazingly reasonable pricing. In addition to Thai massage, treatments include body scrubs, aromatherapy oil massage, and facials. The spas are open until 11 P.M., and you can often walk in without an appointment.

Lavana Spa (4 Sukhumvit Soi 12, Skytrain:

Asok or Nana, tel. 02/229-4510, www.lavana-bangkok.com, 9 A.M.–11:30 P.M. daily) is a serious, professional spa for with scores of treatment rooms, a variety of services and treatments, and probably hundreds of visitors per day. The two-hour Thai massage, at 700B, is a bargain. There are also facials, scrubs, and wraps available as well as half-day and full-day packages. Big tour groups sometimes book here, so make sure to call ahead or you may be turned away.

Potalai Thai Wellness Center (28 Soi Yothinpatta 3, Pradimanuthum Rd., tel. 02/508-1238, www.potalia.com, 90-minute massage 1,200B) is a massive, beautifully decorated compound a little outside the center of the city offering every imaginable treatment at reasonable prices. There is also a spa café where you can sample healthy Thai cuisine. This is a very popular spa with tour groups, so make sure to make an appointment beforehand.

Stepping into the **S Medical Spa** (2/2 Bhakdi Bldg., Wireless Rd., in front of the Nai Lert Park Hotel, Skytrain: Ploenchit, tel. 02/253-1010, www.smedspa.com, 1-hour massage 1,400B) feels a little more serious and professional than indulgent. Here the focus is on holistic health, and you'll be able to consult with a doctor about antiaging treatments, get acupuncture treatments, and even try a little laser skin treatment. If you just want to relax, you can do that too, with one of the massage, scrub, or wrap treatments offered.

Thann Sanctuary (Gaysorn Mall, 3rd Fl., Skytrain: Chit Lom, tel. 02/656-1424, 10 A.M.–8 P.M. daily, 90 minute massage 2,200B), opened by the makers of Thailand's wildly popular Thann spa and home products, is a high-end luxurious indulgence. Many of the massage, body, and facial treatments involve the use of their signature herbal scents. When you're finished, stop at the Thann Native Tea Room on the second floor for a cup of herbal tea.

Shopping

With abundant markets, street stalls on every corner, and giant malls opening up all the time, Bangkok is a shopper's dream. Whether you're looking for international brands or inexpensive souvenirs to take home, nearly every neighborhood has something to offer.

SHOPPING AREAS
◖ Siam Square

Siam Square and the surrounding area is the city's shopping heart, and you'll find the biggest malls here along with Siam Square itself, a cute shopping area just next door to Chulalongkorn University with lots of inexpensive shops catering to students and plenty of places to eat, snack, or grab a cup of coffee. As of 2011, part of Siam Square is being upgraded and renovated, but many of the small shops will remain for the foreseeable future, and smaller stands selling inexpensive clothes and accessories have opened around the construction area. There are a couple of more

upscale boutiques here too, including **It's Happened to Be a Closet** (266/3 Siam Sq. Soi 3, tel. 02/658-4696, 11 A.M.–9 P.M. daily). This unique, offbeat shop, owned by a former designer at one of the big local fashion houses, boasts a collection of vaguely vintage, dramatic handmade pieces. Many of the pieces are one of a kind, and sometimes you'll catch one of the seamstresses at work at the sewing machine upstairs. The store is worth visiting even if you're not looking for any clothing. Designed like the inside of a (very large, three-story) closet, it also has a small café that also sells pastries.

If you're looking for cheaper stuff, take a look at the stalls that have recently sprung up around the construction site. There are plenty of sellers offering trendy 200B pairs of shoes, funky earrings for 80B, and other fun, disposable fashion.

If you want the hectic, crowded feeling of a market with the benefit of air-conditioning and escalators, spend a few hours at **MBK** (444

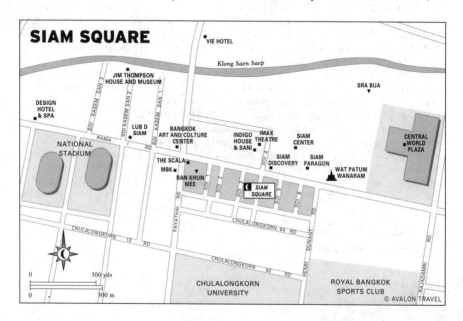

Phayathai Rd., Skytrain: National Stadium, 10 A.M.–10 P.M. daily). The eight-floor mall is packed full of clothing stores, cheap shoes, knockoff leather goods, jewelry, and even electronics. The clothes being sold at the stalls on the ground floor are about the same quality as the stuff you'll find in most markets, although the prices can be a little bit higher. If you're in need of a mobile phone, this is the most convenient place to get one. The fourth floor has literally hundreds of small vendors selling used mobile phones, and you can pick one up for as little as 1,500B. For good deals on digital cameras and accessories, check out **Sunny Camera** (tel. 02/686-3597) on the third floor for Nikon equipment and **Big Camera** (tel. 02/686-3503) on the fourth floor for mostly Canon stuff. Try to avoid the shops on the sixth floor selling souvenirs; prices are generally significantly higher than you'll find elsewhere.

Across the street from MBK are the **Siam Center Mall** and the **Siam Discovery Mall** (989 Rama I Rd., Skytrain: Siam, tel. 02/658-1000, www.siampiwat.com). Siam Center has nearly all of the big Thai designers represented but is also home to plenty of more wallet-friendly clothing and shoe shops. Siam Discovery, connected to Siam Center by a shared courtyard, has mostly mid-range international brands but is home to some great Thai shops too, including **Doi Tung by Mae Fah Luang** (tel. 02/658-0424, 11 A.M.–8 P.M. Mon.–Fri.), part of one of the humanitarian projects of Her Majesty the late Princess Mother, which carries housewares products, furniture, and textiles that are consistently well made and beautifully designed, and a **Thann** (tel. 02/243-2989, 11 A.M.–8 P.M. daily), which carries high-end Thai bath and body products.

This neighborhood is also home to Bangkok's most upscale shopping mall, **Siam Paragon.** Although it's right across the street from the funky, inexpensive shops on Siam Square, Paragon manages to remain a little oasis of high-end shopping surrounded by markets and cheap malls. There are the usual international boutiques, including Prada, Jimmy

a Bangkok market

© SUZANNE NAM

Choo, and Gucci, but the mall takes conspicuous consumption a step further with the luxury-car dealership wing, where you can buy a BMW, Maserati, or Ferrari.

Just a few minutes on foot from Paragon is **Central World Plaza,** which, despite claiming to be the largest shopping mall in the country, doesn't have the frenetic feeling of MBK or the higher price tags of Paragon, though it does have nearly every store imaginable and dozens and dozens of restaurants too. The large branch of department store **Central Zen** was destroyed by fire during civil unrest in 2010; although the rest of the mall has since reopened, as of 2011 Central Zen is still rebuilding.

Petchaburi Neighborhood

While most of the city's most expensive shopping is to be found in the area around Siam Square and Central World Plaza, if you head north just one road to Petchaburi, you'll find a wealth of inexpensive local shopping.

The heart of the shopping district is the **Pratunam Market** (intersection of Petchaburi

TAILOR-MADE

There is nothing as luxurious as getting clothing custom made, and Bangkok is one of the few cities left in the world where you can still afford the luxury. A custom shirt from a Jermyn Street shirtmaker in London will run you more than US$100, and a bespoke suit is probably out of the price range of most people. In U.S. cities, if you can even find a tailor offering such services, custom clothing runs into the hundreds and even thousands of dollars. For women, it's really a chance of a lifetime, as there are few places still making custom women's wear. For half the price you'd pay for an off-the-rack dress or suit, you can go home with something made to your specifications and custom fitted for your body. If you're in need of some new duds, the trip could even pay for itself in the money you save.

There are hundreds of tailors offering their services in Bangkok, and all over the city are signs advertising men's suits custom made in 24 hours for 4,000B along with promoters trying to lure travelers into shops with promises of cheap tailored clothing. Sure, it's tempting to get something as cheap as you can, but if you're in the market for tailor-made clothing, keep in mind that you get what you pay for. You're already saving substantially versus what you'd pay at home; it's foolish to try to find a bargain when you risk being dissatisfied. While the cheaper tailors are often very skilled, the cost savings is usually made up in the quality of the material. Choices in the cheaper shops are usually limited to synthetic blends with few, if any, wools and other natural materials.

To get a suit made of high-quality material in Bangkok, expect to pay 6,000-14,000B. Trousers can cost from 2,000B and up, depending on the material, and shirts around 1,000B. For women, custom suits should run around the same price as men's, and you can pick up a custom evening gown for 6,000B and up, and

even a custom-made silk wedding gown for around 20,000B.

To get the most out of the experience, make sure to give the tailor enough time. All of the good tailors in Bangkok will refuse to make anything if you can't come in for at least two fittings.

At the first fitting, you'll pick out the fabrics, and the tailor will take all of your measurements. If you're not already, you'll become well versed in terms such as flat front, spread collar, slim cut, and notch, because you'll be choosing all of the specifications of your suit and shirt. If that's all too confusing, most good tailors can offer advice and let you know what's likely to look most flattering on your body, or you can even bring in your favorite suit for guidance. When you go in for your second fitting, the clothing won't be finished, but you'll try on the rough pieces for fit. If you're really in a rush, or the clothing fits perfectly at the second fitting, any tailor can arrange for the items to be delivered to your hotel when they're done. But it is always better to try everything on one last time.

Tailors are also expert at copying existing clothing. If you have a dress that fits you perfectly and you'd like to have it in different colors or materials, pack it with you and bring it in. They can even work off of a picture if you've fallen in love with something you saw in a fashion magazine. Whether they're copying or designing from scratch, expect to go in for two fittings as well.

The favorite tailor for diplomats, visiting dignitaries, and even U.S. presidents is **Rajawonse Clothiers** (130 Sukhumvit Rd. near Soi 4, Skytrain: Nana, www.dress-for-success. com, tel. 02/255-3714, 10 A.M.-8 P.M. Mon.-Sat., suit 7,500B). Jesse and Victor say they don't have to advertise their busy little shop in Nana because they have such a good reputation for quality work, and the pictures and business

© SUZANNE NAM

Pick your own fabric at one of Bangkok's tailor shops.

cards of former customers lining the walls (including George Bush Sr. and Tom Ridge) seem to be proof of that fact. The father-and-son duo who runs the shop will shepherd you through the process, offering advice on their extensive selection of fabrics and letting you know tactfully whether something is likely to be flattering. If you have to wait, and you might, given their popularity, you're likely to be offered a beer and a comfortable seat.

Another favorite, and just slightly cheaper, is **Raja's Fashions** (1/6 Sukhumvit Soi 4, Skytrain: Nana, tel. 02/253-8389, 10 A.M.-8 P.M. Mon.-Sat., suit 6,000B) right around the corner. Interestingly, Raja is related to Jesse and Victor, although the two shops seem to be in

tight competition for the best tailor in the city. Raja's shop is slightly bigger, but you can expect the same quality and personal service.

Unfortunately, neither shop does a lot of women's clothes, but a few blocks away at the far end of a little outdoor shopping mall is **N and K Pinky Tailors** (888/40 Mahatunplaza Bldg., Skytrain: Ploenchit, tel. 02/252-9680, 10 A.M.-8 P.M. Mon.-Sat., women's suit with slacks and skirt 6,000B), another popular shop with diplomats and visiting dignitaries. Pinky has three floors of fabrics, turns out excellent quality menswear, and also makes clothes for women. He will happily take even a sketch of something and turn it into a well-made, perfectly fitting dress.

and Ratchaprasong, 24 hours daily), Bangkok's largest clothing market, with many stalls and vendors staying open all day and night. The market starts at the Pratunam intersection and spreads north through covered stalls and small shops at ground level (including at the base of the Bayoke Tower). Here you'll find plenty of inexpensive clothing, much of it geared toward a younger crowd, although if you can wear it, chances are you'll find it at Pratunam. There are also plenty of souvenirs and household goods for sale, and this is the type of market you'll need to wander through for a while. Wednesdays are the busiest, as that's when new shipments typically come in.

Just across the street from Pratunam is the **Platinum Fashion Mall** (542/21-22 Petchaburi Rd., tel. 02/656-5999, 9 A.M.–6 P.M. daily). The multilevel mall feels much like a market with the rows and rows of stalls selling mostly clothing but also accessories and shoes. The best part is that it's air-conditioned and a little less crowded than a typical market. Prices here are usually very reasonable, and most items for sale are in the 200–400B range, although you'll pay a little less if you buy at least three of any item. **Platinum Mall 2,** which will carry much of the same merchandise as the original, is scheduled to open next door in mid-2011.

The Old City

Around Bang Lamphu are a couple of markets worth checking out if you're looking for souvenirs or clothing. The **Bang Lamphu market,** which starts right off of Soi Ram Buttri and extends over Phra Sumen Road, primarily caters to local shoppers, and you'll find everything from socks and underwear to school uniforms on sale at very reasonable prices. Even if you're not in the market for school uniforms or socks, it's an interesting place just to wander around for a while.

Bo Bae Market is another local market that extends for blocks along the Bo Bae canal and is open late into the evening. Surrounding shops are full of clothing and undergarments. Though chances are you aren't going to find lots to buy here, there is a busy commotion around this area that makes it worth walking through.

Khao San Road is full of cheap street stalls and shops selling Thai souvenirs, bathing suits, counterfeit sneakers, sandals, bootleg CDs and DVDs, and anything else young backpackers might be interested in. It is definitely a tourist trap, but just a couple of blocks away there are a handful of lovely boutiques worth checking out.

The first, **OR2K** (106/4 Ram Buttri Rd., tel. 02/629-0400, 11 A.M.–10:30 P.M. Sun.–Thurs., 11 A.M.–7:30 P.M. Fri.) is a little shop just off of Khao San Road on Ram Buttri. The slightly industrial-looking space (originally two standard shophouses) with a glass storefront is filled with lots of hippie-chic finds at reasonable prices. Though there are lots of bright colors and natural fibers here, there's a funkiness to the designs that sets them apart.

Make your way past the madness of Khao San, turn down Soi 32, and you'll enter a little courtyard dominated by a True Internet and coffee café and an old Thai house painted entirely black. Though it's hard to figure out what's going on in there from the outside, it's **Nero** (32 Khao San Rd., tel. 02/629-5271, 1–11 P.M. daily), the sister boutique to the Siam Square It's Happened to be a Closet, filled with locally made creative, colorful clothing, from peasant tops to beaded gowns designed by a local designer. None of it will come cheap, though; items are priced between 1,500B and 15,000B. There's also a café and bakery, and cozy seats everywhere to peruse their library of design books.

On Samsen Road, about 10 minutes on foot from Khao San, is **Bangkoker** (113 Samsen Rd., tel. 02/628-9722, 10 A.M.–8 P.M. Mon.–Sat.), which sells cool, funky shirts in a cool, funky showroom.

Chinatown

The neighborhood shopping here is primarily geared toward shop owners picking up grosses of the latest trends in sandals and pocketbooks. Don't worry, though, if you don't want to buy 12 pairs of shoes at a time; many of the vendors will also sell things individually at a slightly higher price. For shoes, the best place to have a look is in the side streets off of **Yaowarat** heading toward the river, before Surawongse Road. Once you're on **Surawongse,** you'll see scores of small vendors selling pocketbooks, beads, hair bands, and other small, cheap, fun items.

The best part of Chinatown is the silk shopping near **Phahurat.** Inside the covered Phahurat market, you won't find any of the good stuff, and you'll have to be careful to wade through the merchants offering cheap imitation fabrics labeled "Thai silk," but once you come upon the real thing you'll know it. Colors run the gamut from pastel to rich, vivid gem colors, and the slightly nubby texture is the giveaway. Expect to pay anywhere from 300B to 1,100B per meter. Lighter, single-colored fabrics are generally cheaper, and the heavy, traditional, intricate designs are the most expensive. The best place to look is in the **Old Siam Plaza,** a little mall with restaurants and even some gem and gun stores, if you're inclined toward either.

If you're in the market for Thai silk, make sure to stop into **Maeliard Thai Silk** (Old Siam Mall, Room I-205, tel. 02/221-6593, 9:30 a.m.–6 p.m. daily) on the second floor of the Old Siam Mall in Phahurat. The selection of colors is truly unbelievable: There are at least 20 shades of green alone; you may find yourself simply staring at the folds and folds of beautiful richly colored material, all at astoundingly low prices of 250–700B per meter. The family-run shop is the Bangkok outlet of a larger place in Pak Thong Chai, the silk capital of Thailand, and all of the materials are hand-dyed and hand-loomed. You can get the deal of a lifetime if you're in the market for material for home decorating. If you bring measurements or something to copy, they'll even help you find a seamstress or tailor while you're in Bangkok.

Phahurat Road is full of amazing shopping finds, including **Cattleya** (288 Phahurat Rd., tel. 02/222-6272, 9 a.m.–5:30 p.m. daily), which sells ready-made and custom printed cards and invitations as well as picture frames and photo albums. It is a great little store, especially if you need something printed up. The prices are a fraction of what you'd pay back home.

Though you probably won't be able to bring anything home from the **Flower Market** (Pak Khlong Talat, pier: Memorial Bridge, 24 hours daily), it's worth a visit to see the thousands of fresh flowers for sale, including a rainbow array of orchids and roses, all at prices that will make you wish they'd last the flight home. Here you'll also see many devotional flower garlands being made and, if you walk into the side streets, traditional wet markets too. The market is open 24 hours a day and is busiest in the early morning hours, though any time you visit during the day, there will be plenty of activity. The area just north of the market is filled with fabrics and other local goods.

◖ Chatuchak Weekend Market

Covering 14 hectares of land north of the city, the gigantic Chatuchak Weekend Market (Skytrain: Mo Chit, subway: Kamphaeng Phet, 9 a.m.–6 p.m. Sat.–Sun.) is like no other shopping experience in Thailand. Clothing, furniture, scented candles, Thai crafts, dog food, dogs, squirrels—you name it, you can find it among the open and covered stalls that make up the maze that is Chatuchak. Only open on weekends, the market draws in hundreds of thousands of people each week. Old, young, rich, poor, local, traveler, or expatriate, it seems like everyone comes together at Chatuchak with one goal in mind: shopping. And while you'll find plenty of cheap generic stuff here, you're likely to find the best bargains in souvenirs, some funky and creative housewares, and very cool T-shirts and casual tops for women. By noon the place is packed with people, which can be a bit tough if you're carrying lots of packages or it's hot outside. It's always hot in Bangkok, so you're better off getting there early, when the crowds haven't yet arrived and the goods haven't yet been too picked over. When the hordes arrive, don't just leave; instead, head to one of the casual Isan stalls, cafés, bars, or sit-down restaurants in the market.

Like no other place in Bangkok, you'll

need a strategy for Chatuchak. Whatever it is you're hoping to find, chances are that it's there, and you'll be able to get it for a better price than you would pay at a market in the city, but the place is confusing and very big. Don't set out aimlessly wandering around unless you're just there to browse and people-watch. If you're looking to get some shopping done, pick up a map at one of the entrances. The market is broken into sections, and within those, smaller *sois* that are numbered. Similar vendors are generally in the same areas, which are either totally obvious (like the pet area) or at least well signed, like the decorative housewares area. Pick a couple of sections to browse in, and spend some time comparing the goods and the prices. While some vendors may give you a 10–15 percent break, Chatuchak is not a big bargaining market. There's so much competition that prices are already fair. Once you see something you like at a good price, buy it on the spot, as chances are you won't even be able to find the stall again once you walk away.

Although not quite an official guide, www.jatujakguide.com has an online map of the market and some vendor listings. Nancy Chandler's Bangkok map has some fairly detailed information about Chatuchak as well.

HOME FURNISHINGS

Striking a delicate balance between clean, modern lines and traditional intricate designs, Thai-styled home decorations aren't just souvenirs to fill your suitcase with but great decorator items with which to fill your home. While the department stores in the United States might be stocking this stuff at exorbitant prices, in Bangkok you can find some amazing bargains on beautiful serving ware, lamps, pillow coverings, and other items for your home.

Thai Home Industries (35 Oriental Ave., pier: Oriental, tel. 02/234-1736, 9 A.M.–6:30 P.M. Mon.–Sat.) is the place to go if you like exploring as much as you like shopping. Organization is, apparently, an afterthought, judging by the piles of baskets, farming equipment, and other cool curios, although those with more mainstream taste will (eventually) find plenty of great housewares and decorator items. Flatware and other tableware are very popular here.

For everything from small textile accent pieces and picture frames to bookshelves and other large furniture, visit **Pandora Furniture** (Raintree Villa Condominium, 108/196 Sukhumvit Soi 53, Skytrain: Thong Lor, tel. 02/662-7365, 9 A.M.–6 P.M. daily). The shop specializes in wood products made by local craftspeople but also has some Chinese and Indian pieces, and the showroom is a delight to browse through even if you're not looking to buy anything.

Exotique Thai (Emporium Shopping Mall, 622 Sukhumvit Rd., Skytrain: Phrom Phong, tel. 02/269-1000, 10 A.M.–10 P.M. daily) has a huge selection of items for the home, including delicate celadon-colored serving pieces. Though not bargain priced, the shop is more reasonable than its nice digs would otherwise indicate. If you're looking for lighting fixtures and silk lampshades, take a look at **Central Chitlom** (1027 Ploenchit Rd., Skytrain: Chit Lom, tel. 02/793-7777, 10 A.M.–10 P.M. daily).

For some really high-end selections, go to the fifth floor of **Siam Paragon** (tel. 02/690-1000, 10 A.M.–10 P.M. daily), called Paragon Passage. Half the floor is devoted to interior design, and stores such as **Indigo House** and **Sani** have some beautiful modern takes on Thai design.

🅒 Narai Phand

Narai Phand (President Tower Arcade, 973 Ploenchit Rd., Skytrain: Chit Lom, tel. 02/656-0398, 11 A.M.–8 P.M. daily) is the best one-stop shopping spot for all things Thai. This government-run shop sells high-quality handicrafts made in villages across Thailand. Expect to find plenty of Thai silk clothes and linens, enamelware, Bencharong porcelain, bath and body products, and even spirit houses. The shop, behind the Intercontinental Hotel, is very large but doesn't ever feel vibrant or bustling.

◖ Support Foundation

The Support Foundation (The Grand Palace, pier: Chang, tel. 02/225-9421, www.grandpalaceshop.com, 8:30 A.M.–4:30 P.M. daily) is right after the main entrance to the Grand Palace and carries mostly handcrafted goods from all over Thailand. The store is part of the Queen's Support Foundation, and proceeds go toward supporting and sustaining folk arts and crafts in the country; many of the items are made as part of the program. Quality and craftsmanship of everything in the shop tends to be excellent, and prices are very reasonable. This is an excellent place to pick up souvenirs and gifts for home, as you'll also learn something about traditional Thai crafts. Head here after touring the Grand Palace. Even if you're tired from sightseeing, the shop's ice-cold air-conditioning will revive you.

ENGLISH-LANGUAGE BOOKSTORES

Bangkok has a number of bookstore chains selling English-language books at convenient locations throughout central Bangkok, including **Asia Books, B2S,** and **Kinokinuya.** All of the major malls, including Siam Paragon Mall, Central World Plaza, and Emporium Mall, have at least one of these bookstores; some have all three. All Central department stores have small outlets of B2S, often on the top floor.

JEWELRY

Bangkok is full of jewelry stores stocked with everything from inexpensive silver jewelry to precious gems. Buying pricey gems can be a dangerous proposition if you're not already knowledgeable, as you'll have no redress if you don't get what you thought you paid for. **Charoen Krung Road,** starting at the Oriental Hotel until just below Chinatown, is full of gem and jewelry stores.

For silver, **Khao San Road** has more than a dozen shops toward the end of the road, all selling rings, necklaces, earrings, and other jewelry. Some of these shops are wholesale only, so be prepared to buy at least a dozen pieces if you find something you like.

Surawongse Road (corner of Yaowarat and Surawongse, pier: Surawong) has a jewelry market and many small stalls and shops selling mostly inexpensive costume jewelry. Some of these shops are also wholesale only, and although there are no posted hours, they are generally open 10 A.M.–6 P.M. daily.

Two large shops have good reputations, and both are good places to go if you are interested in spending a few hundred to a few thousand dollars on gems set in gold: **Venus Jewelry** (167/1/2 Witthayu Rd., tel. 02/253-9559, www.venus-thailand.com, 11 A.M.–7 P.M. Mon.–Fri., by appointment at other times) caters primarily to visitors associated with the surrounding embassies, and over the years it has garnered a solid reputation and plenty of repeat customers looking for rubies, sapphires, and emerald jewelry. The large shop is right on Witthayu (Wireless) Road between Ploenchit and Lumphini Park and will pick you up from your hotel. Salespeople here tend to be well-informed and very low-pressure. Although many customers come here to buy big-ticket items, Venus also has a good selection of less expensive earrings and rings.

SJ International Joaillier (125/8 Sawankhalok Rd., Dusit, tel. 02/243-2446, www.sjjewelry.com) is another shop with a good reputation and large selection of set gems. It's also a fun experience to visit, as they'll send a driver to pick you up (call ahead), and you'll be greeted with a cold drink and plenty of salesperson attention at their large showroom. Jewelry displayed in the cases tends to be more elaborate and complicated. If you are looking for something simpler, such as a plain pair of sapphire earrings, just ask the saleswoman (for some reason, there don't seem to be any men working here) to show you what else they have. SJ will also make custom rings, earrings, and anything else you want. You'll get to pick out the unset stones and design the setting. If you go this route, things tend to be a little more expensive, and the shop will need at least a few days to make your order. Staff here can be high-pressure, but they are also very good-natured. No one will take it personally if you say no. SJ is in Dusit, and it's a great place to stop after visiting some of the tourist sights in the area.

JIM THOMPSON DESIGNS

Tourists and locals flock to Jim Thompson stores across the city that offer not only the luxurious Thai silk the company is known for but also a collection of furniture and other material for home decorating. The multilevel main store in **Silom** (9 Surawong Rd., tel. 02/632-8100, 10 A.M.–9 P.M. daily), on the corner of Rama IV, carries raw material you can purchase by the meter, in the signature jewel tones the company is known for as well as in modern designs that change every year. If you just want something small, the shops also stock ties, scarves,

handbags, and even stuffed silk elephants. There are other branches around the city, including a large one at the Siam Paragon Mall, and in the international terminal of Bangkok's airport.

The teak furniture at **39 Living** (51/5–6 Sukhumvit Soi 39, Skytrain: Phrom Phong, tel. 02/258-7522, 9 A.M.–7 P.M. daily) is worth a look if you're considering picking up any larger souvenirs. The dining room tables, chairs, settees, and coffee tables are exceptionally well designed and very nicely priced, as are the wooden wall carvings and other decorative items. The manager will help arrange shipping anywhere in the world, but expect those costs to double the price of anything you buy—which might still be worth it.

Accommodations

Whatever time of year you visit, you will find no shortage of accommodations in Bangkok. The city offers excellent options for budget backpackers looking to spend US$20 per night and willing to share a bathroom as well as for high rollers or those on expense accounts.

THE OLD CITY

Bang Lamphu has scores of guesthouses in the 350–700B range, mostly catering to a younger Western crowd. Close to all the major sites in Ko Rattanakosin, it can be a convenient place to stay if you plan on spending all of your time in the Old City and don't want to spend a lot of money on accommodations. If you don't mind the late-night partying, Khao San Road and the surrounding streets are literally packed full of guesthouses (and Western tourists). In the past, they generally offered small guest rooms, shared baths, and no hot water, but the street is slowly going a little more upscale, and nowadays it's not difficult to find private guest rooms, en suite baths, and even air-conditioning. Outside of the Khao San Road area, there are more and more boutique-style small hotels and guesthouses offering visitors

creature comforts along with their immersion into Bangkok life.

Under 1,500B

Sam Sen Sam (48 Samsen Soi 3, pier: Phra Athit, tel. 02/628-7067, www.samsensam. com, 400B) is a colorful, quirky little guesthouse that has great basic guest rooms, a very convenient location, and very helpful and friendly staff. Guest rooms are basic and clean, although the proprietors have made an effort with pretty curtains and bedspreads, and since part of the property is in an old wooden house, it has more personality than other places in this price range. Basic guest rooms have shared baths and are fan-cooled; there are rooms with en suite baths and air-conditioning available. Samsen Soi 3 is just a 10-minute walk from Khao San Road and the river boat, but it is in a more local, less touristy area.

Shambara (138 Khao San Rd., tel. 02/282-7968, 600B) is a lovely guesthouse off Khao San Road, a refreshing surprise in a neighborhood dominated by cheap, characterless rooms. The guesthouse and accompanying restaurant are located in an old wooden house near the

CHAKRABONGSE VILLAS

Although you can't sleep in any former palaces, and you can't even tour the current one, a former royal home on the Chao Phraya, now the Chakrabongse Villas, is available for rent. Once the home of Prince Chakrabongse, it's now open to the public not because the royal family no longer owns it but because they're no longer royalty. Prince Chakrabongse Bhuvanath was born in 1883, the 40th son of King Rama V and the fourth son of Queen Sri Bajarinda. As a child, he was sent off to England to study. During a visit by his father to Russia, Czar Nicolas II invited Rama V to send one of his sons to be educated in Russia under his care. After studying Russian in England, the prince spent his teenage years and early adulthood in Russia and met and fell in love with Ekatrina Desnitskaya, a young, beautiful Russian girl. Afraid of what his parents would say if he asked permission to marry her, he and Ekatrina married in Constantinople, returned to Thailand without announcing their union, and set up a home in a villa on the Chao Phraya.

The king and queen were furious. Although Chakrabongse's mother relented and met Ekatrina, his father never once received her. Despite the sacrifices both had made, the marriage between the two was not fated to last. Ekatrina divorced Prince Chakrabongse and returned to her homeland, leaving behind their son, Chula Chakrabongse. Because of his mixed blood, Chula was passed over for consideration when Rama VII abdicated in 1935. Chula spent much of his childhood in England and, like his father before him, fell in love with a foreigner. He married Englishwoman Elizabeth Hunter in 1938, and in 1956 they had a daughter, Narisa Chakrabongse. The villa stayed in the family and is now owned by Narisa.

---

end of Khao San Road near Thanao Road. Guest rooms are eclectically furnished but charming and clean. Baths are basic.

If you're looking for a more homey feeling and don't mind going without some amenities, **Tuptim Bed and Breakfast** (82 Ram Buttri Rd., tel. 02/629-1535, www.tuptimb-b.com, 700B) is a great choice, and a very cheap one too. On a small side street right near Khao San Road, the front of the building looks like an old wooden house surrounded by flowering plants. The guest rooms themselves are not quite as charming, and there are no en suite baths, but there is air-conditioning, and you can enjoy the included toast and coffee at the downstairs open-air restaurant.

For price and convenience, you can't beat **New Siam II** (50 Trok Rong Mai, pier: Phra Athit, tel. 02/282-2795, www.newsiam.net, 700B). On a side street off of Phra Athit Road, just five minutes from the river and a couple of blocks from Khao San, it's relatively quiet but still centrally located for sightseeing on Ko Rattanakosin or for grabbing a ferry boat right across the street to see the rest of the city. Many guest rooms have air-conditioning, en suite baths, and hot water. The guest rooms themselves are less than stellar, with a sort of aging institutional feeling (fluorescent lighting and shiny paint on the walls probably contribute a lot), but they are clean and very cheap. There's also a small shaded pool on the ground floor and a very casual but decent restaurant.

Bhiman Inn (55 Phra Sumen Rd., pier: Phra Athit, tel. 02/282-6171, www.bhimaninn.com, 1,400B), which opened in 2006 and is located a block from Phra Athit Road, is another inexpensive option in the neighborhood. The exterior looks strangely reminiscent of a Moorish castle, but the guest rooms are clean, new, and comfortable. The ground-floor open-air restaurant, where the hotel serves breakfast daily, is also a plus, as is the small outdoor pool.

1,500-3,000B

A considerable step up from the rest of the street is **Buddy Lodge** (265 Khao San Rd., tel. 02/629-4477, www.buddylodge.com, 2,000B),

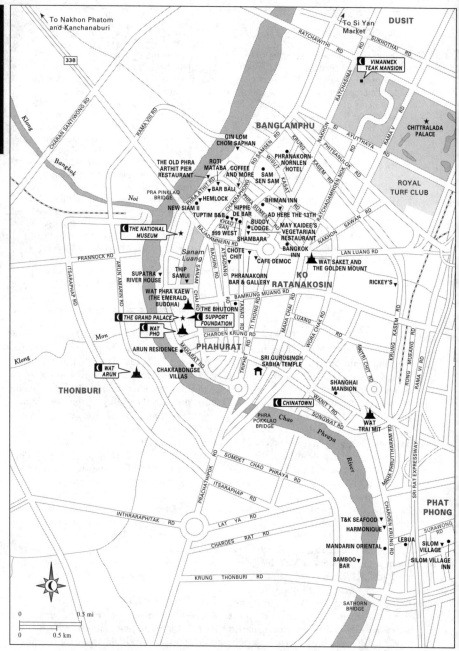

To Nakhon Phatom
and Kanchanaburi

338

Klong

Bangkok

Noi

PRA PINKLAO
BRIDGE

PRANNOCK RD

THONBURI

Klong

Mon

To Si Yan
Market

RATCHAWITHI RD

DUSIT

RATCHASIMA

SUKHOTHAI RD

◖ VIMANMEK
TEAK MANSION

CHARAN SANTIWONG RD

RAMA VIII RD

BANGLAMPHU

GIN LOM
CHOM SAPHAN

THE OLD PHRA
ARTHIT PIER
RESTAURANT

ROTI
MATABA

COFFEE
AND MORE

SAM
SEN SAM

BAR BALI

HEMLOCK

NEW SIAM II

TUPTIM B&B

999 WEST

HIPPIE
DE BAR

KHAO
SAN
RD

BUDDY
LODGE

SHAMBARA

◖ THE NATIONAL
MUSEUM

RAJADAMNERN RD

Sanam
Luang

RACHINI RD

ATSADANG

CHOTE
CHIT

CAFE DEMOC

SUPATRA ▼
RIVER HOUSE

THIP
SAMUI

WAT PHRA KAEW
(THE EMERALD
BUDDHA)

CHAO RD

SANAM

PHRANAKORN
BAR & GALLERY

BAMRUNG MUANG RD

THE BHUTORN

◖ THE GRAND PALACE

SUPPORT
FOUNDATION

◖ WAT
PHO

CHAROEN KRUNG RD

ARUN RESIDENCE

PHAHURAT

◖ WAT
ARUN

CHAKRABONGSE
VILLAS

MAHARAT RD

TRIPHET RD

SRI GURUSINGH
SABHA TEMPLE

PHRANAKORN-
NORNLEN
HOTEL

RD SAMSEN RD

KRUNG

WISUT
KASAI

CHAKRABHONG

PHRA ATHIT RD

PHRA SUMEN RD

BHIMAN INN

AD HERE THE 13TH

MAY KAIDEE'S
VEGETARIAN
RESTAURANT

BANGKOK
INN

NAKHON

SI

AYUTTHAYA

PHITSANULOK RD

RATCHADAMNOEN NOK RD

NAKHON SAWAN RD

LAN LUANG RD

◖ WAT SAKET AND
THE GOLDEN MOUNT

**KO
RATANAKOSIN**

MAHA CHAI RD

MAHA
CHAI

LUANG

TI THONG RD

WORA CHAK RD

KRUNG

KASEM

MAITRI CHIT RD

RONG MUEANG RD

RAMA VI RD

CHITTRALADA
PALACE ★

ROYAL
TURF CLUB

RICKEY'S

SHANGHAI
MANSION

◖ CHINATOWN

PHRA
POKKLAO
BRIDGE

Chao

WANIT 1 RD

SONGWAT RD

WAT
TRAI MIT

Phraya

River

ITSARAPHAP RD

SOMDET CHAO PHRAYA RD

ITSARAPHAP RD

INTHRARAPHITAK RD

LAT YA RD

CHAROES RAT RD

KRUNG THONBURI RD

SATHORN
BRIDGE

MAHA PHRUTTHARAM RD

CHAROEN KRUNG RD

SRI RAT EXPRESSWAY

**PHAT
PHONG**

T&K SEAFOOD ▼

HARMONIQUE ▼

MANDARIN ORIENTAL ▼

BAMBOO ▼
BAR

SURAWONG
RD

LEBUA

SILOM ▼
VILLAGE

SILOM VILLAGE
INN

0   0.5 mi

0   0.5 km

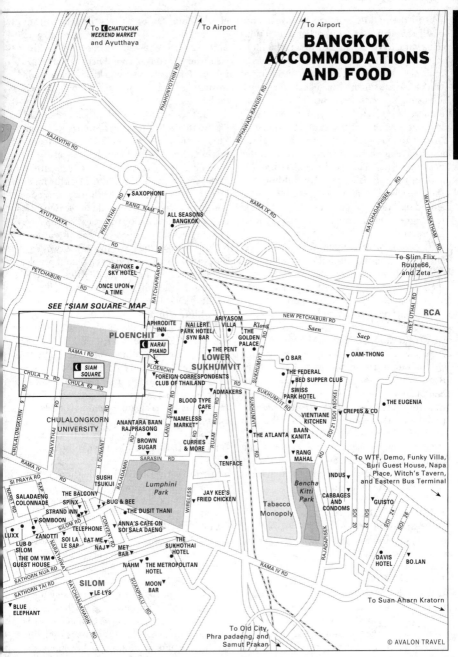

BANGKOK ACCOMMODATIONS AND FOOD

To CHATUCHAK WEEKEND MARKET and Ayutthaya

To Airport

To Airport

PHAHONYOTHIN RD.

WIPHAWADI-RANGSIT RD.

RAJAVITHI RD.

RAMA IX RD.

RATCHADAPHISEK RD.

WATTHANATHAM RD.

AYUTTHAYA

SAXOPHONE

RANG NAM RD.

PRAYATHAI RD.

RATCHAPRAROP RD.

ALL SEASONS BANGKOK

PHI LUTHAI RD.

To Slim Flix, Route66, and Zeta

RCA

PETCHABURI RD.

BAIYOKE SKY HOTEL

ONCE UPON A TIME

NEW PETCHABURI RD.

Klong Saen

Saep

SEE "SIAM SQUARE" MAP

APHRODITE INN

NARAI PHAND

NAI LERT PARK HOTEL/ SYN BAR

ARIYASOM VILLA

THE GOLDEN PALACE

Q BAR

OAM-THONG

PLOENCHIT

RAMA I RD.

SIAM SQUARE

THE PENT

LOWER SUKHUMVIT

THE FEDERAL

BED SUPPER CLUB

THE EUGENIA

CHULA 12 RD.

CHULA 62 RD.

PLOENCHIT

FOREIGN CORRESPONDENTS CLUB OF THAILAND

ADMAKERS

SUKHUMVIT RD.

SWISS PARK HOTEL

SOI 21 (SOI ASOKE)

CREPES & CO

CHULALONGKORN 9 RD.

PHAYATHAI RD.

CHULALONGKORN UNIVERSITY

BLOOD TYPE CAFE

NAMELESS MARKET

LANG SUAN RD.

RUDI

RUAM RUDI

SUKHUMVIT RD.

VIENTIANE KITCHEN

BAAN KANITA

ANANTARA BAAN RAJPRASONG

BROWN SUGAR

CURRIES & MORE

THE ATLANTA

RANG MAHAL

To WTF, Demo, Funky Villa, Buri Guest House, Napa Place, Witch's Tavern, and Eastern Bus Terminal

RAMA IV RD.

H. DUNANT RD.

RAJADAMRI RD.

SARASIN RD.

TENFACE

INDUS

SI PRAYA RD.

SAP RD.

SUSHI TSUKIJI

Lumphini Park

WIRELESS RD.

JAY KEE'S FRIED CHICKEN

Bencha Kitti Park

CABBAGES AND CONDOMS

GUISTO

SALADAENG COLONNADE

THE BALCONY

SPINX

BUG & BEE

THE DUSIT THANI

Tabacco Monopoly

SOI 20

SOI 22

SOI 24

SOI 26

NARET RD.

STRAND INN

SOMBOON

SILOM RD.

TELEPHONE

ANNA'S CAFE ON SOI SALA DAENG

CONVENTO RD.

RAJADAPISEK RD.

LUXX

ZANOTTI

SOI LA LE SAP

EAT ME

NAJ

MET BAR

THE SUKHOTHAI HOTEL

DAVIS HOTEL

BO.LAN

LUB D SILOM

THE OM YIM GUEST HOUSE

NARATHIWAT RD.

NAHM

THE METROPOLITAN HOTEL

RAMA IV RD.

SATHORN NUA RD.

SILOM

LE LYS

MOON BAR

To Suan Aharn Kratorn

SATHORN TAI RD.

RATCHAN KAHRIN RD.

SUANPLU RD.

BLUE ELEPHANT

To Old City, Phra padaeng, and Samut Prakan

© AVALON TRAVEL

right in the middle of Khao San Road. But for all the neon signs and other distractions that characterize Khao San Road, the modern brick building, in a mildly European style, would stand out among the older, disorganized structures that surround it. Nicely furnished, albeit simple, guest rooms with TVs, air-conditioning, and private baths with hot water give this property a bit of a luxury feel compared to its surroundings. On the ground floor are a bunch of retail shops, including a chain coffee shop and a McDonald's. The small swimming pool on the roof is a big bonus, although it can get packed full of people when the hotel is booked up. And if you're not totally exhausted from sightseeing, there's also a small gym on the premises.

◖ Phranakorn-Nornlen Hotel (46 Thewet Soi 1, pier: Thewet, tel. 02/628-8188, www. phranakorn-nornlen.com, 2,200B) is a rare small, lovely hotel in Bang Lamphu. Created around the concept of slowing down life to enjoy it, the hotel staff aim to create a peaceful, relaxed place to visit. Right off busy main Thewet Road, you enter on a side street through a courtyard that serves as a common garden and leads to the reception area. In line with the owner's dedication to preserving the environment, many of the furnishings are restored objects from various eras. The guest rooms, each decorated with the sort of perfected yet casual hand-sewn look usually found in the pages of a Martha Stewart magazine, are equipped with CD players, telephones, and air-conditioning. The included breakfast is vegetarian and features locally grown produce.

3,000-4,500B

◖ Arun Residence (36–38 Soi Pratoo Nok Yoong, pier: Tha Tian, tel. 02/221-9158, www. arunresidence.com, 3,100B) is located in a beautifully restored 80-year-old house on the river. Each of the elegantly decorated guest rooms in this small boutique guesthouse open out to a view of Wat Arun, which is especially stunning at night when the temple is lit up. Inside, each of the five rooms is different, and some of the larger ones have two levels. Try to get the Arun Suite, with its spacious balcony overlooking the river. The restaurant, with outdoor seating on the river, is also worth a visit whether you're staying here or not. Rates include a full sit-down breakfast. If you want to stay on Ko Rattanakosin, there is no better location.

Another small, excellent choice is the **◖ Bangkok Inn** (609 Pra Sumen Rd., pier: Phra Athit, tel. 02/629-1787, www.oldbangkokinn.com, 3,700B). Family run, this small 10-room hotel is filled with teak furnishings. Mosquito netting surrounds the lavishly made beds, and even the baths, with their wood detailing and ceramic basins, add to the romantic environment. Some of the guest rooms have private decks, and one even has an outdoor bathtub. Two of the guest rooms are two-level suites and can accommodate up to four people, a great place for a small family to stay. As if that wasn't enough, the guest rooms all have satellite TV, DVD players, and even a small PC with free Internet.

◖ The Bhuthorn (96–98 Phraeng Bhuthorn Rd., tel. 02/622-2270, www.thebhuthorn.com, 3,200B) is a beautifully restored bank of shophouses near the Grand Palace that houses just a handful of guest rooms, each designed to evoke a sense of Thailand's rich history while giving visitors all the creature comforts one would expect in the 21st century. Wooden armoires, four-poster beds, and ceiling fans mix with Wi-Fi and flat-screen TVs; the result is delightful. The property is very small, so expect a lot of personal attention. If the Bhuthorn is full, ask for a room in the owners' newest property, just a few blocks away.

Over 4,500B

On the banks of the Chao Phraya, across the river from Wat Arun in a leafy garden, is the very small, very lovely **◖ Chakrabongse Villas** (396 Maharaj Rd., no phone, www. thaivillas.com, 10,000B). More like staying in a luxurious but traditional wooden Thai house than staying in a guesthouse or hotel, there is really nothing else like this in Bangkok. The dining *sala* and swimming pool overlook the river, and two of the three villas have small kitchen areas stocked with the basics necessary to prepare a meal. The Riverside Villa has its own private deck with an amazing view of Wat Arun. The staff serve breakfast to guests in the morning and can arrange specially prepared meals served in the *sala*. If you want to take advantage of the river to get around, there's a private boat and captain available. Reservations are through the website only.

CHINATOWN
Under 1,500B
Riverview Guesthouse (768 Soi Panurangsri, tel. 02/234-5429, 450B) isn't for everyone. It's in a very local part of the city on the edge of Chinatown a few minutes from Hua Lamphong Station, surrounded by small car-engine and axle-repair shops, and it's not exactly elegant. Guest rooms are comfortably sized, but the least expensive are rundown and shopworn, and the baths are tolerable. But if you are looking for an authentic Bangkok experience with a view of the river to boot, this is an excellent budget choice. The neighborhood isn't filled with scores of other travelers (even though the guesthouse is right behind a Chinese temple), and it's a great place to wander around before heading out to the nearby sights. There's also a rooftop restaurant with a view of the river that's worth the (small) price you'll pay for a room.

1,500-3,000B
Combine the intimate feeling and attention to detail from a boutique hotel with the pricing you'd normally find in a backpacker guesthouse and set it all in Chinatown, and the result is the **(Shanghai Mansion** (479–481 Yaowarat Rd., tel. 02/678-0101, www.shanghaimansion.com, 2,500B). The moment you enter the hotel, next to a supermarket on busy Yaowarat Road, look up to see colorful Chinese parasols suspended from the ceiling. The theme here is *chinoise,* and the guest rooms and common spaces are filled with boldly colored fabrics, lacquered furniture, and intricate wood carvings. Modern amenities include free

Wi-Fi, cable TV, and a minibar. The hotel also offers complimentary *tuk tuk* shuttle service to other parts of the city and has a spa on the premises. Since the property opened in 2006 it has become very popular, so make sure to book in advance.

Over 4,500B
While hotels catering to the latest trend may come and go, the **Mandarin Oriental** (48 Oriental Ave., tel. 02/659-9000, www.mandarinoriental.com/bangkok, 11,000B), after 130 years, has stood the test of time. The large lobby with soaring ceilings and floors covered in oriental rugs sets the stage for a luxurious, refined experience. Those two themes are consistently reinforced through the swimming pool with individual sitting *salas,* a generous breakfast buffet on the Chao Phraya, and gourmet restaurants on the premises. The guest rooms are spacious and decorated either in neocolonial or traditional Thai style. The Authors' Suites, named for the famous literary figures who've stayed here, including James Michener and W. Somerset Maugham, are lavishly decorated and gigantic at around 102 square meters.

CENTRAL BANGKOK–
SILOM AREA
Under 1,500B
Before Khao San Road became the backpackers' location of choice, the neighborhood south of Sathorn Road surrounding Soi Ngam Dupli was where travelers looking for inexpensive lodging headed. These days there are still many inexpensive guesthouses in the neighborhood, and it's a much quieter and more relaxed place to stay than Khao San Road. If you're looking for a cheap guesthouse but don't want the accompanying backpacker scene, head for this neighborhood. You'll walk 10–15 minutes to the nearest Skytrain or subway station.

Best Living Guesthouse (34/13–14 Soi Sri Bamphen, tel. 08/1616-3542, 500B) is a basic, clean place to stay in the Soi Ngam Dupli neighborhood. Guest rooms are very simple but have air-conditioning, which you'll appreciate after climbing the four flights of stairs to your room.

Only in a city with 10,000 hotel rooms could you find a boutique hostel like 【 **Lub D** (4 Decho Rd., Skytrain: Chong Nonsi, tel. 02/680-9999, www.lubd.com, 400B). Backpackers needn't sacrifice style at this property just off Silom Road. Opened in 2008, it is decorated with muted colors punctuated by bright mandarin-orange furniture. Stay in one of the dormitories if you want to share a room with other cool travelers (there's also a women's-only dorm), or reserve one of the private guest rooms with en suite baths. The communal baths with modern fixtures and concrete are seriously chic and sleek, and like any good hostel, the kitchen-café is where people meet and congregate.

Opened by a young artist from Isan, The **Om Yim Guest House** (72–74 Naratiwat Rd., Skytrain: Chong Nonsi, tel. 02/635-0169, www.omyimgroup.com/omyimhome. html, 990B), between Silom and Sathorn Roads, stands out as an excellent choice in the neighborhood if you're looking for an economical place to stay. The location, right next to the Skytrain and a short walk to busy Silom but away from the noise and commotion, is convenient, and the guesthouse itself, with its well-furnished, clean, modern guest rooms and tile and marble baths, cannot be beat for the money. You also get air-conditioning, hot water, breakfast, and even free Wi-Fi. Like the accommodations, the restaurant is a great value, with a solid selection of very well-prepared Thai dishes. Om Yim is gay-friendly but not to the exclusion of others.

Silom Village Inn (286 Silom Rd., Skytrain: Chong Nonsi, tel. 02/635-6810, 1,400B) is a great budget choice between a guesthouse and hotel. The guest rooms are clean and large, but the real draw is the location. Right on Silom Road but not quite in the noisy, sometimes crazy center of things, the inn also has some great surrounding shops, including a lovely traditional open-air Thai restaurant and a handful of nice and reasonably priced spas.

1,500-3,000B

In the most unlikely of places, right in the middle of the red-light district, is the **Strand Inn** (105 Phat Pong 2 Rd., Skytrain: Sala Daeng, tel. 02/234-4296, www.strandinn. com, 1,600B), a well-designed, inexpensive inn marketing itself as a boutique hotel. "Boutique hotel" might be pushing it a little, but the guest rooms are all nicely appointed with modern furnishings and funky art (in keeping with the theme of the neighborhood, most of the art involves nudity). Try to reserve one of the rooftop bungalows, where you'll have your own private terrace. If the neon lights advertising girlie bars bother you, just keep looking up at the cityscape.

The **Inn Sala Daeng** (5/12 Sala Daeng Rd., Skytrain: Sala Daeng, subway: Silom, tel. 02/637-5533, www.theinnsaladaeng.com, 1,750B), just around the corner from busy Silom Road on a quiet side street, has very clean, stylish guest rooms, modern baths, and Wi-Fi—everything the hip, modern urban traveler could want. There's no pool and little common area to hang out in, but the location is excellent for seeing the city.

Just a block off of busy Silom you'll find 【 **Luxx** (6/11 Decho Rd., tel. 02/635-8800, www.staywithluxx.com, 2,800B), a small, chic designer hotel so well designed that from the outside you might confuse it for someone's studio. The guest rooms are comfortably sized, nicely designed, and appointed with wooden bathtubs and rain showerheads in the glass-walled baths. Lest the overall Zen feeling get to be too peaceful, all guest rooms come with flat-screen TVs and free Wi-Fi throughout. Luxx lacks the common space, swimming pool, and elevators you'll find in larger hotels, however.

Although the charming, upscale **Baan Pra Nond Bed & Breakfast** (18/1 Charoen Rat Rd., Skytrain: Surasak, tel. 02/212-2242, www.baanpranond.com, 3,000B) is a little farther from the center of Silom than other options in the area, it is still very convenient to the river and public transportation. In exchange for a less-than-perfect location, guests get to enjoy staying in a renovated 70-year-old wooden home that has been turned into a lovely, homey bed-and-breakfast with comfortable guest rooms and more amenities, including a small swimming pool, than typically found at this price. Guest rooms and common areas are furnished with tasteful antique furniture.

The **Sala Daeng Colonnade** (21 Soi Sala Daeng, Skytrain: Sala Daeng, Subway: Silom, tel. 02/636-0131, www.saladaengcolonnade-bangkok.com, 3,000B) is a good choice for travelers who'd prefer to stay in what is essentially a very nice apartment while visiting Bangkok instead of a hotel. Units range from oversize studios with separate sitting areas to two-bedroom suites, and all have efficiency kitchens. The lobby area feels much more like an apartment building than a hotel, although there is a small swimming pool and fitness center for guests as well as breakfast service. For the price, this is an excellent value. Plus, Bangkok's best Italian restaurant, Zanotti, is just downstairs, and scores of street food vendors are just a block away on busy Silom Road.

3,000-4,500B

◖ **Lebua at State Tower** (1055 Silom Rd., tel. 02/624-9999, http://bangkok.lebua.com, 4,000B) offers five-star luxury, stunning views, and a great location, which make this all-suite hotel a top choice for business visitors and tourists. Suites are large, light, and airy, decorated with unobtrusive modern furniture. Two- and three-bedroom suites are larger than most apartments and have kitchens. The balconies offer spectacular views (you'll have to sign a liability waiver before they unlock them; guests with small children can opt to keep them locked), but for the best view in town, head upstairs to the Dome at State Tower for cocktails. The hotel is owned by a local businesswoman, so prices tend to be much more reasonable than what you'll find at international luxury hotels.

Over 4,500B

One of the grandes dames of Bangkok hotels, the **Dusit Thani** (946 Rama IV Rd., Skytrain: Sala Daeng, subway: Silom, tel. 02/236-9999, www.dusit.com, 5,000B) is located in busy Silom at the corner of Silom and Rama IV Roads, across the road from Lumphini Park. The five-star hotel is right in the middle of all the business, shopping, eating, and partying that goes on in the neighborhood and right next to both a Skytrain stop and a subway stop. Inside is everything you could ask for in a luxury hotel: well-appointed guest rooms with all the modern amenities and eight different restaurants serving everything from coffee and pastries to traditional Thai food and gourmet French meals. There's also an excellent spa on the grounds. The hotel completed extensive renovations in 2008.

The **Metropolitan Hotel** (27 S. Sathorn Rd., tel. 02/625-3322, www.metropolitan.como.bz/bangkok, 7,500B) embodies what has now become the sleek minimalist design of classic Asia meets Soho. The staff dress in Comme des Garçons uniforms, and everything in the place feels posh and designer, albeit less Thai than some of the other luxury hotels in the city. Most of the guest rooms are very spacious, even by Bangkok five-star-hotel standards, at nearly 46 square meters.

The perfect marriage between traditional Thai style, with its ornate, exotic detailing and modern design, is the ◖ **Sukhothai Hotel** (13/3 S. Sathorn Rd., tel. 02/344-8888, www.sukhothaihotel.com, 12,000B). The grounds are surrounded by small lily ponds and reproductions of statues and pagodas from the Sukhothai period. The guest rooms offer everything you would expect for the price you're paying, and they are more than comfortably sized. Check out the afternoon chocolate buffet.

CENTRAL BANGKOK– PLOENCHIT AND LOWER SUKHUMVIT
Under 1,500B

Lub D Siam (925/9 Rama I Rd., Skytrain: National Stadium, tel. 02/612-4999, www.siamsquare.lubd.com, 1,000B) is a trendy little hostel-guesthouse and a fantastic value find in the middle of Siam Square. It's literally at the foot of the stairs to the Skytrain and a short walk to Siam Square, MBK, and the rest of the area's shopping, food, and attractions. Guest rooms are very basic, but the bright colors, unfinished cement, and funky art make it seem less like a budget hostel and more like a trendy place for travelers to congregate. Some rooms, including the men's and women's dorms, have shared baths, although there are deluxe rooms with en suite baths. There is a courtyard and indoor common area with a bar, and the very friendly staff sometimes organize fun group activities.

With its 1950s theme and rock-bottom prices, the **Atlanta** (78 Sukhumvit Soi 2, Skytrain: Ploenchit, tel. 02/252-6069, www.theatlantahotelbangkok.com, 800B) has become something of a Bangkok institution. It can't be called retro, since the hotel simply has not changed in decades, and although the Atlanta offers amenities such as Internet access, air-conditioning, and a pool, it does have a slightly crumbling feel to it. Still, the location is great, the food at the restaurant is good and cheap (they have lots of vegetarian choices), and the place itself is fascinating. The owners have taken a strong stand against sex tourism, evident from the notices in the hotel and on their website, and won't tolerate the kind of shenanigans that can go on in some of the other hotels in the neighborhood, making it a good place to bring children.

Everyone's favorite mid-range guesthouse in the Siam Square area is **Wendy House** (Soi Kasemsan 1, tel. 02/216-2436, 1,200B), thanks to the clean, pleasant guest rooms, professional service, and great location if you're in Bangkok to do some shopping. This is the quintessential guesthouse experience—lots of young travelers around, a small Internet café in the lobby, and basic guest rooms.

The **Golden Palace** (15 Sukhumvit Soi 1, Skytrain: Ploenchit, tel. 02/252-5115, www.goldenpalacehotel.com, 1,250B) is neither golden nor a palace, but it's a great value if you're looking for a hotel under 1,500B in a quiet but centrally located area. The hotel is reminiscent of an American motor lodge,

with two-story wings on either side of a swimming pool, all covered in stucco and painted aqua. The deluxe guest rooms are big, bright, and airy, but stay away from the standard guest rooms, which don't have any windows. There's also Internet access and a small café serving Thai and Western dishes, but it's so well located, just a five-minute walk from the Ploenchit Skytrain and Sukhumvit Road, that you shouldn't have to eat any meals here.

The **All Seasons Bangkok** (97 Rajprarop Rd., Skytrain: Victory Monument, tel. 02/209-3888, www.accorhotels.com, 1,200B) is a great choice for budget-conscious travelers who want the reliability of an international chain in an interesting urban location. Guest rooms in this large (177 room) property are small and somewhat generic and modern, but they are very clean and comfortable, as are the baths. You won't find a pool here, although there is a restaurant and bar on the premises. The property is just 400 meters from Victory Monument, which is full of food stalls, restaurants, and places to get a beer.

1,500-3,000B

In an area full of five-star hotels and embassies, **Golden House** (1025/5–9 Ploenchit Rd., tel. 02/520-9535, www.goldenhouses.net, 1,650B) stands out as one of the few low-priced options until you get to Sukhumvit Road, a little farther east. The common areas of this small guesthouse are well decorated, and the simple, clean guest rooms and baths are a bargain in the neighborhood, especially if you get one facing the small garden area in the back. The best part is the location, just two minutes from the Ploenchit Skytrain on a very quiet *soi*. Although you're just a 10-minute walk (or two-minute Skytrain ride) to the Nana area, the neighborhood feels worlds apart from the commotion.

Not exactly charming or filled with personality, the **Swiss Park Hotel** (155/23 Sukhumvit Soi 11, Skytrain: Nana, tel. 02/254-0228, www.swissparkhotelbangkok.com, 1,600B) is nonetheless a solid, inexpensive generic hotel in an area where your choices are limited to expensive international chains, really cheap guesthouses, and mediocre mid-range hotels. Guest rooms are clean if a bit basic and dated. There's a swimming pool, a restaurant, and a generous breakfast buffet, all of which give it a slight lead over the competition.

It's nothing fancy, but if you're looking for a hotel in this price range, the **Federal** (27 Sukhumvit Soi 11, Skytrain: Nana, tel. 02/253-0175, www.federalbangkok.com, 1,700B) is a good value. With a small swimming pool, a 24-hour coffee shop, and a location that is perfect if you need to be close to Sukhumvit and the Skytrain, you may not mind the worn feeling—common areas and guest rooms are clean but could use some renovations. It's near some of the bigger clubs, but the area directly around the hotel is not too noisy.

One of the coolest places to spend a night in Bangkok is the newly reopened **Reflections** (244/2–18 Pradipat Rd., Skytrain: Saphan Khwai or Ari, tel. 02/270-3344, www.reflections-thai.com, 1,850B). After losing their lease to a condo development at the old location, the boutique hotel's owner commissioned different Thai and international artists to decorate each of the property's guest rooms once again. The result? Some are filled with modern photography, others are 1970s retro or even communist-Chinese-propaganda themed, and all are funky and expressive. The beds are still comfortable, and the baths clean and functional. The new location lacks a pool but has a good Thai restaurant on the premises; it is becoming a spot to see and be seen.

Across from the enormous Central World Plaza mall and nestled behind another shopping area, the **Aphrodite Inn** (61–65 Ratchadamri Rd., Skytrain: Chit Lom, tel. 02/253-7000, www.aphroditeinn.com, 2,700B) is a rare well-equipped, inexpensive hotel for the area. The guest rooms are a bit sparse (definitely no frills here), but they do have little Thai touches such as colorful pillows and tropical plants.

Baiyoke Sky Hotel (222 Rajprarop Rd., tel. 02/656-3000, www.baiyokehotel.com, 3,000B) is the tallest hotel in Bangkok at 88 stories, and if nothing else, you'll never have trouble explaining to a taxi driver where to go. Just point: You can see the building from anywhere in the city. Though not quite as plush as the many five-star hotels in the city, and decorated in the sort of 1990s generic hotel style you find all over the world, the guest rooms are very large and the view is (as you can imagine) excellent. Take a dip in the outdoor pool on the 28th floor if you want to swim under the stars. Another plus: It's located right next door to the busy Pratunam market. The main drawback is the sheer size of the place. With over 600 guest rooms, it's popular with big tour groups.

C **Tenface** (81 Soi Ruam Ruedi, Skytrain: Ploenchit, tel. 02/695-4242, www.tenface-bangkok.com, 2,800B), a serviced apartment in the Ploenchit neighborhood, features bold modern design, spacious guest rooms, and plenty of in-house amenities. The smallest one-bedroom suites are 60 square meters, but the monthly rates (especially during promotions) make the place a bargain for long-stay visitors compared to similarly luxurious hotels in the area. The downstairs restaurant offers Thai fusion, and there's a swanky little bar too. Extras such as a free Skytrain pass and a local SIM card for your mobile phone are icing on the cake. Some may find the location a drawback, as it is a 20-minute walk from the Skytrain, but there is a complimentary *tuk-tuk* shuttle.

Vie Hotel Bangkok (117/39 Phayathai Rd., Skytrain: Ratchathewi, tel. 02/309-3939, www.viehotelbangkok.com, 2,900B) which opened in 2009, is part of Accor Hotels' upscale designer brand. With more than 150 guest rooms, it's a large property and still feels like part of a chain, but it's exceptionally well maintained, and guest rooms and common areas are clean, comfortable, and predictable. The neighborhood north of National Stadium hasn't traditionally been a big tourist neighborhood, but the opening of Vie and a few other hotels in recent years has proved that it's an excellent base from which to explore both the Old City and modern Bangkok. In addition to being right on the Skytrain, the hotel is just a few minutes by foot to the canal ferry serving historic Bangkok.

3,000-4,500B

Less about tour groups than board meetings, the **Amari Watergate** (847 Petchaburi Rd., tel. 02/653-9000, 3,500B) is an international business hotel in the middle of the busy Pratunam market area. Guest rooms at this high-rise luxury hotel are modern, colorful, and hospitable. The lobby area is spacious and very well furnished, though it feels a little too professional to warrant much hanging out. There's a nice spa on the premises along with a pool, both of which are great for de-stressing after a long day of shopping in the neighborhood.

It's really tough to find any flaws in **(Ariyasom Villa** (65 Sukhumvit Soi 1, Skytrain: Ploenchit, tel. 02/254-8880, www.ariyasom.com, 4,400B), an exceptional small hotel a block away from Sukhumvit Road. The setting, a 1940s-era Thai home, has been perfectly restored and renovated so that it feels both old and authentic as well as modern and convenient (it may be the only property this size in the whole city that's disabled-accessible). There is lots of natural hardwood and Thai silk, but nothing feels overdone or gimmicky. Guest rooms are spacious and modern, and there are also some family suites available. There is even a small swimming pool. The restaurant, Na Aroon, has some of the best Thai vegetarian food anywhere.

Over 4,500B

The **Siam@Siam Design Hotel & Spa** (865 Rama I Rd., tel. 02/217-3000, www.siamat-siam.com, 5,000B), opened in 2007, is another concept hotel, and this time the concept is modern design. With concrete walls and floors, colorful rugs and pillows, and a vaguely Thai aesthetic, it's very modern, a little trendy, and definitely unique. If you're looking for peaceful pastels, this hotel is not for you. Party House One, the bar on the first floor, is bright and funky, with floor-to-ceiling windows so you can watch the traffic whiz or crawl by, depending on the hour. Upstairs, Bar Eleven is a little more chilled out. The coolest part of the hotel

is the infinity swimming pool. Guest rooms are on the small side but come equipped with all the modern amenities.

Just a five-minute walk from the Skytrain, **The Nai Lert Park** (2 Wireless Rd., tel. 02/253-0123, www.swissotel.com, 5,600B) is a well-located five-star hotel. The grounds, including an expansive leafy garden, feature some of the nicest outdoor public spaces in Bangkok. The main lobby is decorated with dark wood and multistory ceilings against the backdrop of the tropical gardens, which you can see thanks to the glass walls in the back. Some of the guest rooms have very modern furnishings; others are more traditional. All are big and airy, though, and some have small balconies overlooking the gardens and swimming pool. It is not quite as fancy as the Oriental or the Four Seasons, but also not quite as expensive.

With its grand stately lobby (look up at the intricately painted ceiling when you enter, and the mural adorning the staircase), spacious and lavishly decorated Thai-style guest rooms, and excellent service, the **Four Seasons** (155 Rajadamri Rd., tel. 02/250-1000, www.fourseasons.com/bangkok, 9,000B) lives up to its name. If your rate includes breakfast, you're in luck—the choice of fresh fruits, dim sum, and traditional American breakfast foods is more than generous. Just five minutes on foot from the nearest Skytrain or the shopping district, the hotel is very well located if you want to avoid dealing with traffic.

Anantara Baan Rajprasong (3 Soi Mahardlekluang 3, Ratchadamri Rd., Skytrain: Ratchadamri, tel. 02/264-6464, www.rajprasong-bangkok.anantara.com, 5,000B), a high-end serviced apartment tucked away in one of Bangkok's most convenient neighborhoods, is an excellent value for those who want a little more space than a regular hotel room without sacrificing luxury. All suites have small kitchens, living rooms, and balconies, and they are the size of a typical one-bedroom apartment. There is a fitness center, a nicely landscaped pool, and a restaurant that serves breakfast daily.

CENTRAL BANGKOK–UPPER SUKHUMVIT
Under 1,500B

For an inexpensive place to sleep on Thong Lor, **Buri Guest House** (58/14–15 Sukhumvit Soi 55, tel. 02/714-1508, www.buribandb.in.th, 500B) is your best choice. Clean, friendly, and five minutes away from the Skytrain, the place even has some cute decorative touches such as satellite TV, art on the walls, and fresh flowers in the guest rooms. But for 500B per night, it's still a guesthouse. The guest rooms are quite small, and there's an Internet café on the premises.

Padi Madi Guest House (2/7 Sukhumvit Soi 53, Skytrain: Thong Lor, tel. 02/662-4272, www.padimadibangkok.com, 1,000B) is a stylish, simple, and friendly guesthouse in trendy Thong Lor, and an exceptional value if you're looking for a nice but inexpensive place to stay in this neighborhood. Guest rooms are small but nicely and efficiently decorated in a universal Ikea-esque style. The location is just a block from the Thong Lor Skytrain station and a couple of minutes to Soi Thong Lor and the food vendors across the street. The owners are very helpful and friendly too.

1,500-3,000B

Three adjacent townhouses right off of Sukhumvit went through extensive renovations to become **Napa Place** (11/3 Napa Place, Sukhumvit Soi 36, tel. 02/661-5525, www.napaplace.com, 2,300B), a unique, personal bed-and-breakfast. Airy and decorated like someone's home, the bedrooms are spacious, sunny, and simple, but a big step above what you'll encounter at any guesthouse. The common spaces include a small library and an area for kids to play. Some baths have whirlpool bathtubs.

A little far from the main road, the **Davis Hotel** (88 Sukhumvit Soi 24, tel. 02/260-8000, www.davisbangkok.net, 2,800B) is worth the extra taxi fare if you're looking for a modern, kitschy pillow to rest your head on at the end of the day. The European-style building looks a little out of place amid the palm trees and plain commercial spaces at the top of the *soi*, and that's a good indicator of what's going on inside. With nearly 250 guest rooms, it's a little too big to qualify as a boutique hotel; nevertheless the common spaces' strange combination of Thai style with modern and neo-Renaissance furnishings creates a sort of quirky luxury feel that is often hard to find in larger properties.

Over 4,500B

Set in a 19th-century colonial mansion, filled with antiques from British and French colonial Burma, India, and Indochina, the ◖ **Eugenia** (267 Sukhumvit Soi 31, tel. 02/259-9017, www.theeugenia.com, 5,800B) is about as lovely a small boutique hotel as you'll find anywhere in Bangkok. Set back from Sukhumvit, each of the 12 spacious suites is decorated with furniture personally collected by the hotel's owner and his family. No detail, down to the light switches, is generic, and you'll feel more like a guest at someone's home than a guest in a hotel. But with deliciously scented bath products, free Wi-Fi, and even a free minibar, you'll miss very little at the Eugenia compared to a larger hotel. Rooms open out onto the rear courtyard and overlook a small dark-green-tiled swimming pool where you can sit beneath swaying palm trees. There is also an excellent restaurant on the premises.

ACROSS THE RIVER

Most visitors like to stay on the east side of the Chao Phraya for the sake of convenience, but just across the river are some good accommodations options too, and crossing over during the day is easy using the many ferries available. At night, you'll need to take a taxi over the closest bridge.

Over 4,500B

Once you leave the busy road and enter the grounds of the **Bangkok Marriott Resort & Spa** (257/1–3 Charoennakorn Rd., tel. 02/476-0021, www.marriott.com, 4,500B) you'll feel like you've really left Bangkok. In fact, the Marriott does the best job of creating a resort atmosphere of all the major hotels in the city. The grounds, overlooking the river, are lush and green, and there are multiple swimming pools to lounge by. Guest rooms are well furnished in modern Thai style. The hotel runs a free shuttle boat across the river during the day that leaves you at Saphan Taksin, where you can catch the Skytrain or Chao Phraya Express Boat.

The newest addition to the other side of the river is the **Millennium Hilton** (123 Charoennakorn Rd., tel. 02/442-2000, www. bangkok.hilton.com, US$175), and the property has a very modern, edgy feel to it. The enormous lobby is decorated in cool light-colored stone, the rooms are likewise light and bright, and many have views of the river. The hotel's dimly lit **Three Sixty Lounge** on the 32nd floor has panoramic views of the city from indoors and is a great place to sip a cocktail and listen to live jazz music as you watch boats travel along the Chao Phraya below. The Hilton also has a free shuttle boat during the day that drops off at River City across the river.

If you're staying at the **Peninsula** (333 Charoennakorn Rd., tel. 02/861-2888, www. bangkok.peninsula.com, US$225) you probably don't care that you're on the "wrong" side of the river, as the grounds and rooms here are among the best you'll find in the country. Rooms are generously sized and elegantly furnished with traditional colonial and Thai accents. The three-tiered pool area has individual lounging *sala* and the spa, **ESPA,** is indulgent to the extreme. The hotel has its own pier on the other side of the river, next to the Oriental Hotel, where its shuttle boat picks up and drops off passengers. The boat will also drop you off at Saphan Taksin, where you can catch the Skytrain, or at River City; it runs 6 A.M.–midnight.

Food

With people pouring in from every region to live, study, and work, Bangkok has the best variety of Thai food you'll find anywhere in the country. And with tens of thousands of restaurants, food stalls, and street vendors, there is plenty of it to be had in the city, whether you are looking to spend 30B or 3,000B on a meal. In addition to regional cuisines such as the coconut-scented southern curries and spicy Isan salads, Bangkok chefs are getting more creative with traditional recipes and flavors, putting new twists on some of the old standards and challenging diners' conceptions of what defines Thai food. All in all, the city is a foodie's dream come true.

Street food in Bangkok is like no other in the world. It's not about greasy hot dogs or overprocessed fast food, despite the fact that it's made quickly out on the street and is often consumed there too. Some of the best food in Bangkok is found in places without addresses or names. Bangkok residents, from construction workers to multimillionaires, eat many of their meals at these casual places. If you're hungry and come upon a crowded street stall with an empty seat, don't be intimidated by your lack of language skills or confusion about the menu (if there is one at all). No one will be offended if you discreetly point to whatever neighboring customers are eating. Then sit down and enjoy your food as you observe Bangkok life surrounding you.

Shophouse restaurants, especially in the Old City, though you'll find them everywhere, are another place to find great food. Most are really just a step above street food, since you'll have a roof over your head while you eat and access to a rudimentary restroom, but there won't be air-conditioning, and you'll still be sitting on plastic stools and putting up with the occasional bug at your feet.

These shops, which probably make up the majority of food places in the country (including in major cities and many tourist areas), aren't always spotlessly clean by Western standards, and some visitors may be put off by the way they look. Many of the suggestions in this book are for just those types of local restaurants, but we've tried our best to adjust expectations by indicating what you'll find inside. If you come across a restaurant falling into this category, don't dismiss it. Prices are always reasonable, and the food is reliable and fresh. Some of the city's oldest and most respected restaurants are in simple shophouses. Two great streets for exploring old-fashioned shophouse eateries are Tanao Road in the Old City and Nakhon Chai Si Road in Dusit, just north of the Old City.

Whatever the hour, you will be able to find something good to eat in Bangkok. Few casual restaurants and even fewer street stalls have posted hours, and closing times will vary depending on the area and the day of the week. In nightlife areas, some vendors will stay open until the last revelers have gone home. On Monday, many street food vendors will be closed, as will smaller restaurants, but larger restaurants will remain open. And there are plenty of late-night and all-night places to eat in the city.

If you're looking for something other than Thai food, the city has some excellent international restaurants. Thanks to thriving expat and immigrant communities, Italian, Indian, and Japanese restaurants are as good as what you'll find at home, wherever that may be, although you'll pay a premium compared to the cost of dining on Thai food.

THE OLD CITY
Cafés
Coffee & More (102/1 Phra Athit Rd., ground floor of Ban Phra Athit, pier: Phra Athit, tel. 02/280-7878, 11 A.M.–7 P.M. daily, 100B) is located in a leafy compound that used to be the Goethe Institute but is now the headquarters of a local newspaper. Grab a comfy seat, enjoy the view afforded by the huge windows facing the street, and order up one of the gourmet coffee drinks the students behind the counter are whipping up. If you're hungry, you can get lunch here too, but the real treat is the desserts: All sorts of cakes and pastries line the shelves.

Grab a table outside of **Rickey's** (22 Phra Athit Rd., pier: Phra Athit, no phone, 9 A.M.–7 P.M. daily, 100B) and sit and watch the busy Phra Athit come to life in the morning. Just a three-minute walk from the Phra Athit boat pier (cross the street, take a left, and head toward the Grand Palace), if you've come by boat, Rickey's is the perfect place for breakfast before hitting Ko Rattanakosin, especially if you're in the mood for Western food. The café has the best French bread in the neighborhood and also serves up omelets, pancakes, caffe lattes, and very good iced coffee. If you're in the mood for *khao phad* or the like instead, it's one of the rare places that does both Thai food and foreign food well, all served in a lovely little *chinoise*-themed shophouse.

Local Cuisine
The most delicious roti (pancake-like flaky fried dough, served with either sweet or savory fillings or dishes) anywhere in Bangkok is at 【 **Roti Mataba** (Phra Athit Rd., opposite Phra Sumen Fort, pier: Phra Athit, tel. 02/282-2119, 7 A.M.–8 P.M. Tues.–Sun., 100B). At any time of day, the women behind the counter will be pounding and rolling out the roti dough, then cooking it on a hot griddle at the front of the small restaurant, just as they have been doing here for years. If you're in the mood for something sweet, ask for a roti stuffed with egg, banana, and sweetened condensed milk. It sounds strange, but the combination is heavenly, especially for breakfast. If you want something a little less sweet, try a roti stuffed with chicken instead. They also serve fragrant soups and stews, but the only thing fancy here is the food. Especially during lunch, the four or five small tables downstairs get packed with people. Try the air-conditioned upstairs if there's nowhere to sit.

During lunchtime, Phra Athit is lined with food vendors selling everything from grilled water buffalo on wooden sticks to sweet bananas. Since many of these vendors move from one place to another depending on the day and the season, it's hard to pin down the best, but one to look for is a pad thai vendor just to the left of Coffee & More and before Roti Mataba. You may notice her by the bamboo hat she's wearing and the sign in English offering pad thai for 30B. Using fresh ingredients and a simple wok on the side of the road, she will whip up a dish of noodles, shrimp, egg, and bean sprouts that's guaranteed to be better than anything you've had before.

On the same side of the street a few blocks toward the Grand Palace is **Hemlock** (56 Phra Athit Rd., pier: Phra Athit, tel. 02/282-7507, 5 P.M.–midnight Mon.–Sat., 200B), one of the first restaurants to open in this neighborhood. Prices are more than reasonable, but this is not quite as casual a spot as the rest of the places that line this street. White tablecloths and Zen rock gardens set the scene at this small restaurant, and you're more likely to find fellow diners sipping glasses of wine than Chang beer. The menu is a solid selection of typical Thai dishes, and the red curry is definitely on the must-try list. Food tends to be a little less

spicy here, which is great if your taste buds have not yet acclimated to the searing heat of Thai chilies. There's also a small Western selection should you be in the mood for, say, garlic bread. On busy nights, expect to wait for a table.

Tucked away on a small street off Thanao Road is **Chote Chit** (146 Prang Pu Thorn, tel. 02/221-4082, 11 A.M.–11 P.M. Mon.–Sat., 200B), which, at more than 80 years old (the owner is unsure exactly when the place first opened), is one of the oldest restaurants in Bangkok. Krachoichuli Kimangsawat, whose grandfather originally opened the place, says the recipes here haven't really changed in all that time, and you'll find some things on the menu that you rarely see in other restaurants, such as banana-flower salad. There is a gigantic selection in this humble spot, but it's better just to ask Krachoichuli what she recommends. She'll size you up, maybe make some small talk, then start naming dishes. If she doesn't say it, ask for the panang curry too. If the restaurant is quiet, Krachoichuli will tell you a bit

There is an endless selection of street food in Bangkok.

© SUZANNE NAM

about the family history with your meal (her English is excellent). Another plus: The beer here is the coldest in Bangkok.

Around the corner from Chote Chit on Thanao Road is a small shop called **Kor Panich** (431 Thanao Rd., tel. 02/221-3554, 8 A.M.–4 P.M. Mon.–Sat., 40B), which has been dedicated to the art of mango sticky rice since the 1930s. Well, they make the sticky rice, which they sell either in bags or small Styrofoam containers, and you've got to buy the mangoes from the surrounding hawkers, who will help you pick the best ones for eating right now (and who can wait any longer?). If you stop by during the day, you'll notice the sheer volume of sticky rice being made and sold. No surprise, many locals will tell you this is the best place for the stuff in the city. It's best to pick out the mango first then hand it over to the sticky-rice folks, who will cut it for you and put it atop the rice with a side of sweet coconut milk and a sprinkle of crunchy, crisped rice. There is a lot of sign language and hand gesturing that will have to occur for this yummy dessert to come together, and then you'll have to eat it standing up as there is no place to sit down, but don't worry, everyone at the shop is friendly and patient, and the result is worth it.

Near Democracy Monument you'll find **Thip Samui** (313 Maha Chai Rd., tel. 02/221-6280, 6–10 P.M. daily, 40B), serving classic pad thai noodles. Surprisingly, pad thai is less popular in Bangkok than dishes such as *guay teow* and *som tam*; still, the sweet, tangy noodles with shrimp are wonderful if you're looking for something familiar and comforting, and they're not spicy. Ask for extra limes to liven up the noodles.

Just a few blocks up the road along the river is **Gin Lom Chom Saphan** (11/6 Samsen Soi 3, at the end of the *soi* on the river, pier: Rama XIII Bridge, tel. 02/628-8382, 11 A.M.–2 A.M. daily, 250B), which literally translates as "eat wind, view bridge" but also means "chill out and enjoy the view." Either of those descriptions is apt for the casual riverside restaurant. There's a gentle breeze coming off the river,

and to the side you have a perfect view of the stunning Taksin suspension bridge as you enjoy an inexpensive seafood meal. It's set on prime real estate, and you'd expect things to be a lot more expensive here, but a full meal with beer will easily run you less than 500B, and that's for two people. The place can get a little noisy later in the evening. The best time to go is early, when you can still get a table right along the river. The restaurant serves mainly seafood, including steamed whole fish with lime and chili sauce, but some nonseafood items are available.

Owners have dropped "Gastronobar" from the name of **The Old Phra Athit Pier Restaurant** (23 Phra Athit Rd., tel. 02/282-9202, 11 A.M.–midnight daily, 400B) along with most non-Thai food from the menu, but it's not just another Thai restaurant thanks to the fantastic location overlooking the Chao Phraya River. The open wooden deck and small indoor dining room both offer comfortable, casual places to eat that are nicer than the average in this neighborhood. If your stomach needs a rest from all the spicy Thai food, skip their delicious curries and opt for the pad thai instead. This is also a lovely spot for an evening cocktail after a day of sightseeing.

Vegetarian

In a small alley off of Khao San Road is the small open-air **May Kaidee's Vegetarian Restaurant** (117/1 Thanoa Rd., pier: Phra Athit, tel. 02/281-7137 or 06/398-4808, www. maykaidee.com, 9 A.M.–11 P.M. daily, 100B) if you're looking for good meatless fare. Serving not just plain rice and steamed vegetables, May takes traditional Thai recipes such as *som tam* and *tom kha* (coconut-milk soup) and revamps them completely so that meat eaters won't feel like they're missing anything. Even if you don't feel like a meal is complete without some flesh, stop by for the black sticky rice with mango and banana for dessert. May also has a location on Samsen Road (this location also has simple, clean guest rooms for 450B and up per night) and runs a cooking school with classes

HOW TO EAT, BANGKOK STYLE

Bangkok is a city that loves to eat. From morning till night there's food everywhere, from street vendors selling fresh fruit for 10B to hole-in-the-wall noodle shops selling *guay teow* noodle soup for 30B to überfancy international restaurants offering up fusion food; you can't walk 10 meters in Bangkok without seeing something to snack on. In fact, many people in Bangkok don't even have full kitchens, as the food is so good and the prices so reasonable out on the street. Why bother spending the time to cook when there's someone a block from your apartment who can make whatever you want better than you can and probably cheaper too?

Chances are your hotel will have more than adequate dining options, and there are plenty of wonderful, accessible sit-down restaurants in the city. But in order to really experience dining in Bangkok, you have to go out to the streets and the food courts. For experimenting and just looking around, the lunch markets in the city center during the week and the crowded dinner markets are perfect. Not only do you get to see the hustle and bustle of urban life, but you can also wander around looking at the different dishes people are eating and take a few chances. Most everything "on the menu"

will be 50B or less, so even if you don't like what you get, you haven't blown your budget, and there's always something else to try.

During the day, the Lang Suan market area and Soi La Le Sap are favorites in central Bangkok. At night, try the Thong Lor Market, the area around Soi Convent, or Sala Daeng Soi 4 in Silom. In Dusit, the Si Yan Market has great food stalls open all day.

Another great place to see and try lots of different things is a mall food court. You won't find any of the tired brands serving up greasy fare in Bangkok. Even at the most expensive malls, food courts are like mini street markets, with an astounding variety of freshly prepared, inexpensive food. Any mall will have good food, but some of the best are MBK for cheap, hectic eats and Siam Paragon for a more refined food-court experience.

Whatever you eat, remember that Thais generally like their food spicy, and many otherwise fantastic dishes can be downright unpleasant if they're too hot for your palate. *Som tam, namtok, tom yam kung,* and *tom kar gai* are all traditionally spicy. If you learn no other phrase in Thai, remember this one – *mai koi phet,* meaning "not very hot." If you can't tolerate chilies at all, say *mai phet.*

Enjoying snacks from street vendors is one of the best ways to experience Thai food.

in Bangkok and Chiang Mai. If you can't make it to one of the scheduled times, she'll even put together private lessons.

DUSIT
Local Cuisine

The **Si Yan Market** (corner of Nakhon Chaisi Rd. and Samsen Rd., 6 A.M.–3 A.M. Tues.–Sun., 40B) is probably one of the best places for eating casual street food in Bangkok. In the morning, Nakhon Chai Si Road is literally packed full of vendors selling everything—noodles, sticky rice, fruits, and other wet-market items. In the evening the street vendors offer amazing *namtok mu* (seasoned and grilled pork salad) and *tom yam kung* made to order. Don't expect to see many foreigners here, and don't expect that most vendors will speak any English. The market is closed on Monday.

The name **Kway Teo Nua Na Sa Paa** (1116/4 Nakhon Chai Si Rd., no phone, 10 A.M.–10 P.M. Wed.–Mon., 40B) means "beef noodles in front of parliament," and that aptly describes the experience you'll have at this large, clean, airy shophouse restaurant a few blocks from Government House. The beef stock, usually served with sliced beef, beef meatballs, and beef tendon, is what has made this place so popular with government workers and people in the neighborhood for decades. If you want something more substantial, order yours with rice or egg noodles. The shop is right next door to a small shoe store (apparently shoemakers to members of the royal family) at the Phi Chai intersection.

Rad Nar (775/1 Nakhon Chai Si Rd., no phone, 10 A.M.–2 P.M. and 5 P.M.–midnight daily, 40B) sticks out because the dining room is substantially nicer than the gritty, worn-down rooms that dominate this old-school neighborhood. Walls and floors have recently been redone in modern concrete, giving the place a funky urban feel. But that's an inconsequential detail, as the food is still old-school (and still prepared and served the old way). The reason to visit is to try their version of *rat na*. Many Thais consider these soft fried noodles covered in gravy and served with vegetables to

a vendor at Si Yan Market in Dusit

© SUZANNE NAM

be the ultimate comfort food, and it's rare to find a restaurant that specializes in this dish.

CHINATOWN

If you're looking for some fast, good dim sum, head to **China Inn** (Yaowarat Rd. at the corner of Trongsawag Rd., 11 A.M.–10 P.M. daily, 50B) on Yaowarat, just across the street from the Shanghai Inn. The waitstaff, armed with wireless handhelds, will take your order from a very helpful picture menu and serve up your dumplings and noodles at lightning speed. It always seems to be busy at this café, despite the fact that there's really no ambience; it must be because the dim sum is delicious and, at 30B per plate, cheap too.

Next to the river on Charoen Krung is the cute, cozy **Harmonique** (22 Charoen Krung Soi 34, tel. 02/237-8175, 11 A.M.–10 P.M. Mon.–Sat., 300B), about 10 minutes from the Oriental Hotel on foot. The menu offers a lot of the standard items you would expect from a Thai restaurant in a tourist neighborhood but is heavier on seafood. One of the standouts is

BANGKOK'S RIVER-CRUISE DINNERS

For combining a traditional Thai meal with a sunset cruise on the Chao Phraya, one of the city's many river-cruise dinners can't be beat. You'll board a boat in the early evening and set off on a journey up and down the river, passing many of the city's historic and cultural landmarks, including the Grand Palace and the *wats* that line the Chao Phraya. Most depart from the Si Phraya pier at the River City shopping center, near the Oriental Hotel (accessible by Skytrain to Saphan Taksin, then a quick cab ride), and include a buffet meal. Some of the larger boats have music and dancing too.

Loya Nava Dinner Cruises (tel. 02/437-7329 or 02/437-4932, www.loyanava.com, departures 6 P.M. and 8:10 P.M., 1,375B adults, half price for children under 15, free children under 5) is a smaller operation with waiter service instead of a large buffet; they serve traditional Thai dishes and lots of seafood. Loya Nava uses refurbished wooden rice barges instead of larger cruise boats, so all tables have direct views of the river, and there is even a small Thai dance performance. This dinner cruise is a little more intimate and romantic than the larger ones. It's a great option for couples or groups with adolescent kids, but those with smaller children might feel a little more secure on a large boat where kids can run around.

You can't miss the large cruise boats run by the *Chao Phraya Princess* (tel. 02/860-3700, www.thaicruise.com, departures 7:30 P.M., 1,200B adults, 900B children under 12) as they float down the river with hundreds of people aboard. This is the quintessential river-cruise experience – lots of people, a huge buffet of food, drinks, dancing, and live music, all on a multilevel boat.

Wan Fa Dinner Cruises (tel. 02/222-8679 or 02/223-8064, departures 7 P.M., 1,200B adults, 800B children under 10, free children under 4) also uses refurbished wooden rice barges, and their boats are ornately decorated and intimate. In addition to the traditional Thai meal, there is Thai classical music and dancing onboard. The company also runs a daily boat tour at 2:30 P.M. (without a meal).

For a more luxurious river-cruise experience, the Banyan Tree Hotel Bangkok has a converted rice barge called the *Apsara* (tel. 02/679-1200, www.banyantree.com/bangkok/facilities/dining/apsara.html, departures 5:45 P.M. for cocktail cruise, 7:45 P.M. for dinner, cocktails 500B, dinner 1,800B). As you would expect from the Banyan Tree, dinner is a more modern affair than the very traditional meals served on the other cruises, but it still focuses on Thai food.

---

the shrimp with orange sauce. The restaurant, with a small courtyard and outdoor veranda seating, is filled with little antiques, set out in a bit of a haphazard way, adding to the charm of the place.

At night, one corner of busy Yaowarat Road is taken over by **T&K Seafood** (49–51 Khadung Dao Rd., subway: Hua Lamphong, pier: Surawongse, tel. 02/223-4519, 4:30 P.M.–2 A.M. daily, 350B). Diners sit at tables on the street, and charcoal grills are set out and filled with fish, crabs, and gigantic shrimp. Whatever seafood you order, get a side of their crab fried rice to go along and, of course, a cold Singha. If it's too hot, you can also sit inside in the air-conditioning, although outside you can enjoy

your meal and observe the never-ending commotion at the same time.

If you're not staying at the guesthouse, try to stop by for dinner at **Arun Residence Restaurant** (36–38 Soi Pratoo Nok Yoong, tel. 02/221-9158, 11 A.M.–10 P.M. daily, tea 3–5:30 P.M. daily, 300B). The half Thai and half Western cuisine, served on the edge of the Chao Phraya, is worth a trip out of your way if only to enjoy the amazing view of Wat Arun from your dinner table. A couple of steps above the casual restaurants that dominate the neighborhood, the experience is only made better by the carefully prepared dishes from the kitchen, including a *yam som o* made with crab meat and roasted rack of lamb. There's also brunch on

© SUZANNE NAM

one of Chinatown's alley restaurants

the weekend, and the restaurant serves a high tea every day, timed so you can watch dusk settle on the river while enjoying your pastries and tea. After you've finished dinner, head a couple of flights up to the small outdoor bar, where you may just have the best view of Wat Arun in the city, and inexpensive cocktails too.

CENTRAL BANGKOK– SILOM AREA
Local Cuisine

About 10 minutes on foot from the Skytrain's Sala Daeng station, on the left side, you'll come across Silom Soi 5, sometimes referred to as ◖ **Soi La Lai Sap** (20–40B). From the street it just looks like a narrow alley next to a bank, but if you walk inside on any weekday, you'll find an outdoor market area with an excellent variety of casual foods, from the ubiquitous *guay teow* to Isan sausage and *som tam*. If you're hungry for lunch but don't want to commit to any particular dish, this is the place to go on a tasting spree. You'll find some of the best variety of street foods here and prices that are right

for sampling. If there's still room left after the main course, look for the *man chueam* hawker. He's the one with a small charcoal grill cooking up chunks of what at first glance looks like an oversized piece of potato. It's cassava (the root used to make tapioca), soaked in sweet syrup and grilled—not a dessert you're likely to find on any restaurant menu.

A 100-year-old colonial-style wooden house filled with palm trees, wooden ceiling fans, and shuttered windows, the building that houses **Blue Elephant** (233 S. Sathorn Rd., Skytrain: Surasak, tel. 02/673-9353, 11:30 A.M.–2:30 P.M. and 6:30–10:30 P.M. daily, 1,300B) alone is worth a visit. And then there's the food: Serving both classic Thai dishes and innovative combinations such as foie gras with tamarind sauce, the menu is creative but stays true to the flavors of Thailand. If the choices are too overwhelming, try the generous set menu. Expensive by Thai standards at 1,300B, it's a bargain for travelers. Blue Elephant is also home to a cooking school, where you'll not only get to attempt to create some of their delicious dishes but also get a chance to go to one of the city's wet markets to select the ingredients first. Since opening in 1980, the restaurant has expanded and now has locations in Europe and other parts of Asia, but there's really nothing like enjoying it in the original location.

Less homey and more formal than Blue Elephant, **Naj** (42 Convent Rd., Silom, Skytrain: Sala Daeng, tel. 02/632-2811, 11:30 A.M.–2:30 P.M. and 5:30–11:30 P.M. daily, 1,200B) is another great choice for a special Thai meal. On Soi Convent between busy Silom and Sathorn Roads, the restaurant is a heavenly oasis set in an old Thai house. Sure, you can get a great *tom yam kung* on the street for 30B, but the attention to detail and the lovely surroundings, not to mention the wine list, make this place worth the expense. Try the *yam som o* (pomelo salad with shrimp), prepared in a way you won't find anywhere else. The restaurant also has a nightly traditional Thai dance and classical music show.

Eat Me (1/6 Soi Pipat 2, off Convent Rd., Skytrain: Sala Daeng, tel. 02/628-8382, 3 P.M.–1 A.M. daily, 1,000B) is a restaurant and a contemporary art gallery set in an old wooden house. Once you step inside, the decor is decidedly modern, with its concrete and exposed beams. The menu is modern too, offering Thai-, Indian-, and Italian-inspired dishes. It's a place to see and be seen but still casual and intimate thanks to the small seating area.

Secret Garden (117/1 Sathorn Rd., Skytrain: Chong Nonsi, tel. 02/286-2454, 11 A.M.–10 P.M. daily, 300B) is a charming restaurant set in a large white house and surrounded by tropical gardens. The menu is full of traditional Thai dishes, all well prepared and nicely presented. Try the *kaeng khiaowan,* Thai green curry, and crispy Thai spring rolls for something indulgent. There is also a large selection of desserts, both Western and Thai, to finish off the meal. While other restaurants like this tend to attract a lot of travelers, this lovely spot is more popular with an upscale local crowd and is a great place for a romantic dinner.

Casual, homey, arty, vegetarian-friendly, gay-friendly, innovative, and unpretentious all at the same time, the **Bug & Bee** (18 Silom Rd., Skytrain: Sala Daeng, tel. 02/233-8118, 24 hours daily, 150B) is all you could ever ask for. Set in the center of Silom, the four-story café is decorated with funky prints and bright pinks and oranges yet somehow still manages to be relaxing. Perhaps it's the totally chilled-out staff who are as happy to quickly whip you up a smoothie as they are to let you sit and sip it for hours while you surf the Net on your laptop or one of their computers (just ask for the Wi-Fi password). On the menu you'll find some creative takes on traditional dishes, such as *rat na* served with sliced crepes instead of rice noodles, or *som tam* with big chunks of papaya accompanied by sticky-rice patties covered in sesame seeds. There's also a vegetarian menu and some vegan dishes. Definitely try one of the extraordinary smoothies, served in either bug (small) or bee (large) size. If you wake up at 3 A.M. from jet lag or are just heading home after a big night and are craving something to eat, hit the Bug & Bee—they're open 24 hours.

It looks a bit like a cafeteria, and it's always packed with tourists, but don't let the linoleum flooring, metal chairs, and tour buses lining the road outside deter you. **Somboon** (169/7–11 Surawongse Rd., tel. 02/233-3104, 4–11 P.M. daily, 400B) has some seriously good seafood. A must-try is the crab curry. You can get it with the crab shells still on, but if you don't feel like working for your meal, ask for it without the shell. The fried rice with crab is a great accompaniment, but if you want something a little different, ask for the fried glass noodles instead. The place is wildly popular, especially with visitors from Japan, as former Japanese prime minister Junichiro Koizumi has eaten here, and there's a photo of him on the first floor. If you're with a large party, you should try to reserve in advance (you'll end up with a table eventually, even if you don't), and ask to be seated in the dining room on the first floor adjacent to the bigger restaurant if you want a setting that's a little more intimate and traditional.

Pretty, airy **The Anna Restaurant and Art Gallery** (27 Soi Piphat, North Sathorn

Rd., Skytrain: Sala Daeng, tel. 02/237-2788, 11 A.M.–10 P.M. daily, 200B), filled with reliable Thai dishes, delicious desserts, and works by local artists, is quickly becoming a favorite among locals and in-the-know experts. That's no surprise, as it's run by the same folks who opened former Bangkok favorite Anna's in Silom. The menu, which focuses on favorite Thai dishes but also includes some fusion food and a few Western items, is similar to the old restaurant. Luckily they've also kept the desserts. The setting, in an old colonial house, is striking enough for special events but casual enough for a relaxing lunch with friends.

Maybe it's just a little bit touristy to sit in the middle of a big modern city watching traditional Thai dance and music while you eat your traditional Thai food served by traditionally dressed staff in an outdoor restaurant meant to look like an old Thai village. Sure, no one really dines that way in Bangkok, certainly no one really dresses that way, and Thai villages probably never really looked like that, but who cares? **Silom Village** (286 Silom Rd., Skytrain: Surasak, tel. 02/234-4448, 10:30 A.M.–11 P.M. daily, 300B) is a fun, charming place, especially if you have picky eaters, as there's a children's menu with some Western dishes. Prices are very reasonable, and you can expect all of the typical Thai foods on the menu. There are also some cute gift shops in the complex if you get bored of the entertainment.

A visit to **Le Lys** (104 Narathiwat Rd. Soi 7, also called Soi Prapinit, Skytrain: Chong Nonsi, tel. 02/287-1898, www.lelys.info, 11 A.M.–10 P.M. daily, 250B) is like going to someone's house for dinner. It's a little bit out of the way, tucked away in a primarily residential corner of the city (but just a few minutes from the Skytrain), and the atmosphere and furnishings feel more like a living room than a restaurant. The manager will happily stop by and chat with you about the menu for a few minutes if it's not too busy. The menu is traditional Thai, and there aren't many surprises here, although the panang duck curry is something you won't find everywhere. This place

definitely isn't as upscale as some of the other restaurants in the neighborhood.

Serious foodies will have to visit Michelin-starred chef David Thompson's restaurant **Nahm** (Metropolitan Hotel, Sathorn Rd., tel. 02/625-3333, 7–11 P.M. daily, 1,500B) at the Metropolitan Hotel. The menu is best described as high-end Thai-inspired, as you won't find any straight classics here, but you will find plenty of classic Thai flavors and Thai ingredients. The decor is somewhat generic and subdued but serves as a good neutral backdrop for the intensely flavored, intensely spicy food.

International Cuisine

If for some reason you want a break from spicy salads and rice noodles and are perhaps craving an Italian meal in Bangkok, **Zanotti** (21/1 Silom Rd., Skytrain: Sala Daeng, tel. 02/636-0002, 11:30 A.M.–2:30 P.M. and 6–10:30 P.M. daily, 700B) is hands-down the best place to go in all of Bangkok. The white dining room, filled with funky modern art, is both family-friendly and formal at the same time. A popular choice is the salt-encrusted fish, especially for the way it's served. Forgot to reserve, or you want to finish off your meal with a cigar while you listen to the live jazz band play? Diagonally across the street is the sister restaurant, Vino, serving the same delicious food in a more casual environment. If you don't see what you want on their menu, ask to see the Zanotti menu. And if you're curious about what types of wines the high-net-worth folks are drinking in Bangkok, they'll happily provide you with a tour of the wine cellar.

Soi Thaniya, off Silom and right next to Phat Phong, is filled with Japanese restaurants catering to a mostly Japanese crowd of tourists and visiting businesspeople. Not surprising given its location, the *soi* is also filled with hostess bars, and there are often scores of working girls hanging around outside trying to lure customers in. But for great sushi, check out **Sushi Tsukiji** (62/19–20 Soi Thaniya, Skytrain: Sala Daeng, tel. 02/233-9698, 11:30 A.M.–2 P.M. and 5:30–11 P.M. daily, 800B), where you can sit at the sushi bar and watch the Japanese sushi chefs prepare your meal, or sit in one of the private rooms upstairs.

Indian Hut (311/2–5 Surawongse Rd., tel. 02/237-8812, 11 A.M.–11 P.M. daily, 300B) looks just like a Pizza Hut from the outside, but don't be fooled—the restaurant is more formal once you step inside. The service is solid, and the northern Indian cuisine is well prepared. One thing you won't find on many menus back home is the *pakoras* in yogurt sauce. These light gram-based dumplings are outstanding. If you're looking for an after-dinner *pon* (tobacco wrapped inside a betel leaf and mixed with different flavors), ask the men at the restaurant to direct you. Otherwise, cross the street, turn left, and then take the next left down what looks like an alley.

CENTRAL BANGKOK– PLOENCHIT AND LOWER SUKHUMVIT
Local Cuisine

In the Siam Square area, there's as much variety in the food as in the shopping. The best bet if you want something quickly is the **Siam Paragon Food Court** on the ground floor of the mall. In the main court with the aquariums, there is a standard food court with noodle soups, chicken and rice, and other basic fare. You'll have to buy tickets for your meal at the counter toward the back, and when you've finished, just return unused tickets for a refund. There are also slews of counters selling *som tam, mu satay,* grilled pork in coconut curry sauce, dim sum treats, and anything else you'd want to try. It is a feast for the eyes if nothing else.

Across the street in Siam Square there are almost as many places to spend your money on food as there are to spend your money on clothing. **Ban Khun Mee** (458/7–9 Siam Sq. Soi 8, tel. 02/658-4112, 11 A.M.–10:30 P.M. daily, 350B), a bigger, homey restaurant that's a little more upscale than most of the other options, serves up some great curries, including a steamed seafood curry in a coconut shell and lots of Thai *kanom wan* (desserts). Although the restaurant looks like a tourist magnet, Ban Khun Mee attracts plenty of locals too.

For a café experience, still filled with college students, try **iBerry Flavors** (Siam Sq. Soi 2, tel. 02/658-4775, 10:30 A.M.–10 P.M. Sun.–Thurs., 10:30 A.M.–10:30 P.M. Fri.–Sat., 200B), the restaurant outlet of the ice cream chain. For lunch or dinner they offer Thai, Italian, and Thai-Italian, if you're in the mood for a spicy tuna salad or spaghetti with *tom yam kung* sauce. For dessert, their ice cream is a must. Local fruits and all-natural ingredients combine into such delightful treats as tamarind and rambutan sorbets and durian ice cream as well as more common flavors.

The ground floor of the posh Erawan Mall is filled with cafés and small restaurants frequented by shoppers and nearby office workers. A real must-try standout is ☕ **Nara** (Erawan Bangkok Mall, 494 Ploenchit Rd., Skytrain: Chit Lom or Rajadamri, tel. 02/250-7707, 10 A.M.–11 P.M. daily, 300B), a traditional Thai restaurant that looks far more expensive than it is. Staff are attentive and friendly, and the decor is casual, elegant, and subtly Thai, but it is really the food that makes it sometimes impossible to get a seat here during lunchtime (call ahead for a reservation). *Som tam mu krop,* traditional *som tam* topped with crispy fried pork, brings new life to a near-staple food; the fresh spring rolls wrapped in crepes are another standout. But the best dish is also one of the cheapest on the menu, at 80B—the Sukhothai noodles, a sweet, spicy noodle soup with ground pork and crispy fried vegetables. Try a bowl even if you're full; it's as good as it gets.

Coffee Beans by Dao (20/12–15 Soi Ruam Rudee, Skytrain: Ploenchit, tel. 02/713-2506, 10 A.M.–10 P.M. daily, 200B) is an immensely popular Thai restaurant with the college crowd, probably thanks to the amazing desserts (including green-tea cheesecake, which is a must-try). It seems like this place's raison d'être is dessert, but don't just go for coffee and sweets. You'll find all of the typical Thai dishes here, including a few Isan favorites, and the food is as good as the sweets.

Try casual, fun **Ad Makers** (65/3 Soi Ruam Rudee, Skytrain: Ploenchit, tel. 02/168-5158, 5:30 P.M.–1 A.M. daily, 200B) if you're looking for a solid Thai meal, cold beer, and live music pretty much any night of the week. Although it's not as casual (or worn down) as the now-closed original location on Lang Suan, the menu, including a delicious panang curry and fried baby soft-shell crabs, is just as reliable, and the crowd is just as fun. If you've just come to have a drink and listen to music, ask for an order of their Isan sausage to snack on. The place always draws a mixed crowd of locals and expatriates, and there's a friendly, casual vibe to the restaurant.

The same folks who own Baan Kanita opened up **Curries & More** (63/2 Soi Ruam Rudee, Skytrain: Ploenchit, tel. 02/253-5408, 11 A.M.–2 P.M. and 6–11 P.M. daily, 500B), a hipper, younger restaurant in the embassy district. The food is as solid as the more formal sister restaurant's, but instead of a traditional theme, the restaurant is decorated with photography and modern art. The outdoor covered veranda is a choice spot to sit.

Sra Bua (Siam Kempinsky Hotel, 991/9 Rama I Rd., tel. 02/162-9000, 6–11 P.M. Tues.–Sat., 1,500B), opened in late 2010 by Henrik Yde-Andersen, the Michelin-starred Dane responsible for Copenhagen's highly acclaimed Kiin Kiin, has a contemporary high-end Thai menu, and the chef uses modern twists that include molecular gastronomy (the table service of the frozen red curry with lobster is awe-inspiring), which you won't find much of in Bangkok. Although the menu is pricey, the prix fixe lunch, at 1,500B, is somewhat of a bargain.

It's hard to find, as it's located on the top floor of an appliance shop, and the name, **Blood Type Cafe** (Verasu Bldg., 83/7 Witthayu Rd., Skytrain: Ploenchit, tel. 02/254-8101, 10 A.M.–7 P.M. daily, 200B), may be a little off-putting, but push aside any assumptions and stop by for a healthy, creative lunch. The concept of the small café is that your blood type dictates the type of food you should eat; the menu offers various suggestions depending on whether your blood type is A, B, AB, or O. No one will mind, though, if you go off-type or even order an appetizer from one list and a main course from another. The chefs have cut back on the sugar and fat and use brown rice, spelt, and brown-rice noodles instead of the typical white-rice stuff you find everywhere, and they pack the plates with fresh vegetables. Two floors down is a little coffee and dessert café run by the same folks.

Between Soi Ton Son and Soi Lang Suan is a **nameless market area** that's packed full of people 10 A.M.–2 P.M. In the maze of connecting side streets, woven between stalls selling trendy T-shirts and tropical fruit by the kilogram, are scores of cheap, yummy dishes to try. There are also a bunch of inexpensive little smoothie shacks if you're in need of a cold drink. Seek out the woman on Lang Suan Soi 6 for Thai sticky-rice desserts wrapped in banana leaves. You'll know it's her if you see a display of little triangular packages that look like they're wrapped in leaves and secured with little wooden skewers. Buy a few and open them up—inside you'll find dollops of sweet, satisfying sticky rice, sometimes topped with custard.

Just a few blocks from Pantip Plaza, across busy Petchaburi Road on a side *soi,* you'll find ◖ **Once Upon a Time** (32 Petchaburi Soi 17, tel. 02/252-8629, 11 A.M.–11 P.M. daily, 400B), the sort of restaurant your fairy godmother might have conjured out of thin air for you had you wished for the perfect dining spot in Bangkok. Serving traditional Thai food in a compound of three old wooden houses with a lovely garden, the restaurant is filled with old pictures of Thai movie stars, a gramophone, and other curious objects that remind you that the country's identity is neither exclusively found in the stereotypical image of kings atop elephants nor in the fast-growing, internationalized urban sprawl that is Bangkok. Owners Pupisit and Pierre have fought a long and hard battle to preserve a bit of the country's history against the tide of modernization. The first restaurant was opened in 1989, but the pair were forced to find new digs when the street they were on was bulldozed to make way for a new road. This is the fourth incarnation of their restaurant. There is a sincerity here that you won't find in other, more expensive restaurants in similar settings. The restaurant serves traditional dishes including curries and rice dishes.

Sometimes called Polo Chicken, ◖ **Jay Kee's Fried Chicken** (137/1–3 Soi Polo, Wireless Rd., subway: Lumphini, tel. 02/251-2772, 10 A.M.–10 P.M. daily, 100B) is so good you may find yourself ordering more after you've finished the first plate. It starts off as juicy, crispy fried chicken but then gets coated with mounds of fried garlic and served with spicy and smoky dipping sauces, sticky rice, and whatever other Isan side dishes you choose. Particularly good are the *moon sen* seafood noodle salad (although it's nearly unbearably hot unless you specify otherwise) and the bamboo-shoot salad, but many people are happy just eating the chicken. This is a very casual joint with Formica tables and metal chairs. If you're not sure how to find it, look for the outline of a chicken in the window.

International Cuisine

Whatever you're in the mood for, from sushi to pizza to Peking duck, you'll find it at the Siam Paragon Mall. The ground floor is not only home to a great food court but also more than a dozen upscale sit-down restaurants. For a Thai take on a French bistro, **Vanilla Café** (Siam Paragon Mall, Skytrain: Siam, tel. 02/714-9652, 11 A.M.–9 P.M. daily, 300B) is the place to go. The mostly Western menu has lots of pastas, salads, and even crepes. The food is good, but the relaxed, upscale environment is the real draw.

CENTRAL BANGKOK–UPPER SUKHUMVIT
Local Cuisine

Just two minutes from the Thong Lor Skytrain station, on the corner of Soi 38 and Sukhumvit, is a little neighborhood that becomes a mecca for **street food** enthusiasts every night. If eating right out in the middle of a crowded street is a little intimidating but you still want to try some of the amazing, inexpensive casual meals Bangkok is known for, this is the place for

you. On the left side of the *soi* are a handful of small, casual shophouse restaurants where you can sit down at a table. Order anything from the menu (even a bottle of beer is sufficient), then head outside to the various stalls and see what else you'd like to try. When you order, just point to the restaurant, and they'll bring the dishes to you at your table. There's usually a *khao kha mu* vendor, serving slow-braised pork leg served with rice and a rich gravy (a dish that's sometimes hard to find in Bangkok and, when you do find it, often sold out for the day), as well as Isan specialties, noodle soups, and desserts. When in season, there's even a mango sticky-rice vendor.

The strange name **Cabbages and Condoms** (6 Sukhumvit Soi 12, Skytrain: Asok, tel. 02/229-4611, www.pda.or.th/restaurant, 11 A.M.–11 P.M. daily, 300B) makes sense once you're inside the place and have had a chance to read the walls. Cabbages are abundant in Thailand, and the founder's wish was that condoms would be too. Created to provide support for the Population and Community Development Association of Thailand (PDA), what would otherwise be just a relaxing, casual traditional Thai restaurant serving great food at reasonable prices has also become a near shrine to safer sex and birth control. Condoms and condom advertisements line the walls, and you'll be given prophylactics with your check. The restaurant was created by Mechai Viravaidya, a former Thai senator and head of the PDA, and money spent here contributes to Thailand's rural development, education and scholarships, HIV/AIDS education, and environmental protection. It's not just a fund-raising gimmick, though; the food is worth the visit. The menu is comprehensive, covering foods from across the country, but for something a little different, try the Yam Cabbages and Condoms, a spicy, sour noodle salad, and the *kai op namphueng,* their special honey-roasted chicken.

Balee Laos (186/6 Sukhumvit Soi 16, Skytrain: Asok, tel. 02/663-1051, 11 A.M.–2:30 P.M. and 5–11:30 P.M. daily, 300B) is a lovely, casual garden restaurant serving Isan food, including an excellent rendition of *namtok* *mu,* spicy grilled-pork salad. If the weather's too hot outdoors, there is an air-conditioned dining room. If the food's too hot, ask for it *mai phet.*

There's a reason **Baan Kanita** (36/1 Sukhumvit Soi 23, Skytrain: Asok, subway: Sukhumvit, tel. 02/258-4181, 11 A.M.–2 P.M. and 6–11 P.M. daily, 500B) is so popular among travelers. The atmosphere in the old Thai house is lovely, and the food is good, particularly because some of the hottest dishes are turned down a notch or two to fit with Western palates. Still, it's not a tourist trap, and dining rooms are both refined and homey at the same time, probably helped by the patient and informative staff who will answer any questions you have about the menu.

From the outside, **Oam-Thong** (7/4–5 Sukhumvit Soi 33, Skytrain: Phrom Phong, tel. 02/662-2804, 11 A.M.–10 P.M. daily, www. oamthong.com, 300B) looks just like the scores of other Thai restaurants in the neighborhood. What sets this place apart is not the white tablecloths or the little Thai dancing performance they offer, but the food. It's actually owned by the same folks who own Naj, although it's not as fancy. Start with one of their delicious *namphrik* dishes (spicy dips served with a selection of fresh vegetables), then try the *pla kra phong thot nampla,* a fried fish prepared with spicy sauce. The fish is served whole, as you'll find in other places, but the chef here prepares it in such a way that you don't have to deal with bones. End with the *bualoi bencharong,* a bowl of tiny, colorful dumplings in sweet coconut milk. It may sound a little strange, but the combination is so good that you may ask for another bowl. The restaurant also has a reasonably priced wine list.

Despite all the hype and the hipster clientele, ◖ **Bo.Lan** (42 Sukhumvit Soi 26, Skytrain: Phrom Phong, tel. 02/260-2962, 6:30 P.M.–midnight daily, 800B), Bangkok's newest innovative modern Thai restaurant, is worth the time and baht you'll spend checking it out. Menu items will mostly look familiar, but flavors have been purified and intensified—no bowls of *tom yam kung* that taste like a muddy mix of lemon grass and chili peppers. The setting is a modernized, open-air home a short taxi ride (or a long walk) from Sukhumvit Road.

Soul Food Mahanakorn (56/10 Sukhumvit Soi 55, Skytrain: Thong Lor, tel. 08/5904-2691, 6:30 P.M.–1 A.M. daily, 300B) is even more proof that Thai food in Bangkok is evolving. This trendy, interesting restaurant is run by an American former food critic, and the menu is ostensibly filled with Thai classics such as *som tam* and curry, although they've been subtly remade and perfected. The tamarind sticky ribs are divine, but you really can't go wrong with anything on the menu. The challenge is just picking a few things. Cocktails are equally creative and delicious but not as reasonably priced. The restaurant can get busy, so try to make reservations, especially for larger groups.

Aside from the street vendors catering to migrants from the northeast, the best Isan food you'll find in Bangkok is at **Vientiane Kitchen** (8 Sukhumvit Soi 36, Skytrain: Thong Lor, tel. 02/258-6171, 11 A.M.–midnight daily, 300B). Sort of like an open shack covered in a thatched roof, with exposed pipes and an eclectic mix of decorations, it nonetheless manages to have a sweet country charm not usually found in Bangkok. Maybe it's the live Isan band playing traditional instruments, or the fact that everyone seems to be having a great time. Maybe it's just because the food is so good. Order up some Isan sausage, some fried fish, and, of course, some *som tam,* which you can get with fermented fish, raw crab, or just plain. If you're feeling adventurous, there are some menu items here guaranteed to test your culinary mettle, including ant-egg salad and grilled duck beaks (just the beaks, no bodies attached).

INTERNATIONAL CUISINE

Right down the road from Baan Kanita is **Guisto** (16 Sukhumvit Soi 23, Skytrain: Asok, subway: Sukhumvit, tel. 02/258-4321, 6 P.M.–midnight daily, 700B), another of the many Italian restaurants in Bangkok. Aside from the more-than-adequate Italian dishes and excellent selection of wines by the glass, the place is generally filled with people from all over the world and has a cosmopolitan vibe that will make you wonder momentarily what city you're in. If you're just in Bangkok for a couple of days, skip Guisto, and all the other non-Thai restaurants, since you want to experience Thailand. But if you're here for an extended period, this is definitely a place to go for dinner and drinks.

Serving crepes and a mostly Mediterranean menu in leafy green surroundings just a short walk from busy Sukhumvit, **Crepes & Co.** (18/1 Sukhumvit Soi 12, Skytrain: Asok, subway: Sukhumvit, tel. 02/653-3990, 9 A.M.– midnight Mon.–Sat., 8 A.M.–midnight Sun., 400B) is a great place to go for lunch or brunch (especially if you're recovering from the night before). The interior, a wooden house, is softly lit and has a partly open kitchen where you can watch the chefs prepare your meal. If it's not too hot, outside is where you really want to be. The tables are set up low to the ground on little *salas* with lounging cushions so cushy you could take a nap. The crepes are very well executed, and the Moroccan, Spanish, and Greek dishes taste just as they should. This is a very popular brunch hangout, and you can get a gigantic brunch with fresh pastries, eggs, crepes, fruit, and coffee for 350B, so booking in advance is a necessity on the weekends.

All of the trendy kids are dining at **Greyhound Café** (Emporium Shopping Mall, 2nd Fl., Skytrain: Phrom Phong, tel. 02/664-8663, 11 A.M.–9 P.M. daily, 400B), a small upscale restaurant serving European pasta dishes and updated Thai favorites. The restaurant is owned by the fashion maven who brought the Greyhound label to Bangkok, so don't show up in a tank top and flip-flops or you'll feel painfully out of place. There's also a branch at the Siam Paragon Mall and one in Thong Lor.

On top of the Rembrandt Hotel sits the city's best northern Indian restaurant, **Rang Mahal** (Rembrandt Hotel, 18 Sukhumvit Soi 18, 26th Fl., Skytrain: Asok, subway: Sukhumvit, tel. 02/261-7100, 11:30 A.M.–2:30 P.M. and 6:30–10:30 P.M. daily, 1,000B). With white tablecloths and extra-attentive waiters, the dining room's ambience is dominated by the view from 26 stories up. It's definitely a special-occasion place, and just about everything on the menu is divine.

The loungey, swanky **Indus** (71 Sukhumvit Soi 26, Skytrain: Phrom Phong, tel. 02/258-4900, www.indusbangkok.com, restaurant and café 11:30 A.M.–11:30 P.M. daily, bar 6 P.M.– midnight daily, restaurant 1,000B, café 400B) in a leafy, quiet part of Soi 26 a few minutes in from Sukhumvit by taxi is definitely the pinnacle of modern Indian dining. There are no stereotypes here—the restaurant is housed in a 1960s art deco house, and the interior is modern but filled with Indian decorations. The food, however, is more traditional, and you'll find some excellent renditions of Kashmir cuisine, including favorites such as tikka masala. There's also a separate bar and dancing area, if you don't feel like leaving after your meal. The adjoining café offers free Wi-Fi during lunch. Just hope your laptop looks cool enough to fit in with the rest of the crowd.

Set in a compound of wooden houses nearly as big as a small village, **Face** (29 Sukhumvit Soi 38, Skytrain: Thong Lor, tel. 02/713-6048, 6–11 P.M. daily, café 10 A.M.–7 P.M. daily, 700B) is part lounge bar, part Thai restaurant, and part Indian restaurant. With spacious dining rooms filled with sculptures, carvings, furniture, and other art from China, Southeast Asia, and India, this is not a place for a fast, casual meal but rather a place to linger over your food for hours, admiring the surroundings. Order a cocktail from the lounge bar, and then take a few minutes to wander the grounds, filled with lily ponds and tropical plants, before sitting down to your meal. Or, stay inside and take a seat on the opium bed, surrounded by *chinoise* curios set in an elegant wooden house. Just keep in mind that the Thai and Indian menus are separate, and you'll have to choose which cuisine to indulge in. There's also a café on the grounds serving tea, coffee, and a selection of French pastries and chocolate.

ACROSS THE RIVER
Local Cuisine

In the Wat Arun neighborhood there are a handful of riverside bars and restaurants, including the **Patravadi Theatre** (69/1 Soi Wat Rakhang, Arun Amarin Rd., tel. 02/412-7287, www.patra-vaditheatre.com), which offers not only nightly shows but also dinner (300B). Another similar outfit is the **Supatra River House** (266 Soi Wat Rakhang, Arunamarin Rd., tel. 02/411-0305, 10 A.M.–2 P.M. and 6–11 P.M. daily, 300B), right on the river across from Sanam Luang. The restaurant serves a classic Thai menu and also offers a generous buffet.

Information and Services

VISITOR AND TRAVEL INFORMATION OFFICES

The **main city tourist office** (17/1 Phra Athit Rd., tel. 02/225-7612 to 02/225-7614, www.bangkoktourist.com, 8:30 A.M.–4:30 P.M. daily) is located in Bang Lamphu near Ko Rattanakosin on Phra Athit Road under the Pinklao Bridge and offers maps and general information about the city.

The main office of the **Tourism Authority of Thailand** (1600 New Petchaburi Rd., tel. 02/250-5500, www.tourismthailand.org, 8:30 A.M.–4:30 P.M. daily) is located in the Lower Sukhumvit neighborhood on Petchaburi Road and offers a myriad of services and information, including maps and general information about Bangkok and other parts of the country. In addition, there are **offices** at 4 Ratchadamnoen Nok Avenue (tel. 02/282-9773 to 02/282-9776, 8:30 A.M.–4:30 P.M. daily) and the Chatuchak weekend market (tel. 02/272-4448, 9 A.M.–5 P.M. Sat.–Sun.) as well as kiosks on Khao San Road and at the international and domestic arrival halls at Suvarnabhumi Airport. When planning your trip, take a look at both www.bangkoktourist.com and www.tourismthailand.org; both have comprehensive information about sights and events. From any phone in Thailand dial **1672** for toll-free information.

The Bangkok Mass Transit System, which runs the Skytrain, has also set up a few **tourist information booths** (8 A.M.–8 P.M. daily) in some of the major Skytrain stations: Siam Square, Nana, and Taksin Bridge. These folks offer maps and basic tourist information and can also help you out if you're lost.

There is also a **tourism police department** set up to protect tourists in the country, mostly from scams. If there's ever a need, dial 02/678-6800, 02/678-6809, or toll-free 1155 from any phone in Thailand.

MEDIA

There are several **local English-language publications** with information about events in the city. Both English-language daily newspapers, the *Bangkok Post* and the *Nation,* have listings of all sorts of events, from small art-gallery exhibits to bigger events, and you can find either newspaper all over the city. *Guru* and *Metro Magazine* are two free monthly magazines aimed at the city's *hi-so* (high society) crowd and the international community. They offer loads of information about current events, from movies to live music, restaurant reviews, and a good insight into what people in the city are interested in. You'll find one or the other at many bars and restaurants, in some hotels, and at most Starbucks throughout the city.

There is a handful of **online information** sources you should check out before your visit. The *Nation*'s website, www.nationmultimedia.com, has entertainment listings as well as reviews of food and shopping. To see what the expats are talking about and to search their recommendations on eating and accommodations, see www.thaivisa.com/forum, an open forum populated by locals and expats with helpful, frank advice.

BANKS AND CURRENCY EXCHANGE

There are ATMs and currency-exchange kiosks in Suvarnabhumi Airport at the international arrivals hall. (As is almost always the case, you will get the best rate if you use your ATM card instead of changing currency or traveler's checks.) The ATMs will all have an English-language option, and the one thing you must do when taking out money the first time is to get small bills. (The best way is to withdraw an amount ending in 900B, instead of an even 1,000B, to get at least four 100B notes.) Taxi drivers generally do not carry change for 1,000B or even 500B notes.

Nearly everywhere in Bangkok you will be able to find banks and ATMs. Stand-alone branches will keep normal banking hours (9 A.M.–5 P.M. Mon.–Sat.), but in some malls you will find banks with extended hours. In general, Bangkok is a safe city, but always be cautious when withdrawing large amounts of money. If you're having problems navigating the foreign machines and attempt to withdraw money too many times in one day, the banks are required to confiscate your card and destroy it. Although you may find a compassionate bank manager willing to break this rule for you (provided you have your passport for identification, of course), you'll be out of luck on evenings or weekends, so make sure to tell your local bank that you will be traveling in Thailand and be careful when entering your PIN and making selections at the ATM.

Branches of all of the major banks offer currency-exchange services in all the heavily touristed areas, including on Soi Ram Buttri near Khao San Road and at all the malls in central Bangkok. Tellers are used to foreigners and are friendly and efficient. Rates will be posted. You may be required to show your passport, so make sure to bring it with you. If you want to exchange traveler's checks, you will be able to do so at any of the bank branches as well.

For picking up wired funds in a pinch, at many branches of Bank of Ayutthaya and Siam City Bank you'll find Western Union services; hours will depend on the individual branch, but check www.westernunion.com for specifics. The post office also offers their services, but you are much more likely to find someone you can communicate with at one of the banks in the center of the city.

While many large stores, restaurants, and hotels will accept American Express, MasterCard, and Visa, most smaller shops, eating spots, bars, and guesthouses are cash-only. Do not expect to be able to charge small amounts. Some establishments, including high-end reputable jewelry and electronics stores, will add a surcharge if you want to use plastic, effectively passing on the fee they are charged by their bank for the service. Though it's technically a violation of their contract with the bank, there's no use arguing. If you want the redress and insurance most credit cards offer for large purchases, you'll have to pay it.

COMMUNICATIONS
Postal Service
The easiest place to get stamps is through your hotel concierge, who will generally sell them to you at face value or just a bit more. If you need to ship something or send it by overnight courier, **DHL** has convenient offices on Soi 12 and on Silom Road. **FedEx** has locations at the Silom Galleria on Silom Road, in Nana Square on Sukhumvit Soi 3, and on Khao San Road under the Buddy Lodge in the basement. **EMS** is another popular international courier service, and you can ship items using this service from the post office.

For full postal services, go to the main post office on Charoen Krung Road, between Surawong Road and Si Phraya Road. It's on the river side of the road and it's huge—you won't be able to miss it.

Internet
All the major hotels offer Internet access, and there are scores of Internet cafés in Bang Lamphu as well as many of the tourist areas, including Siam Square and on many of the side streets of Sukhumvit. **True Coffee,** run by one of the country's telephone and Internet service providers, has locations in Siam Paragon, on Khao San Road, and on Silom, and it is your best bet if you want to do your surfing amid

the hip and cool of Bangkok. They also have great coffee drinks and snacks. If you happen to have your laptop or another Wi-Fi device with you, you're in luck. Bangkok has a slew of free Wi-Fi places at many cafés. Just look for signs reading "Free Wi-Fi" and ask for the password.

Phone Service

If you're in need of local mobile phone service, you can buy a SIM card at any 7-Eleven if you already have an unlocked mobile phone of your own that will work on the same frequencies available in Thailand (900 MHz, 1,800 MHz, and 1,900 MHz). If your phone won't work, the most economical way to get one is to buy a used mobile phone at **MBK Mall,** where you can pick one up for as little as 1,500B, less than the cost of renting a phone for a few days. There are three main mobile-phone service providers: AIS, DTAC, and True Move. You can add value to your SIM card from any of these companies at any 7-Eleven.

EMERGENCY AND MEDICAL SERVICES
Medical

In Bangkok, dial **191** for general emergency services and **199** for fires, but unless you speak Thai, it may be very difficult to communicate your problem to the operator. Dial **1155** for the tourist police, where you're more likely to get an English-speaking operator who may be able to assist you, depending on the emergency.

For medical emergencies, dial **1646** if you need an ambulance in a life-threatening situation, or make your way to the emergency room of the nearest hospital. Private hospitals with English-speaking doctors and nurses offer emergency care and even their own ambulances.

The nicest and most centrally located hospitals are **BNH** (9/1, Convent Rd., Silom, tel. 02/686-2700), **Bumrungrad International Hospital** (33 Sukhumvit 3 Soi Nana Nua, tel. 02/667-1000, emergency tel. 02/667-2999), and **Samitivej Hospital** (133 Sukhumvit 49,

tel. 02/711-8000). Each is a large full-service hospital offering services ranging from emergency care and pediatrics to oncology and even dental care. These hospitals are quite swank by American standards (some of the waiting rooms look more like hotel lobbies than hospitals, and there are attendants who will even bring you tea and water while you wait). Depending on the problem, you can usually get an appointment for the day you call, and the cost will be unbelievably reasonable compared to health care in the United States. If your insurance covers you while abroad, you'll have to pay out of pocket and get reimbursed later.

Dental

If you need dental care while in town (or want to take advantage of the low-cost procedures available), there are scores of dentists in the business districts with storefronts that will be hard to miss. In addition to the regular hospitals offering dental services, **Bangkok Dental Hospital** (Soi Thong Lor/Sukhumvit 55, across the street from the Sizzler restaurant, tel. 02/382-0044, www.bangkokdentalhospital.com) is a large, professional full-service dental hospital.

Pharmacies

There are small pharmacies all over the city if you need a prescription filled. **Foodland** (No. 9 Phat Pong 2, tel. 02/233-2101) in Silom is open 24 hours and has a pharmacy if you can't wait. The English chain **Boots** has locations all over the city with knowledgeable English-speaking pharmacists.

Diplomatic Services

The **American Embassy** (120/22 Wireless Rd., tel. 02/205-4000) can provide guidance in emergency situations. After hours, there is a consular duty officer on call who can provide assistance. The embassy website, http://bangkok.usembassy.gov, provides information about Thai-U.S. relations and events sponsored by the embassy as well as other helpful information.

LAUNDRY SERVICES

While doing your own laundry may prove to be untenable in Bangkok, as most clothing is hung dry and there are few dryers to be found, there are plenty of inexpensive laundry services available in the city. In the Bang Lamphu area you'll see signs for wash-and-fold service, and hotels will routinely provide fast turnaround at inexpensive prices. Nicer hotels, particularly global chains, will charge a premium for laundry service.

LUGGAGE STORAGE

Your best bet for luggage storage is the hotel you're checking out of. Most hotels and even guesthouses will hold onto your bags for a nominal fee (if any) if you are traveling in other parts of the country. If you don't feel confident in the security, however, you can leave luggage at the airport for around 100B per day per item. Look for the **Chubb** counters at the arrival hall on level 2 and the departure hall on level 4.

Getting There

AIR

Bangkok is served by the country's main international airport, Suvarnabhumi Airport, 25 kilometers outside of the city center. Suvarnabhumi Airport was built to replace the outdated Don Muang Airport in 2006, but some regional flights still depart and arrive at Don Muang. If you are flying out of Bangkok on a domestic flight, make sure you check which airport you're leaving from.

Even with Don Muang taking up some of the slack, Suvarnabhumi is one of the busiest airports in Asia, handling up to 40 million passengers per year through one domestic and one international terminal. Generally, check-in and security lines move quickly and efficiently, but you can get caught up at immigration processing. Make sure to allow plenty of time (wait times can be as long as 45 minutes) to get through. Once you're in, there's plenty of food and shopping in the international terminal to keep you busy, although there aren't a lot of comfortable places to just sit and relax.

Taxis from the Airport

Assuming it's not rush hour, the fastest, cheapest way to get to the city center is to take a metered taxi. The airport arrival area is a little confusing, with throngs of people from all over the world pouring out into a cramped area filled with waiting friends, family, and tour guides. You have to go down to level 1 to get to the taxi stand, where you line up and tell the attendant your destination. The attendants are generally helpful and have a list of popular destinations in Thai and English in case you can't get your message across adequately. You'll then be directed to the next available taxi; you must pay 50B in addition to the meter fare as well as any tolls (luggage is free). To the city center, expect the full fare to run 250–350B, depending on traffic. Unless you have time to kill and want to save the equivalent of US$2, ask the driver to take the *thang-duan,* or highway. Drivers will usually ask you to pay tolls as you go, and if you forgot to get small bills at the airport, toll booths can usually break large bills. Sometimes taxis will try to negotiate the fare instead of using the meter. This will never work in your favor, and if one tries to push the point, ask to be returned to the airport (that's usually enough to get them to turn on the meter). As you're making your way to the taxi line, you may be asked if you want a private taxi or limo instead. Do not accept a ride from anyone other than a metered taxi in the official taxi line staffed by airport workers. You'll end up at your destination but you'll pay three or four times the going rate.

Airport Express Train

The **airport rail link** opened in 2010 and offers express service to central Bangkok for

150B, which is a great option if there is traffic and you don't have too much luggage. Board the train in the basement of the arrivals terminal. From there, take either an express train to Makkasan Station and switch to the local line for two stops to connect with Bangkok's Skytrain at Phaya Thai Station, or walk across the street to the Petchaburi subway station.

Airport Buses

There are four public bus lines that run between the airport and the city, making intermittent stops and terminating in Silom, Bang Lamphu, Sukhumvit, and Hua Lamphong Railroad Station. You have to take a free bus from the terminal to the airport bus depot (you can catch the bus on level 2 and level 4), then switch to the shuttle, which costs 150B pp and can take a couple of hours, depending on your destination. Unfortunately for the environment, it's about the same price and much faster to take a taxi if you're traveling with someone else. Buses run 5 A.M.–midnight.

TRAIN

Bangkok has two major train stations, Hua Lamphong and Bangkok Thonburi (sometimes referred to as Bangkok Noi Station), served by the State Railway of Thailand (www.railway.co.th/english/); all international trains terminate at Thonburi. Hua Lamphong (445 Rongmuang Rd., tel. 02/220-4334), on the edge of Chinatown, is easily accessible by subway. Bangkok Noi Station (Rot Fai Road, Thonburi), right across the river from Ko Rattanakosin, serves as a terminating station for trains coming in from Kanchanaburi. There is no direct public transportation except for public ferry to the Rot Fai pier. All of the stations remain open all day and night.

BUS

There are three main bus stations in Bangkok where long-distance buses depart and arrive: the Northern Terminal (Khampeng Phet Rd., tel. 02/936-2852-66), near Chatuchak Weekend Market, serving destinations in the north and northeast; the Eastern Terminal (on Sukhumvit Soi 40, tel. 02/391-2504), serving eastern destinations; and the Southern Terminal (Borom Rat Chonnani Rd., tel. 02/391-2504), across the river in Pinklao, serving southern and western destinations. Buses depart and arrive at these stations at all hours of the day and night.

CAR

Driving into Bangkok can be a disastrous experience for someone not used to traffic signs in a foreign language, driving on the right side of the road, and traffic that turns an eight-kilometer route into a two-hour journey. If you are driving into the city despite all this, you'll find that the major toll roads into the city are well maintained and usually fast until you get to the edge of Bangkok. The city has five major routes coming in from all directions, and the city is encircled by a road that, to oversimplify a complicated situation, is called Ratchadapisek/Asok in the east, Wang Sawang Road in the north, Charan Sanit Wong in the west, and Rama III in the south. Once inside the city center, Bangkok's streets can be very difficult to navigate, with the direction of major roads changing from block to block and winding, narrow side streets that seem to end abruptly. If you make it to your hotel, there will probably be a parking lot, and the price of parking will either be free or a maximum of 200B per day. Guesthouses, however, don't have parking lots.

Getting Around

SKYTRAIN AND SUBWAY

Given the sheer size of Bangkok and its heat and humidity, it is not advisable to try to walk from one neighborhood to another. In the past decade, city authorities have opened both an elevated train, referred to as the Skytrain or BTS (tel. 02/617-7600, www.bts.co.th), with two lines, and a single-line subway system, called the MRT (tel. 02/612-2444, www.mrta. co.th). Both are efficient, modern, and inexpensive, and if you ever have a choice between a taxi and the Skytrain or subway, opt for public transportation.

The Skytrain's Sukhumvit line follows a vague west–east pattern, running along the main artery that changes from Rama I Road to Ploenchit to Sukhumvit Road. The Silom line is north–south, starting at Mo Chit (where the Chatuchak Market and the Northern Bus Terminal are) and then hooking west to cross the Chao Phraya at Taksin Bridge, and then

© SUZANNE NAM

Bangkok traffic jam

continues west for two stops before terminating at Wongwian Yai Station. Trains run every few minutes during rush hour; even during nonpeak times the wait is less than 10 minutes for a train.

The subway makes a sort of backward C, starting at Bang Su in the north, circling the city center, and crossing the Skytrain's Sukhumvit line at Asok (called Sukhumvit on the Skytrain) before turning west and crossing the Skytrain's Silom line at Silom (called Sala Daeng on the Skytrain) before terminating at Hua Lamphong Station.

The fare for either the Skytrain or the subway depends on the number of stops you travel and ranges 20–70B. You can either buy a prepaid card at the staffed counter at any station or go to one of the automated machines and punch in your destination to buy a one-trip card. Although there are interchanges between the Skytrain and the subway, you cannot use the same prepaid card for both, and you have to exit one system completely before entering the other.

The Skytrain and subway run 6 A.M.–midnight daily, and the last train from each station will be announced over a loudspeaker.

RIVERS AND CANALS
Ferries

Given that Bangkok was once a nearly amphibious city, it's no wonder that traveling by boat can sometimes be the best choice for getting around. The Chao Phraya is served by a public ferry system that runs up and down the river, stopping at various piers on either side along the way. If you're taking the Skytrain, you can connect to the ferry at the Taksin Bridge stop, which is Central pier. Just follow the signs for the pier when you exit the station. There are five different types of commuter boats running along the river, all run by the **Chao Phraya Express Boat Company** (www.chaophrayaexpressboat.com/en/home/). The company website offers clear schedules and maps for each pier on the river.

The tourist boat is, as the name implies, for tourists. It's a little bigger than the other boats, so you'll almost always get a seat, and there's a guide at the front who explains historical landmarks along the route. Sometimes it's a little hard to understand, and there may be some historical inaccuracies, but the guides are generally well-meaning tourism students who will answer questions and offer tips if you ask. The tourist boat runs a limited route between Central pier and Phra Athit pier (about 30 minutes either way), and only stops near main attractions, which is probably all you will need. At 100B per day for unlimited trips, it's not a bad deal at all. The first boat in the morning leaves Central pier at 9 A.M., and the last returning from Phra Athit leaves at 3:30 P.M. The tourist boat runs every half an hour on the half hour.

The four other boats are commuter boats, and you may be surprised to see that thousands of people use the boats every day to get back and forth to work or school. The boats can be a little intimidating at first, especially as the staff jump on and off the boats at breakneck speed, tying them quickly to the piers even if they don't seem to have come to a full stop—and they expect you to get on and off just as quickly.

Once on the boat, you'll usually be asked to move to the inside and find a seat, although it's fine to stand in the back where there's a better view if no one asks you to move in. A fare collector will ask you where you're going and collect the correct fare, which varies depending on the number of stops you're going but ranges 9–30B, then hand you a little receipt (sometimes at Central pier you have to buy your ticket before you board). Hold onto your ticket; once in a while someone comes around to make sure everyone's paid. There's a section reserved for monks only, so don't sit in the seats under the sign that reads "Space for Monks."

You can tell the four commuter boats apart by the colored flag at the stern. Most visitors to Bangkok will take either the local line, with a white flag, or the orange line, an express boat

FINDING YOUR WAY

Getting to a specific address in Bangkok can be a little frustrating if you're not used to the road and *soi* system used here. While main roads are generally referred to as "Thanon" (e.g., Sukhumvit Road is Thanon Sukhumvit), the side streets running perpendicular are called *sois* and are numbered consecutively: 16 Sukhumvit Soi 18 means building number 16 on Soi 18 off Sukhumvit Road.

To make things more confusing, sometimes *sois* have names too, such as Soi Polo off of Witthayu Road, or Silom Soi 5, which is commonly referred to as Soi La Lai Sap. If you don't know where you're going, it's best to ask what the nearest numbered *soi* is, the closest Skytrain or subway stop if you're going by public transportation, or, better yet, the closest intersection.

In the city, you'll notice that many intersections are labeled with large green signs in both Thai and English. Sometimes the intersection name corresponds to one of the streets, as is the case at Asok or Nana. Sometimes, of course, they don't correspond, as is the case at Si Yan, the intersection between Nakhon Chai Si Road and Samsen Road in Dusit (where some of the best street food is). Either way, taxi drivers seem to know the name of every single intersection in the city.

that stops at Central pier as well as almost all the stops with nearby major tourist attractions. Blue-flagged boats are long-range express boats with very limited stops going all the way to Nonthaburi, north of the city; you probably won't be using these at all. Express boats with yellow flags also follow a limited-stop express route but don't stop at many of the more touristed piers.

The boats run every 10–20 minutes 5:45 A.M.–7:30 P.M. daily, with the last boat leaving Phra Athit back to Central pier at around 7:15 P.M. The last boat on each of the lines usually flies a black flag.

In addition to the express boats traveling up and down the river, there are small ferries that just travel back and forth across the river from some of the piers. If you want to get to the other side of the river, it's only 2B per journey.

Canal Boats

There are also commuter boats plying some of the major canals in Bangkok, although the service seems to be declining every year. One major convenient route that's still running is along the Saen Saep Canal, which runs right next to Petchaburi Road and goes as far west as the Golden Mount near Democracy Monument and past Sukhumvit Soi 71 to the east. Canal boats are a little more of an adventure than river boats. During rush hour they can be very crowded, and they're smaller and move faster. But they're not only a convenient way to get across the city in areas where there is no other public transportation, they offer a glimpse of life along the canals, and are such an important part of the city's history that it would be a shame to miss out on at least one ride. Boats run from about 6 A.M.–8:30 P.M. and cost 9–13B per ride.

TAXIS

Metered taxis come in a variety of crazy colors, from bright orange to purple to green, but they are all clearly marked, and you won't be able to miss them. If they're available, you'll see a brightly lit red sign on the passenger side of the windshield; just wave one down. On any major road there will be plentiful taxis available, unless it's pouring rain or right around rush hour.

Metered fares start at 35B, and getting across town should run you no more than 80B unless traffic is really bad (which it often is). Although tipping is not required, most people will at least round the fare up. If you're going out of the way, across town, or to the airport, the common etiquette is to ask the driver if he'll take you first, as sometimes they'll turn down a fare if it's too far out of the way or traffic is

abominable. Most taxi drivers in Bangkok are migrants from the northeast and are friendly, personable folks happy to strike up a conversation and practice some English if you break the ice. But some taxi drivers will try to take advantage of visitors by telling them the meter is broken or that the fare is 100B or more per ride. The best way to avoid getting taken for a ride is to just keep repeating "meter" and, if that doesn't work, getting out of the taxi.

You can always arrange transport from your hotel or guesthouse, but if you want a taxi for a few hours or even a full day, most taxi drivers will be happy to have the work, at rates ranging 500–1,000B, depending on the amount of time you hire them for.

MOTORCYCLE TAXIS

Motorcycles are a common mode of transportation in Bangkok and are often the fastest way to get from one point to another, especially if you're going only a few blocks. Motorcycle taxi drivers can either be flagged down on the street or engaged at one of the many stands in the city. You'll be able to spot them immediately; just look for a bunch of guys on motorcycles wearing orange vests. Fares are usually fixed and will run anywhere from 10B for a couple of blocks to 100B to get from one neighborhood to another, but you should ask the driver how much the ride will cost. Once the fare is set, make sure to ask for a helmet, then hop on the back (from the left side only, otherwise you'll burn yourself on the tailpipe) and hold on.

TUK TUKS

The colorful, ubiquitous three-wheeled half motorcycle, half car is another transportation option. These can be a very convenient, quick, fun way to go short distances, but *tuk tuk* drivers, more than anyone else in Bangkok, prey on tourists, sometimes asking exorbitant rates for very short rides. Especially around Hua Lamphong Station, they'll also offer you a very cheap ride if you agree to take a detour to "tour" a nearby gem factory. The best *tuk tuk* strategy is to use them only for short distances off main roads, as it's really no fun to be

© SUZANNE NAM

Motorcycle taxis are a common way of getting around.

stuck in the heat, in traffic, with exhaust fumes pouring into your ride. And if a *tuk tuk* driver starts the bargaining at a high price, just look for another one.

LOCAL BUSES

Under the right circumstances, taking a city bus in Bangkok is convenient and inexpensive. Under the wrong circumstances, it's confusing, time-consuming, and a little scary. The city buses, administered by the Bangkok Metropolitan Transportation Authority (BMTA, www.bmta.co.th/en), cover all of Bangkok and even out into surrounding provinces, so you can get from any place in the city to another by public bus. In fact, this is the most common form of transportation, as the Skytrain and subway systems are very limited in the areas they cover and are prohibitively expensive for most Bangkok residents.

Public buses come in a variety of colors depending on the route, the size, and the comfort level involved. The most common are the orange air-conditioned buses, the blue-and-white and red-and-cream open-air buses, and the small green minibuses (although these are run by private contractors, not the BMTA). Currently there is no bus map available in English, but there is some limited information available on the BMTA website, including bus routes that pass by common tourist sights. Click on the "Travel Guide" link for this information, and be prepared to click through each of the buses listed to determine which one goes from your location to the destination. MapGuideThailand (www.mapguide-thailand.com) also has some bus information under the "Bangkok Bus" tab. Although the search function isn't dependable for non-Thai speakers since spellings vary, if you enter the number of the bus you are considering taking, it will show you on the map the exact route the bus takes.

Bus stops are marked with signs and often have small benches and covered waiting areas. But even if you are standing at the stop, a bus will not necessarily stop for you unless you wave it down, so make sure to be on the lookout for the bus number, and then raise your hand and wave the driver down. Boarding buses happens quickly, and the bus may already be moving before both of your feet are planted inside the bus. If you find the process intimidating, be heartened by all the elderly women who manage to get on safely. Once you're on, take a seat if one is available and wait for the fare collector to come to you. Fares are 7–22B, depending on the distance and the type of bus. When the fare collector approaches you, tell him or her your destination to find out the fare for your specific route.

Bus schedules for specific routes vary, but nearly all routes will be running 5 A.M.–10 P.M. Some very popular routes run 24 hours. Buses are subject to the same traffic as everyone else on the road, and during rush hour can move very slowly, making them a good choice only for those with the luxury of time.

Vicinity of Bangkok

Within the provinces surrounding Bangkok, there are a handful of sights worth seeing, listed below. Generally, these are great excursions if you are traveling with kids and want to get out of the hectic city for a day. Many of the sights have grounds where you don't have to worry as much about traffic or other perils for small children, and many involve animals or have interactive activities, both of which are more likely to keep kids' attention than just touring museums or temples.

Note that while there is public transportation available to each of the sights, taking that route will involve getting to the bus station in Bangkok, taking a bus to the city center in the respective province, and then transferring again to another bus to get to each site. If you're short on time or would rather not have to worry about finding your way, it may make more sense to hire a taxi from Bangkok for the day.

A couple of the best day trips from Bangkok take you out of the city's surrounding provinces. **Ayutthaya,** the country's capital for more than 400 years and home to scores of temple ruins, is in central Thailand. **Kanchanaburi,** with the Bridge on the River Kwai and other historically significant World War II sights, is also in central Thailand; check the *Central Thailand* chapter for more information.

NAKHON PATHOM
นครปฐม
Just over 56 kilometers outside of Bangkok,

Nakhon Pathom is often referred to as the country's oldest city. When the city was settled in the sixth century (some believe it was settled as early as the third century B.C., when travelers from the Indian subcontinent first visited to bring Buddhism to the region), it was the center of the Dvaravati Kingdom. Today, little remains of Nakhon Pathom's glorious past, and the province is largely a suburb of Bangkok.

Sights
Surrounded by porticoes and rising high into the air, the city's imposing **Phra Pathom Chedi,** at more than 100 meters, claims to be the largest Buddhist *chedi* (pagoda) in the world. The current brick structure, covered over in orange stucco, was built during King Rama IV's reign, but inside (although you won't be able to see it) are the remains of a pagoda built in the sixth century. The original pagoda was built during the Dvaravati period, but destroyed by Burmese invaders in the 11th century. Forgotten and left to be claimed by the rainforest, the site was not rediscovered until the 19th century, when Rama IV had Phra Pathom built. Phra Pathom Chedi is also home to the remains of Rama VI.

Food
If you are visiting the Phra Pathom Chedi in the late afternoon or early evening, there is an excellent market right on the edge of the *chedi*'s grounds. Slightly less casual than a typical

market, each of the vendors here has large tables for sitting, and you can find just about anything to eat, including *hoi thot,* oyster omelets, and roti. This dinner market attracts lots of families.

Getting There
You can take public bus 83 from the Southern Bus Terminal in Pinklao on the other side of the river. Buses run frequently, starting at 5 A.M. and ending at 9:30 P.M., and the trip should take about an hour and cost 40B.

DAMNOEN SADUAK FLOATING MARKET
This floating weekend market is a popular draw among tourists. These days the market probably makes more money selling souvenirs to tourists than selling fruits and vegetables, but there's still something fun about climbing into a boat to be guided through narrow canals and watching merchants (mostly older women) paddling gracefully on small wooden boats piled high with fresh produce and other items for sale. The best time to visit the market is early in the morning. By 11:30 A.M. all

you'll find are a few boats and a lot of tourists. If you're heading down the west coast of the gulf to visit Hua Hin, this is a great place to stop since it's on the way.

Getting There
The floating market is in Ratchaburi Province, about 95 kilometers outside of Bangkok. Any tour agency can arrange an early-morning pickup from your hotel (1,000B and up), or you can hire a taxi to take you and return, but if you want to get there on your own, you can take buses 78 or 996 from the Southern Bus Terminal. The ride will take under two hours, but you'll need to catch one of the first ones (they start running at 6 A.M.) if you want to see the market. Once you arrive, you'll need to hire a longtail boat to tour the market by water. Expect to pay 200–500B for the tour.

SAMUT PRAKAN
สมุทรปราการ
Just a 20-minute drive southeast of the city is Samut Prakan (also called Paknam), at the end of the Chao Phraya where the river empties

© SUZANNE NAM

floating market at Damnoen Saduak

BANGKOK

into the Gulf of Thailand. Really an extension of Bangkok, this is where the airport is located. While not historically significant, Samut Prakan has some of the best attractions for children (and adults too) outside the city and is a good destination if you want to take a break from the intensity of Bangkok for a day.

Sights

Ancient City (Km 33, Sukhumvit Rd., Samut Prakan, tel. 02/224-1057, 8 A.M.–5 P.M. daily, 300B adults, 200B children) is an 81-hectare park shaped like the country of Thailand, with replicas of all the historically important buildings, including the Throne Hall of Ayutthaya and even a miniature Grand Palace. There's also a folk museum dedicated to farming culture, and even a recreated floating market. You can rent bikes to get around the park, but you may want to hitch a ride on one of the golf carts if it's too hot. If you plan on spending the day here, there are small cafés serving inexpensive local food on the grounds.

Sure to be breaking some world's record for its large elephant-shaped building, the **Erawan Elephant Museum** (99/9 Sukhumvit Rd., Samut Prakan, tel. 02/371-3135, www.erawan-museum.com, 8 A.M.–5 P.M. daily, 150B) is a spectacular, exceptionally well-crafted 15-story, three-headed bronze elephant with a museum inside. You won't be able to miss it; as you approach from Sukhumvit Road, the elephant will be looming ahead, and even if you're not interested in what's inside the gigantic creature, it's worth a trip just to see the structure. The museum houses a collection of mostly Buddhist artifacts from the founder of the museum, a wealthy Thai who wanted to build a place to house them for the public to see. The interior of the pedestal and elephant are beautifully, intricately decorated, with stairways covered in glittering, colorful mosaics, murals on the walls and ceilings depicting scenes from the life of the Buddha, and even stained-glass windows. The grounds, with lots of vegetation and even a fish pond, are nice to walk around, and there is also a snack bar. The

Erawan Elephant Museum

© SUZANNE NAM

museum closes at 5 P.M., and you'll be denied entry if you arrive after 4 P.M.

Another fun and child-friendly sight is the **Samut Prakan Crocodile Farm and Zoo** (555 Mu 7, Amphoe Muang Samut Prakan, tel. 02/387-0020, 7 A.M.–6 P.M. daily, 300B adults, 200B children). With over 60,000 animals, this is one of the largest crocodile facilities in the world, and there are crocodile wrestling shows and even a scary six-meter crocodile. There's also a small zoo with elephants, tigers, monkeys, and turtles.

If you are up for an adventure that may or may not work out, **Wat Khun Samut,** also called the Temple in the Sea, in Khun Samut Chin village (located southeast of Samut Prakan on the coast) is a fascinating day trip. The temple has been covered by the international media because it's slowly being subsumed by the surrounding Gulf of Thailand, stark evidence of the effects of rising sea levels. The *wat* is located on a promontory that was once connected to a village in an area surrounded by canals and shrimp farms. Much of the village has since been subsumed, and villagers are continually forced to relocate farther and farther inland, but the *wat* remains. Getting there is a little difficult, as so far there are no organized tours (although no doubt this will come soon), and you need to get to the beginning of the promontory by boat and then walk about 1.5 kilometers out to the temple. There is one daily boat to the village of Khun Samut Chin leaving the Paknam Market pier at 9:15 A.M. and returning at 3 P.M., so if you go this route, you'll have to make a day of it. Plan on bringing a picnic lunch with you, as this may be the one part of the country where you won't be able to find anything to eat. Another option is to try to hire a longtail boat from Paknam Market pier itself, though you will have to wing it a bit and ask around for someone to take you and bring you back. You can also get a car to Sakhla, a small town on the other side of the river, and then look for a boat from there. This day trip is definitely not for those who have limited time, need to follow a set schedule, or feel uncomfortable trying to communicate with people who do not speak English. If you believe that the journey is as important as the destination, you will be rewarded by not only seeing a part of the country few others visit, but also visiting the temple itself. If you come during low tide, you'll find a simple temple complex at the end of a long concrete walkway surrounded by mud flats. You'll notice that the floors have been raised by about one meter, meaning you'll need to duck quite a bit going through the doorways. During high tide, the water nearly reaches the new floor level, and if you come during a storm, you may see the waves washing in the temple windows.

Food

For some fun and interesting eating experiences, head to Samut Prakan's neighbor, Bang Na Town, where you'll find a wet market in the center of the city and plenty of food stalls serving quick, cheap meals. Given its location right on the water, even the simple noodle soups will be filled with fresh seafood instead of the usual pork, chicken, or beef. A wild, wacky dining option is **Suan Aharn Kratorn** (99/1 Bang Na-Trad Rd., Bang Na, tel. 02/399-5202, 5 P.M.–1 A.M. daily, 200B), sometimes referred to as the flying-chicken restaurant. The menu has lots of standard Thai fare, except for the first item on the list—flying chicken. When you order a flying chicken, before it's served at the table it's set on fire and then tossed across the outdoor restaurant, to be caught on the spike of a hat worn by a man riding a unicycle. Sometimes there's a little kid sitting on the shoulders of the man riding the unicycle, and he gets to wear the hat and catch the chicken. It is totally bizarre, but lots of fun. There's also a small outdoor playground for kids and karaoke stalls if you feel like belting out a tune or two after your meal.

Getting There

Samut Prakan is south of Bangkok; you can follow Sukhumvit Road all the way there if you are driving (although Sukhumvit runs northwest–southeast in the city, it turns south later). If you are taking public transportation, buses 507, 508, and 511 run from Sukhumvit in central Bangkok all the way to Samut Prakan, though with traffic in the city the journey of less than 16 kilometers will probably take well over an hour. A taxi to any of the destinations listed will cost under 200B.

THE EASTERN SEABOARD

Just a few hours' drive from Bangkok, Thailand's eastern seaboard is home to virtually every type of beach attraction that the kingdom has to offer. From the infamous nightlife and crowded beaches of Thailand's most popular beachside resort town, Pattaya, to the secluded bungalows and more upscale hangouts on Ko Chang, the seaside options in this part of the country cover a full spectrum of choices.

In addition to the sun and sand, Thailand's eastern seaboard is also home to plenty of idyllic countryside where you can see the way of life in small Thai towns where travelers rarely venture. And if you're into glistening baubles, you won't want to miss Chanthaburi's teeming gem market, where buyers and sellers from the world over congregate every weekend to deal in rubies, sapphires, and other precious gems.

Apart from Pattaya, this region is most often left unexplored by foreigners and travelers. While the hustle and bustle of Bangkok and the islands in the south often steal the limelight, Thailand's eastern seaboard has been left largely untouched—and it's as authentic today as it has always been.

PLANNING YOUR TIME

For people visiting Thailand on a short vacation, this region should be a lower priority. Although it's extremely convenient to visit from Bangkok, the beaches and islands pale in comparison to those along the lower part of the southern peninsula, and there aren't many sights of historical or cultural significance. The primary attraction of this region is that it's close to Bangkok, and many of the

© SUZANNE NAM

HIGHLIGHTS

☾ Ko Samet: Just a few hours' drive from Bangkok, this little island is surrounded by warm water and has plenty of inexpensive places to stay (page 129).

☾ Ko Man Nok: With just one recently refurbished resort on this tiny little private island, half an hour by boat from the mainland, there's nothing to do but relax and enjoy the view of the Gulf of Thailand (page 134).

☾ Chanthaburi: Gem dealers, the largest Catholic church in Thailand, and plenty of noodles to eat make this a quirky but charming little town (page 136).

☾ Ko Chang: This large, quiet island boasts breathtaking scenery thanks to rugged mountains and smaller islands speckling the horizon (page 144).

LOOK FOR ☾ TO FIND RECOMMENDED SIGHTS, ACTIVITIES, DINING, AND LODGING.

THE EASTERN SEABOARD

destinations can be visited in a day from the capital. But even if you have limited time in Thailand, getting on a plane to Phuket or Krabi on the Andaman coast or Samui would be worth the time and money for a more satisfying beach experience.

For those who do make it to this region, Ko Samet, with its warm waters and plentiful moderate accommodations, is a good choice if you're looking to get your toes in the sand as quickly as possible, although it's small and most visitors find it a little boring after just a few days. Ko Chang is much larger and offers remarkable scenery and enough other activities to keep you busy for a while. It's a growing destination, so expect it to continue to develop. Those looking for something off the beaten path should pay a visit to the town of Chanthaburi, the center of the local gem trade.

The seasons in Pattaya and Chonburi Province are similar to the rest of Thailand. The most pleasant time of year in the southeast of the country is in November–early January, when the tropical temperatures are somewhat cooler and it rains the least. It's steaming hot February–May, but it doesn't rain very much. And then, June–October, it's hot and wet, with monsoon rains becoming a near-daily occurrence.

The northern hemisphere's wintertime—due to holiday breaks there and the cooler temperatures in the kingdom—is high season for Thailand's tourism industry. Hotel, service, and transportation rates are universally increased during this time and into Songkran in April to reflect higher demand, and it's necessary to book ahead to secure flights, hotel rooms, and so on. Rates are often reduced in the May–September low season.

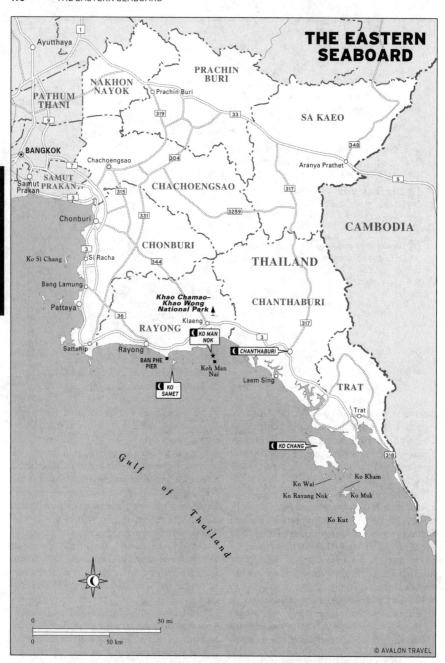

THE EASTERN SEABOARD

Pattaya and Chonburi Province พัทยา/จังหวัดชลบุรี

The city of Pattaya, just 147 kilometers southeast of Bangkok, was once a typical fishing village. Not anymore: U.S. servicemen began to popularize Pattaya in the late 1950s when GIs started flocking to its beaches from the U.S. base in Nakhon Ratchasima in northeastern Thailand. As troop levels surged throughout the Vietnam War years, Pattaya turned into a "red-light city" and became infamous for its raucous nightlife. Today, the war is long over, but the strip bars and general seediness of the city remain and have been amplified by the region's increase in tourism.

Today's Pattaya is seemingly disorganized, overdeveloped, and endlessly tacky. American soldiers have been replaced by (mostly male) tourists, but otherwise the vibe is probably pretty much the same as it has been for the past 50 years: lots of drinking, loud music, and sex for sale. It has been referred to as the world's largest brothel, and while that might not be factually correct, it probably is at least Thailand's largest.

What is so perplexing is that in recent years, Pattaya's popularity has skyrocketed. It's one of Thailand's most popular beach resorts, with hordes of foreigners arriving daily, especially from Europe, Russia, and the Middle East. Tourism figures indicate that fully one-third of all tourists who come to Thailand visit Pattaya, most as part of package tours sold through travel agents. Another figure that might make you scratch your head: 5 million, the number of tourists that arrive in Pattaya every year.

Despite its popularity, Pattaya City is dirty, depressing, and definitely not fit for families. Pattaya Beach and the surrounding beaches and islands are mediocre, especially compared with the beaches farther down the coast or on the other side of the gulf. It's just not clear why so many tourists flock here, other than for the sex tourism and because it's an easy drive from Bangkok.

That's the bad news, and there's no sugarcoating it. The good news is that the local government's attempt to broaden Pattaya's appeal, coupled with an increasing diversity of holidaymakers who visit the region, have led to a diversity of accommodations and attractions. The city and developers have really been pushing to make the area more family-friendly. While there may be plenty of cheap guesthouses above bars and lurid nightlife catering to the bachelor set, there are also plenty of luxe resorts and increasingly good shopping and other attractions. It's not easy to avoid the go-go bars, night clubs, and prostitution, since no one seems to be doing anything to really cover them up, but if you stick to the upscale resorts and family-friendly activities, you can keep your exposure to a minimum.

However, be aware that even in the nicest resorts, you may very well see other guests bringing in overnight visitors (i.e. prostitutes). If you find this offensive, it may be best to stay away completely. There's just no way to avoid it. And if you're visiting Pattaya but on a tight budget, you will most likely end up in the belly of the beast, as there are very limited inexpensive accommodations that are not in the center of the city.

Just south of Pattaya lies Jomtien Beach, which offers visitors decent beaches, plenty of accommodations, and fewer go-go bars and prostitutes than Pattaya.

Meanwhile, the rest of Chonburi, with the exception of the small and charming island Ko Si Chang off of Si Racha just north of Pattaya, is fairly unremarkable. Much of the region's coast has been developed into industrial and manufacturing areas; the rest is not special enough to draw visitors looking for a glimpse of everyday life in rural Thailand.

ORIENTATION

Chonburi Province starts just east of Bangkok, and while the inland areas offer little for visitors, the coast, which runs north–south along the Gulf of Thailand, offers a few stretches of sandy beach, the most popular of which is Pattaya Beach. Jomtien Beach lies to the south,

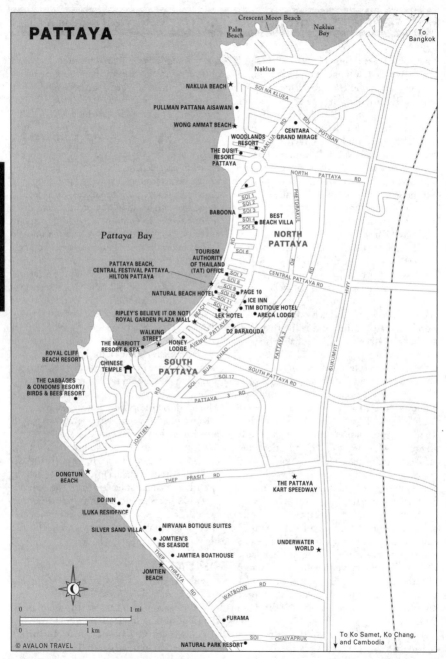

PATTAYA

Crescent Moon Beach

Palm
Beach

Naklua
Bay

To
Bangkok

Naklua

SOI NA KLUEA

NAKLUA BEACH ★

PULLMAN PATTANA AISAWAN ●

WONG AMMAT BEACH ★

WOODLANDS
RESORT ●

CENTARA
GRAND MIRAGE

THE DUSIT
RESORT
PATTAYA ●

NAKLUA RD

SOI POTISAN

NORTH   PATTAYA   RD

PHETBRAKUL RD

SOI 1
SOI 2
SOI 3

BABOONA ●

SOI 4
SOI 5

BEST
BEACH VILLA

NORTH
PATTAYA

Pattaya Bay

SOI 6

TOURISM
AUTHORITY
OF THAILAND
(TAT) OFFICE ●

PATTAYA BEACH,
CENTRAL FESTIVAL PATTAYA,
HILTON PATTAYA

SOI 7

CENTRAL PATTAYA RD

SOI 8

SOI 9

NATURAL BEACH HOTEL ●

SOI 10

PAGE 10 ●

BEACH RD

SOI 11

● ICE INN

SOI 12

● TIM BOTIQUE HOTEL

LEK HOTEL ●

● ARECA LODGE

RIPLEY'S BELIEVE IT OR NOT!
ROYAL GARDEN PLAZA MALL ★

● D2 BARAQUDA

AVENUE PATTAYA

PATTAYA 2 RD

WALKING
STREET ★

THE MARRIOTT
RESORT & SPA ★

HONEY
LODGE ●

SOI BUA KHAO

SUKUMVIT HWY

ROYAL CLIFF
BEACH RESORT ●

CHINESE
TEMPLE 🛕

SOUTH
PATTAYA

SOI 17

SOUTH PATTAYA RD

THE CABBAGES
& CONDOMS RESORT/
BIRDS & BEES RESORT ●

PATTAYA   3   RD

JOMTIEN RD

DONGTUN ★
BEACH

THEP   PRASIT   RD

★ THE PATTAYA
KART SPEEDWAY

DD INN ●

ILUKA RESIDENCE ●

NIRVANA BOTIQUE SUITES
●

SILVER SAND VILLA ●

● JOMTIEN'S
RS SEASIDE

UNDERWATER
WORLD ★

THEP   PHRAYA   RD

● JAMTIEA BOATHOUSE

JOMTIEN
BEACH

WATBOON   RD

0   1 mi

0   1 km

● FURAMA

© AVALON TRAVEL

SOI   CHAIYAPRUK

To Ko Samet, Ko Chang,
↓ and Cambodia

NATURAL PARK RESORT ●

© SUZANNE NAM

The Eastern Seaboard beaches are popular with visitors.

and Naklua Beach and Wong Ammat are to the north. Between Jomtien Beach and Pattaya Beach is a small strip called Dongtan Beach, though it's really just an extension of Jomtien, it's different enough to warrant consideration on its own. Although the whole Pattaya area, including the beach, is technically called Pattaya City, the built-up urban commercial area to the east of the beach is considered by most to be the city. Sukhumvit Road is the main connecting road in Pattaya City, running just outside the center of the beach area a couple of kilometers. A small area on the west end of Pattaya Beach, very close to the water, is Walking Street, the big strip of nightclubs, bars, and go-go clubs that seem to attract tourists like magnets. At night, this is ground zero for partying, and you'll also find plenty of similar spots along the side *sois.*

SIGHTS

There's not a lot of truly Thai stuff going on in the Pattaya area. Most of the sights are geared toward visitors and designed to give you

something to do while you wait for the sun to set and the partying to begin.

Pattaya Elephant Village
หมู่บ้านช้างพัทยา

The Pattaya Elephant Village (54/1 Mu 2, Tambon Nong Prue, Pattaya City, tel. 03/824-9818, www.elephant-village-pattaya. com, 9 A.M.–4:30 P.M. daily), located seven kilometers from Sukhumvit Road, offers elephant rides and rainforest walks as well as daily shows. Although the Pattaya Elephant Village bills itself as a nonprofit sanctuary for elephants, it appears to be exactly like other for-profit elephant camps in Thailand. Shows at 2:30 P.M. daily (500B adults, 400B children) feature training methods, and various treks (900–1,900B adults, 700–1,300B children) are available.

Ripley's Believe It or Not!
อันเดอร์วอเตอร์เวิลด์

Ripley's Believe It or Not! (3rd Fl., Royal Garden Plaza, Pattaya 2nd Rd., South

Pattaya, tel. 03/824-9818, www.ripleysthailand.com, 11 A.M.–11 P.M. daily, 380B adults, 230B children) may be over-the-top, but it can also be quite fun, especially for children. The "museum" features various gory and sensationalistic "exhibits." There are also theme rides to choose from. The Ripley's Haunted Adventure (380B extra for children and adults) is a sort of haunted house with animatronics, while the Infinity Maze (also 380B extra) consists of various mirrored hallways and other illusions. The Moving Theater is a simulator ride with a 3-D movie and vibrating seats (200B extra).

Underwater World

Underwater World (Sukhumvit Rd., less than 1 km south of Tesco Lotus, Pattaya City, tel. 03/875-6879, www.underwaterworldpattaya.com, 9 A.M.–6 P.M. daily, 400B adults, 200B children) is a popular—and prominently advertised—private aquarium. There are nurse sharks, leopard sharks, rays, and a host of other creatures that include batfish, angelfish, and sea dragons, all congregating around the artificial reefs.

Pattaya Kart Speedway

Pattaya Kart Speedway (248/2 Mu 12 Thep Prasit Rd., tel. 03/842-2044, www.pattayakart.com, 9:30 A.M.–6:30 P.M. daily, 250–700B per session, depending on type of kart), just outside of the center of Pattaya, has two go-kart racing tracks and an all-terrain-vehicle course to keep you entertained. They also offer bungee jumping and paintball.

Pattaya Park Water Park

This water park (345 Jomtien Beach, Pattaya City, tel. 03/825-1201, www.pattayapark.com, 11 A.M.–9 P.M. daily, 200B adults, 100B children, plus cost of rides), right at the top of Jomtien Beach, has massive waterslides and other water rides where the kids can cool off and have some fun. There are also a few traditional amusement park rides. During high season, October–April, the park is often packed with families.

Flight of the Gibbon

Looking for some outdoor adventure? Flight of the Gibbon (Khao Kheow Open Zoo, Chonburi, tel. 08/9970-5511, www.treetopasia.com, daily beginning with hotel pickup at 9 A.M., 2,600B) lets you fly through the rainforest suspended on a zip-line, stopping at 24 different treetop platforms along the way to catch your breath and view the flora and fauna. Their site in Chonburi, a short drive from Pattaya, also has suspended bridges, supervised jumps, and swings.

BEACHES AND ISLANDS

Don't expect crystal-clear azure seas around this part of the Gulf of Thailand. The water tends to be murkier and the beaches more crowded and noisy than you'll find in other parts of the country. All of the popular beaches in this area tend to be crowded and very commercial, with back-to-back rental chairs set up along the beach and hawkers selling everything from boiled crab and Chang beer to cheap textiles and souvenirs. Still, if you're looking for an action-packed beach vacation that's convenient to Bangkok and you enjoy all of the commotion, the beaches are a good place to spend a few days.

Pattaya Beach
หาดพัทยา

Pattaya Beach—otherwise known as Hat Pattaya—is the city's main beach. It follows the curve of Pattaya Bay (Ao Pattaya, อ่าวพัทยา) and contains some relatively scenic features: The sand is decent, and the water is clean, if a bit cloudy, although the fervent activity and loud whine of Jet Skis is far from idyllic. Pattaya Beach is decidedly not the place to go if you're searching for solitude. Because there's so much boat traffic in the area (mostly speedboats taking tourists on trips to nearby islands), limited safe swimming areas are set off with brightly colored buoys. The whole strip just behind the beach is packed with restaurants, bars, hotels, shopping centers, and other commercial establishments, and the sand is lined with beach chairs and umbrellas right on top

© SUZANNE NAM

Pattaya Beach

of each other. Right behind Pattaya Beach is a very well-developed strip of commercial property, where you'll be able to find anything from small shopping malls to street vendors and international fast food chains. If you're looking for beach activities, you can Jet Ski, water ski, banana boat, or even go parasailing. You can rent equipment on the beach. Although Pattaya Beach itself isn't completely nonfamily-friendly, everything around it and its proximity to Walking Street might make it uncomfortable for travelers with children.

Jomtien Beach
หาดจอมเทียน

Jomtien Beach, located a little more than 1 kilometer south of Pattaya Beach, is more serene than its northern neighbor—and much more family friendly. The stretch here is less densely packed, so you're likely to find some peace and quiet relative to Pattaya. However, it is a very popular beach for European vacationers and locals (including local college kids), so chances are you won't find any idyllic scenes here either,

especially if you're visiting over the weekend or during a Thai holiday. The water and sand are slightly less disturbed, and you'll find all of the same water-sport activities available on Jomtien as you would on Pattaya Beach.

Dongtan Beach
หาดดงตาล

Between Jomtien Beach and Pattaya Beach is a small strip of coast called Dongtan Beach. Part of the beach is closed to traffic, making it quieter and a little less hectic than the neighboring beaches on either side, though the water and the condition of the sand are essentially exactly the same. There are even public restrooms and showers, which you won't find on the other beaches. Dongtan is known by locals and visitors as a gay beach, but it's not exclusively gay.

Wong Ammat Beach
หาดวงศ์อำมาตย์

Wong Ammat is Pattaya's most undeveloped beach. Located around the Dusit Thani hotel,

PATTAYA: THE FUTURE OF THAILAND'S SIN CITY

Pattaya attracts a staggering number of tourists every year, and the city is brimming with foreigners. It's estimated that one-third of all visitors to the kingdom go to the beachside resort city during their stay. There are a multitude of hotels, resorts, restaurants, bars, clubs, and shops. And just as varied as the range of commercial establishments is the diversity among the visitors themselves: You might see a tour bus full of German retirees one minute and a group of Middle Eastern travelers the next. You might encounter a married Russian couple crossing the street, while a group of 20-something Australians hang out in a restaurant nearby.

But perhaps most striking for first-time visitors to the city is that a great proportion of the tourists you'll see in Pattaya are foreign men. What brings them to the seaside has less to do with Thailand's traditional charms, such as *wats* and *tom yam kung*. Although prostitution is illegal in the kingdom, many of these visitors are drawn to Pattaya's neon-lit go-go bars, dimly lit pubs, and various other pursuits. Pattaya has been attracting this type of crowd ever since the late 1950s, when U.S. servicemen started flocking to the city for R&R. What

does the future have in store for Thailand's very own red-light city?

Analysts say – or perhaps hope – that the city is, and will continue to become, more family-friendly and upscale. While there are increasing numbers of diversions for kids, it's hard to imagine families feeling at home on Walking Street (where the greatest number of go-go bars are located) or, for that matter, in many parts of Pattaya, where seediness can seem pervasive.

It's true that Pattaya has seen a rise in luxury developments. There's speculation that several five-star hotels, for instance, are considering coming to Pattaya. And in the south, Jomtien Beach may soon be home to Thailand's tallest building, a planned 367-meter-high luxury condo building.

While the seedier parts of the city will likely continue to thrive, new hotels and resorts are being constructed farther outside of town, many of them with top-notch golf courses. And with the forthcoming completion of a new expressway from Bangkok directly to Pattaya, it will soon be possible to visit Pattaya and stay at a self-contained resort – and never once set foot on Pattaya Beach Road or Walking Street.

Wong Ammat is much quieter than Pattaya's other oceanfront strips and has neither the booming nightlife of its neighbor nor as many beach activities. It's about 0.5 kilometers north of Pattaya Beach, separated by a headland.

Naklua Beach
หาดนาเกลือ
Family-friendly Naklua Beach is located just north of Wong Ammat Beach. There are some hotels clustered here, so this area is a good option for those looking for a more laid-back scene and who don't mind missing out on raucous beach activities as the trade-off.

Surrounding Islands
About seven kilometers off the coast of Pattaya are three small islands that have become hot

spots for visitors on mostly day trips: **Ko Krok** (เกาะครก), **Ko Lan** (เกาะล้าน), and Ko Sak (เกาะสาก). The tiny Ko Lan, which is also referred to as "Coral Island," is the most popular of these. It has a variety of restaurants and activities such as parasailing and glass-bottom boat rides. Ko Krok is a tiny, mostly rocky island with just a 100-meter-long strip of beach. There's little to do here except sit in a beach chair and take in the scene, but it's definitely more tranquil than the main beaches on the coast. Ko Sak is not far from Ko Lan, and like Ko Krok, it's minuscule. Ko Sak has two beaches, one in the north and one in the south, but there aren't many restaurants or other facilities.

The islands are so close to the mainland that you can see them from the shore (and vice versa).

To get to these islands, you can take a ferry from **Balihai Pier** (ทาเรือแหลมบาลีฮาย), at the south end of Pattaya Beach. Boats leave every two hours 8:30 A.M.–4:30 P.M. daily and cost 20B. There are also numerous tour operators offering day tours to the islands (most spend most of their time on and around Ko Lan and will be marketed as "Coral Island tours") that include hotel pickup and a simple lunch and allow guests to add on parasailing, diving, snorkeling, and even windsurfing, depending on conditions. These tours offer virtually identical services and are competitively priced. To find a tour, ask at your hotel or a nearby travel agent; either can book for you a day in advance. Private speedboats are also available. You'll have to negotiate with the captain, but you can usually get a one-way ride for 500B pp. The price per person becomes significantly lower if you are traveling with a group.

ENTERTAINMENT AND EVENTS

If you're uncomfortable with the seediness and overt sexuality on display in the Pattaya area, it can be really tough to find things to do at night. Even if you're not looking to party at a go-go bar or nightclub, it's virtually impossible to find a bar or pool hall where there aren't so-called "bar girls" hanging around and patrons talking to them.

Bars

All manner of bars—go-go bars, strip joints, and everything in between—can be found by taking a stroll down Walking Street and its surrounding *sois*. If you're searching for live music in an environment devoid of sexual content, be sure to check out **The Blues Factory** (131/3 Mu 10, Soi Lucky Star, off Walking St., tel. 03/830-0180, www.thebluesfactorypattaya.com, 8:30 P.M.–2 A.M. daily, free). You can find bands playing there every night, and it might just be the only spot in Pattaya where the main attraction doesn't revolve around flesh.

Pattaya's vibrant gay nightlife is centered on Pattaya Beach Road Soi 3. The road is lined with numerous bars and clubs that are every bit as raucous as the places on Walking Street.

THE EASTERN SEABOARD

© SUZANNE NAM

Pattaya's bars get crowded at night.

Nightclubs

Walking Street, located at the southern end of Pattaya Beach Road, contains the city's largest concentration of beer bars, go-go clubs, strip joints, dance clubs, and other such establishments. Even if you're not interested in stopping for a drink or two, strolling down neon-lit Walking Street—which becomes pedestrian only at night—makes for an interesting trip. The beer-soaked, music-blaring ground zero for Pattaya's nightlife is, after all, what some call "Phat Phong by the Sea." Though no one will stop you from bringing kids along for the walk, remember that this is definitely an R-rated (and once in a while X-rated) area.

Cabaret

Tiffany's (north end of Pattaya 2nd Rd., tel. 03/842-1705, www.tiffany-show.co.th, 500–800B, depending on seat location) is a classy cabaret show. The self-described "first ever truly transvestite cabaret show in southeast Asia" has been putting on extravagant, though tasteful, performances since 1974. Show times are 6 P.M., 7:30 P.M., and 9 P.M. Tiffany's is also home to the annual **Miss International Queen** pageant, a transvestite and transgender beauty contest attracting contestants from all over the globe. This good natured, G-rated event is billed as the largest such event in the world and is usually held in November. Tickets are available on the website.

SHOPPING

Pattaya has plenty of pharmacies, eyeglass stores, and mom-and-pop beach shops selling flip-flops and floatation devices, so you'll be able to find any of the necessities you might need while you are here. There are a few outdoor markets in central Pattaya, both on the beach and on Pattaya Second Road. These cater almost exclusively to tourists and carry the typical selection of T-shirts, sundresses, backpacks, and souvenirs, but it isn't necessary to seek out one of these markets to shop. Tourist items can be purchased virtually anywhere in the city—small shops, vendor's carts,

stands, etc. The area along Pattaya Beach Road is especially fully of vendors.

The opening of the large, upscale **Central Festival** (Pattaya Beach Rd. between Sois 9 and 10, Pattaya, tel. 02/635-1111, www.centralfestival.co.th, 10 A.M.–10 P.M. daily) right in the center of Pattaya Beach has made a huge impact on the area's once bleak and overpriced shopping scene. The mall has a large Central department store, numerous local and international brands, sports stores, banks, and plenty of places to eat at every budget. There is also a supermarket on the bottom floor with both local and international foods.

The **Avenue Pattaya** (Pattaya Second Rd. at Soi 14), just a couple of blocks from the beach, is a nice outdoor mall with a small selection of name-brand shops and lots of merchants selling everything from costumes to mobile phones on the upper floors. There is a small selection of fast food, a Starbucks, and a Villa Market that offers international and imported foods.

The **Royal Garden Plaza Mall** (218 Pattaya Beach Rd., tel. 03/871-0294, www.royalgardenplaza.co.th, 10 A.M.–midnight daily), located between the southern end of Pattaya Beach Road and Pattaya Second Road, is right on the beach and is home to some local boutiques as well as international chain shops. Those looking for diversions in addition to shopping can occupy their time at the Ripley's Believe it or Not Museum located here.

Walking Street is home to an inordinate number of jewelry stores. Items in these shops can be quite expensive, and bargaining is mandatory if you're plunking down a few thousand dollars for some sapphire or ruby gems.

SPORTS AND RECREATION
Diving and Snorkeling

The quality of the scuba and snorkeling off the coast of Pattaya pales in comparison to what can be had elsewhere in Thailand. Even in the outer islands, visibility is generally about 5–15 meters. But there's no shortage of dive shops and expeditions to choose from if you're interested in exploring the underwater world, and visitors based in Bangkok often get certified around the islands off of Pattaya because of its proximity to the capital. The islands of Ko Krok, Ko Lan, and Ko Sak tend to attract those who are new to the sport, while divers with more experience will want to head for islands farther afield, such as **Ko Rin** (เกาะริน) and **Ko Man Wichai** (เกาะมารวิชัย). Given their greater distance from the mainland, these islands are less disturbed by activity closer to shore.

While there are several shipwrecks in the area, a particularly popular advanced diving spot for viewing a variety of marinelife is **Samaesan Hole** (แสมสาร). The decommissioned ammunition dump goes down to a depth of more than 80 meters. This dive is not for beginners. Most local dive companies specialize in trips to the shipwrecks, but some organize outings to Samaesan Hole.

Two of the best-known dive shops in Pattaya include **Paradise Scuba Divers** (Siam Bayview Resort, Pattaya Beach Rd., Pattaya, tel. 03/871-0567, www.tauchenthailand.de) and **Mermaid's Diver Center** (Soi White House, Jomtien Beach, tel. 03/823-2219, www. mermaiddive.com). Both of these companies, as well as most of the other shops in the area, do day trips to the outer islands as well as to Samaesan Hole.

Water Sports

Everything from windsurfing to waterskiing, Jet Skiing to parasailing can be done all along Pattaya Beach and Jomtien Beach. Rates vary according to the season, but generally you'll spend about 1,200B per hour to rent a Jet Ski. Waterskiing costs 500–1,000B, depending on how long you go for and what season it is. Parasailing is 300B per ride (about five minutes in the air). If you rent a motorized personal watercraft and there's an accident, be warned that you will be held financially responsible for any damage that occurs. Also be aware that fatal Jet Ski accidents have happened on Pattaya Beach, so be careful and stay clear of their path.

ACCOMMODATIONS

Given the number of visitors who descend on Pattaya every day, there's a wide range of lodgings available, although quality and value are harder to come by in Pattaya than in other popular tourist spots in the Kingdom. Hotels and resorts run the gamut from inexpensive guesthouses to large mid-range hotels to luxury resorts. If you're immune to noise and don't mind a certain element of seediness, there are numerous small hotels on the little streets off the beach and around Walking Street. The high-end resorts have compounds right on the beach, farther away from the hustle and bustle. Prostitution, although illegal in Thailand, goes on blatantly in Pattaya. Most guesthouses and hotels, especially around Walking Street, allow guests to bring in overnight visitors. More upscale accommodations (which tend to be in the northern part of Pattaya, around Naklua Beach and farther away from Walking Street) try to discourage such activity, but even so you may still see signs of it.

Since Pattaya attracts more middle-of-the-road tourists looking for mid-range lodging, the city doesn't have as many inexpensive guesthouses catering to backpackers to choose from as Bangkok or Chiang Mai. There's really no budget-traveler neighborhood in Pattaya and virtually no backpacker scene to speak of. Nevertheless, guesthouses in Pattaya with rooms under US$20 should still offer air-conditioning and, if you're lucky, perhaps a few more creature comforts. The key is finding a place that's far enough away from the nightlife that you're able to get a good night's sleep, and that's not an easy bill to fill.

Pattaya Beach

The very basic but economical **Honey Lodge** (597/8 Mu 10 Pattaya 2nd Rd., South Pattaya, tel. 03/842-9133, 500–600B) offers simple guest rooms, a pool, and an attached restaurant.

Ice Inn (528/2–3 Pattaya 2nd Rd., tel. 03/872-0671, www.pattayacity.com/iceinn, 300–700B) is a popular place. Its rooms are well maintained, and, like most options in this price range, you get no more than a bed, a TV, air-conditioning, and a refrigerator. Ice Inn stands out from the rest of the competition in this price range because it's exceptionally clean and tidy. There's also an Internet café on the premises with several computers.

Natural Beach Hotel (216 Mu 10, Soi 11, tel. 03/842-9239, naturalbeach@excite.com, 850B) is rather serene despite the chaos of Pattaya that surrounds the hotel. The guest rooms are typical for this price range: white walls, air-conditioning, and satellite TVs. It has a pool that is surrounded by trees, and it's in close proximity to the beach, which is just across Pattaya Beach Road.

Lek Hotel (284/5 Pattaya 2nd Rd., tel. 03/842-5552, http://lekhotel.tripod.com, 850B) has a regular following and is known for its personal touch and affable staff. The large guest rooms have air-conditioning and satellite-enabled TVs. The large high-rise hotel is located just off Pattaya Beach Road, right in the center of all the action, and it's just a short walk from the beach. There's a pool on-site as well as a restaurant that serves Thai, Chinese, and continental dishes.

The large **Areca Lodge** (198/23 Mu 9, Soi Diana Inn, Pattaya 2nd Rd., tel. 03/841-0123, www.arecalodge.com, 1,450B), just a few minutes from the main drag, has decent amenities for the price. It has a hot tub, two pools, and well-appointed guest rooms with dark-wood furniture and large TVs with cable. There's also a gym, a sauna, a beer garden, and a sports pub.

Best Beach Villa (362 Mu 9, Soi 5, Pattaya Beach Rd., tel. 03/841-4666, www.bestbeach-pattaya.com, 1,500B) is a similar large, mid-range property with good amenities and clean, comfortable guest rooms. Guest rooms and decor are slightly dated but well maintained and not run-down. Don't be fooled by the name, though; it's a block away from the beach and it's a high-rise hotel, not villas.

Baboona (119/3 Mu 9, North Pattaya Beach Rd., tel. 03/848-8720, www.baboonabeach.com, 1,700B), which opened in 2009, is one of Pattaya's newer small boutique hotels. The hotel is located right on the beach road, and most rooms have great views of the ocean. Decor is very modern, and the guest rooms, though not huge, are very well organized and maintained. The lobby-level café is comfortable enough for hanging out, and there is a spa on the premises for those looking for a little pampering. The only drawback is that there's no pool, though since it's right across the street from the beach, you may not miss it.

Conveniently located a block from the beach and a block from Central Festival Mall is the newly opened **Page 10** (365/3 Mu 10, Soi 10, Pattaya 2nd Rd., tel. 03/842-3245, www.page-10hotel.com, 1,700B), another small boutique hotel. The small lobby and restaurant-bar on the ground floor are airy and comfortable, and the rooftop pool is well maintained. Guest rooms are spotless and nicely decorated in a generic modern style, but inattention to small finishing details means this hotel isn't quite in four-star territory. It's still an excellent value for the price, especially for those looking to be in the center of things but who want to stay in a slightly more family-friendly place.

The **Amari Orchid Resort** (Naklua Rd. and North Pattaya Rd., North Pattaya, tel. 03/841-8418, www.amari.com/orchid, 2,100B) is well established, very upscale, and very large. The Amari is divided between a high-rise hotel (the Ocean Tower) and a Garden Wing. Guest rooms make use of Thai fabrics and dark-wood accent paneling and offer Internet access. As at other resorts in this price range, visitors have various pools, spas, and restaurants at their disposal. There's also a huge swimming pool and various family-friendly diversions, like miniature golf and a playground.

Just a couple of blocks from the beach is the very popular **Tim Boutique Hotel** (397/42 Mu 10, Soi 14, Pattaya 2nd Rd., tel. 03/872-3349, www.timboutiquehotel.com, 2,200B). Though some might find the decor a little too funky and colorful, this well-maintained midsize hotel is a great value for those who want some five-star amenities at three- or four-star prices. Guest rooms are clean, modern, and stylish. There's a lovely rooftop swimming pool with a bar and a restaurant on the premises. The immediate surroundings outside the hotel feel a bit urban and run-down, but it's just a five-minute walk to the beach.

The [C] **Cabbages & Condoms Resort/ Birds & Bees Resort** (Phra Tamnak Rd., Soi 4, South Pattaya, tel. 03/825-0035, www. cabbagesandcondoms.co.th, 2,500B) not only has 50 guest rooms set on grounds with streams and ponds, its own semiprivate beach, and a swimming pool, it's also a resort with a noble mission: It provides financial support for Thailand's Population and Community Development Association (PDA). The PDA teaches the importance of condoms in preventing the spread of HIV/AIDS and does other rural development work in Thailand. The individually decorated guest rooms have Thai motifs, such as elephant prints on the walls. Thai MP Mechai Viravaidya created this resort, along with its affiliated Cabbages & Condoms restaurants throughout the country. His quest to promote safer sex has been quite successful—so much so that today the Thai slang word for condom, *mechai,* is taken from his first name.

Located in the slightly quieter North Pattaya area, the **Dusit Resort Pattaya** (240/2 Pattaya Beach Rd., North Pattaya, tel. 03/842-5611, www.dusit.com, 4,000B) is a classic favorite for those who'd like to get pampered, Pattaya-style. As stately and well-respected as any upscale place to stay in the city, the sprawling compound offers a huge number of plush guest rooms (each with high-speed Internet access), various pools, a spa, and a semi-private beach. The eating options are diverse, with separate Chinese, Italian, and European-Asian restaurants in addition to a bakery. One of the pools has a swim-up bar, and there are also tennis courts and fitness facilities.

The [C] **Marriott Resort & Spa** (218 Mu 10, Pattaya Beach Rd., South Pattaya, tel. 03/841-2120, www.marriott.com, 4,100B) is a good choice if you are looking for an upscale, secluded (and sea-facing) resort near all of the Walking Street shenanigans. In contrast to its high-energy location, the resort's meticulously manicured surroundings, done in the traditional Thai style, convey a sense of calm. All of the guest rooms are sleek and modern, with lots of dark wood, and also contain Thai accents

such as traditional art. There are numerous on-site amenities: movie theaters, a truly gargantuan pool, several bars, restaurants (including a Benihana), a fitness center, and a spa.

Part of the Dusit chain's younger, hipper brand is the **D2 Baraquda** (485/1 Mu 10, Pattaya 2nd Rd., tel. 03/876-9999, www.dusit. com, 4,500B), a block away from the beach. The large hotel has a stunning open lobby, and all of the hotel's common areas have lots of modern art and dramatic furniture. Guest rooms are a little more subdued—still stylish, but more relaxing. The hotel's immediate surroundings aren't stylish enough to match the hotel, but this is Pattaya, after all.

Another urban five-star hotel is the **Pattaya Hilton** (333/111 Mu 9, Pattaya Beach Rd., tel. 03/825-3000, www1.hilton.com, 5,000B), part of the upscale Central Festival Mall. The asymmetrical exterior design is striking and modern, but guest rooms are typical generic Hilton style. Still, the hotel, which just opened in late 2010, is one of the nicest, if not the nicest, in central Pattaya, and service is excellent.

The posh **Royal Cliff Beach Resort** (353 Phra Tamnuk Rd., South Pattaya, tel. 03/825-0421, www.royalcliff.com, 6,120B), at the southern end of Pattaya Bay, features various types of guest rooms, from smaller rooms to suites, in its four distinct sections. The Royal Cliff Terrace section, opened in 1973 and renovated in 2006, is built into the side of a cliff, so all guest rooms have views of the sea; some are decked out in Thai silks. The 20-story Royal Cliff Grand and Spa section is a conventional high-rise luxury hotel. And in the überupscale Royal Wing and Spa, all guest rooms are suites and have views of the ocean. The smaller ones have king beds and marble baths with hot tubs, while the larger suites are essentially small apartments that come with dedicated butlers. The Royal Cliff Beach Hotel has mostly standard high-end hotel rooms with ocean views.

Jomtien Beach
The unpretentious **Jomtien Boathouse** (380/5–6 Jomtien Beach Rd., tel. 03/875-6143, www.jomtien-boathouse.com, 900B)

offers guests clean rooms and a great view of the ocean. Although the decor is a bit dated, it's a great choice because of the location. There is a popular on-site bar and restaurant that attracts lots of other visitors and residents, but try to get a seat that doesn't directly overlook the parking lot.

For those who don't need lots of amenities or a name brand but want to stay somewhere personal, comfortable, and clean, **ILUKA Residence** (413/6 Thappraya Rd., Soi 1, Jomtien Complex, tel. 08/8215-6866, www.iluka-residence.com, 900B) is a great choice. Guest rooms at this very small property are minimally furnished and clean. It tends to attract a gay crowd and is very close to area nightlife and bars.

Tui's Place (318/77-78 Mu 12, Thap Phraya Rd., tel. 03/825-1432, www.tuisplace.com, 1,000B) on Dongtan Beach is a good pick for budget travelers looking for basic, tidy lodgings on the beach. Most of the guest rooms at this gay-run guesthouse consist of simple beds, desks, TVs, and white walls, but everything is clean, and the proprietors are friendly. There is a small bar and restaurant attached too.

The relatively secluded **Silver Sand Villa** (97 Mu 12, Jomtien Beach Rd., tel. 03/823-1289, www.silversandvilla.com, 900B) has two swimming pools and good-size guest rooms with simple wooden furniture. The hotel's furnishings are somewhat aging, but the compound is spacious and offers big-hotel facilities at guesthouse prices. There's also a salon and a Thai massage facility.

Jomtien's RS Seaside (125/9 Mu 10, Jomtien Beach Rd., tel. 03/823-1867, www.rs-seaside.com, 1,100–2,300B) is located at the south end of the beach strip. It's renowned for offering a good value and is a great alternative to a guesthouse if you're willing to pay just a little more. The guest rooms are clean and well lit, and at the top price range, you'll get views of the sea. There's also a pool, a hot tub, and an espresso bar.

The decor at **Nirvana Boutique Suites** (75/187–190 Mu 12, Soi 14, Jomtien Beach Road, tel. 03/875-7014, www.

nirvanaboutiquehotel.com, 1,200B) is a little over-the-top (think lots of reds and golds and excessive use of animal motifs), but the hotel is clean and well maintained, and all suites have small efficiency kitchens, making it a great place for longer stays. There is a small pool on the premises, but it's just a couple of short blocks to the beach.

Jomtien Chalet (57/1 Mu 1, Jomtien Beach Rd., tel. 03/823-1205, bungalows 1,300B) is the place to go if you're looking for novelty. Guest rooms that sleep two or six people are available in a converted railroad car. For a more conventional setup, there are also regular bungalows available. Guest rooms are clean, but the furnishings are basic.

Jomtien's Natural Park Resort (412 Mu 12, tel. 03/823-1561, www.naturalparkresort.com, 2,500B) has a main building with arched rooflines done in the traditional Thai style. The guest rooms feature large beds, wood paneling, and Thai tapestries. The lush grounds contain a Thai *sala* (covered sitting area) and two pools, one for children and one for adults.

Furama Jomtien (457 Mu 12, Soi 13, Jomtien Beach Rd., tel. 03/841-8999, www.furama.com/jomtienbeach, 2,500B), a large high-rise hotel right on the beach, was refurbished in 2010 and is a great-value property for those who want a convenient location and resort-level amenities. This is not a five-star hotel, so service isn't always flawless, but guest rooms are modern and clean, and there is a large and well-kept swimming pool.

The massive four-star **Ravindra Beach Resort and Spa** (246 Mu 4, Jomtien Beach, tel. 03/823-5777, www.ravindraresort.com, 3,500B) on Jomtien Beach offers just about everything—large grounds and swimming pool, well furnished, modern rooms, a spa and small fitness center. The property, which opened in 2009, still feels new and well-maintained, but that may not last long as it also seems to attract lots of big groups.

Spacious guest rooms and pretty grounds make **Dor Shada Hotel** (256 Mu 4, tel. 03/823-5870, www.dor-shadaresort.com, 3,500B) on Jomtien a great choice for families. There are two pools and even a small golf course and playground. Generic Thai decor and decent service don't stand out among the competition, but it's a family-friendly value property.

Sea Sand Sun Resort and Spa (78-4 Mu 8, 163 Jomtien Beach Rd., tel. 03/843-5163, www.seasandsunpty.com, 4,000B) is a traditional resort with both stand-alone pool villas and regular hotel rooms, all decorated with traditional Thai furnishings. The grounds are large and nicely manicured, and there is an expansive pool overlooking the ocean, plus a separate children's pool, an on-site restaurant, and a bar.

Palm Grove Resort (245/96 Mu 3, Jomtien Beach Rd., tel. 03/870-9444, www.palmgroveresortpattaya.com, 5,000B) is another traditional resort with large private villas, lush grounds, and multiple swimming pools. The property is well designed, and the Thai decor feels luxurious, although it's not quite up to par with fully five-star hotels. Many villas have their own pools, and the beach is about 10 minutes away on foot.

Naklua Beach

An excellent choice for families is **Woodlands Resort** (164/1 Naklua Rd., tel. 03/842-1707, www.woodland-resort.com, 2,100B). The place has stylishly decorated guest rooms with light-wood accents, sleek baths, and hardwood floors. There are also two pools, a fitness center, a spa, a French bakery, and a restaurant.

Pullman Pattaya Aisawan (445/3 Mu 5, Naklua Beach, tel. 03/841-1940, www.pullmanpattayaaisawan.com, 3,500B) is a self-contained resort with a slightly edgy, modern feel to it that makes it seem a little more cosmopolitan than neighboring resorts. Rooms are breezy and minimalist, and the grounds offer plenty of places to lounge by the pool or enjoy a cocktail.

Centara Grand Mirage Beach Resort (277 Mu 5, Naklua Beach, tel. 03/830-1234, www.centarahotelsresorts.com, 5,000B) is a self-contained, lush, family-friendly resort away from the madness of downtown Pattaya. Guest rooms are large and contemporary but have subtle Thai design elements. There are multiple restaurants, swimming pools, a water park with water slides, and a fitness center. The "Lost World" theme gives the resort an Atlantis–Jurassic Park feeling, but somehow it isn't tacky or over-the-top. This is a great resort for families.

FOOD

Don't expect to be bowled over by the dining selections in Pattaya. The vast majority of visitors come here to party, and most of them aren't obsessed with finding authentic Thai—or any other—culinary experiences. And when it comes to atmosphere, many of the restaurants in the boisterous Walking Street area—home to the prime drinking, go-go club, and strip-club scene—necessarily suffer from a somewhat less-refined feel that spills over from the streets.

That said, just as lodging in Pattaya is so diverse that there's something for virtually every visitor's taste, the city's eating options are also so varied that if you look hard enough, you can probably find what you're looking for. The **Central Festival Mall** has brought some much-needed high-quality variety to Pattaya. In the basement is a large food court with everything from basic inexpensive Thai dishes to Russian and Indian fare. Upstairs is the **Central Food Loft**, essentially a more upscale food court with pan-Asian and European cuisine and stunning views of the ocean. And inside the mall is a handful of local and international chain restaurants, so finding a decent meal in a normal environment shouldn't be a problem.

Walking Street is home to a handful of seafood restaurants that serve Thai and Western dishes as well as fresh fish and shellfish made to order. Some have views of the water, and though it's hard to call the atmosphere at these popular restaurants romantic, given the surroundings, they can be nice.

If you're looking for a quiet meal, some of Pattaya's more upscale hotels, including the **Royal Cliff Beach Resort, Cabbages & Condoms Resort,** and the **Marriott Resort & Spa** have lovely formal restaurants that tend

© NEWLEY PURNELL

outdoor market, Chonburi Province

to be substantially more insulated from the carousing that takes place outside. Both the Royal Cliff Beach Resort and the Marriott restaurants offer both traditional Thai menus and European menus; expect to pay around 2,000B per couple for dinner, not including wine or cocktails.

Upscale Thai and International

◖ **Mantra** (Amari Orchard Resort, near Naklua Rd. at the extreme northern end of Pattaya Beach Rd., North Pattaya, tel. 03/842-9591, www.mantra-pattaya.com, 5 P.M.–1 A.M. daily, 300–1,000B) continues its reign as on of Pattaya's coolest restaurants. Everyone is buzzing about its well-executed pan-Asian dishes and its very slick design. Indeed, the sparkling restaurant has brought a much-needed breath of fresh air to the city's dining scene. The place serves Indian, Japanese, and Thai fusion—and it does all of them quite well. The interior features bold colors and is a sight to behold. The bar area makes a comfy place for a drink or two in a swanky environment, while the interior

dining area is sprawling—and also very cool. The basic Indian food—naan, samosas, and dal, especially—is particularly delectable.

Cabbages and Condoms Restaurant (Soi 4, Phra Tamnak Rd., South Pattaya, tel. 03/825-0035, www.cabbagesandcondoms. co.th, 5–11 P.M. daily, from 600B) offers reliable Thai classics in a breezy open-air dining room with nice views of the ocean. If you're looking for a nice meal in a comfortable environment, it's worth the taxi ride to get here. Flavors tend to cater to foreign palates, so those wanting extra spice should ask for it.

Markets

As is the case all over Thailand, casual street food is always a good bet for fresh, cheap snacks or meals. While food stands can be found all over the city, there's a conglomeration of vendors along Pattaya Beach Road. Here you'll find a typical selection of *som tam,* noodle soups, and grilled meats. And while high-quality grub and food courts are mutually exclusive in the West, that's not the case in the kingdom. If you're looking to sample a wide variety of authentic Thai food, head to the food court in the **Carrefour** (Pattaya Klang Rd., Pattaya, 11 A.M.–10 P.M. daily, 100B and up). This hypermarket is a popular destination for Thais themselves who are looking for good, cheap eats. You can get everything from rice and noodle dishes to fish and other meat curries. This is also true of the Tesco Lotus stores as well.

INFORMATION AND SERVICES
Tourist Information
The office of the **Tourism Authority of Thailand** (TAT, 609 Mu 10, Phra Tamnak Rd., tel. 03/842-8750, tatchon@tat.or.th, 8:30 A.M.–4:30 P.M. daily) can be found to the southeast of Walking Street at the top of Pattaya Beach. You can find information about hotels, restaurants, and other Pattaya attractions. Staff can help answer any questions you might have.

Money
Changing or withdrawing cash is not a problem in Pattaya. ATMs that accept international cards as well as banks and currency exchange facilities can be found all over the city.

Hospitals
The 15-story **Bangkok Pattaya Hospital** (301 Mu 6, Sukhumvit Rd., Naklua Beach, tel. 03/842-9999, www.bph.co.th, 24 hours daily) is Pattaya's most renowned medical center and has English-speaking staff. In addition to 24-hour emergency services, the hospital has extensive elective and cosmetic treatment options.

Internet Cafés
Pattaya is a very well wired city, and nearly every café and many restaurants offer free wireless Internet for patrons. In fact, many hotels and other establishments don't bother password-protecting their networks in Pattaya, so you can often pick up a signal sitting outside. If you haven't brought your own computer or

smart phone, there are a few Internet cafés along the main strip of Pattaya Beach Road downtown, as well as along Jomtien Beach Road to the south.

GETTING THERE AND AROUND
Car
If you are driving from Bangkok, you can make the trip to Pattaya in 2–3 hours, depending on traffic. There are two popular routes: You can take Highway 34 or the Bangkok–Chonburi Motorway. The latter is faster but is a toll road. If you plan to get a car once you arrive, try **Holiday Rent-A-Car** (Pattaya 2nd Rd., across from Royal Garden Plaza, tel. 03/842-6203, www.pattayacar-rent.com, 9 A.M.–5 P.M. daily). The Dusit Resort contains a branch of **Avis Rent-A-Car** (240/2 Pattaya Beach Rd., tel. 03/836-1628, www.avisthailand.com, 9 A.M.–5 P.M. daily).

Bus
You can take a bus from Bangkok's Suvarnabhumi airport directly to Pattaya. The journey typically takes less than three hours (depending on traffic) and costs 106B. The bus, number 389, departs from the airport about eight times per day, 6:30 A.M.–8:30 P.M. If you're coming from elsewhere in Bangkok, you can catch a bus from the Eastern and Northern terminals. Buses leave every 30 minutes, 6 A.M.–9 P.M., and costs 124B for the two-hour trip. You'll arrive at the Pattaya bus station on Pattaya Neua Beach Road in North Pattaya. From there, you can take a *song thaew* or taxi to your destination.

Song Thaew
Song thaew run between the north end of Pattaya Beach and Jomtien all day. If you are hopping on one of the trucks on its scheduled route, you should pay about 10–50B, depending on how far you're going. Ask the driver for the fare cost when you get off. If you happen to grab an empty *song thaew* and are going to a location that's not on the route (i.e., you ask to be taken directly to your hotel or another

destination, instead of just hopping off on the main road), you must negotiate the price in advance, and you may be asked to pay a few hundred baht.

Motorcycle

Since taxis aren't as abundant in Pattaya as they are in Bangkok, some visitors prefer to rent motorcycles to get around town. This is indeed a convenient means of transport, as motorcycles are immune to traffic jams, since splitting the lanes is permitted, and they're cheap to rent. Small 100 cc four-speed motorcycles, which can often be shifted without a clutch, start at about 150B per day (with a deposit in the neighborhood of 500–1,000B). Larger motorcycles—up to 1,000 cc—cost about 500–1,000B per day.

Before renting a motorcycle, beware of two things. First, it's not a good idea to try motorcycling in a foreign land unless you're an experienced rider at home. This commonsense advice may seem obvious, but a surprising number of travelers get carried away and throw caution to the wind. Secondly, be sure to play it safe and drive with caution, even though you may see everyone else breaking the traffic laws. The police in Pattaya have been known to enforce the traffic laws vigorously. If you're ticketed, your passport may be confiscated by the officer who issues the ticket while you're made to go pay a small fine at Pattaya's central police station. The fine is generally not expensive, but unless you have several hours to spare, this is likely an experience you'll want to avoid.

SI RACHA
ศรีราชา

South of Bangkok and just 32 kilometers north of Pattaya is the coastal town of Si Racha, home of the popular red-colored hot sauce *namphrik si racha*. It's a great place to witness an authentic Thai seaside scene, with its piers and markets by the waterfront. It makes for an excellent place to spend the afternoon or evening, either as a day trip from Bangkok (it's just 105 kilometers from the Thai capital) or as a stop while making your way farther south.

The town's seafood is the main draw: It is flavorful and abundant, and it can be found in many casual restaurants. There's a very popular for-profit Tiger Zoo in Si Racha—you won't be able to miss the signs—but its reputation over the past decade has not been stellar (either as a safe place for visitors or a humane place for animals).

To get to the charming coastal part of Si Racha, though, you'll have to pass through the developed urban part first. Don't be put off by the blocks of concrete buildings, big shopping mall, and fast-food joints.

Food

Running perpendicular to the town's waterfront area, starting from the east and ending at the waterfront, **Si Racha Nakon Third Road** is home to a proliferation of food stalls, vendors, and restaurants serving fresh seafood. The area is home to one of Thailand's famous exports: Si Racha hot sauce, the fiery red sauce used as an Asian condiment in the United States. Another conglomeration of eateries can be found on **Jermjompol Road,** which runs parallel to the coast. Here you'll find a café, a bakery, and a beer bar.

Grand Seaside Restaurant (Soi 18, Jermjompol Rd., tel. 03/832-3851, lunch and dinner daily, 100–250B) is a stylish place perched over the water. You can't go wrong with virtually any selection here, and the lovely water view makes all the food taste that much better. The seafood, naturally, given its proximity to the water, is excellent, and the seafood-rice clay pot is a popular dish. Another typical seafood restaurant is **Bang Phra Seafood** (Bang Phra, tel. 03/834-1674, 1–9 P.M. daily, 250B), which also serves traditional Thai meals with fresh seafood. The atmosphere is not very fancy, but it is nonetheless a very popular place with visiting Thais.

You can also find a number of very basic, sit-down seafood stalls on tiny **Ko Loi (เกาะลอย)**, an island that you can walk to via a jetty from downtown. The prices range 50–150B, so just peruse the offerings and let your nose guide your way.

Getting There

If you are traveling by **car,** Si Racha is just a little over an hour from Bangkok on the Bangkok–Chonburi Motorway. If you don't want to pay tolls, you can also take Highway 36, which will add a minimum of 10 minutes to the drive, more if you are driving during rush hour. If you're coming from Pattaya, the trip is about 30 minutes, depending on traffic.

You can charter a **taxi** to Si Racha from Bangkok; fares and drive time will depend on your driver. The ride usually takes less than 90 minutes; expect a price range of 1,000–2,000B each way. You should arrange for the taxi to wait for you as you explore the town in order to have a ride back.

You can also get to Si Racha by **bus.** Most buses from Bangkok's Eastern bus station going to Pattaya stop in Si Racha on the way and run at least every hour, 6 A.M.–9 P.M. The ride costs less than 100B and takes 1.5 hours. Some buses en route to Pattaya will only stop on the main road in the developed part of town. It can be difficult to get a taxi from the highway, so make sure to ask at the bus station whether the bus will drive into Si Racha itself before you board. The buses that go into town will stop at the bus station, where you can pick up a taxi to get to your destination.

KO SI CHANG
เกาะสีชัง

Ko Si Chang—not to be confused with the larger and much more developed Ko Chang—is an interesting little island that was once King Rama V's summer residence. It is quite close to the mainland and has a somewhat commercial feeling, so don't expect crystal-clear waters, quiet serenity, or undisturbed beaches. In fact, don't expect it to be anything like Ko Samui or Ko Samet, as it's not a resort island. Nevertheless, Ko Si Chang, covering only 18 square kilometers, has a rich history and is quirky and charming enough to warrant a day trip.

Throughout history, three Thai kings have visited the island as a getaway. The first was

Rama IV, who stopped through periodically in the mid-1800s. Later, Rama V and Rama VI also stayed on the island, and the latter convalesced here for the better part of a year while ill.

Rama V Palace Ruins
พระจุฑาธุชราชฐาน

The Vimanmek Teak Mansion, originally constructed on Ko Si Chang for convalescing royals, was moved by King Rama V to Bangkok around 1900 (and can be toured in the capital). There are a few remaining structures on the complex's original site (9 A.M.–5 P.M. daily, free), but you'll have to use your imagination to envision the grandeur of the teak mansion, as only the foundation remains on the island's east coast. Still, the grounds and the few structures that remain, including the elegant, austere white palace temple, **Wat Asadang,** are worth walking through.

Saan Chao Paw Khao Yai Chinese Shrine
ศาลเจ้าพ่อเขาใหญ

According to local legend, the Saan Chao Paw Khao Yai Chinese Shrine has been around for hundreds of years, dating back to before the days of the Rama kings, when Chinese traders plied the Gulf of Thailand. The shrine, built around a cave atop a large hill where traders saw a mystical light shining, includes a Chinese-style structure and a series of caves filled with statues, other paraphernalia, and during the Chinese New Year season, hundreds of visitors. If you continue up, there is also what is purported to be a **Buddha Footprint** enclosed in a small pagoda.

Tham Yai Phrik Vipassana Monastery
วัดถ้ำยายปริก

The Tham Yai Phrik Vipassana Monastery (tel. 03/821-6104, www.wat-thamyaiprik. com, dawn–dusk daily) is a meditation center in the middle of the island that is famous for its caves, where monks and nuns cloister themselves. Outsiders are welcome to visit and meditate, but guests should be sure to comport themselves with appropriate piousness.

Beaches

Although given Ko Si Chang's proximity to the mainland, the beaches are far from deserted, they are pleasant and pretty. For those tired of rows of beach chairs and nonstop commerce on more popular beaches and islands, Ko Si Chang is actually a welcome break. It's not really set up for classic sunbathing and water sports, but it is wonderful for walking. **Tham Phang Beach,** on the west side of the island, has limited facilities for visitors, but you can at least rent a chair and umbrella.

Accommodations

Sichang Palace Hotel & Resort (81 Asdang Rd., tel. 03/821-6276, www.sichangpalace. com, 1,200B) is the island's only true hotel, right in the center of town. There's a swimming pool and small café-restaurant, and guest rooms are clean and functional but quite basic and uninteresting design-wise. You can also see the Gulf of Thailand from most of the guest rooms.

The pretty, pleasant **Si Chang View Resort** (91 Mu 6, Hat Khao Kat, tel. 03/821-6210, www.sichangview.com, 900B) on the island's west coast is a basic motel-style resort with just a dozen guest rooms and well-manicured gardens.

Food

Billed as an Italian-Thai place, the popular traveler hangout **Pan & David Restaurant** (167 Asdang Rd., tel. 03/821-6075, 11 A.M.–9:30 P.M. Mon. and Wed.–Fri., 8:30 A.M.–10 P.M. Sat., 8:30 A.M.–10:30 P.M. Sun., 200B) is really worth visiting for the seafood. The Thai fish dishes, including *tom yam kung* and steamed sea bass, are traditionally prepared, but if you want to go Italian, the restaurant also offers pasta dishes and inexpensive wine. The atmosphere here is casual, and there's outdoor seating too.

Getting There

Ferry boats to Ko Si Chang depart from Si Racha's Ko Loi jetty hourly, 7 A.M.–8 P.M. The last boat leaves Ko Si Chang at 6 P.M. The ride costs 40B one-way. When you arrive, Ko Si Chang's Thaa Laang pier is on the east side of the island, facing the mainland. It's not within walking distance from the island's sights, but transport to the center is available for 40–50B.

Getting Around

Ko Si Chang is so small that most of the touring involves three-wheeled motorized *samlor* (rickshaws) instead of motorcycles or taxis. You can pick these up at the pier or any of the tourist sights during the day. Expect to pay 60–100B, depending on how far you are going.

Rayong Province   จังหวัดระยอง

Rayong is a mix of industrial buildings (mostly supporting the petrochemical industry) and fruit orchards. While there's really nothing much for travelers to do in Rayong, it serves as a departure point for some of the smaller islands in the upper Gulf of Thailand.

BAN PHE
บ้านเพ

This little town is home to the pier from which you'll depart to Ko Samet but isn't otherwise particularly interesting or scenic. If you time things right, you'll be in town for just a few minutes to provision up for Samet on your way to the ferry. If you time things wrong and the ferries have stopped running, you can either spend the night in Ban Phe or persuade one of the speedboat taxis to take you to Samet after-hours. (Speedboats are not supposed to travel the route at night, but you may be able to persuade one to bend the rules.)

Along Ban Phe's main road, facing the pier, are a couple of markets and liquor stores that sell a small selection of local and foreign goods. Prices will seem exorbitant but will be that much more expensive once you get to the island, so it's probably worth it to grab that bottle of wine now.

Accommodations and Food

Sleeping options are limited in Ban Phe, but there are a couple of guesthouses available if you need to spend the night here. **Tan Tan Two** (Soi 2, across from the pier, tel. 03/865-3671, 400B) is a traditional guesthouse with rooms that look like they've accommodated their share of local students and folks who missed the last ferry. The place is very clean, and the guest rooms are large. There is an Internet café on the ground floor and even a travel agent.

Christie's Restaurant and Guesthouse (280/92 Soi 1, tel. 03/865-1976, 100B) has everything from stir-fried vegetables to cheeseburgers. The food is not fantastic, but later in the evening, the place becomes the town's main (or perhaps only) bar spot and is a good place to grab a drink. There is also a guesthouse above it with basic air-conditioned guest rooms available for 600B per night. The guesthouse is small, so rooms are often booked up if you try to get one later in the evening.

Getting There

Most travelers get to Ban Phe by bus, either from the Eastern (Ekkamai) Bus Terminal in Bangkok or from Khao San Road, where buses are advertised as "Ko Samet" buses. If you are taking a government bus from the Eastern Terminal, you'll pay around 175B for the 3–4-hour ride, and buses leave hourly 5 A.M.–8:30 P.M. Return buses leave 4 A.M.–6:30 P.M. From Khao San Road, most of the buses are minivans and cost about 250B. All buses will take you directly to the pier for Ko Samet.

Ban Phe is just off Highway 36, past Pattaya on the way to Rayong. The drive from Bangkok is at least three hours but can take longer if traffic is bad.

◀ KO SAMET
เกาะเสม็ด

Ko Samet's blessing is also, some would say, its curse. It's a sizable island located a mere four hours from Bangkok. The weather there is usually dry, and it has plenty of good-quality beaches. These attributes have generated a lot of development in recent years, and some of it is now trending upscale, causing some to be nostalgic for the days when it was a much quieter, more backpacker-centric destination. Nevertheless, much of the island retains a laid-back vibe and still contains some excellent, if increasingly crowded, beaches. Since the island is close to the mainland, don't expect pristine waters. Much of Ko Samet is already developed, and unobstructed views of the ocean—free of hotels, guesthouses, bars, and restaurants within your line of sight—can be hard to come by. So far, there are no high-rises on the island, so at least what you're looking at won't be blocking out everything else.

Samet definitely pales in comparison to some of Thailand's more popular island destinations. The beaches aren't quite as nice, the water not as clear, and the food and accommodations choices not as varied. But it's an excellent place to go if you're looking for a place you can travel to quickly and easily. Ko Samet is usually populated by an eclectic mix of visitors, from young Western backpackers looking for an inexpensive spot to enjoy the beach, to Bangkok residents, both Thai and expat, on quick weekend getaways. Unlike many of Thailand's other beaches and islands, there's not actually too much to do in Samet other than relax and enjoy the cold Singha beer. Unless you've got a stack of novels or enjoy just chilling out for days on end, Samet is best enjoyed as a short break instead of a weeklong vacation.

Beaches

The vast majority of beaches and resorts are on Ko Samet's eastern shore. The northeastern coast, in particular, is densely packed. For the sake of convenience, the island is broken into about a dozen beaches, each with a different

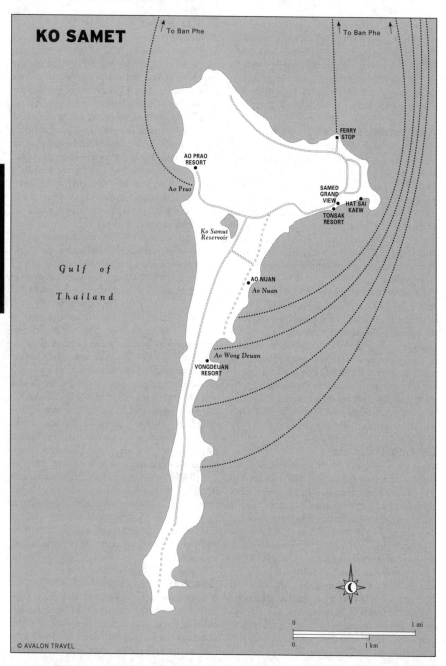

KO SAMET

To Ban Phe

To Ban Phe

FERRY
STOP

AO PRAO
RESORT

Ao Prao

SAMED
GRAND
VIEW

HAT SAI
KAEW

TONSAK
RESORT

Ko Samut
Reservoir

Gulf   of

Thailand

AO NUAN

Ao Nuan

Ao Wong Deuan

VONGDEUAN
RESORT

0   1 mi

0   1 km

© AVALON TRAVEL

© SUZANNE NAM

Ko Samet beach

name, but if you're on the east coast, you won't really notice that you've passed from one beach to another. For the most part it's one continuous strip of beach, broken by occasional headlands. If you want to stay on one beach and hang out on another, don't worry about the inconvenience unless they're on extreme opposite ends of the island. Ko Samet is only a few kilometers long, and since there is a mostly dirt road that runs along the entire coast just behind the beach, getting from one beach to another, on foot or otherwise, is easy.

Hat Sai Kaew (หาดทรายแก้ว), located on the northeast part of the island, is the Grand Central Station of Ko Samet's beaches since it's closest to the main ferry pier, and it's also the island's nicest beach. The name means "Diamond Sand Beach," and although you won't see any diamonds here, the sand is soft and light. The area surrounding the beach is clustered with various hotels and restaurants, and if you want to play on a personal motorized watercraft or ride a banana boat, this is the spot for you. This long stretch of beach is very popular with Thais and others with families.

Ao Phai (อ่าวไผ่) is located on Ko Samet's east coast, south of Hat Sai Kaew and north of Ao Nuan. This is one of the most popular areas, with a wide beach that can become crowded during the day.

The relatively cloistered **Ao Nuan** (อ่าวนวล), a bay just down the coast from Sai Kaew Beach, is a good choice for those who'd like more secluded surroundings. The beach is actually a very small, curved bay backed by trees. In terms of activities, there are no water sports here except swimming.

Ao Wong Deuan (อ่าววงเดือน), midway down the east coast, is a very popular beach and has lots of places to eat and sleep. However, there is also a lot of ferry, motorboat, and Jet Ski traffic, which makes it less than ideal for swimming in the gulf.

Ao Prao (อ่าวพร้าว) is the only developed beach on the west side of the island and is home to a handful of high-end resorts. The upside of Ao Prao is that it's quieter than most of the other beaches. You won't be disturbed by Jet Skiers or speedboats, and the west-facing view means good sunsets when the weather cooperates. The downside is that the beach itself isn't spectacular. The sand is rougher and darker than that on Hat Sai Kaew, and it's shallow for a long stretch, meaning you have to do a lot of walking to get to a swimmable depth.

Nightlife

Ko Samet is a pretty laid-back spot, and the nightlife seems to follow that trend. Most of the bars adjacent to the beach in Hat Sai Kew and Ao Wong Deuan set up mats on the sand lit with candles. Come nightfall, everyone just grabs a mat and hangs out drinking and listening to music. As the night wears on and the buckets of beer and mixed drink are consumed, the party scene tends to get a little more energetic. A few of the beach bars, including **Ploy Talay** (Hat Sai Kaew, tel. 03/864-4212), have fire dancing displays with techno music.

Sports and Recreation

There are facilities on Ko Samet that offer scuba diving, snorkeling, and other water sports. Many resorts also rent kayaks by the hour or for the day. Hat Sai Kaew and Ao Phai have concentrations of shops, but most diving and snorkeling here is going to be mediocre compared to other parts of the country. The surrounding waters are just too turbid to offer good visibility. Banana boating and even parasailing are also common on Samet, and you can arrange them right on the beach.

Accommodations and Food

When booking accommodations, keep in mind that Ko Samet is popular year-round. Be sure to reserve in advance of arriving if you've got a specific hotel or resort in mind. Since weekends draw such a high number of visitors, there's decreased demand during the week, and discounts are often given. Also, rates are often increased in the October–April high-season.

There is not a lot of standout food in Samet, and no real restaurant scene to speak of. Most people either eat at their resorts or grab roti on the beach or another quick, inexpensive snack from one of the vendors on the beach or the

kayaking off the coast of Ko Samet

© LINDA TRUE

road behind it. Many resorts and bars have very casual open-air restaurants right on the beach (basically just mats or tables in the sand) and serve popular Thai and Western dishes such as papaya salad, noodles, club sandwiches and french fries.

Ao Nuan (Ao Nuan, no phone, no reservations, 500B) is the place to go if you want to rough it on the beach and get away from it all. Bungalows have little more than a bed, but there's a restaurant-bar to hang out in at night.

Naga Bungalows (Ao Hin Khok, tel. 03/864-4035, 500B) is the sort of one-stop shop that relaxed travelers who aren't too picky will appreciate. There are a variety of guest rooms, a big restaurant, and even a proper bar, and although the guest rooms themselves are not directly on the beach, they are just a couple of minutes away. The on-site bakery is a big draw, and the food in general is better than typical resort fare.

Although ◖ **Tubtim** (Ao Tubtim, tel. 03/864-4025, www.tubtimresort.com, basic concrete bungalows with fan 600B to air-conditioned wood bungalows 3,000B) started out decades ago offering just basic thatched-roof beach huts, a series of renovations means that there are now a variety of different accommodations options, from very basic older bungalows in the back of the complex to stylish wooden bungalows with direct beach views. Aside from lots of options, what probably keeps expats and locals returning here again and again is the friendly attitude of the staff and the fact that Tubtim is the only resort on the beach, meaning you and other resort guests are likely to have it all to yourselves.

Vongdeuan Resort (Ao Wong Deuan, tel. 03/865-1777, www.vongdeuan.com, 1,500B) has two guest-room options: bungalows set back off the beach, and teak houses closer to the water. Some of the bungalows are done in a rustic beach style with thatched roofs, and some look like small contemporary houses.

Samed Grand View (Hat Sai Kaew, tel. 03/864-4220, www.grandviewgroup.net, bungalows 2,000B) is a well-kept, tidy place right in the thick of things in Hat Sai Kaew. The

snacks on Ko Samet beach

bungalows, some of which are all-wood and built in the traditional Thai style with angled roofs, have air-conditioning and clean, new bath fixtures.

Samed Villas (Ao Phai, tel. 03/864-4094, www.samedvilla.com, bungalows 2,000B) has modern semi-attached bungalows facing the beach. The decor of the small resort is generic but pleasant, the baths are spotless, and the air-conditioning is cold. The lobby and open-air restaurant areas are comfortable and have a nice view of the ocean, and the beach itself is very neatly maintained. Although it's not located on a private beach, it feels somewhat secluded and a little more "grown up" than some of the other resorts on the island.

Tonsak Resort (8/5 Ko Samed, Mu 4 Tambon Phe, Hat Sai Kaew, tel. 03/864-4314, www.tonsak.com, 2,000B) has wooden bungalows and a restaurant-bar close to the beach. The bungalows are wood throughout, imparting a log-cabin-on-the-beach vibe, complete with tables made out of tree trunks and tree-stump chairs.

For something a little cooler and more stylish than most of the competition, **Lima Coco** (Ao Prao, tel. 02/938-1811, www.tubtimresort.com, 2,600B) is the only option. Guest rooms and public spaces are colorfully decorated though not over the top. Guest rooms range from clean and basic to luxuriously fitted, depending on how much you're willing to spend. The large covered public space is great for big groups who want to hang out together in the evening. Though room rates are pricey compared to the east coast, Lima Coco is actually the most economical resort on the west coast's Ao Prao, and it benefits from that beach's lack of crowds.

(**Ao Prao Resort** (Ao Prao, tel. 02/438-9771, www.samedresorts.com, 5,700B) has hillside bungalows and is next to a scenic beach on the more secluded west coast of the island. The guest rooms are sumptuously appointed with dark-wood furniture and large bathtubs. There's also a restaurant, Seaview, that serves up tasty eats—both Thai and international cuisine—as well as liquor and wine.

The upscale **Le Vimarn** (Ao Prao, tel. 03/864-4104, www.kohsametlevimarn.com, 7,000B) is one of the nicest resorts on Ko Samet. In addition to private bungalows furnished with mostly wooden furniture and breezy textiles, the property also has a large infinity pool and a spa, both rare on the island. Le Vimarn feels more secluded than most resorts on Ko Samet.

Getting There

Catch a ferry to Ko Samet from Ban Phe, the mainland gateway for the island. Tickets can be purchased from the tourism information center (on the pier, tel. 03/889-6155, 7 A.M.–5 P.M.) in Ban Phe and cost 50B for the 30-minute ride. Boats go to Ko Samet frequently during the day but do not usually leave until full, so if you get there early, you'll wait around for an hour or more. The last ferry leaves Ban Phe at 5 P.M., and if you miss it, you can also arrange for a private speedboat to take you to the beach of your choice. The boats cost 1,200–1,600B, but they take small groups and deposit you directly

where you're going. If you arrive late in Ban Phe, speedboats are not supposed to travel the route at night, but you may be able to persuade one to bend the rules, as long as you're willing to pay on the high end of the scale.

Ko Samet's main pier, Na Dan Pier, is located on the north side of the island. There are also ferries that run throughout the day from Ban Phe to Ao Wong Deuan, on Ko Samet's east coast. Visitors should check with their hotels on Ko Samet to see which pier is best. Some hotels can arrange for private speedboats as well.

Getting Around

There are only two transport options in Ko Samet—*song thaew* and motorcycles. *Song thaew* circle the island and cost 20–80B depending on distance. Like all *song thaew*, the fares only apply along their standard route. Once you ask a *song thaew* to take you to a specific spot, you'll pay a couple of hundred baht for the ride instead. You can also rent a motorcycle to get around the island for about 300B per day, but keep in mind that much of the island has only dirt roads, and riding a motorcycle (or even sitting in a *song thaew*) can be uncomfortable. Many foreigners wipe out on Ko Samet, so make sure to wear your helmet.

(KO MAN NOK
เกาะมันนอก

If you're looking for that private-island experience without spending a ton of money or having to travel for hours, Ko Man Nok (also spelled Ko Man Nork and Ko Mun Nork) is a great place to head for a few days. It's so small that it barely qualifies as an island, and there's only one resort here. Aside from hanging out and reading, there is not really anything else to do on Ko Man Nok except watch the sunset.

The only resort on this gorgeous island, **Mun Nork Island Resort** (Bangkok office tel. 02/860-3025, www.munnorkislandresort.com, packages from 3,590B pp depending on number of guests and type of bungalow) is an incredibly tranquil, private place. It consists of just a scattering of bungalows with

sala (pavilion) on the beach at Ko Man Nok

© SUZANNE NAM

Rayong Sea Turtle Sanctuary
สถานีอนุรักษ์พันธุ์เต่าทะเล

The Rayong Sea Turtle Sanctuary (Ko Man Nai, tel. 03/865-7466, 8 A.M.–6 P.M. daily) is a breeding and research center for sea turtles and can be visited during the day. The sanctuary has resident adult sea turtles used for breeding, and once eggs are laid in the sand, they are taken into the nursery where they hatch. The baby turtles remain there for a year, when they can be set free. You can tour the facilities and, if there happen to be baby turtles on-site, visit them too. Otherwise, you can swim on the small island's beach.

Getting There
You can get to Ko Man Nai by arranging transportation from Christie's Restaurant and Guesthouse in Ban Phe. Or you can come from Ko Samet, where boat tours to the sanctuary can be booked via **Jimmy's Tours** (Hat Sai Kaew, tel. 08/9832-1627). The cost is 400B, and the trip takes about 50 minutes. During low tide, you can walk to Ko Man Nai from Hat Kai Bae in Ko Chang.

KHAO CHAMAO
เขาชะเมา

Located inland between Rayong Town and Chanthaburi Town is **Khao Chamao-Khao Wong National Park** (อุทยานแหงชาติเขาชะเมา เขาวง, tel. 03/889-4378 or 02/562-0760, reserve@dnp.go.th, 400B). The park contains wild animals such as bears, elephants, wild pigs, deer, and 53 species of birds. The topography here is dramatic: There are limestone cliffs as well as the **Khao Chamao** (น้ำตกเขาชะเมา), and **Khlong Pla Kang** (น้ำตกคลองปลากาง) waterfalls. The latter is considered the most beautiful waterfall in the park. From the park headquarters, it is possible to hike to either waterfall. The Khao Chamao waterfall is just over three kilometers from the headquarters on a marked trail, and the Khlong Pla Kang waterfall is about two kilometers past it on the same trail.

air-conditioning and outdoor showers along with a central restaurant. Packages—the shortest is two nights, but longer stays are possible—include all meals. The food is simple but well-prepared Thai cuisine. Best of all, the small beach is dotted with *sala* (pavilions) with walkways that stretch out over the sand. These make perfect locations for relaxing, having a drink, reading a book, or doing nothing at all. Ko Man Nok is pure, unadulterated relaxation. In order to reserve a spot, call or email the Bangkok office. A deposit must be made to secure rooms. The package fee includes the boat ride from the Laem Tarn Pier near Rayong. The resort will provide you with driving directions and a map to get to the pier.

KO MAN NAI
เกาะมันใน

Tiny Ko Man Nai has just one beach, there are no lodgings, and camping is prohibited due to the abundance of sea turtles. It does, however, house the Rayong Sea Turtle Sanctuary.

Accommodations and Camping

For just a 50B fee, you can camp in the park at designated grounds near the headquarters. You can also rent sleeping bags and tents for a nominal fee, although during weekends and holidays these can run out. The park also has bungalows that sleep 2–8 people. These are basic wooden bungalows, but many have hot water, air-conditioning, and refrigerators. The cost is 400–1,200B per night per bungalow. If you're planning on sleeping in the park, make sure to contact the park in advance to reserve a space, or you can make reservations through the national park website (www.dnp.go.th).

Getting There

You can take a *song thaew* from Ban Phe to the point where the park meets the road, and then another one from there to the park entrance. The cost is under 100B per segment, but the trucks only run during the day. *Song thaew* only make the trip when there are sufficient passengers, so service is irregular. To go by car, take Highway 3 east from Ban Phe to the Km 274 marker, then drive 17 kilometers north to the park.

Chanthaburi Province   จังหวัดจันทบุรี

With its national parks, quiet coastline, and abundant tropical fruit orchards, rural Chanthaburi Province is an idyllic place to visit, either in its own right or when passing through to Trat Province. A highlight is the sleepy city of Chanthaburi, located on its eponymous river. It is the provincial capital, and its name means "city of the moon."

Chanthaburi Town has various French influences—the French occupied it 1893–1904—and this gives it a different feel from the rest of the kingdom. While many visitors simply skip through Chanthaburi Province on their way to Trat and the island hotspot of Ko Chang, curious outsiders will find that Chanthaburi Town and the surrounding area make an attractive destination. More than anything, the area offers something unique: a glimpse of Thai life far away from the bright lights of Bangkok and the kingdom's well-developed Western visitor–oriented beach resorts.

Chanthaburi Town, located 330 kilometers southeast of Bangkok, is also the center of the region's gem trade, with scores of dealers and shops selling rubies, sapphires, and other gems in the city every weekend. And this region is fertile ground for a wide variety of tropical fruits, including jackfruit, rambutan, mangosteen, and—perhaps most famously—durian. Known as the king of Thai fruits, this distinctive, yellow, melon-shaped fruit with a spiked skin is by equal turns beloved and reviled for its pungent odor. If you've never tried durian before, there's no better place to do so than Chanthaburi Province, as some say the region produces the best specimens of the fruit in the world.

◖ CHANTHABURI
จันทบุรี
Gem Market
ตลาดพลอย

Operating Friday–Sunday morning, the gem market comprises various stalls and shops located along Si Chan Road in downtown Chanthaburi. The gem market is a serious affair: Masses of buyers from all over the world convene here to conduct their business. There are more than 300 registered gem dealers in the city, and the market is often hot and crowded. Buyers and sellers gather around tables and hammer out deals, with sacks of stones trading hands. Sapphires and rubies from Laos, Cambodia, and Africa are the main draw.

If you'd like to purchase gem stones, insiders suggest making friends with the merchants who run their own tables. If you're lucky, you can sit in with these regulars. Otherwise, if you're forced to walk around searching out the best deals, chances are you'll either be totally

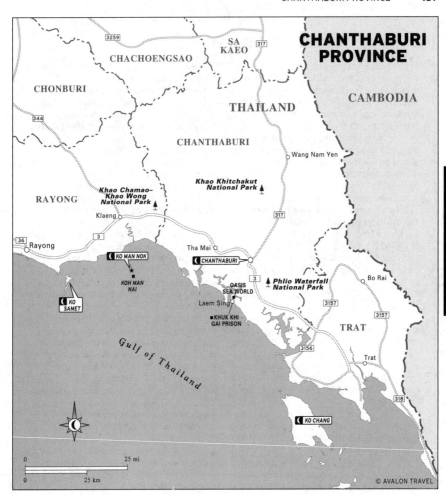

ignored or targeted as an obvious neophyte and subjected to inflated prices.

Also keep in mind that verbal agreements are often binding, so if you offer a price on a whim, be prepared to pay it. The merchants here often conduct their business with verbal negotiations and expect that agreed-upon prices will be honored. Don't be scared off, however. Many of the cut gems available at the market are selling for hundreds, not thousands of baht, making it possible to buy something.

Other Sights

The **Cathedral of the Immaculate Conception Chanthaburi** is a surprising sight to encounter in a land of *wats:* Located across a footbridge from downtown Chanthaburi, it's a 60-meter-tall French-style cathedral and Thailand's biggest church. The construction is full of the requisite stained glass windows and murals. The city has long been a destination for Christians fleeing Vietnam, and construction of the cathedral began in 1906—though

BUYING GEMS IN THAILAND

The typical Bangkok gem scam goes something like this: An unwitting foreign tourist is approached on the street, often outside a well-known sight like the Grand Palace. It's the king's birthday (or some other such fabricated holiday), the line goes, and today – only today – gems at a particular shop are being sold at a massively reduced rate. The tourist agrees to go and peruse the goods, and along the way to the shop, he or she might even be approached by another foreigner – in cahoots with the scammers – and told about this special sale.

The endgame is, unfortunately, predictable: The tourist purchases some costly goods for anywhere from several hundred to several thousand U.S. dollars at the shop. They're told that they can be sold, in turn, for an enormous profit back at home. Only after arriving in his or her native land does the victim discover that the "gems" he or she bought are worth significantly less than the price paid.

The good news is, in Chanthaburi – home to Thailand's largest gem market – people probably won't be trying to rip you off. But buying gems in this market requires a different type of savvy. It's an interesting place to sit out on the sidelines and observe, but if you want to take home some baubles, follow this advice.

First, get a sense of what's sold at the market. Sapphires and rubies are the main attraction in Chanthaburi, for example. In fact, it's said that at least half of all of these gems in the world make their way through Chanthaburi. They come from Southeast Asia and other places; sellers often buy them rough and then have them cut before they're sold. It's also a good idea to get a sense of typical prices. It's best to be as well informed as possible, not only to know when you're being

offered a good deal, but also to know when a price you're being quoted is too high.

You'll also want to conduct yourself in a professional, conservative manner when dealing with merchants. You may be a traveler passing through town, but don't dress that way. Smart attire will help convey your competence, while shorts, sandals, and a T-shirt may mark you as an out-of-town neophyte who can't be taken seriously. Before entering into negotiations, you should also try to get a sense of how the market operates. For example, in Chanthaburi, verbal commitments are often taken as seriously as handshakes or signatures. If someone offers you a price for a bag of gems and you agree to it, your word should be honored. If a seller asks you to name your price and you do so, be prepared to lay your cash on the table if he or she accepts. It's poor form – and will provoke anger – if you try to wiggle your way out of a deal.

And finally, as in many other endeavors, it's enormously helpful to solicit guidance from a seasoned pro. If possible, make friends with buyers or sellers you encounter at the market. Over time, if you gain their trust – and if you behave in a trustworthy manner as well – they'll give you some insider tips. And if you're lucky, you might even be invited to sit in at a seller's or buyer's table. This will give you credibility and shield you from the higher prices you might be subject to should you walk around the market on your own.

Unless you already have some expertise in gems, it may be wiser to sit this one out or just spend a few thousand baht on items you're buying for decorative purposes instead of as an investment. Either way, it's a great place to spend a few hours.

various Christian buildings have existed at this location since 1711—and continued for many years as various elements of the building were added. Note that although its doors are often left open to visitors during the day, there have been times when visitors are not allowed to climb up the cathedral's tower. Lining the

path from the footbridge that connects the cathedral to the downtown area are some striking Vietnamese-style houses that are also worth a look.

Just four kilometers outside of Chanthaburi on Sukhumvit Highway is **Wat Thong Thua** (วัดทองทั่ว), which is remarkable for its Khmer sculptures. Not far away is an archaeological site with additional Khmer remains.

Wat Khao Sukim (วัดเขาสุกิม, www.khaosukim.org, 6:30 A.M.–5 P.M. daily) is a temple and meditation center in Tambon Khao Bai Si, approximately 20 kilometers north of Chanthaburi along Route 3322. Known for its tranquil setting and its many Buddha statues and artwork, it's a good destination if you'd like to see the countryside surrounding the provincial capital. Wat Khao Sukim is on a hillside, and its rooftop provides vistas of the lush surrounding area. You can reach the temple via taxi from Chanthaburi Town; expect to pay about 100B. The drive takes 20–30 minutes.

Accommodations

Just a block away from the gem market, **The River Guest House** (3/5–8 Si Chan Rd., tel. 03/932-8211, 250B fan-cooled, 350B air-conditioned) is popular due to its low cost and homey, backpacker-friendly feel. The open-air lobby is close to the Chanthaburi River and makes for a pleasant place to lounge. The hotel's rooms are tidy but quite bare-bones, with little more than a bed and a desk.

Muangchan Hotel (257–259 Si Chan Rd., tel. 03/931-2909, 280B fan-cooled, 600B air-conditioned) is a good mid-range option for visitors who'd like to be close to the gem market. The vast building, however, is somewhat creaking, and the lobby feels gloomy. The guest rooms have basic furnishings, such as simple wooden desks and tables, but are tidy.

Just outside of town is the **Maneechan Resort** (110 Sukhumvit Rd., tel. 03/934-3777, www.maneechan.com, 1,500B), a surprisingly lovely resort with large, comfortable guest rooms, a big pool, and nicely maintained grounds. Although you will need to take advantage of the hotel's shuttle or find other transport into the center of town, the commute is worth it for those who would like to stay somewhere nice. Most visitors who stay here are local tourists exploring the area, but the staff works hard to make everyone feel comfortable.

Food

When it comes to cuisine, Chanthaburi is known principally for its fruit and its rice noodles (the main ingredient in pad thai).

If you want to sample Chanthaburi's distinctive cuisine, make a beeline for ◖ **Chanthorn Phochana** (98/2 Benjamarachutis Rd., tel. 03/931-2339, 9 A.M.–9 P.M. daily, 80–150B), located just north of the Kasemsarn Hotel. The restaurant is the perfect place to soak up Chanthaburi's local flavor and meet some of the city's enthusiastic citizens. Signature dishes—which range from Thai to Vietnamese to Chinese cuisine—include Chanthaburi's special noodles with crab, stir-fried chicken with cardamom stems, and fried Vietnamese-style spring rolls. If you're lucky enough to visit when it's available (approximately May–Oct.), the mangosteen salad is also a popular dish.

Baan Puan (33/4 Saritidet Rd., tel. 03/935-0849, 6:30 A.M.–5:30 P.M. daily) means "friend's house" in Thai, and the mood at this unpretentious coffeehouse and snack bar is indeed collegial. Dismiss any notions you might have of an establishment proffering overpriced macchiatos or extra-hot, no-foam, half-caf lattes: This is the kind of place that serves delectable, incredibly sweet Thai-style iced coffee, thick with condensed milk, for a mere 10B. The various snacks on offer include dainty dessert cakes, various sweet rolls, and sandwiches. The friendly owner, Khun Oratai, couldn't be more welcoming to outsiders. Baan Puan is popular with students, so they strive to keep the prices low.

Sony Yadaw (Si Chan Rd., just before the river) is a tiny restaurant that serves vegetarian Indian food and caters to Chanthaburi visitors from the subcontinent. It's located just before the river, across Si Chan Road from the River Guest House. The place is easy to miss, since its unassuming entranceway opens up onto just three or four tables. The samosas are excellent, as is the hot *chai* tea.

Getting There

Chanthaburi is a 4.5-hour bus journey from Bangkok's Eastern Bus Terminal. The ride

THE DURIAN: KING OF THAI FRUITS

No other fruit in the world evokes such strong feelings as the durian – or requires as prominent signage prohibiting its consumption in public places. The heavy, yellow, melon-shaped fruit with the woody, razor-sharp spiked skin is worshipped and reviled in equal measure in Thailand and throughout Asia. And it can be hard to tell who feels more fervently about the issue.

There are those who love the durian and proclaim its exotic, custard-like flesh to be simply divine. And then there are the durian-haters who decry the devil fruit's powerful taste, odd, fleshy texture, and – most of all – its pungent odor, so strong that some have compared it to the smell of dead bodies or garbage dumps.

From a nutritional standpoint, the durian is high in protein and fat and often eaten raw or used as ice cream flavoring. Thais tend to like their durians to taste sweet, which sets them apart from other consumers in the region. The fruit is considered an aphrodisiac and is thought to be "heating" to the body – thus, people say, it should never be consumed with alcohol. Indeed, should you ever be foolhardy enough to eat durian and then drink beer, you're likely to suffer some significant gastro-intestinal distress (as well as some distinctive burping).

When Thais buy durians on the street, you'll often see vendors bang the fruits with a small mallet, as the resulting sound can indicate ripeness. Sellers will then often crack the fruit open and offer their customers a chance to take a whiff to ensure suitability. The durian, in fact, takes several months to mature. The most expensive specimens can cost hundreds of dollars. Chanthaburi Province, with its many fruit farms, is considered the heart of the country's durian production. Fans of the fruit say some of the world's best durians are grown in the kingdom.

A Thai scientist's recent work underscored the many thorny issues surrounding the fruit. By virtue of genetic crossbreeding, he was able to produce – of all things – an odorless durian. His objective, he said, was to make the durian more acceptable to the general public – and make it more likely to be exported to places where such strong-smelling produce is frowned on. He also wanted to ensure the fruit's survival among the next generation of durian consumers. That's because today, many young people here don't fancy the fruit as much as older Thais.

But will the project succeed? Will Thais – or foreigners, for that matter – take to the odorless durian? Many hardcore fans of the divisive fruit are decidedly dubious. They say an odorless durian essentially misses the point – the smell is among the fruit's most critical components.

costs about 200B, and scheduled buses leave Bangkok regularly throughout the day. Buses can also be taken from Trat to Chanthaburi, which is a one-hour trip. The ride costs 200B each way, and buses run every 30 minutes during the day. Passengers are dropped off at the Chanthaburi bus station, which is east of town, less than one kilometer from downtown. Taxis and *tuk tuks* can be taken from the bus station to other parts of town. A more informal—and economical—way of traveling is by minivan. These can be hailed on the street and usually carry 3–10 passengers. The ride from Trat to Chanthaburi, for example, will only set you back about 70B. To recognize these minivans, it's best to ask at hotels, bus stations, or restaurants. Local people can usually tell you where to hail a minivan or find one preparing to depart.

You also can hire a taxi—rates are negotiable—to take you from Chanthaburi, Trat, or points farther afield, but doing so will be substantially more expensive than traveling by bus. The cost of a taxi ride from Chanthaburi to Bangkok varies widely, but a ballpark figure might be 2,000–4,000B. To drive to Chanthaburi from Bangkok, take Highway 315 south, then Highway 344 southeast to Highway 3. Highway 3 runs to Chanthaburi and then continues on, farther east, to Trat.

SOUTH OF CHANTHABURI
Chanthaburi Horticultural Research Center
ศูนย์วิจัยพืชสวนจันทบุรี

Located 15 kilometers southeast of Chanthaburi Town along Highway 3 is the Chanthaburi Horticultural Research Center (Tambon Ta Pon, near Phlio, tel. 03/939-7030, 9 A.M.–4 P.M. daily for large groups who call ahead). It contains information on various agricultural development initiatives as well as various fruits grown in the region. It's designed to accommodate groups of more than 10 visitors and is open daily. Call ahead to arrange a visit.

Phlio Waterfall National Park
อุทยานแห่งชาติน้ำตกพลิ้ว

Phlio Waterfall National Park (tel. 03/943-4528, reserve@dnp.go.th, 8:30 A.M.–4:30 P.M. daily, 400B) is 14 kilometers from Chanthaburi Town on Highway 3. It is known for the plethora of wild animals living in its dense rainforest. The park's namesake Phlio Waterfall empties into a fish-filled pool. Visitors can also take in the Alongkorn Chedi, which was built in 1876 and affords good views of the falls. Phlio Waterfall and Alongkorn Chedi are located near the main entrance to the park, along Highway 3. Overnight guests may stay at the park's campsite (50B pp plus 10B for the site). Visitors can also sleep in the bungalow, which has six guest rooms, each of which cost 1,800B. Guest rooms are available individually, but visitors must phone or email the park before arriving.

Oasis Sea World
Oasis Sea World (48/2 Mu 5 Paknam, Laem Sing, tel. 03/939-9015 or 03/936-3238, www.oasisseaworld.net, 9 A.M.–5 P.M. daily, admission 180B, 400B to swim with dolphins), located 25 kilometers south of Chanthaburi Town, puts on dolphin shows in which bottlenose and other species of dolphin perform standard tricks like bouncing balls and jumping through rings. Shows are at 9 A.M., 11 A.M., 1 P.M., 3 P.M., and 5 P.M. Monday–Friday; there's an additional show at 7 A.M. Saturday and Sunday. You can swim with the creatures here as well, and the grounds include a garden and a restaurant. The center is also a breeding and conservation station. Tour operators run trips here from Pattaya, Rayong, and Ko Chang. Taxis can be hired for negotiable rates—the distance isn't great, so the meter price might be 750–1,500B. To drive from Chanthaburi, take Highway 3 south and follow the signs to Oasis Sea World.

Laem Sing
แหลมสิงห์

Laem Sing is a quiet, laid-back beach area. The small town of Laem Sing itself is approximately 30 kilometers due south of Chanthaburi Town, where the Chanthaburi River meets the Gulf of Thailand. The town is a traditional fishing village and has limited tourist-related amenities, but there are a few attractions to take in.

The **Khuk Khi Gai Prison** (คุกขี้ไก่), a small brick building near the Laem Sing pier, was built by the French in 1893 to detain unruly Thais. The building contains slits in the walls for windows and, oddly enough, was built to facilitate a strange form of torture: Droppings from chickens were placed on the roof and fell through onto the prisoners below (hence the name Khi Gai, which means "bird droppings"). The prison is quite small, but if you are in the area and have an hour to kill, it is worth the visit.

Laem Sing Beach sits close to the mouth of the Chanthaburi River. Restaurants, bungalows, and trees line the wide, clean beach, which is free from throngs of travelers. It is possible to rent a kayak (expect to pay around 300B for two hours) or charter a longtail boat if you're interested in exploring surrounding islands.

To get to Laem Sing from Chanthaburi, you can drive south on Highway 3 or take a taxi, which will cost approximately 750–1,500B.

KHAO KHITCHAKUT NATIONAL PARK
อุทยานแห่งชาติเขาคิชฌกูฏ

Khao Khitchakut National Park (tel. 03/945-2074, reserve@dnp.go.th, 8:30 A.M.–4:30 P.M. daily, 400B) is one of Thailand's smallest national parks at just 59 square kilometers. The park is located 28 kilometers northeast of Chanthaburi Town on Highway 3249, and the scenery is mostly lush green low mountains. Its principal attraction is the popular **Krathing Falls** (น้ำตกกระทิง), which draws approximately 2,000 Thai tourists each weekend. The waterfall, fueled by the Chanthaburi River, has 13 levels, and its pools are deep enough for swimming. The trail to the falls starts at the park headquarters, but to get to the top, you'll have to follow a very steep path, so come equipped with substantial footwear. Butterflies congregate around the 13th tier.

Accommodations
For those interested in accommodations (tel. 02/562-0760, reserve@dnp.go.th) in the park, **campsites** are available (50B pp). **Bungalows** that sleep two people are available for 600B per night. Arrangements should be made in advance of arriving, especially if you plan to visit during the weekend.

Getting There and Around
If you're not driving, you can take a *song thaew* from Chanthaburi Town to the park. The ride costs 40B and takes approximately 45 minutes. Visitors are dropped off within walking distance of the park entrance. Taxis can also be hired in Chanthaburi Town, but plan ahead as a driver might not be immediately available, and the charge may be steep. To drive to Khao Khitchakut National Park from Chanthaburi Town, follow Highway 3249 northeast for 28 kilometers.

As in all of the country's national parks, it is unfortunately virtually impossible to get around the park without your own transport.

Trat Province   จังหวัดตราด

Trat Province is located in the kingdom's far southeast, on the Gulf of Thailand's east coast. Bordered by Cambodia to the east and Chanthaburi Province to the west, the area contains some serene and infrequently visited beaches on its mainland, as well as the sleepy and welcoming provincial capital of Trat City. Most visitors venture to the region merely to use it as a transit point for trips to the larger islands off its coast, such as Ko Chang. But the area provides an interesting look at how life is lived in Thailand's rural regions.

TRAT CITY
ตราด

Trat City stands out for what it lacks: travelers. Small, rather undeveloped, and fairly unremarkable, the city is much less frequently visited by foreigners than Chanthaburi—and is certainly farther off the beaten path than Ko Chang. But that's not to say Trat is devoid of charm. It has an interesting *wat* and thriving day and night markets that are worth a look. Seafood is a big draw here, given the city's proximity to the gulf. Succulent fruits from the surrounding area are also on offer, and you'll find plenty of them in the markets and being displayed on carts throughout the city.

Sights
Just two kilometers outside town is **Wat Buppharam** (วัดบุปผาราม) or **Wat Plai Khlong** (วัดปลายคลอง), a 350-year-old temple with a lush garden. Situated on a hill, the *wat*'s grounds contain wooden houses in the traditional Thai style. The most interesting part of this Ayutthaya-period *wat* is the *wihan*. It's the country's oldest surviving *wihan,* according to the resident monks, and is also an excellent example of wooden construction of the era. The

© SUZANNE NAM

Locals repair fishing nets off the Gulf of Thailand.

temple also houses a small museum with devotional items as well as some interesting Chinese and European pottery pieces.

Food

Eating in Trat City centers on its **food markets,** and a wide variety of street food is readily available. During the day, head for the indoor market on Tat Mai Road, where you'll find various authentic Thai dishes. In the evening, the night market can be found just to the north.

Getting There

Bangkok Airways (tel. 02/265-5555, www. bangkokair.com) offers three daily flights from Bangkok to Trat and vice versa (6,200B roundtrip, depending on the season). Trat's recently constructed—and charmingly Lilliputian—airport is really pleasant, as it's beautifully manicured and quite peaceful. Virtually the entire tiny complex is open-air, and meticulously trimmed plants and flowers line the facility. It's 40 kilometers southwest of Trat City,

and Bangkok Airways runs a shuttle service to town for 300B pp. It takes approximately 30–45 minutes to get to town.

Visitors who are traveling from Trat's airport to Ko Chang can book buses that will take them from the airport, to the vehicle ferry that departs from **Tha Thammachat pier** (ทาธรรมชาติ) in **Laem Ngop** (แหลมงอบ), and on to their chosen destination on Ko Chang. The small tourist information desk in the airport, from which buses can be booked, can also arrange for reservations at the hotel or resort of your choice. Brochures and maps are available for travelers who've not yet decided where to stay. Bookings can be made for Ko Chang only.

You can get to Trat from Bangkok's Eastern and Northern Bus Terminals—or vice versa. In Trat, you can book with **Cherdchai Tours** (Sukhumvit Rd., 300 meters south of the Trat bus station, tel. 03/951-1062, 7 A.M.–11 P.M. daily). The service has buses that go in each direction hourly. The journey takes about 5.5 hours and costs roughly 250B. Taxis can be hired from the bus station for visitors arriving in Trat who want to travel elsewhere in town.

Taxis can be chartered from Bangkok to Trat or vice versa, but this option is obviously much slower than flying, and the round-trip taxi journey is likely just as expensive as round-trip flights.

KO CHANG
เกาะช้าง

Ko Chang, first and foremost, boasts visually stunning topography. Situated on Thailand's eastern seaboard, near the Cambodian border, its craggy peaks seem to rise straight up out of the water. And the sprawling island—it's Thailand's second-largest, after Phuket—is packed with dense, lush, abundantly green rainforests.

The island's allure, however, goes beyond simply lazing in the sun. What draws many visitors to Ko Chang—and more and more of them seem to be arriving every year—is the island's eminently laid-back vibe coupled with its eco-adventure pursuits, which include snorkeling, diving, and tropical hiking and trekking.

Ko Chang's diversity of offerings is sufficient to meet nearly every visitor's expectations. Some parts of the island cater to the young party-centric demographic (think nighttime fire shows), while other sections are quieter and more family-friendly. Recently development has come to Ko Chang, and over the last several years it has come at a faster pace than many other beach destinations in the kingdom. You'll see new construction everywhere; the effort seems to be focused on turning the island into a more upscale destination.

Occasional construction sites and more travelers have longtime visitors who've been coming for years bemoaning the end of an era; they fear Ko Chang is becoming just another Phuket. That might be true, but the development so far has done nothing to diminish the island's striking geographic attributes. Spend enough time on Ko Chang and you'll catch vistas as dramatic as any in Thailand. A twist in the road here, up and around a hill there, and it hits you: a sweeping view of the deep-blue sea framed by steep hillsides and palm trees rustling in the wind.

Beaches and Islands

Ko Chang's beaches are of varying quality: Some are narrow and somewhat rocky, while others are wide and welcoming. Swimming can be dangerous in some places due to powerful riptides. In terms of sand, water clarity, and views, the island's beast beaches are on the west coast.

In fact, the vast majority of Ko Chang's development is along the west coast, while the east coast contains fewer resorts, and these tend to cater to Thai package tourists. The west side of the island has a paved road that runs its entire length, and the west coast is divided into villages and their accompanying beaches. **Hat Sai Khao** (หาดทรายขาว), commonly known as White Sand Beach, located in the northwest near the ferry pier, has the island's highest concentration of hotels, restaurants, and shops. While other parts of Ko Chang seem to cater to younger crowds, Hat Sai Khao is more middle-of-the-road and attracts an older clientele. To the south is **Hat Kai Mook** (หาดไข่มุก), a quieter village with a sleepy feel. To the south, about midway down the coast, a slew of more upscale resorts is clustered in **Ao Khlong Prao** (อ่าวคลองพร้าว). **Hat Kaibae** (หาดไกแบ), the next village to the south, contains a range of accommodations but can feel crowded, depending on the season. Next comes **Hat Tha Nam** (หาดทานํา), otherwise known as Lonely Beach, where younger visitors looking for late nights and more raucous nightlife generally head. The prevailing truism is that a spate of recent development has rendered the beach lonely no more. **Bailan Bay** (อ่าวใบลาน), to the south, is more subdued and is a popular choice for a quieter feeling. At the southwestern tip of Ko Chang is **Bang Bao Bay** (อ่าวบางเบา), with its pier, many dive shops, and a spate of upscale developments.

Ko Wai is just off the southern coast of Ko Chang. The island has limited lodging but boasts high-quality diving and snorkeling.

© LINDA TRUE

cliffs along the coast of Ko Chang

Diving and Snorkeling

While other locations in Thailand—notably the Similan and Surin Islands, as well as Ko Tao—are arguably home to higher-quality diving, Ko Chang is increasingly popular. That's because its waters are relatively clear, with good reefs located at the fairly shallow depths of 5–25 meters. Visibility depends on the time of year but can reach distances of 30 meters. Though diving is possible year-round, ideal conditions exist October–May.

Several seamounts (underwater mountains that rise toward the ocean's surface) are situated off Ko Chang's southern tip, between Ko Chang and Ko Kut. Coral reefs on these seamounts attract a large number of sea creatures. Popular dive sites include **Hin Luk Bat** (หินลูกบาศก์) and **Hin Rap** (หินราบ).

Many snorkeling and dive shops are located along the west coast of the island; there's a concentration at the southernmost village, Bang Bao Bay. A popular dive shops is **Ploy Scuba Diving** (tel. 08/1451-1387, www.ploys-cuba.com). Ploy's main office is in Bang Bao,

but there are also Ploy Scuba Diving shops all along Ko Chang's west coast, as well as on the outlying islands of Ko Kut, Ko Mak, and Ko Wai. Another popular shop is **BB Divers** (tel. 03/955-8040, www.bbdivers.com), a Belgian-run outfit that also has its main office in Bang Bao. Their training pool and other facilities are located in Lonely Beach.

Scuba-diving courses for neophytes typically cost about 3,500B, while PADI Open Water certification will set you back about approximately 11,500B. The shortest courses take just a few hours, while the longer ones last a few days. Overnight trips are also available.

Other Sports and Recreation

Ko Chang means "elephant island" in Thai, although it's named that because of the island's physical appearance, not the fact that elephants roamed freely here. A few operators have brought pachyderms to their eponymous locale, though, and offer elephant trekking and visits to elephant camps: **Chang Chutiman** (near Hat Kaibae, tel. 08/9939-6676, 8 A.M.–5 P.M.

daily) and **Ban Kwan Elephant Camp** (near Ban Khlong Son, just inland from Ao Sapparot pier in the north, tel. 08/1919-3995, chang-tone@yahoo.com, 8:30 A.M.–5 P.M. daily). Packages, some of which include an educational session and a short ride, typically cost 500–900B. Transfers from hotels to the camps can be arranged.

A major portion of the island is devoted to the **Ko Chang National Park** (อุทยานแหงชาติหมูเกาะชาง). Ko Chang's mountainous interior and dense rainforests make for excellent day hikes and treks. In addition, several waterfalls provide scenic destinations to visit. These cascades are usually active year-round, but ask around before setting off to ensure that low water levels haven't dried them out. Popular falls include Namtok Than Mayom and Namtok Khlong Plu. The **Namtok Than Mayom** (น้ำตกธารมะยม) waterfall is located midway down the east coast and affords striking views from its peak. The **Namtok Khlong Plu** (น้ำตกคลองพลู) waterfall, in the center of the island, is the island's biggest cascade and is accessible from the central west coast. Both can be accessed independently or with tours that can be booked through various agencies. Other waterfalls exist on the island, but these two are administered by the national park.

An outfit called **Evolution Tour** (Ao Khlong Prao, tel. 08/9603-9642, www.evolutiontour. com) offers guides and tours to various waterfalls. Another tour operator, **Jungle Way** (Ao Khlong Prao, tel. 08/9223-4795, www.jungle-way.com) runs daylong and overnight treks to Ko Chang's interior that range 600–1,800B in price. Approximately 75 percent of Ko Chang is rugged rainforest, so there's plenty of terrain to explore.

Accommodations

The entire west coast of Ko Chang is lined with all manner of lodging, from cut-rate bungalows to high-end resorts. Like most other parts of Thailand, Ko Chang is slowly but surely moving upmarket, so it's harder and harder to find the cheap beachfront bamboo huts that made travelers in the past fall in love with the island.

That's not to say that they don't exist; it's just that they are being supplanted by nicer and more expensive accommodations.

€ Bailan Family Bungalows (Bailan Bay, 800 meters south of Lonely Beach, tel. 08/9051-2701, www.bailanfamilybungalow.com, 350B) is a good choice for clean budget lodgings at a family-run, family-friendly property. Basic Thai-style huts include a fan, hot water, and a bathroom. Bungalows with air-conditioning, TVs, and fridges are also available.

€ Paradise Cottage (Hat Tha Nam, tel. 08/1773-9337, www.paradisecottagekohchang. com, 400B) on Lonely Beach is an inexpensive resort with a variety of different types of bungalows to choose from. The cheapest, at 400B during high season (Oct.–Apr.), are as basic as it gets—fan-cooled only, basic plumbing, and set back from the views, but they are still a good value considering the beachfront location. The open-air bar and restaurant have a minimalist concrete-meets–*Gilligan's Island* theme going, which sets Paradise Cottage apart from other run-of-the-mill bungalow developments and makes it feel a little more trendy and younger. Air-conditioned bungalows with ocean views are also available.

Blue Lagoon Resort (Ao Khlong Prao, tel. 08/1940-0649 or 03/955-7243, 500B) is perhaps better known for its adjoining—and quite popular—**Ko Chang Thai Cookery School** (1,000B for a 5-hour class). Bungalows at Blue Lagoon are set on a lagoon not far from the beach. Some bungalows are fan-cooled while others have air-conditioning. The most basic huts, right on the lagoon, feature private balconies.

The family-run, middle-of-the-road **Garden Resort** (Hat Kaibae, tel. 03/955-7260, www. gardenresortkohchang.com, 1,800B) is an excellent choice for those who don't want basic backpacker bungalows but don't need five-star service or amenities. The resort has clean, comfortable air-conditioned bungalows, a large swimming pool, and pretty gardens on the grounds. The bungalows are furnished with lots of bamboo and other tropical materials but aren't particularly stylish on the inside.

Cookies Hotel (Hat Sai Khao, tel. 03/955-1105 to 03/955-1107, www.cookieskohchang.com, 2,000B) is a bit more conventional than many of Ko Chang's more bohemian-oriented budget hotels and bungalows. Cookies feels less like a secluded spa than a standard beach hotel. It is, however, a well-established place, and its location is decent if you'd like to be in the commercial hub of White Sand Beach. Guest rooms across the street, away from the beach, cost less but aren't as well-appointed as the ones near the lobby. The hotel also has a large, clean pool and access to the beach.

Koh Chang Tropicana Resort (Ao Khlong Prao, tel. 03/955-7122, www.kohchangtropicana.net, 4,000B) on Khlong Prao is a cluster of stand-alone bungalows amid a traditional hotel amid a lush beachfront garden. The pool area is large and stylishly designed; bungalows lack the common areas' aesthetic appeal but are large and furnished with Thai-style wooden furniture.

⬛ GajaPuri (Hat Kaibae, tel. 03/955-7300, www.gajapuri.com, 4,200B) is an elegant, chic resort catering to those who want to enjoy Ko Chang without having to rough it. Wooden bungalows are open, airy, and have subtle Thai design elements without being over-the-top. There's a pretty pool, and some villas even have their own pools. Different structures are interconnected by wooden walkways, which give the property a romantic, adventuresome feeling. The resort has a restaurant, bar, and spa, but guests looking for some diversity can walk just a few minutes to the main Kaibae beach area.

Food

Visitors on the prowl for high-end restaurants might well be disappointed at the range of eating options in Ko Chang. But what's lacking in sophistication is made up for in personality and quirkiness.

India Hut Restaurant (Hat Sai Khao, opposite Grand View Resort, tel. 08/1441-3234, 10 A.M.–11 P.M. daily, 300B)—not to be confused with the similarly-named Bangkok establishment—serves a variety of dishes from the subcontinent in an upbeat, fun atmosphere. A scene such as a staff member holding court and entertaining guests with card tricks as the restaurant's resident dog, an aging golden retriever named Julian, dozes just outside the kitchen is not uncommon. The owners are ethnically Punjabi, and dishes from that region of India are your best bet.

If you're in the mood for Italian, try **Invito** (Hat Sai Khao, tel. 03/955-1326, www.whitesandsthailand.com/invito, 10 A.M.–11 P.M. daily, 350B), an upscale eatery that specializes in wood-fired pizzas. They also have Italian classics like homemade pasta, seafood and meat dishes, and wine. Delivery (noon–10 P.M.) and catering are also available.

Jinda's Resort and Restaurant (north end of Hat Sai Khao, tel. 03/955-1548, 6 A.M.–10 P.M. daily, 100B) makes for an enjoyable vantage point from which to take in the Ko Chang scene. The restaurant, which draws foreigners and locals alike, serves traditional Thai food and a host of international dishes, like Western breakfasts, sandwiches, and pasta. The *kaphrao mu* (stir-fried pork with basil) is particularly good. Also on offer are fruit shakes, beer, coffee, and a few unconventionally named cocktails, such as the Lang Island and Sex in the Hot Spring. Best to avoid, however, are the "plank steak" and a rather profane misinterpretation of chicken cordon bleu.

Although it's only open in the October–April high-season months, **⬛ Thor's Palace** (Hat Sai Khao, tel. 08/192-72502, 9 A.M.–11 P.M. daily) has earned rave reviews thanks to its tasty Thai food, lavish decor, views of the sea, and upbeat music. High tea and various coffees are also available.

Getting There and Around

If you're coming from Bangkok, you can fly into the Trat airport on one of Bangkok Airways' daily flights, then book a bus to the ferry pier for 300B. There is regular **ferry service** between the small town of Laem Ngop and Ko Chang and points farther afield. Laem Ngop is 20 kilometers south of the city of Trat, and its piers serve the outlying islands. Various boats depart from Laem Ngop's piers at varying times, but the most reliable is the hourly vehicle ferry from Laem Ngop's newest pier, Tha Thammachat, which runs 6 A.M.–7 P.M. daily during October–April high season. The cost is 100B pp or 150B per car for the journey, which takes 20–30 minutes.

Ko Chang's ferry pier is located at Ao Sapparot, at the very north of the island. Buses booked through the info desk at the Trat airport take all passengers from the airport, via the ferry, directly to their hotels on Ko Chang. Once you've reached the island, *song thaew* can be hailed for cheap journeys around the island; rides cost 40–100B, depending on the length of the journey. Small motorcycles can also be rented for about 200B per day, but inexperienced riders should be cautious, as many of Ko Chang's roads are very steep and dotted with corkscrew turns.

KO MAK
เกาะหมาก

Many of Ko Chang's outlying islands—the most sizable of which are all located to Ko Chang's south—contain minimal development, and all are quieter and more secluded than Ko Chang. But they can be difficult to access during the May–September low season, with many of their lodging facilities closing down. Even during the October–April high season, the islands are more welcoming to package tourists.

Ko Mak (also spelled Ko Maak), 16 kilometers south of Ko Chang, is a 16-square-kilometer island that London's *Times* newspaper listed, in 2006, as one of the world's Top 10 Secret Beaches. The island contains many coconut and rubber plantations, and the year-round population is only about 500. If Ko Chang seems overly developed, Ko Mak might just fit the bill as the quintessential desert island. And while Ko Chang is mountainous, Ko Mak is low-lying and thus easily navigable on foot. Ko Mak is definitely up-and-coming, and some of the island's businesses have got together and created their own website (www.kohmak.com), which not only offers listings but also details very specific instructions on how to get to the island.

Surrounding Islands

Ko Kham (เกาะขาม) is a tiny island just to the north of Ko Mak. It's renowned for its good snorkeling. You can get there via boat or sea kayak from Ko Mak—the distance is so short that walking to it is even possible during low tide. There's just one aging resort on Ko Kham, so it is best enjoyed as a day trip.

Ko Rayang Nok (เกาะระยังนอก) is another small island near Ko Mak. It has just one resort, and the entire island can be rented, it's said, for 500 euros per day.

Accommodations

Right now Ko Mak has just a few dozen different lodgings to choose from, ranging from very basic bungalows to mid-range resorts and moderate villas. **Suchanari Bungalows** (Ao Suan Yai, tel. 03/953-2351, 400B) are a flashback to a time when most travelers to Thailand stayed in wooden bungalows on the beach and there were no full moon parties or discos next door. The bungalows are very plain, fan-cooled structures but are located on a nearly deserted stretch of beautiful beach in the northwest part of the island. At the high end is **Koh Mak Villas** (Ao Kao, tel. 08/1925-6591, www.kohmakvilla.com, 2,500B), which offers two large houses with rooms that can either be rented separately or as part of the whole house. The rooms are nicely decorated using lots of natural wood and elegant but simple details. The bedrooms are very comfortable, and the baths are modern. From the upstairs rooms you can see out to neighboring islands, and the grounds are well kept.

Getting There

Ko Mak can be reached by taking a boat from Laem Ngop pier, near Trat. The trip costs 300B and takes three hours. Boats run at 3 P.M. daily and stop at Ko Wai along the way. Boats make the return journey from Ko Mak at 8 A.M. Ko Mak can be reached from Ko Chang October–May via the Bang Bao pier, in the south of Ko

Chang. Boats depart at 8 A.M. and noon daily, and the trip costs 350B per segment. Boats return from Ko Mak at noon daily.

KO KUT
เกาะกูด

Ko Kut (sometimes spelled Ko Kood) is the biggest of Ko Chang's outlying islands. It's also the farthest away, located an hour's speedboat ride to the south. Ko Kut is very quiet, with little in the way of infrastructure. The water is a striking crystal blue color. Most resorts are on the west side of the island, and they tend to be more upmarket than many of Ko Chang's. Be sure to make travel arrangements ahead of time, as the island is a popular destination for package tourists, and hotels and restaurants can be inaccessible for those traveling independently.

Sports and Recreation
Ploy Scuba Diving (tel. 08/1451-1387, www.ployscuba.com) has two shops on Ko Kut. Snorkeling on Ko Kut is also good due to the clarity of the water.

Accommodations
Budget accommodations on Ko Kut can be hard to find, but a good option is **KohKood-Ngamkho Resort** (Ngamkho Bay on the southwest coast, tel. 08/1825-7076, www.kohkood-ngamkho.com, fan-cooled huts or bungalows 650B). The basic huts are situated among coconut trees and offer views of the water. There's running water and modern plumbing, but not much else. They also rent tents for those who want to sleep right on the beach.

Siam Beach Ko Kood (Ao Bang Bao, tel. 08/1945-5789, www.siambeachkohkood.net, 1,200B) has a private beach and is a good mid-range option. The guest rooms are clean and funky, with some bright decor.

Shantaa Ko Kood (Ao Tapao, midway up the west coast, tel. 08/1817-9648, www.

shantaakohkood.com, 3,500B) is a idyllic resort with Thai-style wooden bungalows surrounded by dense trees and rainforest foliage. The cliff-top setting provides dramatic views. Book ahead, as this place is popular.

By far the nicest spot on the island, and perhaps the whole region, is **Soneva Kiri by Six Senses** (tel. 03/961-9800, www.sixsenses.com/Soneva-Kiri/, from 30,000B). Guests stay in massive private villas decorated with elegant natural materials and every imaginable amenity and comfort, including private swimming pools. Rates include an individual butler and flights from Bangkok's international airport on the resort's Cessna.

Getting There
Ko Kut Seatrans (Laem Ngop, tel. 03/959-7646) runs boats between Laem Ngop, on the mainland, and Ko Kut. If you're flying in from Bangkok, you can catch an airport shuttle from the airport to Laem Ngop for around 300B. The 2.5-hour boat ride runs at 9 A.M. Tuesday and Saturday–Sunday and costs 500B. You can catch the boat back from Ko Kut to Laem Ngop at 12:30 P.M. Thursday–Saturday.

If you're coming from Ko Chang, **Island Hopper** (tel. 08/1865-0610, http://island-hopper-kochang.com) ferries leave daily from the Bang Bao pier, on the southern end of Ko Chang. The ride from Ko Chang to Ko Kut costs 600B each way. The ride takes 1–2 hours, depending on the weather. Rough seas mean a longer journey. Visitors are taken directly to the hotel or resort where they're staying on Ko Kut. There's no central pier on Ko Kut from which to taxi or walk to hotels: Much of the island is only reachable by boat, so reservations with resorts must be made ahead of arriving.

Remember that all schedules are subject to change—particularly in the May–September low season, when fewer boat trips are made, so be sure to check all times when making your plans.

THE UPPER SOUTHERN GULF

While most international visitors overlook this part of Thailand in favor of the more popular destinations on the Andaman coast or the Samui Archipelago, the beaches of the upper southern gulf are some of the best in the country if you're looking for a relaxed place to throw down a towel, experience some real Thai culture, or see some beautiful landscapes. In fact, the area surrounding Hua Hin has been the first choice for the Thai royal family for more than 100 years. Perhaps it's the ease with which you can get there from Bangkok, or the calm seas of the Gulf of Thailand, or the strong Thai identity that remains despite the development. For myriad reasons, it's easy to see why kings and queens have chosen to vacation here over the years. And with the explosion of new boutique resorts in Pranburi, just south of Hua

Hin, the region is attracting not just families looking for an easy place to spend the weekend, but a younger, hipper crowd too. Although the region may not hold your attention for a full week's vacation, it's a great destination for travelers who've already exhausted the more popular beach areas or who are just looking for a less touristy experience.

In the southern part of the region, the land mass thins out considerably, and there's not much to see aside from the beaches that line the coast, the adjacent villages and cities, and the mountains to the west (which border Burma, also called Myanmar). If you travel south into Chumphon, you'll find a completely different experience awaits you. Some of the beaches are as nice or nicer than those you'll find farther north, and there are beautiful views of nearby

HIGHLIGHTS

◖ **Phra Nakhon Khiri:** Petchaburi's celestial city on a mountain offers a striking *wat*, a royal palace, a national museum, and an excellent view, all in one place. Plus you can see it in a day (page 153).

◖ **Hua Hin Beach:** This scenic, relaxed beach is just a couple of hours by car from Bangkok. If you get bored of the water, head for one of the area's many seafood restaurants to enjoy some local fish, Thai-style (page 161).

◖ **Pranburi:** This upscale, pretty beach town a short drive from Hua Hin is the perfect place for a relaxing getaway (page 169).

◖ **Khao Sam Roi Yot National Park:** Hundreds of dramatic limestone peaks, freshwater marshes, and rugged coastline make up this magnificent national park. Inside you'll find more than 300 bird species, crab-eating macaques, and other wildlife that will amaze and amuse (page 172).

◖ **Arunothai Beach:** So far undiscovered by the crowds of vacationers farther north, this wide beach next to a fishing village has a beautiful view of the islands off the coast (page 177).

◖ **Mu Ko Chumphon National Park:** Just off the coast of Chumphon are more than 40 small islands that make up this marine national park. Spend a day or two island-hopping, snorkeling, and exploring (page 177).

LOOK FOR ◖ TO FIND RECOMMENDED SIGHTS, ACTIVITIES, DINING, AND LODGING.

THE UPPER SOUTHERN GULF

islands from the mainland, but there's none of the generic, concrete development that's present all over the Hua Hin area.

And this region is not all coastline and mountains. In the northern reaches, you'll find Petchaburi, an ancient city filled with temples but refreshingly untouristed by foreigners despite its proximity to Bangkok.

PLANNING YOUR TIME

While the upper southern gulf may not have beaches as spectacular as those along the Andaman coast, it has some of the best weather in the kingdom. The northern part of the area has some of the lowest rainfall levels in the country, and even if you're visiting during rainy season (July–Oct.), you won't often experience the deluges that can occur to the north and south. Once you get to Chumphon, however, the opposite seems to hold true—the province can be hit with flash floods and is best avoided during rainy season. During the hot season (Mar.–June), temperatures can reach into the mid-30s Celsius, although the nights are generally a little cooler. This time of year also tends to be windier, so if you're

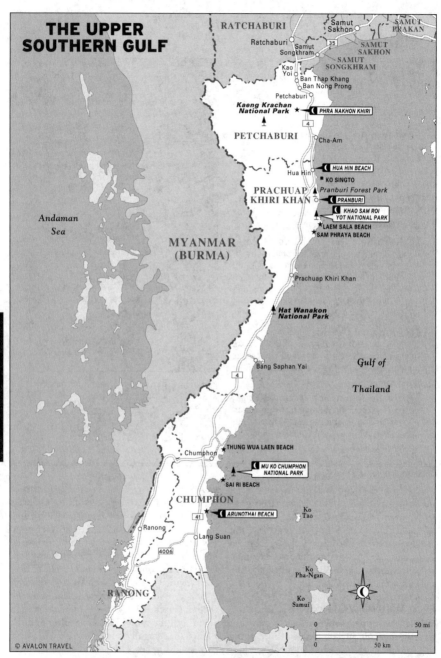

THE UPPER SOUTHERN GULF

RATCHABURI

Samut Sakhon

SAMUT PRAKAN

Ratchaburi

Samut Songkhram

35

SAMUT SAKHON

SAMUT SONGKHRAM

Kao Yoi

Ban Thap Khang

Ban Nong Prong

Petchaburi

Kaeng Krachan National Park ★ ◖ PHRA NAKHON KHIRI

4

PETCHABURI

Cha-Am

◖ HUA HIN BEACH

Hua Hin ▪ KO SINGTO

PRACHUAP KHIRI KHAN

▲ *Pranburi Forest Park*

◖ PRANBURI

▲ KHAO SAM ROI YOT NATIONAL PARK

★ LAEM SALA BEACH

SAM PHRAYA BEACH

Andaman Sea

MYANMAR (BURMA)

Prachuap Khiri Khan

▲ *Hat Wanakon National Park*

Gulf of

Thailand

4

Bang Saphan Yai

★ THUNG WUA LAEN BEACH

Chumphon

▲ ◖ MU KO CHUMPHON NATIONAL PARK

★ SAI RI BEACH

CHUMPHON

Ko Tao

41

◖ ARUNOTHAI BEACH

Ranong

Lang Suan

4006

Ko Pha-Ngan

RANONG

Ko Samui

0   50 mi

0   50 km

© AVALON TRAVEL

planning to do any kite surfing or windsurfing, this is probably the best time of year to come. Like the rest of Thailand, November–February are the mildest months, with temperatures in the 20s Celsius on most days. This is also the most popular part of the year to visit, and accommodations are priced accordingly. Accommodation prices are listed here for the high season, but if you are visiting during the hot or rainy season, the cost may be as low as half off. If you are planning on doing any serious diving in the area, it's better to come during rainy season, as April–October affords the best visibility.

Although just a few hours' drive from Bangkok, this region is best enjoyed not as a day trip but over at least a few days so you can enjoy some of the beaches and national parks. The upper southern gulf extends for more than 160 kilometers north to south, but don't expect that it will provide enough diversions to keep you there for weeks. Realistically, you can tour Petchaburi in a day if you prioritize the sights. The beaches and mountains can take as little or as much time as you want, although you won't find the same breadth of water sports and diversions as you would on the Andaman coast or the Samui Archipelago.

Petchaburi Province   จังหวัดเพชรบุรี

THE UPPER SOUTHERN GULF

Petchaburi Province became known as a local destination after King Rama VI built his summer palace here. The current king still spends much of his time in Cha-Am.

PETCHABURI CITY
เพชรบุรี

The city of Petchaburi is one of the country's lesser-known historically important ancient cities. Although it was never a seat of power, it has been inhabited since at least the Dvaravati period and was considered a major city during both the Ayutthaya and Sukhothai periods. The surrounding region borders Burma to the west, so during the frequent periods of strife, it served as a stronghold against invaders and afterward became a favorite among Chakri Dynasty kings.

Petchaburi means "diamond city," after the stones once found in the area. Although there are no more diamonds to be found, a quick stroll through the small city to view the striking *wats* and royal palace makes clear that this was once a rich and endowed place.

Few Western travelers spend a lot of time here, but it's full of interesting historic and cultural sights that are easily accessible for foreign visitors. It's perhaps not exciting or large enough to spend even a few days here, but if

you're heading to Hua Hin from Bangkok, it's a great one-day layover on your way.

◖ Phra Nakhon Khiri
พระนครคีรี

The city's most famous landmark, referred to locally as Khao Wang, or Palace Hill, is home to Phra Nakhon Khiri Historical Park. Phra Nakhon Khiri means "celestial city on a mountain," and although most visitors won't find it quite as dramatic as the name suggests, it is still an interesting and scenic place to visit. Within the park's borders are not only a summer residence built by King Rama IV but also numerous temples and other buildings that together make up a large royal compound.

Architecturally, the site is interesting because of the sometimes-unexpected combinations of Thai and Western design. If you're looking for some Thai history, the king's former residence and observatory have been turned into the **Phra Nakhon Khiri National Museum** (Phra Nakhon Khiri, tel. 03/240-1006, 9 A.M.–4 P.M. daily, 40B), which houses objects from the former palace, including household furnishings, sculpture, and ceramics. In addition to the museum and other royal buildings, there are also several *wats* on the compound, including **Wat Maha Samanaram,** which was

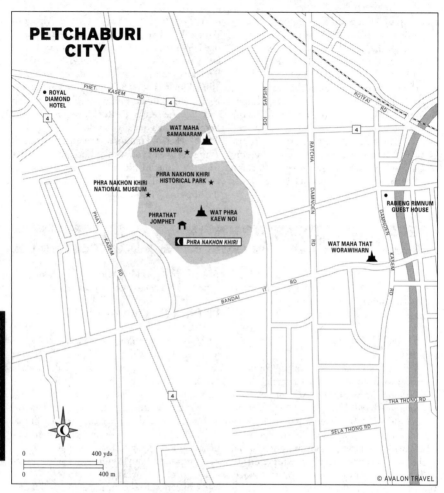

originally built during the Ayutthaya period and is decorated with interesting mural work; **Wat Phra Kaew Noi,** built in a style similar to the style of Bangkok's Grand Palace and Wat Phra Kaew; and **Phrathat Jomphet,** a large white *chedi.*

Although some visitors walk up the hundreds of stairs to visit the compound and museum, there is also a cable car that runs 8:15 A.M.– 5:30 P.M. daily and costs 50B.

Other Sights

In the city center, alongside the Petchaburi River, is the impressive **Wat Mahathat Worawiharn** (corner of Damnoen Kasem Rd. and Phrasong Rd., west side of the Petchaburi River), a temple consisting of five white *prang* built in the late Ayutthaya–early Rattanakosin styles. The largest *prang* is over 46 meters tall, making the *wat* not only an important religious and cultural site but an unmistakable landmark in the city. Like many *wats* in Thailand, the sacred site has been built and rebuilt over time, and although historians are not certain as to the date of the original structure, there is evidence that it was built around the 11th century.

Inside the *wat* are relics said to be from the Buddha, gifted by the current king in the 1950s. The *wat* is a beautiful site to take in from a distance, but the detailed stuccowork on the *prang* is more impressive up close. While you're here, take a look at the nearby hall with murals depicting life in Thailand and a small museum housing devotional works of art.

Just a short drive outside of town is the **Khao Luang cave,** set inside a small mountain right behind a train station called Khao Yoi. It's about 25 kilometers north of Petchaburi off Highway 4. The area is a popular picnic spot for local families and was a favorite of King Rama V, who commissioned the casting of a large image of the Buddha for the cave. There are also scores of other Buddhas inside. An opening atop the large cave allows sunlight to spill in onto the images, creating a dramatic scene. The cave is a very popular attraction and is easy to get to by taxi, *samlor,* or motorcycle taxi. The ride should cost 30–60B pp.

Accommodations

Within the city of Petchaburi, the accommodations options are limited. There are few guesthouses catering to international travelers and even fewer mid- to high-end sleeping options. It's unfortunate, as a tour of the city could easily be done over a couple of relaxed days if there were good places to stay. If you need to spend the night, the **Rabieng Rimnum Guest House** (1 Chisa Rd., tel. 03/242-5707, www.rabiengrimnum.com, 120B) offers very cheap, basic guest rooms with shared baths right in the center of town overlooking the river. Looked at in the right light, the old wooden house is a romantic throwback to an era when Southeast Asia was exotic and untouristed by Westerners, although cynics might find it just another shabby old guesthouse. Guest rooms offer little more than a bed to sleep in, but the Thai restaurant downstairs is excellent and very traveler-friendly. Rabieng Rimnum also offers tours and hiking trips in the area and is generally a great resource. For those looking for something a little nicer, a good bet is the **Royal Diamond Hotel** (555 Mu 1, Phet Kasem Rd., Tambon Rai Som, tel. 03/241-1061 to 03/241-1070, www.royaldiamondhotel.com, 800B). Although the hotel is not in the middle of town, it is within walking distance of Khao Wang in the northwest part of the city. The large, mid-range property has clean, comfortable guest rooms and modern baths as well as restaurants on the premises. Aside from the location (it's about three kilometers from the center), the only drawback here is that the Royal Diamond is quite a generic place.

Getting There and Around

If you're driving from Bangkok, head toward Samut Songkhram Province on Highway 35, then switch to Highway 4, which will take you through the city. The distance is about 113 kilometers, and when there's no traffic and you can get out of Bangkok quickly, the ride will take well under two hours.

There are frequent buses (at least every hour during the day) from Bangkok's Southern Bus Terminal, and the trip will take around 2.5 hours. Tickets cost a maximum of 125B for a seat on an air-conditioned express bus. Buses will drop you off at the bus station on the northern edge of town, just across the street from the Night Market on Ratwiti Road. There are *samlor* and motorcycle taxis at the bus station, but the city is small enough that you can walk to most sights from here without a problem.

There are also nine daily trains on the southern line that will stop at Petchaburi. Trains leave Bangkok 8 A.M.–10:50 P.M. daily. The ride takes three hours, and a normal second-class air-conditioned seat will cost under 200B.

Petchaburi is one of the few cities left in Thailand where *samlor* (three-wheeled rickshaws) are still common, and a ride in town should cost 40B or less. There are also motorcycle taxis with similar pricing, although they are not as common here.

CHA-AM
ชะอำ

About 32 kilometers south of Petchaburi is Cha-Am, a scenic, relaxed beach town with wide, flat stretches of sand and plenty of resorts catering to local vacationers and foreign travelers. Although Cha-Am is not as well known to international travelers as Hua Hin, it is a popular resort town and has plenty of the necessities—good accommodations, restaurants, and beach chairs and umbrellas.

Cha-Am is a favorite among groups of college students and, somewhat incongruously, European retirees, so it can feel a little sleepy. In fact, it's one of the few big beach towns in Thailand where you won't have to contend with lots of go-go bars or discos. Otherwise, Cha-Am is normally weekend beach, with average-joe appeal and popularity.

Accommodations

Nana House (208/3 Ruamchit Rd., tel. 08/9883-5279, www.nanahouse.net, 800B) is a standout in the cheap, clean, and comfortable category. The small guesthouse, a short walk from the beach, is very well maintained, and the guest rooms are spacious if not chic. There's also a coffee shop on the first floor.

The **Baan Pantai Hotel & Resort** (Ruamchit Rd. at Soi Cha Am North 2, tel. 03/243-3111, 2,000B) is right on the main beach road and has pretty Thai-style guest rooms and grounds and a very nice swimming pool. The property is small but has everything necessary for a nice beach weekend, including an on-site restaurant and bar as well as a spa.

The **Cha-Am Methavalai Hotel** (220 Ruamchit Rd., tel. 03/243-3250, www.methavalai.com, 3,000B) exemplifies what Cha-Am is all about. The hotel is a little too big and confusing, and it feels anachronistic and modern at the same time. It is also on some of the best real estate in the area, and every one of the many guest rooms has a beautiful view of the

ocean. The rooms are clean and tastefully decorated, and the grounds are well manicured, with two large swimming pools. This is a very family-friendly resort.

Designed by renowned Thai architect Duangrit Bunnag, the **Alila Cha-Am** (115 Mu 7, Bangkao, tel. 03/270-9555, www.alila-live.com, 7,800B) opened in February 2008 to great acclaim. The white stone steps leading to the reception and common areas make quite a first impression. The property is starkly modern, but guest rooms are spacious and airy and come with all the accoutrements one would expect from a luxury resort. A spa and a rooftop restaurant are also on-site.

Information and Services

Cha-Am has a **Tourism of Thailand** office (500/51 Petchkasem Rd., tel. 03/247-1005, 8:30 A.M.–4:30 P.M. daily) about 10 minutes on foot outside of town. The office is the regional headquarters, covering both Prachuap Khiri Khan and Petchaburi Provinces, and if you decide to trek out here, you'll get plenty of helpful information on all of the destinations in these provinces. There are plenty of Internet cafés along Cha-Am's main beach road, Ruam Chit Road.

Getting There

Cha-Am is an easy three-hour bus ride from Bangkok, and buses run every half hour 5 A.M.–midnight daily from the Southern Bus Terminal. Seats on air-conditioned buses cost less than 120B; if you are taking one, make sure to ask whether or not it is an express bus. If it's not, it will make many local stops, adding a significant amount of time to your journey. Buses heading for Cha-Am Beach stop right on Ruam Chit Road, the main beach road, but if you're taking a bus bound for Hua Hin and beyond, and Cha-Am Beach is not a designated stop, you'll be let off close to the train station. You can also take a train to Cha-Am. Not all trains on the southern line will stop at Cha-Am, but currently at least two, one departing Bangkok at 9:20 A.M. and the other departing at 3:35 P.M., stop here. The fare for a second-class air-conditioned seat is under 200B, and the ride will take 3–4 hours. Trains will drop you off on Narathip Road about 1.6 kilometers west of the beach. You can either walk to your hotel from there or grab a taxi or *song thaew* to the beach.

Cha-Am is less than 250 kilometers from Bangkok, right off the north–south Highway 4 on the way to Hua Hin. You can take Highway 4 directly, but it's often faster to take Route 35 past Samut Songkhram before getting onto Highway 4. The journey should take about 2.5 hours if there's not too much traffic.

LAO SONG VILLAGES
หมู่บ้านลาวโซ่ง

Although the true origins of the Lao Song people are unknown, they are believed to hail originally from northern Laos and Vietnam, possibly as prisoners of war during the reign of King Taksin more than 200 years ago. Their descendants eventually settled in Petchaburi, Ratchaburi, and Suphan Buri Provinces. Although many Lao Song people have integrated into mainstream Thai society, there are still Lao Song villages where their distinctive forms of language, dress, song, dance, and food are preserved. In Ban Nong Prong and Ban Thap Khang, there are Lao Song villages that can be visited as an easy excursion from any of the nearby beach areas.

Getting There

The villages in Ban Nong Prong and Ban Thap Khang are close to Kao Yoi Station, between Ratchaburi and Petchaburi, and you can easily charter a taxi to take you; the ride is about 20 minutes from Petchaburi and will cost around 100B. From Cha-Am the trip is about an hour by taxi, and the round-trip costs about 1,000B. Before going, make sure to contact the **Yiem Ruan Yuan Yao Project at Kao Yoi** (tel. 03/249-9393) to enquire about specific activities and to arrange a tour.

KAENG KRACHAN NATIONAL PARK
อุทยานแห่งชาติแก่งกระจาน

This national park is one of the country's largest and covers nearly 3,000 square kilometers of land in Petchaburi and Prachuap Khiri Khan Provinces. In the park you'll find lakes, waterfalls, evergreen forests and rainforests, rivers, mountains, and caves. Flora and fauna include a wide variety of plants and trees as well as butterflies, rare birds, barking deer, gibbons, wild pigs, and even wild elephants. The park is also home to the Kaeng Krachan Dam. If you plan on doing a multiday hike or going off the main trails, you'll need to get permission from the park's main headquarters, and depending on your plans, you may need to hire a guide. In fact, if you're planning on spending more than a day at the park, it's wise to hire a guide, as the park is vast and has much to offer visitors. Although the park is open year-round, some of the trails and caves close during the August–October rainy season due to flooding.

Sights and Recreation

The **Kaeng Krachan Dam** was constructed in 1966 to manage water flow from the Petchaburi River. The large earthen dam created the **Kaeng Krachan Reservoir,** which can hold up to 710 million cubic meters of water. The dam serves its irrigation purpose but also offers a stunning view of the reservoir and surrounding area. The dozens of small mountains and hills in the area are now mostly submerged, but the peaks of some have become islands scattered through the reservoir. The park's headquarters are near the banks of this reservoir, and you can rent a boat from the parks department to explore them. There are also bungalows available for rent nearby.

The park has a number of mountains worth hiking, including **Panoen Thung Mountain,** at more than 1,200 meters above sea level. The top of Panoen Thung, instead of a sharp peak, is a flat grassland area where you can camp for the night or just relax and enjoy the cooler temperatures and the view. If you're planning this hike, be prepared for 5–6 hours (depending on your fitness level) of moderate to difficult hiking.

As a watershed for two large rivers, the park is also home to many waterfalls, most of which require some hiking to view. The most popular is the **Pala-U Waterfall,** a 16-level cascade in the southern part of the park. The waterfall gets a little messy (some of the levels seem more like rapids than neat cascades of water), but it's quite large and scenic, and there are ample opportunities for bird-watching, hiking, and exploring nearby. The **Thornthip Waterfall** has nine levels flowing through the lush forest and a nearby campground. The **Tharnthip and Hinlad Waterfalls** are cascading falls in the deep forest and are stunningly set amid lush trees. In order to see Tharnthip and Hinlad Waterfalls, however, you'll have to arrange a multiday hike, as they are too far from the main trails to be reached in a day.

If you're looking for a waterfall you can see in one day, the **Pranburi Waterfall** is a good choice. It is less picturesque than some of the others but still offers a chance to get out into the forest on a moderate hike. Some parts of the park are off-limits during rainy season (Aug.–Oct.), so make sure to call first before arriving.

Accommodations and Food

Campgrounds are scattered throughout the park. The cost for a site is 50B, and you can rent a tent and sleeping bags if necessary, although they can run out if you get there too late. All campgrounds have adjacent baths with cold-water showers as well as basic food. There are also a number of **bungalows** available for 1,200–3,000B that sleep 4–10 people. The best bungalows in the park are near the reservoir; many of these have beautiful views and also hot water, heating, and even refrigerators. You must book and pay for bungalows in advance with the park service (tel. 02/562-0760, www.dnp.go.th) to ensure you'll get one when you arrive. The park service requires that foreign

visitors pay via wire transfer; details can be found on their website.

The national park has **canteens and small shops** scattered near headquarters and satellite offices throughout the park. This is a national park, and it's very large, so remember to bring provisions with you if you're venturing away from the main areas. You'll be able to stock up on snacks and water at headquarters and park offices, but if there's something particular you want for your journey (peanut butter, trail mix, or energy bars), you'll need to bring it with you, as the park's canteens cater to more local tastes.

There are two casual **cafeteria-style restaurants** in the park, one at the headquarters near the reservoir and the other on Panoen Thung Mountain. As is the case in all of the country's parks, the food is simple, inexpensive, and good. You'll find a limited selection of standard Thai fare at every meal for less than 50B per plate.

Getting There

The park is approximately 32 kilometers directly east of Cha-Am, about 36 kilometers northeast of Hua Hin, and around 113 kilometers from Bangkok, making it an easy journey should you decide to take a car. If you are driving from Bangkok, take Highway 4 heading south until you see signs for Petchaburi. Follow the Petchaburi road to Route 3499, which will take you straight to the park headquarters. If you are coming from Hua Hin, the entrance to the park is about 36 kilometers from the beach, and the best way to reach it is to take Route 3219 from Hua Hin heading east, then Route 3419 heading north. The drive from Hua Hin is one hour or less; from Bangkok, it's three hours.

Hua Hin   หัวหิน

This beach town is a favorite among locals, and over the past decade has increasingly become a destination for international tourists from Europe as well. If you're arriving by train, you'll be pleasantly surprised by the train station: Built in the 1920s under King Rama VI, the small, elaborately decorated buildings are a cross between Victorian gingerbread houses and Thai *sala*.

The town of Hua Hin is a laid-back beach town with plenty of places to eat, drink, and relax, but it is not visually remarkable aside from the coast itself. There's a lot of concrete development as well as the typical guesthouses, coffee shops, motorcycle rental stores, and the like. Most of your time will be best spent on or very near the beach.

The beach, Klai Kangwon Palace (if you can get in), and a couple of scenic mountains are Hua Hin's main attractions, but the town also serves as a good base for visiting some of Thailand's most beautiful national parks, such as Kaeng Krachan National Park and Sam Roi Yot National Park. These parks, at less than an hour's drive away, are easily accessible and can make a great day trip if you're looking for something to do to break up time on the beach.

SIGHTS
Khao Krailat and Khao Takiab
เขาไกรลาส และ เขาตะเกียบ

These are two small mountains just adjacent to Hua Hin Beach, about four kilometers from the center of the beach. On Khao Takiab you'll find a small Buddhist monastery, an 18-meter golden Buddha, and a collection of hungry monkeys happy to take whatever they can get from you. The view from the top (305 meters) is beautiful—you can see not only the beach below and Ko Singto, but the ethereal peaks of Khao Sam Roi Yot off in the distance. The best way to

THE UPPER SOUTHERN GULF

© SUZANNE NAM

greedy monkey on Khao Takiab

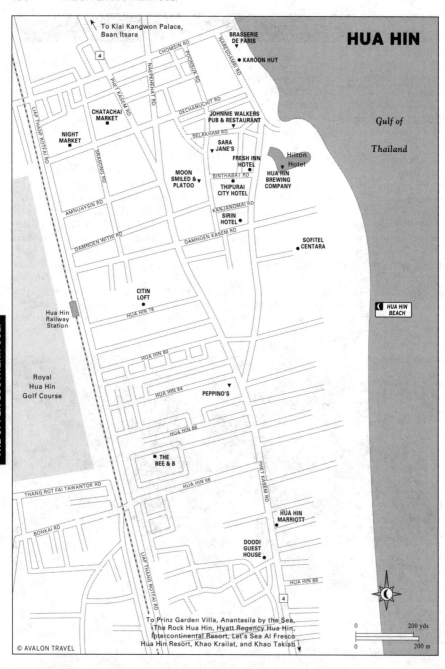

HUA HIN

To Klai Kangwon Palace,
Baan Itsara

CHOMSIN RD
POONSUK RD
NAEBKEHAT RD
NARESDAMRI RD

BRASSERIE
DE PARIS

KAROON HUT

4

PHET KASEM RD

DECHANUCHIT RD

JOHNNIE WALKERS
PUB & RESTAURANT

CHATACHAI
MARKET

NIGHT
MARKET

SELAKHAM RD

SARA
JANE'S

FRESH INN
HOTEL

Gulf of

Thailand

Hilton
Hotel

SPASONG RD

LIAP THANG ROTFAI RD

AMNUAYSIN RD

MOON
SMILED &
PLATOO

BINTHABAT RD

THIPURAI
CITY HOTEL

HUA HIN
BREWING
COMPANY

KANJANOMAI RD

SIRIN
HOTEL

DAMNOEN WITHI RD

DAMNOEN KASEM RD

SOFITEL
CENTARA

Hua Hin
Railway
Station

CITIN
LOFT

HUA HIN 78

HUA HIN
BEACH

HUA HIN 80

Royal
Hua Hin
Golf Course

HUA HIN 84

PEPPINO'S

HUA HIN 86

THE
BEE & B

HUA HIN 88

THANG ROT FAI TAWANTOK RD

PHET KASEM RD

HUA HIN
MARRIOTT

BONKAI RD

DOODI
GUEST
HOUSE

LIAP THANG ROTFAI RD

HUA HIN 69

4

To Prinz Garden Villa, Anantasila by the Sea,
The Rock Hua Hin, Hyatt Regency Hua Hin,
Intercontinental Resort, Let's Sea Al Fresco
Hua Hin Resort, Khao Krailat, and Khao Takiab

0   200 yds

0   200 m

© AVALON TRAVEL

visit is simply to walk from the beach then climb the mountain, as the road is paved and some parts even have steps. The whole trip there and back should only take a few hours. Otherwise, you can take a local bus heading south from Hua Hin town and ask the driver to let you off at Khao Takiab. (You'll walk a few minutes from the main road once you get off the bus.) The most fun way to go is to hire one of the many horses on the shore to take you up. Even if you don't ride, the guide will walk along with you. Prices are entirely negotiable, but expect to pay around 500B per hour, and the ride to Khao Takiab and back will be a couple of hours. There are a handful of small, casual restaurants at the base of the mountain.

Klai Kangwon Palace
วังไกลกังวล
Klai Kangwon means "far from worries," and it's easy to understand why King Rama VII gave such a name to this palace (Petchkasem Beach Rd., tel. 03/251-1155, 9 A.M.–4 P.M. daily when unoccupied, 20B). Originally built as a summer home just north of Hua Hin, the palace is far less palatial and immense than the royal family's official residence in Bangkok. It looks more like a large, comfortable seaside mansion, devoid of any pomp and circumstance. The palace is technically open for visitors when the royal family is not there, but King Bhumibol spends much of his time in Hua Hin, making it unlikely that you'll be able to catch a glimpse of the family's living quarters. Call ahead, though, and you might get lucky.

BEACHES AND ISLANDS
◖ Hua Hin Beach
หาดหัวหิน
Hua Hin Beach is a wide, open swath of sand backed by high-end resorts and the town of Hua Hin itself. Although you won't find palm trees in abundance and there are a few tall buildings, there isn't the same rampant development here as you'll see in places like Phuket or Pattaya. Most of the year, the water is relatively calm

and flat, making it difficult to do many water sports but great if you're with small kids.

Water quality in and around Hua Hin is generally good, although there is not enough visibility or coral to do anything more than very casual snorkeling. The beach can sometimes be plagued by stinging jellyfish, especially during the August–October rainy season, in numbers plentiful enough to ruin an otherwise lovely day at the beach.

Despite the thousands of foreign travelers who visit every year, the beach remains relatively relaxed and laid-back. There are beachside bar-restaurants offering inexpensive Thai food, drinks, and lawn chairs and towels for rent (expect to pay about 200B for the day). Horses and their keepers trot up and down the beach, offering rides and lessons. Families with small children are some of the most frequent visitors. Although there are some bars where you might not want to take your mother, for the most part there's nothing going on in Hua Hin that isn't appropriate for all ages.

Ko Singto
เกาะสิงโต
Less than 500 meters off the coast is the small Ko Singto, a nice diversion if you want to get off Hua Hin Beach but don't want to venture too far. The rocky outcropping resembles a crouching tiger, hence the name *singto*. There's no real beach here and no accommodations, but you can arrange a group tour from any travel agency in town and head out to the island for a day of fishing, rock climbing, or swimming. The day trips usually last about five hours and cost under 1,000B pp, including lunch.

NIGHTLIFE
For the most part, Hua Hin lacks the debauched nightlife that other beach areas seem to attract. What you will find are hotel and resort bars, a handful of outdoor bars where people congregate for cocktails, and a few hidden hole-in-the-wall joints. So far, there are no real discos in this beach town and no big bar scene either, although there is a small sprinkling of bars with names such as **Lolita's, Octopussy,**

fishing boats near Hua Hin

© SUZANNE NAM

or **Romantic Bar** that seem to attract working women and their potential customers.

Along Naredamri Road are a handful of open-air bars serving cocktails and playing pop music. At the end of the street is the **Hua Hin Brewing Company** (Hilton Hotel, 33 Naredamri Rd., Hua Hin, tel. 03/251-2888, 6 P.M.–1 A.M. daily), which has the best selection of bottled and draught beer in the area and has live music every night. The atmosphere is a little on the generic side despite the Thai fishing decorations, but it's a nice relaxed place to enjoy a beer.

The indoor outdoor **Johnnie Walkers Pub & Restaurant** (Soi Selakam, Hua Hin, 9 A.M.–1 A.M. daily) has just about everything you could want in a bar—live music, a casual atmosphere, a pool, inexpensive drinks, and a mix of local and expat customers.

SHOPPING

Although you won't find any one-of-a-kind objects at the **Hua Hin Market** (Dechanuchit Rd., which runs perpendicular to the ocean

in the northern part of town), it's a vibrant, fun place to wander around or do some souvenir shopping. Every night crowds of shoppers and eaters gather at the market to check out the wares (mostly inexpensive Thai household items, kitschy T-shirts, and knockoff designer goods) and sample the food at the many street food stalls.

SPORTS AND RECREATION
Golf

The Hua Hin area has a number of established golf courses catering to local and international visitors. Greens fees are reasonable, especially compared to Phuket, and the courses are generally well maintained. At nearly all of the courses, rental clubs are available, and you'll be required to hire a caddie for the day. Many tour companies offer golf packages, but you may be able to save money by just calling yourself to schedule a time.

Opened in 1924, **The Royal Hua Hin Golf Club** (Damnernkasem Rd., Hua Hin, tel. 03/251-2475, 5 A.M.–6 P.M. daily, 1,500B) is the country's first golf course. The course is right by the railroad station and offers some nice views of the Gulf of Thailand. Some of the wide fairways are lined with topiaries shaped like animals and creatures from Thai mythology.

Surrounded on three sides by hilly forest, the **Hua Hin Seoul Country Club** (200 Mu 1, Praknampran, Pranburi, tel. 03/257-2500, 5 A.M.–6 P.M. daily, 1,500B) has a compact, challenging 18-hole course. The club is located in Pranburi, about 20 minutes by car from the center of Hua Hin, and when you call to reserve a time, the club can also arrange transportation for you.

Horseback Riding

At the center of Hua Hin Beach you'll find horses and their keepers, who will let you go out on your own if you are an experienced rider or escort you up and down the beach (or even as far as Khao Takiab). Prices are negotiable, but they generally run about 500B per hour and a little less if you are renting a horse for more time.

Kite Boarding

Hua Hin and the coast near Sam Roi Yot National Park are among the few areas in Thailand with good conditions for kite boarding (sometimes called kite surfing). More and more schools seem to be opening up, but as the sport can be a little dangerous and very challenging for beginners, it's best to stick with a teacher who's been at it for a while. **Kiteboarding Asia** (tel. 08/1591-4593, www. kiteboardingasia.com) offers lessons in Hua Hin November–June for about 4,000B per day. They also rent equipment to experienced boarders.

In March every year, Hua Hin holds a **Kiteboard World Cup** (www.pkraasia.com) that's open to qualifying competitors from around the world.

Elephants

If you're interested in seeing how elephants navigate through the forest or want to hitch a ride on one yourself, the **Elephant Village** (38/47 Khaonoi Village, behind Wat Etisukatow, Hua Hin, tel. 03/251-6181, www.thaielephant-village.com, 9 A.M.–5 P.M. daily) has daily shows and offers guided rides on the friendly beasts. Mahouts will take you around a little circuit, which goes through some forest and even a small lake while you sit on your elephant's head. It's not quite a wild ride, as the animals are well trained and the mahouts keep a careful eye on them. Still, for all but the most jaded traveler, it's a fun, once-in-a-lifetime experience.

ACCOMMODATIONS

Hua Hin has a variety of accommodations options, from cheap, basic rooms for travelers to expansive luxury suites plus a good number of mid-range hotels. The nicest rooms in Hua Hin are going to be found right on the water and mostly in larger international chain resorts. If you are looking for something less expensive or with a little more character, there are plentiful guesthouses and small hotels in the town itself. Although you won't be directly on the water, the town is small enough that walking to the beach takes 10 minutes or less. Brand-name hotels and resorts tend to fill up quickly during high season (Oct.–Apr.), and it can be difficult to find a room in one if you're making your plans just a few weeks in advance. As with all of the beach areas in Thailand, prices can be significantly cheaper during low season, especially if you book through a website such as www.agoda.com, www. asiarooms.com, or www.sawadee.com.

Under 1,500B

Although most of the cheaper options are found away from the beach, there are a handful of hotels on and around the fishing pier just north of the main beach. The location can't be beat if you are looking for something on the water for cheap, but the rooms tend to be bleak: very small and bare-bones, with simple bedding and fans instead of air-conditioning. If you are looking for something really cheap or want to experience sleeping on a pier, they

HUA HIN HILLS VINEYARD

About 32 kilometers outside Hua Hin is something most would be surprised to find anywhere in Thailand – a winery. So-called "new latitude wines," named because the grapes from which they're made are grown in nontraditional regions, are booming, and Siam Winery was one of the first in Thailand to start producing and selling their own reds, whites, and rosés.

You can pick up a bottle of shiraz or Siam rouge at most high-end supermarkets in the country, but if you're in Hua Hin, you can also head right to the source. The Hua Hin Hills Vineyard (tel. 03/252-6351, www.huahinhillsvineyard.com) is the Siam Winery's showcase vineyard and education center, and it's open for tours Tuesday–Sunday. Aside from a pretty vineyard (which you can tour atop an elephant!), there is a bistro offering Thai and Western food, a wine bar, and a gift shop. Visitors are welcome to stop in for a meal or to arrange a tour of the vineyard, which includes wine tasting. The vineyard also offers daily pick up from central Hua Hin.

are worth a night (at most) of your time. If you're looking for something comfortable or spacious, you need to go elsewhere. One pier guesthouse is **Karoon Hut** (80 Naresdamri Rd., tel. 03/253-0242, 500B), typical of the choices you'll find here.

If you're looking for something inexpensive but well-kept and comfortable, the **Citin Loft Hua Hin** (20/22 Soi Hua Hin 78, Petchkasem Rd., tel. 03/253-3778, www.royalasiahuahin.com, 1,100B) is a good compromise. The mid-size hotel has clean, large guest rooms decorated in a contemporary Thai style with TVs, free Wi-Fi, and balconies. There's also a small swimming pool on the roof and a café. The best deals are in the court wing rooms; other rooms can run more than twice as much.

If staying right on the beach isn't a priority, **Narawan Hotel** (250/131 Soi Hua Hin 94, Petchkasem Rd., tel. 03/252-6390, www.narawan.com, 1,300B) is a good value. The property doesn't offer a lot of bells and whistles, but the basic guest rooms are clean and modern, and there is a small, pretty swimming pool. The property has only been open since 2009, so although it's not fancy or trendy, everything is in very good condition.

The clean, basic, inexpensive **Thipurai City Hotel** (8/5–7 Soi Kanjanomai Poonsuk Rd., tel. 03/253-3555, www.thipuraicityhotel.com, 1,400B) has all the necessities—clean guest rooms, modern baths, a decent buffet breakfast, a swimming pool, and an urban location walking distance from the beach. It's not the most stylish hotel in Thailand, but it's a good value property in the price range.

1,500-3,000B

Sirin Hotel (6/3 Damnernkasem Rd., tel. 03/251-1150, www.sirinhuahin.com, 1,500B) is a reliable, friendly property with comfortable standard hotel rooms, a central location just a few minutes from the beach, and a small swimming pool. This is another good-value property; although there's not much personality here, the price, cleanliness, and location make up for it.

◖ Fresh Inn Hotel (132 Naresdamri Rd., tel. 03/251-1389, 1,700B) is one of the best values among mid-range hotels in Hua Hin. It's located just across from the Hilton and only a few minutes from the beach. The property is less than 10 years old, and the guest rooms are all stylishly decorated, with an abundance of dark wood and colorful Thai silk, as well as modern baths. Common areas are also well designed and clean. Guest rooms can be a little small, but you won't find a nicer hotel for the money and location.

Staying at **The Bee & B** (226/32 Petchkasem Rd., tel. 08/7089-0606, www.beeandb.com, 1,800B) is more like staying in someone's home than in a large hotel or a typical guesthouse. There are only a handful of guest rooms, but each is fitted with a very comfortable bed and a funky, nicely designed en suite bath. Guest rooms and common areas are spotlessly clean, and there's even a jetted tub (no swimming pool) in the small garden. The property is just a couple of blocks from the beach and the center of town. In fact, there's not much you'll miss compared to staying in a guesthouse, except the anonymity.

Doodi Guest House (256/10–11 Petchkasem Rd., tel. 03/251-2501, www.doodiguesthouse. com, 2,000B) is a small, basic guesthouse with clean guest rooms that have TVs and balconies. Although the property won't win any awards in the style category (think wicker and bedspreads), it is a good place to stay if you are looking for something that's not quite in the middle of everything but easily accessible from the beach or town.

If you are looking for something that's comfortable, well maintained, and in a good location, the **Prinz Garden Villa** (8/30 Soi Hua Hin 98, tel. 03/251-1720, http://en.prinz-garden-villa.de, 2,100B) is a good option. It is located just south of the center of Hua Hin and a few minutes away from the beach. The guest rooms are basic but comfortable and have TVs, DVD players, and some even come with kitchens. There's also a pool and a small area for eating and hanging out. This property is particularly family-friendly, as there are apartments and larger suites available. There is also a small restaurant on the premises serving Thai and Western dishes.

3,000-4,500B

Although the size, layout, and design of the guest rooms at **Anantasila by the Sea** (Khao Takiab, tel. 03/251-1879, www.anantasila.com, 3,500B) vary within the property from large and homey to typically sized and modern, this is one of the few places directly on the beach where you'll be able to find guest rooms for under 4,000B per night. The grounds are well maintained and include a 25-meter swimming pool and dining area overlooking the ocean. There are also larger apartment-style guest rooms with kitchen facilities for families and larger groups. The Anantasila is located just outside Hua Hin, past Khao Takiab.

The **Anantara Resort & Spa** (43/1 Petchkasem Rd., tel. 03/252-0250, www.huahin.anantara.com, 4,500B) combines luxury, excellent service, a great location, and unmistakable Thai style. Guest rooms are spacious and have modern amenities, although they are full of traditional Thai detailing. The surrounding gardens are lush and private, and some guest rooms have direct beach views.

Over 4,500B

The Rock Hua Hin (4/44 Mu Ban Takiab Rd., tel. 03/253-7100, www.therockhuahin. com, 5,500B) is a luxury boutique hotel on the beach just south of the main area. Although the property itself is small, containing fewer than 40 guest rooms, the guest rooms stand out as some of the largest and best equipped in the area. Minimalist and modern with an Asian flavor, each guest room has an enormous bath with a soaking tub, and most have direct views of the ocean. There is a nice outdoor lounging area and infinity pool, but that is the extent of the communal amenities. It's a great weekend spot for couples.

Although it's sometimes hard to distinguish among the beachfront international resorts in the area, the **Hyatt Regency Hua Hin** (91 Hua Hin–Khao Takiab Rd., tel. 03/252-1234, http:// huahin.regency.hyatt.com, 5,800B) is a favorite among international travelers because of the airy, modern guest rooms, extra-large pool, and long stretch of beach in front of the hotel. This is a large property with more than 100 guest rooms and suites, so there will be plenty of activities, restaurants, and places to hang out without having to leave the compound. The spa, set on 1.6 hectares of land, is stunning.

The **Hua Hin Marriott** (107/1 Petchkasem Beach Rd., tel. 03/251-1881, www.marriott. com, 5,900B) is a comfortable resort right near the center of the beach, with large grounds fronting on the ocean. The property does not have a private beach, but there are deck chairs set up in front of the hotel for guests. As is typical among the international resorts in the country, the buildings housing the guest rooms are set up around a central common area that has a swimming pool, restaurants, and plenty of lush green spaces to create a secluded feeling. The most inexpensive guest rooms can feel a little small, but all have balconies and are well equipped, furnished with dark wood and Thai detailing. There are also tennis courts and a beautiful spa with open-air treatment rooms. This property is very popular with European tourists and families with small children. Although it may be a little worn around the edges, it is a good value if you are not paying rack rates.

Built in the 1920s, the ◖ **Sofitel Centara** (1 Damnernkasem Rd., tel. 03/251-2021, www. sofitel.com, 7,000B) is the hotel that started it all for Hua Hin. Originally the railroad hotel, and the only place to stay on the beach, the magnificent two-story colonial-style property has been thoroughly modernized, with all of the facilities you would expect in a five-star hotel. It still maintains such details as verandas that open out onto the lush gardens and wooden shutters and ceiling fans in the guest rooms. The massive grounds include multiple restaurants and swimming pools as well as a spa. The area has really developed around this hotel: It is right in the center of the beach and just on the edge of Hua Hin Town.

Stunningly modern but undoubtedly Thai, the **Intercontinental Resort** (33/33 Petchkasem Beach Rd., tel. 03/261-6999, www.ichotelsgroup.com, 6,000B) is Hua Hin's newest, nicest five-star resort. Guest rooms have everything one would expect from an international five-star hotel—plenty of space, flat-screen TVs, DVD players, and iPod docks. Some guest rooms have spacious balconies overlooking the grounds and gulf. Common areas have a minimalist feel to them but still offer lots of soft, comfortable places to relax.

The urban, modern design at ◖ **Let's Sea Al Fresco Hua Hin Resort** (83/188 Soi Talay 12, Khao Takiab, tel. 03/253-6888, www.

letussea.com, 9,000B) can't be ignored, but the main attraction is the narrow 100-meter swimming pool in the center of the property. The guest rooms are ultra-hip and fitted with modern, minimalist furnishings as well as large baths with extra-large bathtubs. There's a spa, a restaurant, and a bar on the premises, but all of the common spaces are tranquil and chilled out, as are the guests and the attentive staff. Located south of the center of the beach toward Khao Takiab, you'll have to walk a few kilometers or take a hotel shuttle if you are looking for activities, such as horseback riding or getting a massage on the beach. This is not a very family-friendly place, and the manager gently suggests that it may not be suitable for children under 12. It is a good choice for couples looking for a chic, quiet retreat.

Trust-fund babies, movie stars, and everyday folks willing to spend a substantial amount of money to relax and rejuvenate on the beach should head for the **Chiva-Som** (73/4 Petchkasem Rd., tel. 03/253-6536, www.chivasom.com, about 50,000B for 3 nights, additional nights 16,000B). There are 2.8 hectares of perfectly manicured grounds and large, sunny guest rooms with light, modern Thai furnishings. Perhaps the nicest property in the area, the Chiva-Som is also an amazing holistic spa. You'll start your stay with a wellness evaluation where health consultants will design a personalized program for you, which may include fitness, yoga, tai chi, meditation, and massage, depending on your goals and physical condition. Although it's a pricey place to stay, all meals and a daily massage are included, as are scheduled classes. You can also take spa cooking classes and have private lessons. The staff-to-guest ratio is nearly three-to-one, so expect a lot of personal attention.

FOOD

Because of the largely European clientele, Hua Hin probably has more Italian and German restaurants than casual Thai cuisine. But if you look past the multitude of Western restaurants (most of these have Thai menus also), especially on Naresdamri Road, you'll find some nice local restaurants catering mostly to Thai vacationers. As Hua Hin is a seaside town and there are active fishing villages all around, the big star on menus is fresh seafood. Most of the restaurants listed below serve excellent seafood, but they all also have chicken, pork, and beef dishes, should you be looking for something different.

All of the nicer hotels have upscale Thai restaurants, often with excellent locations right on the beach. They're not listed here as they're easy to find, but if you are looking to splash out a little on a special dinner, they are a great option, although aficionados of Thai cuisine may complain that the dishes are "dumbed down" for Western palates.

Markets

Chatachai Market (Petchkasem Rd., 5 A.M.–5 P.M. daily), like the local markets in all parts of Thailand, is where you are likely to find the freshest, cheapest, and most fun eating experience. You may have to eat your fried squid standing up or on a plastic chair amid crowds of shoppers, but it's worth it. Hua Hin Town can get a little confusing once you get off the beach, so the best way to get here is to take Dechanuchit Road east (away from the water) until you get to Petchkasem Road. Take a left, and keep walking until you see all the stalls. The walk from the market is about 1.6 kilometers and should take about 15 minutes.

In the evening, the **Night Market** on Dechanuchit Road, which runs perpendicular to the water from the northern part of town, not only has souvenirs, pirated DVDs, and other tourist stuff but many food stalls as well.

Thai

Sara Jane's (28/1 Poonsuk Rd., tel. 03/253-2990, 11 A.M.–10 P.M. daily, 400B) is the kind of restaurant every beach town should have. It's pretty, comfortable, foreigner-friendly, and offers a variety of Thai and Italian dishes (for travelers who want some comfort food). There

is a small, very casual open-air dining room and a garden in the back with plenty of seating. The restaurant is very popular, and though nothing here is going to knock your socks off, it's a smart choice if you're looking for something relatively easy that will satisfy everyone.

Baan Itsara (7 Naeb Kehardt Rd., tel. 03/253-0574, 11 A.M.–10 P.M. daily, 500B) has a well-deserved reputation among locals and returning vacationers as a favorite spot for dinner. The restaurant, sometimes called "Baan Issara" or "Baan Isara," is set in a charming old wooden house, and there's indoor and outdoor seating available. The menu is full of seafood choices, including favorites such as steamed whole sea bass and stir-fried mussels. Baan Itsara isn't as fancy as some of the hotel restaurants in the area, but you might still be uncomfortable if you show up in shorts and a T-shirt. If you want a table on a weekend night or during a local holiday, make sure to book in advance; the restaurant can fill up quickly.

For an authentic Hua Hin–style meal and an authentic dining experience, head to **Chao Talay Seafood** (15 Naresdamri Rd., tel. 03/251-3436, 10 A.M.–10 P.M. daily, 500B). Set right out on the water, the casual restaurant has an extensive menu, and you can pick your fish or crustacean from the tanks out front. The restaurant feels a little run-down on the edges, but don't be bothered—just take in the view of the water or the food on your plate. Servers may not speak fluent English, but there's a picture menu available.

Just across the street from Sara Jane's is the wonderfully named **Moon Smile & Platoo** (23 Poonsuk Rd., tel. 03/251-1664, 11 A.M.–10 P.M. daily, 400B), a very homey Thai-style open-air restaurant. Thai and Thai-Chinese dishes are reliable and fresh. Lately Moon Smile & Platoo has become a European-tourist magnet, so be prepared to wait for a table for dinner.

International

If you are looking for local seafood with European flavor, the Belgian-run **Brasserie**

de Paris (3 Naresdamri Rd., tel. 03/253-0637, 10 A.M.–2 P.M. and 6–10 P.M. daily, 700B) is a nice elegant choice. Although there is plenty of fish on the menu, such as the bouillabaisse made with local catch, you can also find steaks. Located near the pier in Hua Hin Town, the restaurant is also easy to get to.

If you are craving well-made pasta, **Peppino** (214 Petchkasem Rd., tel. 03/251-1664, 11:30 A.M.–10:30 P.M. daily, 500B) has an extensive selection of Italian dishes, including standard Italian fare. There is indoor and outdoor seating. The restaurant serves excellent Italian food and is a great value, especially if you stick to the inexpensive wine.

Maharaja Restaurant (25 Naresdamri Rd., tel. 03/253-1122, 10 A.M.–11 P.M. daily, 150B) offers typical northern Indian cuisine, including favorites such as chicken tikka masala and tandoori shrimp as well as a good selection of curries. The food here is well prepared, and the service is attentive. The restaurant is located past the large Hilton Hotel, toward the fishing pier on the main road.

INFORMATION AND SERVICES

The closest official Tourism Authority of Thailand (TAT) office is in Cha-Am (500/51 Petchkasem Rd., Cha-Am, tel. 03/247-1005, 8:30 A.M.–4:30 P.M. daily), not particularly convenient or worth the trek unless there's something you need to find out that you cannot get from them over the telephone. If you're just looking for maps and bus or train tickets, Hua Hin has a **tourist information center** (corner of Petchkasem and Damnoen Kasem, tel. 03/251-1047, 8:30 A.M.–4:30 P.M. daily), but because it's not an official TAT office, the information you get may not be totally unbiased.

GETTING THERE
Train

If you're a fan of the rails and coming from Bangkok, Hua Hin is the perfect place to take the train. The ride from Hua Lamphong

Hua Hin train station

© SUZANNE NAM

Station takes 3–4 hours (depending on whether you get an express train), and there are 12 departures throughout the day, starting at 7:45 A.M. The second-class express train that leaves first thing in the morning has comfortable air-conditioned cars, and you'll even get breakfast and lunch served (not with silver cutlery, mind you—meals come in Styrofoam containers), all for around 200B; third-class tickets on other trains run around 95B pp. The train station is about 500 meters out of town on Damnoen Kasem Road, which runs perpendicular to the beach. It's an easy walk without heavy bags; otherwise there are plenty of *tuk tuks* to cart you to your hotel.

Bus

There are frequent buses from Bangkok's Southern Bus Terminal to Hua Hin, which cost around 150B and take about three hours, depending on traffic. The government buses run at least hourly throughout the day, but if you do not have hours to kill, make sure you get on an express bus and not a local bus (nearly all the air-conditioned buses are express buses). The bus drops you off on Sra Song Road, near the corner of Dechanuchit Road, less than 500 meters from the northern part of the beach. When you're returning from Hua Hin to Bangkok, you can take a government bus, but many tour companies also offer shared minibus service that goes directly from the beach to Bangkok. You'll have to wait till the minibus is full before it departs (or, on very busy nights, wait in line for an available bus); the cost is around 300B pp.

Car

Hua Hin is about 275 kilometers from Bangkok, right off Highway 4, which runs north–south. Although you can take Highway 4 directly, it's faster to take Route 35 past Samut Songkhram before getting onto Highway 4. The journey should take about three hours if there's not too much traffic.

GETTING AROUND

Hua Hin Beach and the surrounding town are quite small, so if you're planning on just

hanging out in the area for a few days, a pair of flip-flops will probably be the best form of transportation.

Motorcycle

There are plenty of motorcycle rental shops in Hua Hin where you can pick up a 100–125 cc semiautomatic scooter for about 200B per day. If you're comfortable on a bike, it's an easy ride to Pranburi or even Sam Roi Yot National Park, but keep in mind that you'll spend a little time on main roads with multiple lanes of traffic.

Car

It's also easy to drive if you're going from one part of the region to another. Getting to the main Highway 4 from Hua Hin is straightforward, and there's not too much traffic to contend with in town. If you want a car to venture out of town but don't feel like driving or dealing with parking, any travel agent in town can arrange a car and driver for about 1,500–2,000B per day. This is a great option for families or small groups, as most agencies also rent minivans that can seat up to seven people.

Prachuap Khiri Khan Province จังหวัดประจวบคีรีขันธ์ตอนกลาง

The central Prachuap Khiri Khan Province is the country's thinnest, stretching barely 11 kilometers at its narrowest point between the Gulf of Thailand to the east and the Burmese border to the west. Hua Hin and Pranburi are Prachuap Khiri Khan's main attractions, and the rest of the province is less well traversed. The coast and the state parks are worth visiting for the diversity of wildlife and quiet beach towns.

◧ PRANBURI
ปราณบุรี

Thailand's hottest new beach isn't on a deserted island, and you don't even need to fly

to get here from Bangkok. Pranburi is just south of the popular middle-class beach town of Hua Hin, and it's just a few hours by car from the capital.

Just a decade ago, Pranburi was an undeveloped strip of beach, but the opening of the Aleenta in 2002, one of the first boutique resorts in the area, started a trend. Other small, high-end luxury resorts have followed, including the superluxurious Villa Maroc in 2009, and today Pranburi is a high-end boutique-hotel destination. You won't find any budget guesthouses, and the only large chain resort is the upscale Evason.

Though Pranburi has become more

© SUZANNE NAM

Pranburi's coastline with islands beyond

developed over the years, it's nothing like neighboring Hua Hin or any of the country's popular islands, so you won't feel any of the hustle and bustle that goes along with popular tourist destinations. You won't be constantly harassed by hawkers selling souvenirs, and there won't be throngs of other tourists on the beach. The downside is that it's less convenient. There aren't many places to eat in Pranburi that aren't attached to existing resorts, and there's virtually no shopping or other entertainment to speak of.

As for being family-friendly, in the past Pranburi had a reputation for being a romantic retreat for couples, but it has definitely expanded to a broader audience over the years, and many of the resorts have larger suites for families and even some activities for children.

Sights and Beaches

The lovely **Pranburi Forest Park** barely qualifies as park as it's just over 2.5 square kilometers in size. The park is part mangrove forest and part evergreen forest, with the Pranburi River running through it. This may not be the

place for a long hike, but it's a nice spot to go for a picnic or a (short) walk if you're staying in Pranburi. To get here, follow Highway 4 (called Phetchakasem Road in the area) from Hua Hin for about 16 kilometers. You'll see a sign for the forest park on the left. You may also be able to arrange a ride through your hotel or resort, but other transportation options are limited in the area.

The beach is wide and calm and similar to Hua Hin, except that there are very few people and no activities.

Accommodations

The area has developed around small, high-end resorts, and there are very few bargain accommodations to be had in Pranburi.

Dolphin Bay Resort (223 Mu 4, Phu Noi Beach, Prachuap Khiri Khan, tel. 03/255-9333, www.dolphinbayresort.com, 1,490B) is the most inexpensive place you'll find in the area. This midsize resort has all of the basics you'll need, including a couple of well-maintained swimming pools, clean and comfortable (if uninspired) guest rooms, and a good location

the Aleenta Reort in Pranburi

on the beach with a magnificent view of the nearby islands. There is also a restaurant and a spa with limited services. Unlike most of the other places in the area, this resort, which has lots of places for kids to play, is a great choice for families.

Less expensive and, perhaps, less pretentious than the other small resorts along the Pranburi Coast, **Lazy Beach** (79 Mu 4, Paknampran, tel. 03/263-0555, www.huapleelazybeach.com, 3,500B) is a delightful, laid-back place to spend a few days. Each guest room is different, but all feature lots of windows, private balconies, open-air baths, and eclectic beach-themed furnishings. Many also have sitting areas. But Lazy Beach isn't dowdy or tacky: The thatched roofs and white stucco structures have a relaxed, chic feeling. There is no pool here, so any swimming has to happen in the ocean, which is right at the resort's doorstep.

Thatched-roof bungalows on stilts in a paddy field by the gulf, polished concrete showers, abstract mobiles . . . **La A Natu Bed & Bakery** (234 Mu 2, Samroiyod, tel. 03/268-9941, www.laanatu.com, 4,900B)

defies definition, other than that it's a very stylish, small, ecofriendly resort with a chic rooftop pool. The resort offers a variety of different types of bungalows and villas that vary both in style and size. There's also a bakery serving homemade treats such as carrot cake, brownies, and scones.

The 🌙 **Aleenta Resort** (183 Mu 4, Paknampran, Pranburi, tel. 02/508-5333, www.aleenta.com, 5,500B) is a very small beachside boutique resort that looks and feels exclusive and indulgent. The villas and guest rooms are designed in a Mediterranean style—clean lines and white stucco abound. Come here to relax, read a book, or go for a swim, but go elsewhere if you're looking to party. Guest rooms are equipped with modern amenities such as iPods, but TVs are conspicuously absent. All have their own spacious decks for watching the waves or enjoying a private dinner. Villas have their own plunge pools. The common pool is barely the size of a large bathtub, which is one of the only downsides of this property.

The cozy 🌙 **Purimuntra Resort and Spa**

(97 Mu 4, Paknampran, Pranburi, tel. 02/392-2522, www.purimuntra.com, 5,500B) is yet another small boutique resort on the coast in Pranburi. Guest rooms are comfortable and chic, although more colorfully decorated than the austere Aleenta, and here you'll also find TVs. The resort has well-appointed common spaces, including a small spa and a medium-size pool overlooking the ocean.

The **Evason Hua Hin & Six Senses Spa** (9 Mu 5 Paknampran Beach, Pranburi, tel. 03/263-2111, www.sixsenses.com, 5,500B) is a large resort with nearly 200 guest rooms but holds true to the brand's upscale, pampering reputation. Guest rooms have a Spartan uncluttered feeling but aren't lacking in comfort, featuring sitting areas, balconies, open baths with bathtubs, and TVs. The swimming pool is enormous and has plenty of deck chairs. There are also eight tennis courts and a fitness center. Although the Evason is a grown-up property, it's definitely child-friendly. They even arrange supervised overnight camping. Don't be thrown off by the name of the resort: It's in Pranburi, not Hua Hin.

◖ **Villa Maroc** (165/3 Mu 3, Paknampran, Pranburi, tel. 03/263-0771, www.villamarocresort.com, 8,000B), a Moroccan-themed luxury resort, is one of Pranburi's most stunning spots. The expansive property overlooks the Gulf of Thailand and offers some beautiful views both inside and out. Guest rooms are individually decorated in bright colors, with plenty of natural materials meticulous carved, sewn, and hewn to create a perfect, if idealized, vision of North African luxury. The large infinity swimming pool dominates the main common area, but it's the indoor hammam that really impresses. In addition to typical spacious guest rooms, there are also two-bedroom family villas.

Food

Aside from the restaurants at the resorts in the area, there aren't many dining choices in the immediate vicinity. There are, however, some great **outdoor beachfront seafood restaurants** with traditional Thai food and grilled fish and shellfish. These are nothing fancy (bamboo or plastic tables and chairs are out on the beach), but the food will be fresh and the beer will be cold.

Getting There

Unless you're driving, the best way to get to Pranburi is to go to Hua Hin and arrange transport from there. Pranburi is about 30 minutes south of Hua Hin by car, and it's possible to arrange a taxi or have your resort pick you up. Expect to pay around 400B for the ride, either by taxi or by pickup.

If you are driving, take Highway 4 south from Hua Hin and follow the road to Route 3168, where you turn left and head toward the coast.

Getting Around

There is little public transportation in the area, so if you want to tour the area, you can either arrange a car and driver with your resort or rent a car or motorcycle. The cost of hiring a car and driver starts at about 1,000B for half a day. Most of the resorts have motorcycles for rent or can arrange to have them brought to the resort for you.

◖ KHAO SAM ROI YOT NATIONAL PARK
อุทยานแห่งชาติเขาสามร้อยยอด

With its soft, irregularly shaped mountain peaks, Khao Sam Roi Yot National Park (Mu 2, Ban Khao Daeng, Kuri Buri, tel. 03/261-9078, 400B) has one of the most distinctive skylines of any national park in the country, and some consider the park's physical landscape to be among the most beautiful in the country. The park's name means "mountain of 300 peaks," and while there may not quite be that many, there are certainly scores of majestic gray limestone mountains to be seen and climbed. In this coastal park, which is easily reachable from Hua Hin, Cha-Am, or Pranburi, you'll also find salt flats, freshwater marshes, and caves as well as a canal where you can rent a boat and explore a mangrove forest. There are also quiet beaches and bungalows for rent should you decide to stay for longer than a day.

Sights and Recreation

If you're in the park in the early morning, start off with a hike to the **Khao Daeng Viewpoint.** From the top, about 152 meters above sea level, there is a panoramic view of the park's mountains, marshes, and coastline. The hike is moderately difficult but should take 30–45 minutes for reasonably fit hikers. The trailhead is about 500 meters from the park headquarters; you can either drive to it or walk along the paved road till you see a sign for the trail.

Laem Sala Beach is a small cape surrounded by water on three sides, backed by casuarina pine trees. The coast here is wide but slopes very slowly, so it's a great place to take small children and new swimmers. You may find yourself walking out for a while to hit deeper water. There are beach bungalow facilities and campsites, a small cafeteria-style restaurant, and restroom and shower facilities.

To get to the beach, you'll have to hike about 30 minutes along a well-marked but at times steep trail. You can also arrange to hire a boat (100B pp) from nearby Bang Pu Village.

Sam Phraya Beach is a small pine tree–backed beach with a small restaurant and camping facilities for visitors. This beach has a shallow drop-off similar to Laem Sala and is a few kilometers north of the main park headquarters.

Perhaps Thailand's most photographed cave, **Phraya Nakhon Cave** is a 30-minute hike from Laem Sala Beach. The cave complex is actually two large sinkholes whose roofs have collapsed, allowing sunshine to pour into the structure and creating a skylight effect during the day. Inside is a royal pavilion built for a visit by King Rama V in 1890, which, in the right light, takes on an eerie and mystical appearance. The uphill trail that leads to the cave starts just off the beach and is a steep 400-meter uphill climb. Make sure to wear appropriate footwear—no flip-flops.

Birding fans will love this park. More than

Soft mountains create a stunning landscape in the Upper Southern Gulf.

300 species of bird have been recorded at Khao Sam Roi Yot, which becomes even more impressive when you consider that the park covers less than 105 square kilometers. The park attracts plenty of wetland birds, including Malaysian plovers, and the best place to find them is at the freshwater marshes throughout the park. You'll also find Caspian terns, white-bellied sea eagles, greater spotted eagles, and Oriental hobbies. There have also been sightings of the endangered spoon-billed sandpiper.

Macaques, dusky langurs, and slow lorises are among the primates that call the park home, as do deer, fishing cats, mongooses, and goat-antelopes. Offshore, dolphins have been spotted near the park's beaches. One of the best ways to see animals in their natural habitat is to take a boat trip on the **Khao Daeng Canal.** The loop takes about an hour, and if you go in the early morning or around sunset, you're likely to see plenty of bird life. The start of the route is about 1.5 kilometers from the park's headquarters. Stop in to arrange a boat tour, which will cost around 1,000B for the whole boat. For those who'd rather propel themselves through the water, there are kayaks available for rent at park headquarters; they cost around 200B for the day.

Getting There

There are no buses that go directly to the park, so if you are trying to get here without your own wheels, the best bet is to get yourself to Hua Hin and then take a motorcycle or taxi the rest of the way. A taxi from Hua Hin to the park will run 300–500B, but like all national parks, arriving without transportation makes it very difficult to enjoy the park.

If you are going by car, follow Highway 4 south past Hua Hin until you get to Pranburi. At the main junction in the town, turn left, then follow the road another 1.6 kilometers until it forks to the right. After another 1.6 kilometers, you'll see a small police kiosk, at which point you turn right and continue down the road for another 19 kilometers until you

see a sign for the park. Although the park is right on the coast, it's a little tricky to get to unless you are familiar with the roads. From Pranburi you can see the mountain peaks in the distance, and they are a good way to orient yourself if you get lost. From Pranburi, the trip will take about 40 minutes; from Hua Hin, about an hour.

HAT WANAKON NATIONAL PARK
อุทยานแห่งชาติหาดวนกร

Hat Wanakon National Park (Mu 7, Huai Yang, tel. 03/261-9030) is a very small park (39 square kilometers) covering beach forest, coastline, and small islands. The park is less impressive than Khao Sam Roi Yot, as it has less diversity of landscape and wildlife. It is, however, an excellent place to camp right on the coast.

Wanakon Beach has wide, soft sands and clean water, and most signs of commercial activity are conspicuously absent. You will be able to find a few vendors out during the day selling snacks and beverages and a small cafeteria-style restaurant just south of the beach at the park's headquarters. The beach bungalows rented by the National Park Department, which have air-conditioning and hot water, are some of the best-equipped in the country. Some of the larger bungalows also have TVs and refrigerators, making them a great choice for large groups or families.

Getting There

Hat Wanakon is located about 50 kilometers from Hua Hin, just off of Highway 4 in Thap Sakae. If you are taking a car from Hua Hin, head south on the main road until you see signs for the park. The drive will take around an hour with moderate traffic, and you'll pass Pranburi and Kuri Buri on the way.

You can also take a train to **Wang Duan** station from Bangkok or Hua Hin. From Bangkok, the trip is about three hours. From Hua Hin it is about 20 minutes. From Wang Duan station to the park is about five kilometers; a motorcycle or taxi should cost anywhere from 50B, and it's a quick ride to the park.

BANG SAPHAN YAI
บางสะพานใหญ่

Bang Saphan Yai is a peaceful, relatively un-touristed local beach town at the southern end of the upper Gulf of Thailand. The beaches are clean and offer wide stretches of sand and rela-tively clear water (depending on the weather). Frankly, they are nicer than those you'll find in Hua Hin, Cha-Am, or Pranburi, and the area has little of the large-scale mid-market development seen in Hua Hin and Cha-Am and none of the exclusivity seen in Pranburi. Bang Saphan Yai also has a handful of resorts on small private islands and offers a chance to enjoy idyllic, relaxing days in the sun with very few crowds. Although the area doesn't specifically cater to the backpacking crowd, neither does it serve those looking for all-out luxury. There also isn't really a lot to do on the beach except swimming and lounging. Close to the coast, the water is not clear enough for snorkeling, and there are no merchants offer-ing water sports. The best way to describe Bang Saphan is comfortable and casual. In fact, it may be the best bet for both enjoying the natu-ral environment and getting a glimpse of how people in Thailand really live without having to travel too far off the beaten track.

Just off the coast of Bang Saphan Yai are a three small, lush green islands—**Ko Thalu, Ko Sang,** and **Ko Sing**—surrounded by some nice coral clusters and good visibility January–May. The islands can be visited as part of a daylong snorkeling or diving trip, but for a private is-land experience, stay over at Ko Thalu. Ko Thalu, technically in Chumphon Province, is a mostly rocky island with an interesting "bridge" caused by the erosion of soft rock by the waves. There is a small white-sand beach fringed with palm trees to swim or lay out on. The islands are close enough to the shore that they don't really feel deserted, but as a consola-tion, they are easy to get to (less than 30 min-utes by boat). Day trips to these islands can be arranged as part of a package tour and will cost around 1,400B.

Chumphon Province
จังหวัดชุมพร

Just south of the thinnest point on the Kra Isthmus is Chumphon Province, the gateway to southern Thailand. For many travelers, the area is just a convenient embarkation point for boats to Ko Tao and other island desti-nations in the Gulf of Thailand. However, the slightly different flavor of the Malay and Muslim influences of the south make it a more interesting place to explore than most would think at first glance. The area is also home to some peaceful, scenic beaches, beautiful little islands close to the shore, and good spots for diving, snorkeling, and kite surfing.

Chumphon is a long, thin province, flanked on the west by a mountainous region leading to the border with Burma and on the east by the Gulf of Thailand. The city of Chumphon, after which the province is named, doesn't offer much for tourists, either in terms of accommo-dations or things to see, unless you're interested in looking at what life in a small, semiurban area is like in the country. The beaches and is-lands are the real draw here.

The most popular destination around Chumphon is Ko Tao, the northernmost island in the Samui Archipelago. Closer to Chumphon are a number of nice beaches and islands that have not yet become stars of the tourist indus-try. Many of the small islands in the area tech-nically belong to Mu Ko Chumphon National Park but can be easily visited by making ar-rangements with a local travel agent or through the resort you're staying at. Although many find the beaches north of Chumphon pleasant, some say the best beaches on the gulf are to be found in Chumphon and below. The tourist development here is not to the degree of that in and around Hua Hin, so those looking for beautiful beaches without too many of the generic tourist trappings typically associated with world-class vacation spots should find Chumphon a perfect fit. The downside is that the lack of development (particularly that geared toward international non-Thai-speaking visitors) can make it more difficult to get around, especially if you are relying on public transportation. And the quality of the beaches can be hit or miss—some are lovely and clean, others less well maintained. If you go with the right state of mind, however, and take advantage of the general friendliness and helpfulness that pervades this region, you'll enjoy yourself even if you do run into some problems. Chumphon is also prone to flooding and has been hit hard in recent years. It is best to avoid it during the July–October rainy season, unless you are up for wading around in knee-deep water.

Getting There

There are more than 10 daily trains from Bangkok to Chumphon Town (480B), which take 5–8 hours, depending on the type of train.

There are also frequent buses from Bangkok to Chumphon (350B); the ride takes about six hours. Whether taking a train or a bus, you'll be dropped off in the middle of Chumphon Town, and you'll have to make your own way to your beach or other destination. Some of the smaller resorts and hotels offer pickup service, so make sure to ask when reserving your room. Otherwise you can arrange a taxi from the bus or train station.

If you're driving, Chumphon Town is right off of Highway 4 and an easy drive if you're coming from the Hua Hin area. Once you get to the province, you'll see signs indicating where to turn off for particular beaches. Some signs will be in Thai, however, and it may be better to get specific directions if you are staying in a hotel or resort in the area.

THUNG WUA LAEN BEACH
หาดทุ่งวัวแล่น

This beach, just north of Chumphon Town, has a wide stretch of light sand that slopes slowly toward the sea. Waves are generally calm here, so it's a great place for kids and others not looking to do too much strenuous swimming but rather to enjoy the surroundings and the warm water. There are pines and palm trees fringing the coast, and it's usually completely devoid of beach umbrellas, chairs, or any motorized water sports, making for beautiful, relaxing views. There is also some decent casual snorkeling to be done just offshore, and the water can be surprisingly clear for the gulf. Although the area is relatively undeveloped, there are a couple of resorts, some dive shops, and plenty of casual beach food.

Accommodations

Chumphon Cabana Beach Resort and Diving Center (69 Mu 8, Thung Wua Laen Beach, Pathiu, tel. 07/756-0245 or 02/391-6859, www.cabana.co.th, 1,500B) is a large resort complex with private bungalows and guest rooms in an attached building. The resort has a large swimming pool, a restaurant, and a dive center. The gardens are nice, and the location right on the beach leaves little to be desired, but the property feels a little weary. If you're looking for something really fancy, this is not the place for you, but it's definitely a few steps above the other options in this price range. The resort is one of the few in the country with ecofriendly elements, including a water-treatment center.

Baan Talay Thungwualaen (54/13 Mu 8, Thung Wua Laen Beach, Pathiu, tel. 07/762-2887, www.baantalay-thungwualaen.com, 1,000B) just opened in 2009 and offers clean, modern guest rooms right on the beach. The hotel is very small, with just nine rooms, so there are limited public facilities, but the guest rooms themselves are very well decorated and constructed. There are some family guest rooms available.

Getting There

To get to the beach, take Highway 4 heading south from Bangkok or Hua Hin or north from Chumphon Town. Turn east onto Route 3180 in Chumphon Province, and follow the road toward the water until you see Saplee Village, then take a right and follow the road to the beach.

SAI RI BEACH
หาดทรายรี

Hat Sai Ri, on a small jut of land sticking out into the gulf, is one of the region's nicest beaches. Located on a small bay, the coast gently curves and offers some nice views of the small islands in the distance, and the sand is soft and clean. During high season and on the weekends you'll find plenty of places to rent a lawn chair, buy a cold beer, or get a snack, although don't expect too much in the way of service in English; most visitors are local.

Getting There

The beach is about 19 kilometers southeast of Chumphon. From Highway 4, take Route 4119 or 4098 to reach it. On the way to Sai Ri Beach, you'll also pass Hat Paradorn, the area's most popular beach. The coast at Hat Paradorn is wide and is backed by palm trees. It can get crowded here during the weekends, so if you're looking for something quieter, keep heading south to Sai Ri.

◖ ARUNOTHAI BEACH
หาดอรุโณทัย

A clean, relaxed beach set next to a working fishing village, Hat Arunothai is a relatively unknown gem of a beach and a great place to spend a day or a few days. The beach has soft sand, palm trees, and a stunning view of neighboring limestone islands. Although there are a couple of resorts, including one of the nicest in the province, the area still feels very local and relaxed.

Accommodations

Rungaroon Villa Beach Resort (262/6 Paknum Tako, Arunothai Beach, tel. 07/757-9161, 1,200B) is an inexpensive resort on Arunothai Beach. The cluster of bungalows is set on the beach, and the guest rooms are Spartan but clean and air-conditioned. There is a swimming pool and a restaurant on the premises.

The nicest resort in the region is **Tusita Haven Resort and Spa** (259/9 Mu 1, Paktako, Tungtako, tel. 07/757-9151, www.tusitaresort. com, 6,900B). Here you'll find everything you need: guest rooms and villas furnished in an elegant, modern Thai style, all the amenities you could possibly need, a pool with an ocean view, a beachside restaurant, beautiful grounds and common areas for lounging, and a full-service spa. All of the accommodations are generously sized; the two-story, two-bedroom villas are perfect for families or groups traveling together.

Getting There

Arunothai Beach is about 40 kilometers south of Chumphon. If you are driving, take Highway 4 to Khao Peeb/Tako then turn east toward Arunothai Beach.

◖ MU KO CHUMPHON NATIONAL PARK
อุทยานแห่งชาติหมู่เกาะชุมพร

This national park comprises over 40 limestone islands off the coast of Chumphon. The islands vary from small rock formations with little or no vegetation to lush, green islands with sandy beaches. Surrounding the islands are some of the best diving in the upper gulf (although you will still find better if you travel south or head to the Andaman coast).

The best diving in the area is around the islands farther away from the coast. Freshwater flowing from rivers into the gulf creates an environment less suitable for coral and marine-life, so the closest islands don't offer the most beautiful things to see. If you're planning on diving or snorkeling in the park, Ngam Yai, Ngam Noi, Lak Ngam, Thalu, and Mattra are the best places to go.

Although there is no real beach nor accommodations, the rock formations known as **Ko Ngam Yai, Ko Ngam Noi,** and **Ko Lak Ngam** are surrounded by some nice coral reefs and have underwater caves. Ko Ngam Yai and Ko Ngam Noi are also home to swallows whose nests are gathered and used to make soup. The nests, set atop the stone islands, make for a scenic view from above the water. To get here, you can arrange for a fishing boat or tour guide at Thung Wua Laen Beach.

Ko Mattra is one of the larger islands in the park and has some small patches of sandy beach surrounding the otherwise rocky and green interior. Ko Mattra is home to the *pu kai,* or chicken crab, a rare crab that climbs trees and makes a chirping sound. Surrounding the islands are some nice patches of coral. Many of the dive companies listed for Ko Tao offer trips to the islands in the national park. These are group tours and will cost 1,200–1,500B.

THE ANDAMAN COAST

If paradise were a place on earth, it would be somewhere on the Andaman coast of Thailand. The region is astoundingly beautiful—bright, clear, warm water teeming with wildlife from tropical fish to magnificent coral, even occasional sea cows and reef sharks (the kind that don't eat people). The coast and islands have sandy beaches, and there are hundreds of small islands and limestone rock formations rising up out of the ocean to stay on, dive around, or just gaze out to at sunset. Inland, there are tropical rainforests, mangrove swamps, mountains, and waterfalls. If it's an active vacation you're looking for, there are abundant opportunities to snorkel, dive, sea kayak, or hike, especially in the numerous national parks.

But it's not just the physical beauty and activities that make the area such a great traveling experience. The region still offers a chance to glimpse rural and small-city life in Thailand. While Phuket has attracted residents from all over the world as well as transplants from Bangkok and other parts of the country, and largely feels like a commercialized tourist destination, if you travel north to Phang Nga Province, you'll find small fishing villages along the coast where fishing families can often be found clearing nets at the end of the day or setting out squid to dry in the sun. To the south, in Satun, you'll find a largely Muslim population and a fascinating blend of Islam and Buddhism evidenced in the houses of worship and the dress of the local people.

In the past few decades, Phuket has really blossomed into a world-class destination for

© MING THIEN

HIGHLIGHTS

◖ **Surin Beach:** This beautiful beach on the northwest coast of Phuket is quiet and relaxed but still offers plenty to do and great accommodations options (page 189).

◖ **Kata Yai and Kata Noi Beaches:** These two beaches on the southwest coast of Phuket have clean, white sand and beautiful views, without the big crowds (page 191).

◖ **Rai Le Beach:** Dramatic limestone cliffs along with warm, clear, emerald-colored water and plenty of outdoor activities make the beach on the west side of Rai Le in Krabi perhaps Thailand's best beach destination (page 223).

◖ **Ton Sai Bay:** This is the most popular area of Ko Phi Phi, and even with the crowds of day-trippers, the scenery of the little island is amazing, as are the diving and snorkeling options surrounding it (page 230).

◖ **Khlong Dao Beach, Ko Lanta:** This beach is beautiful and quiet, and it has just enough amenities and accommodations choices, with none of the overcrowding found at some of the more popular island destinations (page 238).

◖ **Ko Kradan:** Arguably the prettiest island in Trang, Ko Kradan offers amazing views of neighboring islands and accessible reefs for snorkelers (page 245).

LOOK FOR ◖ TO FIND RECOMMENDED SIGHTS, ACTIVITIES, DINING, AND LODGING.

vacationers from all over the world, with all of the pros and cons that go with it. But traveling either north to Phang Nga or south to Krabi and Trang, things slow down again, although even in Trang there are more and more bungalows, resorts, and hotels for visitors being built every year. Though many travelers go to one spot on the Andaman and plant themselves there for the duration, if you want to both indulge and explore, it's an easy place to be a little more adventurous. Public and private buses can take you from Phuket or Krabi either north or south along the coast, and if you rent a car, you'll find the highway system exceptionally

well maintained and generally navigable, even if you can't read a word of Thai.

The Andaman coast is also perfect for island-hopping, and the best way to do that is by boat. There are plenty of ferries, speedboats, and longtails to take you from island to island and beach to beach. You can fly into Phuket, spend a few days on one of the nearby beaches, then take a boat to Phi Phi, Ko Lanta, or one of the other numerous islands in Phang Nga Bay, or hit 3–4 islands in one trip; there are hundreds of islands in the region to choose from. Some, such as Phi Phi, are arguably overpopulated with travelers and resorts. But there are

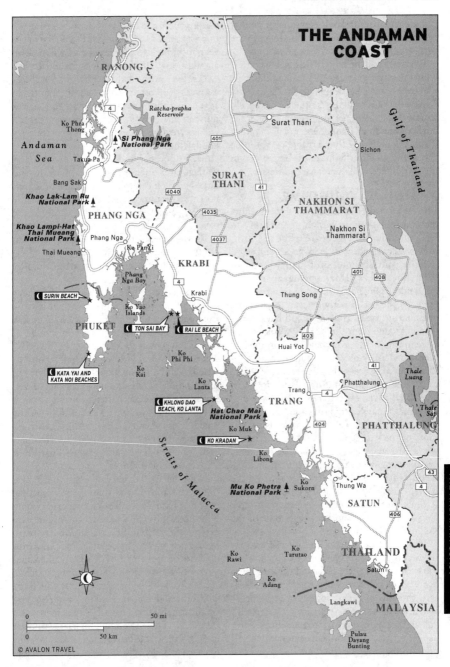

THE ANDAMAN COAST

RANONG

Ko Phra Thong

Ratcha-prapha Reservoir

Andaman Sea

Si Phang Nga National Park

Takua Pa

Surat Thani

Sichon

Bang Sak

SURAT THANI

Khao Lak-Lam Ru National Park

PHANG NGA

Khao Lampi-Hat Thai Mueang National Park

Phang Nga

Thai Mueang

Ko Panyi

Phang Nga Bay

KRABI

Krabi

SURIN BEACH

Ko Yao Islands

TON SAI BAY   RAI LE BEACH

PHUKET

Ko Phi Phi

KATA YAI AND KATA NOI BEACHES

Ko Kai

Ko Lanta

KHLONG DAO BEACH, KO LANTA

Hat Chao Mai National Park

Ko Muk

KO KRADAN

Ko Libong

Straits of Malacca

Mu Ko Phetra National Park

Ko Sukorn

NAKHON SI THAMMARAT

Nakhon Si Thammarat

Thung Song

Huai Yot

Trang

Phatthalung

TRANG

Thale Luang

Thale Sap

PHATTHALUNG

Thung Wa

SATUN

Satun

Ko Rawi

Ko Tarutao

Ko Adang

Gulf of Thailand

THAILAND

Langkawi

MALAYSIA

Pulau Dayang Bunting

0   50 mi

0   50 km

© AVALON TRAVEL

4

401

41

4040

4035

4037

4

401

408

403

41

4

404

406

43

4

still some beautiful islands you can stay on that feel less exploited by tourism and kinder to the natural surroundings.

Prices are still amazingly reasonable considering the physical landscape. Even in the most coveted areas, you'll be able to find simple accommodations, sometimes right on the beach, for less than US$40 per night, even cheaper the farther away from Phuket you are. Of course, if you're looking for five-star luxury, you'll be able to find that too. Some of the best resorts in the world have Andaman coast addresses.

PLANNING YOUR TIME

The region is not so much filled with must-sees and must-dos as it is an opportunity to relax on beautiful beaches, explore the stunning physical landscape, enjoy local foods, and pamper yourself in a bit of luxury. You can spend three weeks island-hopping, diving, hiking, and playing golf, or spend just a few days lying on the beach without even touring the neighboring areas, and you'll still have something of value from the region. While it may be tempting to idle your days away in the immediate vicinity of your hotel, if you are on Phuket, make sure to set aside at least one day to explore the surrounding islands by boat. The small islands you'll pass on the way create scenery that's enchanting and like nothing in North America. Off the smaller islands is some of the best scuba and snorkeling in the world. If you've never dived before, Phuket is the place to start. There are numerous dive schools that offer PADI certification, and the courses are inexpensive and a lot of fun. Even if you're not interested in diving, set aside a couple of hours to snorkel above some of the shallow coral reefs.

Phuket is open year-round for visitors, but the best time to go is November–March, when the weather cools off a little and the Andaman Sea is at its calmest. This is peak tourist season, though, so expect lots of other international tourists sharing your beach space with you and enjoying the 30°C temperatures. Also, expect to pay more for accommodations. All prices listed in this chapter are based on peak

season, but in the two-week period starting before Christmas and ending after the first of the year, most hotels and guesthouses will tack on an additional 20 percent or more above peak prices. Even with the higher prices, the choicest places will often be booked full months in advance of this season. If you are in the area during Christmas or New Year, many resorts will also require that you pay for a compulsory holiday dinner.

May–October is the rainy season, and while it rains often, the showers generally end quickly. If you can tolerate getting a little wet, it can be pleasantly cool, the island is a little quieter, and prices can be half of peak-season prices. If you like to surf, it's the best time to go, as the waves can be quite dramatic. If you are there primarily to dive and snorkel, however, stick with the high season, when visibility is at its best.

If you choose to explore some of Phuket's surrounding islands, remember that getting from one place to another can often take a few hours and involve taking land transportation to a pier and then a sometimes-long boat ride, especially if you are relying on public transportation. Many tour operators offer day trips to surrounding islands, and these can be an excellent way to see many different places at once, although you won't have any control over the schedule or itinerary. If you really want to explore each island (or stay overnight), your best bet is to take one of the large ferry boats from Phuket to Ko Phi Phi, Ko Lanta, or Krabi and then use the smaller longtail boats to take you to other islands in the vicinity. Some people prefer to base themselves on one of the more built-up islands (Ko Lanta or Ko Phi Phi) and explore the surrounding islands on day trips, but it's just as easy to sleep on different islands or even camp at one of the island national parks. If you plan on island-hopping, make sure to pack light. Longtail boats, which are colorful wooden boats used for short trips, are small, usually not covered, and sometimes a little leaky. There's no room for a large suitcase or even a very large backpack. It is also possible to charter a sailboat or speedboat to island-hop, but the cost is in the thousands of dollars for a multiday trip.

If you've come to the region primarily to dive, you'll actually find it much easier to get around, as there are numerous large dive boats offering live-aboard, multiday dive trips that will take you to some of the best diving sites in the country. Trips generally depart from Phuket, Krabi, and Khao Lak.

HISTORY

During prehistoric times, Phuket was inhabited by indigenous people sometimes referred to as Negritos, a group of hunter-gatherer pygmies who were, like many indigenous Southeast Asians, displaced and assimilated during waves of successive migration. Although no clear records exist, the last of the pygmy tribes was probably wiped out in the 19th century.

Although Phuket, then called Jang Si Lang or Junk Ceylon, shows up in some of Ptolemy's maps and writings, the island's history is largely unknown until about 800 years ago. Phuket's main natural resource, tin, was mined by prehistoric inhabitants, but what is now known as Phuket didn't come to the attention of the Thai people until the 13th century, when they arrived for trading and tin mining.

Word spread of the abundant natural resources, which included not only tin but also pearls, and by the 15th–16th centuries Talang, as the island was then known, became a popular trading center, attracting the Dutch, Portuguese, and French. While Thailand has never technically been colonized, the Dutch set up trading posts in the region in the 16th century and parts of the island were governed by tin traders under a concession. Phuket was even under the administration of the French between 1681 and 1685.

At the end of the Ayutthaya period, after the Burmese had sacked the capital city and were pushed back by General Taksin, they set their sights on Phuket and the surrounding region, invading the island and trying to take it over in 1785. The island's governor was killed by the intruders, but Phuket did not fall, according to the story told by nearly every islander. The

rubber tapping

© SUZANNE NAM

governor's widow and her sister, both disguised as men, led a force against the siege and succeeded in repelling the Burmese after weeks of fighting. In recognition of their heroism, the two women were granted noble titles by King Rama I, and today there is a statue dedicated to them in the middle of the island.

After that dramatic high point in Phuket's history, the island continued to be used primarily as a tin-mining area, and later for rubber plantations, attracting thousands of Chinese immigrants in the 19th century, many of whom remained and, with the Muslim fisherfolk who immigrated from what is now Malaysia, constitute much of the modern indigenous population.

It wasn't until the 1970s that intrepid foreign travelers "discovered" Phuket's beauty and began to visit the island to enjoy the mountainous rainforests and pristine beaches. Starting with some small bungalow developments on Patong Beach, the island has boomed into a world-class tourist destination over the past three decades. Urban Thais in their 50s and

60s will often laugh and reminisce about what the Andaman coast used to be like before travelers and developers realized it was a natural tourist destination, when they'd head down on motorcycles to the largely untouched island for some adventure. Fast-forward 30 years, and the dirt roads and simple local folks have since been replaced by an exceptionally sophisticated infrastructure with easily navigable roads, hospitals, shopping malls, and an international airport.

Nowadays Phuket's "local" population is not just the Chinese immigrants and Muslim fisherfolk but thousands of Thais who've moved here to open hotels, restaurants, and other tourism-related businesses. The mining industry is virtually gone, but rubber tapping remains one of the island's income generators. The island's identity is tourism, attracting millions of visitors each year and accounting for the majority of the island's revenues.

Phuket   ภูเก็ต

It's no wonder millions of people visit Phuket each year. If you're in the market for the perfect beach vacation and don't mind sharing your space with others, nothing can beat it. The landscape, with its hilly, green, forested interior and clean sandy beaches, is awe-inspiring. The vibes of the beaches and their surrounding areas vary from spring break fun to secluded romantic getaway to family-friendly. The accommodations range from unbelievably cheap to unbelievably luxurious. The tourism infrastructure is solid, and anything you want— perhaps a spur-of-the-moment diving trip, a midday massage on the beach, or a bespoke suit made in 24 hours—is available with no hassle. As if that weren't enough, nearly all of the clean, inviting beaches face west, so picture-perfect sunsets are a given. On an island this popular and this built-up, there are no more absolutely deserted places, but the northern and southern parts of the west coast offer some surprisingly quiet, quaint, and relaxed places to pull up a beach chair and chill out.

Phuket, Thailand's largest island, is about 48 kilometers long and 16 kilometers across. Imagine an elongated star with extra points and you'll have a rough idea of what Phuket looks like from above. The points are promontories, rock formations jutting out into the ocean and separating the island into numerous individual beaches with curving coasts. The road system on the island is very well maintained, and there

is both a coastal road that encircles nearly the whole island and large multilane inland roads as well. Off the main island, the Andaman Sea is littered with small islands and elegant rock formations jutting out from the sea. Many of the surrounding islands could be destinations in their own right, if not overshadowed by the main island.

Phuket and the surrounding areas rebuilt quickly after the 2004 tsunami, but the momentum from the redevelopment seems not to have slowed once all of the damage was repaired. There are new resorts and villas popping up in every corner, and more visitors coming every year to stay in those new places. If you want to experience some of what Phuket became famous for, hurry up and come now: Even the most remote beaches and islands will surely become developed in the next few years.

SIGHTS

If you can drag yourself away from the beautiful beaches, the island is actually full of interesting places to see. Aside from sights geared for visiting tourists, Phuket and the surrounding islands are home to some amazing natural sights, including rainforests, mangrove swamps, karst rock formations rising out of the ocean, and marine areas with colorful fish and coral. Since it is a vacation town, there are tons of fun or silly ways to spend your afternoons,

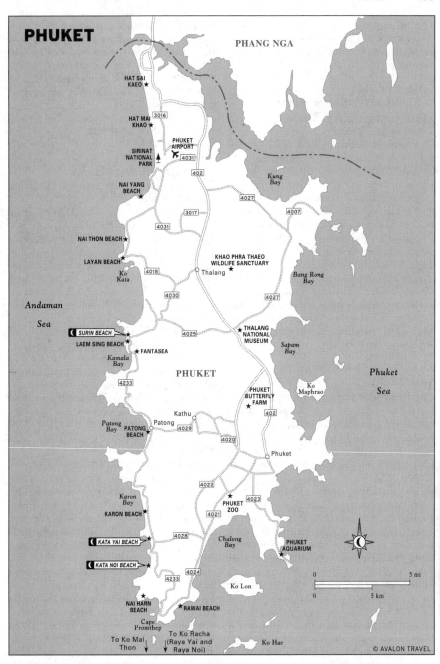

PHUKET

PHANG NGA

HAT SAI KAEO ★

HAT MAI KHAO ★

3016

PHUKET AIRPORT

SIRINAT NATIONAL PARK

4031

402

Kung Bay

NAI YANG BEACH

4027

4007

3017

4031

NAI THON BEACH ★

KHAO PHRA THAEO WILDLIFE SANCTUARY ★

LAYAN BEACH ★

Ko Kata

4018

Thalang

Bang Rong Bay

4030

Andaman

Sea

4025

4027

◖ *SURIN BEACH* ★

LAEM SING BEACH ★

★ FANTASEA

THALANG NATIONAL MUSEUM

Sapam Bay

Kamala Bay

PHUKET

Ko Maphrao

Phuket

Sea

4233

PHUKET BUTTERFLY FARM ★

Kathu

402

Patong Bay

PATONG BEACH

Patong

4029

4020

Phuket

4022

4023

Karon Bay

PHUKET ZOO ★

KARON BEACH ★

4021

◖ *KATA YAI BEACH* ★

4028

Chalong Bay

PHUKET AQUARIUM ★

◖ *KATA NOI BEACH* ★

4024

4233

Ko Lon

0   5 mi

0   5 km

NAI HARN BEACH ★

★ RAWAI BEACH

Cape Promthep

To Ko Mai Thon ↓

To Ko Racha (Raya Yai and Raya Noi) ↓

Ko Hae

© AVALON TRAVEL

whether taking in a cabaret show or seeing captive butterflies. They may not be all that culturally significant, but they'll certainly keep you distracted on a rainy day.

Inland Phuket
THALANG NATIONAL MUSEUM
พิพิธภัณฑสถานแห่งชาติถลาง

The Thalang National Museum (Mu 3, Si Sumthon, Thalang, tel. 07/631-1426, 8:30 A.M.–4:30 P.M. daily except national holidays, 30B, free under age 7), eponymous with one of Phuket's historical names, houses a number of exhibitions demonstrating Phuket's history and includes some prehistoric artifacts such as stone tools as well as religious items. The museum isn't vast or particularly comprehensive, but there are some entertaining displays reenacting life on the island throughout the ages, including a reenactment of the famous Battle of Thalang, involving the two sister-heroines. The highlight of the museum might be a ninth-century statue of the Hindu god Vishnu, discovered in the forests of Phang Nga about 200 years ago.

KHAO PHRA THAEO WILDLIFE SANCTUARY
อุทยานสัตว์ป่าเขาพระแทว

Instead of taking the kids to the zoo, where they'll see animals in captivity, or to monkey, elephant, and crocodile shows bordering on exploitation, bring them to the wildlife sanctuary (Bang Pae Waterfall, Pa Khao, tel. 02/896-2672, 9 A.M.–4 P.M. daily). Covering the only remaining virgin rainforest on the island, the sanctuary is home to barking deer, wild boars, monkeys, lizards, and a host of other creatures as well as some lovely waterfalls such as **Namtok Ton Sai** and **Namtok Bang Pae.** The sanctuary is also home to the **Gibbon Rehabilitation Project,** an organization that takes in formerly captive gibbons and rehabilitates them for return to the wild. Gibbons have been poached to extinction in Phuket but are now kept in captivity on the island, often to lure visitors into bars. The project has been working to reintroduce gibbons

to Phuket and has set up a facility at the wildlife sanctuary staffed by volunteers from all over the world who come to feed, care for, and train the animals. The project is open for visitors during the day and also accepts volunteers year-round. There's no admission fee, but they do accept donations.

Phuket Town and the East Coast
PHUKET AQUARIUM
สถานแสดงพันธุ์สัตว์น้ำภูเก็ต

This aquarium (Cape Panawa, 51 Sakdi Det Rd., Phuket Town, tel. 07/639-1126, 9 A.M.–5 P.M. daily, 100B adults, 50B children), a part of the Phuket Marine Biological Center, has a collection of ocean and saltwater fish as well as sharks, rays, and sea turtles housed in over 30 tanks. It's a great opportunity to see some of the exotic tropical fish that might have swum by you in the ocean (except for the gigantic cod, which you'll be hoping aren't swimming anywhere near you). The coolest part of the aquarium is a clear tunnel through one of the large tanks, which you can walk through to see the sharks, fish, and rays. For kids, there's a touch pool where they can experience firsthand what a sea cucumber feels like. The center, located at Cape Panawa on the southeast part of the island, also has a research vessel you can visit when it's not out at sea.

PHUKET BUTTERFLY FARM
สวนผีเสื้อและโลกแมลงภูเก็ต

If you can't get enough of flying insects during your tropical vacation, check out the butterfly farm (71/6 Samkong, Phuket Town, tel. 07/621-5616, www.phuketbutterfly.com, 9 A.M.–5:30 P.M. daily, 300B adults, 150B under age 10), which is home to tens of thousands of butterflies fluttering around its outdoor garden. There's also an insectarium, with bugs of all types to see, including giant grasshoppers, bugs that look like leaves and sticks, and even tarantulas. The farm is also home to a domesticated otter the staff adopted from its former owner and keeps on the grounds to protect it from the wild. The butterfly farm

© SUZANNE NAM

Phuket Town

can arrange to pick you up from your hotel for a small fee.

PHUKET ZOO
สวนสัตว์ภูเก็ต

This private for-profit zoo (23/2 Mu 3, Soi Palai, Chaofah Rd., Phuket Town, tel. 07/638-1227, www.phuketzoo.com, 8:30 A.M.–6 P.M. daily, 400B adults, 200B children) is not the greatest in the world, but it's a decent place to take children if they want to see tigers, rare birds, camels, and other animals while on vacation. There are also daily monkey shows (9 A.M., noon, 2:30 P.M., and 4:45 P.M.), crocodile shows (9:40 A.M., 12:45 P.M., 3:15 P.M., and 5:30 P.M.), and elephant shows (10:30 A.M., 1:35 P.M., and 4 P.M.).

BEACHES AND ISLANDS

While there are plenty of other sights that can fill your day, Phuket really is all about hanging out on the beaches and exploring the surrounding islands. Phuket is ringed with beaches, each with its own distinct personality. If you don't

like one, go up a kilometer or two to the next one to find your perfect spot. Almost all of the sandy beaches on the island face west and look out onto the clear blue Andaman Sea, they are all clean, and they all offer at least minimum amenities (restrooms and small shops or food vendors for drinks and snacks) close by. Due to the island's topography, most of the beaches are separated from each other by rocky outcroppings, creating a natural curving bay at each. What really sets the beaches apart aside from size is what's going on behind them. A cozy beach chair with a great view will feel a lot different depending on whether there are copses of pine and palm trees behind you or a big street lined with shops, cafés, and restaurants. Luckily, whether you're looking for some action or just want peace and quiet, Phuket has both.

For most people, it's a good idea to pick the beach first, then the accommodations. Phuket has a main road running down the west coast, making all beaches easily accessible by car or scooter. On the island, the *sabai sabai* attitude

DROWNING HAZARDS

During high season, the Andaman Sea is often calm and clear, with few waves and no dangerous tides. But during the April-October monsoon season in the low season, the sea can become deadly, especially if there is a storm in the surrounding area. Dozens of people drown in Phuket every year, both locals and visitors.

Phuket has a flag system on all of its beaches, and anytime you see a red flag, it means authorities have decided that the waves and undercurrent are too dangerous. Swimming is not advised at these times, although during low season there are generally no lifeguards around to enforce this rule on even the most popular beaches.

For surfers, this is the best time of year to be in Phuket, as the waves are great, particularly on Nai Harn and Kata Beaches. It's also a great time to learn how to surf, as you can rent a board for a few hundred baht at Kata

Swimmers are warned of rough seas during the rainy season on Kata Beach in Phuket.

© SUZANNE NAM

and even take some lessons at one of the many casual surf schools that set up shop on the south end of the beach. But if you are not a strong swimmer, stay out of the water or remain very close to shore.

tends to take hold quickly, and although all of the beaches are easy to access, it's a lot nicer to be able to walk to your favorite spot in a few minutes instead of taking a taxi or driving.

Patong and Vicinity
ป่าตองและบริเวณใกล้เคียง
PATONG BEACH
หาดป่าตอง

Not quite the desert-island paradise you may have imagined, Patong is a built-up, bustling beach community filled with Starbucks, McDonald's, scores of hotels and restaurants, a full-fledged shopping mall within walking distance of the beach, and a vibrant nightlife scene. For some, Patong is the only place to go in Phuket; for others, it's the worst-case scenario for a tropical vacation. If going out till the wee hours of the morning then rolling onto the beach to sleep it off with your fellow revelers is your thing, pick Patong. If you're looking for a quiet place to relax away from the hustle and bustle of urban life, stay away. The white-sand beach is generally covered

with beach chairs and umbrellas by day but, despite being crowded, is a wide, clean beach with soft sand and clear water. It is one of the island's nicest beaches, if you don't mind lots of people or Jet Skis. The beach is one of the largest in the area, and the wide sidewalk has some small playgrounds and some interesting sculptures too, if you get bored of the natural scenery.

LAEM SING BEACH
หาดแหลมสิงห์

Just 20 minutes north of Patong is Laem Sing Beach, which feels worlds away from the crowds and development. To access the small, curved beach, you'll have to walk down a steep path, and the shore is hidden from the main road. There are still some vendors selling fruit, snacks, and random souvenirs at Laem Sing, places to rent chairs, and even a few casual shops to grab lunch, so don't worry about amenities. Laem Sing also has some granite rock formations along the shore, making it a nice place to do a little casual snorkeling.

Northern West Coast

Aside from the more popular Kamala Bay, this part of the island is home to some of the more serene and secluded beaches, for now at least. The beaches of Kamala, Surin, and Pansea along the curving Kamala Bay are a nice compromise between secluded and overcrowded. A little farther north, private villas for wealthy expatriates and high-end hotels seem to be coming up in nearly every village.

KAMALA BAY
อ่าวกมลา

Not quite like Patong, but with a little more going on than Laem Sing, The relatively undeveloped stretch of wide beach, shaded by trees, is large compared to other beaches. In the hills above the bay are a handful of small upscale hotels, and part of the beach is bordered by protected lands. Kamala Bay also houses Kamala village, a former fishing village with some residents still plying the ocean in their colorful longtail boats. Kamala village has a number of inexpensive guesthouses and places to get fresh seafood meals.

◖ SURIN BEACH
หาดสุรินทร

The perfect balance of secluded and interesting, at Surin Beach there's plenty to do, if you want, but none of the fast-paced activity you'll find on other popular beaches. The small, clean beach is backed by large green lawns and tall trees with only a small road behind it. Although there's no boardwalk, a pedestrian lane between the palms and pine trees is lined with small shops and restaurants, many of which set up dining areas right at the edge of the sand. Surrounding the beach area are some nice modern luxury resorts and some excellent dining options. But what really makes Surin special is that it still feels like a local family beach, and it still feels like Thailand. There's a sort of small town–meets–Miami Beach vibe here—local school kids playing volleyball on the lawn behind you while you sip a glass of wine on a comfy beach chair and watch the sun set. If you want modern luxury without the feeling of a sterile, generic resort town, Surin is the place.

© SUZANNE NAM

sunset on Phuket's west coast

THE ANDAMAN COAST

SIRINAT NATIONAL PARK
อุทยานแห่งชาติสิรินาถ

This small national park (89/1 Mu 1, Ban Nai Yang, Amphoe Thalang, tel. 07/632-8226 or 07/632-7152, 8 A.M.–6 P.M. daily, 50B) is actually located right on the coast of the Andaman Sea, near the Phuket International Airport, and covers **Hat Mai Khao, Hat Nai Thon, Hat Sai Kaeo, Ko Kata,** and **Hat Nai Yang.** Aside from the little islands, the park comprises white sandy beaches shaded by casuarina pine trees; thin forest full of birds, including magpie robins, spotted doves, and Asian fairy bluebirds; and a small mangrove forest. Although it is just a few kilometers from the airport, the park is tranquil and quiet, except for the sounds of the birds and the waves. The beach is a small curving coast, and because there are no big developments around, it feels more secluded. The park is a great destination to bring a picnic or to hang out for the day on the beach. Off the coast, and technically part of the park, are a collection of coral reefs just under one kilometer out, if you're up for some snorkeling (and are a strong swimmer, since the coral is out quite far).

If you're really looking to check out and unplug for a while, you can also camp on **Mai Khao** and **Nai Yang** Beaches in designated areas. There is a visitors center in the middle of the park along the main lane where you can rent a tent and some supplies or, better yet, one of the park's very rustic bungalows. You'll be sleeping closer to the beach than at most of the high-end luxury resorts on the island for just a couple of hundred baht per night. If you choose that path, bear in mind that the bungalows sell out very quickly, and you have to reserve and pay in advance. The parks department has an impressively sophisticated system that allows you to transfer funds either from a local ATM or via wire transfer. Call 02/562-0760 to make reservations; you can also email reserve@dnp.go.th but you may not get a response. There are clean, basic showers and bath facilities and a few very casual canteens open 8 A.M.–9 P.M. as well as a couple of vendors who set up small stalls and sell water, soft drinks,

the coast at Sirinat National Park, Phuket

beer, and even *som tam.* If you're looking for something a little more substantial, just outside the park there are plenty of shops selling whatever you might need.

NAI THON BEACH
หาดในทอน

Another small, simple, quiet beach heading toward the airport is Nai Thon Beach. The golden sand beach is quite deep, so there's plenty of room to lay out a towel (it's one of the few beaches where there are no beach chairs for rent, very few vendors, and no restroom facilities). The area surrounding the southern part of the beach has just a couple of hotels and restaurants, but to the north, Nai Thon is part of Sirinat National Park, so the area behind it remains in its natural state.

NAI YANG BEACH AND
MAI KHAO BEACH
หาดในยางและหาดไม้ขาว

Just below Nai Thon are Nai Yang and Mai Khao Beaches, separated by a small outcropping of trees. The beach is home to endangered giant leatherback turtles who lay their eggs in the sand during the cool season. When they hatch a few months later, usually in April, the babies make their way to the ocean en masse, a fascinating spectacle if you happen to be around when it happens. In recent years, community groups have beefed up protection of the turtles, restricting access to the beach during nesting and hatching periods. Although much of it is still a part of the national park and therefore undeveloped, not all is protected. There's a large resort on the southern part of Nai Yang, but otherwise accommodations options are limited in this area. There are two coral reefs 1.5 kilometers out that can easily be seen with just a snorkel.

LAYAN BEACH
หาดลายัน

During the April–October low season, this pristine beach is nearly deserted, and it may be as close to the desert-island experience as you'll find on Phuket. There's really nothing in the area aside from a couple of simple beach-front restaurants serving local food. Behind the beach is a more residential area, although there are numerous villas being built in the vicinity.

Southern West Coast

South of Patong Beach are a group of picturesque beaches that aren't as crowded as neighboring beaches but still have plenty of accommodations, food, and activities.

KARON BEACH
หาดกะรน

Karon is a big, wide beach, another popular spot for visitors but much less built up than Patong. For some it's a perfect balance between amenities and quiet. Karon is one of the largest beaches on the island, and instead of being bordered by trees or a quiet street, there is a fairly main road adjacent and numerous shops across the street. There will still be some loud water sports such as Jet Skis, but the beach is large enough that noisy activities are confined to the southern end.

◖ KATA YAI AND KATA NOI BEACHES
หาดกะตะใหญ่และกะตะน้อย

What's so great about Kata Beach is what it's missing. Most of the land directly in front of Kata Yai, separated by a narrow lane, is used by an enormous but discreet Club Med, virtually ensuring that there will be no high-rise hotels or other development on the spot for years to come. Kata Yai's beach is used by another high-end hotel (the beach is not private, but some access points are only for hotel guests). As a result, Kata, just south of Karon Beach, is one of the few large beaches on the island without a built-up boardwalk of sorts. That doesn't mean there are no amenities, however. *Som tam,* pad thai, and roti vendors set up stalls in the parking lot every day, there are public showers and restrooms across the lane, and some of the nicest waterfront restaurants on the island are right on the beach. In the low season, the beach attracts surfers looking to take advantage of

© SUZANNE NAM

view of Karon and Kata Beaches

the waves as well as surf instructors and board-rental stands. The Kata and Karon area also has some great relaxed nightlife if you're looking for a place to have a drink and listen to live music. Behind the beach area is a small hilly village filled with everything you would expect from a beach town—restaurants, cafés, small shops selling local products, and many tailors trying to lure in passing travelers.

NAI HARN BEACH
หาดในหาน

Nearly at the southern tip of the island is the secluded Nai Harn Beach, with a small coastline set off by long strips of land on either side. The area right behind the beach is a patch of casuarina pine trees, offering shade and further enhancing the feeling of seclusion. In front, there's a beautiful view of some of the rock formations just off the coast. Compared with some of the other beaches in the center of the island's west coast, Nai Harn is a little more difficult to access, but the drive, through winding country roads and past rubber plantations, is worth the

extra time involved (there's also a bus that goes directly from Phuket Town for 100B). Perhaps because it's at the end of the island, the beach is less crowded, even during high season. During the monsoon season, Nai Harn often has the biggest waves on the island, thanks to a quick drop from shallow to deep water. It's a popular spot for surfing, but the waves can be treacherous during parts of the year for inexperienced swimmers. The area right behind Nai Harn is steep, stony cliffs, and there are no big roads or built-up areas in the immediate vicinity, just a couple of resorts and a Buddhist monastery. Although there's no boardwalk and no nightlife to speak of, there are still a handful of small shops right next to the beach and even a couple of little restaurants.

CAPE PHROMTHEP
แหลมพรหมเทพ

The southernmost point of the island is a small headland jutting out into the sea like the point of a star. It's not a place to go and swim for the day, rather a place to take in the view. This is a popular place for enjoying the sunset.

© SUZANNE NAM

fishing boats on Rawai Beach

RAWAI BEACH
หาดราไวย์

It's tough to lay out a towel or beach chair and spend the day at this beach, as many longtail fishing boats are moored here during the day, and the coral fragments on the coast make it really uncomfortable on bare feet for wading in the water. But the area surrounding it is a small fishing village with a wet market selling lots of fresh seafood as well as some touristy souvenirs made from shells, making it a pleasant little excursion if you happen to be in the neighborhood. This is one of the few beaches not facing west, something to keep in mind if you're looking for a sunset view.

KO RACHA (RACHA YAI AND RACHA NOI)
เกาะราชา (รายาใหญ่ และ รายานน้อย)

Made up of two islands, **Racha Yai** and **Racha Noi,** about 13 kilometers off the southern coast of Phuket, Ko Racha is generally visited on diving and snorkeling trips. There are no accommodations on Racha Noi, but now

a handful of little bungalows and resorts dot Racha Yai. On Racha Yai the most popular spot to go is Tawan Tok Bay, sometimes called **Ao Bungalow.** The sand here is very fine and soft. When the seas are calm and the water is clear, this is a great place for snorkeling, especially as it's so close to the mainland. Racha Noi, which can only be visited on day trips, has some excellent diving at the hard coral reefs off the northern and southern coasts of the island, and it is not uncommon for divers to see manta rays and even occasional whales. There's also a relatively new shipwreck off the southwest coast. Not yet overgrown with sealife, it nonetheless attracts lots of fish and is a fun thing to do if you've never wreck-dived before. Diving off of Racha Noi, however, is not for beginners because of the depths and strong currents. Newbies should stick with Racha Yai, which has some great coral reefs of its own and can easily be viewed by novice divers and even snorkelers. Many dive, snorkel, and touring companies offer day trips to the islands; otherwise you can get a longtail boat from Chalong Bay if you're interested in going there on your own.

Phuket Town and the East Coast

Less visitor-oriented, Phuket Town offers a quick glimpse into the region's history and a bit of normal city life in Thailand. Although most of the small city is not particularly interesting for visitors, Phuket Town has some excellent examples of Sino-Portuguese architecture, a reminder that although Thailand was never colonized, European influences nevertheless have seeped into the country. The turn-of-the-20th-century buildings, many with porticoes on the street, were actually built by wealthy Chinese merchants who took their design cues from places such as Penang in Malaysia and Singapore, where the Portuguese did have a presence. A handful of those mansions have been converted into inexpensive guesthouses, which, though not full of amenities, are quite charming places.

KO LON
เกาะโหลน
Just a few minutes by boat from the mainland is the chilled-out Ko Lon. There's not a ton to do here, but if you're looking for a bit of that desert-island feeling that's easy to get to, it is a good option. There's just one resort on the island, although you can take day trips if you're just interested in hanging out on their sandy beach.

CHALONG BAY
อ่าวฉลอง
The bay is not suitable for swimming, but it serves as the launching point for a number of charter and tour boats heading to different islands off the coast. In the morning the pier is filled with visitors getting ready for excursions, and in the afternoon you'll see the same folks heading back. The little streets surrounding the bay have a relaxed atmosphere and some inexpensive guesthouses, as well as diving and other marine-activity supply shops. In the afternoon and at night, there are a couple of modern restaurants with outdoor seating and

great views, perfect if you've just returned from an excursion and are looking for a place to unwind and watch the sunset.

KO MAI THON
เกาะไม้ทอน
Ko Mai Thon is known for some excellent coral formations within snorkeling distance of the shore and can be reached from the mainland in less than an hour. This small island is home to a private resort, so any visits have to be arranged through them.

ENTERTAINMENT AND EVENTS
Fantasea
ภูเก็ตแฟนตาซี
More a Las Vegas spectacle than a mellow evening, Fantasea can put on a show (99 Mu 3, Kamala Beach, tel. 07/638-5000, www.phuket-fantasea.com, 5:30–11:30 P.M. Fri.–Wed., dinner 6–8:30 P.M., show begins 9 P.M., show and dinner 1,200B): Special effects, scores of acrobats and other performers in costume, and even dancing elephants make for quite an event at this nightly performance. There's also a buffet dinner, carnival games, and shopping to keep you busy after the program. It's not quite a romantic night out, but great for families with children.

Nightlife
Much of the island's nightlife is centered around Patong Beach, which becomes a sort of red-light district meets frat party come nightfall. There are scores of bars and discos packing in the travelers, and music and people seem to pour out of every doorway into the streets surrounding Bangla Road. The music is almost always pop, Top 40, or techno. If that's not your scene, it can be tough to find live music venues or sophisticated places to hang your hat, get your drink on, or do a little dancing. Although there are plenty of high-end accommodations, this trend historically has not spilled over into the nightlife choices, and many visitors not interested in extreme partying tend to spend their nights hanging out at

the bars in their hotel or resort. That may be changing, as small bars sans working women or eardrum-bursting music are beginning to appear in small numbers.

The nightlife scene in Phuket is very fluid, and bars and clubs that were popular a year ago may already be closed down, or reincarnated with a different name, by the time you visit. Bars generally close at 1 A.M., nightclubs at 2 A.M., although those rules are sometimes less strictly enforced in Phuket.

PATONG BEACH

It's hard to understand why **Tiger Entertainment** (Bangla Rd., tel. 07/629-2771, 7 P.M.–2 A.M. daily) is always so crowded. Imagine about a dozen small bars and discos bunched together in an area that looks like a large fake cave, then add go-go dancers, throngs of people, and strange animal figures, and you'll have a good idea what the place looks like. Perhaps it's the beer goggles or the fact that most who visit just won't remember in the morning, but everyone always seems to think they had a good time at Tiger. Music tends to be very pop-oriented.

Banana Disco (96 Thawiwong Rd., tel. 08/1271-2469, 7 P.M.–2 A.M. daily, cover 200B) is one of the area's most popular nightclubs. Despite (or maybe because of) the name, it seems to attract lots of young, single local women. Though it is known as a pickup joint, it doesn't feel too sleazy, especially compared to the choices on Bangla Road. The music selection is techno and pop, and the cover charge includes one drink.

There are plenty of gay nightclubs in the Bangla area, but for something a little more interesting, check out **Paradise Kiss Club** (123/809 Paradise Complex, Rat-U-Thit 200 Pee Rd., tel. 08/6944-2423, 6 P.M.–2 A.M. daily, no cover). This house-music venue also has live dancing and singing cabaret performances every night.

If you're looking to party on Patong Beach but want something a little more . . . decent, **Club Lime** (Patong Beach Rd. at the corner of Soi Namyen, tel. 08/5798-1850, www.clublime.

info, 9 P.M.–2 A.M. daily, no cover) is a relatively new nightclub that's about as urban and hip as one can be on an island. Local and international guest DJs are usually playing house and techno mixes to the young and beautiful. It may not be the smartest way to spend an evening, but Monday and Thursday, pay 900B to drink all you can 8–11 P.M. There's also a free buffet on those nights to help keep all the booze down.

SOUTHERN WEST COAST

Perched in the rocks at the far southern end of Kata Beach is **Ska Bar** (no address, tel. 07/893-4831, 4 P.M.–1 A.M. daily). Stop in for a drink and you may think you're vacationing in Jamaica instead of Thailand. The DJ at this casual outdoor bar is always spinning reggae music, and there's plenty of Bob Marley paraphernalia around; no surprise that the vibe here is always relaxed and friendly. There is no dancing, but later in the evening the staff put on a fire show. It's either totally trippy or just really cool, depending on your state of mind.

Decked out with photos of Peter Fonda and old motorcycles, **Easy Rider** (87/4 Taina Rd., Kata Town, no phone, 8 P.M.–1 A.M. daily) looks a little scary from the outside, but once you enter, it is a fun and laid-back live-music venue. The local cover band is usually playing soft-rock covers (lots of Guns N' Roses and Aerosmith) to a slightly older crowd.

Karon's nightlife ambience is somewhere between that of Patong Beach and Kata. You'll find some rowdy bars filled with working women, especially on Luang Poh Chuan Road, but it doesn't dominate the area, so if you just want to go for an evening stroll, you won't feel bombarded by loud music. One spot worth grabbing a drink in is **Bang Bar II** (Patak East Rd., no phone, noon–1 A.M. daily). Similar to Ska Bar in its reggae-oriented music and decor, the inland bar is relaxed and comfortable.

SHOPPING

If you're just looking for small souvenirs to take home, every village near every beach has small items such as seashells or Thai-styled handicrafts, although after you've seen the same products over and over again, they start to look less appealing. There are some small shops throughout the island selling items that are a little more authentic, as well as some high-end antiques stores, some gem stores, and even full-fledged shopping malls.

If you're shopping for gems or antiques on the island, it's difficult to ensure you are getting a good deal unless you have some amount of expertise to evaluate the merchandise. Although there are some good deals to be had, there is no redress should you get home and realize you are unhappy with your purchase.

There are a couple of large shopping malls on the island, serving both visitors and the year-round folks—a real convenience if you find you've forgotten something from home.

Patong and Vicinity

Jungceylon (181 Rat-U-Thit 200 Pee Rd., Patong, tel. 07/660-0111, 11 A.M.–midnight daily) is about a 10-minute walk from Patong Beach up Soi Bangla. The mall, which opened in 2007, is a considerable step up from the shopping that was previously available in the area. There's a full-sized **Robinson Department Store**, a **Carrefour** hypermarket stocked with food, appliances, electronics, and everything in between, and many other stores to fulfill your shopping needs. The mall also has a nice little food court in the basement, serving up noodle and rice dishes, smoothies, and even fresh seafood. Aside from the food court, the bottom level also houses That's Siam. This shop, really a group of small shops, carries scores of Thai handicrafts and other decorative items, including home textiles, silk products, and delicious-smelling bath and body goodies.

Northern West Coast

This area is where you'll find lots of antiques shops and galleries, catering mainly to people who are furnishing villas they've purchased on the island.

Oriental Fine Art (106/19-20 Bangtao Rd., Thalang, tel. 07/632-5141, 9 A.M.–8 P.M. daily)

is a large multistory shop that feels more like a gallery for Asian sculpture, except that you can buy everything on display. They also carry furniture, mainly with classic Chinese styling, and will arrange worldwide shipping.

Songtique (8/48-49 Srisoontorn Rd., Cherngtalay, tel. 08/1668-2555, 9 A.M.–6 P.M. Mon.–Sat.) carries mostly original-period Buddha images and reproductions. Some of the pieces are stunningly larger than life, although the owner also stocks images small enough to take home with you. There is also a selection of antique Chinese furniture. This store is worth dropping by just to see the beautiful Buddhas.

On the road to Laguna Phuket, there are a handful of furniture and antiques stores. **Heritage Collection** (60 Phuket Laguna Rd., tel. 07/632-5818, 9 A.M.–8 P.M. daily) has an inventory of beautiful antiques from China and Southeast Asia. There are Chinese chests, paintings, sculptures, and plenty of Buddhist objects in this large shop.

For more contemporary items, **Ceramics of Phuket** (185/6 Mu 7 Srisoontorn Rd., Talang, tel. 07/627-2151, 8 A.M.–5 P.M. Mon.–Sat.) carries vases, display bowls, and decorative figures, all from a local designer.

Located in the swanky Plaza Surin, **Ginger Shop** (Plaza Surin, 5/50 Mu 3, Cherngtalay, Thalang, tel. 07/627-1616, 10 A.M.–8 P.M. daily) is a fun shop carrying everything from cushions to glassware and even spa products. What really sets the shop apart, though, is the clothing and women's accessories. There's a lot of beading going on in their collection of tops, dresses, bags, and scarves, but since they design their clothes with contemporary lines, the result looks modern and just a little funky.

Phuket Town

Just outside of the center of Phuket town is the large, convenient **Central Festival Mall** (74/75 Mu 5, 5 Vichitsongkram Rd., tel. 07/629-1111, 10:30 A.M.–11 P.M. daily), which has a large high-end department store, a sports store, a bookstore, and plenty of other shops carrying both local and international products. The mall also has a large movie theater, multiple restaurants, and a food court.

Ban Boran Textiles (51 Yaworat Rd., tel. 07/621-1563, 10:30 A.M.–6:30 P.M. Mon.–Sat.), a funky little shop in Phuket Town, sells a nice selection of mostly handwoven textiles from Thailand and other countries in the region. Offerings include wall hangings as well as clothing, and prices are quite reasonable. There are also some small curios and decorative jewelry.

Rasada Handmade (29 Rasada Rd., tel. 07/635-5439, 9:30 A.M.–7 P.M. Mon.–Sat.) is another little shop specializing in textiles and small objects for the home that stocks items such as bed covers, tablecloths, and Buddhist figures.

For more upscale decorator objects, stop in at **Fine Orient** (51/20 Chaofa West Rd., tel. 07/622-3686). The shop specializes in reproduction and antique furniture from China but also carries furniture and other items from neighboring countries. Many of the things sold here are beautiful, expensive, and too big to fit in a suitcase. The shop will arrange shipping for anything you buy there.

Kai Tak Interior Designs (Royal Phuket Marina, 63/202 Thep Kasattri Rd., tel. 07/636-0891, 9 A.M.–7 P.M. Mon.–Sat.) carries some beautiful furniture and decorator items from all over the region. The prices here are on the high to very high end, but the shop is worth visiting if only to look at what they've got.

Fortune Shop (12–16 Rasada Rd., tel. 07/621-6238, 9:30 A.M.–7 P.M. Mon.–Sat., 10 A.M.–3 P.M. Sun.) has lots of small Thai souvenir items, including Thai silk decorative pillows and wall hangings, pottery, jewelry, and spa products. This is a great one-stop shop if you're looking to pick up some nice gifts to bring home.

SPORTS AND RECREATION
Snorkeling
If you're not a diver, there is still a lot to see in relatively shallow waters if you're armed with a snorkel and a mask. The **north end of Patong, the north end of Kata, the south end of Karon,** and the **north end of Kamala** beaches have lovely coral or rocks just off the coast, and you'll definitely see some tropical fish around most of the beaches even if the bottom of the sea is sandy. Otherwise, you can arrange a day trip to tour some of the islands in **Phang Nga Bay,** which will include some snorkeling time. Most tour providers will rent snorkels and fins too. These tours are almost exclusively sold through travel agents, and there are scores of them in Phuket. If you're buying a snorkeling trip, make sure to ask how much time you'll spend on the boat versus in the water, the type of boat you'll be traveling on, and the islands you will visit.

Sailing and Speedboat Charters
There are a number of sailing companies that offer everything from just the sailboat to a whole crew. If you have the time and money, spending a week sailing around the Andaman coast is a luxury adventure you'll never forget. For large groups, the cost of chartering a sailboat and doing some private island-hopping can be even cheaper than staying on a resort, and all the charter companies will take care of food, supplies, and fuel. Chartering a sailboat or speedboat will cost 15,000–100,000B per day, depending on the type of vessel and whether it has a crew. **Phuket Sailing** (20/28 Soi Suksan 2, Mu 4, Tambon Rawai, Amphoe Muang, tel. 07/628-9656 or 08/1895-1826, www.phuket-sailing.com) offers both crewed and noncrewed boats and will help you design an itinerary. **Yacht Pro** (adjacent to Yacht Haven Marina, tel. 07/634-8117 to 07/634-8119, www.sailing-thailand.com) has day sailing trips and also offers lessons.

If you're interested in sailing in the area around Phuket and you have your own boat, there are three separate marinas, the **Phuket Boat Lagoon, Royal Phuket Marina,** and **Yacht Haven Phuket Marina,** with year-round anchorage.

Golf
Phuket boasts a handful of well-maintained golf courses open to visitors. Playing on courses surrounded by palm trees and overlooking the

ocean is a real treat. Although you can walk on during the low season, it is essential to make reservations as far in advance as possible during the high season, when the cooler weather makes a day on the greens that much more enjoyable. Caddies are obligatory at all of the clubs.

Located closer to the east coast near Phuket Town, the **Phuket Country Club** (80/1 Mu 7, Vichitsongkram Rd., Kathu, tel. 07/631-9200, www.phuketcountryclub.com, 3,000B) has an 18-hole par-72 course over a former tin mine. The course is great for less-experienced players, although it's not as challenging for low-handicappers.

Set between Phuket Town and Patong Beach in the middle of the island, the **Loch Palm Golf Club** (38 Mu 5 Vichitsongkram Rd., Kathu, tel. 07/632-1929, www.lochpalm.com, 3,000B) is a hilly course but otherwise good for beginner golfers.

One of the island's newest courses, **Red Mountain Golf Course** (38 Mu 5 Vichitsongkram Rd., Kathu, tel. 07/632-1929, 4,500B), in the middle of the island, opened in 2007 on another former tin mine. This course is well designed for shorter hitters, and there are lots of slopes and water to contend with.

Located at the Laguna Phuket, home to a handful of luxury resorts, the **Laguna Phuket Golf Club** (34 Mu 4, Srisoonthorn Rd., Cherngtalay, tel. 07/627-0991, www.lagunaphuket.com/golfclub, 3,400B) has an 18-hole par-71 course with great views of the Andaman Sea.

Although **Thai Muang Golf** (157/12 Mu 9, Limdul Rd., Thai Muang, Phang Nga, tel. 07/657-1533, www.thaimuanggolfcourse.com, 2,200B) isn't the fanciest course in the area, it does have the only course set right next to the beach. But for the view, you'll have to travel a bit, as the course is actually about an hour's drive off the island in Phang Nga.

Blue Canyon (165 Mu 1, Thep Kasattri Rd., Talang, tel. 07/632-8088, www.bluecanyonclub.com, canyon course 5,600B, lakes course 4,000B) has two separate 18-hole courses. The lakes course, as the name implies, is surrounded by small water hazards on 17 of the 18 holes. The canyon course, home to the Johnnie

Walker Classic, is the nicest in Phuket and has been played by the likes of Tiger Woods and Ernie Els.

The Nicklaus Design **Mission Hills Phuket Golf Club** (195 Mu 4, Pla Khlock, Talang, tel. 07/631-0888, www.missionhillsphuket.com, 3,800B) has both an 18-hole and a separate nine-hole course and is located in the northeast part of the island. This is a favorite course among regular golfers on the island, with not only great views of the ocean but challenging sea breezes to contend with.

Go-Karts

If you get really bored staring at the beautiful views or island-hopping and want to try something a little more adventurous on land, check out the **Patong Go Kart Speedway** (118/5 Vichitsongkram Rd., Mu 7, Kathu, tel. 07/632-1949, 10 A.M.–7 P.M. daily Nov.–May, from 1,000B). You can spend your time circling the course or practice a few times before you compete in a Grand Prix race with other participants. Kids have to be at least age 16 unless they're participating in one of the kids-only races. Make sure to book ahead, as the course is very popular.

Cycling

If you're interested in touring the island on two wheels, **Action Holidays Phuket** (10/195 Jomthong Thani 5/4 Kwang Rd., Phuket Town, tel. 07/626-3575, www.biketourstailand.com) offers full-day (2,400B) and half-day (1,400B) bike tours around the island. Most of the tours will keep you in the less-touristed eastern part of the island and are a great way to see some smaller villages and rubber plantations. They also offer tours of a neighboring island, Ko Yao Noi, that start in Phuket and involve a short boat ride.

Sea Kayaking

Most of the sea kayaking and sea canoeing trips that originate in Phuket will involve taking a motorboat to **Phang Nga Bay,** where you'll explore the smaller islands, lagoons, and caves for the day before being shuttled back to the big island. Paddling around Phang Nga Bay is a spectacular way to see the area. You can get up close to many of the smaller islands with no beaches to land on, and as opposed to a speedboat tour, you'll be traveling slowly enough to look closely at the nature around you. Most guides will require only that you are in reasonably good shape to participate. Some will also even paddle for you, should you wish to just sit back and enjoy the scenery. If you're already an experienced paddler, these group tours may feel a little slow, but all of the tour guides can arrange personalized itineraries if you give them enough notice. **Sea Canoe** (367/4 Yaowarat Rd., Phuket Town, tel. 07/621-2172, www.seacanoe.net) has trips that run from one day to one week and has been running trips in the Andaman every day for nearly 20 years.

Andaman Sea Kayak (tel. 07/623-5353, www.andamanseakayak.com) also has one-day and multiple-day trips from Phuket, which they combine with camping in a national park. Day trips start around 3,200B pp.

Experienced paddlers may want to rent their own kayaks to explore the islands. **Paddle Asia** (tel. 07/624-0952, www.paddleasia.com) rents well-maintained, high-quality kayaks, although they will only rent to experienced kayakers. If you are not experienced or familiar with the area, unguided kayaking is not recommended unless you're paddling around close to the shore. Many area beaches are filled with Jet Skis and speedboats, and fishing boats travel frequently between beaches and islands.

ACCOMMODATIONS

Phuket already has hundreds of accommodations options along the coast, and new ones are being built every year. While it may be hard to find that secluded beach feeling when all you can see around you are hotels, guesthouses, and cranes building them, the competition keeps costs very competitive, especially during the low season. If you're willing to pay for it, there are still quiet places on the island, and some of the high-end resorts even have small private or semiprivate beaches. And if you stay in the northern part of the island, around the airport,

you'll find the beaches much less crowded. If you're traveling with children, bear in mind that Patong Beach can get pretty seedy at night. There are plenty of discos and clubs catering to both gay and straight clientele, and passing through the nightlife neighborhood at night is difficult to avoid if you're staying here.

While you'll still be able to find a few inexpensive bungalows on the beaches in the northern part of the island, if you're basing yourself in the southern part of Phuket or anywhere around Patong Beach, inexpensive accommodations are almost exclusively guesthouses set inland from the beach, and you'll need to walk at least a few minutes to get to the water. In those areas, waterfront rooms are only available at mid-range and high-end resorts.

Patong and Vicinity
UNDER 1,500B

A great option in Patong if you don't want to stay in the thick of it all and don't want to sleep in a generic or messy guesthouse is the **《 Little Buddha Guest House** (74/31 Nanai Rd., Patong Beach, tel. 07/629-6148, www.littlebuddhaphuket.com, 500B). Rates are an exceptionally good value considering the very clean guest rooms, nice baths, and tasteful furnishings. There's even a small lobby done in muted colors and natural materials. Located behind the Jungceylon Mall, it is about a 10-minute walk to the beach. The economy guest rooms are small but inviting. For two people, upgrade to a standard guest room.

Set right against the hills in Patong, **Jinny** (87–89 Phisitkoranee Rd., Patong Beach, tel. 07/634-2457, www.jinnyphuket.com, 1,000B) is a small, simple hotel with comfortable, airy guest rooms, all with balconies and a small common swimming pool. Baths are just a bit more than basic, but certainly a step above what you can usually get in this price range. It's a short walk to the beach and the middle of all the action.

The small, cheap, pleasant **FunDee Boutique Hotel** (232/3 Phung Muang Sai Gor Rd., Patong Beach, tel. 07/636-6780, www.fundee.co.th, 1,200B) is a few blocks from Patong Beach but worth the walk if you're looking for something a little nicer than the average guesthouse. The property is only a few years old, spotlessly clean, and somewhat stylishly decorated with modern Thai furnishings and textiles. It's not really a boutique hotel and doesn't have a pool, but there is a very small bar and café as well as plenty of food and drink options just outside the door.

Cheap and chic **SleepWithMe** (39/119 Prabaramee Rd., Patong Beach, tel. 07/634-3044, www.sleepwithme.co.th, 1,200B), has small, stylish guest rooms and very cheap prices. Beds are decked out with crisp white sheets and duvets, and the modern baths are equally minimalist and stylish. The lobby area is very small but so well-decorated it looks totally out of place in the neighborhood. The downside is that you'll have to walk about 20 minutes to the beach (or take a taxi or *tuk tuk*), but for those who would rather save their money for martinis, it's not such a bad trade-off.

1,500-3,000B

The slightly more grown-up cousin of Little Buddha (they're owned by the same people) is **Nirvana Hotel** (241/17–18 Rat-U-Thit 200 Pee Rd., Patong Beach, tel. 01/080-1365, www.nirvanaphuket.com, 1,850B). Although not quite expensive enough to qualify as a boutique hotel, it's certainly a great, cheap urban property in the middle of the tropics. Nirvana has modern guest rooms more spacious than a typical guesthouse and a small restaurant with Italian and Thai food. They'll also set up very reasonably priced spa treatments in your room if you'd like.

3,000-4,500B

If you get a guest room in the newer, low-rise wing, **Royal Paradise** (135/23 Rat-U-Thit 200 Pee Rd., Patong Beach, tel. 07/634-0666, www.royalparadise.com, 3,300B) is a great value since the simple but modernly decorated guest rooms are only a few years old; the tower rooms definitely feel like a generic high-rise hotel. It's right in the middle of everything going on in Phuket, and for some it is a perfect place to relax after partying. For others, being right next to some of the nightclubs might feel a little uncomfortable.

Closer to the center of the action is **Thara Patong Beach Resort and Spa** (170, 170/1 Thaweewong Rd., Patong Beach, tel. 07/634-0135, www.tharapatong.com, 3,200B), another good choice if you're looking to stay on a larger property near the beach but not pay international-resort prices. The guest rooms are nicely decorated with Thai-style furnishings, and the swimming pool in the center of the property is large and nicely maintained. The resort is also very kid-friendly, with a couple of large restaurants on the property and a separate children's swimming pool.

The hip, retro **Album Hotel Patong** (29 Sawatdirak Rd., Patong Beach, tel. 07/629-7023, www.thealbumhotel.com, 3,500B) fills its spotlessly clean guest rooms with crisp white sheets and creative but understated art. Although this isn't a luxury property, there is breakfast service in the morning and even a small rooftop swimming pool. The location, just two blocks in from the beach, is idea for some because it's so convenient to everything, but it can get a little noisy at night. Published rates are significantly discounted, so if you are booking here, make sure to check other booking websites.

The large **Phuket Graceland** (190 Thaweewong Rd., Patong Beach, tel. 07/637-0555 or 02/655-1736, www.phuketgraceland.com, 3,800B) is more of a hotel than a resort. Although there are some nice grounds, a spa, and a restaurant, the ratio of guests to common space is high, and it can feel a little crowded during the high season. Graceland is still a great value for the price if you're looking for amenities and comfort a step above the guesthouse offerings. And the guest rooms are well furnished, albeit in a more generic modern style than Thai style. It's located just north of the center of Patong but right across the street from the beach, and the guest rooms are spacious and well maintained.

OVER 4,500B

The lovely **Baan Yin Dee** (7/5 Muean Ngen Rd., Patong Beach, tel. 07/629-4104, www.baanyindee.com, 4,500B) resort has only 21 guest rooms, so it feels less like a generic resort and more like a boutique hotel, but it has many of the amenities, such as a large pool and restaurant, that you'd find in bigger properties. Set in the hills behind Patong, the hotel is designed like a Thai wooden house on the outside, and the guest rooms themselves are furnished with modern Thai-style furnishings and decorations. The only downside is that it's located right on a main road, but if you're looking to stay in the Patong area, it's much quieter than anything you'll find in the main center.

Northern West Coast
UNDER 1,500B
With all of the development going on, it's surprising that simple beach bungalows such as **Mai Khao Beach Bungalows** (Mai Khao Beach, tel. 08/1895-1233, www.mai-khao-beach.com, 800B) still exist. The very basic thatched-roof huts don't have air-conditioning—only fans—but do have their own very basic baths with coldwater showers. Mai Khao Beach is a very quiet spot with limited amenities, but there is a beachfront restaurant on the premises serving good inexpensive Thai food. There's also camping available, and the bungalows close during low season (May–Nov.).

Though it's a bit of a walk to the beach, **Wong Lee House** (65/15 Mu 5, Nai Yang Beach, tel. 08/6276-1908, 800B) is an excellent budget option. Most of the guest rooms in this house have air-conditioning and are clean, although the furnishings are simple. Guest rooms are reasonably sized and baths are basic but functional and maintained. This is a small family-run operation and not the place to go if you are looking for an anonymous hotel experience.

1,500–3,000B
Near a quiet, pretty beach is the comfy **Golddigger's Resort** (74/12 Surin Rd., Nai Yang Beach, tel. 07/632-8424, www.golddigger-resort.com, 2,100B). This very small resort has clean, basically furnished guest rooms and some larger family accommodations that can

sleep four people. There's also a nice swimming pool on the grounds, but if you want to go to the beach, it's only a five-minute walk. The decor leaves a lot to be desired, but this is an excellent deal in the off-season, when rates are just over half price.

Kamala Beach Resort (96/42–3 Mu 3, Kamala Beach, tel. 07/627-9580, www.kamalabeach.com, 2,000B) is a large mid-range resort right on Kamala Beach. Guest rooms are clean and modern and share the same subtle Thai style seen in most hotels in this price range. The decor isn't particularly charming, but it is inoffensive and practical. This is not a five-star luxury resort but has most high-end amenities, including minibars, satellite TV, and high-speed Internet in the guest rooms. The common grounds have multiple swimming pools, bars, and restaurants. Overall, Kamala Beach Resort is a very convenient and easy place to stay, especially for those traveling with children or large groups.

Courtyard Marriott Kamala Beach (100/10 Mu 3, Kamala Beach, tel. 07/630-3000, www.marriott.com, 2,800B), an all-suites resort about 10 minutes on foot from Kamala Beach, offers clean guest rooms and grounds as well as consistent, friendly service. Suites are comfortably furnished with modern, generic furniture, and some have nice views of the surrounding gardens. The property's main pool is kid-friendly, and there is a kid's club with activities and babysitting services. There is also a large restaurant for those who do not want to venture out. The oversized suites tend to attract mostly families and groups.

OVER 4,500B
Laguna Phuket (390/1 Mu 1, Srisoonthorn Rd., tel. 07/636-2300, www.lagunaphuket.com, 4,000B) is an expansive compound with six separate world-class resorts set around a small lagoon just off the coast. With about 240 hectares of shared space along with private beaches, the resort feels like a large village of its own instead of part of the rest of the island. The land it sits on, now prime property on Bang Tao Bay, was once a tin mine that

had been abandoned, the land left fallow for years. In the 1980s the land was reclaimed at a cost of US$200 million. There's also an 18-hole golf course, tennis courts, activities for children, and even a wedding chapel, should you choose to tie the knot on a romantic vacation. The upside of Laguna Phuket is that it's completely enclosed and has everything you'll need for a relaxing vacation. But that can be a downside too, as there's little chance to experience Thailand when you're there unless you venture off the compound.

The Bill Bensley–designed **Indigo Pearl** (Nai Yang Beach, tel. 07/632-7006, www.indigo-pearl.com, 5,500B) is a standout in the luxury-resort category. Designed to convey Phuket's mining history, the property has cement flooring, exposed beams, and thatched roofs juxtaposed against colorful, modern design elements in addition to verdant landscaping throughout. The guest rooms are as funky as the common space. Expect modern modular furniture and color combinations not often seen in generic hotel rooms. There are also tennis courts, a library, and activities for children.

The swankiest, and most expensive, of the resorts is **Banyan Tree Laguna** (33, 33/27 Mu 4, Srisoonthorn Rd., Nai Yang Beach, tel. 07/632-4374, www.banyantree.com, 14,000B), filled with large luxury villas with small private pools and beautifully manicured grounds. Individual Thai-style villas are decorated with modern furnishings and have separate sitting and sleeping areas. The villas are exceptionally well maintained and feel more like five-star hotel rooms than beach bungalows.

Situated in Surin, just across the main road from the beach, **❿ Twin Palms** (106/46 Mu 3, Srisoonthorn Rd., Surin Beach, tel. 07/631-6500, www.twinpalms-phuket.com, 5,000B) is the perfect blend of urban chic and tropical resort. The guest rooms look out onto two big, beautiful pools and perfectly landscaped grounds, and inside is a blend of dark woods and clean whites—it's definitely designed for the jet-set crowd. What really makes the property stand out is the location. Though you could spend all your time lazing around the pool and

eating at their restaurants, it's two minutes to the shore, and the resort has a small area reserved for guests, so you can enjoy comfortable chairs and great service on the beach too.

Right next door to the Twin Palms is the **Manathai** (121 Srisoonthorn Rd., Surin Beach, tel. 07/627-0900, www.manathai.com, 4,000B). Not quite as swanky or expansive, the Manathai still has pleasant, well-designed, modern guest rooms and excellent friendly service. Neither of the two pools is large, but they are beautifully laid out with indigo-blue tiles. The common lobby and bar area, which has soaring ceilings and plenty of plush and comfortable sitting areas, almost makes up for the fact that the pools and other common areas are just too small for the number of guest rooms.

The **Allamanda Laguna** (29 Mu 4, Srisoonthorn Rd., tel. 07/632-4359, www.allamanda.com, 3,000B) is a more down-to-earth property and has very spacious suites that are perfect for families or larger groups traveling together. There are three large pools on the property and three separate pools for children; it's hard to get bored hanging out on the property. Although the Allamanda is not directly on the beach, it offers a shuttle to its own beach area with sun chairs and changing rooms.

Dewa Phuket (Nai Yang Beach, tel. 07/637-2300, www.dewaphuket.com, 5,000B), a pretty, pleasant hotel resort just south of the airport, has spacious suites and villas—essentially luxury serviced apartments with living rooms and small kitchens. The property is right across the street from the beach, and there is also a very large swimming pool on the premises. This is a great place for families. Though Dewa Phuket is right near the airport and guests can sometimes hear airplane activity, it feels much quieter and more secluded than most other places on the island.

The **Anantara Phuket Villas** (888 Mu 3, Mai Khao Beach, tel. 07/633-6100, www.phuket.anantara.com, 15,000B), on the relatively quiet and peaceful Mai Khao Beach, has luxurious large villas with private pools. The lush property is unmistakably Thai; all the villas are filled with traditional Thai furnishings but are still modern and stylish. The Anantara spa is likewise luxurious and traditional, and though treatments can be pricey, the surroundings make it worth the cost. Service is discreet, but staffers are very focused on making sure guests are well taken care of. For an indulgent, romantic vacation in a secluded spot on a beautiful beach, the Anantara will not disappoint.

A world-class resort with just about every luxury you could ask for, the **J. W. Marriott** (231 Mu 3, Mai Khao Beach, tel. 07/633-8000, www.marriott.com, 9,000B) is on the northwest coast of Phuket. There are large, modern guest rooms, a gigantic swimming pool and two other pools, a spa, 10 restaurants, and plenty of activities to fill the day. All of the guest rooms face the ocean, and the property is set on its own private beach. It's a great property if you want to spend most of your time on the grounds; otherwise you'll have to rely on the hotel's shuttles or rented transportation to explore the rest of the island. The property is also very family-friendly and attracts parents with young kids.

Set in the hills above Kamala Beach, the **Paresa** (49 Mu 6, Layi-Nakalay Rd., Kamala Beach, tel. 07/630-2000, www.paresaresorts. com, 20,000B), offers guests high-end, jet-set luxury in a convenient central location. The property's style—modern and minimalist—isn't oozing Thai character, but since the views of the island and the ocean are so stunning, guests won't be able to forget they are on Phuket. The large main infinity pool is set right in the cliffs over Kamala Beach. Villas and suites are spacious, and many have private pools and indoor and outdoor areas for entertaining.

Perhaps the most beautiful and luxurious resort on the island is **Trisara** (60/1 Mu 6, Srisoonthorn Rd., Nai Thon Beach, tel. 07/631-0100, www.trisara.com, 22,500B). The guest rooms are larger than most city apartments and furnished with impressive teakwood pieces. The multibedroom villas are pricey but come with their own waitstaff, private pools, and amazing views of the ocean. There is also a larger pool at the resort right on the edge of the coast, and a very small private beach for guests.

Southern West Coast
UNDER 1,500B

A great budget option in Karon is the **Pineapple Guesthouse** (261/1 Patak Rd., Karon Plaza, tel. 07/639-6223, www.pineapplephuket.com, 700B), with very clean, basic guest rooms just a few minutes' walk from the beach. The outside is unimpressive and blends in with the overly aggressive signage in Karon Plaza, but the owners have added some little extras inside, including colorful walls and decorations, to make the guest rooms stand out among so many competitors in the area. There are also shared dorms for those who want to save some cash or solo travelers looking to meet people.

Karon Café Inn (526/17 Patak Rd., Karon Beach, tel. 07/639-6217, www.karoncafe.com, 800B) is a typical Karon Beach guesthouse—set inland a few minutes on foot from the beach on the upper floors of a commercial shophouse. Rooms are clean and well-furnished and come with hot-water showers, air-conditioning, cable TV, and refrigerators. There's a restaurant on the lower floor and Wi-Fi Internet access. There are also larger family rooms available if you need to sleep more than two people.

Karon Living Room (39/119 Patak Rd., Karon Beach, tel. 07/628-6618, www.karonlivingroom.com, 900B) is what an inexpensive guesthouse should be—clean, comfortable, and very friendly. Guest rooms are spotless and have simple but attractive wooden furnishings, and baths are modern and very clean too. Rates include a basic but sufficient breakfast, although there are plenty of places to eat a few minutes away. The location, a few minutes inland from the beach, isn't perfect, but you probably won't find a better value in Karon.

Tony and Eak Guest House (213-215 Khoktanot Rd., Kata Beach, tel. 07/633-0425, www.kataguesthouse.com, 1,200B), just a few of minutes on foot to Kata Beach and the center of Kata, has basic, modern, comfortable guest rooms, very clean baths, and friendly owners. Those who want no frills but require some style and good service will love this property. The guesthouse is very small, and there is no bar or restaurant on the premises, but everything you'll need is very convenient.

1,500-3,000B

The ◖ **3rd Street Cafe and Guest House** (4 Kata Rd., Karon Beach, tel. 07/628-4510, www.3rdstreetcafe.com, 2,200B) is almost too stylish for the neighborhood and the price. With hardwood floors, concrete bathtubs, flatscreen TVs, and modern, urban furnishings, this six-room guesthouse is a great choice in this price range if you want to feel like you're staying in a boutique hotel without breaking the bank. The guesthouse is less than 10 minutes from the beach.

3,000-4,500B

The **Phulin Resort** (10/2 Patak Soi 18, Karon Beach, tel. 07/639-8327, www.thephulin. com, 3,300B) is a great-value property if you want the amenities of a larger resort but are looking for the more reasonable prices of a three- or four-star property. The compound offers many of the things you'll find in the big brand-name spots, such as a nice large swimming pool, a spa, well-landscaped grounds, and Thai-themed design throughout, but the guest rooms are a bargain—especially during the low season. The property is set back about a 20-minute walk from the beach, but there is a frequent shuttle to bring you to Karon Beach.

Metadee Resort (66 Kata Rd., Kata Beach, tel. 07/633-7888, www.metadeephuket.com, 3,500B), a modern, full service resort a 10-minute walk from the beach, has a stunning, massive, free-form central swimming pool. The modern, spacious villas and guest rooms are clustered around the pool, and some have direct access from their balconies, though some have their own smaller, private pools. The overall design at the resort is clean, light, and minimalist, with some small Thai details. There is a fitness center, a spa, and a restaurant on the premises, and it's just a short walk to town. This is not quite a five-star property, but if

you're able to book it at a discount, it's a great value in a great location.

For a larger family-friendly property near Kata Beach, try **Kata Palm Resort** (60 Kata Rd., Karon, tel. 07/628-4334, www.katapalmresort.com, 3,500B). The resort is just a few minutes on foot to Kata Beach but also has a very large pool area with a funky little artificial waterfall and a bar in one of the pools, should you wish to remain at the resort for the day. Guest rooms are a mix of traditional Thai with a nondescript large hotel; it's nothing stunning from a design point of view but definitely nicelooking, clean, and comfortable.

OVER 4,500B

Set on a small lagoon close to Karon Beach, the **Front Village Resort** (566 Patak Rd., Karon, tel. 07/639-8200, www.frontvillage. com, 4,500B) is a great choice for families because of the large swimming pool and the extra-large family rooms available. Although it's close enough to Karon Beach and Karon village to walk, it's not in the center of all the action, though you will hear the busy main road, depending on which way your room is facing.

The ◖ **Evason Phuket & Spa** (100 Vised Rd., Rawai Beach, tel. 07/381-1010, www.sixsenses.com/Evason-Phuket, 5,000B) has its own stretch of private beach right near Rawai, and airy guest rooms with minimalist furnishings and beautiful views. The property is a full-scale resort with beautiful tropical grounds, three swimming pools, its own spa, and even its own small private island off the coast, where you can hang out for the day or just have lunch. There's nothing much to do right around the resort, and if you want to go out exploring, you'll need transportation.

Mom Tri's Boathouse (Kata Beach, tel. 07/633-0015 to 07/633-0017, www.boathousephuket.com, 6,500B) is a beautiful small hotel in a fantastic spot right at the end of Kata Beach. The comfortably appointed guest rooms are decorated in a modern Thai style, and many have views looking right out onto the ocean. There is an excellent restaurant on the premises, and a spa and small swimming pool too. This is a great place to stay if you're looking for something a little more upscale right on Kata Beach.

Phuket Town and the East Coast

Staying in Phuket Town has its benefits and drawbacks. You'll be in a more historic area than the beach spots, and you'll generally pay less for your accommodations. But you'll also be far from the beach, which is the main reason most visitors come to Phuket. There are buses that go from the market to the popular beaches every day, but you'll spend about 30 minutes each way, depending on traffic,, making it a good choice only if you're not interested in the ocean or have a lot of time on your hands to spend commuting.

UNDER 1,500B

If **Talang Guest House** (37 Thalang Rd., Phuket Town, tel. 07/621-4225, www.thalangguesthouse.com, 350B) were ever to be renovated, the family-owned and run guesthouse has the potential to be a lovely old Sino-Portuguese shophouse boutique hotel. For now, it's just a comfortable, inexpensive place to sleep with quite a bit of character. Some guest rooms have air-conditioning, and all have private baths, but the property is definitely wearing its decades. Nevertheless, it is a very friendly place to stay, and it is also conveniently located and very inexpensive.

If there ever was a reason to stay in Phuket Town, it would have to be **Phuket 346** (15 Soi Romanee, Thalang Rd., Phuket Town, tel. 07/625-8108, www.phuket346.com, 1,300B), an art gallery–guesthouse in an old Sino-Portuguese shophouse in the center of the city. Each of Phuket 346's three guest rooms are quirky and funky but have big, comfortable beds, TVs, and Wi-Fi. The lobby, gallery, and attached café are very modern but have incorporated Phuket Town's historic architecture.

1,500–3,000B

The **Phuket Merlin Hotel** (158/1 Yaowarat Rd., Phuket Town, tel. 07/621-2866, www.merlinphuket.com, 1,500B) is a large, modern hotel and offers some nice amenities, including a swimming pool and a restaurant. Guest rooms are clean and comfortable but not charming or unique. This hotel seems to be very popular with tour groups. Although it's very far from the beaches, there are daily shuttles to Patong. Of course, if you're spending the money for this property, you might as well stay at their sister resort in Patong or another place closer to the beach.

OVER 4,500B

The Vijitt Resort (16 Mu 2, Vised Rd., Rawai Beach, tel. 07/636-3600, www.vijittresort.com, 6,000B) on Phuket's southeast coast, has beautiful spacious stand-alone villas scattered in the mountains overlooking Rawai Beach. The villas are elegantly furnished with modern minimalist furniture made mostly from natural materials, are airy and spacious, and take advantage of surrounding views of the ocean and grounds. The only downside is that Rawai is lovely but really isn't a swimmable beach, so guests will have to travel to the west coast for the beach.

Nearby Islands

Rayaburi Resort (Racha Yai, tel. 07/629-7111, www.rayaburigroup.com, 3,000B) is one of just a few hotels on the island of Racha Yai, and though it's a little bit of a hassle to get here, it definitely has the relaxed desert-island feeling most find lacking in bustling Phuket. Bungalows are clean and well-designed, with simple but pretty Thai furniture and lots of lush foliage in the surrounding gardens. Some but not all of the spacious guest rooms have access to a semiprivate swimming pool, and some guest rooms are designed to accommodate families with children.

FOOD

You'll find that although the island is packed full of beautiful resorts and beaches, food offerings are simply not up to par with what you'll find in Bangkok and other urban areas in the country, although things have been improving over the past few years. Nearly all restaurants in tourist areas offer some sort of hybrid menu combining Thai food and Western food, whether it's German, French, Italian, Swiss, or just cheeseburgers and french fries to go with your pad thai or fried rice. Unfortunately, most places do neither cuisine particularly well but manage to stay in business because they're located on the beach or because visitors are happy enough to be in such beautiful surroundings that they're not so bothered by the lack of excellent food.

Patong and Vicinity

Patong Beach has everything, and lots of it. Hundreds of guesthouses, hotels, and resorts, hundreds of little shops to spend your money in, and hundreds of places—from small street stalls to sit-down restaurants and familiar Western-brand fast food—to find something to eat. Quantity aside, Patong is unfortunately not known for quality dining. To find the best places, you'll have to venture out a little bit. If you're looking for some authentic Thai food and are not too picky about where you eat, venture over to the **night market** on Rat-U-Thit Road, parallel to the beach, between Soi Bangla and Sawatdirak Road. You'll find plenty of seafood and other stalls set up, catering to hungry visitors and locals alike.

Right in the center of all the action, across the street from the beach, is the **Ban Thai Restaurant** (94 Thaveewong Rd., Patong Beach, tel. 07/634-0850, 11 A.M.–1 A.M. daily, 500B). The outdoor dining area is lovelier than one would expect in the middle of Patong Beach, and the seafood is fresh and well prepared. The restaurant is great for people-watching, but it's not a place for a quiet romantic dinner: There's often loud live music playing in the background and plenty of commotion to be heard from the streets of Patong.

Unpretentiously serving up solid Thai food, **Kaab Gluay** (58/3 Phrabaramee Rd., Patong Beach, tel. 07/634-0562, 5 A.M.–2:30 P.M. daily, 200B) is always a favorite among local residents. The simple restaurant up the road from Patong Beach has many of the Thai dishes you'll see all over the country, including

tom yam kung, but also fresh local fish dishes, all for very reasonable prices.

An excellent choice for high Thai cuisine is **Baan Rim Pa** (223 Prabaramee Rd., Patong, tel. 07/634-0789, noon–10 P.M. daily, 600B), in the cliffs adjacent to Patong Beach, overlooking the ocean. The view is wonderful, and the food is solid, although the menu may feel a little touristy. The atmosphere is relaxed but much more formal than most beachfront restaurants. It's not the type of place to walk into in flip-flops after a day at the beach, but it's a great choice for a special night out on the island.

If you're in the mood for Indian, **Navrang Mahal** (58/11 Bangla Rd., Soi Patong Resort, tel. 07/629-2280, noon–midnight daily, 300B) off Soi Bangla is unpretentious and relaxed but has fantastic food. They have both northern and southern dishes on the menu and you'll find good curries and dals as well as many dishes with fresh seafood.

For something a little more chic, with a great view and a relaxed vibe, **◖ Joe's Downstairs** (223 Prabaramee Rd., Patong, tel. 07/634-4254, noon–1 A.M. daily, 600B), right below Baan Rim Pa, is a fun tapas bar–cocktail lounge–restaurant with an international menu. The modern white interior is a nice backdrop to the view of the ocean and the colorful, artfully arranged dishes.

White Box (247/5 Prabaramee Rd., Kalim Beach, Patong, tel. 07/634-6271, noon– 11 P.M. daily, 800B), a slick modern restaurant just north of Patong Beach, has great views of the ocean from the glass-enclosed indoor dining room or the terrace. The trendy restaurant's menu, which includes French, Thai, and fusion dishes, is a bit pricey, but the atmosphere, views, and attentive service make it worth the price. Those who don't want to dine here can stop in for rooftop cocktails and live jazz instead.

At the southern end of Kamala Beach is **◖ Rockfish** (33/6 Kamala Beach Rd., tel. 07/627-9732, 8 A.M.–10 P.M. daily, 500B), one of the most popular restaurants on the islands. No wonder it gets kudos: The menu, split into Thai, Western, and fusion sections, has something for everyone but does everything well, apparently a difficult task considering the quality of fare served up at many tourist-oriented restaurants in the area. The restaurant-bar also has a nice casual atmosphere and, set right on the beach, a beautiful view of the Andaman Sea.

White Orchid (18/40 Mu 6, Kamala Beach, tel. 08/1892-9757, 11:30 A.M.–11 P.M. daily, 250B) offers inexpensive but well-prepared classic Thai dishes in a pleasant setting on the beach. The restaurant, essentially a large thatched-roof roadside shack on Kamala Beach, also has tables on the sand. Service is very friendly and relaxed. Eating here feels a little like Phuket used to be—full of character and less crowded and commercialized.

Sure, you're not in Cabo, but if you're in the mood for some Mexican food, head to **Coyote** (94 Beach Rd., Patong Beach, tel. 07/634-4366, 11:30 A.M.–11 P.M. daily, 350B) on Patong. Like their locations in Bangkok, the decor is bright and colorful, the margarita menu huge, and the food surprisingly good considering how far you are from Mexico.

Northern West Coast

Tatonka (382/19 Mu 1, Srisoontorn Rd., Cherngtalay, Thalang, tel. 07/632-4399, 6 P.M.–midnight Thurs.–Tues., 600B) just outside of the Laguna Resort area, offers innovative global cuisine in a Native American–themed restaurant with an open kitchen where you can watch chefs prepare your Thai bouillabaisse or Peking duck pizza. This is some of the best fusion food you'll find on the island, and the dining room and outdoor dining areas have a casual elegance to them.

 Silk (Andara Resort and Villas, 15 Mu 6, Kamala Beach, tel. 07/633-8777, www.silkphuket.com, 6 P.M.–1 A.M. daily, 600B) recently relocated from its Surin Plaza location to more central Kamala Beach, but it's still as swanky and chic as ever. No wonder: It's owned by the same group that owns the popular bar area Lan Kwai Fong in Hong Kong. The interior is stunning, with soaring ceilings, red silk, and dark wood throughout, and you can have

your meal served at one of the dining tables or, if you're feeling indulgent, lounging on one of the opium beds. The menu has many typical Thai dishes with a little extra flair, such as the panang curry with duck and asparagus.

Right on Surin Beach, there are a number of small restaurants serving up seaside meals and offering menus of both Thai and Western food. Everything is pretty much predictably decent and inexpensive. If you come around dusk and sit at one of the tables on the beach, you'll feel like you're dining like royalty regardless of what you're eating—the view from the tables is magnificent during sunset. In the parking lot of the beach, a number of **street vendors** begin setting up in the late afternoon, and there is plenty to choose from there if you're looking for something more casual.

Twin Brothers (Surin Beach, tel. 09/591-1274, 11 A.M.–10 P.M. daily, 200B) is a little fancier than most of the choices on the beach. They have a mixed Thai and Western menu, including pizza. In addition to the food, they've set up a free Wi-Fi zone, so you can surf the Net and eat at the same time.

For something a little more upscale right on the beach, **Catch Beach Club** (Surin Beach, directly across from Twin Palms, 11 A.M.–11 P.M. daily, 500B), the beach restaurant of the Twin Palms, has indoor and outdoor seating that opens right onto the beach. The restaurant, done in stark white with an amazing array of cocktails and a good wine list, is more Miami Beach than Surin. They also have live-music performances on the weekends. It's a jet-set spot on an otherwise totally unpretentious beach. But despite appearances, it is a laid-back and friendly place to have food or drinks.

In keeping with the upscale urban trendiness that characterizes many of the best resorts in Surin, **Kindee** (71/6 Mu 5, Mai Khao Beach, tel. 07/634-8478, www.kindeephuket.com, noon–11 P.M. daily, 250B) offers authentic, flavorful Thai dishes in an unpretentious, relaxed outdoor restaurant. The atmosphere, basic bamboo furniture in lush surroundings, is casual but very pretty. The vast menu includes familiar dishes such as pad thai and some, such as banana flower salad, that new visitors to Thailand may not have tried before. The owner also offers cooking classes.

The attractive, high-end **Thai@Siam** (82/17 Mu 5, Nai Yang Beach, tel. 07/632-8290, 11:30 A.M.–11 P.M. daily, 450B) features mostly Thai seafood dishes served in a lovely setting—an expansive old wooden Thai house surrounded by lush gardens. In addition to Thai classics such as fried spring rolls and *yam talay* (seafood salad), there are also some Western dishes and fusion dishes. This is really a restaurant for travelers, so those who want more intense flavors should make that clear when ordering.

Southern West Coast

Set inside the Aspasia Phuket, **Malina's** (1/3 Laem Sai Rd., Kata Beach, Karon, tel. 07/633-3033, 7 A.M.–11 P.M. daily, 500B) has a chic contemporary feeling thanks to lots of stainless steel and glass, and it offers a Thai menu as well as Mediterranean fare. The food is less edgy than the decor, but expect the Thai dishes, such as seafood in tamarind soup, to be more interpretive than what you'll find at traditional restaurants. The best part of the place, aside from the view to the sea from the outdoor seats, is the desserts.

The Boathouse (Kata Beach, tel. 07/633-0015, www.boathousephuket.com, 10:30 A.M.–11 P.M. daily, 800B), right on Kata Beach, is the restaurant next to Mom Tri's and has one of the best wine selections on the island. This is definitely a place to trade the flip-flops for nicer garb. The kitchen serves both Thai and Western food, and although the restaurant is technically indoors, it opens out onto the beach, and there's a wonderful view to accompany your meal.

Locanda (Bougainvillea Terrace Resort, 86 Patak Rd., Kata Beach, tel. 07/633-0139, www.locanda-phuket.com, 2 P.M.–2 A.M. daily, 1,000B) in Kata is part Argentinean *churrascaria,* part Thai restaurant that is owned by Swiss people and has an Italian name, but the combination works well. It's one of the best

places on the island to get a steak. A big plus for those balking at the sorry selection of wines on the island, there's also a wine cellar with Old World and New World wines to choose from. If you're not totally stuffed by the grilled meats, the restaurant has a small but well-prepared Thai menu.

The entrance to **Kampong Kata Hill** (4 Karon Rd., Kata, tel. 07/633-0103, 6–11 P.M. daily, 500B), in the center of Kata, is easy to miss, but if you walk up the hill on the (many) outdoor stairs, you'll find one of the nicest Thai restaurants in the area. The decor, filled with Thai antiques and Buddha images, might seem a bit over-the-top to some, but it's pretty and pleasant. The menu includes just about every Thai dish imaginable, from Thai salads to curries plus plenty of seafood.

Two Chefs Bar and Grill (526/7-8 Patak Rd., Karon Beach, tel. 07/628-6479, www.twochefs-phuket.com, 8 A.M.–11 P.M. daily, 450B) probably comes the closest to American chain-restaurant dining on Phuket. The restaurant serves a mixed menu of Tex-Mex, Thai food, sandwiches, and burgers in a comfortable, modern setting. Though the Thai food is definitely toned down for Western palates, it's consistent, and most find the flavors plenty intense. They also serve some hearty breakfast dishes in the morning. In addition to the Karon location, there are two locations in Kata.

Phuket Town and the East Coast

The **night market** in Phuket Town, on Ong Sim Fai Road near the bus station, probably has the best casual food in the vicinity. Although Phuket Town attracts a number of travelers, the diners here are mostly locals, and the food is consequently reasonably priced and freshly prepared.

◖ **Raya Thai** (48 Deebuk Rd., Phuket Town, tel. 07/621-8155, 10 A.M.–11 P.M. daily, 300B) is a must if you're anywhere near Phuket Town around lunch or dinnertime and prefer excellent local food and charming atmosphere to Westernized menus and slick decor. The elegant yet unpretentious restaurant is in an old Chinese-style home, and there's also outdoor seating in the small courtyard. Madam Rose (as the restaurant is sometimes called) has been running things for decades, and she offers deliciously prepared traditional Thai cuisine, with lots of fresh seafood on the menu. The *tom yam kung* is particularly good. This is one of those gems that's more popular with out-of-town Thais on vacation than with hordes of Westerners. It is a very family-friendly restaurant too.

Even if you're not staying in Phuket Town, **Siam Indigo Bar & Restaurant** (8 Phang Nga Rd., Phuket Town, tel. 07/625-6697, www.siamindigo.com, 6:30 A.M.–11 P.M. daily, 500B) is reason enough to make the trip. The restaurant, set in a nicely restored old Sino-Portuguese building, offers a mixed menu of Thai and French fusion dishes as well as creative cocktails. The decor is fresh and modern, and the space also doubles as a modern art gallery to showcase local artists' work.

The stately, expansive **Baan Klung Jinda Restaurant** (158 Yaowarat Rd., Phuket Town, tel. 07/622-1777, 11 A.M.–2 P.M. and 5–10 P.M. Mon.–Sat., 350B) is set in an old colonial-style house, complete with porticoes and shuttered windows, a definite step up from most of the dining options on the island. Inside, the menu is deliberately traditional and typical, although there are some more exotic ingredients such as venison. Expect to find lots of curry and seafood dishes, all well prepared and presented. The restaurant also has a good wine selection, another plus if you're looking for a special place to dine.

Blue Elephant Cooking School and Restaurant (96 Krabi Rd., Phuket Town, tel. 07/635-4355, 11:30 A.M.–10:30 P.M. daily, 650B), set in the old Phuket governor's mansion, has been serving royal Thai cuisine to patrons for years. Dishes, including curries and *tom yam kung,* will seem familiar to most who know Thai food, but presentation here is meticulous. The physical setting, another old colonial mansion, is stunning and makes for a very special spot for lunch or dinner. Like the Bangkok location, the Blue Elephant in Phuket also offers cooking classes.

There are several seafood restaurants along Chalong Bay, but **Kan-Eang Seafood** (9/3 Chofa Rd., Chalong Bay, tel. 07/638-1323, 10 A.M.–midnight daily, 400B) is a favorite among returning visitors to the island. Originally opened in the 1970s as a small fish stand, Kan-Eang has grown into a large open-air restaurant facing the bay. Try the steamed fish with lime and chili sauce and crab-fried rice for an authentic local seafood meal. This restaurant is insanely popular with large tour groups, but don't be put off by the big buses in the parking lot.

Wood-fired pizza, fresh seafood, Thai food, and a great view are what draw travelers and expats to **Nikita's** (Rawai Beach Rd., tel. 07/628-8703, 10 A.M.–1 A.M. daily, 250B) night after night. You might not get that cultural experience you've been craving if you come for dinner, but you'll definitely satisfy any pizza urges. The view from the tables on Rawai beach, the cold beer on tap, and the relaxed atmosphere only add to the experience.

INFORMATION AND SERVICES
Tourist and Travel Information

The **main island tourist office** (191 Thalang Rd., Phuket Town, tel. 07/621-2213 or 07/621-1036, www.tourismthailand.org) is located in Phuket Town and offers maps and general information about the island. There's also a Tourism Authority of Thailand office right in the airport, and it's a convenient place to grab some maps and get general information.

There is also a noticeable presence of tourist police in Phuket, especially during the high season. If there's ever a need, dial 02/678-6800, 02/678-6809, or toll-free 1699 from any phone in Thailand.

Banks and Currency Exchange

As long as your local bank is on one of the international networks, such as Cirrus, you should have no problems getting access to money anywhere on Phuket, although many of the outlying islands don't have ATMs or banks.

There are ATMs and currency-exchange kiosks in the Phuket International Airport.

You will get the best rate if you use your ATM card instead of changing currency or traveler's checks. The ATMs will all have an English-language option. Remember that Phuket is a pretty casual place, and you'll most likely be spending a lot of time swimming, away from your valuables or on a boat with other travelers you don't know, so it's better not to carry wads of cash with you. If your hotel doesn't have a safe that you feel confident with (and most casual bungalows don't), take out only as much as you need for a day or two.

Branches of all of the major banks offer currency-exchange services in Phuket Town and the larger beach areas. Rates are always posted, and after you calculate in fees and commissions, they will be better than anything you'll get from someone offering to exchange money for you on the street or out of a shop front. You may be required to show your passport, so make sure to bring it with you. If you want to exchange traveler's checks, you will be able to do so at any of the bank branches as well.

As in Bangkok, international hotels and restaurants will take American Express, MasterCard, and Visa cards, but smaller guesthouses and virtually all casual restaurants are cash-only.

Communications

The best place to get stamps is at your hotel, and even the smallest guesthouses will arrange to send postcards home for you.

The region abounds with **Internet cafés,** so unless you're out hiking in the rainforest or on one of the smaller islands, you will be able to check in from anywhere for 100B per hour and up. Increasingly and conveniently, cafés and inexpensive guesthouses are offering **free Wi-Fi** on their premises. Even if you're staying in an 800B-per-night guesthouse, you may find a solid Wi-Fi signal in your guest room.

Emergency and Medical Services

Phuket has two major private hospitals with English-speaking staff. While the level of service may not be as high as in the swanky international hospitals in Bangkok, these institutions do cater to foreigners, and staff are well trained and professional. If there is an emergency or you need to be seen by a doctor before you head off the island, do not hesitate to stop into one of these hospitals. Both have 24-hour walk-in services for a fraction of what you'd pay back home. **Bangkok Hospital Phuket** (2/1 Hongyok Utis Rd., Phuket Town, tel. 07/625-4425) is located in Phuket Town. **Phuket International Hospital** (44 Chalermprakiat Ror 9 Rd., tel. 07/624-9400) is on the airport bypass road. Both hospitals have emergency services. If you want help from Bangkok Hospital, dial 1719 from any local phone. The Bangkok Hospital has a 24-hour emergency response, including ambulance service. The emergency number for Phuket International Hospital is 07/621-0935, and they also have 24-hour emergency service. If you are using Phuket as a base and heading out to one of the surrounding islands, remember that you may be hours away from medical care.

There are small **pharmacies** all over the island if you need a prescription filled. If you need something that isn't commonly used in Thailand, you may have trouble getting it. Antibiotics and oral contraceptives are very easy to find, but make sure you know the generic name of the drug you need, as many pharmaceutical companies brand their products differently in different countries.

The American (tel. 02/205-4000), British (tel. 08/1854-7362), and Australian (tel. 02/344-6300) **embassies** do not have consular offices on the island, but each can be reached by phone in case of emergency or to provide guidance.

Laundry Services

There are no real wash-and-dry launderettes on the island, but there are plenty of places to get your laundry done inexpensively. If you are staying in any of the popular beach towns, including Patong, Kamala, Kata, or Karon, there will be plenty of shops offering laundry services, sometimes as a side business to a convenience store or even a coffee shop, so keep an eye out for little signs, and ask if necessary. Nearly every hotel, even cheap bungalows, will have some laundry services too. Take advantage of this when planning your packing. Expect to pay 50–100B per kilogram. Prices will be substantially higher in larger resorts, however.

Luggage Storage

There is luggage storage at the Phuket airport at a rate of 60B per day per item; it's to the left just after you exit the baggage-claim area.

GETTING THERE

Although Phuket is an island, it is connected to the mainland by a short bridge, making boat travel unnecessary unless you are coming from one of the smaller islands in the region (such as Phi Phi or Lanta). Many people take advantage of the inexpensive flights from Bangkok, but it is also easy to travel overland to the island.

Air

Phuket has one international airport, the **Phuket International Airport** (tel. 07/632-7230 to 07/632-7237) located in the northwest part of the island on Thep Kasattri Road, serving passengers arriving from all over the world.

If you're coming from Bangkok, it's cheap and easy to get to Phuket by air. Between regular and low-cost airlines, there are more than 20 flights per day, and even during peak travel it is unlikely you won't be able to find a flight on the day you want to leave (although you're better off making reservations in advance if you are traveling in December–January). The low-cost carriers, including **Nok Air** and **Air Asia,** often have same-day flights available for less than 2,000B each way. Unless it's peak season or Sunday night (when Bangkok residents are returning from weekend getaways), you can literally show up at the airport and ask for the next available flight. Flights are just over an hour from the city, making Phuket an easy place to go even for a weekend.

Flights from Bangkok to Phuket and Krabi are still running from both the new

Suvarnabhumi airport and the old airport, Don Muang, which was supposed to be decommissioned after the new airport was built, but was reopened for domestic flights while repair work was being done on the new airport and seems to be lingering. The situation is supposed to be temporary, and the old airport feels makeshift, with very limited food or modern airport comforts. There is only one terminal open, so you won't have to worry about going to the wrong place, but if you're taking a taxi to the airport in Bangkok, make sure the driver understands which one you are going to. Make sure you understand too. It's not uncommon for carriers to book you on a flight from Don Muang going to Phuket but returning to Suvarnabhumi.

Train

Phuket does not have rail service, but you can take a train to Surat Thani (actually Phun Phin, about 10 minutes by car outside of Surat Thani), and then switch to a bus for the remainder of the journey. An overnight second-class sleeper to Surat Thani will cost around 650B, and there are also a couple of trains leaving during the day. The train ride is around 14 hours, then you'll switch to a bus, which you need to pick up in town, although there are cheap buses from the train station to Surat Thani. The bus from Surat Thani to Phuket is about five hours and costs under 200B. The whole journey will take around 20 hours, making taking a bus directly from Bangkok a little more appealing (and less expensive).

Bus

There are frequent buses to Phuket from Bangkok and other parts of the country. If you're coming from Bangkok, you can take a bus straight from the **Southern Bus Terminal** into Phuket. The journey takes around 12 hours and costs 625B baht for the air-conditioned luxury bus run by **Phuket Central Tour** (tel. 02/434-3233 or 07/621-3615). Other air-conditioned government express buses cost around 500B. If you're heading to Phuket from Bangkok, watch out for tour companies running their own buses, especially those originating in the Khao San Road area. They can be cheaper than government buses and seem more convenient since they leave from the center of the city. But oftentimes you'll arrive at the departure point at the scheduled time only to have to wait another hour or more as other passengers arrive. Government buses leaving from the Southern Bus Terminal are generally prompt, and the air-conditioned buses are surprisingly pleasant. Seats are comfortable and recline, there is a bath on board, and you'll be given a blanket if you take an overnight bus.

If you're coming from Krabi, there are frequent daily buses to Phuket; the cost is less than 200B, and they take about four hours. You can also travel between Phuket and Phang Nga by bus. The ride is about 2.5 hours and it costs under 150B.

Car

Depending on where you're coming from, it's easy to drive into Phuket (the island is connected by bridge to Phang Nga), and since getting around once you're there can be expensive, a car could come in handy. Phuket is best reached from Highway 4, which runs north–south down the peninsula. To get to Phuket, you have to travel through Phang Nga Province to get to the Surin Bridge, and the turnoff from the highway is at Route 402, which is well signed in English indicating that it's the route to take to get to Phuket. Route 402 is called Thep Kasattri Road; it runs inland down the island and is where the airport is located.

GETTING AROUND

Transportation on the island is the one thing that's relatively expensive and can sometimes account for more of your budget than your accommodations.

Taxi

Metered taxis are generally hard to come by in Phuket, but you will be able to find them at the airport, and they will probably be cheaper than any car service you're offered. Expect to pay 400–700B to get from the airport to your hotel. The **official taxi stand,** which is on the right of the arrivals terminal once you exit the building, has posted estimates of the cost to various beaches. Although there will be many people offering you taxis the minute you step out of the terminal, just walk to the taxi stand and take one from there, as it's almost always a better deal. Once outside the airport, though, there are no metered taxis.

In every beach village, there are taxi stands for unmetered taxis with prevailing prices posted. These prices are somewhat negotiable but are always shockingly expensive compared to Bangkok. Expect to pay at least 300B for any trip you take with one of these cars. If you're traveling farther than the next beach town, prices will be higher. To get back to the airport from your hotel will generally run around 700B if you're in the southern part of the island and slightly less the closer you are to the airport.

Tuk Tuk

The most common way to get around the island is by *tuk tuk*. Not quite like the three-wheeled version seen all over Bangkok and Chiang Mai, the Phuket version is more like a small pickup truck with seats in the back facing backward and forward. They're often painted in bright colors or carry advertisements for local businesses, and some of them also have bright neon lights. You can't miss them—they look like mini disco buses. In Patong, you'll find rows of *tuk tuks* lined up on the main road waiting for customers. When none are waiting, you can just flag one down. It's best to settle on a price before you get into the *tuk tuk,* and generally it's around 200B to get to a nearby beach, more for farther destinations. They don't have seat belts—nor doors, for that matter—so if you're traveling with small kids, be advised.

Motorcycle Taxi

Motorcycles are less common in Phuket than in Bangkok, but they can be found in very developed areas such as Phuket Town and Patong. Drivers wear brightly colored vests, often with white numbers on the back, and will negotiate fares to take you where you need to go. Prices range anywhere from 50B to get from one part of a beach to another to a few hundred baht if you are traveling farther.

Motorcycle Rental

Many people rent motorcycles to get around Phuket. Mostly you'll find 100 cc and 110 cc Honda Waves, which have a clutchless shift system (you still have to change gears with your left foot, but you don't need to squeeze a clutch to do so), but there are also lots of places renting newer scooters that are totally automatic. At around 250B per day (slightly more in high season or if you're in a remote area), it's the cheapest form of transportation you'll be able to find on the island. It's also a great way to see the island, since you're totally mobile and you can come and go as you please. The downside is that some of the roads are windy and hilly, which can be challenging or scary for new riders. Also, riding a motorcycle anywhere is dangerous. If you rent one, make sure you know what you are doing, and always wear your helmet. You may feel like the only person on the island with one on, but you'll be the safest. You will also avoid potentially expensive and inconvenient traffic tickets, as the Phuket police occasionally crack down on helmetless riders.

Car Rental

There are numerous international and local car rental companies on the island. While a car isn't necessary, this is a great option if you have children. Although not all of the agencies will require this, it's best to go to a auto club office at home to get an international driver's license before arriving. You can legally drive in Thailand without one, but for insurance reasons some companies will ask that you have it anyway.

Avis (arrival terminal, Phuket International Airport, tel. 07/635-1243, www.avisthailand.com, 8 A.M.–9 P.M. daily) has a rental counter right at the airport, and you can book online and pick up your car when you arrive.

Andaman Car Rent (51/11 Mu 3 Cherngtalay Rd., Surin Beach, tel. 07/632-4422, www.andamancarrent.com, 9 A.M.–9 P.M. daily) is located on Surin Beach and has a good selection of Jeeps and other sport vehicles as well as regular cars. They'll pick you up from the airport if you arrange it ahead of time.

Via Phuket (120/18 Rat-U-Thit Rd., Patong Beach, tel. 07/634-1660, www.via-phuket.com, 8 A.M.–5 P.M. Mon–Sat.) has off-road vehicles in addition to normal cars and will pick you up and drop you off wherever you are staying.

Braun Car Rental (66/29 Soi Veerakit, Nanai Rd., Patong Beach, tel. 07/629-6619, www.braun-rentacar.com, 9 A.M.–9 P.M. daily) is on Patong Beach and will do pickup and drop-off at the airport or at your hotel. Braun also rents baby seats for a small fee.

Phang Nga Province   จังหวัดพังงา

Phang Nga Province, north of Phuket on the mainland, is home to the spectacular Phang Nga Bay, which overlaps with Phuket and Krabi. But aside from this well-known tourist spot, traveling north along the west coast, the region has beautiful beaches and a mountainous, forested interior. It's also home to the Surin and Similan National Marine Parks off the coast. With plentiful coral, this is some of the best diving and snorkeling in the country. The mainland beaches are arguably as top-notch as those in Phuket and Krabi, and the area is more visited by travelers every year. Although there are world-class resorts, and the lower part of the region is easily reached from the Phuket airport (to Khao Lak it's about the same drive as to parts of southern Phuket), it's definitely quieter. There's nothing even close to the density of Phuket's Patong Beach, so it is perfect for those looking for a slightly off-the-beaten-track experience without having to cut out any amenities.

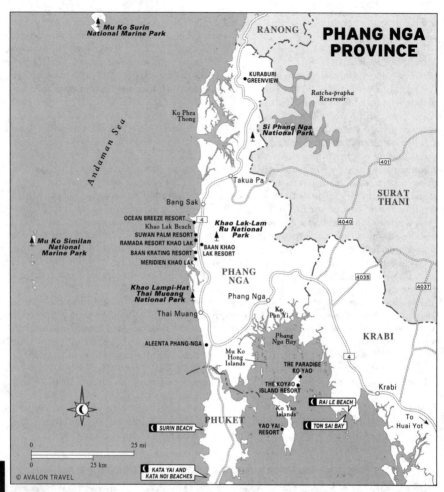

PHANG NGA BAY
อ่าวพังงา

Surrounded by Phuket to the west, Phang Nga Province to the north, and Krabi to the east, Phang Nga Bay is filled with small islands and rock formations rising out of the sea, creating breathtaking scenery that, for many, is what the Andaman coast is all about. There are more than 100 islands in the bay; some, such as Ko Yao Noi, are large enough for accommodations, and some, such as "James Bond Island," are so small that they're barely more than rocks. In addition to some sandy beaches, the bay's islands and surrounding coasts are also home to verdant mangrove swamps. You may be able to sight egrets, kingfishers, and herons. There are hidden lagoons inside some of the islands where you can snorkel or swim in sheltered waters, and caves on some of the islands from the continued erosion of the limestone material they're primarily made of. The relatively shallow waters create amazing ocean colors, from light blue when the sun is shining to deep emerald, and despite the fact that you'll probably be plying the waters and exploring the caves with thousands of visitors from all over the world, it's worth the crowds and the slightly commercialized feeling of the area just to enjoy the physical landscape.

There is only one public ferry to the bay, traveling from the east side of Phuket to Ko Yao Noi. To tour the bay, you'll either need to arrange a group tour with one of the many travel agents in the region or hire a private boat from Phang Nga. There are many agencies offering tours, and it can be a convenient way to see the area.

Islands

Ko Pan Yi (เกาะปันหยี, Sea Gypsy Island) is really a large cluster of houses, shops, and even a mosque built on stilts right over the water next to a small rocky island, a sort of Water World–esque village in the middle of the sea. The people living in the village are primarily Muslim fisherfolk, who used to make their living plying the surrounding waters but now have seen much of their existence subsidized by the thousands of tourists who visit each day and who buy food and drinks on the island. The island is quite picturesque, but it's not inhabited by the traditional sea gypsies of the region, called Moken, a nomadic people who spend months at a time at sea.

About one hour by boat from Krabi, the **Mu Ko Hong Islands** (หมู่เกาะห้อง) are a stunning group of limestone formations surrounded by coral reefs with some sandy beaches. Although the islands are too small to have any accommodations, they can be visited during day trips and for snorkeling, canoeing, or kayaking. One of the larger islands in the group, Ko Hong, has a small hiking trail.

The **Ko Yao** islands (เกาะยาว) are the largest islands in Phang Nga Bay and comprise the larger **Ko Yao Yai** and the smaller **Ko Yao Noi** to the north. Just a couple of hours by ferry from the mainland, the Ko Yao islands are amazingly untouched by the rampant tourism that seems to have changed even the smallest

islands from places supported by local industry and quiet refuges for indigenous animals to bungalow- and bar-laden resort spots. Here it's dirt roads, water buffalo, and dense green forest. Perhaps this is because the beaches are not as beautiful as some of the others in the area—at low tide it's just too rocky to swim. Still, if you are looking to get away somewhere quiet and feel like you're actually in Thailand, these islands are a truly special experience. The local culture is primarily Muslim Thai, and there's much less of a party scene; it can even be hard to find a beer at the handful of small restaurants. Both islands have accommodations, even a couple of luxury resorts, although the smaller Ko Yao Noi has the most options for places to stay. So far, there are no ATMs on the island (although this may be changing soon), so bring plenty of cash from the mainland if you're planning on hanging out here. To get to Ko Yao, you can take a longtail boat from the Bang Rong pier on the east coast of Phuket. There are daily ferries at 9:30 A.M., noon, and 5 P.M.

Sea Kayaking

Phang Nga Bay is a great kayaking destination. You can explore the smaller islands that have lagoons, caves, and no beaches to land on. Many kayaking trips originate from Phuket, where you can make arrangements for a day-long or multiple-day trip to the area.

Accommodations and Food

If you want to stay on Ko Yao but are looking for something in the budget category, the **Yao Yai Resort** (Mu 7, Ban Lopareh, tel. 08/5784-3043, www.yaoyairesort.com, 1,000B) has some very cheap little wooden bungalows with their own small outdoor sitting areas. The guest rooms are not spectacular, but they are clean, and many of them have air-conditioning. There's no pool, but there is a small restaurant on the premises and a nice beach.

The **Paradise Ko Yao** (24 Mu 4, Ko Yao Noi, tel. 07/623-8081 or 08/1892-4878, www.theparadise.biz, 7,500B) is a contemporary but casual bungalow resort with very well-

JAMES BOND ISLAND

When the James Bond thriller *The Man with the Golden Gun* came out in 1974, Phang Nga Bay was barely known by anyone outside Thailand. The tiny island where Roger Moore stood is formally called Ko Phing Kan, but it's often referred to as James Bond Island. Like many of the islands in Phang Nga Bay, it has spectacular karst topography and a small but beautiful beach.

Fast-forward three decades, and little Ko Phing Kan has become a staple on the tourist trail. During high season, literally hundreds of people visit the island each day, a trip that's often combined with a visit to Ko Pan Yi to see the "sea gypsies" of Thailand. Instead of a deserted beach in paradise, as seen in the film, the beach is now crammed full of vendors selling postcards and other tourist items. And everyone, it seems, wants to have their picture taken on the island, against a backdrop of the spectacular Ko Tapu. Ko Tapu, which means "nail island" in Thai, is a beautiful karst formation towering about 180 meters straight out of the water; it can also be seen in the film.

Many tour companies will encourage visitors to take this day trip, and if you're a big James Bond movie buff, you might enjoy it despite the crowds being herded on and off the island. But bear in mind that although the islands of Phang Nga Bay are beautiful and worth visiting, marine ecosystems are fragile. There are plenty of stunning islands to see, and it's better to spread the impact of our visits around instead of piling it all onto one tiny island.

---

designed, open, airy guest rooms, many with their own sitting rooms that open to the surrounding landscape of Phang Nga Bay. Some of the guest rooms even have whirlpool tubs. The grounds are set in the hills, which are speckled with the thatched roofs of the bungalows, and they also have a very chic infinity swimming pool.

This is the place to go if you want to experience that secluded desert-island feeling with a little luxury. **The Koyao Island Resort** (24/2 Mu 5, Ko Yao Noi, tel. 07/659-7474 to 07/659-7476, www.koyao.com, 8,000B) has some beautiful villas set right on the beach, each with a charming rustic feeling but without compromising on amenities such as air-conditioning or nice baths. There's also a small spa and a beautiful swimming pool.

If you want a lot of luxury, **Six Senses Yao Noi** (56 Mu 5, T. Ko Yao Noi, A. Ko Yao, tel. 07/641-8500, www.sixsenses.com, 12,000B) is an indulgent, beautiful, discreet five-star resort set on massive lush grounds. Most accommodations are spacious private pool villas; there are also some larger villas available or groups or those who want even more room. Like other Six Senses properties, the decor looks very understated and blends with the surrounding environment but is luxurious at the same time—thatched-roof bungalows done in mostly natural fibers but with amazingly comfortable beds, ice-cold air-conditioning, large baths, and private swimming pools. The resort has several restaurants and bars to choose from as well as staff to prepare meals in your villa if you prefer.

Since most of these islands are visited as day trips, the only food you'll find is very casual beach dining. Ko Pan Yi, a popular lunch stop for boat tours, has some reasonable restaurants right on the water, serving seafood and other Thai dishes, and Ko Yao has some similar spots to eat.

If you're staying at one of the resorts, meals are not included, but each of the accommodations listed has a reasonable restaurant on-site.

Getting There

As Phang Nga Bay is bordered by Phuket, Krabi, Phang Nga, and Trang to the south, there are a number of different launching points from which to see the islands. If you are flying into Phuket airport, it's actually easier to get a boat from Phuket than to drive to Phang Nga and seek sea transportation from there. Phuket is so heavily visited that many of the tours around Phang Nga Bay will originate at one of the Phuket marinas. Krabi is also a very popular launch point, and if you fly into Krabi, you'll most likely be taking a boat from Ao Nang.

If you are staying at one of the island resorts, they will advise you of the best way to get there (the nicer ones will arrange transportation for you). If you're going for a day trip, you'll most likely do it as part of an organized tour leaving from Phuket or Krabi; these tours almost always pick you up from your hotel and bring you back in the evening. Tours advertising trips to Ko Pan Yi or "James Bond Island" are good for viewing the bay, and if they don't include snorkeling or other activities, they will cost around 500B pp. Many of the small islands don't have consistent ferry service, so if you want to spend the day on one of them without a tour, you will have to hire a boat to take you out. You can hire a boat from Phuket marina, but you'll probably pay hundreds of dollars, since the only boats that can access the bay from there are speedboats. If you're coming from Phang Nga, you'll be able to hire a private boat for a couple of hours from the Ao Phang Nga Marine National Park visitors center in Tha Dan. Expect to pay around 1,000B for two hours.

If you're driving, the only island in the bay you'll be able to access is Ko Lanta. Otherwise, plan on driving to Tha Dan, Krabi, or Phuket and leaving your car there to switch to sea transportation.

KHAO LAMPI-HAT THAI MUANG NATIONAL PARK
อุทยานแห่งชาติเขาลำปี-หาดท้ายเหมือง

The Khao Lampi-Hat Thai Muang National Park (Mu 5, Amphoe Thai Muang, Phang Nga, tel. 08/4059-7879 or 07/641-7206, 8:30 A.M.–6 P.M. daily, 400B) is a small national park on just over 7,200 hectares of land and water that is best known for some spectacular waterfalls, including the **Namtok Lampi,** a three-tiered waterfall that runs all year. The waterfall is about 13 kilometers from the park headquarters on the beach; to get there you'll need to drive most of the way along the main road (there are plenty of signs for the waterfall) and then take a short walk to the falls.

Another great waterfall to explore is **Namtok Ton Phrai,** the largest in the park (although like most waterfalls in the country, it will be less impressive during dry season). These falls are about 11 kilometers from the park's headquarters on the beach, and there are marked roads from there. There is also a ranger station here and a canteen, as it is one of the most popular spots in the park. If you're looking for a quiet beach, **Hat Thai Muang** is a 13-kilometer stretch of sandy beach with clear blue waters. If you visit November–February, you may see **sea turtles** coming to lay their eggs on shore at night, and park rangers collecting the eggs to incubate them safe from poachers or predators in their nursery (this is the main reason the beach is a protected national park). In March there's a festival in which locals and visitors watch the little baby turtles make their way to the sea after hatching.

The park has both bungalows for rent and camping areas where you can pitch a tent. There are some small food vendors around during the day in addition to the canteen at Namtok Lampi.

Getting There

By car from Phuket airport or anywhere on Highway 4, head straight north to Phang Nga on Highway 4 for about 56 kilometers to the Tai Muang Market, where you'll see a sign for the national park. Turn off the main road onto Route 401 for about 6.5 kilometers.

There are frequent buses from Bangkok to Phang Nga, which often traverse the popular Highway 4 and terminate in Phuket; they cost 400–500B for an air-conditioned bus. From Phang Nga to the park, you can pick up a normal local bus for about 30B or an air-conditioned bus for 45B.

BO DAN HOT SPRINGS
น้ำพุร้อนบ้านบ่อดาน

If you want a hot-spring experience without going to a spa, the Bo Dan Hot Springs

THE ANDAMAN COAST

(6 A.M.–9 P.M. daily, 10B) are hot mineral springs that locals swear will relieve arthritis and mental and physical stress. Even if it's not the cure-all it's hyped to be, bathing in the springs is a fun experience, and the surrounding greenery is relaxing.

Getting There
The springs are on a side road a few kilometers off of Highway 4. When you reach Khok Kloi, look for the turnoff; there will be a sign for the hot springs. A taxi from Takua Pa costs at least 1,000B.

TAKUA PA
ตะกั่วป่า
Just an hour's drive from the Phuket airport is Takua Pa Province, although it's often referred to as Khao Lak (the name of a part of the province). Despite being literally washed away by the 2004 tsunami, the area is once again an up-and-coming resort area with beautiful beaches, scenic mountain ranges with rainforest in the background, and some luxurious resorts and quaint bungalows. Although more travelers are visiting the area every year, especially in Khao Lak, and you'll see some big brand-name accommodations, it still feels much quieter and more relaxed than any beach you'll find on Phuket.

Khao Lak-Lam Ru National Park
อุทยานแห่งชาติเขาหลัก-ลำรู่
Spanning four provinces, the Khao Lak-Lam Ru National Park (8:30 A.M.–6 P.M. daily, 400B), named after the large mountain within its borders, Khao Lak, has kilometers of pristine beach and thick forest. There are a number of small waterfalls, including the Lam Ru waterfall, a five-tiered waterfall hidden amid thick trees. During the day the park is populated not only with visitors but also with beautiful butterflies and exotic birds. If you feel like camping, there is a campground with some limited facilities and just a few bungalows available for rent. Khao Lak Beach is also part of the park, and although parts of the beach are too rocky for swimming, there are some sandy patches

where you can lay out a towel and enjoy the view of the Andaman Sea.

Beaches and Islands
The **Khao Lak Beach** region, close to the bridge connecting Phuket with the mainland, offers clean, quiet stretches of beach with amazing crystal-clear waters. From north to south, there are three beaches in the stretch called Khao Lak—Bang Niang, Nang Thong, and Sunset—and together they take up about eight kilometers of coastline. Khao Lak has traditionally been a hangout for divers, since it's an easy place to set off to the Similan or Surin Islands, and thus remains a laid-back, rustic place to visit. There are lots of dive shops, a handful of restaurants, and the Andaman Sea to keep you occupied.

About 32 kilometers north of Khao Lak is **Bang Sak,** even less developed than its neighbor to the north, which has attracted some luxury resorts in the past few years. There's no nightlife in the area, but if you're looking for a place to be based for some diving or looking to enjoy the water and the convenience of the Phuket airport without dealing with crowds, this is a great spot. The beach is really spectacular: The shore is wide and flat, and the white sands are smooth and relatively unmarred by rocks.

Accommodations
Ocean Breeze Resort (26/3 Mu 7, Kuk Kak, Takua Pa, www.gerdnoi.com, tel. 07/648-5145, 1,800B), formerly called Gerd & Noi Bungalows, isn't very fancy, but it is located right on the beach and has clean, very family-friendly accommodations. The larger bungalows can easily sleep a small family, and there's a small swimming pool and a restaurant serving Thai and European food. The vibe is like old Khao Lak—laid-back and unpretentious.

If you plan to spend some time doing a live-aboard diving trip to the outer islands, the **Kuraburi Greenview** (140/89 Mu 3, Kura, Kuraburi, tel. 07/640-1400, 1,900B) has some charming cabins in which to base yourself at super-budget prices. The cabins and guest rooms look like they would be more appropriate in New England than Southeast Asia, with lots of exposed wood and rocks along with views of the grounds. The hotel runs lots of dive and snorkeling trips and can arrange live-aboards on their boats, but the hotel itself is not right on the water.

Just south of Bang Sak, **Baan Khao Lak Resort** (26/16 Mu 7, Phetchakasem Rd., Kuk Kak, Takua Pa, tel. 07/648-5198, www.baankhaolak.com, 3,500B) is a great value, even during the high season. All of the guest rooms and villas are modern, stylish, and well maintained, and the grounds of this resort on the beach are lushly landscaped and have lots of amenities you wouldn't expect for the price, including a pool right on the beach, restaurants, and an outdoor beach bar. This is a family-friendly property and also one of the rare resorts in the country that have wheelchair-accessible rooms and grounds.

Set on Bang Niang, **La Flora** (59/1 Mu 5 Kuk Kak, Takua Pa, tel. 07/642-8000, 5,500B) is a surprisingly large resort, with over 100 guest rooms and villas set on a quiet stretch of beach. The guest rooms are spacious and designed with a modern Thai theme, and the best are the villas on the beach. While the area may be quiet, the resort's restaurants, spa, gorgeous swimming pool, and even free Wi-Fi will keep you occupied.

For a smaller resort experience, **Baan Krating Resort** (28 Mu 7, Kuk Kak, Takua Pa, tel. 07/648-5188 or 07/648-5189, 2,000B), next to Khao Lak National Park, has rustic grounds set in the cliffs overlooking the ocean and peppered with wooden bungalows connected via walkway. Each of the guest rooms is individually decorated, but you won't have to do without nice sheets and decent baths if you decide to stay here, as the bungalows, although not brand new, are definitely not in the budget category. The pool and common areas are small, as is the resort, but there's a restaurant on the premises, and the view of Khao Lak Bay is amazing. This is definitely a place for the young and agile: Depending on where your bungalow is, you may be climbing stairs.

The **Suwan Palm Resort** (30/27 Mu 7, Kuk Kak, Takua Pa, tel. 07/648-5830, www.suwan-palm.com, 3,000B) is on the same beach as some of Khao Lak's most expensive properties, and although it's not a luxury chain, it does offer guests clean, modern guest rooms, a nice swimming pool, a bar and restaurant on the premises, and even a small spa. The facilities are small but sufficient for those whose primary goal is to enjoy the beach. Low season rates can be an excellent value.

The **Ramada Resort Khao Lak** (59 Mu 5, Kuk Kak, Takua Pa, tel. 07/642-7777, 3,500B), though not quite as nice as Le Meridien, is a nice new resort set on a beautiful strip of beach. The guest rooms are large and modern, and some have unobstructed views of the Andaman Sea. Pool villas are compact but a great value for those who want some privacy. The property's main swimming pool, which is just behind the beach, is massive. There is also a spa, a fitness center, and an activity program for kids.

◖ **Le Meridien Khao Lak** (9/9 Mu 1, Kuk Kak, Takua Pa, tel. 07/642-7500, www.starwoodhotels.com, 5,000B) is one of the nicest resorts in the area. The nine-hectare grounds are lush and well manicured, with a large child-friendly pool and direct beach access. The guest rooms are modern, airy, and comfortable, with dark-wood details and crisp linens. The villas are spacious, although they can cost significantly more than the rooms. There's a beautiful spa on the premises and a charming Thai restaurant. Although this is a large chain resort, there's no generic feeling here.

The small, luxurious **Sarojin** (60 Mu 2, Kuk Kak, Takua Pa, tel. 07/648-5830, www.sarojin.com, 7,000B) resort, located right on the beach, has large, comfortable guest rooms and suites filled with modern Thai-style furnishings. The grounds are lush and spacious and include shaded *salas* for lounging at the large modern pool as well as a high-end spa. The resort's restaurant and bar options are a little pricey, but the breakfast, included in most rates, has lots of variety and is served till late. Service in general is excellent and attentive, and this is a great choice for a romantic getaway or honeymoon.

Just south of the Khao Lak area, and only a few kilometers from the Sarasin Bridge to Phuket, is the 🄲 **Aleenta Phang-Nga** (33 Mu 5, Khok Kloi, Takua Pa, tel. 02/508-5333, www.aleenta.com, 12,000B), at the top of the class of small boutique resorts in Thailand. The villas are swanky and contemporary, with a blend of Mediterranean and Thai styling; some are full apartments with living areas and small private pools. The common areas are small, but the restaurant has an excellent East-West menu. Little touches, including iPods in every guest room and scented oil burners, will make you feel pampered. This is definitely a place you're likely to find incognito movie stars.

Getting There

The easiest way to get to Phang Nga is to fly into Phuket International Airport. Since the airport is in the northern part of the island, it's less than an hour's drive from the Sarasin Bridge to Phang Nga. Metered taxis from the airport will drive you to Phang Nga for 300–1,000B, depending on where you're going. If you're heading for Khao Lak, expect to pay around 700B.

If you're driving, Phang Nga is best reached by car by driving along Highway 4 until you reach Phang Nga, which will be well signed in English.

Buses running from Bangkok to Phuket will always stop in Phang Nga along the way as long as you let the driver know that's where you're going (since Phang Nga is the only land crossing to the island).

KO PHRA THONG

เกาะพระทอง

Separated from the mainland by a channel, mudflats, and mangroves, this little island, just 90 square kilometers, is named Phra Thong, or golden Buddha, based on a legend that shipwrecked pirates buried a gold statue of the Buddha somewhere on the island. These days, there are no pirates around, and the treasure

has never been found, but the island is home to a handful of fishing villages and just a couple of ecofriendly resorts. The beaches on the west side of the island are beautiful, serene, and relatively untouched by commercialism. In addition to the mangroves, sea grass, and patches of rainforest, the island is home to macaques, otters, and lemurs, to name just a few of the small animals you might run into. It's also home to sea turtles that come to bury their eggs on the shore every year. Although the island and neighboring Ko Ra together form one of the newest national parks in the country, there are no national park amenities.

Sports and Recreation

There are plentiful opportunities to hike and walk the island, although there are no established marked trails. If you are staying on the island, the resort will provide you with a map of the areas you can safely explore.

Accommodations

The Golden Buddha Resort (tel. 08/7055-4099, 3,500B) is a small, quiet, ecofriendly resort on the west coast of the island. Here you'll find beach yoga and wooden bungalows close to the water, without the typical crowds or prices. You have to forgo luxuries such as air-conditioning and reliable Internet access, but if you're looking for a quiet, remote place on the shore, this is a beautiful spot to relax and unwind. There are also larger houses available for groups.

You can also camp on the island, as it's a national park, although right now there are no bungalows, tent rentals, or canteens, so you have to bring everything you need with you, including water.

Food

There's really no tourism infrastructure set up on the island, so finding food is challenging. If you're staying at the island's resort, they'll make sure to feed you. Otherwise, you may be able to find someone to prepare a meal for you in the villages, slightly inland. If you're coming for the day or camping, pack food and water.

Getting There

To get to Ko Phra Thong, you'll first have to find your way to the Kuraburi pier. If you're driving, take Highway 4 to the Kuraburi district, which is south of Ranong Province and north of Takua Pa and Si Phang Nga National Park. From the pier in Kuraburi, there are no scheduled boats. You can either negotiate with a longtail captain to take you, or if you are staying at the Golden Buddha Resort, they will arrange to have someone pick you up. Expect to pay 1,000–1,500B each way, even if you arrange it through the hotel.

SI PHANG NGA NATIONAL PARK
อุทยานแห่งชาติศรีพังงา

Mostly rainforest on a rugged mountain range, Si Phang Nga National Park (8:30 A.M.–6 P.M. daily, 400B) has the 60-meter-high **Namtok Tam Nang** waterfall and a number of smaller waterfalls. There are a limited number of marked trails in the park; on them are ample opportunities to spot rare birds, including hornbills. There are small bungalows for rent as well as a camping ground, but this park, unlike most others in the region, does not have a beach. Although the names are similar, this is not the same park as Ao Phang Nga National Park.

Sports and Recreation

There are a few short marked hiking trails in the park. The nicest is actually the shortest, at just over 1.5 kilometers, starting at the **Tam Nang waterfall.** From there, you head up to a viewpoint in the forest where you can see the mangrove swamps edging out into the sea.

Getting There

The national park is located between Kuraburi and Takua Pa on Highway 4. If you're driving, you'll see signs from the highway for the national park and the Tam Nang waterfall. Follow signs for either, as the park's headquarters are right next to the waterfall. The park is east of Highway 4.

Krabi
กระบี่

With a rugged coastline and white sandy beaches, the former fishing area of Krabi is probably the most beautiful province on the mainland of Thailand if you're looking for a beach destination. Like the island of Phuket, Krabi has a mountainous green interior broken up by highlands and some plains as well as an irregular coastline creating lots of small bays and beaches. Right off the coast of Krabi are some of the most beautiful limestone rock formations in the Andaman Sea, which offer great opportunities for rock climbing, if you're feeling adventurous, or sea kayaking through some of the caves worn into the rocks, if you prefer a less strenuous approach. The best beaches in Krabi are located in the center of the province, around Rai Le and Nang, and you'll have to see them to understand just how beautiful a simple beach can be. It's not just the water and the sand, although the crystal-clear blue Andaman Sea and clean, fine sand certainly help. It's the surrounding cliffs and luxuriant tree greenery as well as the view to the small islands off the coast that create a landscape like nowhere else in the world. Krabi Province is also technically home to some of the best islands in region—Ko Phi Phi and Ko Lanta—although many people will travel to these from Phuket or Trang, as they are about halfway between those locations and Krabi. Although Krabi certainly has its share of luxury resorts catering to vacationers' every whim, the region is nowhere near as built-up as Phuket is. Getting to some of the popular beaches involves taking a boat from the mainland—although Krabi is not an island, there are many spots where no roads go. Maybe because it is slightly less accessible, Krabi also has a more rugged feel to it.

THE ANDAMAN COAST

© SUZANNE NAM

mainland Krabi

KRABI TOWN
เมืองกระบี่

Most people pass through Krabi Town on their way to the beaches or skirt it entirely on their way from the Krabi airport to the boat pier. While there's no reason to stay in Krabi Town unless you're on a really tight budget, as it's not close to the beach and the available accommodations are not quite up to international standards, it's an interesting place to spend a few hours, if only to see what life is like away from the beaches. The town is set on the Krabi River, an estuary that empties into the Andaman Sea farther down, and there are some picturesque wooden houses built on stilts, although you may find some of the town less charming and appealing due to its urbanized feel. Krabi Town does have some of the most interesting and creative statues–cum–traffic lights in Thailand. If that's not enough to hold your attention for very long (they're not *that* interesting), there's also a **night market** (Khong Kha Rd., right next to the Chao Fa pier, 6–10 P.M. daily) where visitors often stop to take photos or grab a snack from one of the curry stalls or *satay* vendors. The **Maharat Market,** on Maharat Soi 9, opens at 3 A.M. and closes by midday daily. It's one of the largest indoor markets in the country, and although you probably won't be taking home any of the seafood or produce on offer, it's worth looking at.

BEACHES
Ao Nang Bay
อ่าวนาง

The large, sweeping Ao Nang Bay is the most popular beach area in Krabi, with scores of accommodations, including many large international chains. Although nowhere near as hopping as Patong, Ao Nang is nonetheless a very touristy, slightly generic resort area. Still, the physical landscape surrounding the bay is impressive—there are scores of different small islands and rock formations in view. Ao Nang also serves as a jumping-off point for day trips to the surrounding islands. Unfortunately, the beach itself is not swimmable all the time because of the boat traffic.

© SUZANNE NAM

Rai Le Beach

◖ Rai Le Beach
หาดไร่เลย์

The small Rai Le Beach, surrounded by lime-stone cliffs behind and large rock formations rising from the sea in front, is the most beautiful of the beaches in Krabi and arguably one of the most beautiful in all of Thailand. Since Rai Le is an isthmus jutting off the mainland, there are actually two Rai Le beaches, one to the east and one to the west. With crystal-clear blue waters, soft sand, and only a handful of resorts and small restaurants right near the beach, **West Rai Le** is both breathtaking and totally relaxed. **East Rai Le** also has lovely surrounding scenery, but it's actually mostly mudflats, and there's no sand and nowhere to lay out a towel. But that's not a problem, as you can easily walk to sandy West Rai Le in 10–15 minutes if you're staying on the east side, where accommodations are generally less expensive.

Noppharat Thara Beach
หาดนพรัตน์ธารา

Just adjacent to Ao Nang is Noppharat Thara, a long sandy beach that's technically part of a national park. Lined with casuarina trees and just a handful of amenities, this is a great beach for hanging out if you're looking for something quiet and peaceful but close to the more happening Ao Nang.

Tham Phra Nang Beach
หาดถ้ำพระนาง

Just a short walk from Rai Le at the end of the peninsula, this small, secluded beach is bordered by a rocky headland on one side and limestone cliffs on the other. There's also a mystical cave here—**Tham Phra Nang Nok,** or Princess Cave—believed by local fisherfolk to house a sea princess. Although so far she hasn't been sighted by any travelers, you can check out the interesting offerings that are left for her in the cave.

SPORTS AND RECREATION
Rock Climbing

Krabi has the best rock climbing in the country, thanks to the beautiful limestone mountains

THE ANDAMAN COAST

and the built-up rock climbing industry. There are hundreds of bolted routes that will take you as high as 300 meters at varying levels of difficulty. This is not a sport to try without some training or proper equipment, but fortunately there are at least half a dozen rock-climbing shops offering lessons, rentals, and guided tours. Total beginners can take either full-day (2,000B) or half-day (1,000B) lessons, which include on-the-ground training and climbing. Those with experience can either hire a guide to explore the many routes in the area or just rent the necessary equipment and pick up a map from any of the shops.

Wee and Elke of **Basecamp Tonsai** (Ton Sai Beach, next to Ton Sai Bay Resort, www.basecamptonsai.com), formerly Wee's Climbing School, literally wrote the book on rock climbing in Krabi. You can buy their newly updated guide at their shop or take one of the half-day, full-day, or multiple-day classes they offer. Their shop also sells and rents an extensive selection of equipment. **Hot Rock** (Rai Le Beach West, tel. 07/562-1771, www.railayadventure. com) is also highly recommended because of the professionalism and personalities of their guides. They offer instruction for beginners and tours for advanced climbers. Their shop also sells and rents equipment.

Kayaking

The uneven coastline, mangrove forests, and scores of rock outcroppings and islands make Krabi an excellent area to explore with a kayak. Many guided kayaking tours (around 1,500B for a full day) leave from Ao Nang. On a typical tour, you'll spend some time paddling through the nearby mangrove forests and also set out to explore some of the small islands and sea caves that have been created through thousands of years of erosion. **Sea Canoe Thailand** (Ao Nang, tel. 07/569-5387) is one of about half a dozen companies offering daily kayak tours.

On Rai Le Beach West, there are rental kayaks available right on the beach(400B for the day). Inexperienced kayakers should be aware that currents can be surprisingly strong and that longtail boats, speedboats, and larger vessels are frequently in the water and may not see you.

Snorkeling

The islands around Krabi, including Ko Phi Phi, have some of the best snorkeling in the country, and it's quite possible to see not only amazingly colorful tropical fish and coral gardens with just a snorkel and a mask, but you might even spot some reef sharks. While many people choose to enjoy snorkeling on one of the day tours offered by dive shops and travel agents in Krabi, it is also possible to charter a longtail boat to take you out on your own. If you're going the prepackaged-tour route, **Kon-Tiki Thailand Diving & Snorkeling Center** (61/1 Mu 2, Ao Nang, tel. 07/563-7675, www. kontiki-krabi.com) offers snorkel-only excursions (850B) instead of the usual boat tour of the area with snorkeling tacked on. Their tours will take you to Ko Phi Phi and the Mu Ko Hong islands, and since they're focused on snorkeling you'll spend as much time as possible in the water.

If you'd prefer to go out on your own, longtail boats can take you out to the smaller islands around Ao Nang and will generally know where you'll be able to see fish or coral. There are scores of private longtail captains in Ao Nang and West Rai Le available; prices for personalized trips are entirely negotiable, but you should expect to pay at least 1,000B for a few hours on the sea. Longtail boats are smaller, less comfortable, and slower than speedboats (and life preservers are generally nonexistent), so if you are planning on going out on one, it's best done for shorter distances.

ACCOMMODATIONS
Ao Nang

If you want to avoid the big properties, **The Buri Tara Resort** (159/1 Mu 3, Ao Nang, tel. 07/563-8277, www.buritara.net, 3,500B), with only 69 guest rooms, is a smart, stylish choice in the budget-luxury category. The pool isn't as large as what you'll find at other resorts, and it's a few minutes' walk to the closest beach, but the property opened at the end of 2006 and the guest rooms are nicely decorated in a modern dark-wood style with some Thai touches.

The small, charming **Alis Hotel** (125 Ao Nang, tel. 07/563-8000, www.alisthailand. com, 2,500B) has a unique Mediterranean design and comfortable guest rooms with luxurious baths. For nice guest rooms and a good location about 10 minutes from the beach, it's a good choice. There's a nice rooftop pool and a bar on the premises, but the grounds aren't massive, and the lack of things like elevators are a reminder that it's not quite a boutique resort but rather a small hotel.

Although not as beautifully kept up as the Centara Grand, the large **Krabi La Playa Resort** (143 Mu 3, Ao Nang, tel. 07/563-7015 to 07/563-7020, www.krabilaplaya.com, 5,100B) has a great pool area and roomy, well-furnished guest rooms done in a modern Thai style. It is right on the beach and an easy walk to town. Some of the guest rooms have swim-up access to the pool.

The **Cliff Ao Nang Resort** (85/2 Mu 2, Ao Nang, tel. 07/563-8117, www.k-bi.com, 8,000B) is a beautiful property with many design elements from traditional bungalows but completely modern, comfortable guest rooms. Although there are some rustic elements, they're purely aesthetic—there's not a trace of backpacker to be found. The semi-outdoor baths are spacious and have rain showerheads, the restaurant is elegant, and the pool is large and minimalist so as not to detract from the natural beauty found in the surrounding cliffs and ocean. This is definitely a hip, romantic resort designed for couples, although kids are welcome.

The **Centara Grand Beach Resort and Villas** (396–396/1 Mu 2, Ao Nang, tel. 07/563-7789, www.centralhotelsresorts.com, 8,000B) has large, beautiful guest rooms with stunning ocean views, top-class resort amenities, and excellent service, all set on its own small private bay with a small beach right next to Ao Nang. If you don't feel like leaving the compound, there are five different places to eat within Centara as well as a spa and multiple swimming pools. If you're looking for a big resort experience in Krabi, this is probably the best price you'll find in the category, and especially in the off-season, when you'll pay about half the price; it's a bargain.

Rai Le Beach

Since it's set on the mudflats side of Rai Le, you'll have to walk about 15 minutes to get to the good part of the beach from **Sunrise Tropical Resort** (39 Mu 2 Ao Nang, Rai Le Beach, tel. 07/562-2599, www.sunrisetropical.com, 3,500B), but it is a great value if you want to stay in a well-appointed beach bungalow without paying five-star resort prices. The bungalows are modern, spacious, and clean, the baths have outdoor showers and are nicely fitted, and the grounds are leafy. The larger villas are enormous for the price. Although it's a small property with only 28 bungalows, there's a pool, a small restaurant, and an Internet café.

If you can get one of the bungalows at **Railei Beach Club** (Rai Le Beach, Ao Nang, tel. 07/562-2582, www.raileibeachclub. com, 5,000B), consider yourself lucky. A cluster of houses set right on the beach, this is neither a resort nor a hotel. Each of the homes is individually owned and rented out by owners when they're not in town, and they vary in size from cozy bungalow to four-bedroom house. The design of each is a little different, but they're all wooden bungalow houses with clean, comfortable bedrooms and baths. Some have elegant dark-wood furnishings; others are a little more rustic. The larger buildings have their own kitchens and entertaining space, perfect for a family or larger group, or a couple that wants to spend an extended time. There's no pool, although it is set on what is arguably the most beautiful part of the beach. Although it's not a resort, there's daily maid service, and if you want, they'll arrange to have someone come to your bungalow and cook dinner for you.

"Beach bungalow" doesn't do the **Rayavadee Premier** (214 Mu 2, Ao Nang, tel. 02/301-1850, www.rayavadee.com, 15,000B) justice. The individual accommodations are more like small luxury homes set in a quiet, secluded part of the beach. This is one of the most indulgent places to stay on Rai Le, as is clear from the hefty rates you'll pay. The property has nearly 100 bungalows, so there are lots of amenities, including tennis courts, a fitness center, and a handful of restaurants. While most people staying on Rai Le have to arrive at the pier on the east side of the beach and walk to their resort, the Rayavadee will arrange to have a private boat pick you up from Krabi Town and deliver you straight to the resort. Despite the high prices, peak season fills up months in advance, so book quickly if you're interested in staying here.

FOOD
Krabi Town
Hands down the best Thai restaurant in Krabi Town, both for food and ambience, is **(Ruen Mai** (315/5 Maharat Rd., tel. 07/563-1797, 11 A.M.–10 P.M. daily, 200B). It may be filled with travelers, but don't be put off. It's worth feeling like a lemming to enjoy a meal in this verdant garden setting. The curries and other typical Thai dishes are well executed, but for something different, try the crunchy *plai sai* fried fish snacks or *kaeng som* sour curry with fish. This is also a great place for vegetarians. Although there aren't many straight veggie offerings on the menu, the kitchen will prepare just about anything you want without meat.

For a distinctly southern-Thailand breakfast dish, head to **Kanom Jin Mae Weaw** (137 Krabi–Khao Thong Rd., next to the PTT gas station, tel. 07/561-2666, 7 A.M.–noon daily, 50B) for some *kanom chin*—curry served over thin rice noodles. This very casual place has three different varieties and serves them spicy. For Western palates it may feel more appropriate to have this for dinner, but it's a morning meal, so get there early to try it.

Ao Nang
For seafood on the beach, **Wangsai Seafood Restaurant** (98 Mu 3, Ao Nang, tel. 07/563-8128, 10 A.M.–10 P.M. daily, 300B) is a good relaxed restaurant with a view of the ocean and a large deck right on the beach. The large sign is in Thai (it's the only place with no English sign), but the menu has English translations for all the typical Thai seafood dishes, including seafood fried rice and braised fish in lime, chilies, and garlic. The restaurant is quite popular among foreign visitors.

Another popular, solid choice for seafood on the beach is the **Salathai Restaurant** (32 Mu 2, Ao Nang, tel. 07/563-7024, 9 A.M.–10 P.M. daily, 300B). The menu has both traditional Thai dishes with seafood and some Western fare. Better to stick with the local food and seafood, which you can select yourself, and enjoy the view at this charming thatched-roof restaurant right on the water. It's not very fancy, by any standard, but the food and location are just right.

Krua Thara (82 Mu 5, Ao Nang, tel. 07/563-7361, 11 A.M.–9:30 P.M. daily, 200B) has great seafood dishes, whether part of a traditional Thai meal or just plain grilled or fried with Thai sauce. Like most of the places to eat in Krabi, it's nothing fancy to look at, but the food is good.

Rai Le
While Rai Le has some of the best beachfront property in Thailand, it's definitely not a contender for best dining options, and Krabi Town and Ao Nang have much better dining. That's not to say the food is bad, but there isn't much selection—most of it is from bungalow and resort restaurants and the roti vendors on the beach in the afternoon.

GETTING THERE
When planning your trip, remember that Krabi Town is more than 16 kilometers away from the area's main attraction—the beaches.

Air
The Krabi airport has frequent flights from Bangkok and is served by **Thai Airways** and **Bangkok Airways** as well as the budget airlines **Nok Air, Air Asia,** and **One-Two-Go.** If you're coming in from Singapore, **Tiger Airways** also has direct flights from that city. Although the

airport is comfortable and modern, it's very small, and the services inside, including food, are very limited. From the airport, it's about a 30-minute drive to Ao Nang; there are plenty of taxis on hand to take you (400–600B). There is also a private airport shuttle that runs at least every hour (more frequently during high season) between the airport and Ao Nang. The fare is 150B, so if you're traveling with a group, it can be more economical (and faster if you happen to be staying at the last hotel on the route) to take a taxi.

It's also possible to fly into Phuket International Airport and then make the three-hour drive to Krabi. There is a minibus from the Phuket airport that goes to Krabi Town. It leaves three times daily 9 A.M.–1 P.M. for 350B per person.

Boat

If you're coming from Phuket, there is a boat that heads to the **Noppharat Thara pier** next to Ao Nang at 8 A.M. daily and goes back to Phuket at 3 P.M. The ride is about two hours and costs 350B.

Boat connections between Phi Phi and Krabi are frequent, especially during high season. There are ferry boats from Noppharat Thara pier that are currently running once daily at 3 P.M. The ride is about three hours and costs 550B. To get to Krabi from Phi Phi, there are frequent boats during high season, leaving at 9 A.M., 10:30 A.M., and 2:30 P.M.

If you're on Phi Phi, there are also ferries that leave Phi Phi at 9 A.M. for Ao Nang in Krabi and take a little under three hours.

If you are coming from Ko Lanta, boats only run during high season; otherwise you'll have to take a minivan, which involves two short ferry crossings. During high season, ferries from Ko Lanta to Krabi leave at 8 A.M. and 1 P.M. daily, returning at 10:30 A.M. and 2:30 P.M. The cost is 300B pp and takes about 1.5 hours.

Even if you're coming by air or ground transportation to Krabi, if you're staying in Rai Le, you'll have to take a boat to get to your ultimate destination. Although Krabi is on the mainland, there are no roads to Rai Le; you have to take a longtail boat from Ao Nang or Krabi Town. There are frequent boats from the Saphan Chaofa pier that should run around 80B pp (unless you arrive after the scheduled boats have stopped running, in which case you will have to negotiate with the owner of the boat). Your hotel in Rai Le will be able to arrange the transfer for you. The short trip to Rai Le can be a little treacherous, depending on the weather conditions and what you're carrying. The boats stop on Rai Le East beach, and if the tides are in when you arrive, the pier may be partially submerged in water. You have to walk, carrying your luggage, through sometimes knee-deep water, so it is essential that you pack only what you can comfortably lift over your head while walking. Once you get onto dry land, if you're staying on Rai Le West, you'll need to walk about 15 minutes to get to your final location. There are no cars or motorcycles—another reason to pack light. If you happen to be staying at the Rayavadee, they'll arrange a private boat to take you directly to the hotel—they'll even carry your stuff for you.

Bus

There are overnight buses leaving from Bangkok's Southern Bus Terminal at 5:30 P.M. daily for the 12-hour overnight drive to Krabi. Tickets on air-conditioned luxury buses cost 850B and terminate in Krabi Town. Regular air-conditioned buses leave Bangkok at 7 A.M., 4 P.M., and 5:30 P.M. daily and cost 450–600B. There are also frequent buses to Krabi from Phuket, Ko Pha-Ngan, Surat Thani, Trang, and Hat Yai.

Car

It's relatively easy to drive to Krabi. Highway 4, which runs south down the peninsula, is the best way to go and is well signed in English for the correct turnoff to Ao Nang. Once you're in the area, many people find cars totally unnecessary, as most time is spent either on the beach or at one of the many marine sights that can't be reached by road anyway.

THAN BOK KHORANI NATIONAL PARK
อุทยานแห่งชาติธารโบกขรณี

Mostly mountainous rainforests and mangroves, the small Than Bok Khorani National Park (8:30 A.M.–6 P.M. daily, 400B) also has a number of ponds, caves, and streams that seem to disappear under the limestone mountains as well as, of course, sandy beaches. There are also more than 20 small islands, really just rocks jutting out of the ocean, that are a part of the park. The best way to visit the islands is by canoe or kayak, but most do not have beaches, so it's difficult to disembark. Camping is allowed in the park, but amenities are very limited, so you'll have to bring everything with you.

Inside the park is the **Tham Phi Hua To,** which is believed to have been a shelter for prehistoric people living in the area; it has some prehistoric paintings of people and animals. The cave got its name, which means "big-headed ghost cave," because of the number of abnormally large human skulls found in the cave. It is also used by Buddhist monks as a temple and for meditation retreats. The cave is not accessible by land; to visit you have to take a boat. If you aren't already exploring the area by boat, or just want to visit the cave, you can pick up a longtail boat to take you there from the Bo Tho pier in Ao Luek.

Getting There

If you're staying in Ao Nang, you can get to the park either by land or by sea. It's a one-hour drive to the Bo Tho pier in Ao Luek, where you'll be able either to rent a canoe or kayak or charter one of the local boat captains to take you around. If you don't have a car, you can charter a longtail boat from Ao Nang to take you to the park and tour you around the islands (expect to pay around 1,000B for the trip, regardless of the number of passengers), making it a great day trip if you're hanging out in one of the more touristed areas in Krabi.

KHAO PHANOM BENCHA NATIONAL PARK
อุทยานแห่งชาติเขาพนมเบญจา

Another small national park worth visiting for a few hours because of the waterfalls and peaks is Khao Phanom Bencha National Park (8:30 A.M.–6 P.M. daily, 400B). There are some short hiking trails, including one that will take you to the highest point in the area, at more than 1,200 meters, and another that will bring you to a three-tiered waterfall called **Namtok Huay To,** where the water collects into 11 large pools at the base. The Tham Khao Phueng cave has stalagmites and stalactites typical of caves in the region. You can pick up a map of the park at the ranger station; the trails are easy to moderate.

Getting There

Less than 32 kilometers from Krabi Town, Khao Phanom Bencha National Park is best accessed either by car, *tuk tuk,* or motorcycle. If you get a ride from Krabi Town or Ao Nang, it's better to arrange round-trip transport, since when you're done exploring the park, there may not be anyone around to bring you back. If you are driving, take Pracha U Thit Road north out of Krabi Town, until you see Ban Thap Prik Health Center, where you take a left and continue heading north to the ranger station.

KHLONG THOM
คลองท่อม
Sights

The **Khlong Thom hot spring** (10B pp) is worth a visit if you happen to be in the area, particularly for the so-called **Emerald Pool,** where springwater collects in the forest, creating a strangely deep emerald or turquoise color, depending on the time of day. To see the pool at its best, come when the light is soft, either very early in the morning or just before dusk.

Right near the Emerald Pool is the **Ron Khlong Thom Waterfall,** in a part of the forest with lots of small hot springs that flow into cold streams, creating a warm-water waterfall.

The **Khao Pra-Bang Khram Wildlife Sanctuary** (เขตรักษาพันธุ์สัตว์ป่า เขาประ-บางคราม, 8:30 A.M.–6 P.M. daily, 200B), also commonly referred to as Khao Nor Chuchi, has some small trails through lowland forests and past the Emerald Pool. The sanctuary is considered the single richest site for birds in the whole region, and you're likely to spot black hornbills and kingfishers. Gurney's Pitta, of which there are less than 100 pairs estimated to exist on the planet, are known to nest in this area. There is also camping in the sanctuary, although unlike the national parks, there are no tent rentals, so you have to come equipped.

If you're interested in archaeology, the **Wat Khlong Thom Museum** at Wat Khlong Thom houses numerous items found during an excavation of Kuan Luk Pat, commonly referred to in English as the bead mound. Items on display include tools from the Stone and Bronze Ages, pieces of pottery, coins, and colored beads said to be more than 5,000 years old.

Getting There

To get to Khlong Thom, drive on Highway 4 heading south from Krabi Town; Khlong Thom will be marked at the junction of Highway 4 and Route 4038. From there, you will see well-marked signs directing you to the Emerald Pool or the wildlife sanctuary. You can also take a public bus headed for Trang from the bus terminal outside Krabi Town and tell the driver when you board that you want to get off at Khlong Thom. These buses run nearly hourly during the day, and you'll spend less than 30B to get to Khlong Thom. You'll end up in a small town area and will have to find transport to the surrounding sites, but during the day there are plenty of motorcycles that will take you. Although you can sometimes find a ride back from the sanctuary or the Emerald Pool, it's best to arrange round-trip transport at least back to Khlong Thom, where you can catch a bus heading for Krabi or Trang for the rest of your journey.

Mu Ko Phi Phi หมู่เกาะพีพี

In recent years it seems the rest of the world has discovered what residents and intrepid travelers knew all along—the Ko Phi Phi islands, a small group of islands in Krabi Province about 40 kilometers off of the west coast of the mainland and just south of Phang Nga Bay, are lush and beautiful, the surrounding waters warm and clear, and the marinelife astounding. The discovery may have something to do with the Leonardo DiCaprio movie *The Beach,* which was filmed in the area. Certainly the movie helped put the islands on the map, but it's the physical beauty and ease with which you can go from lazing around on the beach to snorkeling or scuba diving that will make sure it stands the test of time.

The largest island of the group and the only one with tourist accommodations, Ko Phi Phi Don is shaped like two separate islands connected together by a thin strip of land with sandy beaches on each side. The beaches along that isthmus, Ton Sai Bay on the south and Loh Dalam Bay on the north, have become very popular for day-trippers and those staying on the island. The island is only about 16 kilometers long, and there are no roads or motorized transportation to take you from one part to another. Instead, there are plenty of longtail boats that function like shuttle buses and taxis. The rest of the islands in the group can easily be visited via a short ride on a longtail boat taxi from Phi Phi Don, or on a longer two-hour ferry or tour boat if you're coming from Phuket or Krabi.

Originally inhabited by Muslim fisherfolk, Phi Phi Don has changed dramatically in recent years. Ton Sai Bay is jam-packed with restaurants and small shops selling everything from sunglasses to T-shirts. Where there were once only a few simple bungalows, there are now full-scale resorts with swimming pools, spas, and anything else a traveler might be interested in, although in a much lower-key manner than you'll see on Phuket. If you're visiting Phi Phi or one of the surrounding islands for the day, you'll notice scores of speedboats and ferries moored close to the shore, all bringing in visitors who can crowd the beaches during high season. Residents and enlightened guests do their best to keep the island clean, but at times you will notice some wear and tear from the hundreds of visitors that come to the island every day. It's a shame, because Phi Phi is probably one of the most beautiful islands in the Andaman region, and it increasingly feels like its beauty is on the edge of being spoiled by overly eager tour operators and irresponsible visitors.

Neighboring, smaller Ko Phi Phi Le is a stunning limestone island encircling emerald-green Maya Bay. There are no accommodations on Phi Phi Le, but it has become a huge tourist draw, with day-trippers visiting by the hundreds per day during high season. With the throngs of other people and scores of motorboats in the bay, it's amazing that the island continues to look as beautiful as it does.

BEACHES
◖ Ton Sai Bay
หาดต้นไทร
The beaches along Ton Sai Bay, including **Hin**

Khom Beach and Long Beach (Hat Yao), are stunningly beautiful, with white sand and mountain ranges off in the distance as well as some great opportunities for viewing the coral just off the coast. This beach area, however, is the most popular, and right behind the beach there are scores of guesthouses, bungalows, and even some bars and shops. If you want a budget backpacker experience in paradise, this is where you'll probably end up. This is also a popular place for day visitors to hang out, meaning it can become very crowded during high season.

Ranti Beach
อ่าวรันตี
Off the east coast of the larger part of Phi Phi Don, this beach has fewer accommodations and can only be reached from Ton Sai Bay on foot, or by speedboat or longtail, so pack light if you are planning on staying here. The beach itself is as beautiful as the rest of the island, and there is plentiful coral to view right off the coast. If you're looking for budget bungalows but want to avoid Ton Sai, Ranti is a great place to stay.

boats along Ton Sai Bay

© SUZANNE NAM

Maya Bay, Ko Phi Phi Le

Phak Nam Beach
อ่าวผักหนาม

Phak Nam has the same clear blue water and soft sand but is even more secluded than Ranti, with very few accommodations, though this will probably be changing soon in light of all the development going on in the region. To get to this beach, you can either hike to the east side of the island or take a water taxi.

Laem Thong Beach
หาดแหลมตง

Way at the northern tip of the island, Laem Thong is one of the quieter areas, with a long white-sand beach and only a few accommodations. This area, at a point when the island thins out to only about 200 meters wide, has a quiet, peaceful atmosphere and a handful of high-end resorts. It can be a little difficult to get to if you're coming from Ton Sai Bay, as it's too far to walk, and you have to travel by water, but the beach has its own pier, so you can skip the crowds and commotion and head straight here from the mainland instead.

Ko Phi Phi Le
เกาะพีพีเล

On Phi Phi Le there are no accommodations but some beautiful places to visit either from the mainland or from Phi Phi Don.

Amazing emerald-colored waters and large rock formations characterize **Maya Bay** (อ่าวมาหยา), a tiny bay on the east side of Phi Phi Le. Once you enter the bay, you'll be astounded by the beauty of the surrounding physical landscape. There's a small beach for swimming with rocky outcroppings overhead and even a tiny bit of rainforest to walk around in. There are no overnight accommodations on Maya Bay, but the place gets packed with day-trippers, so try to arrive early to enjoy a bit of the beauty without the crowds. You can go by longtail boat or speedboat, or paddle over on your own. The bay itself is not great for snorkeling (especially because it's usually filled with boats), but if you walk across the island and through a small cave (you can't miss it, as there's only one path you can walk on), there's some better snorkeling off of that

DIVING ON THE ANDAMAN COAST

The waters surrounding the Andaman coast and its islands offer an amazing diversity of marine-life and dive sites from beginner to advanced, some considered among the best in the world. Hundreds of dive shops offer courses, equipment rental, day trips, and live-aboards (where you live aboard a boat for a few days). If you're planning on diving in the region, don't worry too much about where you are staying relative to the areas where you want to dive; most diving shops (especially in Phuket) offer dives to all of the most popular sites in the region. When deciding where to dive, take advantage of the many resources on the Internet. One excellent resource is **Dive Guide Thailand** (www.dive-guidethailand.com), which offers a free downloadable guide to diving in the region.

PHUKET AREA

The area surrounding the main island offers some good diving day trips. **Ko Racha Noi** is a popular place to visit on a day trip and has a nice mix of both colorful coral and challenging, rocky terrain. Another very popular destination is **Shark Point,** about 32 kilometers east of Chalong Bay. There are three rock outcroppings that attract – as the name implies – sharks (mostly leopard sharks). Just under one kilometer away is **Anemone Reef,** with lots of anemone, coral, and plenty of colorful small fish. If you're interested in wreck diving, close by is **King Cruiser Wreck,** a sunken car ferry in Phang Nga Bay. This site is appropriate for most divers and attracts lots of fish. Other wrecks near Phuket, including **SS Petaling, HMS Squirrel,** and **HMS Vestal,** are considered technical dives and can only be visited by experienced divers.

KO PHI PHI AREA

The waters surrounding Ko Phi Phi offer both nice diving and excellent snorkeling. The biggest attraction here is the colorful coral and vibrant fish. Most of the dives are not difficult, but divers looking for more of a challenge can check out the wall diving at **Ao Nui.**

KO LANTA AREA

South of Ko Lanta are some excellent (and con-venient) dive sites. The Mu Ko Lanta National Marine Park is a group of 15 small islands, many with good diving in surrounding areas. You'll find lots of rocky terrain attracting colorful fish, some underwater caves to explore, and beautiful coral. The **Ko Kradan Wreck** is now an artificial reef.

MERGUI ARCHIPELAGO

This archipelago, technically in Burma's waters, has only been open to international visitors for a decade and offers some interesting off-the-beaten-path diving opportunities. The draw of these islands is in the very rocky underwater terrain and interesting marinelife. You'll have lots of opportunities to swim with sharks, including hammerheads, reef, nurse, and bull sharks, as well as plenty of rays. These dive sites are only accessible on live-aboard trips.

SURIN ISLANDS

These islands are part of the Mu Ko Surin National Marine Park and are best known for the excellent coral surrounding them. The biggest draw is **Richelieu Rock,** a rock pinnacle jutting out of the ocean that's known to attract giant, gentle whale sharks. These islands are accessible by live-aboard trips from Phuket, but if you're staying in Khao Lak, you can visit on a day trip.

SIMILAN ISLANDS

These nine granite islands make up the Mu Ko Similan National Marine Park and are considered by most to offer the best diving in Thailand and some of the best diving in the world. Here you'll find plenty of colorful reefs and plankton blooms (during the hot season) attracting sharks, rays, and plenty of tropical fish. Other parts of the island grouping are more rugged, with boulder formations offering more adventurous diving. There are also great night-diving spots where you'll see squid, crustaceans, and other creatures. These islands can be visited on day trips from Phuket and Khao Lak, but many people choose multiple-day live-aboards.

CERTIFICATION

In Thailand most diving instruction courses offer

PADI (www.padi.com) open-water diver certification. These courses take 3-4 days, at the end of which you'll be certified to dive all over the world. You'll spend time in the classroom first learning about safety and dive theory, take your first dive in a swimming pool, and advance to supervised open-water dives. Expect to pay 10,000-15,000B for the full course, including equipment and dives. If you can't imagine wasting hours inside a classroom while you're on vacation, and assuming there is a PADI training center where you live, you can do the classroom and pool-diving components of your training at home and bring your referral paperwork with you to Thailand, where you'll be able to complete the open-water portion of the certification.

Certified divers looking to advance their skills can also take **dive master** courses, become certified diving instructors, and arrange training internships at some of the larger training centers. These programs are at least two weeks long and cost 30,000-40,000B.

DIVE SHOPS AND CENTERS

When choosing a company to go diving with, first check the PADI website, which lists all of the PADI-certified dive shops across the globe and is searchable by country. There are many excellent dive shops and training centers throughout the Andaman region, and Thailand in general has an excellent safety record when it comes to diving. Instructors and dive masters are both local and foreign, and all are fluent in English. To pick a dive shop, it's best to drop in to some in your vicinity and spend a few minutes talking to staff before deciding who to dive or train with. The following dive centers are all certified by PADI to offer open-water diving certification, dive master training, and instructor training. All also offer one-day trips and multiple-day live-aboard diving trips.

- **Ao Nang Divers** (Krabi Seaview Resort, 143 Mu 2, Ao Nang, Krabi, tel. 07/563-7242, www.aonang-divers.com)

- **Dive Asia** (24 Thanon Karon, Kata Beach, Phuket, tel. 07/633-0598, www.diveasia.com)

- **Kata Diving Service** (Kata Garden Resort, 121/1 Mu 4, Thanon Patak, Karon Beach, tel. 07/633-0392)

- **Marina Divers** (45 Thanon Karon, Karon Beach, Phuket, tel. 07/633-0272)

- **Moskito Diving** (Tonsai Bay, Ko Phi Phi, tel. 07/560-1154, www.moskitodiving.com)

- **Oceanic Divecenter** (30 Thanon Karon, Karon Beach, Phuket, tel. 07/633-3043, www.oceanicdivecenter.com)

- **Pro-Tech Dive College** (389 Thanon Patak, Karon Beach, tel. 07/628-6112, www.pro-techdivers.com)

- **Sea Dragon Dive Center** (5/51 Mu 7, Thanon Khuek Khak, Khao Lak, Phang Nga, tel. 07/648-5420, www.seadragondivecenter.com)

- **Sea Fun Divers** (Katathani Beach Resort, 14 Kata Noi Rd., Kata Noi Beach, tel. 07/633-0124, www.seafundivers.com)

- **Sea World Dive Team** (177/23 Soi Sansabai, Patong Beach, tel. 07/634-1595, www.seaworld-phuket.com)

- **Sunrise Diving** (49 Thanon Thaweewong, Patong Beach, Phuket, tel. 07/629-2052)

- **Visa Diving** (77 Mu 7, Ko Phi Phi, tel. 07/560-1157, www.visadiving.com)

- **Warm Water Divers** (229 Thanon Rat-U-Thit 200 Pee, Patong Beach, Phuket, tel. 07/629-2201, www.warmwaterdivers.com)

- **West Coast Divers** (120/1-3 Rat-T-Tit 200 Pee Rd., Patong Beach, tel. 07/634-1673, www.westcoastdivers.com)

RECOMPRESSION CHAMBER

Although accidents and the bends are quite rare, **Badalveda Diving Medical Center at Bangkok Hospital Phuket** (2/1 Thanon Hongyok Utis, Phuket Town, tel. 07/625-4425, 24-hour emergency hotline tel. 08/1989-9482) has a hyperbaric chamber and medical staff who specialize in diving injuries.

coast, including views of sea urchins and tropical fish.

Monkey Beach (Hat Ling, หาดลิง) is a fun place to visit if you want to hang out with the scores of monkeys populating this pretty little strip of sandy coast that can be reached by canoe, speedboat, or longtail boat. If you go, make sure you bring something for the monkeys to snack on—as a result of thousands of tourists visiting every year, they've grown to expect some compensation in exchange for the entertainment they're providing, and they can get a little surly and even aggressive if you disappoint them.

SPORTS AND RECREATION
Diving
Phi Phi has some of the best diving in Thailand, made even better by the fact that it's so accessible and inexpensive. There's no need to set out on a boat for days or even to stay on Phi Phi. With all of the organized dive trips from Phuket, you can easily schedule full-day trips and return to the main island at night. Most of the outfitters listed for the Andaman coast offer trips to Phi Phi.

Boating
Most of the boating that goes on around Phi Phi is through chartered speedboats that take visitors from island to island during the day. These trips are hugely popular, as evidenced by the number of charter boats that line the coast of Phi Phi. Many of these tours include some snorkeling as well as lunch and depart from either Phi Phi or Phuket. There are a handful of companies that offer tours, although they sell almost exclusively through third-party tour agents, and you can arrange a tour through any travel agency on the mainland or Phi Phi, or from your hotel. Because of the intermediaries, prices for the trips can vary and are negotiable, although the agent may not tell you that it's not actually their company putting together the package. Prices for a day trip around Phi Phi should run about 1,200–2,000B, depending on the type of vessel you're on and the number of other passengers.

If you want to cruise around the surrounding islands at your own pace, at almost any beach you can hire a longtail boat to take you from one place to another. It's quite an experience to sit back and take in the view of the Andaman Sea from one of the long, thin, colorful boats while the captain steers from behind. Compared to speedboats, longtail boats are a lot smaller and less agile in choppy waters, so they're best enjoyed if you're only doing limited island hopping. When longtail boats are used as taxis, prices are usually fixed, and you should expect to pay 40–100B per trip. Chartering a boat for a fixed amount of time can cost anywhere from 400B, depending on the number of people and the time of year.

Kayaking
The area around the Phi Phi islands offers excellent opportunities for sea kayaking to explore the hidden bays and mangrove forests surrounding the islands. If you're just looking to paddle around close to shore, there are plenty of kayaks on the beaches available for rent. More-experienced kayakers can rent boats and arrange to have them pulled by longtail from Phi Phi Don to Maya Bay on Phi Phi Le. You can also request that the boat's captain pick you up at a designated time and place when you're ready to return. It's possible to cross from one island to another by kayak, but weather conditions can change rapidly, and only experienced kayakers should attempt the venture.

If you're kayaking, bear in mind that Phi Phi is a very popular destination for speedboats and larger tour boats, and by midday in high season the whole area can get very crowded with larger vessels. What may seem like just an annoyance can become dangerous if you're not seen by another boat, so pay close attention to the waters around you. The quietest time for kayaking is early in the morning, before the rest of the world arrives.

ACCOMMODATIONS
Phi Phi Don was long a favorite of travelers on a budget, thanks to the cheap bungalows,

especially along Ton Sai Bay, that had few amenities but the prime real estate on the island. The island was devastated during the tsunami in 2004, and most of the bungalows, resorts, and hotels have had to rebuild. Like everywhere else in Thailand, tourism is moving upscale, and the rebuilding seems to have shifted the island's focus from budget backpacker upward. Although there are still opportunities to sleep in a small shack on the beach without air-conditioning or hot water for just a few hundred baht per night, you'll find those accommodations increasingly packed together in smaller and smaller areas (namely Ton Sai), with mid-range hotels and more expensive resorts popping up on the island in their place. On the luxury front, the island is increasingly getting its share of high-end resorts too. Perhaps because Phi Phi is so beautiful and so popular, hoteliers don't seem to be trying too hard to compete with one another or to woo guests. The most common complaint that travelers have about the island is that where they stayed was overpriced and mediocre, regardless of whether it was a cheap bungalow or a high-end resort.

Ton Sai Bay

With scores of guesthouses in the area, Ton Sai Village, the small strip of flat land in the middle of the island, is a popular spot for visitors to stay. Here's where you'll find most conveniences; the majority of the island's restaurants and small shops are here, but you'll find less peace and calm.

J. J. Guesthouse (Ton Sai Village, tel. 07/560-1090, www.jjbungalow.com, 700B) offers very basic fan-cooled guest rooms in their small guesthouse. Guest rooms are clean and comfortable, and definitely good value for the money. There is a small restaurant on the property. For a little more money, you can stay at one of their bungalows, which are all air-conditioned and spacious, though simple.

If you want to stay right near Ton Sai Bay but still feel a little pampered, the **Phi Phi Island Cabana Hotel** (58 Mu 7, tel. 07/560-1170, 4,200B) is a nice choice for a not-too-expensive resort. The guest rooms are well maintained, and the grounds are nicely designed. The guest rooms are all decorated in a modern Thai style and feel much less rustic than bungalows you'll find scattered along the beach, and there's a nice large swimming pool with comfortable chairs. The hotel is also very well located on Ton Sai between two beaches, so visitors can take advantage of the more inexpensive longtail boats in the area to hop from place to place. The only trade-off is that with more than 150 guest rooms, it's not quite a small resort.

Laem Thong Beach

At the northern tip of the island, in secluded Laem Thong Beach, is **Phi Phi Natural Resort** (Mu 8, Laem Tong Beach, tel. 07/561-3010, 3,300B). The standard guest rooms and cottages have a rustic feel to them, with lots of exposed wood and simple, basic furnishings. It's nothing luxurious or fancy, but there's air-conditioning and a small swimming pool with an ocean view. The resort is tucked away from any crowds and feels secluded and relaxed, more like a summer vacation at camp. There are also larger cottages that are great for families.

For something a little more predictable, if with slightly less personality, the **Holiday Inn Phi Phi Island** (Mu 8, Laem Tong Beach, tel. 07/562-7300, www.phiphi.holidayinn.com, 4,000B) has nice individual bungalows, many with ocean views. The swimming pool is not huge but opens onto the beach. Bungalows are decorated in a modern, somewhat generic style but have some small Thai details. Many have their own small balconies or porches.

Ao Lo Bakao

This beach's only resort, **Pee Pee Island Village** (Ao Lo Bakao, tel. 07/621-5014, www.ppisland.com, 6,500B), is definitely on the higher end of the beach bungalow experience, although it's not quite a five-star luxury resort. The bungalows and villas are done in a traditional Thai design with thatched roofs that fade into the surrounding palm trees and are designed to let in as much light and ocean view as possible. There is a spa and a few restaurants on the premises as well as a fantastic swimming pool looking out onto the Andaman Sea. This is a great place to stay if you're looking for seclusion and are happy to idle your vacation away reading books and listening to the waves, although at low tide the shore is too rocky and shallow to swim. Getting off the resort during the day can be a little tricky—the resort has infrequent shuttle boats running to Ton Sai Bay, but if you miss them and need to charter a private boat from the hotel, the prices are steep.

Ao Toh Ko

Ao Toh Ko Bungalows (Ao Toh Ko, Phi Phi Island, tel. 08/1731-9470, 350B) offers supercheap, basic sleeping accommodations with lovely beach views in a quiet, secluded beach on the east coast of the island. If you're on a budget, or just want to experience what Phi Phi was like before all the other travelers came, these little bungalows will feel charming and quaint, and the little bar and inexpensive restaurant on the premises will feel like an added extra. If you're higher maintenance, this is not the place for you, however: There's no air-conditioning or hot water in most of the guest rooms.

FOOD

Come nighttime, Ton Sai Bay is ground zero for food and entertainment, and if you're staying on one of the more remote beaches, the action can be a welcome change from all that peace and quiet. Almost all of the resorts on the island have small restaurants serving Thai food. Western food tends to be more than well represented at the stand-alone shops, perhaps to feed all the hungry Americans, Europeans, and Australians who flock here.

Even if you'll feel a little guilty eating baked goods on a tropical island, ◖ **Pee Pee Bakery** (Ton Sai Bay, 7 A.M.–8 P.M. daily, 40B) is hard to resist. The shop's glass display cases of doughnuts, breads, and cakes seem to beckon every traveler, especially around breakfast time. The bakery also serves Thai food, sandwiches, and pizza, all of which are well prepared.

During the day, the seafood restaurants right on the edge of the beach overlooking Ton Sai Bay are usually filled with day-trippers on arranged tours. At night, these restaurants feel less like food conveyer belts and are pleasant places to drink a cold Singha over dinner and enjoy the view. **Chao Koh** (tel. 07/560-1083, 11 A.M.–9 P.M. daily, 250B) is one with good seafood and a nice view. Cuisine here is traditional Thai seafood dishes. The food is good, but don't expect anything too creative.

Although some visitors, particularly the over-30 crowd, seem perplexed as to the reason, **Hippies** (Hin Khom Beach, tel. 08/1970-5483, 8 A.M.–late daily, 200B) is a wildly popular restaurant, bar, and party spot right on Hin Khom Beach. The menu, which features Middle Eastern food, pizza, and plenty of Thai dishes, seems designed to offer something for everyone. The food is actually pretty good (although if you want authentic Thai food, make sure to ask for it extra spicy), but it's really the beachfront location, charming thatched roofs and bamboo furniture, and laid-back vibe that are the draws here.

GETTING THERE

The only way to get to the island is by water. In the past, intrepid tour operators have tried using seaplanes for the short flight from Phuket airport, but they have not managed to make that business model work.

Boat

Phi Phi Don is easily reached by ferry boat or speedboat from Phuket or Krabi. There are no public ferries per se, only private operators, and when you buy a ticket, most will include a ride from your hotel in Phuket or Krabi to the pier. Schedules change frequently, especially in the low season, but during high season there are least two boats from Chalong Bay in Phuket to Ton Sai Bay on Phi Phi Don, one in the morning and another in the afternoon, and returning boats on a similar schedule. The trip should take around two hours, depending on the weather conditions. From Krabi, there are boats leaving from Ao Nang and Rai Le

© SUZANNE NAM

Ko Phi Phi Le's streets are lined with shops and stalls that cater to tourists.

Beaches daily, also in the morning and afternoon. Fares run from 350B upward, depending on the time of day and the season. If you're with a large group of people, it can sometimes be more economical to charter your own speedboat from Chalong Bay or Krabi to Phi Phi. In a small, fast vessel, the trip can take half as long as the larger boats, but you should expect to pay a few thousand baht per journey.

Given the cost of the trip, if you have some time to spare, it may be worthwhile to take one of the package tours that will not only bring you to Phi Phi but also provide a tour of neighboring islands and sights while you're on the way. Just make sure the boat will stop at Ton Sai Bay (if that's where you're going), as some tours skip this spot entirely.

Many of the hotels on Phi Phi can arrange your transport from either Krabi or Phuket for you if you're staying on their property. Otherwise, you can buy tickets from any travel agent, but when purchasing, make sure to ask about the size of the boat and the number of passengers if you have a preference for the type of vessel. Larger ferries and speedboats generally take 90 minutes from either Krabi or Phuket. During the low season, it's fine just to show up at the pier and buy a ticket, but during high season ferries can sometimes sell out, so the best bet is to find a travel agency and buy a ticket as soon as you can.

GETTING AROUND

There are no taxis or *tuk tuks* on Phi Phi; for the most part there aren't even any roads. Most of the getting-around involves walking or traveling from Ton Sai Bay to other spots on the island by longtail boat, the area's taxi service. You'll pay 40–100B pp per trip from one part of the island to another, depending on the distance and whether you are traveling alone. From one island to another, expect to pay around 100B pp for the boat trip. Your hotel will be able to arrange a boat for you, but if you're picking one up from the beach, make sure you agree on the cost in advance.

THE ANDAMAN COAST

Ko Lanta

เกาะลันตา

Just off the coast of Krabi is Ko Lanta, really two adjacent islands—**Ko Lanta Yai** and **Ko Lanta Noi.** Ko Lanta Yai, generally referred to just as Ko Lanta, is a large, thin island with limestone cliffs, a jungly interior, mangroves, and some good coral beaches. Although there are mangroves along much of the coast, there are also some great sandy beaches on the west side of the island, and that's where you'll find plenty of bungalows and small resorts. The interior has some great hiking trails through rainforests and some waterfalls worth checking out in Lanta's national park, which covers nearly half the island. Ko Lanta is arguably nearly as blissfully beautiful as Phi Phi, but Ko Lanta has yet to explode with the same popularity as its neighbor, and it has a strange half-backpacker, half-luxury vibe to it that some visitors find a perfect balance. You'll see this interesting dichotomy in the choice of accommodations as well—there are some great choices at both the upper and lower ends. Ban Saladan, a small village on the northeast corner of the island, functions as Ko Lanta's Main Street. This is where many of the ferries arrive, and there are also some limited amenities such as ATMs, Internet cafés, and supermarkets, but some of the more popular beach areas will have similar amenities as well. Ko Lanta Noi, adjacent to Ko Lanta Yai, has no beaches and has therefore not become a big destination, but depending on how you get to Ko Lanta, you may end up passing through the island.

SIGHTS
Lanta Old Town
หมู่บ้านเก่าแก่เกาะลันตา
Located on the east side of southern Ko Lanta, Lanta Old Town is a quaint fishing village that now serves as the island's capital. It's picturesque, with little teakwood houses on stilts above the water and brightly colored fishing boats set against the backdrop of an enticing blue ocean speckled with islands that seem to emerge as you watch. But Lanta Old Town is also a fascinating place to observe the cultural diversity in southern Thailand that's often difficult to discern in heavily touristed areas. The town, once a major fishing port in the middle part of the 20th century, is home to Chinese immigrants, descendants of nomadic seafarers, and Thai Muslims who've created a comfortable, peaceful town blending all of their cultures together.

BEACHES AND SURROUNDING ISLANDS
◖ Khlong Dao Beach
หาดคลองดาว
Khlong Dao, closest to Ban Saladan, is a long stretch of wide, sandy beach on the southwest tip of the island backed by casuarina and palm trees. The waters in this crescent-shaped beach are generally quite calm, but this is the island's most popular tourist spot, so expect more of everything—more accommodations, more places to eat, and more people. It's still Ko Lanta, though, so even during peak season, you won't see any overcrowding at Khlong Dao.

Pra Ae Beach
หาดพระแอะ
Also called **Long Beach,** Pra Ae is another stretch of wide, sandy beach, with a nice selection of bungalows and resorts right on the water nestled among the trees. Just a few kilometers down from Khlong Dao, Long Beach is rarely crowded.

Khlong Khong and Khlong Nin Beaches
หาดคลองโขง และ หาดคลองนิน
As you move farther down the island, there are still plenty of bungalows right on the coast, but the beaches become less crowded with accommodations or people. Both Khlong Kong and Khlong Nin Beaches are served by a little village called Ban Khlong Nin, where you'll find all the basics, including an ATM, some places to eat, and small shops.

Kan Tiang Bay and the Southwest Coast
อ่าวกันเตียง

With less usable beach in relation to mangrove or rocky shore, this is where the island starts to feel remote. Kan Tiang Beach, with white sands and just a scattering of resorts, is nearly deserted in the low season, making it a great choice if you're looking for a quiet, romantic getaway. **Mai Pay Bay** is sometimes nicknamed "Last Beach" because it's at the end of the island and feels like the last beach in Thailand that hasn't been discovered. With simple bungalows and little going on other than the beautiful scenery and warm blue waters, Mai Pay Bay feels off the beaten path, and it attracts the backpacker crowd and other adventurers seeking scenery as well as peace and quiet.

Ko Ha
เกาะห้า

A group of five small rocky islands off the coast of Ko Lanta, Ko Ha is a popular place for diving and snorkeling due to the abundant coral and exotic sealife surrounding the islands as well as the excellent visibility in the water. There are no accommodations on the island, but it's often visited on day trips. To get to Ko Ha, you'll need to charter a speedboat or sailboat or go with an organized tour.

Ko Hai (Ngai) Lanta
เกาะไหง

With just a handful of resorts and very limited amenities, Ko Hai offers the quintessential desert-island experience if you're willing to give up a few luxuries in exchange for a laid-back, secluded vacation. The small island, mostly hilly rainforest, has a stretch of beautiful beach with views of karst rock formations rising from the sea and some great coral snorkeling just off the coast. The island is in Krabi Province just south of Ko Lanta Yai, but it's more convenient to get there by taking a boat from Trang instead. If you're staying on the island, the resort will arrange transportation for you.

Ko Ta Lebeng and Ko Bu Bu
เกาะตะละเบ็ง และ เกาะบูบู

Off the east coast of Ko Lanta, Ko Ta Lebeng is a limestone island with dramatic limestone cliffs and lush mangroves as well as a small bit of sandy beach. The island is very popular among sea kayakers and is a great place to go if you're not confident in open waters—the smaller Ko Ta Lebeng is protected by the main island, and the waters are a little calmer.

If you want to stay on a small island, Ko Bu Bu has only one resort with a handful of bungalows and clear warm waters for snorkeling. "Chilled-out" might be too exciting to describe the place—there's some great sandy beach and not much else to occupy your time other than sitting in a hammock and reading a book. The island is even too small for any long hiking.

NIGHTLIFE

Club Ibark (Khlong Nin Beach, Ko Lanta Yai, tel. 08/3507-9237, www.ibarkkrabi.com, 6 P.M.–late daily, no cover) bills itself as the country's freshest and funkiest club and, while that's definitely not true, it is the hottest thing going on Ko Lanta. Of course, Ko Lanta is a small island, and the nightlife pickings are pretty slim. Still, during high season the club pulls in a good crowd, and the DJs spin music that's head and shoulders above the typical Western pop classics you'll hear at most venues. There's a casual, fun vibe at this open-air dance club, and since everyone is on vacation, the partying can go on till late at night.

SPORTS AND RECREATION
Ko Lanta National Marine Park

The National Marine Park covers Hat Hin Ngam and Hat Tanod Beaches at the southern tip of Ko Lanta as well as a handful of surrounding small islands and rock formations. There are no resorts on the beaches, and like the other national parks with beaches, there are some camping amenities. **Tanod Beach,** at the bottom of Ko Lanta, is covered in rugged mountain terrain and sugar palms, giving way to a beautiful beach. There are hiking trails throughout this area filled with birdlife, and at the end is the Lanta lighthouse, where you can climb up and view the island from above. There are campgrounds as well as many bungalows that can be rented from the parks authority. Approaching the lighthouse and surrounding area by road can be really tough without a 4WD vehicle, and depending on the weather, it may be easier to charter a longtail boat to take you.

Snorkeling

If you're looking to do some serious snorkeling, the area surrounding Ko Lanta has some great coral reefs and marinelife to see. You can swim out on your own, but to really see what's going on in the sea, arrange a boat trip around the island and neighboring islands. **Freedom Adventures** (70 Mu 6, Khlong Nin Beach, Ko Lanta Yai, tel. 08/4910-9132 or 08/1077-5025, www.freedom-adventures.com), based on Khlong Nin Beach, runs group day trips for about 1,500B from Ko Lanta on their charming wooden motorboat and can also create a personalized itinerary for you depending on your interests and abilities. This is a great excursion for nondivers who are interested in seeing the coral and tropical fish, as these folks specialize in snorkeling and not diving, so they'll only take you places you can enjoy viewing the underwater world without need of breathing gear.

ACCOMMODATIONS
Under 1,500B

Bu Bu Island Resort (Ko Bu Bu, tel. 07/561-8066, 350B) is a throwback to the days when simple bungalows on quiet beaches dominated the now mostly built-up Andaman coast. Guest rooms are very basic thatched-roof bungalows with private coldwater baths. There's also a small restaurant here, making it a great place to just chill out and enjoy the view.

1,500-3,000B

If you want to pay backpacker prices but don't want to forgo things such as a swimming pool and a restaurant on the premises, the **Andaman Lanta Resort** (142 Mu 3, Khlong Dao Beach, Ko Lanta, tel. 07/568-4200, www.andamanlanta.com, 2,100B) is a decent midrange option. The guest rooms are clean, if a little weary, but the resort is relaxed and child-friendly. Located on the north part of the island, it's definitely in a more crowded neighborhood, but the nearby beach stays mellow even during high season. It sort of looks like a group of IHOP restaurants, since all of the buildings have similar blue roofs.

Right nearby, at the southern end of Khlong Dao Beach, **Lanta Villa Resort** (14 Mu 3 Saladan, Ko Lanta, tel. 07/568-4129 or 08/1536-2527, www.lantavillaresort.com, 1,900B) is a similar property with clean, basic guest rooms and a nice swimming pool right on the popular beach. The bungalow-style rooms are a little too close together to feel secluded, but for this price and this location, it really is a bargain.

Ancient Realm Resort & Spa (364 Mu 3 Saladan, Ko Lanta, tel. 08/7998-1336, www.ancientrealmresort.com, 1,800B) is a solid midrange beach resort with excellent service and good-value guest rooms. Some might be aesthetically offended by the liberal use of Buddhist and Southeast Asian images in the decor, but if you can get past that, the guest rooms are very comfortable and clean, and the beach location is excellent. All guest rooms have air-conditioning and hot water. The resort also feels less businesslike than some other properties, so staff and guests are more relaxed and friendly.

LaLaanta Hideaway (188 Mu 5, Ko Lanta, tel. 07/566-5066, www.lalaanta.com, 2,800B) is quiet, secluded, and relaxing, and though the bungalows are not at the five-star level, they are clean, nicely furnished, and comfortable enough that you won't miss much. There is a hotel restaurant and bar, plus a large swimming pool overlooking the Andaman Sea. The beach the resort is located on feels very secluded, and those who are looking for a place that feels like a deserted island will enjoy their time here.

3,000-4,500B

The small **Baan Laanta** (72 Mu 5, Kan Tiang Bay, Ko Lanta Yai, tel. 07/566-5091, www.baanlaanta.com, 3,500B) resort has only 15 bungalows, which straddle the line between rustic and luxurious. Terra-cotta tiles and lots of wood and bamboo give the guest rooms a very natural feeling, but things like a mini-bar, bathrobes, and private balconies with excellent views add bits of pampering and in-dulgence. The dark-tiled pool, spa *sala,* and outdoor bar are small but swanky-feeling and well maintained.

A boutique resort of the best kind, (**Sri Lanta** (111 Mu 6 Khlong Nin Beach, Ko Lanta Yai, tel. 07/566-2688, 3,800B) is both aestheti-cally pleasing and geared toward connecting visitors to the beautiful surroundings of Ko Lanta. This is not a place designed to make you forget where you are: The individual thatched-roof villas have wall-length shutters that you can open out onto the grounds, and the interi-ors are rustic but comfortable and deliberately don't have TVs. But things like the amazing black-tiled swimming pool, Wi-Fi, and good iced coffee mean you won't feel like you're missing out on much during vacation.

Over 4,500B

With bright, beautiful guest rooms set on a property that creeps into the surrounding rain-forest along with lots of things to do, the **Rawi Warin Resort & Spa** (139 Mu 8, Ko Lanta, tel. 07/560-7400, www.rawiwarin.com, 7,800B) has more personality and charm than most large re-sorts. The guest rooms are modern but have an airy, clean tropical style to them, and the stucco exteriors give the resort a more Mediterranean feel than a Southeast Asian island feel. Some of the gigantic villas have their own swimming pools, but the common areas, which include multiple swimming pools, tennis courts, and a gym, are more than sufficient to keep you oc-cupied. One of the restaurants also has free Wi-Fi. The property is very child-friendly, although some of the guest rooms are located up in the hills and will require a little bit of walking.

If you're looking for more amenities, the (**Pimalai Resort** (99 Mu 5, Ba Kan Tiang Beach, Ko Lanta, tel. 07/560-7999, www.pim-alai.com, 12,000B) is a larger property with more than 100 guest rooms nestled in the hilly

rainforest above a beautiful, quiet stretch of white-sand beach. All of the guest rooms are in small bungalow buildings, giving the property a less crowded feeling despite the fact that there may be hundreds of guests and staff around during peak season. Inside, the guest rooms are a little more generic but still have some nice Thai design elements. The 35-meter infinity swimming pool overlooking the ocean is nearly as beautiful as the beach below.

FOOD

If you're just looking for casual food, you'll find lots of roti vendors around, selling the traditional Muslim rolled and flattened pan-cakes. They're traditionally served with savory curries, but these guys will stuff them with all sorts of sweet treats, including chocolate and bananas, for around 30B.

Gong Grit Bar (Khlong Dao Beach, 176 Mu 3, T. Saladan, A. Ko Lanta, tel. 08/9592-5844, 8 A.M.–10 P.M. daily, 300B) is one of the many places you'll find on Khlong Dao Beach serving up local fare and seafood dishes on the beach. This one isn't very fancy—none of them are—but the food is well done and the service is good. Gong Grit is at the southern end of the beach.

GETTING THERE
Boat

During high season, there is a twice-daily ferry boat from Krabi's new pier on **Tharua Road,** just outside Krabi Town. Remember that there are two piers in Krabi: **Chao Fah** pier, which is now used for travel immediately around Krabi, and the new pier, which is used for larger vessels. The ferry for Lanta leaves at 8 A.M. and 1 P.M., takes about 90 minutes, and costs 300B. It's best to arrange transport to the pier through your hotel in Krabi. There are also daily boats during high season from Ko Phi Phi to Ko Lanta, departing at 11:30 A.M. and 2 P.M. daily. That trip takes 90 minutes and also costs 300B.

Bus

Although Ko Lanta is an island, you can do much of the journey there by land, using two ferry crossings that can accommodate vehicles. In the low season, this is the only option, and there are numerous minivan services that will take you from Krabi to Ko Lanta. If you take one of the scheduled vans with **Lanta Transport** (tel. 07/568-4121), which run every few hours and take about 90 minutes, you'll pay 250B pp. You can also arrange to have a private minivan with any tour company, which should cost around 1,000B.

Car

If you're driving to Ko Lanta, head south on Highway 4 toward Trang (if you're coming from the Phang Nga area). Turn off at Route 4206 at Khlong Thom, about 32 kilometers from Krabi Town, and follow that road heading south all the way to the Hua Hin pier on the mainland. That leg of the journey is about 29 kilometers. From there you'll take your first ferry crossing to Ko Lanta Noi. The second ferry, about eight kilometers after the first, will bring you to Ko Lanta Yai; each will cost 100B.

GETTING AROUND

Ko Lanta does not have a public transportation system; to get around you'll have to rely on occasional motorcycle taxis and the shuttle buses and trucks run by the island's resorts. If you're driving on your own, by car or motorcycle, the island has a main road on the west coast that runs north–south and will allow you access to those beaches.

Trang and Satun Provinces จังหวัดตรัง และ จังหวัดสตูล

The two southernmost provinces on the Andaman coast before Thailand becomes Malaysia, Trang and Satun have not yet become popular tourism destinations, although direct flights from Bangkok to Krabi and Trang make them readily accessible for those looking for something off the beaten path. Both share much of the topography of neighboring Krabi—limestone cliffs, beautiful beaches, mangrove swamps, and a verdant interior, but are less commonly visited by travelers, most likely due to the plethora of amazing places to see so close to Phuket and its well-maintained tourism infrastructure. If the idea of flying into a big international airport and staying in a place where you'll most definitely see other foreign travelers is unappealing, these two provinces are worth the extra effort it takes to get here, if only for the chance to see what Thailand is really like while at the same time enjoying beautiful beaches and islands. The provinces are home to some spectacular small islands off the coast, most protected by two large national marine parks and easily accessible from the mainland either for day trips, if you're in a hurry, or extended stays, if you're looking for a desert-island experience. Off the coast of Trang is the Mo Ko Phetra National Park, comprising about 30 islands you can dive and snorkel around, or enjoy the gray-white sandy beaches and do some bird-watching. Off the coast of Satun are the Tarutao Islands, which, compared to their northern neighbors, are more visited, although still nothing like what you'll see in Phang Nga Bay. The national park comprises more than 50 islands where you can see coral and go snorkeling and scuba diving.

The mainland also has its share of natural beauty, and although there are scant tourist sights to see, there's still plenty to keep you busy should you decide to stay here for more than a day or two. Trang was the first area in Thailand where rubber trees, now an important part of the economy of the south, were planted, and Satun is home to a majority Muslim population, making both provinces culturally and historically interesting places to visit in addition to their physical beauty.

Compared to Phuket or Krabi, you won't find the same number or quality of accommodations on the mainland of either Trang or

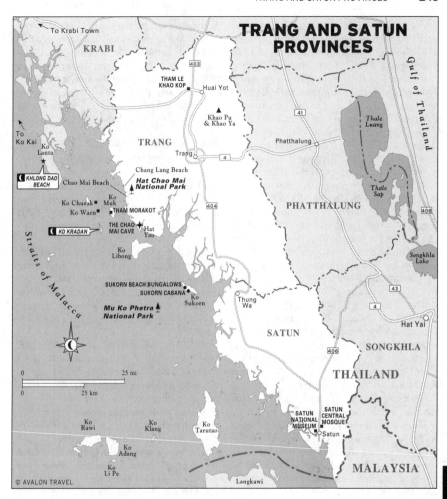

Satun, although a couple of resorts have sprung up in the area as well as some very budget, very simple beach bungalows.

TRANG
Trang Town
เมืองตรัง

Trang Town isn't so much a tourist town as just a small town going about its daily business: Although there are travel agencies that can set up dive expeditions to the nearby islands, hardware stores and noodle shops are the rule instead of tailor shops and bars. It's not a physically beautiful town, and most travelers will see it only in transit from the mainland to the beaches, but if you're interested in what semi-urban life looks like in this part of the world, it's a pedestrian-friendly place where you can wander around for a while observing the mundane without fear of getting lost. While it's sometimes difficult to discern small cultural differences among regions in foreign countries,

Trang feels distinctly different from more northern areas of Thailand. Like other parts of southern Thailand, the distinct mix of Thai-Chinese and Malay cultures can be fascinating to observe, plus there is some Sino-Portuguese architecture. Other than that, there isn't too much to see except for the markets and the governor's house, set on one of the area's hills.

Here you'll also find some of the best coffee shops. Say goodbye to instant and order a *kopi* instead. Just like the coffee you'll find in cafés in Malaysia and Singapore, this is the strong cloth bag–filtered version with a generous helping of sweetened condensed milk to make it go down smoothly. Trang is also known for two other culinary specialties—dim sum, which you can find at many coffee shops and which is especially popular for breakfast, and *mu yang Trang,* Trang-style crispy roasted pork. **Ton Noon Dim Sum** (202 Pad Sathani Rd., 6 A.M.–9 P.M. daily, 30B) and **Khao Chong Coffee** (Phatthalung Rd., tel. 07/521-8759, 6 A.M.–9 P.M. daily, 30B) are two traditional *kopi* shops with excellent dim sum choices.

Nok Air is the only airline offering flights to Trang from Bangkok, currently leaving from Don Muang airport. If you book far enough in advance on Nok Air, tickets are as cheap as 2,800B round-trip with tax. Otherwise, you may pay a little under 4,000B for a ticket.

There's an **overnight train** from Bangkok to Trang that leaves Hua Lamphong Station at 5:05 P.M. and arrives in Trang at 7:55 A.M. the next day. The tickets cost under 800B for a first-class sleeper ticket, so if you're comfortable sleeping on trains, it's a really economical and adventurous way to get to the region.

There are buses for Trang that leave the Southern Bus Terminal in Bangkok around 6 P.M.; call 02/435-1199 for the latest schedule. Buses take 12–14 hours. Expect to pay in the neighborhood of 800B for a ticket on an air-conditioned luxury bus, less than 550B for an unair-conditioned bus.

If you're driving from the surrounding areas, Highway 4 cuts through Trang in a zigzag pattern, making it the most accessible route for inland travel in the province. For the beaches

in the southern part of the province, however, you'll have to turn onto secondary road 404. Although Trang is close to Phuket, Krabi, and Phang Nga as the crow flies, the drive can take hours due to the mountainous terrain. The drive from Krabi Town to Trang takes two hours; from Phuket to Trang, it takes 4.5–5 hours, so plan accordingly.

Mu Ko Phetra National Park
อุทยานแห่งชาติหมู่เกาะเภตรา
Mu Ko Phetra, a marine park in Trang, is a small grouping of islands just north of the Ko Tarutao area that feels even more remote than the rest of the province. The scenery, including the craggy limestone rock formations jutting out from the ocean and rainforest-covered islands, is spectacular. Under the surface of the sea surrounding many of the islands there's coral at relatively shallow depths, making this a great destination for snorkeling. The only way to stay in the national park is either to camp or to rent one of the national park bungalows on Ko Phetra.

Ko Khao Yai means "large mountain island." Although that could adequately define many of the islands in the Andaman Sea, Ko Khao Yai stands out because, thanks to erosion and tectonic forces, one of the large chunks of limestone jutting off the island has been worn through and forms a sort of natural bridge that can be rowed under during low tide.

The much smaller **Ko Lidi,** which covers less than 10 square kilometers, doesn't have great beaches for swimming, but it has some caves within the limestone cliffs that are nesting grounds for swallows, along with a campground where you can rent tents.

Ko Muk
เกาะมุก
Just off the coast of Trang, across from Chang Lang Beach, Ko Muk is a small inhabited island with some beautiful beaches backed by limestone cliffs on the west coast, coral clusters to snorkel around (particularly nearby Hat Sai Yao), and a scattering of bungalows and resorts catering to travelers. To the south, the eastern

part of the island is mainly a fishing village, and the local economy is also dependent on the rubber plantations in the center of the island. But to the north, on the west coast, lies one of the coolest physical attractions in the region—the **Tham Morakot** (Emerald Cave). If you visit during low tide, you can access the cave and interior lagoon by boat, but the more fun way to go is during high tide, when the entrance to the cave is nearly filled with water and you have to swim through the limestone passage. When you reemerge, you'll be in a beautiful emerald lagoon surrounded by cliffs. During high season this is a popular place, so don't expect to have it to yourself.

To get to Ko Muk, you can take a longtail or speedboat from the Kuan Tungku pier, which is about 30 minutes from Trang Town. If you're flying into the Trang airport, there are frequent *song thaew* traveling this route during the day; expect to pay around 50B pp. At the pier, you'll have to negotiate with the captain, but a trip to Ko Muk will take around 30 minutes on a longtail boat and will cost around 400B.

Hat Chao Mai National Park
อุทยานแห่งชาติหาดเจ้าไหม
The Hat Chao Mai National Park (Mu 5, Ban Chang Lang, Amphoe Sikao, tel. 07/521-3260, 8:30 A.M.–6 P.M. daily, 200B) is a large protected area covering 19 kilometers of rocky and sandy coastline north of Hat Yao and south of Krabi Province. The interior of the park includes mangrove swamps, mountains, and rivers. The park also technically extends to the adjacent islands of Ko Muk, Ko Kradan, Ko Waen, Ko Cheaung, Ko Pring, and Ko Meng, although you won't necessarily notice that you've entered the park or even have to pay an entrance fee if you're visiting one of these islands. Although the park is a beautiful nature preserve and includes some amazing coral reef offshore, what Hat Chao Mai is best known for is the **dugong,** or sea cows, that live in the ocean territory covered by the park. This endangered species, similar to a manatee, was once hunted but has now been adopted by the locals as the region's unofficial mascot. The

sweet, awkward-looking dugong can sometimes be spotted during snorkeling or diving trips along the coast or islands covered by the park. If you're looking to explore the mainland part of the park, there are simple bungalows for rent as well as areas to camp with restrooms and canteens serving up tasty, casual local food.

◀ Ko Kradan
เกาะกระดาน
Partially under the protection of the Hat Chao Mai National Park, Ko Kradan is often called the most beautiful island in Trang. It's no surprise, given the beautiful view of Ko Muk and other neighboring islands that seem to emerge magically from the Andaman Sea, the pristine soft-sand beaches, and the surrounding coral reefs. For snorkelers it's particularly alluring: The water is clear, and you'll only need to swim out to shallow depths to see some amazing coral and tropical fish. Although there are some rubber plantations on the island, it's largely undeveloped and usually visited by tourists as part of a tour to Ko Muk. If you want to stay over, there are a few bungalows on the island, and you can also camp on the island through the parks department.

Hat Yao and Surrounding Islands
หาดยาว
The longest stretch of beach in the province, Hat Yao has some clear sandy swaths punctuated by rock formations and rocky cliffs backed by pine and palm trees. Off the coast in the warm, clear-blue waters of the Andaman Sea are some islands and rock formations where you'll be able to do some snorkeling and diving away from the crowds a little farther north. There are very limited accommodations on the beach; it's definitely quiet and secluded. For budget travelers it's a great option if you feel like you've been squeezed out of the more popular tourist areas as they've gone upscale—you can still find accommodations for less than US$15 per night in the area.

Just off the coast of Hat Yao is **Ko Libong.** The largest island in Trang is a very short trip by longtail boat from the pier at Yao Beach and has a handful of small fishing villages and rubber plantations populated by the mostly Muslim Thais living in the area. The island itself has some beautiful sandy beaches and rugged, hilly rainforest in the middle, and there is snorkeling right off the coast, although not as much coral to be seen as you'll find in and around Phi Phi. Ko Libong also has a handful of quaint resorts if you're looking to stay on the island overnight.

South of Ko Libong is **Ko Sukorn,** one of the southernmost islands in Trang Province. This island has a handful of small villages mostly engaged in fishing and working on small rubber plantations on the island. The brown sandy beaches are surrounded by clear waters, and the island is mostly flat and without many of the rock formations characteristic of the region. The island is small enough that you can walk around it in a few hours, and close enough that it only takes about 20 minutes in a longtail boat from the mainland; you'll get a chance to see how people in the region make a living while enjoying the laid-back atmosphere on the island.

There are some relaxed bungalow resorts here, although nothing is fancy. If you're looking for an off-the-beaten-path island getaway, this is a great place to stay for a few days. **Sukorn Beach Bungalows** (Ko Sukorn, tel. 07/526-7707, www.sukorn-island-trang.com, 1,000B) is casual and unpretentious. This is definitely a place to stay for the location and the price, and for now you won't have to worry about being overrun by other travelers, since Ko Sukorn hasn't made it big yet. The guest rooms are filled with simple bamboo furniture and are a very short walk to the beach; most have air-conditioning. There aren't many amenities available here, but there is a small restaurant serving Thai food.

Sukorn Cabana (Ko Sukorn, tel. 07/511-5894, www.sukorncabana.com, 1,000B) has airy, basic, but pretty bungalows. This is not a high-end resort—many of the bungalows don't have air-conditioning or hot water—but they're just minutes from the beach.

Ko Chueak and **Ko Waen,** just adjacent to each other off the coast of Trang, are two very small islands with some of the best casual snorkeling in the region. Aside from some exotic, colorful fish, there is plenty of deep and shallow-water coral to view.

On the mainland, the national park area covers **Khao Pu** and **Khao Ya** mountains, which have thick forest cover, caves, and plenty of waterfalls to hike around in. Tha Le Song Hong—Lake of Two Rooms—is a fascinating and beautiful physical phenomenon to view. The large, clean lake is nearly divided by a mountain rising from the middle, creating two separate bodies of water. To get there by car, take Phetchakasem Road (Huai Yot–Krabi) to Ban Phraek, then turn right and drive about 13 kilometers. There will be signs in English pointing the way. If you want to rough it a little, there's a Boy Scout campground (tel. 07/522-4294) nearby. When it's not filled with kids, they rent out the houses.

Chang Lang Beach
หาดฉางหลาง

This beach has all of the spectacular scenery typically found along the Andaman coast—limestone cliffs, sandy beaches, and casuarina pine trees. One of the campsites, as well as the main headquarters for Hat Chao Mai National Park, is located on the beach.

At the tip of a forested headland is **Chao Mai Beach,** a wide stretch of sandy beach covering about three kilometers of coastline. Both of these beaches are beautiful and feel much more remote and less populated by visitors than the national parks to the north; if you come during the low season, you may well be the only person around.

The **Chao Mai Cave** is one of the larger caves in the region, with extensive stalactites and stalagmites, fossils, and multilevel chambers. There's also a spring inside one of the chambers, and some of the stalactites and stalagmites have joined, creating strange-looking pillars and an altogether otherworldly feeling inside. Although the cave is on the grounds of the national park, it's easier to access from Yao

Beach. From here, you can rent a rowboat to row into the cave from the ocean.

Another cool cave to visit is **Tham Le Khao Kop,** which has pools of water and a stream flowing through it as well as steep interior cliff walls, plus more than three kilometers of stalagmites and stalactites. During the day there are guides who'll row you through the cave in a little boat. At one point the passage is so low you have to lie on your back in the boat, which feels like a bit of adventure. To tour the cave with a boat and guide, the fee is 200B per boat or 30B pp. Take Highway 4 from the Huai Yot district heading toward the **Wang Wiset district** (อำเภอวังวิเศษ). After about six kilometers, you will see Andaman intersection; continue for 460 meters, and you will see another intersection with a temple on the right; turn left, drive about 640 meters, and you'll see a bridge to the cave.

SATUN
Satun Town
เมืองสตูล

As untouristed as Trang Town is, Satun Town is even more so. The center of the southernmost province on the Andaman coast before Malaysia, the town of Satun, as with the whole province, is primarily Muslim, having been a part of Malaya until the early 19th century. Sectarian violence has infected the three southernmost provinces on the east side of the peninsula, but even though Satun is nearly right next door, there have been no reports of insurgent activity here, and it's a great opportunity to catch a glimpse of a culture different from what you'll see to the north. To better understand Islam in Thailand, visit the **Ku Den Mansion,** the Satun National Museum. Housed in a colonial-style former palace that once housed King Rama V, this museum for Islamic studies has interesting displays on the lives of Muslims in the area through the ages. There's also the large **Satun Central Mosque.** Although it's not going to win any architectural awards, having been completed in the late 1970s, you can visit to pray or watch others do so.

If you're heading to Satun, you can take a train to Hat Yai (there's no train station in Satun), but then you have to travel by land for the remaining 95 kilometers.

Satun is on the same bus line as Trang. Buses leave the Southern Bus Terminal in Bangkok around 6 P.M.; call 02/435-1199 for the latest schedule. Buses will take 12–14 hours to reach Satun. Expect to pay in the neighborhood of 800B for a ticket on an air-conditioned luxury bus, less than 550B for an unair-conditioned bus.

If you're driving through Satun, Route 416 travels down the coast slightly inland, and from there you'll turn off onto country roads depending on your destination. Although Satun is close to Phuket, Krabi, and Phang Nga, keep in mind that the drive can take hours due to the mountainous terrain. If you are driving from Krabi Town to Satun, it will take three hours. From Phuket to Trang, the drive will take 5.5–6 hours.

Ko Tarutao National Park
อุทยานแห่งชาติหมู่เกาะตะรุเตา

Ko Tarutao National Park in Satun is the highlight of region if you're looking for a place to do some diving and snorkeling. The park comprises more than 50 islands off the coast of Satun and just north of Malaysian territorial waters, some barely a speck on the map and some, such as Ko Tarutao, covering dozens of square kilometers of land. Within the island group you'll find rainforests, clean quiet beaches, mangroves, coral reefs, and plenty of wildlife. Many people visit these islands on chartered tours from the mainland. As in other parts of the region, these tours are generally done on speedboats with other visitors from around the world and include lunch, a chance to enjoy the scenery, and some snorkeling. On the larger islands, there are a small number of decent accommodations, if you are looking to hang out in the area for a few days as you island-hop from one sight to the other. If you're on a budget or really want to enjoy the natural environment unfettered by modern distractions, try camping at one of the many campgrounds or renting a bungalow from the national parks department.

The largest island, **Ko Tarutao**, is a mountainous, forested island with limestone cliffs, mangrove swamps, and white-sand beaches. The island formerly housed a detainment center for political and other prisoners, but these days it's home to some of the national park facilities as well as the biggest selection of bungalows and resorts. If you're interested in seeing the darker side of the country's history, you can visit the old prisons at **Talo Udang Bay** in the southernmost part of the island and Talowao Bay in the southeastern part of the island. They're connected by a trail that was built by prisoners before the site was abandoned during World War II.

Mu Ko Adang Rawi comprises two islands, **Ko Adang** and **Ko Rawi,** both characterized by light-sand beaches, verdant interiors with limestone cliffs, and some coral reefs offshore that can be easily viewed when snorkeling or diving. Many people visit these islands as part of a day trip, but if you want to stay overnight, there are some bungalows available through the parks department, or you can rent a tent from them or bring your own to camp on the beach.

Ko Kai and **Ko Klang** in the center of the marine park are also both popular spots for snorkeling and hanging out on the clean sandy beaches. There are no accommodations here, and tour groups will often add these islands to a multiple-island day tour.

Ko Li Pe
เกาะหลีเป๊ะ

Just below the national park is Ko Li Pe, a small, charming island just 40 kilometers from Malaysia's Langkawi Island. Populated by sea gypsies and a smattering of unpretentious resorts and bungalows, every year the island is becoming more popular with adventurous vacationers looking for something a little off the beaten path. Still, it's small enough that you can tour the whole island in two hours,

and you won't find any big partying or even ATMs on Ko Li Pe, just a handful of beautiful beaches and some dive shops catering to those who want to enjoy the underwater life around the island.

There are three beaches on Ko Li Pe, which is shaped roughly like a boomerang pointing northeast. The eastern beach is called Sunset Beach, the northern beach is Sunrise Beach, and the southwestern beach (the inside of the boomerang) is called Pattaya Beach. Sunrise Beach and Pattaya Beach are connected to each other by a road that functions as the island's main street.

Many resorts close up shop during low season, but there are some that remain open year-round. **Idyllic Concept Resort** (Sunrise Beach, tel. 08/8227-5389, www.idyllicresort. com, 3,500B) features modern, funky guest rooms and bungalows right on the beach, plus a resort restaurant. The resort is only a few years old and is very clean and well-maintained.

Sita Beach Resort and Spa Villa (Pattaya Beach, tel. 07/475-0382, www.sitabeachresort. com, 3,500B) is a full-service mid-range resort with a swimming pool, a restaurant, a bar, and a small spa. Guest rooms are comfortable and have flat-screen TVs and vaguely Thai decor. The pool area is spacious and surrounded by guest rooms and villas. The resort is very family-friendly too. It's the location, and the view of the beach, though, that are the big attraction here.

The cool, popular, and ecochic **Castaway Resort** (Sunrise Beach, tel. 08/3138-7472, www.kohlipe.castaway-resorts.com, 2,000B) is a collection of stand-alone bamboo bungalows on the beach, plus an outdoor bar and restaurant. The accommodations are basic—there's no air-conditioning or hot water, although because the bungalows are right off the water, ceiling fans keep everything cool enough. Most bungalows have an upstairs and a downstairs plus a small balcony for lounging and enjoying the view.

THE LOWER SOUTHERN GULF

Visit the lower southern Gulf of Thailand for the idyllic islands of the Samui Archipelago, off-the-beaten-path beaches on the mainland, and some charming small historical cities where you can learn about the culture and history of the region.

White sandy beaches, coconut trees, and green rolling hills, as well as excellent diving, make the Samui Archipelago islands off the coast of Surat Thani a top choice if you're looking for a beach vacation in Thailand. Although some mistakenly consider the Samui Archipelago second-best when compared with the Andaman coast, the region has plenty to offer that you won't find on the other side of the Kra Isthmus. The landscapes are not as dramatic as the karst cliffs that pepper Phuket, Krabi, and Trang, but thanks to an abundance

of coconut trees and a softer, more rolling topography, the islands are greener and lusher. The resorts can be as posh as those on the Andaman coast, and at the cheaper end, the selection is better. The rainy season is much shorter, lasting from only mid-October–mid-December. Plus, the Ang Thong National Marine Park, comprising 40 islands, is much less touched by tourism than any of the marine national parks in the Andaman region.

The islands of Ko Samui, Ko Pha-Ngan, and Ko Tao, sometimes called the pearls of the gulf, were once considered a backpacker haven, but at least Ko Samui is moving upscale, with five-star resorts and plenty of indulgent spas. Ko Pha-Ngan, just north of Ko Samui, has more luxury lodgings every year but is still one of the few popular islands left in the country where

© SUZANNE NAM

HIGHLIGHTS

◖ Mu Ko Ang Thong National Marine Park: These lush, green islands near the Samui Archipelago are easy to visit on a day trip and offer snorkeling, kayaking, and camping (page 255).

◖ Lamai Beach, Ko Samui: This pretty beach on Thailand's popular resort island offer everything you could ever want, including soft sand, peace and quiet, and five-star resorts (page 258).

◖ Nakhon Si Thammarat: The coolest city you've never heard of is the center of Thai Buddhism, and it offers plenty of culture, great food, and not a lot of other travelers (page 283).

◖ Khanom and Sichon: These are two relatively undiscovered beaches with clear, clean, warm water, soft sand, and friendly people (page 287).

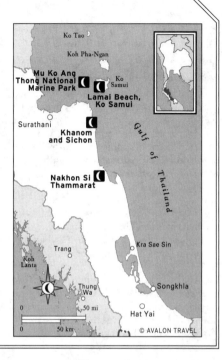

LOOK FOR ◖ TO FIND RECOMMENDED SIGHTS, ACTIVITIES, DINING, AND LODGING.

designer suitcases might get some funny looks among fellow travelers and cheap bungalows remain the norm.

If you want to get away from the crowds of travelers and the indulgent atmosphere you'll find on Samui or the party atmosphere on Ko Pha-Ngan, visit some of the mainland beaches north of Nakhon Si Thammarat. Although they aren't as slick and foreigner-friendly as the more popular beach spots, the natural landscape is mostly unmarred by development, and the area still retains the typically Thai culture that's often harder to see in more popular destinations.

South of Nakhon Si Thammarat, the coast along the Gulf of Thailand changes significantly. You'll still find stretches of beach and plenty of friendly people, but once you enter Songkhla Province, Islam begins to be more

apparent. Hat Yai, the area's economic hub, attracts hordes of visitors, but mostly people from Malaysia, who come for shopping and to take advantage of Thailand's more permissive culture. This makes it a very interesting place to people-watch, if you happen to be passing through, although it's probably not going to be a primary destination for most.

PLANNING YOUR TIME

Many visitors to the gulf spend all of their time on Ko Samui, and it's easy to do so with direct flights to the island from Bangkok. On Ko Samui you'll find there are few cultural and historical sights to visit, as the island has really only developed around the travelers that have come to visit in recent decades, but there are plenty of beach activities to fill your time. If you plan on seeing more than one of

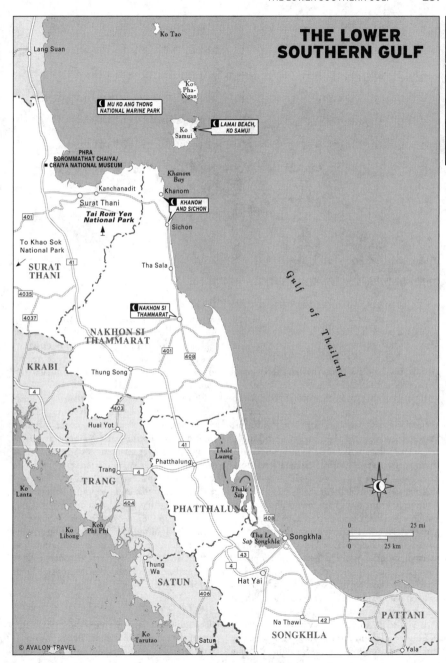

THE LOWER SOUTHERN GULF

Ko Tao

Lang Suan

Ko Pha-Ngan

🌙 MU KO ANG THONG NATIONAL MARINE PARK

🌙 LAMAI BEACH, KO SAMUI

Ko Samui ★

PHRA BOROMMATHAT CHAIYA/ ■ CHAIYA NATIONAL MUSEUM

Khanom Bay

Kanchanadit

Khanom

Surat Thani

🌙 KHANOM AND SICHON

Tai Rom Yen National Park

Sichon

401

To Khao Sok National Park

SURAT THANI

41

Tha Sala

4035

4037

🌙 NAKHON SI THAMMARAT

NAKHON SI THAMMARAT

401   408

KRABI

4

Thung Song

403

Huai Yot

41

Phatthalung

Thale Luang

Trang   4

TRANG

Thale Sap

404

Ko Lanta

Koh Phi Phi

PHATTHALUNG

408

Ko Libong

Tha Le Sap Songkhla

Songkhla

Gulf of Thailand

0   25 mi

0   25 km

Thung Wa

SATUN

43

406

Hat Yai

4

PATTANI

Ko Tarutao

Satun

Na Thawi   42

SONGKHLA

Yala

© AVALON TRAVEL

© SUZANNE NAM

fishing boat off of Ko Samui

the islands in the archipelago, give yourself at least a week, especially if you want to get some diving in. Hopping from Ko Samui to Ko Pha-Ngan to Ko Tao is simple but time-consuming, and there are frequent ferry boats between the islands.

If you're flying into nearby Surat Thani and taking a ferry to one of the islands, expect to spend about half a day getting from the airport to the ferry pier and then to the island itself. It's not as convenient as flying into Ko Samui, but you may save yourself quite a few thousand baht. There are only two airlines—Bangkok Airways and Thai Airways—that fly into Ko Samui from Bangkok. Bangkok Airways, which owns the Samui airport, is known for great service and convenient flight schedules, but not cheap prices. Since Thai Airways started flying to Samui a few years ago, many thought prices would go down. So far, they haven't, so travelers on a budget usually opt to take one of the low-cost carriers to Surat Thani and transfer from there.

If you're planning on a visit to the cities of Nakhon Si Thammarat or Songkhla, you can easily see most of the important sights in a day

or two, leaving plenty of extra time to relax on one of the beaches up north. With direct flights on Nok Air to Nakhon Si Thammarat, it's surprisingly easy to get to the city or nearby Songkhla without spending hours transferring from one place to another.

Although Islam and Buddhism have coexisted in this part of the country for centuries with few problems, sectarian violence currently gripping Yala, Pattani, and Narathiwat has recently spilled over into parts of Songkhla. Hat Yai, the province's capital, has had multiple bomb attacks in the past decade that have targeted hotels, pubs, and shopping centers. The violence so far has been limited to Hat Yai and has been very sporadic, but it's something that cannot be ignored if you're traveling to this part of the country. There have been no incidents, however, in any of the popular tourist spots and no indication that there is a threat of violence there.

HISTORY

Although these days the mainland cities in this part of the country look more like semi-industrialized towns and transport hubs for travelers moving onto the beaches and islands, Surat Thani was once the seat of the Srivijaya empire in Thailand. Though little is known about the lost empire, historians speculate that it existed from somewhere between the third and fifth centuries to the 13th century. The center of the Srivijaya empire's power was on the island of Sumatra, in present-day Indonesia, but the empire spread throughout the Indonesian archipelago and northward, encompassing the Malay Peninsula up to present-day Surat Thani. Although the kingdom was Hindu, Buddhist, and then Muslim, remains from the Surat Thani area are Mahayana Buddhist, and there are temple ruins in the city of Chaiya, outside of Surat Thani, as well as the Chaiya National Museum.

In some sense, Thailand became its own kingdom in the 13th century when the region became ruled by Thai people instead of outsiders, but the country as it is known today did not exist until the 20th century. Southeast Asia had for centuries been under the influence of innumerable empires bearing little relation to current national borders, and it was the Anglo-Siamese Treaty of 1909 that put the last pieces of the puzzle (at least in the south) together for the Kingdom of Siam. It was then that Siam got the provinces of Satun, Songkhla, Pattani, Narathiwat, and Yala in exchange for giving up claims to provinces farther south that are now part of Malaysia. While the country as a whole identifies with the Kingdoms of Sukhothai and Ayutthaya, the south has always had a somewhat different history.

Since the Srivijaya period, Nakhon Si Thammarat emerged as its own kingdom of sorts, existing independently but paying tribute to the Sukhothai and then Ayutthaya Kingdoms. By the 18th century, the region was ruled by the Kingdom of Siam, although at least with respect to Songkhla, that rule was challenged until the 1909 treaty.

Nakhon Si Thammarat has become an important city for Buddhists, and you'll see plenty of *wats* if you visit. Just south, in Songkhla, the predominant religion is Islam.

The island of Samui was first officially recorded by the Chinese around 1500 in ancient maps but was probably settled more than 1,000 years ago by mariners from Hainan in southwest China. While the mainland was a part of the Srivijaya Kingdom, Samui and neighboring islands were not a significant part of the kingdom. Until the 1970s, Ko Samui was just a simple island relying on ample coconut trees and fishing for commerce. During World War II, Ko Samui was briefly occupied by the Japanese, but otherwise it stayed below the radar.

Three decades later, the island and neighboring Ko Pha-Ngan arrived on the backpacker trail and slowly grew from quiet tropical refuges to international tourist destinations.

Ko Samui and the Samui Archipelago   เกาะสมุย

Once just a quiet island happily going about its business farming coconuts, Ko Samui is now one of the most popular vacation spots in Thailand. Filled with palm trees and rimmed by white sandy beaches, the island has all the ingredients necessary for a gorgeous holiday retreat. If you're arriving by plane to Ko Samui, the moment you step off the airplane and onto the tarmac you'll understand what the island is all about. There's no steel or glass at the international airport. Instead, it's a group of thatch-roofed huts where you check in and pick up your luggage. To get to and from the planes, passengers are taken by open-air buses akin to large golf carts. If you're arriving by ferry from the mainland, you'll get to enjoy the spectacular view of the surrounding islands during the 90-minute ride.

The island is not all huts and coconut trees, however. Since its debut as a budget destination, Samui has grown up. Although there are still beach bungalows to be found, there is also

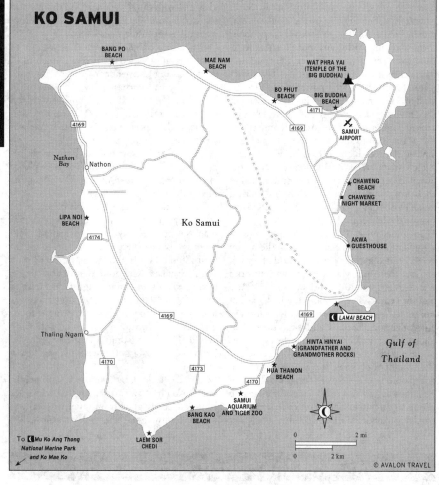

KO SAMUI

BANG PO BEACH

MAE NAM BEACH

WAT PHRA YAI (TEMPLE OF THE BIG BUDDHA)

BO PHUT BEACH

BIG BUDDHA BEACH

4171

4169

SAMUI AIRPORT

Nathon Bay

Nathon

CHAWENG BEACH

CHAWENG NIGHT MARKET

LIPA NOI BEACH

4174

Ko Samui

AKWA GUESTHOUSE

4169

LAMAI BEACH

Thaling Ngam

4169

HINTA HINYAI (GRANDFATHER AND GRANDMOTHER ROCKS)

Gulf of Thailand

4170

4173

4170

HUA THANON BEACH

SAMUI AQUARIUM AND TIGER ZOO

BANG KAO BEACH

To Mu Ko Ang Thong National Marine Park and Ko Mae Ko

LAEM SOR CHEDI

0   2 mi

0   2 km

© AVALON TRAVEL

a large selection of five-star resorts as well as lots of spas and retreats and a dining scene that gets better every year. Thanks to a ring road that circles the entire island, there's plenty of built-up infrastructure, and you'll have easy access to things such as medical care and rental cars. Every beach has at least one Internet café, and many hotels and cafés in more built-up beach areas have Wi-Fi. The development hasn't come without a price. Although the beaches are still beautiful, parts of the island

can seem like a messy, incoherently developed mass of cheap concrete buildings and tangled power lines. Covering nearly 260 square kilometers, Samui is a large island and can sometimes feel like a small city instead of desert paradise.

Just north of Samui, Ko Pha-Ngan is still mostly a backpacker haven, with a good selection of inexpensive places to stay and plenty of cheap drinks and all-night partying. The island's famous full moon parties, which seem

© SUZANNE NAM

small islands off the northern tip of Ko Samui

to take place every weekend regardless of the lunar phase, are what has given Ko Pha-Ngan this reputation, although there are more high-end resorts opening up and attracting a different type of independent traveler. The physical landscape of the island, with gentle hills covered in trees and white sandy beaches, is as beautiful as Samui, and perhaps even more so, as it's less developed. Part of this is certainly due to the fact that there are no flights to the island. If you are visiting Pha-Ngan, you'll need to take a ferry boat from Surat Thani or Ko Samui, making it a good choice if you have the luxury of time but not money. Ko Tao, the northernmost main island in the archipelago, is still largely a base for divers but shares the same topography as its larger neighbors.

SIGHTS
◖ Mu Ko Ang Thong National Marine Park
อุทยานแห่งชาติหมู่เกาะอ่างทอง

This national park, spanning a cluster of more than 40 small islands in the Samui

Archipelago, is the gem of the region. The relatively small, amazingly green islands are really limestone mountains rising out of the sea, so there are plenty of caves and interesting rock formations to explore while you're there, as well as a handful of sandy beaches, rare birds, and macaques.

What really sets this group of islands apart is that they are virtually undeveloped and uninhabited, something you won't see on the Andaman coast. Before being declared a national park in 1980, the area was used by the Royal Thai Navy, and thus there are no bungalow developments or other commercial activity to disturb the natural environment. Getting to the islands is not a problem, though: There are plenty of tour companies on Samui and in Surat Thani who do daily day trips.

If you're into snorkeling or scuba, this is probably not the place for you, however. The water can be less than crystal clear, and there is only limited coral. This has nothing to do with the cleanliness of the water in the gulf; it's just that the islands are located in relatively shallow

© SUZANNE NAM

islands within Mu Ko Ang Thong National Marine Park

waters, and sediment that runs off from mainland rivers into the gulf doesn't settle quickly. If you're planning on visiting the park, remember that it is closed for most of November–December because of the monsoon season.

The national park headquarters are on the island of **Ko Wua Talap,** and this is a great place to start your tour of the islands (many guided tours stop here for a couple of hours). In addition to a white-sand beach right in front of the headquarters, there is also a hiking trail to a lookout point with a fantastic view of the surrounding islands. If you take the hike, expect to spend at least an hour going up and down, and do not attempt it in flip-flops. At certain points the trail becomes very steep (and very slippery if it has recently rained), and you'll need to rely on the ropes to pull yourself up. Although there are no commercial accommodations on any of the islands in the park, there are simple but charming fan-cooled bungalows and a campground on Ko Wua Talap as well as a drinks concession and a small restaurant.

Ko Mae Ko also has a nice beach to spend some time on, but if you're visiting this island, make sure to hike up to Thale Nai, a large emerald-green saltwater lake in the middle of rising cliffs. Much of the path is lined with stairs, which can be very steep at times, and as long as you go slowly, the 10-minute climb is fine even for moderately active people. For clear water, sandy beaches, and good snorkeling by the shore, **Ko Samsoa,** just across from Ko Mae Ko, is also a nice island on which to spend some time. If you're on a tour, you'll be provided with snorkel gear, though many boats don't bring fins.

Most visitors to the national marine park start from Ko Samui, where there are a number of tour operators that do the trip.

Samui Aquarium and Tiger Zoo
พิพิธภัณฑ์สัตว์น้ำสมุยและสวนเสือ

The aquarium and zoo (33/2 Mu 2, Maret, tel. 07/742-4017, www.samuiorchid.com, 9 A.M.–5 P.M. daily, 250B) are part of the private Samui Orchid Resort, and the animals are there as entertainment, not part of a conservation effort or scientific endeavor. In the tanks you'll see lots of colorful coral as well as exotic tropical fish and even a couple of sharks. In the cages are tigers, monkeys, and birds, and you can even have your picture taken with one of the tigers if you're brave enough.

Wat Phra Yai (Temple of the Big Buddha)
วัดพระใหญ่

At the northern tip of the island is Wat Phra Yai, an outdoor temple with an immense 10-meter golden statue of Buddha. Although it's right near the eponymous Big Buddha Beach, it's a very peaceful place to visit and hear the resident monks pray and get a nice panoramic view of the surrounding area, especially at sunset (since you'll have to climb quite a few stairs to get to the Buddha). When you visit, you have to toll the bells surrounding the Buddha for good luck. If you're anywhere in the area, you won't be able to miss the big Buddha on the mountain. To get here, you'll need to take Route 4171 heading east, or arrange a ride with an off-duty *song thaew*.

HinTa HinYai (Grandfather and Grandmother Rocks)
หินตาหินยาย

Near Lamai Beach, HinTa HinYai is a very famous natural phenomena—strange rocks look like human sex organs when viewed from a certain angle. The locals discreetly refer to them as grandfather and grandmother. When you visit, make sure to bring a camera to capture the view. When you're done, make sure to buy some *kalamae* from one of the nearby vendors. It's a type of Thai toffee and it's creamy, not too sweet, and comes packaged in little triangles. The rocks are just a couple of kilometers south of Lamai Beach off of the ring road. If you are on Lamai, you can either walk there or catch a *song thaew* the short distance (make sure to tell the driver you are going to HinTa HinYai).

Laem Sor Chedi
เจดีย์แหลมสอ

On the southern tip of the island is Laem Sor Chedi, a seldom visited, peaceful place with a large, ornate *chedi* right adjacent to the beach. Although you won't find much to do here,

that's sort of the point. Next to the *chedi* is a small forest clearing often referred to as the meditation forest, where visitors can go and sit and ponder existence (you can even arrange to spend a few days at the *wat* learning how to meditate, but you'll need to work that out in person with the resident abbot). Laem Sor Chedi is about 1.5 kilometers off the main Ring Road around the island, so it is possible to take a *song thaew* and then walk the rest of the way. You can also take a taxi, but if you do not want to walk the 1.5 kilometers back to the main road, consider asking the driver to wait for you. The round-trip will cost you around 500B depending on which beach you are coming from. If you are driving, on the way to the *chedi* is a secret viewpoint. All of the signs are in Thai, so to get there your best bet is to enlist the help of a local (taking a taxi might be even better). You'll have to follow the turnoff to the Rattanakosin Chedi, up an extremely steep road to a beautiful viewpoint where you can see the southern part of the island.

BEACHES
East Coast

Chaweng Beach, on the island's east coast, is the most famous beach in Samui, and it always draws more than its fair share of visitors, especially those traveling from other countries. The beach itself is a beautiful, long strip of light, soft sand backed by palm trees, and the water is warm, clear, and generally calm. Although Chaweng is one continuous bay, it's broken into three different sections—North Chaweng, Central Chaweng and Chaweng Noi, and Coral Cove just below it. There's a reef just offshore that serves to break most incoming waves. During high season, you can't avoid feeling a little hustle and bustle here, and visitors flock to the numerous resorts that line the beach. It's the most built-up area on the island, which makes it a very convenient place to stay, and in addition to the bungalows you'll find fronting the shore, there are also lots of restaurants and vendors. The main road runs parallel to the shore just behind the beach, and it feels more like a little city than

© SUZANNE NAM

busy Chaweng Beach

a quiet beach town. Here you'll see lots of familiar brands, such as McDonald's, Pizza Hut, and Starbucks. In fact, it might be hard to notice you're in Thailand at all, as most of the signs are in English.

【 LAMAI BEACH
Lamai Beach, just south of Chaweng, is the island's second most popular beach. In Thai, Lamai means "sweet" and "smooth," and that's a good description of Lamai Beach. Although Chaweng Beach has the softest sand and arguably the best view, Lamai is a close second. It's also second to Chaweng in terms of development and, for lots of visitors, represents a happy medium between development and seclusion. There is a good selection of resorts and ample places to eat, but it's also a bit more *sabai* than its neighbor to the north. There are still plenty of conveniences here, though, as central Lamai just behind the beach is full of shops and restaurants. The beach itself is typical of Samui—a gently curving bay, bathwater-temperature water, and lots of surrounding coconut

trees swaying in the wind. Lamai Beach has rougher water, as there's no reef to break the waves as they come in. At the southern end of the beach is the strange rock formation HinTa HinYai, which draws daily crowds of visitors.

South Coast
Hua Thanon and **Bang Kao** beaches on the south of the island are the least developed on Samui. Some of this part of the coast is rocky, although there are plenty of places were you can comfortably spread out a towel or open a beach chair and enjoy the peace and quiet. There are not many accommodations on this part of the island, but the few that are here are quite nice and have private beaches. The village at Hua Thanon is a picture-perfect, charming little Muslim fishing village with a small market that adds to the overall beauty of the physical surroundings.

West Coast
The west coast of the island is dominated by **Nathon Bay,** where most ferries from Ko Pha-

DETOX RETREATS

The colonic-irrigation trend is still popular in Thailand, and Ko Samui has more than a handful of spas offering the service as part of a multiday detox program. The programs vary from spa to spa, but in general, participants consume only water, fruit juice, special low-calorie shakes, and vitamin supplements for the duration. In addition to twice-daily colonics, the spas offer meditation, yoga classes, and massage.

Colonics have been viewed with skepticism by the traditional medical community, but there are thousands of people from across the globe who flock to Samui's spas every year for their detox programs, hoping to get a little healthier and maybe drop a few kilograms in the process. Whether it works in the long term is up for debate, but people who've spent a week at one of the island's detox retreats say they come away feeling good.

Although the focus of many spas is colonic detox, and many require fasting as part of the program, they also offer regular retreats with healthy low-calorie meals, meditation, and yoga.

Absolute Yoga, one of the upscale yoga studios in Bangkok, has a spa called **Absolute Yoga & The Love Kitchen** (Fisherman's Village, Bo Phut Beach, tel. 07/743-0290, www.absoluteyogasamui.com) offering a variety of programs from weekend detox retreats to 10-day intensive programs that include yoga, meditation, and colonics. Some of the programs involve juice fasting, but they also have programs where you dine on vegetarian food from their Love Kitchen. The programs run around 1,400B per day, which includes food and classes. If you're not interested in the detox regimen, you can buy an unlimited yoga pass for a week for just 1,500B. The resort itself is a charming, boutique-style small hotel with colorful but elegant guest rooms and a nice swimming pool.

The **Spa Resorts** (Lamai Beach, tel. 07/742-4666, www.thesparesorts.net) has been around for more than 15 years and has a number of programs centered on detox and cleansing as well as meditation and yoga. The program runs around 1,500B per day, not including accommodations. The spa also has a basic bungalow resort with a nice swimming pool and gardens. The vegetarian menu at the spa is one of the best on the island.

Ngan and Surat Thani arrive. The town of Nathon is definitely worth some time, as it's home to many of the local residents of the island and offers a chance to see what life is like in Thailand, but bear in mind that Nathon is the business end of Samui, and the beach itself is much less beautiful than what you'll find at Lamai, Chaweng, or Big Buddha Beaches.

South of Nathon Bay are two wonderful small beaches. **Lipa Noi Beach** is nestled amidst coconut trees. The water is shallow for quite a way offshore, making it a great place for kids to play. There are a few cheap bungalows and resorts here, and a handful of places to eat, but otherwise it's a very quiet, almost sleepy beach area. May through November, the water is too shallow for swimming except at high tide. **Thaling Ngam** is a small, secluded beach backed by cliffs and ubiquitous coconut trees. The scenery is beautiful, but parts of the beach are rocky and the sand has lots of coral fragments, so it's not as soft as other beaches on the island.

North Coast

On the northern part of the island, the largest stretch of beach is at **Bang Po Beach.** This four-kilometer-long beach has clear water, soft, light sand, and coconut trees as well as a coral reef just off the coast. It's backed by green hills and has a beautiful, secluded feeling. Despite all the draws, the beach is generally quite quiet, and there are only a handful of resorts and visitor amenities in the area. If you're looking to do a lot of swimming, this is not a great spot, as the water is very shallow until you pass the reef, and this may be why it's less popular. It's a good beach for snorkeling, however, since the reef is in shallow water, and you'll usually see at least a handful of people out looking at the reef and marinelife.

Mae Nam Beach, Bo Phut Beach, and **Big Buddha Beach** (also called Bangrak Beach) are all adjacent to each other on the northern coast, and some consider this the best part of the island. Each of the beaches is in a softly curving cove, and although there's no view of either sunset or sunrise, the beach, the water, and the surrounding greenery are beautiful. There are a handful of inexpensive bungalows here along with some of the nicest resorts on the island and some trendy, upscale places to eat. Although not nearly as busy as Chaweng Beach, there are still dive shops and travel agencies if you're looking to schedule an excursion. Some spots on these beaches won't be easily swimmable April–November due to seasonal tides that make the water too shallow. Mae Nam Beach is the quietest of the three and could be a great choice if you want to feel like you're in a quiet area but have access to more of the action. Plus it has the best selection of cheap bungalows. Bo Phut Beach is particularly charming, especially due to the adjacent fishing village with charming wooden shophouses. If you're looking to Jet Ski, it's one of the places on the island you can rent a Jet Ski on the beach. If you're looking for peace and quiet, however, all the activity can be annoying. Big Buddha Beach, right near the airport, has the most action. Although it's named after the large golden Buddha that sits on a nearby hill overlooking the island, it's not quite the tranquil spot the name would imply. There are scores of cheap bungalows here, and the beach tends to attract a younger crowd. Although there are no discos or true nightclubs, there are plenty of bars with live music lining the beach at night.

SHOPPING

Most of the tourist shopping you'll find on the island is in the street stalls surrounding the beaches, which sell everything from sarongs to kitchenware made of coconut shells. If you're looking to drop a few baht, find that you've forgotten your flip-flops, or want casual and inexpensive beachwear, the best bet is Chaweng Beach. The nearby roads are lined with stalls and small shops, and it's an especially vibrant and bustling scene after dark. It's sometimes referred to as the **Chaweng Night Market,** although it is technically open all day too. When you buy, make sure to barter, as prices tend to start high. Although there are some more upscale shops in Chaweng as well, prices are generally not that competitive if you're comparing them to what you'll find in Bangkok, or in any major city around the world, for that matter.

The shopping scene for necessities is a little better. Chaweng has a **Tops Market** with international and local groceries, and there are similar shops in Lamai. The **Tesco Lotus** on the ring road between Bo Phut Beach and Chaweng Beach has everything from household appliances to staple groceries, plus fresh meat and produce. It's in a mall surrounded by smaller local shops, pharmacies, restaurants, and a movie theater.

SPORTS AND RECREATION
Kayaking and Snorkeling Tours

Day tours to Ang Thong National Marine Park or neighboring Ko Tao and Ko Nang Yuan are some of the most popular activities for visitors to Samui. There are a handful of companies offering these tours, which almost always include either snorkeling or kayaking. Some also include elephant trekking. Tickets are almost always sold through tour agents scattered across the island. Tours are very similar to one another and competitively priced, so expect to pay 1,200–1,500B for a day tour. Even though many brochures have prices printed on them, agents will almost always offer at least a 10 percent discount, so ask if you haven't been offered it. Also make sure to look over the tour brochure and ask the travel agent what your tour includes. Each usually includes pickup from your hotel or guesthouse; you'll be dropped of at the pier, where you'll board either a **speedboat** or a **ferry** with other passengers. Speedboat tours have the benefit of less time in transit and are a little more adventurous, but a ride on a larger boat allows for more relaxing and lounging. Regardless of the type of vessel, you'll be given a light breakfast (coffee and fruit or pastry) and you'll also be served lunch either onboard or on one of the islands you'll stop at. Make sure to bring a swimsuit, towel, and good shoes for hiking, as many tours include stops on islands with good viewpoints.

Samui Island Tour (349 Mu 3, Ang Thong, tel. 07/742-1506, www.samui-islandtour.com) offers daily tours of Ang Thong National Marine Park on large ferries, with stops at Ko Mae Ko and Ko Wua Talap (national park headquarters). They also offer kayaking with a guide on their tours. Expect to pay 400–500B extra to use their kayaks.

Seahawk Speedboat (14/1 Mu 2, Chaweng Beach, tel. 07/723-1597) offers speedboat tours of both Ang Thong National Marine Park and the islands surrounding Ko Tao. The marine park tours are similar to those offered by Samui Island Tours with the addition of a stop at Ko Paluay, where you can snorkel or use one of their kayaks. Their Ko Tao day tour takes you to Ko Tao for snorkeling, then to Ko Nang Yuan (the three connected islands) for sunbathing and sightseeing.

Another speedboat tour is **Grand Sea Discovery** (187 Mu 1, Mae Nam Beach, tel. 07/742-7001, www.grandseatours.com), which offers tours to Ko Tao and Ko Nang Yaun, Ang Thong National Marine Park, or Ko Pha-Ngan. Their Ko Tao trip follows basically the same route as Seahawk Speedboat's, and their marine park tour is similar to that of Samui Island Tour. They also offer a one-day tour of Ko Pha-Ngan, where you'll do some sightseeing, visit an elephant camp, have lunch, and swim and snorkel.

Sea Safari by Speed Boat (tel. 07/742-5563, www.islandsafaritour.com) offers a typical tour of Ang Thong National Marine Park, which includes sea canoeing, but also adds elephant trekking or ATV biking in the afternoon, making for a long but full day.

Island Tours

If you're interested in staying on dry land, there are also a few outfits offering island tours. **Sita**

Tour 2000 (9/13 Mu 2, Chaweng Beach, tel. 07/748-4834) offers half-day tours of the island's sights, and includes stops at the Big Buddha, HinTa HinYai rocks, and even a monkey show. These trips cost less than 500B for a half day, but they do not include meals, and since the island's sights and attractions aren't all that spectacular, they are probably best left for a rainy day. **Mr. Ung's Safari** (52/4 Mu 3, Chaweng Beach, tel. 07/723-0114, www.ung-safari.com) offers full-day tours of the island's sights but throws in some trekking, four-wheeling, and elephant rides.

Boating

Lately Samui has become a popular place for sailors—not the type on shore leave from long journeys abroad but the jet-set kind who like to travel in multimillion-dollar yachts. Much of this popularity may be due to the **Samui Regatta** (www.samuiregatta.com), an annual five-day sailboat race held in late May–early June, pulling in competitors from all over the world. If you find yourself without your own boat on Samui, there are a handful of sailboat rental agencies, including **Samui Ocean Sports** (Chaweng Regent Beach Resort, 155/4 Mu 2, Bo Phut Beach, tel. 08/1940-1999, www.sailing-in-samui.com) and **Sunsail Thailand** (www.sunsailthailand.com). If you're lucky enough to be staying at the posh Anantara Resort, they have a number of craft available for rent, including Hobbies and Lasers, as well as sailing lessons and other sailing activities.

ACCOMMODATIONS
Under 1,500B

For a quintessential beach bungalow experience, try **New Huts** (Lamai Beach, tel. 08/9729-8489, 200B). Here you'll get a small, very basic wooden bungalow just a few steps above a shack and share a basic bath with other travelers. Oh, and there's no air-conditioning, but for 200B it's hard to complain, especially considering the location a short walk from a nice part of Lamai Beach. If you can't get a room here, **Beer's House Beach Bungalows** (161/4 Mu 4, Lamai Beach, tel. 07/723-0467, www.beerhousebungalow.com, 600B) is another excellent option in the budget category. Here most of the bungalows have private baths with coldwater showers, and there is a small restaurant on the premises.

While there are plenty of beach bungalows in the 400–500B range on Mae Nam Beach, **Moon Huts** (67/2 Mu 1, Mae Nam, tel. 07/742-5247, www.moonhutsamui.com, 500B) tend to be a little cleaner and nicer than the competition. At this price they won't deliver luxury, but you will get a private bath, fresh sheets, and a spotless guest room a short walk from the beach and the property's bar-restaurant. Nicer bungalows on the beach have air-conditioning instead of fans; expect to pay around 1,000B for these. There are also large two-bedroom family bungalows available.

The **Akwa Guesthouse** (28/12 Chaweng Beach Rd., tel. 08/4660-0551, 800B) is head and shoulders above the typical guesthouse experience in Thailand, and if you're looking for an edgy, comfortable place on Samui, and there happens to be a room available, you can't go wrong here. The guesthouse, just a two-minute walk from quieter northern Chaweng Beach, is clean, funky, and inexpensive, and the management and staff are excellent. The guest rooms are all decorated with pop art prints and colorful, thoughtfully placed furnishings, starkly contrasting against the white-duvet-covered beds. There's free Wi-Fi throughout, and standard guest rooms come equipped with DVD and MP3 players; some have nicely decorated wooden decks too. If you want to have an urban palace in the middle of the tropics, the 65-square-meter penthouse is also available, and it has an amazing deck. The downstairs restaurant, which offers very reasonably priced Thai and Western dishes all day, has the same design theme and friendly attitude. Aside from the fabulous decor, reasonable prices, and good food, everyone who works at the Akwa is sincere and will go out of their way to make your stay memorable, from arranging airport transfers to setting up excursions. Although there's no pool here and it doesn't have the typical resort amenities, this is the type of place you

rarely find in touristy areas and one you'll want to return to again after your first stay.

Beachfront bungalows are tough to find in this price range on this beach, but **Thong Ta Kian Villa** (Thong Ta Kien Bay, 146 Mu 4, Maret, tel. 07/723-0978, 1,300B) offers some exceptionally clean, large, stand-alone guest rooms. Design is simple, and this is certainly not a resort, but extras such as air-conditioning, small fridges to keep your beer cold, and TVs put this property well above the typical beach bungalow offerings.

Though not right on the beach, **Cocooning Hotel and Tapas Bar** (6/11 Mu 1, Bo Phut Beach, tel. 07/742-7150, www.cocooninghotelsamui.com, 1,000B) is a lovely, intimate, well-designed guesthouse with some of the prettiest guest rooms you'll find on the island. There are only a handful of guest rooms here, and each has its own color and design theme against a backdrop of white walls and modern concrete flooring. This is not a resort, and it's quite small, so the only amenities available are a very small swimming pool and a tapas bar serving drinks and light snacks. Still, the property has a very chic European feel to it, probably thanks to the French owner.

Ampha Place Hotel (67/59 Mu 1, Mae Nam, tel. 07/733-2129, www.samui-ampha-hotel.com, 1,200B) has cheap, clean guest rooms just 10 minutes on foot from Mae Nam Beach. Ampha Place is a no-frills property but isn't old or run-down. Guest rooms are small but surprisingly well-equipped, have small balconies, and are accented with Thai decor. There is also a small but pretty swimming pool in the middle of the property.

NovaSamui Resort (147/3 Mu 2, Chaweng, tel. 07/723-0864, www.novasamui.com, 1,200B) has cheap, clean guest rooms, a large swimming pool, and nicely maintained common areas. Although the NovaSamui has some resort-level amenities, it's not a luxury resort, and it's not right on the water, but just a short walk from Chaweng Beach. For about one-third of the price, however, it's an excellent choice.

Like other Ibis properties in Thailand and all over the world, **The Ibis Bophut** (197/1

Mu 1, Bo Phut Beach, tel. 02/659-2888, www. ibishotel.com, 1,400B) offers guests a good location and spotlessly clean, reliable guest rooms and common areas. Guest rooms at this large hotel are very small, but the bar, restaurant, and large pool area give guests plenty of other options for hanging out. There are also family rooms available with bunk beds for kids, although they are also small.

Marina Villa (124 Mu 3, Lamai Beach, tel. 07/742-4426, www.marinavillasamui.com, 1,400B), right on Lamai Beach, is a small, pleasant, family-friendly resort with comfortable, clean guest rooms and a good location. This is not a luxury resort but does have two swimming pools and a restaurant.

1,500-3,000B

Choeng Mon Beach Hotel (24/3 Mu 5, Choeng Mon Beach, Bo Phut, tel. 07/742-5372, www.choengmon.com, 1,500B), on Choeng Mon Beach just northeast of Bo Phut Beach, is a somewhat generic midsize tourist hotel but has amenities and facilities, including a swimming pool, a small gym, and a restaurant that make it a good value for guests who want resort perks but do not want to pay resort prices for them. Guest rooms at this beachfront property are clean, simple, and comfortable. Larger groups can also rent one of their bungalows.

A good location and reasonably priced guest rooms are what make **Samui Hacienda** (98/2/1 Mu 1, Bo Phut Beach, tel. 07/724-5943, www. samui-hacienda.com, 1,800B) such a good value. Guest rooms, many of which have beach views, are simple but clean and comfortable, and the whole property is well maintained. The design theme—a fusion of Mediterranean and Thai styles—surprisingly does not seem out of place in Bo Phut. There is a very small rooftop pool, not big enough to get any exercise but a wonderful place for a cocktail or just to cool off.

The **Lamai Wanta** (124/264 Mu 3, Lamai Beach, tel. 07/742-4550, www.lamaiwanta. com, 1,800B) is right on Lamai Beach and has modern, comfortable, well-maintained guest

rooms and a small but very pretty pool overlooking the ocean. There are both traditional hotel rooms and stand-alone villas, some with two bedrooms. The location, just walking distance from Lamai's restaurants, is convenient, but the hotel is big enough that it still feels quiet and private.

Montien House (5 Mu 2, Chaweng Beach, tel. 07/742-2169, www.montienhouse.com, 2,500B) is another great property on Chaweng if you're looking for a resort environment but don't want to pay five-star prices. The Montien is right on the beach but far enough away from the center that you'll be able to enjoy some peace and quiet. There's a lovely small pool and a beachside restaurant, and the traditional Thai-style grounds are well maintained. The standard guest rooms are clean and well maintained, if a little Spartan. The beachfront guest rooms, housed in small cottages, are a little more expensive but feel a little more luxurious and are great for small families.

The guest rooms and villas at **The Waterfront Boutique Hotel** (71/2 Mu 1, Bo Phut Beach, tel. 07/742-7165, www.thewaterfrontbophut.com, 2,900B) are simple and unpretentious, and the setting right next to the beach, with the requisite coconut trees shading the sun, is as good as it gets. What sets this property apart is the relaxed environment, the friendly staff, and the great value for the money. There's a pool and also a small restaurant on the premises where you can enjoy a complimentary fresh-cooked breakfast and Wi-Fi, but it's not quite luxurious enough to be a boutique hotel. It is, however, a very family-friendly place—there are larger suites available as well as babysitting services.

Another inexpensive gem on Chaweng is **Tango Beach Resort** (119 Mu 2, North Chaweng Beach, www.tangobeachsamui.com, 2,700B). This is not five-star luxury, but nonetheless it's an amazing value for the price. The small resort has pretty, simple grounds with a nice, if small, swimming pool, a beachfront bar and restaurant, and their own chair-and-towel service on the sand. The guest rooms are surprisingly well furnished in a modern

Thai style, and some even have views of the ocean. Baths are on par with more expensive resorts and feature rain showerheads and glass bowl sinks. The hotel is located in northern Chaweng, which is a more relaxed and quiet area of the beach, although it's not as easy to swim here because there are sandbars at low tide. If you're looking to get to the bustling center, expect a 15-minute walk or five-minute motorcycle ride.

The Maryoo Hotel Samui (99/99 Mu 2, North Chaweng Rd., tel. 07/760-1102, www. maryoosamui.com, 2,700B), a modern mid-size hotel near Chaweng Beach, has very clean, comfortable guest rooms and a big, beautiful swimming pool. There is also an average Thai restaurant and a spa on the property. This won't be the right choice for those looking for lots of personality, but those who want cleanliness and comfort at a reasonable price will find it a great value.

3,000-4,500B

Villa Nalinnadda (99/1-4 Mu 1, Maret, tel. 07/723-3131, www.nalinnadda.com, 3,500B) is a small luxury boutique hotel on Lamai Beach that seems like it was expressly designed for honeymoons and romantic getaways. All of the eight bright, airy guest rooms on the property face the ocean, they'll serve you breakfast in bed whenever you want it, and the guest rooms also come equipped with private whirlpool tubs. There's also a definite Greek Mediterranean feeling to the property, thanks to the bright white buildings, but you won't forget that you're still in Thailand. The beach it's on is very quiet, but if you travel down to the center of Lamai Beach, you can find some more action.

Over 4,500B

The **Ⓒ Anantara Samui** (101/3 Bo Phut Bay, tel. 07/742-8300, www.anantara.com, 6,000B) has all the luxury, style, and generous Thai hospitality that has made Samui famous the world over. The grounds are perfectly manicured and filled with exotic details such as fire torches and reproductions of ancient sculptures. The

pool area, with a large infinity pool that seems to spill out into the Gulf of Thailand, and the main lobby look like the grounds of a royal palace. The guest rooms are modern and luxurious, and there's also an indulgent spa and lots of great restaurants to eat and drink at. The staff is professional and friendly. If you're looking for a place to splash out, perhaps for a honeymoon or an anniversary, you will not be disappointed here. The Anantara offers lots of the typical activities and excursions, but they also have windsurfing lessons on Bo Phut Bay as well as sailboat rental.

The **Scent Hotel** (58/1 Mu 4, Bo Phut Beach, tel. 07/796-2198, www.thescenthotel. com, 6,000B), a high-end, intimate boutique hotel right on the beach, has beautifully furnished guest rooms with European or Asian decor (you can specify, depending on availability). Regardless of decor, guest rooms are spacious and many have balconies with enough space to dine. The common areas are not large, but all guest rooms open onto the property's pleasant beachfront infinity pool and are reminiscent of an old Chinese shophouse.

If you want to stay in a large resort hotel with lots of amenities and facilities as well as nicely appointed guest rooms, the **Centara Grand** (38/2 Mu 3, Chaweng Beach, tel. 07/723-0500, www.centarahotelsresorts.com, 6,500B) is a great choice on Chaweng Beach. The resort has more than 200 guest rooms, so although it doesn't quite feel secluded, there is plenty of pool space, a beautiful full-service spa, and bars and restaurants on the premises. There are also tennis courts and even a small Jim Thompson Thai Silk outlet. The guest rooms are all modern Thai with dark hardwood flooring and private balconies. The property has just undergone refreshing and renovation, so the guest rooms and grounds feel new and fresh despite the fact that the resort has been around for a while. Although it's quiet and peaceful on the grounds, just outside on Chaweng Beach it can get crowded and noisy, especially during high season.

Napasai (65/10 Mu 10, Mae Nam Beach, tel. 07/742-9200, www.napasai.com, 10,000B), one of the Orient Express branded hotels, is also one of the island's most luxurious and indulgent properties. The villas and guest rooms are scattered among the surrounding hills and are spacious and private. Some also have kitchens where guests or staff can cook. Expansive common areas, including an infinity pool, a spa, two restaurants, and two bars, mean guests don't need to leave the property for anything if they don't want to.

The Library (14/1 Mu 2, Bo Phut Beach, tel. 07/742-2767, www.thelibrary.co.th, 12,600B) is centered around the property's immense, übertrendy library filled with books and magazines, but guests may find it hard to focus on anything other than the superb modern design of the resort. It's just too cool here. The buildings are white minimalist cubes, and the grounds are filled with modern sculpture. The best part is the red-tiled swimming pool. Inside the enormous guest rooms and suites, expect to find sleek wood furniture, lots of sunlight, and sparse decorations; they share the same clean, modern design as the rest of the resort. You'll still find the same types of amenities, such as a beachside restaurant and cozy lounge chairs on the beach, as you would in other similarly priced resorts.

Sila Evason Hideaway & Spa (9/10 Mu 5, Ban Plai Laem, Bo Phut Beach, tel. 07/724-5678, www.sixsenses.com/SixSensesSamui/, 17,000B) looks like it was built specifically with the jet-setting movie-star crowd in mind. The private thatched-roof villas come complete with personal butlers available to answer your every need. Each also has a small private dip pool and lounge area. And the views, which you can easily enjoy from the comfort of your bed, are amazing. The public parts of the property, including the large swimming pool and open-air restaurant, are equally swanky, although the style of the grounds and buildings is subdued, sleek, and modern.

FOOD

Whatever you're in the mood for, you won't go hungry on Ko Samui. The island seems to have an inordinate number of restaurants for its size.

Although there are plenty of uninspired, overpriced tourist restaurants, there are more and more excellent places to eat, whether you're looking for quick, inexpensive street food, international fare, or a special Thai meal in a romantic setting overlooking the ocean. On Ko Samui, it's important to remember that the quality of the food sometimes has no relationship to the appearance of the restaurant. Some of the best meals to be found are at very casual places that almost look like holes-in-the-wall. Although you'll find the most restaurants on and near busy Chaweng Beach, if you're looking for a place to enjoy a meal and watch the sunset, head to Nathon Beach on the west coast of the island.

Markets

The **Lamai Food Center,** about 2.5 kilometers from HinTa HinYai Rocks in front of the Wat Lamai School, has a handful of small casual restaurants with great inexpensive Thai food. This is a very relaxed local spot, so expect great food but not a lot of amenities. Many of these restaurants stay open till the wee hours of the morning. If you're in the mood for some *kanom chin* (rice noodles with curry), try **Sophita** (tel. 08/6954-8861, 9 A.M.–3 A.M. daily, 40B). For simple but hearty *guay teow* or *khao mu dang* (red pork with rice), try **Chakangraw Noodle** (tel. 08/9868-8515, 40B). If you're in the mood for freshly made seafood, **Chaophraya Seafood** (tel. 07/741-8117 or 08/6345-9647, 80B) has excellent *gang thot kratiem* (extra-large fried shrimp with garlic and pepper).

Right near Chaweng Beach, close to the Island Resort and Chaweng Villa Resort, is a food center with different food vendors where you can find fresh fruit, the typical selection of noodles and rice dishes, and lots of seafood.

Thai Food

If you're near Lamai Beach, stop at **Sabiang Lae** (tel. 07/723-3082, 10 A.M.–10 P.M. daily, 200B), between Lamai Beach and Ban Hua Thanon, for seafood Samui style. This casual open-air beachfront restaurant is a great place to watch the sunset and enjoy some *kung yai thot* *rad nam manao* (fried lobster with lime juice) and *yum sabiang lae* (spicy seafood salad).

Bang Po Seafood (10 A.M.–10 P.M. daily, 300B) on Bang Po Beach is another great seafood restaurant with a similar atmosphere to Sabiang Lae. This is a popular spot among international and Thai visitors to the island, perhaps because of the *kei ji* appetizer they offer for free. It's a delicious blend of shrimp paste and coconut, and you won't find it anywhere in Bangkok.

Another great casual open-air spot for good, inexpensive food is **Sunset Restaurant** (Nathon 175/3, Mu 3, Tambon Ang Thong, tel. 07/742-1244, 4–10 P.M. daily, 300B) on Nathon Beach. Although it's not right on the beach, as the name implies, it's a great place to watch the sunset overlooking Nathon Pier, and the Thai food is fresh, fast, and cheap. Try the rice in coconut if you're looking for something hearty and not spicy; it's great comfort food. This is definitely a casual place to eat, so don't worry about showing up in flip-flops and a T-shirt.

K-Siri (4169 Mu 1, Bo Phut Ring Rd., no phone, 6–10 P.M. daily, 150B), a modest restaurant serving Thai seafood, is the perfect spot for those looking for a place to eat that's basic and simple but doesn't skimp on quality ingredients or preparation. The open-air restaurant, just a short walk from the beach, is a step above a basic shophouse (they even serve wine!) but is definitely pleasant enough for a casual dinner.

Fusion and International

If you're on Chaweng Beach for breakfast, head straight to **Akwa Guesthouse** (28/12 Chaweng Beach Rd., tel. 08/4660-0551, 7 A.M.–11 P.M. daily, 300B). Their breakfast combos are generous and delicious; no tiny slices of toast and hot dogs masquerading as sausages here. Instead, you'll get real sausage, fresh bread, omelets, pancakes, and even hash browns. All of that comes on one plate if you order the Canadian breakfast. Their imported coffee is also excellent, and the bright colors and friendly staff will definitely help wake you up.

Poppies (Chaweng Beach, tel. 07/742-2419, www.poppiessamui.com, 6:30 A.M.–midnight daily, 600B) has become something of an island sensation in the past decade, thanks to the elegant setting at the resort of the same name, the beach view, and the excellent food. The restaurant serves Thai and international dishes, and both sides of the menu offer innovative interpretations of standard fare. Try the *kai pad met mamuang* (stir-fried chicken with cashew nuts) or the roast-duck spring rolls if you're looking for something familiar with a creative twist. Or try the ostrich in panang curry for something really unexpected. Poppies also has an extensive selection of seafood and grilled meats as well as a very good vegetarian menu. The vegetarian green curry with pumpkin is excellent and something you won't be able to find meatless in many places.

Top Ten (98 Mu 2, Chaweng Beach Rd., tel. 07/723-0235, www.toptenrestaurantsamui. com, 5–11 P.M. daily, 400B), a nicely decorated, upscale modern restaurant, serves a mix of straight European flavors, fusion, and some standard Thai dishes, including a clever *tom yam* pasta. The restaurant wins on decor and service, and it's a great choice if you want to eat somewhere a little nicer than the typical Chaweng Beach restaurant.

Sala Thai (12/12, Mu 1, Tambon Mae Nam, tel. 07/742-5031 to 07/742-5038, 6–11 P.M. daily, 700B) is another excellent choice for an upscale Thai meal. The restaurant is part of the Santiburi Resort but attracts plenty of people who aren't staying there. The setting—traditional Thai architecture, lily ponds, pathways lit with tiki torches, and a luxuriant garden—is about as romantic as it gets. The food is mostly traditional Thai cuisine, and it's all expertly prepared and presented. The *tom yam kung* is as good as you'll find anywhere, as are other classic dishes such as *kai phat* (stir-fried chicken) and *pha kung* (spicy shrimp salad).

The chef at **Zazen** (Zazen Boutique Resort and Spa, 177 Mu 1, Bo Phut Beach, tel. 07/742-5085, 5–11 P.M. daily, 600B) mixes fresh local ingredients with foreign flavors to create interesting and innovative modern Thai and fusion cuisine. The elegant restaurant, with a nice view of the Gulf of Thailand, serves dishes such as five spices–marinated barracuda, sesame and wasabi–crusted shrimp, and *neua pla nam deng* (caramelized roasted fish) in addition to some traditional Thai and European favorites. For dessert, the banana flambé in Mekhong whiskey is both entertaining and palate-pleasing.

Betelnut (43/4-5 Mu 3, Soi Colibri, Chaweng Beach, tel. 07/741-3370, 6–11 P.M. daily, 700B) is a top contender for best restaurant on the island. The California-Thai fusion menu is filled with the dishes of crab cake, seared tuna, and duck breast you'll find at upscale international dining spots around the world. To spice things up a bit, the U.S.- and European-trained chef also features dishes such as New England clam chowder with green curry and softshell crab with mango and papaya salad. Although there are lots of culinary risks being taken in the kitchen, the food is too good to be gimmicky. The restaurant is light and airy, with plenty of modern art on the walls.

Another great choice for a special dinner on Chaweng Beach is **Eat Sense** (11 Mu 2, Chaweng Beach, tel. 07/741-4242, 11 A.M.– midnight daily, 700B). The upscale beachside restaurant has lots of seating with great views of the Gulf of Thailand, and there are plenty of little patios at different levels to make the large space feel a little more intimate. The cuisine is international, and there are lots of seafood dishes to choose from. The Thai food, which includes a variety of seafood dishes such as the classic *pla thot ta khrai* (fried whole fish with lemongrass, garlic, and lime juice) is definitely made for Western palates. If you're looking for something a little spicier, make sure to ask.

The cliff-top **Dr. Frogs** (103 Mu 3, Chaweng Beach Rd., tel. 07/741-3797, www.drfrogssamui.com, noon–2 A.M. daily, 400B), a Thai and Italian restaurant, has some of the nicest views on the island and for that reason alone is worth visiting for drinks or dinner. Food is well-prepared and presented, and while their pizzas may not remind you of your vacation in Italy, considering the island location, they are pretty good. Pastas and seafood entrées are consistently delicious.

The dark wood furnishings, lounge music, and trendy patrons make 【 **Rice** (167/7 Mu 2, Chaweng Beach, tel. 07/723-1934, www.ricesamui.com, 6 P.M.–midnight daily, 400B) feel more like the type of Italian restaurant you'd find in a trendy city neighborhood instead of on the main strip in Chaweng Beach. The food is among the best European fare you'll find on Samui. In fact, the brick oven–baked pizza is unparalleled. Ditch the flip-flops, or you'll definitely feel underdressed.

The small, unpretentious, but well-put together **Barracuda** (216/2 Mu 2, Soi 4, Mae Nam Beach Rd., tel. 07/724-7287 or 07/792-1663, www.barracuda-restaurant.com, 6–11 P.M. daily, 400B) offers high-quality seafood dishes that take advantage of Thai flavors, such as lobster tortellini and salmon with a *tom yam* sauce, and other mostly Western fare. The interior feels more like a nice fish shack than a shophouse restaurant.

While combining Greek and Thai cuisine in one restaurant seems like a recipe for mediocrity, **Fi Kitchen & Bar** (75/1 Mu 1, Mae Nam Ring Rd., tel. 08/9607-2967, 6–11 P.M. daily, 300B) pulls off the combo surprisingly well, and it's a fun, casual place to go, especially if you're craving Greek food. Fresh vegetables and lots of flavor seem to be the hallmarks of the Greek dishes, and the small stand-alone restaurant, which opened in early 2011, already has a following among expatriate and vacationing Greeks on Samui.

The sexy, shabby chic **Boudoir** (Soi 1, Mae Nam Beach, tel. 08/5783-1031, 6 P.M.–midnight daily, 450B), offers casual French cuisine in a relaxing, fun atmosphere. This is a good place to go for inexpensive wine and cheese platters before dinner, although the full meals are also a great value.

Homesick for cheesecake, brownies, and a Western breakfast? Head to **Angela's Bakery and Café** (64/29 Mu 1, Mae Nam Beach, tel. 07/742-7396, 7 A.M.–3:30 P.M. daily, 150B) for some of the best desserts and baked goods on the island. The very basic restaurant has been around for years, and they even have bagels and lox and sandwiches, although those looking for Thai food will find a few dishes.

For well-prepared, great-tasting vegetarian food, **Radiance** (Spa Samui Resort, 71/7 Mu 3, Maret, tel. 07/723-0855, 7 A.M.–10 P.M. daily, 300B) is the best choice on the island and might even be the best in the country. The extensive menu has mostly meatless and vegan dishes made with lots of fresh fruits and vegetables, but it features a few fish and chicken meals too. It can be difficult to find vegetarian versions of most Thai dishes, but here the kitchen can make just about anything, including *tom kha* (coconut soup) and *tom yam* (spicy, sour soup) without any meat products. Spa Samui also has a large breakfast menu featuring items such as french toast made with homemade whole-grain bread and veggie sausages. There's even a large selection of raw dishes for raw foodists. This is a casual place, with open-air seating on the spa's verdant grounds.

A Cajun restaurant in the middle of a tropical island in Southeast Asia seems a little strange, but when you enter **Coco Blues** (161/9 Mu 2, Chaweng Beach Rd., tel. 07/741-4354, 5 P.M.–midnight daily, 300B) on Bo Phut Beach, it all makes sense. The spicy dishes, including blackened fish and Cajun crepes, taste just right in the heat, and the live blues music creates a decidedly comfortable atmosphere. The three-story restaurant opens onto the street and has New Orleans decor and vibe. If you've already eaten, drop in to listen to some music and have a draft beer or two.

For a casual beer and some barbecue, stop in to **Bill's Beach Bar** (near Hua Thanon Beach, just south of Lamai Beach, tel. 08/4778-9145, 9 A.M.–10 P.M. daily). Imagine an open-air beach shack, add running water, a mix of Thai-, Australian-, and Western-style grilled meats, and plenty of foreigners, and you'll get a good idea of what to expect here. The bar holds a barbecue party every Sunday for just 100B pp.

A pretty beachside location, nice Mediterranean fare, and a relaxing atmosphere make **Ad Hoc Beach Cafe** (11/5 Mu 1, Bo Phut Beach, tel. 07/742-5380, noon–11:30 P.M. daily, 450B) a perfect spot for a casual meal or a snack and cocktails while watching the sunset. The menu, mostly typical Italian dishes, is reliable and not too expensive, but it's the view that keeps people coming back.

◖ **The Farmer** (1/26 Mu 4, Mae Nam Beach, tel. 07/744-7222, www.thefarmerrestaurantsamui.com, noon–11 P.M. daily, 550B), surrounded by paddy fields with mountains in the background, is one of Samui's nicest new restaurants. The interior of the large open-air restaurant is upscale but understated, so it doesn't compete with the beautiful view outside. The menu, mostly European dishes but including some Thai classics, spotlights local and organic produce. It's definitely worth the taxi ride.

INFORMATION AND SERVICES

The regional **Tourism Authority of Thailand office** (TAT, 5 Talat Mai Rd., Surat Thani, tel. 07/728-2828) is located on the mainland in Surat Thani, but you can call either the office or the TAT hotline (1672, 8 A.M.–8 P.M. daily) for information about ferry schedules and other travel-related issues.

Internet access is available at Internet cafés on most beaches. All large resorts and even many small guesthouses now offer at least Wi-Fi too.

GETTING THERE
Air

Samui has its own charming little airport owned by **Bangkok Airways** (www.bangkokair.com), which runs as many as 17 flights per day during high season. Although Bangkok Airways has just opened the airport to **Thai Airways,** they are only running limited flights, mostly for international passengers connecting in Bangkok and traveling on to the island, but between the two, if you are booking even a few days in advance and are flexible with your travel times, you should be able to get a flight. The big exception to this is during

© SUZANNE NAM

Ko Samui's airport

high season, especially in December, when you should book as far in advance as possible. With limited competition, airfares to Samui from Bangkok are generally higher than for similar distances to other parts of the country, where budget airlines such as Nok Air can fly. Expect to pay 5,000–9,000B for a round-trip ticket to the island. The cheapest fares sell out quickly. If you're flying in from Bangkok, the flight is just over an hour.

Boat

If you have a little more time, it's easy to fly into Surat Thani on Nok Air or Air Asia and then take a fast boat to Samui. Flights to Surat Thani can cost as little as 3,000B round-trip with tax, and once you arrive at the Surat Thani airport, you can buy a combination bus-ferry ticket for around 300B that will take you from the airport to the pier, and then from the pier to the island. The **Pantip Ferry Company** (tel. 07/727-2906) has a booth in the Surat Thani airport. From the airport to the ferry pier is about 90 minutes; from the time you leave the

airport, expect the whole trip to take about 4.5 hours to your hotel.

Bus or Train

You can also take a bus from Bangkok's Southern Bus Terminal or an overnight train from Hua Lamphong to Surat Thani (actually Phun Phin, about 16 kilometers outside downtown Surat Thani). If you are coming by train, you'll need to take a bus to the Donsak pier from the station, and then transfer to the ferry. Whatever time of day or night you arrive, there will be touts selling combination bus-train tickets to the islands; they should cost no more than 300B. If you are taking a government bus from Bangkok, the ride to Surat Thani is around 12 hours, but you'll then have to get from downtown Surat Thani to the pier. You can either take a local bus, which you can get at the bus station, or a taxi to Donsak pier. The better way may be to take a Samui express bus from Bangkok, using one of the private bus companies that leave from the Southern Bus Terminal. These buses will travel directly to the pier, and some include the ferry ride in the price. **Transportation Co.** (tel. 07/742-0765) and **Sopon Tours** (tel. 07/742-0175) both run VIP buses to the ferry, and fares are under 700B for the trip.

GETTING AROUND

Ko Samui has frequent *song thaew* that circle the island's main road from early morning into the evening. There are no fixed stops, so if you want a ride, just give the driver a wave and then hop in the back. When you want to get off, press the buzzer in the back (it's usually on the ceiling) and then pay your fare after you get off. Fares are set, and rides cost 20–60B if you are going from beach to beach. For trips from the pier to Chaweng, expect to pay 110B, less if you are traveling to a closer beach. There are also plentiful taxis and motorcycle taxis on the popular beaches in the area (if you are staying somewhere more secluded, your guesthouse can call one for you).

KO PHA-NGAN

เกาะพะงัน

If you're looking for a beautiful island with nice beaches that's cheap and full of folks who want to party all night long, this is the spot to pick. Although Ko Pha-Ngan is physically similar to Ko Samui, except that it's about half the size and has smaller sandy beaches instead of Samui's large, sweeping ones, and is just a short ferry trip away, it definitely feels a world apart. You won't see as much development here, or even any main roads. Instead, the island is rimmed by stretches of clean white sand, and the interior mountainous rainforest is peppered with inexpensive bungalows and, more and more, secluded resorts.

Although there is one long strip of coast on the west side of the island, which gives the added benefit of beautiful sunsets, many of the beaches on Ko Pha-Ngan are set in small coves backed by cliffs and thick forest. The physical landscapes are truly beautiful, and they are often the more secluded-feeling areas, but they can be really tough to access. Weather and tidal conditions permitting, you can take a longtail

boat from one beach to another. Many of the roads leading to these beaches are dirt roads; there are some 4WD vehicles on the island that can take you, and many visitors also rent motorcycles to get from one beach to another. If you go that route, be aware that some of the dirt roads can be treacherous on two wheels, especially if it has been raining.

In many ways, Ko Pha-Ngan is a breath of fresh air since it's so much less developed than other popular spots in the region. It tends to attract visitors such as young backpackers and aging hippies, all looking to enjoy the beauty of the region without spending a lot of money. For better or worse, the island has become something of an international party zone, probably thanks to the many young travelers who visit every year. During high season, the all-night full moon parties have given way to half moon parties and black moon parties—any excuse to have a few drinks and dance around on the beach to music more fit for an urban rave than a tropical paradise. Don't bother wearing a watch, as the drinking tends to start as soon as the haze from the night before has cleared sufficiently to open a bottle of beer. If you're in the right mood, it can be a lot of fun, particularly because you can sleep your hangover off on one of the beautiful beaches come morning. If you're not into the scene, avoid Hat Rin, the island's party beach.

Beaches and Islands

The beaches in the northern part of the island on **Ao Chaloklum Bay** are the least desirable on the island. The sand is darker and a little coarser, and the tides make it difficult to swim unless you're doing so at high tide. It's also not a great place for snorkeling as most of the coral surrounding the bay is dead. It's not paradise, but it is home to a fishing village, so while you may not be able to enjoy the swimming too much, you will be able to hang out and watch the colorful longtail boats on the water. If you travel just a little east to **Hat Khom,** you'll find a prettier beach with some vibrant coral in relatively shallow water (great for snorkeling). This beach, however, is not easily swimmable at low

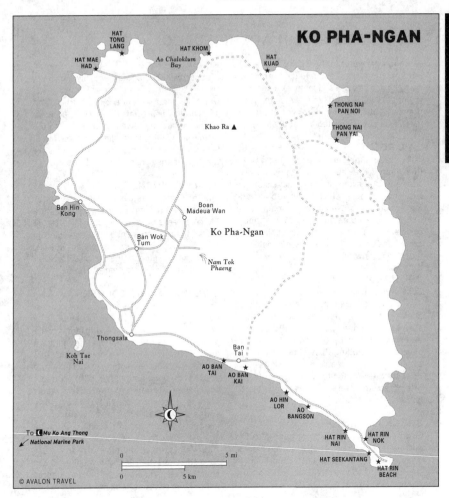

tide either. **Hat Kuad,** just to the west, is one of the island favorites. A wide swath of sand backed by green mountains and surrounded by a cove, it's one of the prettier beaches on the north side of the island. It's difficult to get to by land, so it's only crowded by those willing to take a longtail or endure a bumpy ride in a 4WD vehicle to get here. Although there's no coral, you can swim regardless of the tide thanks to a steep drop-off close to shore. **Hat Tong Lang** is in a small cove surrounded by leafy green foliage. There's a coral reef close to shore, and its presence creates a lagoon of sorts. This beach is also tough to access and hence calm and quiet. You can take a long-tail boat from Chaloklum Bay, but if you go by land, the dirt road leading to the beach is pretty rough.

The east side of the island has just a handful of beautiful small beaches interspersed among the green hills and mountains. Thanks to the geography, there's a definite wild and natural

DIVING THE SAMUI ARCHIPELAGO

Although the water in the Gulf of Thailand is not as clear as what you'll find on the Andaman coast, there are still many excellent diving opportunities. Ko Tao is by far the most popular spot for diving, thanks to its proximity to some of the region's best diving sites.

SAIL ROCK

This rock pinnacle between Ko Tao and Ko Pha-Ngan is the region's most popular dive spot and is appropriate for all levels of divers. The pinnacle, which towers about nine meters above the surface, is a magnet for fish, so there's plenty of colorful marinelife to be spotted. The swim-through chimney, a cavernous tunnel through the pinnacle, is a must-do for anyone visiting Sail Rock.

CHUMPHON PINNACLE

Just under 10 kilometers northwest of Ko Tao is Chumphon Pinnacle, a very popular granite pinnacle that does not break the surface. The base is covered with colorful anemones and attracts plenty of large and small fish (including little clownfish, which everyone in the area refers to as "Nemos" after the Disney movie). Large whale sharks are often spotted here, as are leopard sharks.

SHARK ISLAND

Southeast of Ko Tao is a grouping of rocks surrounded by colorful coral and anemones. Snappers, rays, and angel fish congregate in the rocks and, as you might suspect from the name, so do sharks.

KO MA

Just north of Ko Pha-Ngan (actually connected to it by a strip of sand at low tide) is Ko Ma, which has some vibrant and healthy hard and soft coral as well as lots of colorful marinelife swimming around. Given its proximity to the main island and its suitability for divers of all levels, this is often where beginning divers are taken when they are getting certified.

KO NANG YUAN

The three interconnected islands also offer some nice snorkeling and diving opportunities. The coral reef attracts plenty of smaller fish (no sharks, though) and is a nice place for beginning divers and for snorkelers. Nang Yuan pinnacle, a small granite pinnacle below the surface, attracts larger fish who've come to feed.

DIVE SHOPS AND COURSES

There are many dive shops in the area, especially on Ko Tao, which has dozens. Safety records across Thailand's diving industry are good, but make sure to inspect equipment and talk to the instructors and dive masters you'll be with before signing up to make sure you're comfortable with them. Also ask about environmental awareness. PADI divers should follow a strict no-hands rule, but some dive shops have been known to be somewhat lax about it (touching or even brushing up against coral can damage it).

On Ko Tao, especially, many dive shops also have small guesthouses, and you'll get a discounted rate (sometimes just a few hundred baht) if you're taking lessons or going out on

feeling here. There's no coral on this side of the island, but if you happen to be awake in time, the sunrises are beautiful. **Thong Nai Pan Noi** and **Thong Nai Pan Yai** are the most popular beaches on the east side of the island, and there are some simple bungalows and a few more upscale resorts if you want to stay here. The two curved beaches are set in coves and have soft white sand. Thong Nai Pan Noi has a little

village with restaurants, bars, and a few places to spend money, while Thong Nai Pan Yai is a little less developed.

Hat Rin Beach in the southern part of Ko Pha-Ngan is the island's most popular. Located on a small peninsula on the southern tip of the island, Hat Rin is actually two bays—**Hat Rin Nok** and **Hat Rin Nai** (also called Hat Rin Sunrise and Hat Rin Sunset, since the beaches dives with them. Accommodations run the gamut from basic and clean to luxurious. You'll be surrounded by fellow divers if you choose to stay in one of these guesthouses.

There are also plenty of dive shops on Ko Samui and Ko Pha-Ngan who offer diving trips and equipment. You can also take 3-4-day PADI diving certification courses that can be arranged at any of the diving shops and schools listed below. Live-aboards tend to be less popular in this part of the country; instead, most diving is done on day trips or multiday trips where divers sleep in basic accommodations on one of the islands in Ang Thong National Park.

Ko Samui

- **Blue Planet Dive Centre** (119 Mu 2, Chaweng Beach, tel. 07/741-3106, www.blue-planetdivers.net)

- **Calypso Diving** (27/5 Chaweng Rd., Chaweng Beach, tel. 07/742-2437, www.ca-lypso-diving.com)

- **Samui Diving Service** (80/3 Mu 3, Chaweng Beach, tel. 07/723-0053)

- **Samui Easy Divers** (locations on Bo Phut, Chaweng, Lamai, and Big Buddha Beaches, tel. 07/723-1190, www.easydivers-thailand.com)

- **SIDS-Samui International Diving School** (Malibu Beach Resort, Chaweng Beach, tel. 07/742-2386, www.planet-scuba.net)

- **Silent Divers** (101/7 Mu 2, Bo Phut Beach, tel. 07/742-2730, www.silentdivers.com)

Ko Pha-Ngan

- **Asia Divers Koh Phangan** (44/42 Mu 1, Thongsala Pier, tel. 07/737-7274, www.asia-divers.com)

- **Haad Yao Divers** (Sandy Bay Bungalows, Hat Yao, tel. 07/734-9119, www.haadyaodivers.com)

- **MTF Diving** (Weangthai Resort, Ban Tai Bay, tel. 07/737-7247, www.mtfdiving.com)

Ko Tao

- **Ban's Diving Center** (Sairee Beach, tel. 07/745-6466, www.amazingkohtao.com)

- **Blacktip Diving** (40/5 Mu 3, Tanote Bay, tel. 07/745-6488, www.blacktipdiving.com)

- **Buddha View Dive Resort** (45 Mu 3, Chalok Ban Kao, tel. 07/745-6074, www.bud-dhaview-diving.com)

- **Coral Grand Divers** (15/4 Mu 1, Sairee Beach, tel. 07/745-6431, www.coralgrand-divers.com)

- **Crystal Dive Resort** (7/1 Mu 2, Mae Hat, tel. 07/745-6107, www.crystaldive.com)

- **Easy Divers – Koh Tao Island** (10/3 Mu 2, Mae Hat, also located on Ko Nang Yuan, tel. 07/745-6321, www.kohtaoeasydivers.com)

- **Sairee Hut Dive Resort** (14/45 Sairee Hut Resort, Mu 2, Sairee Beach, tel. 07/745-6815, www.saireehut.com)

- **SIDS-Planet Scuba Koh Tao** (9 Mu 2, Mae Hat, tel. 07/745-6110, www.planet-scuba.net)

face east and west, respectively). At the bottom of the peninsula is **Hat Seekantang,** a small, slightly quieter beach. All of the beaches on the peninsula have clean, light sand and clear water and are fringed with palm trees. Since they're so popular among travelers, there are plenty of bungalows and plenty of bars. Hat Rin Nok and Hat Rin Nai are home to the island's infamous full moon parties, so expect

a lot of partying if you're hanging out or staying here.

Traveling up the west side of the island from the Hat Rin peninsula, there's a long stretch of beach broken only by an outcropping of verdant hills. Here you'll find **Ao Bangson, Ao Hin Lor, Ao Ban Kai,** and **Ao Ban Tai.** The beaches are long and look idyllic thanks to the coconut trees, views of Samui, and fishing boats on the water. The swimming is not always great, however. There's a coral reef just off the coast, and there are some sandbars that pop up at low tide, making it difficult to do more than walk or wade. Around Ao Ban Kai and Ao Ban Tai, you'll find lots of inexpensive to moderately priced bungalows as well as beach bars and restaurants.

Around the ferry pier at **Thongsala** is a stretch of beach more than five kilometers long with plenty of bungalows to choose from (and some of the cheapest on the island). Right at the beach, the land is mostly flat, and there are plenty of surrounding coconut trees that help create the tropical-paradise vibe. Perhaps because they're so close to the ferry, the bungalows tend to be cheaper and also to attract a younger crowd.

The upper western part of the island has a number of beaches close together, although separated by cliffs or hills and mostly accessible by dirt road. **Hat Yao** and **Ao Chao Phao** to the west are some of the most popular beaches on the island. The beaches are about a kilometer long, the sand is white, the western views spectacular, and the surrounding green hills an added bonus. Here you'll find a variety of accommodation options, from simple 200B-per-night bungalows with fans to more upscale small resorts.

Hat Mae Had is another beautiful white-sand beach fringed with coconut trees, but what really sets this beach apart is neighboring **Ko Ma,** a small island that's connected to the main island by a thin sandbar. The snorkeling around Ko Ma is great, as there is a lot of healthy coral and marinelife to look at, so it's also a popular dive site.

Sports and Recreation

If you're staying on Ko Pha-Ngan, expect to do quite a bit of hiking, unless you park yourself on the beach and don't leave till it's time to go home. Much of the island's interior is rugged, and some of it is rocky, so you'll need to be agile to get from one place to another. The island's highest peak is at **Khao Ra,** just over 600 meters above sea level. To hike there,

start in the village of **Ban Madeua Wan** in the center of the island. The trail will take you past **Namtok Phaeng** and lead to the top of the mountain, where there's a viewpoint from which you can see the whole island. The trail is steep at times and not always clearly marked, so use caution when climbing, and expect to spend a couple of hours going and coming back if you are in good physical shape.

The west side of the island has some coral reefs, sometimes just a few hundred meters from the coastline. The water is generally very shallow until the reefs, so you'll be able to see the reefs without having to swim out too deep.

The best diving in the area is around Ko Tao, but the west side of Ko Pha-Ngan has some good diving too. Most of the diving is relatively shallow, at around 15 meters, but there's plentiful hard and soft coral to see as well as lots of colorful marinelife swimming around. Local dive companies also do daily trips to dive sites around the region.

Accommodations

Most of what you'll find on Ko Pha-Ngan is casual beach bungalows and mid-priced small resorts. Unlike neighboring Ko Samui, the island isn't filled with luxurious amenities, although there are more small, high-end resorts opening every year. If you are on a tight budget and looking for simple accommodations, you'll be able to find something inexpensive and comfortable. If you want to get away from it all and enjoy a little luxury, there are a handful of resorts that are not in the middle of all of the action.

Coco Garden Bungalows (100/7 Mu 1, Bang Thai Beach, tel. 07/737-7721, www. cocogardens.com, 400B) is as good a bungalow resort as you're going to find on the island. The small compound is right next to a beautiful strip of the beach, the bungalows are cute and well maintained, and the interiors are furnished in a simple Thai style. Only a handful of the bungalows come with air-conditioning, so if that's a priority, book early and make sure you confirm you are not in a fan-only guest

FULL MOON PARTIES

While it's tempting to think that celebrating the full moon by dancing out on the sand is part of some ancient Thai ritual, the truth is that it's a relatively new tradition and one that's primarily fueled by foreign visitors.

No one can agree on exactly how the tradition was started, but as the prevailing legend would have it, the full moon parties that Ko Pha-Ngan has become famous for were started by a small group of backpackers who celebrated the full moon one night by throwing a party on Hat Rin. The party was such a success that on the night of the next full moon, they threw another party, and more visitors joined them, then another and another until the attendees packed the beach.

Whatever its origins, during peak season the full-moon parties on Hat Rin now attract thousands of partiers, and coming down to the beach for one of the outdoor all-night music-filled soirees is an unforgettable experience. There are DJs, fire-eaters, fireworks, and lots and lots of booze. The all-night outdoor raves also tend to feature illicit drugs of various sorts and sometimes undercover police.

room. There's a small, relaxed restaurant and bar on the premises serving inexpensive and well-made food and drink; if you're looking to enjoy some of the partying that goes on, you'll be close to the black moon and half moon parties on Hat Rin—but not so close that you won't be able to get some sleep if you want.

If you're on the island to enjoy the rugged beauty and peace and quiet, the **Coconut Beach Bungalows** (Hat Khom Beach, Chaloklum, no phone, 400B) on Hat Khom is an excellent choice. The bungalows are very simple and very cheap, and what they lack in amenities, such as hot water and air-conditioning, they make up for in the friendliness of the staff and the secluded, peaceful feeling that

seems to permeate the area. The beach is good for snorkeling, and the staff has snorkel sets available. There is a small restaurant attached, but if you're looking for more action, it'll be tough to get there—you have to travel about 15 minutes on an unpaved road to get back to civilization (the bungalow will arrange to pick you up at the pier and take you back when you depart). Better to pack a bunch of books and enjoy their cold beer without having to leave.

Seaview Bungalows Thansadet (Thansadet Beach, no phone, www.seaview.thansadet.com, 400B) is an excellent choice for cheap, clean bungalows. Thansadet Beach, south of Thong Nai Pan, is small, rugged, and secluded and has beautiful clear water. Fan-cooled bungalows are very basic wooden structures but have comfortable beds and modern baths (albeit with cold water only). Although there isn't lots to do on the beach, there is a small restaurant on the property, and most people come just to relax anyway.

The rustic but comfortable **Sunset Cove Resort** (Ao Chao Phao, www.phangansunset.com, 1,200B), on popular Ao Chao Phao on the west coast, has pretty, lush grounds, a great pool, and a fantastic location right on the beach. Guest rooms are clean, and though not opulent, are well-coordinated and calming. Staff are super friendly and helpful, and they set the tone everyone else at the resort seems to follow—happy and relaxed. There is a restaurant and bar on the property, but this is really more a place to chill out and have a few beers with friends while enjoying the view than to party.

Palita Lodge (119 Mu 6, Bang Thai Beach, tel. 07/737-5170, www.palitalodge.com, 2,000B) isn't a high-end resort but offers guests nearly every amenity that more expensive properties do, including a very pretty, well-maintained swimming pool as well as clean, stylish guest rooms with flat-screen TVs and minibars and spotless modern baths. The modern Thai style is subtle but consistent throughout the property. Palita Lodge is right on Hat Rin and in the middle of full moon madness, and it tends to attract partygoers.

The Green Papaya Resort (64/8 Mu 8, Salad Beach, tel. 07/737-4230, www.greenpapayaresort.com, 4,600B) is a beautifully designed small resort on the northwestern part of the island. The property is filled with modern Thai furnishings, a beautiful pool overlooking the ocean, a couple of restaurants, and not much else to distract you from the scenery or the sunsets. Most of the accommodations are in new wooden bungalows with all the amenities you could want inside, including large sleek baths, DVD players, and minibars. There are also two-bedroom family villas on this property.

Another option for a bit of remote luxury is the **Panviman Resort** (22/1 Mu 5, Thong Nai Pan Noi Bay, Bantai, tel. 07/744-5100, 4,500B) on Bantai. Like the Santhiya, it's in a location that's well away from the crowds and the partying, and it has a beautiful pool, restaurants, and a bar to keep you fed, quaffed, and entertained. The guest rooms are done in a Thai style, and the baths are large, well equipped, and nicely designed. This is a great resort for families since there are a few large family villas that can accommodate more than two people comfortably. Some of the guest rooms and villas are in the hills, so when booking, make sure to take that into consideration; the hillside rooms have a nicer view, but you'll need to climb some stairs to get to them.

For a more upscale Ko Pha-Ngan experience, try the **Santhiya Resort & Spa** (22/7 Mu 5, Thong Nai Pan Yai, tel. 07/742-8999, www.santhiya.com, 10,000B), which opened in 2006 and has some of the nicest guest rooms on the island. The resort is done in a traditional Thai style, with plenty of carved woodwork and colorful textiles as well as luxuriant grounds. The guest rooms are all nestled in the cliffs surrounding the beach, and the views are beautiful, although it can be difficult to get from one place to another, especially if you're in one of the higher-level guest rooms or you're not agile. The grounds, in the middle of lush tropical foliage, have multiple swimming pools, including one with a waterfall. For those who want to stay out of the sun, there is also a fitness center and a library. The Santhiya offers reasonably priced guests transfer by catamaran or speedboat from Samui, which makes it considerably more convenient. The beach itself is not quite as smooth on your feet as others you'll find on the island, but if you're just there to sunbathe and kayak, it's not a problem.

Food

If you're looking for something authentically Thai, you'll probably be disappointed in the offerings on Ko Pha-Ngan. The island is so overrun by young Western travelers looking for pizza and falafel that it's nearly impossible to find great Thai food. Western food varies from mediocre to pretty good, and most of the restaurants are around "Chicken Corner" in Hat Rin, the area's crossroads.

The street parallel to Hat Rin Beach is full of places advertising foreign food of all types, but **Fair House Restaurant & Bar** (119/1 Hat Rin Rd., 9 A.M.–10:30 P.M. daily, 100B) has just about anything Western you could be missing. From potatoes (baked, mashed, or fried) to pasta dishes, steaks, bacon rolls, plus a wide selection of Thai options and even burritos, the menu here is massive, but the pizza is a winner. They also have some creative and appetizing salads on the menu (pumpkin-tofu), and drinks cover the rounds, from *lassis* to whiskey fruit shakes and cocktails. Try a carrot-honey *lassi.* The only downside to this casual spot is that you will have to endure season after season of the TV series *Friends,* although they sometimes play movies at nighttime.

In a location that's too convenient to be good, **Pla-Bla Restaurant** (Hat Rin Rd., 36 Mu 6, next to Sunrise Resort, 9:30 A.M.– 11 P.M. daily, 100B) actually does get patrons returning for their tasty and satisfying meals. Better known as the "Family Guy restaurant," they play episodes of the U.S. comedy series *The Family Guy* continuously. The menu here is almost as extensive as Fair House's, with options for everyone. All of the following got seriously good reviews: shrimp pad thai, green curry chicken or seafood, and the *yam* salad with chicken: a Thai dish with plenty of chicken and a light spicy dressing. For Western fare, the burgers and hot sandwiches are popular. The large drink selection, including alcoholic drinks and shakes, will quench any thirst. Besides the food, it seems that no matter what the nationality, the crowd drawn to "Family Guy" is a friendly sort, and it is an overall pleasant dining experience, especially after a day in the sun.

The baked goods alone will force you to peek into **Nira's Deli Sandwich Bar & Restaurant** (right off Hat Rin Rd., on the way to Chicken Corner, sit-down meals 7 A.M.–11 P.M., bakery and deli 24 hours, 200B), just a few meters off the main drag. If you can tear your eyes away from the food on display, you will see the build-your-own-sandwich board. What better for a place that has the best bread in town? (We suspect they supply all other restaurants offering "fresh bread.") The options range from spreads—cheese, hummus, even Mexican salsa—to more hearty fillings such as boiled egg, smoked salmon, and even turkey. The deli shares dining space with their full-service restaurant, offering Thai food as well as thin-crust individual pizzas baked in the oven just behind the counter. Whatever you fancy, they have a delicious breakfast menu, and you don't have to be a vegetarian to order the vegetarian sandwich (scrambled eggs with tomato, onion, and cheese on your choice of bread). Nira's opens early, making it a great option before a ferry trip or if your night runs into morning. In their fridges they have premade sandwiches and foods and usually squares of deep-dish pizza at the bakery. They also sell their hummus and salsa. Even with all the sweets that make you forget about any other food you ate, this place definitely has a healthy vibe; whole grains and fresh fruit juices such as carrot-ginger abound.

If you're craving Middle Eastern food, **Paprika Mediterranean Restaurant** (Chicken Corner, 11 A.M.–10:30 P.M. daily, 150B) is as good as it gets. It's also why you'll hear mostly Hebrew chatter here. The service also sets this place apart, and they can pop out a delicious Israeli salad in three minutes. On Saturday they offer a special beef-tomato stew, but the hummus and falafel dishes are so good it can be difficult to order anything else. Paprika's also serves schnitzel (it comes out steaming hot) and *shawarma*, so everyone can be satisfied. There is Thai food on the menu too, but it is quite possible nobody has ever tried it. Perhaps the true reason this place always has customers is their 80B deal: a full pita with falafel and hummus and a fruit shake. The best of both regions? Judge for yourself.

Palita Lodge (119 Mu 6, Hat Rin, tel. 07/737-5170, 8 A.M.–10 P.M. daily, 150B) will make you wish your breakfast wasn't included in the cost of your accommodations. Their menu has seven different sets to choose from, such as eggs, porridge, or pancakes. Each set comes with a choice of hot drink (tea, chocolate, or fresh coffee), plus fresh fruit or juice. The fruit plate is a better option and very generous. If you want a traditional Thai breakfast, opt for the rice soup. There are also plenty of Thai and Western choices for lunch and dinner. It is a very pretty spot, a bit away from the main entrances to the beach, so it is surprisingly quiet without being out of the way. Digest afterward by their pool in the comfortable sun chairs.

The Lighthouse (Leela Beach, Hat Rin, 8 A.M.–11 P.M. daily, 200B) gets an A for atmosphere. The isolated corner it is located on is an easy walk from the hedonistic side of Hat Rin Beach, but it feels like it is the opposite side of the island. Perched on the very southern tip of Ko Pha-Ngan, the panorama-windowed eating-lounging area looks straight out to sea. If you go by beach, you walk to the end and then follow a lovely boardwalk that wraps around the corner of the island. Come lounge in the hammock and admire the view over fruit shakes; it has an atmosphere that feels like an afternoon nap. The scenery is especially beautiful at sunset, but at any point during the day, the peaceful atmosphere dissipates tension as well as any Thai massage. It has the familiar menu with Western and Thai options along with very hearty breakfasts, from porridge to a Thai stuffed omelet. The Thai food is the cheapest option, and you aren't charged extra for picking a back-road location. They have a choice of salads, plus a more obscure Western taste that found its way to the menu: the cheese plate—four different types of cheese (including brie) with salad. Order this if it's to your liking, with a glass of 100B wine, and looking out at the ocean, you may decide you have achieved the pinnacle of all Euro-Asian ideals.

Far up the hill, **Sunsmile Restaurant and Guesthouse** (Hat Rin Beach, 8 A.M.–9:30 P.M. daily, 100B) occupies a scenic spot overlooking Hat Rin Nok (Sunrise Beach). An everlasting breeze blows here. They definitely cater to backpackers, and you can either dine outside with the view or inside with a host of movies to choose from. It is a hike—at least a 10-minute walk up a heavily rutted rocky and sandy road—so if you need to escape and really just avoid people for a bit, this is the place. The curries and Thai food are very good deals. Western food is on the menu but is more limited. During full moon party weeks, it can be fun to watch the party from a distance and still be able to hear the music. The rest of the month, it's one of the quietest places in all of Hat Rin.

Getting There

The closest airport to Ko Pha-Ngan is on Samui, so if you want to spend as little time as possible getting to the beach, you can fly to the neighboring island and then take a ferry boat to Ko Pha-Ngan.

Since the island mostly attracts a younger crowd with tighter purse strings, most people arrive by boat from Surat Thani. If you're arriving in Surat Thani by air, you can buy a combination bus-ferry ticket right at the airport, and the whole trip should run around five hours. If you're coming to Surat Thani by train or bus from Bangkok, you'll need to make your way to the Donsak pier outside of town and then catch a ferry to Ko Pha-Ngan. The ferries that travel from Surat Thani to Samui then make their way to Ko Pha-Ngan; you'll spend another couple of hours on the ferry and pay an additional 150B on top of the

Samui fare. There is no direct ferry to Ko Pha-Ngan from Surat Thani—you have to stop in Samui first.

Getting Around

Ko Pha-Ngan is less built-up than Ko Samui but has some roads in place, and during the day there are *song thaew* running from the pier in Thongsala to other beaches. You should pay under 80B for most rides (unless you charter the *song thaew* to take you to a specific destination that is not on the route, in which case you'll need to negotiate a price). Many visitors also rent motorcycles or mountain bikes, both of which are available at most beaches. Expect to pay around 200B per day regardless of whether you're getting a pedal-powered or gas-powered bike.

KO TAO
เกาะเต่า

Ko Tao means turtle island, although that's not so much about its shape (it looks more like a kidney bean) as the fact that the waters around the island used to be filled with sea turtles. They've since mostly moved on, but there's still lots of amazing marinelife to explore around Ko Tao. The waters surrounding the island are relatively shallow and have little current, except during monsoon season. In fact, the island is one of the best launching points for scuba diving in the Gulf of Thailand and a great place to do some snorkeling right off the beach. The island is full of dive shops and dive schools, so if you're looking to get PADI certified, this is a great place to pick—courses tend to be a little cheaper than the rest of the country, and you can really shop around for the dive instructor you feel most comfortable with. In fact, the island issues more PADI certificates than any other spot in Thailand and most other spots in the world. If you visit, you'll find bungalow resorts and a few up-market offerings, and they are mostly geared toward divers. Every resort, up-market or otherwise, has a dive shop attached.

Even if you're not into diving, Ko Tao is a beautiful little island to enjoy the scenery and the beaches, although you might feel a bit like the odd man out. The island itself is surrounded by some stretches of sandy shore surrounded by rocky promontories and backed by shady palm trees. The center of the island is mostly jungly rain forest, although there's enough development here that you'll be able to find a post office and a few places to spend your money. Getting around the island, however, can be a little tough. It's a great place for hiking, but the road system is not well developed. If you're not staying near Mae Had (on the island's west coast, where the ferry arrives and departs), expect a long and bumpy ride, especially if you're going across the island. Despite the challenging transport, don't write off Ko Tao—its remoteness gives it a distinct *sabai* attitude.

Beaches and Islands

For a clear stretch of sandy beach, **Sairee Beach,** closest to the ferry pier, is your best bet on the island. The nearly 3.5-kilometer beach faces west, so you not only get the view of the mainland but beautiful sunsets too. This is the most populated beach on the island, and there is a good selection of accommodations and places to eat, although you could hardly call it overcrowded, even in high season. Since the island itself is so small—just a couple of kilometers across—it's a good base from which you can hike around the rest of the island. Just south of Sairee Beach and adjacent to it is **Mae Had,** where the ferry pier is located and probably the only part of the island that could ever legitimately be described as crowded or busy. The area right around the pier isn't optimal for relaxing, but to the south the beach gets nicer and there are some decent places to stay.

Aside from the long stretch of sand on Sairee Beach and Mae Had, the rest of Ko Tao is made up of about a dozen small bays on the north, east, and south of the island. Popular ones include **Hin Wong Bay** on the east coast and **Mango Bay** on the north coast. Both have spectacular views and excellent snorkeling and diving, but the beaches are often quite rocky. Neighboring **Ko Nang Yuan,** just off the

northeast coast of Ko Tao, is perhaps the coolest-looking island in the area. It's actually three separate small islands connected together by a thin stretch of sand you can walk across during low tide. The cluster of small islands also lends itself well to snorkeling and diving, as the interconnecting islands create three separate shallow bays that are mostly protected from strong currents. The beaches are also very shallow unless you walk out pretty far, making it a great place for families. If you're looking for something to do on land, the mountainous island is filled with boulders to climb and a couple of short hiking trails.

From Sairee Beach on Ko Tao you can charter a longtail boat to take you to Ko Nang Yuan for about 150B each way. During high season there are plenty of people going back and forth, so it won't be a problem to get a ride back to Ko Tao. During low season you should arrange a round-trip ride. There is also a ferry that runs from the main pier in Ko Tao once a day during high season; make sure to check at the pier for the current schedule and price. If you are coming from Ko Samui, you can take the ferry to Ko Tao, and then transfer to another boat (either a small ferry or longtail), but you may want to consider spending at least one night on Ko Tao if you're doing that, as you'll spend at least five hours traveling back and forth. There is one resort on the island, Three Paradise Islands, and if you're staying there, they'll help you arrange transport.

Accommodations and Food

For simple, rustic, charming bungalows, the **Sai Thong Resort & Spa** (Mu 2, Sai Nuan Beach, tel. 07/745-6868, 350B) cannot be beat. It's in a remote spot on the southwestern part of the island, so the only way to get there is either by boat taxi or a bumpy ride in a 4WD vehicle. Once you're there, the view to the Gulf of Thailand is gorgeous, as is the surrounding verdant scenery. The bungalows are very simple wooden shacks with mosquito netting and fans. There's a small restaurant that's open all day, and even Internet access, but no pool, and the spa has limited services. It's not a luxury choice, by any means, but if you're looking for that *Survivor* feeling on a budget, you'll be very satisfied here.

If you're just on the island to do some diving, **Khun Ying House** (15/19 Mu 1, Sairee Beach, tel. 08/0620-5527, 450B) is a cheap, clean, and comfortable hotel. The guest rooms are well maintained, although they aren't the most stylishly designed. Some have shared baths and fans, and you can use their kitchen facilities if you feel like cooking up a meal yourself. There are limited facilities here; it's definitely just a place to store your flippers and sleep.

Koh Tao Simple Life (Sairee Beach, tel. 07/745-6142, www.kohtaosimpleliferesort. com, 1,500B) has a good location on popular Sairee Beach, a big swimming pool, a popular restaurant and bar serving Thai and Western food, and nicely furnished, stylish, modern guest rooms. Despite the name, though, it's not a luxury resort and really more like a well-run midsize hotel.

The **Mango Bay Grand Resort** (11/3 Mu 2, Mae Had, tel. 07/745-6097, www.kohtao-mangobay.com, 1,500B) isn't quite grand, and it's not really a resort either, since there's no pool and limited facilities. Still, it's a great place because of its location and the clean and well-maintained bungalows perched on stilts on the rocks above the bay. The interiors of the bungalows are simple and clean, and each has comfortable beds and stunning views to the water. The interior design in the baths may cause you to wonder who picked the paint and tile colors, but everything is modern and works well despite the fact that it's not entirely fashionable. The snorkeling in the area is excellent when it's not monsoon season, and this alone might be reason to stay here. From the resort you can swim out to see excellent coral and other marinelife.

For small-resort luxury, the **Jamakhiri Spa & Resort** (19/1 Mu 3 Chalook, Ban Kao, tel. 07/745-6400, www.jamahkiri.com, 2,500B) is an exceptional property set on the rocks and just a few minutes' walk to the beach. The guest rooms are all large and well kept, with comfortable modern Thai-style furnishing and hardwood floors. All have views to the Gulf of Thailand and large bay windows. There's a beautiful pool, a small spa, and even a fitness center, although unless it's pouring outside, there's really no reason to stay indoors. The resort seems to cascade down the rocks, which means there's quite a bit of walking involved if you're staying on one of the higher levels. As at many other secluded places on the island, you'll have to contend with difficult roads to reach the Jamakhiri, although the hotel will arrange transportation for you from the pier.

The small, upscale **Chintakiri Resort** (19/59 Mu 3 Chalook, Ban Kao, tel. 07/745-6391, www.chintakiriresort.com, 2,500B) has beautiful views of the Gulf of Thailand and clean, nicely furnished Thai-style bungalows. The property is built into the hills behind the beach on one of the island's southern bays near the Jamakhiri Spa & Resort, which makes for amazing views, lush landscaping, and a secluded feeling, but those with any mobility issues might have trouble getting up and down to their guest room. The infinity pool is not huge but also has a beautiful view, and since the property is so small, it rarely gets full.

Anankhira Boutique Villas (15/3 Mu 1, Sairee Beach, tel. 08/7719-7696, www.anan-khira.com, 3,500B) is a little more luxurious than the typical Sairee Beach accommodations. Each of the charming thatched-roof villas has a big bedroom, large outdoor lounging area, and its own small plunge pool. The style, which management calls "ecoconscious," is rustic but very clean and well-maintained. Those who want more space and privacy will find these an excellent value. The villas are not right on the beach, but they are a 10-minute walk away from the northern part of Sairee Beach.

If you want to stay on Ko Nang Yaun, the set of three islands joined by sandbars just off the coast of Ko Tao, your only choice is the **Three Paradise Island Resort,** sometimes also called the **Nang Yuan Island Dive Resort** (tel. 07/745-6088, www.nangyuan. com or www.3paradiseislands.com, 1,500B). The resort has accommodations scattered across the three islands, from simple fan bungalows to larger air-conditioned cottages. None of the options are luxurious, but there's a small restaurant and a dive shop, and staying on a private island might be worth giving up a few amenities.

Getting There

The only way to get to Ko Tao is by boat, either from Chumphon on the mainland or from Ko Samui and Ko Pha-Ngan, using the normal ferries. A high-speed ferry from Chumphon or Samui takes just under two hours and costs around 550B; an overnight ride on a cargo boat takes six hours and costs half the price. There are a number of different companies offering ferry services, including **Lomprayah High Speed Ferries** (www.lomprayah.com), **Ko Jaroen Car Ferry** (tel. 07/758-0030), **Seatran Ferry** (tel. 02/240-2582, www.seatrandiscovery.com), **Songserm Express Boat** (tel. 02/280-8073, www.songserm-expressboat.com) and the **Talay Sub Cargo Night Boat** (tel. 07/743-0531), and the schedules change from year to year, but from neighboring islands there are at least two boats per day each way.

Mainland Surat Thani สุราษฎร์ธานี

Surat Thani isn't a place most tourists end up spending too much time, given the beautiful islands just offshore. It's more or less a run-of-the-mill city going about daily life despite the throngs of foreign visitors that pass through. But just outside the city is Chaiya, the former seat of the Srivijaya Empire, which has an excellent museum. There are also a couple of nearby national parks worth visiting if you are in the area.

TAI ROM YEN NATIONAL PARK
อุทยานแห่งชาติใต้ร่มเย็น

The Tai Rom Yen National Park (Amphoe Ban Na San, Surat Thani, tel. 07/734-4633, 8:30 A.M.–6 P.M. daily, 400B), covering part of the Nakhon Si Thammarat mountain range, is covered in dense forest, with beautiful waterfalls to visit and well-marked trails for hiking. The 22-step **Dard Fa Waterfall** is the region's largest, and one of the levels is a 75-meter cliff drop. To get here, you must drive to the base of the trail at the park headquarters (once you enter the park you'll see signs), where you can also pick up a map to get to **Khao Nong,** the highest point in the province at over 1,370 meters. In addition to the beautiful natural scenery, the park is also home to a couple of significant historical landmarks worth visiting.

In the 1970s and 1980s, the area was a communist-rebel stronghold, and there are a couple of former hideout camps that can now be visited. There are bungalows and a canteen at the park headquarters near the Dard Fa Waterfall.

Getting There

From Surat Thani there's a direct bus that will take you to the entrance of the park on Route 4009 (ask for buses headed south toward the Phin Phun train station; the 15-minute trip should cost around 20B), but once you arrive, it is impossible to get around the park without transportation. If you're driving, take Route 4009 south from Surat Thani about 24 kilometers to Ban Chiang Phra, then look for the signs for the national park.

KHAO ŞOK NATIONAL PARK
อุทยานแห่งชาติเขาสก

Khao Sok National Park (8:30 A.M.–6 P.M. daily, 400B) in Surat Thani Province is covered with rainforest, limestone cliffs, and lakes. It's the wettest national park in the country, thanks to an abundance of rain in the region, and it's also often referred to as the most beautiful. The frequent rainfall keeps the park lush and green, and there is plentiful exotic flora, including palm trees, fig trees, lots of bamboo, and vine trees. There's also the

Rafflesia. At nearly one meter wide, the flower is one of the largest in the world and is quite rare. You'll also find pitcher plants, which are large insect-eating plants shaped like pitchers to trap unsuspecting bugs. You can tour the park's waterfalls and caves and canoe on the Chong Kaeb Khao Ka Loh lake, the result of a dam built to generate hydroelectric power for the region.

Accommodations and Food

The park offers simple accommodations in dormitory-style rooms and very cool but basic floating huts near two of the ranger stations. The huts, which have beds but shared toilets, are only 400B per night but are popular with large tour groups and book up quickly; you must reserve your place in advance. The park's website (www.dnp.go.th) has instructions on reserving accommodations (click on "National Park Online Reservation" in the English version of the site). Near the ranger station are also a couple of small restaurants that are open for breakfast, lunch, and dinner. These canteens serve only Thai food, but it is fresh and inexpensive.

Getting There

If you are coming from Surat Thani, you can pick up a bus to the park's entrance. The bus ride takes an hour and costs 70B, but they only run two a day, one in the morning and one in the afternoon (make sure to check at the bus station for current schedules). Once you are in the park, as with all national parks in Thailand, you will have a very difficult time getting around unless you either plan on hitching rides with other visitors or renting a car. If you are driving on your own, the park's entrance is on Route 401, which runs east–west between Surat Thani and Takua Pa. The park is about 97 kilometers east of Surat Thani.

PHRA BOROMMATHAT CHAIYA AND THE CHAIYA NATIONAL MUSEUM
พระบรมธาตุไชยา และ พิพิธภัณฑสถานแหงชาติไชยา

Located about 48 kilometers north of the city, Phra Borommathat Chaiya is an ancient *chedi* said to house relics of the Buddha. The *chedi* itself is small but has amazingly detailed carvings. It was probably built around 1,200 years ago during the Srivijaya Empire. On the grounds you'll also find the Chaiya National Museum (Raksanorakit Rd., Tambon Wiang, Amphoe Chaiya, tel. 07/743-1066, 9 A.M.–4 P.M. Wed.–Sun., 30B). This small gem of a museum has an excellent collection of prehistoric artifacts such as tools, pottery, and housewares found in the region as well as regional art from the sixth century to the present. Here you'll be able to see a large collection of Srivijaya art, mostly devotional figures of the Buddha, but also Hindu art such as sculptures of Vishnu from before Buddhism took hold in the region.

The museum also has a collection of items found in shipwrecks in the Gulf of Thailand, left by sailors from China and beyond.

Getting There

If you're driving, Chaiya is 48 kilometers north of Surat Thani on Route 41. To visit without a car, you can take one of the frequent *song thaew* that depart from Surat Thani's bus terminal during the day. The trip will take about 45 minutes and costs 50B.

Nakhon Si Thammarat Province จังหวัดนครศรีธ

The Nakhon Si Thammarat region might just be one of the best untouristed places to visit in Thailand. The city is well organized, easy to navigate, and filled with museums and *wats*. The beaches have the clean, warm waters of the Gulf of Thailand but none of the crowds, and the inland national parks are filled with fertile rainforests and scores of waterfalls. There's also an airport with direct flights from Bangkok, and you can pick up a ticket for a song on Nok Air. Best of all, if you enjoying traveling to places where you're not likely to run into folks just like you, there are still very few Western travelers coming this way. The area is frequented by visitors from other parts of Thailand and Southeast Asia, however, so there are adequate accommodations and other tourism infrastructure.

◖ NAKHON SI THAMMARAT
นครศรีธรรมราช

Nakhon Si Thammarat is one of the oldest cities in the country and has a great collection of interesting historical and cultural sights to visit. If you're looking for an urban break in a small city after soaking up the sun and sea, spend a day visiting the museums and religious buildings. As a whole, the city isn't beautiful. The newer parts suffer from a type of generic urbanization that seems to know no international boundaries. But in the older part of the city you'll find Wat Phra Mahathat, one of the oldest and largest *wats* in the country, and some charming streets to wander around.

Despite the charm and cultural significance, the city is not a typical tourist trap. There are a couple of Tourism Authority of Thailand offices (one in city hall and one near the Ta Chang market), but other than that, the city is pretty much oblivious to travelers. You won't find lots of signs in English or even lots of taxis. To get around, it's best to grab one of the visitor maps from your hotel or the TAT office and set out on foot.

© SUZANNE NAM

mountains in Nakhon Si Thammarat Province

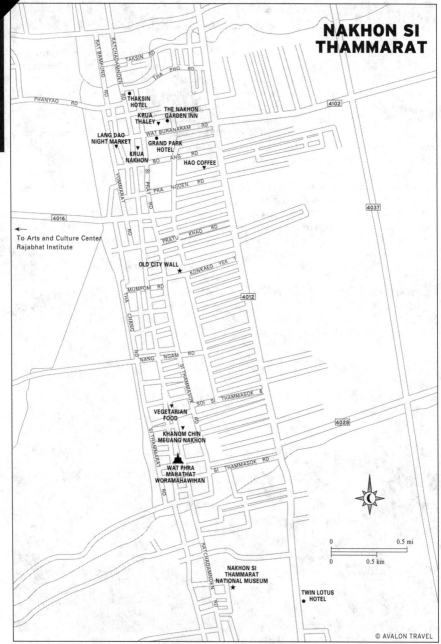

NAKHON SI THAMMARAT

THAKSIN HOTEL

THE NAKHON GARDEN INN

KRUA THALEY

LANG DAO NIGHT MARKET

GRAND PARK HOTEL

KRUA NAKHON

HAO COFFEE

PHANYAO RD

TAKSIN RD

RATCHADAMNOEN RD

RAT BAMRUNG RD

THA PHO RD

WAT BURANARAM RD

BO ANG RD

SI PRA NGOEN RD

SI PRAT RD

YOMMARAT RD

4102

4037

4016

To Arts and Culture Center
Rajabhat Institute

PRATU KHAO RD

OLD CITY WALL

KONKAED YEK

MUMPOM RD

THA CHANG RD

4012

NANG NGAM RD

SI THAMMASOK RD

SOI SI THAMMASOK 6

VEGETABIAN FOOD

KHANOM CHIN MEUANG NAKHON

4028

WAT PHRA MAHATHAT WORAMAHAWIHAN

SI THAMMARAT RD

SI THAMMASOK RD

RATCHADAMNOEN RD

NAKHON SI THAMMARAT NATIONAL MUSEUM

TWIN LOTUS HOTEL

| 0 | 0.5 mi |
| 0 | 0.5 km |

© AVALON TRAVEL

Sights

Nakhon Si Thammarat is one of the oldest cities in the country, and although only fragments of the **Old City Wall** from the 13th century remain, they give a glimpse of what the city must have been like hundreds of years ago. The wall once enclosed the center of the city.

Located in such a historic city, the **Nakhon Si Thammarat National Museum** (Ratchadamnoen Rd., 9 A.M.–4 P.M. Wed.–Sun., 30B) does a nice job of exhibiting artifacts from prehistory through modern times, many relating to Buddhism. You'll find exhibits of local crafts through the ages and also some excellent examples of fine art. The niello ware (engraved metalwork) pieces are worth extra time perusing. There are also some more fun exhibits in the museum's new wing relating to Thai life, marriage rituals, and local food. The museum is 2.4 kilometers out of the center of town, heading south on Ratchadamnoen Road. You can grab a local *song thaew* or public bus from the main road, which will cost about 10B.

Nearly every postcard you see in the city will have an image of the imposing *chedi* at **Wat Phra Mahathat Woramahawihan** (Ratchadamnoen Rd., 8 A.M.–4:30 P.M. daily, 30B, museum 20B extra), which indicates how important the *wat* is to the city and the country. The original structure is believed to have been built between the sixth and eighth centuries, during the Srivijaya period, as a monastery and school. The ornately decorated *ubosot* (coronation hall), from the 18th-century Ayutthaya period, is relatively new, but the foundation of the large Phra Borom That Chedi is believed to have been built when the *wat* itself was founded. There is also a small museum on the premises with Buddhist reliquaries and other objects. While the historical significance may be difficult to grasp for someone unfamiliar with the spread of Buddhism in the region, the grounds themselves are quite stunning, and just wandering around for an hour or two is worth the time. The *wat* is 1.5 kilometers south of the center of town: Grab a local *song thaew* or public bus

on Ratchadamnoen Rd. or, if the weather is good, walk.

The Nakhon Si Thammarat **Arts and Culture Center Rajabhat Institute** (Nakhon Si Thammarat–Phrom Khiri Rd., Hwy. 4016, 9 A.M.–4 P.M. daily), 13 kilometers east of the center of town, has numerous archaeological exhibits of artifacts found in the region, including tools and other objects from the Srivijaya Empire. The center, which is unfortunately mostly signed in Thai, also preserves and catalogs local customs, languages, and literature.

Accommodations

Although the city has a lot to offer travelers, the accommodations have yet to catch up (or catch on), and you'll find very limited options in Nakhon Si Thammarat. If you're looking for a place to indulge in a little luxury, or even a charming guesthouse with decent facilities, you're out of luck. If you just want a clean and comfortable place to sleep, there are a few options.

The top-of-the-line hotel in the city is the **Twin Lotus Hotel** (97/8 Pattanakarn-Kukwang Rd., tel. 07/532-3777, www.twinlotushotel. net, 1,500B). The guest rooms are spacious and well equipped, and the property is clean and maintained. Since it's a large city hotel, it's not a particularly interesting place to stay, however. Think beige curtains, Formica, and floral bedspreads. It does have a large pool, a fitness center, and other amenities you won't find anywhere else in the city. The hotel is not quite in the center of all of the action, so if you're looking for a place from which you can easily walk to all the sights, this may be a little far.

The **Thaksin Hotel** (1584/23 Si Prat Rd., tel. 07/534-2790 to 07/534-2794, www.thaksinhotel.com, 600B) and the **Grand Park Hotel** (1204/79 Pak Nakhon Rd., T. Klang, tel. 07/531-7666, www.grandparknakhon.com, 600B) are more central but still suffer from a lack of character that's even more pronounced in a city that's so culturally rich. Thaksin is a large, clean, modern place, just off of the main Ratchadamnoen Road and close to the train station. The guest rooms are well-kept and comfortable, and the price is more than reasonable, but generic decor and a business-conference vibe make it more of a utility choice than anything else. The Grand Park Hotel is similar to the Thaksin—clean, large, comfortable, and generic.

The guest rooms at **The Nakhon Garden Inn** (1/4 Pak Nakhon Rd., tel. 07/534-4831, 700B) are set around a leafy courtyard. This property has perhaps the most character of all the places you'll find in the city, although it's definitely not as modern and tidy as the other options.

Food

Downstairs at the Robinson Ocean Department Store is the highly popular **Hao Coffee** (Robinson Ocean, Pak Panang Kukwang Rd., tel. 07/534-6563, 10:30 A.M.–8:30 P.M. daily, 35–120B), which is actually two restaurants together, and the Ligor Bakery next door, which offers a choice of cakes and pastries. There are plenty of seats, but these restaurants do get busy at lunchtime, especially on the weekend, although chances are you will be able to find a free table among the knickknacks and curios on display and get to try some of their acclaimed food. The English menu has many one-dish choices from just 35B, such as prawns in chili sauce or chicken with holy basil, 10 different types of fried rice, and a wide choice of larger meals featuring curries, *tom yam,* and the intriguing fried Chinese kale with shellfish sausage. There are 16 coffees and eight types of tea to choose from, along with fresh fruit juices and ice cream or desserts from the Ligor Bakery to finish. The *khao gluk gapee* (fried rice with shrimp paste) is just right for a light lunch, with a glass of the wonderfully sweet *nam makaam* (tamarind juice) on the side. There is also a Hao Coffee at Bavorn Bazaar, but they have no English menu. Neither location has English-speaking staff.

Set centrally in a large open-air *sala* at Bavorn Bazaar is **Krua Nakhon** (Bavorn Bazaar, off Ratchadamnoen Rd. near Thawang Junction, no phone, 6:30 A.M.–2 P.M. daily, 25–100B), well known for the southern specialty *kanom chin*—a type of thin rice noodle served with dishes of fish curry, *kaeng tai pla* (fish-stomach curry), and vegetables. This is available in a small size for 1–2 people for 180B, or in a large size for five or more people for 250B. Also available are a selection of premade curries on rice for just 25B, and *khao yam*—another local dish of fried rice mixed with herbs, lemongrass, and pomelo. There's no menu, and English isn't spoken, so this really is a "choose and point" restaurant. A small shop at the back of the restaurant sells a small selection of local handicrafts and sweets, and the whole place is decorated with old farming and cooking implements, including a rather naughtily shaped coconut grinder.

Out toward Wat Mahathat you can find the spotlessly clean **Vegetarian Food** (496 Ratchadamnoen Rd., on the left about 300 meters before the Provincial Court, 7:30 A.M.–4 P.M. daily, 40–80B) restaurant and store. Each day there are a choice of around 12 premade vegetarian stir-fries and curries, along with a selection of meat-free sausages and cutlets as side dishes. Everything here is free of animal products, so the curries are made with tofu or textured vegetable protein (TVP), and even the fish sauce contains absolutely no fish. Everything used to prepare the food is for sale, and each table has a price list in English of the TVP products for sale including fish balls, sausages, pig intestines, mock duck, and many others. There's no menu, and though the owner speaks English, the staff do not. They will provide a larger helping of food, however, for a few extra baht if you let them know you're hungry.

If you only go to one restaurant in Nakhon Si Thammarat, this is the one. Within walking distance of Wat Mahathat is the specialty **C Khanom Chin Meuang Nakhon** (23 Soi Panyum, left off Ratchadamnoen Rd. about 500 meters before the temple, tel. 07/534-2615, 7:30 A.M.–3:30 P.M. daily, 25B), which serves mountains of freshly made *kanom chin* every day. There are a few premade curries named in English available, but the *kanom chin* is a bargain at just 50B for a set meal for two, or 100B for a meal for four. For the money, you'll get a basket of *kanom chin*, light fish curries with and without coconut milk, a sweet curry with tamarind and peanuts, a plate of local herbs with cucumber salad, fried morning glory, and pickled cabbage with bean sprouts on the side. Get a dish of the *kaeng tai pla* (fish-stomach curry) as well and experiment a little—add a little fish curry to your *kanom chin*, maybe a few spoonfuls of *kaeng tai pla*, tear up a few herbs, add some bean sprouts, mix it all up with some cucumber salad, and enjoy. It's the perfect place to come for lunch when visiting Wat Mahathat, especially if you finish with some *kanom jak* (shredded coconut with sugar wrapped in long thin palm leaves and slow grilled until it all caramelizes) from the stalls offering sweets outside.

In the area where most of the places to stay are situated, **Krua Thaley** (1204/29–30 Pak Nakhon Rd., opposite VDO Town video, next to Nakhon Garden Inn, tel. 07/534-6724 or 07/531-7180, 4–10 P.M. daily, 50–250B) is locally recommended for its choice and quality of seafood. The mussels, crabs, prawns, oysters, clams, and fish are all on display, but in the kitchen they're transformed into dishes such as green mussels with hot and fragrant herb salad and steamed butterfish with Chinese plum sauce. The English menu has some cheaper simple Thai food too, but there's a good chance there will be something in the pages of seafood offerings that will appeal. If not, every day there are also 12 specials on the board in Thai, though the owner may need to translate these as the staff do not speak English. The front of the restaurant is decorated with Buddha images, antiques, and collectibles and has a very "old Thai" feel to it, whereas the back room is a little farther from the road, and the trees and plants make for a different atmosphere. Recommendations here are the *tom yam kung* and the southern specialty *kaeng som pla grapong* (orange curry with flakey whitefish).

Around the area in front of the railroad station, the **Lang Dao Night Market** (Yommarat Rd., 4:30–9:30 P.M. daily) has many stalls selling fresh fruit and cheap packet food for a few baht, but this is really the place to come for some proper local food. Pots of steaming curries almost line the road in places, and you can sit and eat a bowlful with rice for just 25B. It's definitely a place to experiment. Noodle stalls and *khao man kai* (chicken and rice) are easy to find, but do look out for the stall selling *hoi thot* (deep-fried shellfish wrapped in egg) for something a bit different. Walking food comes by way of *luk chin* stalls selling skewered fish balls, crab sticks, tofu, quail eggs in batter, and others that are grilled or deep-fried, depending on the stall, then drowned in a bag of spicy chili sauce. For dessert, try the exotic fruit in sickly sweet syrup, or the *bpatong goh* (deep-fried batter), maybe washed down with a bag of sugarcane juice. It's a great place to see what takes your fancy, but if you need to know exactly what you're eating, it's unlikely you'll find many people able to explain in English.

Getting There

The easiest and fastest way to get to the city is to fly from Bangkok, and there are a couple of carriers that have direct flights at least once per day. If you're going by land, the city is about 800 kilometers south of Bangkok, so expect a long ride. By bus, it's about 12 hours from Bangkok, and there are frequent buses, including an overnight bus that leaves from the Southern Bus Terminal in the early evening. Another option is to take the train from Bangkok's Hua Lamphong Station; there are a couple of direct trains that take a little over 14 hours.

◖ KHANOM AND SICHON
ขนอม-สิชล

If you're in the area to enjoy the beaches, these two towns in the northern part of the province are where you want to be. Here you'll find kilometers of beautiful sandy beaches fringed with palm trees and surrounded by mangrove forests and occasional limestone cliffs. If you want to experience the country's physical beauty and feel like you're in a foreign country while you're doing it, this area is unrivaled. In fact, you'll hear from a lot of

© SUZANNE NAM

river near the coast of Sichon

people that this is one of Thailand's undiscovered gems. The truth is, development is happening, just at a very slow pace. You won't find lots of resorts or tourist diversions compared to Samui, Phuket, or Krabi, but there are a handful of places to stay. You also won't find discos, go-go bars, or much evidence of the sex industry. Although the beaches of Khanom and Sichon are adjacent to each other, for now you cannot go directly from one to the other on a paved path, as there is no road connecting them near the coast. From Khanom to Sichon (or vice versa) you'll have to get out onto the main highway and circle around, which takes about 45 minutes.

Beaches

Starting from Khanom at the northernmost part of the region, the first beach to visit is **Hat Na Dan,** a long stretch of clean, clear beach. Khanom's eastern border is the Gulf of Thailand, and unlike most of the coastline in the region, this beach is undisturbed by many promontories or cliffs. Although the area is

referred to as **Khanom Bay,** most of the coastline isn't curved; it's just one long stretch of sea and sand for kilometers. This is the area's most popular beach, and it can get a little busy during weekends or holidays, although the crowds are nothing like you'll see in Samui.

At the bottom of Hat Na Dan is a small bay where you'll find **Hat Nai Pret** and then, separated by a grouping of boulders, **Hat Nai Phlao.** The gently curving coastline is what makes these beaches so attractive. To add to the charm, just around the beach are coconut plantations. The shore is rocky, though, so it's not the greatest place for swimming.

Just south of Hat Nai Phlao are **Ao Thong Yi** and **Ao Thong Yang,** two small secluded bays with excellent beaches for swimming, snorkeling, or just lying around and reading a novel. Ao Thong Yi has some coral just off the coast that's easy to view by swimming out. These beaches are quite isolated and a great place to go if you're looking for a bit of the desert-island feeling without having to trek out for kilometers. You'll be able to reach Ao Thong Yi from

© SUZANNE NAM

a beach in Khanom

Hat Nai Phlao, but because of some mountains in the way, to get to Ao Thong Yang you can either travel by boat from Hat Nai Phlao or by road from Sichon in the south.

In Sichon, a small coastal town on the way to Nakhon Si Thammarat, there are a few beaches worth visiting—**Sichon Beach, Hat Hin Ngam,** and **Hat Piti.** Hat Sichon and Hat Hin Ngam are beautiful and quiet, but there are lots of rocks on the shore, especially in Hat Hin Ngam. Hat Piti (also called Hat Ko Khao) has a smooth, sandy coast and also a few restaurants and resorts. Both Hat Nin Ngam and Hat Piti can be reached easily from Hat Sichon using the small service road that follows the coast.

Accommodations

There's not much in the way of five-star luxury in Sichon and Khanom since the area is still largely unknown by foreign visitors. There are a handful of modest, simple bungalows and small resorts that offer enough amenities and comfort for most travelers.

The basic white wooden bungalows at **Krua Poy Beach Resort** (625 Mu 3, Hin Ngam Beach, Sichon, tel. 07/553-6055, www.kruapoybeachresort.com, 550B) are clean and air-conditioned and even have simple private baths. The small resort fronts a beautiful stretch of beach, and the young manager, Palm, whose family has owned the resort for decades, also gives windsurfing lessons. There is a nice open-air restaurant on the beach and plenty of chairs to lounge on if you're not windsurfing with Palm.

Next door, **Prasarnsook Villas** (Hin Ngam Beach, Sichon, tel. 07/553-6299, www.prasarnsookresort.com, 1,500B) is owned by the grandmother of the family, and the villas, which opened in 2008, are very nicely designed, spacious stand-alone structures with modern baths and small outdoor verandas. Depending on your budget, either choice is a great value for the money. Visitors here are mostly urban Thais on vacation, but staff speak English and are happy to accommodate foreign guests.

© SUZANNE NAM

Krua Poy Beach Resort in Sichon

The **Ekman Garden Resort** (39/2 Mu 5, Tumble Saopao, tel. 07/536-7566, www.ekmangarden.com, 1,200B) is a small family-run resort with clean, basic guest rooms and bungalows, a swimming pool, and a good location on the beach in Sichon. The sunny guest rooms are not luxurious, but they are well-decorated, if simple, and have air-conditioning, comfortable beds, and modern baths. The wooden buildings and thatched roof give the resort a relaxed, unpretentious feeling, and it's family-friendly as well.

Set on a beautiful open stretch of coast is the **Khanom Golden Beach Hotel** (59/3 Mu 4, Nadan Beach, www.khanomgoldenbeach.com, tel. 07/532-6688, 1,200B). This large modern hotel is a great choice if you want hotel amenities (in fact, it's the only hotel in the area), and the guest rooms are clean and well maintained though not particularly interesting. There is also a nice beach bar and a swimming pool. This property tends to attract families, and there are plenty of little kids at the beach and pool.

The **Piti Resort** (Hat Piti, tel. 07/533-5301, 1,500B) is another clean, simple resort right on the beach in Sichon. The guest rooms feel a little more modern and less traditional but still have a basic budget feeling you'd expect for the price and considering the location. The resort also has a small swimming pool and a good inexpensive restaurant with lots of local dishes.

Khanom Hill Resort (60/1 Mu 8, Khanom Beach, tel. 07/552-9403, www.khanom.info, 2,500B) is set on a hill overlooking Khanom Beach, with bungalows and guest rooms dotting the hillside. The guest rooms vary from simple and clean to beautifully decorated with modern Thai touches and nicer-than-usual baths, depending on the rate. The newest guest rooms, which are across the road from the beach, are the nicest, and there's a small swimming pool on that side, but the older guest rooms have a better view of the water. There is direct beach access and a nice restaurant overlooking the water that serves Thai and Western food. Staff and management are friendly and helpful.

Aava Resort & Spa (28/3 Mu 6, Nadan Beach, tel. 07/530-0310, www.aavaresort.com, 2,500B), which opened in 2010, is the area's nicest resort. The minimalist Thai design and massive swimming pool seem almost out of place in otherwise sleepy Khanom, but those who enjoy flashpacking and off-the-beaten-path beaches will love it (as do, it appears, the Finnish, who seem to be most of the guests). The resort is set right on the beach, and there are a couple of high-end restaurants serving Thai and Western food.

Food

There is very limited food in the area, but all of the resorts and bungalows listed above have restaurants serving fresh, well-prepared Thai food, and all also have outdoor areas with beach views to enjoy your meals.

Halfway along the Nadan Beach Road, you will find **Taalkoo Beach Resort and Restaurant** (23/9 Mu 2, Nadan Beach, just south of Golden Beach Resort, tel. 07/552-8218, 7 A.M.–10 P.M., jantima_manajit@yahoo.com, 60–150B) right on the beach surrounded by its 42 bungalows. Sit inside on the heavy gnarled wooden chairs, or head for the veranda in the afternoon after the sun has passed behind the trees and sit with a clear view of the long, empty beach. The English menu is quite small, but the usual Thai stir-fries, *tom yam,* and curries are secondary to the choice of "by-weight" fresh fish and seafood. The fresh fish sold in this restaurant has a good reputation locally; the *yam takrai* (spicy lemongrass salad), *thot man kung* (deep-fried mashed prawns), and *pla lui suan* (fish with cashew nuts and lemongrass) make a great meal for two. The staff generally cannot speak English, but the manager will be able to help.

At the northernmost end of Hat Ko Khao, on the right where the road hits the beach, are 10 **food stalls** (Hat Ko Khao, no phone, 11 A.M.–8 P.M. daily, 50–150B), all serving similar menus based on Isan food and grilled seafood. The food is great with *yam, larb, som tam, tom yam,* and sticky rice, but it's really the low-key atmosphere that appeals here. Small bamboo-roofed *salas* that look like they should've blown away years ago sit above the beach covering concrete seats or haphazard wooden benches, while a dilapidated jukebox plays Thai music at an unreasonably loud volume just far enough away so you don't really care. Get a bucket of ice and a bottle of something appropriate to pour over it, get a plate of the excellent *namtok mu* (marinated grilled pork salad with ground chilies) to start with, and prepare yourself for a slow afternoon grazing the menus—which will all be in Thai, and it's unlikely anyone will speak much English, but if you're not sure, just point.

Another Thai experience can be had at the Music Kitchen, or **Krua Dondtree** (Talaad Seeyaek, Khanom, tel. 08/6952-7835, 11 A.M.–11 P.M., 40–80B), where Isan food meets with country-and-western and 1970s easy-listening music. It's on the right about one kilometer north out of Khanom Town; look for the green-fronted *sala* 500 meters after the Honda dealer. There may not be many places in Thailand where you can eat your *som tam* accompanied by "Puff the Magic Dragon" or "Tie a Yellow Ribbon," but this is definitely one of them. As well as *som tam, larb mu,* and *larb pla duk,* numerous kinds of *yam, namtok mu, tom yam kung,* and grilled meat and seafood, there is a daily specials board with another five dishes to supplement the small two-page menu. The specials are not in English, however, and the owner does not speak English, so it might be easiest to ask for her most popular meal: *yam pak grut* (spicy local-vegetable salad) with *larb pet* (duck *larb*), another combination you're unlikely to see in many places.

The last restaurant on the beach road before Piti Resort is **Sichon Seafood** (Beach Rd., Hat Sichon, tel. 08/9586-9402, 7:30 A.M.–10 P.M. daily, 80–250B), offering the basic Thai fare of curries, stir-fries, and *yam,* but specializing in seafood dishes such as grilled lobster, crab with plum sauce, and deep-fried sea bass with mango salad, which comes highly recommended. The open-air *sala* has a cozy feel with aged-wood tables, and a veranda projects over the rocky beach while remaining shaded from the afternoon sun. It's a nice place for a long, relaxed evening meal, possibly taking advantage of the wide range of local spirits on offer at the bar. Menus are in English, and a little English is spoken.

Positioned fairly centrally on Hat Hin Ngam is the **Prasarnsook Resort** (625/4 Hin Ngam Beach, tel. 07/553-6299 or 07/533-5601, 6:30 A.M.–9:30 P.M. daily, www.prasarnsookresort.com, 50–250B), a fairly standard resort-based restaurant set in pleasant cultivated gardens and immediately overlooking the sea. The extensive menu runs from breakfasts, with a choice of Thai food, through more Western-oriented Thai food with cream or wine sauces, with fresh seafood being the most expensive of the options. That said, there are lots of choices around 80B. There are also five specials, in Thai only, on the otherwise English menu, but the restaurant manager will be able to explain them to you. The *kung gati jaan rorn* (prawns in coconut milk) is definitely worth a try, especially if you don't like your food too spicy. There's the choice of eating in the large, impressive *sala* or at one of the small tables on the beach itself.

Raan Nong Wee (Hin Ngam Beach, tel. 08/9287-1522, 10 A.M.–7 P.M. daily, 30–100B) is at the southern end of Hat Hin Ngam just before the Isra Beach Resort (turn left at the bottom of the only small *soi* off the Beach Road down to Hat Hin Ngam). It is a place well worth hunting out. You can eat in the small *sala* in front of the owner's house, but it's more enjoyable to sit on a mat on the beach under the trees with a cold beer and a few choice plates of Isan food. There is a only a Thai menu, and don't expect any English to be spoken, but all of the essentials are here— *som tam*, different kinds of *larb*, many different *yam* spicy salads, sticky rice, deep-fried fish cakes, grilled fish and other seafood, fried rice, and simple stir-fries. It's so cheap and delicious that you can get a selection of dishes, and then grab a table and get to chatting with the locals. A good choice for two people would be *som tam pla rah* (papaya salad), *yam wun sen pla muek* (spicy salad of squid and glass noodles),

thot man pla (deep-fried fish cakes) and *pla duk yahng* (grilled catfish). Add a couple of Chang beers to keep the chilies under control.

Back in Sichon Town on the way to the main highway, opposite the police station, the **Kotone Restaurant** (6/1 Talaad Sichon, tel. 07/553-6259 or 07/553-5242, 7 A.M.–9 P.M. daily, 35–150B) comes highly recommended by local people. A 15-page English menu gives ample choice among one-dish Thai food such as curries on rice and stir-fries for just 35B, soups, spicy *yam* salads, and other Isan food, along with southern curries such as *kaeng som pla* (orange curry with fish) and Massaman curry, lots of pork dishes that are the general specialty of this restaurant, and, of course, fresh local fish, crabs, and prawns. The particular specialty here is *khao mu kotone*—leg of pork cooked in the three-flavor "sweet, sour, and salt" style. Well-served tables are available outside on a decked area, inside at street level, or in an air-conditioned room on the upper floor, and the duty manager will help if your waitress doesn't speak English. Not surprisingly, this restaurant is so popular they have opened another one on the main highway, about two kilometers toward Khanom, called **Kotone Restaurant 2.**

Getting There

Sichon and Khanom are between Surat Thani and Nakhon Si Thammarat, and you can take a plane, car, bus, or train to either city and then make your way to your final destination. The cheapest and easiest way is to get to the bus station in Surat Thani or Nakhon Si Thammarat and take a bus for less than 100B. There are frequent buses (at least hourly 8 A.M.–6 P.M. daily) to Sichon and Khanom from both Surat Thani and Nakhon Si Thammarat. If you're driving, Sichon and Khanom are both off Highway 401, which you can access from either Surat Thani or Nakhon Si Thammarat.

KHAO LUANG NATIONAL PARK
อุทยานแห่งชาติเขาหลวง

This national park is named for Khao Luang mountain, at nearly 1,830 meters the highest mountain in southern Thailand. You can hike to the summit and back in two days if you hike 7–8 hours per day. You can also do the hike over three days and include a stay in **Kiriwong Village** (tel. 07/530-9010, 05/394-8286, or 08/1642-0081), which includes basic accommodations in the village and meals, for 1,500B per person. The views from the peak are spectacular—you'll be able to see the tropical cloud forest and the rest of the mountain range from above. The park is also home to more than 300 species of wild orchids, some of which aren't found anywhere else in the world. But this inland park is best known for its waterfalls, and there are 10 major falls in the 570-square-kilometer national park. The Krung Ching waterfall is one of the most spectacular, and there's also a nearby ranger substation and visitors center you can drive to, and then walk to the waterfall, just a few minutes away. To get here, take Route 4016 from Nakhon Si Thammarat until you reach the junction with Route 4140. Turn left onto 4140 until you reach Ban Rong Lek, where you'll turn right onto Route 4186 to Route 4188. Turn left on this road, and you'll find a sign for the visitors center after about six kilometers.

If you're interested in staying in the park, there are bungalows for rent and campgrounds where you can pitch a tent. You must reserve accommodations in advance; check the park's website (www.dnp.go.th) for details.

For a real off-the-beaten-path experience, you can also base yourself in one of the neighboring villages. Kiriwong Village, at the base of Khao Luang in the southern part of the park, is not technically in the park but has become something of an ecotourism destination, and for good reason. The village's primary industry is growing fruit, but instead of clearing forests, the villagers have interspersed their mangosteen, jackfruit, and durian trees within the natural ecosystem. You can tour their organic *suam somron* garden or arrange a homestay with one of the village families. They've been taking in visitors from all over the world for years, so although you won't be in luxurious surroundings, you'll be comfortable, well taken care of, and get a chance to get to know some of the villagers. The **Thailand Community Based Tourism Institute** (tel. 07/530-9010, 05/394-8286, or 08/1642-0081) is a not-for-profit organization that arranges homestays and tours of the area as well as to other places in the region, many of which are once-in-a-lifetime opportunities.

Getting There

If you're driving to the park's main headquarters, take Route 4015 from Nakhon Si Thammarat for about 24 kilometers to Lanksaka. Just past the town, you'll see a turnoff for the park headquarters.

You can also take a *song thaew* from Nakhon Si Thammarat that stops right after the turnoff on Route 4015.

Songkhla Province   จังหวัดสงขลา

Just north of the three southernmost provinces in Thailand, Songkhla Province is bordered on the east by the Gulf of Thailand and on the west by the state of Kedah in Malaysia. It was part of the Srivijaya Empire, then came under the rule of neighboring Nakhon Si Thammarat. It's in this part of the country that you'll feel the dominance of Buddhism give way to Islam, as evidenced in the mosques and attire of many of the people living in the province. Many people in Songkhla Province speak Yawi as their primary language instead of Thai, and although it may be difficult to discern, the Thai speakers here have a markedly different accent from their compatriots up north.

SONGKHLA
สงขลา

Bordered to the west by the large **Tha Le Sap Songkhla** lake and to the east by the Gulf of Thailand, the coastal city of Songkhla is surrounded by magnificent physical scenery.

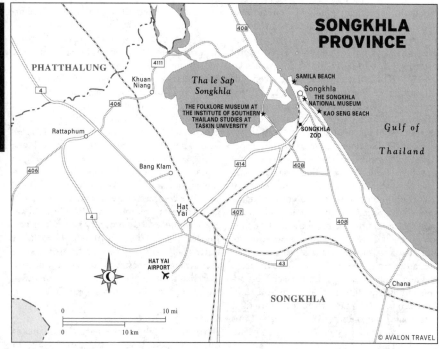

PHATTHALUNG

Khuan
Niang

*Tha le Sap
Songkhla*

THE FOLKLORE MUSEUM AT
THE INSTITUTE OF SOUTHERN ★
THAILAND STUDIES AT
TASKIN UNIVERSITY

Rattaphum

Bang Klam

Hat
Yai

HAT YAI
AIRPORT

SAMILA BEACH

Songkhla
★ THE SONGKHLA
NATIONAL MUSEUM
★ KAO SENG BEACH

SONGKHLA
ZOO

**SONGKHLA
PROVINCE**

Gulf of

Thailand

Chana

SONGKHLA

0   10 mi
0   10 km

© AVALON TRAVEL

Thanks to its location, it was once a thriving port city attracting merchants from Persia, the Arabian Peninsula, and India. Nowadays it's considerably sleepier, although you'll still find a thriving fishing industry and remnants from its trading past in the city's Sino-Portuguese architecture. This small city offers a great opportunity to observe urban life in Thailand and learn a bit about the culture and history of the southern region as well.

Sights

The city's old quarter, centered around Nang Ngam Road, has a collection of historic buildings and small shops selling everything from snacks to religious wares for monks. Although not vast, it's a nice area to wander around for a while.

The **Songkhla Zoo** (189 Mu 5, tel. 07/433-6268, 8 A.M.–6 P.M. daily, 50B adults, 30B children) covers more than 140 hectares in the hills just outside of the city limits—it's almost necessary to rent a motorcycle to see the whole thing. Inside the confines you'll find a typical selection of animals that includes tigers, camels, primates, and bird species. This public zoo is also a breeding center for endangered tapirs—large mammals that look like a cross between a rhinoceros and an anteater. In addition to visiting the animals, you'll get a great view of the city from above.

The **Folklore Museum at the Institute of Southern Thailand Studies at Taksin University** (Ko Yo Hill, 9 A.M.–4 P.M. Tues.–Fri., donation) has a wide collection of materials and exhibits on the culture of southern Thais. There are some exhibits on the history of the area in the museum, but the most interesting things to see are the exhibits relating to the everyday life of the people in this part of the country, featuring local art and handicrafts, shadow puppetry, and traditional medicines.

The museum is worth visiting just for its location: It's on the small Yo Island on Songkhla lake, one of the country's largest natural lakes, and the grounds are filled with local plants.

Housed in a sweeping Chinese-style mansion originally built by the deputy governor of Songkhla in 1878, **The Songkhla National Museum** (Vichianchom Rd., Bo Yang, tel. 07/431-1728, 9 A.M.–4 P.M. Wed.–Sun., 30B) now displays a large collection of art and artifacts from the region from prehistoric times to the present. The small collection of prehistoric artifacts includes terra-cotta, pottery, and small beads. The Srivijayan collection has both Buddhist and Hindu art and illustrates the transition the kingdom made from one religion to another. The Dvaravati Buddhist art section has some beautiful examples of 16th–17th-century Buddhist imagery from the Nakhon Si Thammarat School of Art. In addition to the art based on the cultures of the region, the museum also houses a large collection of art from China along with some pieces (mostly ceramics) from Vietnam, Japan, and Europe, illustrating the region's former importance as a trading port.

Accommodations

As in the rest of the region, the accommodations in Songkhla aren't up to international standards. There are some large, generic hotels in the city with basic accommodations but no character, and just a couple of resorts on the water. As the area's charms and attractions become better known, this might change, but for now it's a challenge to find good places to stay in the city and environs.

The **Hat Kaew Resort** (163/1 Km. 5, Ching Ko, Singhanakhon, tel. 07/433-1058-66, 1,200B) on Samila Beach is a large property with clean, comfortable guest rooms, a large swimming pool, and well-maintained grounds. If you're not looking for a five-star experience, this property will be more than adequate. The resort isn't full of local character, however—beige and floral prints seem to dominate the decor. It's also a popular place for conventions, thanks to the large banquet hall and meeting areas.

The **Pavilion Songkhla Hotel** (17 Palatha Rd., tel. 07/444-1850, www.pavilionhotels. com, 1,200B) is another large, generic hotel in the city. It's often bustling with organized tours, and the tour buses can be a little off-putting. But it is inexpensive and right in the city if you're looking for a place to stay while you set out to explore Songkhla.

Food

Coffee Peak (95/5 Somrong Junction, Songkhla–Natave Rd., tel. 07/431-4682, 11 A.M.–9 P.M. daily, 100B) is a casual restaurant with a small outdoor seating area in town. In addition to coffee, the menu also offers a nice combination of Thai food and international dishes. This is not a restaurant that tries to please Western palates: International dishes are geared toward Thai tastes, so some items may not taste as you would expect them to, so it's best to stick with the Thai dishes and the delicious desserts.

Another great place for Thai food and coffee is **Crown Bakery** (38/1 Tai Ngam Rd., tel. 07/444-1305, 11 A.M.–8 P.M. daily, 100B). The atmosphere is casual but is much more upscale than your typical noodle shop or shophouse eatery. The menu has typical Thai and Chinese-Thai dishes—there's no standout here, but everything is well prepared, and the atmosphere is nice.

If you don't mind trading atmosphere for taste, **Pajit Restaurant** (1/25 Saiburi Rd., tel. 07/432-1710, 11 A.M.–8 P.M. daily, 40B) has excellent *guay teow* (traditional noodle soup). This is a typical shophouse with outdoor seating, mismatched dishes, and toilet-paper rolls for napkins—a very casual, inexpensive place for a quick meal.

For more Isan fare, stop at **Deeplee's** (211 Nakornnai Rd., tel. 08/9463-3874, 11 A.M.–10 P.M. daily, 80B). You'll find *som tam, kai yang* (grilled chicken with smoky, spicy sauce), and sticky rice. The atmosphere is very local and casual, making it another great place for a quick, inexpensive meal. Another Isan restaurant, **Rotsab** (39/11 Mu 1, Pawong, tel. 07/433-4602, 11 A.M.–9 P.M. daily, 100B), offers similar dishes but is a little larger and fancier. This spot is very popular with families and large groups in the evening.

Getting There

To get to Songkhla by rail or air, you'll have to arrive in neighboring Hat Yai and make your way the 30-something kilometers to Songkhla either by bus (there are numerous daily buses between the cities) or by car. If you're taking the bus from Hat Yai, make your way to the city's main bus terminal to get to Songkhla.

HAT YAI
หาดใหญ่

Until the construction of a railroad line linking Thailand with Malaysia in the 20th century, Hat Yai was just a small village with nothing particularly special going on. When the railroad station came, the city seemed to develop around it, and while Songkhla is the provincial capital, neighboring Hat Yai has become the economic hub of the area and is a much more bustling, urban, industrialized city. If you spend time in Hat Yai, you might thing that Songkhla got the better end of the deal, and that's probably an accurate assessment. Some southern Thais half-jokingly refer to Hat Yai as the ugliest city in Thailand. It's not so much the concrete buildings, traffic, and generic urban feeling in Hat Yai that makes it unappealing, but the seedy feeling the city seems to have. There's a lot of neon and plenty of nightclubs, and it's a big spot for visitors from neighboring countries. Unfortunately, it seems like most people are visiting the city as sex tourists. In Hat Yai there's no ambiguity about what's going on—you'll see plenty of massage parlors, strip clubs, and bordellos, and also plenty of people frequenting them. Use Hat Yai as a transit hub (since it's the southernmost airport currently connected to Bangkok) and spend your time in the regions outside of the city.

Sights

Just on the edge of Hat Yai is **Samila Beach,** a surprisingly quiet and uncrowded stretch of coast given its proximity to the center of the city (you can easily walk there from the main market in about 20 minutes). The water is shallow and fine for swimming, although you won't see many people swimming here, and it's not as beautiful as some of the beaches you'll find in Sichon and Khanom to the north. You'll also find Hat Yai's unofficial symbol on Samila Beach—a large sculpture of the Hindu goddess Mae Thorani as a mermaid.

About three kilometers south of Samila Beach is **Khao Seng Beach.** Like its neighbor, Khao Seng is relaxed and uncrowded. The shoreline has some very large rocks, one of which is said to have treasure buried beneath it. As the legend goes, a wealthy merchant was bringing some treasure to a *wat* in Nakhon Si Thammarat but had to stop on Khao Seng Beach. He left the treasure here under a large rock and promised that anyone who could move the rock would get the treasure. The Muslim fisherfolk at Kao Seng village ply the waters with colorfully painted Kolae boats, which you'll be able to see if you're at the beach.

Accommodations and Food

Selection is bleak in Hat Yai. If you've arrived late and need to spend the night before heading out, you'll have to choose among sometimes dicey-looking small hotels, guesthouses, and mediocre large hotels.

Laem Thong Hotel (46 Thamnoonvitti Rd., tel. 07/435-2301, 500B) isn't really stylish or modern, but it's well located in the city and doesn't seem to have too much brothel activity going on in the area. Guest rooms look like they haven't been updated in decades (nor has the lobby), but they do look like they were cleaned this morning. Another inexpensive guesthouse is **Cathay Guesthouse** (93/1 Niphat U-Thit 2 Rd., tel. 07/424-3815, 300B). Cathay is a longtime favorite of backpackers, so if you're craving some conversation in a language you're fluent in, you'll definitely find it at the hotel's downstairs café-restaurant.

There's also plenty of tourist information available here. Guest rooms are pretty shabby, but you can't really complain for the price. The only drawback, which may be a showstopper for some, is the squat toilets.

The most reliable and nicest hotel in the city is the **Hotel Novotel Hat Yai Centara** (3 Sanehanusorn Rd., tel. 07/435-2222, 2,000B). You'll welcome the slightly generic, very clean guest rooms with crisp sheets and modern baths compared to the musty digs in the other large hotels in this area. The hotel also has a pool, a fitness center, and a good restaurant.

Getting There

Hat Yai is well served by an international airport with flights from Malaysia and Singapore as well as Bangkok, a large train station, and buses from Bangkok's Southern Bus Terminal as well as surrounding localities. If you're planning to fly from Bangkok, Air Asia, Nok Air, and Thai Airways all have direct flights to Hat Yai. The train station is one of the largest in the region, and there are five daily trains from Bangkok as well as daily trains from Butterworth in Malaysia if you happen to be coming from the south.

CENTRAL THAILAND

Central Thailand is the kingdom's cultural heartland. This is an agriculturally fertile region steeped in rich history and dotted with crumbling remnants from a time when the region was politically dominant. The area contains not one but two major ancient capitals—Ayutthaya and Sukhothai—that provide excellent opportunities for glimpsing Thailand's past architectural and artistic glories in a relaxing and laid-back environment.

Located less than two hours by car north of Bangkok, Ayutthaya, with its famous temple ruins, is one of central Thailand's most-visited attractions, especially as a day trip from the Thai capital. Ayutthaya stands out as the place where Thai power was consolidated for more than 400 years, before the capital was moved to Bangkok.

To the west of Bangkok are the thick rainforests and rolling limestone hills of laid-back Kanchanaburi Province. It's in the sleepy river town of Kanchanaburi itself that you'll find the infamous River Kwai Bridge, part of the notorious World War II "Death Railway" that resulted in the deaths of 115,000 Allied POWs and local laborers.

Sukhothai, farther to the north, was Thailand's first capital, an area that today is home to the ruins of 40 *wats* that date to the 13th century. Although Sukhothai isn't visited as frequently as the more-accessible Ayutthaya, many argue that its ruins are more impressive. To be sure, the temples here occupy an important place in the Thai psyche: Sukhothai is where the Thai people first coalesced as a nation in 1238.

© SUZANNE NAM

HIGHLIGHTS

◖ Ayutthaya Historical Park: This UNESCO World Heritage Site is filled with ruins from the country's former capital (page 303).

◖ Thailand-Burma Railway Centre: An interactive museum tells the painful history of the Thailand-Burma railway (page 311).

◖ Bridge on the River Kwai: The bridge built by Allied POWs is now part of an idyllic setting in Kanchanaburi (page 312).

◖ Sukhothai Historical Park: Another UNESCO World Heritage Site, this park contains temple and palace ruins from the 13th and 14th centuries (page 326).

◖ Ramkhamhaeng National Museum: Located inside Sukhothai Historical Park, this museum has an amazing collection of detailed carvings found in Sukhothai (page 327).

LOOK FOR ◖ TO FIND RECOMMENDED SIGHTS, ACTIVITIES, DINING, AND LODGING.

PLANNING YOUR TIME

The weather in central Thailand largely mirrors that of the nation at large. February–June is the hot season. It rains frequently July–October. The cool season runs November–January. Due to the pleasant weather during this time—and because it's winter in the northern hemisphere—this is Thailand's high season for tourism.

Because the sights in central Thailand are scattered throughout the region, many visitors use Bangkok as a base and travel to the area's attractions on separate trips instead of as part of a regional tour. Both Kanchanaburi and Ayutthaya are just a few hours away from the capital, but far away from each other, making a multiday journey to visit these sights together unnecessary and a little inconvenient. Ayutthaya can easily be visited on a day trip

from Bangkok. You won't be able to see everything in an afternoon, but since the temple ruins are clustered in a central area, you can cover quite a lot of ground if you arrive in the late morning and leave in the early evening. Kanchanaburi is also doable during a day trip, although because some of the sights are far from the center, most people opt to visit for at least a couple of days. Fortunately there are plenty of inexpensive places to stay if you decide to take that route.

A multiday trip is a good idea if you're really interested in temple ruins and are planning on seeing both Ayutthaya and Sukhothai Historical Parks. Sukhothai is at least five hours from Bangkok by car, and Ayutthaya is on the way—plus you won't have to feel like you're rushing through the sights. Don't expect either place to hold your attention for more than a

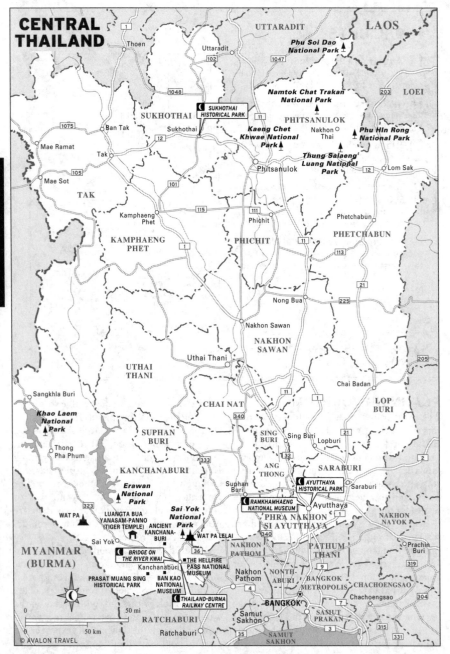

CENTRAL THAILAND

LAOS

UTTARADIT

LOEI

Phu Soi Dao National Park

Thoen

Uttaradit

Namtok Chat Trakan National Park

SUKHOTHAI

SUKHOTHAI HISTORICAL PARK

PHITSANULOK

Ban Tak

Sukhothai

Nakhon Thai

Phu Hin Rong National Park

Kaeng Chet Khwae National Park

Mae Ramat

Tak

Thung Salaeng Luang National Park

Lom Sak

Mae Sot

Phitsanulok

TAK

Kamphaeng Phet

Phetchabun

Phichit

PHETCHABUN

KAMPHAENG PHET

PHICHIT

Nong Bua

NAKHON SAWAN

Nakhon Sawan

Uthai Thani

Chai Badan

UTHAI THANI

LOP BURI

Sangkhla Buri

Khao Laem National Park

CHAI NAT

Thong Pha Phum

SUPHAN BURI

SING BURI

Sing Buri

Lopburi

KANCHANABURI

ANG THONG

SARABURI

Erawan National Park

Suphan Buri

AYUTTHAYA HISTORICAL PARK

Saraburi

WAT PA

RAMKHAMHAENG NATIONAL MUSEUM

Sai Yok National Park

Ayutthaya

LUANGTA BUA YANASAM-PANNO (TIGER TEMPLE)

ANCIENT KANCHANA-BURI

WAT PA LELAI

PHRA NAKHON SI AYUTTHAYA

NAKHON NAYOK

Sai Yok

BRIDGE ON THE RIVER KWAI

NAKHON PATHOM

Prachin Buri

MYANMAR (BURMA)

Kanchanaburi

THE HELLFIRE PASS NATIONAL MUSEUM

PATHUM THANI

PRASAT MUANG SING HISTORICAL PARK

BAN KAO NATIONAL MUSEUM

Nakhon Pathom

NONTH-ABURI

BANGKOK METROPOLIS

CHACHOENGSAO

THAILAND-BURMA RAILWAY CENTRE

Chachoengsao

0   50 mi

BANGKOK

RATCHABURI

Samut Sakhon

SAMUT PRAKAN

0   50 km

Ratchaburi

SAMUT SAKHON

© AVALON TRAVEL

couple of days, though. Some of the ruins are impressive, but there aren't lots of them to see, especially in Sukhothai, where you could realistically see everything in a day but for the fact that it's so far from everything.

HISTORY

While Ayutthaya draws far more tourists every year, the ruins of the Sukhothai Empire are just as important to Thailand's cultural history. This is, in essence, where Thai history and culture began. Founded in 1238 and lasting until the 14th century, Sukhothai was the first independent kingdom dominated by ethnic Tai people.

The earliest Tai people are believed to have lived in what is now southern China. Around the fifth century A.D., they migrated to present-day southern Laos, driven there by the expanding Vietnamese and Chinese empires. This group then moved to what we now call northern Thailand around the late seventh century. Here they founded their first sizeable empire, Sukhothai. The Sukhothai Kingdom would last until the 14th century and be ruled by nine kings. Sukhothai is the place where the Tai people—and the Thai nation—first began to coalesce. The city's name translates as "dawn of happiness."

The city of Sukhothai was previously a frontier outpost of the Khmer Empire. The Khmers, based in Cambodia, controlled all of Thailand, but Tai soldiers wrested control of Sukhothai in 1238. At this time, two Tai tribal leaders—Pho Khun Pha Muang and Pho Khun Bang Klang Hao—forged their independence from the Khmer Empire and formed the Sukhothai Kingdom. The kingdom's third and best-known leader, King Ramkhamhaeng, was on the throne from 1278 until 1299, when he died.

History has judged Ramkhamhaeng as a just and equitable ruler, and he is credited with developing the first Thai script, drawing on Mon and Khmer writing systems. (The Mon ethnic group had a kingdom in what is now Burma and Thailand from the sixth to the 11th centuries, while the Khmer Kingdom lasted from the ninth to the 11th centuries.) The script was designed to convey the tones of the Thai language to non-Thai speakers, who had begun to migrate to the area for trading purposes. Ramkhamhaeng's stone etchings became what is today known as the first Thai literature—and the alphabet that he created is more or less the same as the one used today. He also used a royal code of law to bring together disparate Tai peoples—this paternalistic monarchical system is still in place today. In was during this time that Theravada Buddhism was established as the unifying religion, and its peace-loving influences have paved the way for centuries of harmony within the country.

Under Ramkhamhaeng's leadership, the empire spread out to incorporate all of present-day Thailand. He even established a relationship with the Chinese, making two trips to China and bringing Chinese artisans home with him to teach the Tais their skills in creating fine pottery.

The Sukhothai Kingdom is viewed as the golden age of Thai politics. A stone inscription bears the following description of Ramkhamhaeng's reign and provides insight into what daily life was like under his rule:

> This realm of Sukhothai is good. In the water there are fish; in the fields there is rice. The ruler does not levy a tax on the people who travel along the road together, leading their own oxen on the way to trade and riding their horses on the way to sell. Whoever wants to trade in elephants, so trades. Whoever wants to trade in horses, so trades. Whoever wants to trade in silver and gold, so trades.

Architecturally, Sukhothai is where the original, classical Thai style began. Previously, the Khmer Bayon style, with its bulky stone monuments and Hindu-inspired accents, was prominent. But in Sukhothai, artisans ushered in something new altogether: wood structures and what would come to be known as the Buddhist temple, with its characteristic sweeping, pointed roofs. Ornamental features, such as brightly colored tiles, were also introduced at this time.

The rise of Buddhism naturally saw a related surge in Buddha-themed art, as evidenced in Sukhothai. This is symbolized by round Buddha faces and sculptures portraying the Buddha sitting or standing. Sculptors also drew inspiration from Sri Lankan sources, creating *chedi*—bell-shaped stupas or pagodas. The many famous Buddha statues in Bangkok—such as the reclining Buddha and the emerald Buddha—have their origins in what sculptors first did in Sukhothai.

By the mid-14th century, the Ayutthaya Kingdom took control of Sukhothai, which had been on the wane after Ramkhamhaeng's death. When Sukhothai was abandoned in favor of Ayutthaya, the area was forgotten and became overgrown. Today it has been restored, and the Sukhothai Historical Park, which contains the ruins, is a UNESCO World Heritage Site.

While the Sukhothai Kingdom was the first truly Tai state, the Ayutthaya Kingdom is recognized as being the seat of Siamese power for 400 years. Its artistic and architectural legacy—evident throughout Thailand today—was great.

The city of Ayutthaya was founded in 1350 by King Ramathibodi, when the Sukhothai Kingdom was still active. But Sukhothai was soon folded into Ayutthaya. Ayutthaya grew over the years from a small town into a magnificent regional capital. The rise in trade in the mid-14th century brought an influx of foreign merchants—and riches—to Ayutthaya, as it was positioned fortuitously between China and India.

In many ways, Ayutthaya blazed a trail for modern-day Bangkok. Ayutthaya was established where three rivers meet in a flood plain. This setting, along the lower Chao Phraya basin, made sense both militarily and from a transportation standpoint: A defensive moat was created, and there were easily navigable canals. There was fertile agriculture output as well. Bangkok, like Ayutthaya, is situated along a bend in the Chao Phraya River.

In 1516, a treaty with Portugal helped established a relationship with Europe. Ayutthaya was overrun by the Burmese in 1569, but the Tais regained the city less than 20 years later. King Naresuan ruled over the regained empire and expanded its sphere of influence to the north and south of Thailand, Laos, and Cambodia. The Dutch and British began making inroads in Thailand in the early 17th century. When King Narai came to power in 1657, Ayutthaya was a bustling and impressive city with a population of 1 million.

King Narai, who would rule until 1688, welcomed the French, who were granted land on which to construct schools and churches. Thailand and the court of King Louis XIV had strong relations, with a Thai embassy arriving in France in 1684.

François-Timoléon de Choisy arrived in Ayutthaya with the first French embassy in 1685. In a memoir, he spoke not only the grandeur of the city but also its international influences:

We went for a walk outside the town. I paused frequently to admire the great city, seated upon an island round which flowed a river three times the width of the Seine. There rode ships from France, England, Holland, China and Japan, while innumerable boats and gilded barges rowed by 60 men plied to and fro. No less extraordinary were the camps and villages outside the walls inhabited by the different nations who came trading there, with all the wooden houses standing on posts over the water, the bulls, crows, and pigs on dry land. The streets, stretching out of sight, are alleys of clear running water. Under the great green trees and in the little houses crowd the people. Beyond these camps of the nations are the wide rice fields. The horizon is tall trees, above which are visible the sparkling towers and pyramids of the pagodas. I do not know whether I have conveyed to you the impression of the beautiful view, but certainly I myself have never seen a lovelier one.

Ayutthaya's artistic importance is immense, and its varying styles were byproducts of the various cultural influences brought about through trading with Asian kingdoms, the Chinese, and the Europeans. There are many such foreign styles visible in Ayutthaya. St. Joseph's Church, for example, was a Catholic house of worship for three centuries. Wat Phra Si Sanphet has arches done in a European style. And there is also a Chinese-influenced *chedi* at Wat Mahathat.

Other characteristically Thai architectural elements came to the fore in Ayutthaya. The temple buildings have sloped roofs with spiked, curved flourishes at their peaks. At its height, Ayutthaya was also home to many examples of sublime arts and crafts. The **Chao Sam Phraya National Museum** contains a number of exquisite salvaged pieces, such as cabinetry with gilt lacquerwork and mother-of-pearl inlay as well as other gold artifacts.

Ayutthaya fell to marauding Burmese troops—this time for good—in 1767. The Burmese looted the city and then burned it to the ground, returning home to Burma with more than 30,000 captives. The future King Taksin ultimately forced the Burmese to relinquish control of Ayutthaya, but the capital was in total ruins. The capital was moved south along the Chao Phraya to Thonburi, and then finally across the river to Bangkok. Ayutthaya is now a UNESCO World Heritage Site.

Ayutthaya and Vicinity   พระนครศรีอยุธยา

Historically rich and visually stunning Ayutthaya—or Phra Nakhon Si Ayutthaya, as it's officially called—is a well-worn stop for travelers. Buses and trains ferry visitors north from Bangkok day in and day out, discharging passengers with guidebooks in hand to be met by tour guides and taxi drivers hoping for a day's work. Visitors all end up wandering the same ruins and temples for the day, then packing up and heading back to the capital. But don't let that deter you from visiting. There's a reason so many people flock to Ayutthaya, and it's an interesting and pleasant way to spend a day or two.

Most of the sights are located "on the island"—that is, in the middle of the old city, which is surrounded by the Chao Phraya River on the south and the Lopburi River on the north. Though the island is less than two kilometers across, because of the heat and the fact that the sites are scattered around, you're much better off renting a bike or hiring a taxi or *tuk tuk* than trying to see everything on foot.

The island itself is also more developed than most people expect, so discard images of green grassy footpaths, scattered ruins, and nothing more (you'll see that in Sukhothai), if that's what you expect. Ayutthaya has its share of concrete buildings, roads, and even banks, shops, and guesthouses interspersed among the ruins and concentrated in the eastern part of the island. There are some idyllic spots, but that's not all there is.

◖ AYUTTHAYA HISTORICAL PARK
อุทยานประวัติศาสตร์อยุธยา

The Ayutthaya Historical Park (7:30 A.M.–6:30 P.M. daily), a UNESCO World Heritage Site, covers the ruins of the old capital and contains an impressive collection of crumbling temples. The park is contained within the island. Most of the temples are on the west side of the island, with the town itself on the east side. Some of the ruins are close enough to each other that you'll be able to walk from one to another, but to see everything the park has to offer in a day, you'll need at least a bicycle to get around. At 7 P.M. the flood lights go on, illuminating all of the ruins. Although you can't climb around the park at night, if you are in Ayutthaya after sundown, the view is striking.

There are actually three different museums within the historical park: the Ayutthaya Historical Study Center, the Chao Sam Phraya

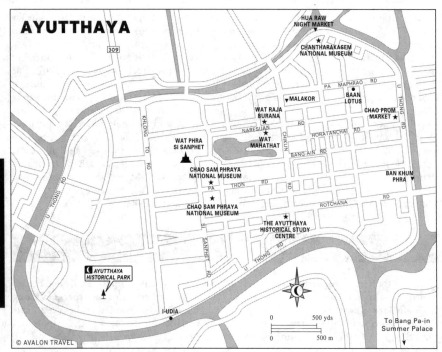

AYUTTHAYA

National Museum, and the Chantharakasem National Museum. Those interested in understanding Ayutthaya's history should spend an hour or so here first to get an overview before venturing out into the ruins. The island's other two museums house exhibits specific to a particular *wat* or palace but are nonetheless worth spending a little time in to gain an understanding of what went on inside these amazing structures when they were still standing.

Chao Sam Phraya National Museum
พิพิธภัณฑสถานแห่งชาติ เจ้าสามพระยา

The Chao Sam Phraya National Museum (tel. 03/524-1587, 9 A.M.–4 P.M. Wed.–Sun., 30B), in the middle of Ayutthaya, has on display an extensive collection of gold items that were once kept in Wat Phra Mahathat and Wat

Rajaburana. Many items here are more than 500 years old, dating from the Ayutthayan Empire. There are various bronze Buddha images and altars here. Particularly impressive is a lacquered book cabinet that portrays the Buddhist cosmos.

The Ayutthaya Historical Study Centre
ศูนย์ศึกษาประวัติศาสตร์อยุธยา

The Ayutthaya Historical Study Centre (Rotchana Rd., tel. 03/524-5123, 8:30 A.M.–4:30 P.M. Mon.–Fri., 8:30 A.M.–5 P.M. Sat. and Sun., 100B adults, 50B students), funded by the Japanese government for research into Ayutthaya's history, has impressive models and exhibits that provide a good overview of Ayutthaya's time as capital of Siam. This is a good place to visit to get a sense of historical context before striking out to the ruins.

© SUZANNE NAM

Ayutthaya Historical Park

Wat Phra Si Sanphet
วัดพระศรีสรรเพชญ

Wat Phra Si Sanphet (8:30 A.M.–5 P.M. daily, 30B), which dates from 1491, is located inside what used to be the **Royal Palace,** just northwest of the center of the island. It served as the royal chapel, much like Wat Phra Kaew in Bangkok. Wat Phra Si Sanphet is one of the most popular temples due to its line of three picturesque *chedi,* or pagodas, that are emblematic of Ayutthaya. These *chedi* contain the ashes of three of Ayutthaya's kings.

Chantharakasem National Museum
พิพิธภัณฑสถานแหงชาติ จันทรเกษม

The Chantharakasem National Museum (U-Thong Rd., tel. 03/525-1586, 9 A.M.–4 P.M. Wed.–Sun., 30B), in the northeast corner of the island, contains a small collection of art and artifacts in the former Chan Kasem palace. Some of the items on display are personal effects of King Rama IV and are unrelated

to the history of Ayutthaya (as the Chakri Dynasty did not begin until Ayutthaya had already been sacked). There are some interesting Ayutthaya period pieces, including devotional Buddhist artwork, weaponry, and plenty of ceramic containers used by traders during the time. The elephant armor and weapons tend to be favorites among visitors.

Wat Rajaburana
วัดราชบูรณะ

Wat Rajaburana, one of the best restored *wats* in the park, also has an interesting history. As lore would have it, two brothers, both princes, fought to the death on the grounds of the temple, and the third brother then had the *wat* erected. Most of the items once held at the base of the temple are now on display at the Chao Sam Phraya National Museum, but there are some remaining murals of life in Ayutthaya to see. The main temple building is roofless, but most of the walls are intact, and the detailing on the main *prang* is in very good condition, including statues of mythical creatures and carved flora detailing.

Wat Mahathat
วัดมหาธาตุ

There is little left of 14th-century Wat Mahathat other than rows of headless statues, a majestic corncob-shaped redbrick *prang,* and some crumbling walls. Still, this is one of the most visited *wats* in the park, probably because of the nearby tree that's grown around a broken Buddha statue, creating an ethereal effect. Wat Mahathat is across the road from Wat Rajaburana.

Wihan Phra Mongkhon Bophit
วิหารพระมงคลบพิตร

Wihan Phra Mongkhon Bophit is a modern *wat* that's architecturally unremarkable but is home to one of the most sacred Buddha images in Ayutthaya. Inside the white and red *wihan* sits a large golden Buddha that was probably made during the 16th century and, according to common lore, was struck by

CENTRAL THAILAND

© SUZANNE NAM

some of the thousands of Buddhas in Ayutthaya

lightning soon after its creation. Later, when the capital was sacked by the Burmese, it was damaged again and sat unrestored for nearly 200 years. In the 1950s, the current *wihan* was built to house the Buddha, and it was later covered in gold leaf. Most Buddhists visiting Ayutthaya will make a pilgrimage to visit Phra Mongkhon Bophit.

Wat Phanan Choeng
วัดพนัญเชิง

Wat Phanan Choeng, built before the establishment of the Ayutthaya Kingdom, is the oldest *wat* in the area and houses an 18-meter Buddha, which was made in the 14th century. Thousands of worshippers visit the *wat* every week to pay homage to the Buddha and the hundreds of smaller Buddha figures that line its walls. Pilgrims visiting the *wat* can take part in a graceful, elaborately choreographed ritual changing of the statue's orange robe. The *wat* is located just across the Chao Phraya River from the island on the southeastern corner.

Wat Yai Chai Mongkhon
วัดใหญ่ชัยมงคล

Wat Yai Chai Mongkhon was built in the 14th century, but the main attraction is the main *chedi* that was built by King Naresuan in the 16th century. You can climb up the many stairs of the *chedi* to enjoy the view. In fact, there were three other large bell-shaped *chedi* built, although only one remains standing, as well as some smaller, similarly shaped *chedi* on the *wat*'s grounds. The *wat* is just outside the island on the southeast corner, about a 15-minute walk from Wat Phanan Choeng.

Wat Chai Wattanaram
วัดชัยวัฒนาราม

Just on the other side of the river from the southwest corner of the island is perhaps one of Ayutthaya's most impressive temple ruins. At just under 400 years old, Wat Chai Wattanaram is younger than many of the temples in the area but is one of the best-preserved and largest complexes. The Khmer-style *prang* is surrounded by half a dozen smaller structures, and there are more than 100 seated Buddha images on the grounds. This temple is definitely worth the extra time and expense to visit.

OTHER SIGHTS
Bang Pa-in Summer Palace
พระราชวังบางปะอิน

Located 20 kilometers south of central Ayutthaya along the Chao Phraya in the Bang Len subdistrict, Bang Pa-in Summer Palace (8 A.M.–4 P.M. daily, 50B) was remade by King Rama V, who vacationed here in the mid-19th century. It was originally used by kings of Thailand as a summer retreat in the 17th century, but it was abandoned after Ayutthaya fell in 1767. There are bridges lined with statues, various buildings, and ponds. The Summer Palace makes for a tranquil afternoon getaway from central Ayutthaya. You can get here by *song thaew*, which takes about an hour and costs 20B.

ACCOMMODATIONS

The vast majority of visitors who come to Ayutthaya do so as part of a day trip from Bangkok. If you arrive in the morning from the Thai capital, as most visitors do, the temples can easily be taken in during the day before heading back by sundown. However, if you'd like more time in Ayutthaya, there are some options for staying overnight. Most lodgings cater to budget travelers.

Situated in three Thai-style antique wooden houses, **Bannkunpra Guesthouse** (48 U-Thong Rd., tel. 03/524-1978, www.bannkunpra.com, 500B) is a good low-cost option if you'd like to be close to the temples. There are male and female dorms as well as some private guest rooms that have shared baths and are fan-cooled and some private guest rooms that have private baths, air-conditioning, and hot water. There's a restaurant and a large wooden terrace; much of the property was renovated in 2010, significantly increasing the charm and comfort.

Baan Lotus (20 Pamaphrao Rd, tel. 03/525-1988, 600B) is a clean, basic place with a famously friendly owner. Some guest rooms have

gilded Buddhas at one of Ayutthaya's living temples

shared baths and are fan-cooled, while others have private baths and air-conditioning. The namesake lotus-filled pond in the back provides a tranquil touch.

Located a few kilometers outside the center, **Chow Praya Hut** (45/1 Mu 8, Baanmai, tel. 03/539-8200, www.chowprayahut.com, 900B) has quaint, romantic wooden bungalows right on the river. The guest rooms are simple but clean and come with basic "necessities" such as air-conditioning and en suite baths. Aside from the relaxed atmosphere and romantic setting, which are very nice, the biggest benefit to staying here is the outdoor waterfront restaurant that serves traditional Thai food.

Right in the center of the island and a stone's throw from the historical park is ◖ **I-udia** (11/12 Mu 4, U-Tong Rd., tel. 03/532-3208, www.iudia.com, 2,500B), a moderately priced small boutique hotel that caters to a more up-scale crowd. Decor is modern Thai with a bit of Persian and Chinese thrown in, although it comes together nicely. The landscaped grounds with pools and gardens are beautiful, as is the view of the ruins across the way.

Baan Thai House Ayutthaya (119/19 Mu 4, Pailing, tel. 03/524-5555, www.baanthaihouse.com, 2,100B) is just outside the old island and rents old-style wooden Thai houses that have been transformed into comfortable villas. The grounds are green and pretty and include a swimming pool.

FOOD
Markets
Located between Bang Ian Road (ถนนบางเอียน) and Naresuan Road (ถนนนเรศวร) is the **Chao Prom Market** (ตลาดเจาพรหม), which begins in the morning and continues until the afternoon. Here you'll find stalls with vendors selling everything from standard Thai dishes—noodles, soups, and curries—to Chinese dishes.

In order to sample a local Ayutthaya treat, head to the *roti sai mai* stalls on U-Thong Road. *Roti sai mai* (โรตีสายไหม) is a Muslim dessert consisting of melted sugar wrapped in a flour pancake.

If you stick around town into the evening, the **Hua Raw Night Market,** on U-Thong Road, is the place to go for Muslim dishes like Massaman curry—beef in coconut milk with spices. There are tables next to the river.

Restaurants
Malakor (Chee Kun Rd., 11 A.M.–9 P.M. daily, 50–100B) offers standard Thai food—curries, Thai salads, and noodles—as well as other Asian dishes, and its location affords glimpses of nearby Wat Rajaburana. **Ban Khun Phra** (48/2 U-Thong Rd., tel. 03/524-1978, 11 A.M.–9 P.M. daily, 70–80B), next to the river, is popular for dishes like winged bean soup with prawns. There's indoor and outdoor seating. The smoked snakehead fish at (**Ban Watcharachai** (9 Mu 7, Ban Pom, tel. 03/532-1333, 200B) has an international fan following, but nearly everything on the seafood-heavy menu is worth trying. The restaurant is set in an old wooden house, with a garden and even a boat moored on the river you can dine on.

INFORMATION
There is a visitor information center (Si Sanphet Rd., tel. 03/532-2730, 8:30 A.M.–4:30 P.M. daily) on the west side of the island that can provide information.

GETTING THERE
Train
You can get to Ayutthaya from Bangkok's downtown Hua Lamphong Station in 1.5 hours for only 30B if you take a nonexpress train and sit in third-class seats; otherwise, expect to pay a little more. There are 11 scheduled trains running 7 A.M.–10 P.M. daily. Once you arrive in Ayutthaya, on the east side of the river, you can take a boat from the nearby pier across to the inner part of the island, or pick up a taxi for the day at the train station (prices are fixed and prominently posted).

Bus
The bus ride from Ayutthaya from Bangkok takes 1.5 hours and costs 45B. Buses leave at least every hour throughout the day 5 A.M.–9 P.M. from Mo Chit Station in Bangkok. You'll arrive right in the middle of the island. There are also minibuses from Bangkok's Victory Monument BTS station 5 A.M.–8 P.M. that go directly to Ayutthaya and take 1.25–2 hours, depending on traffic. These buses cost 60B and leave frequently, but only once filled with passengers, so you may have to wait around for a departure.

Boat
There are no public boats that run from Bangkok to Ayutthaya, but you can book a private tour. This typically includes the journey via the Chao Phraya River to Ayutthaya, a tour, and then a bus ride back to Bangkok.

One such outfit is **Asian Oasis** (end of Chan Rd., Chok Tran, tel. 02/651-9101, www.mekhalacruise.com, 2-day trip from 8,670B) in southern Bangkok, near the river in the Menam Riverside Hotel, which runs trips to Ayutthaya on refurbished rice barges. Guests sleep on the boat at night.

Another tour operator is the upscale **Manohra Cruises** (Bangkok Marriott Resort and Spa, Thonburi, tel. 02/477-0770, 3-day trip 3,750B), which runs two-night, three-day trips on magnificently restored teak rice barges. This is an all-inclusive package that includes candlelit dinners.

Car

If you're driving to Ayutthaya, take the Don Muang Tollway heading toward the old airport, and then continue driving north on Highway 1. The Highway will end just before Bang Pa-In, but continue driving north on local roads, as the route is well marked with signs for Ayutthaya.

GETTING AROUND

Tuk tuks are good for quick trips. Prices can be negotiated, but start at about 10B per passenger, and drivers can usually be hired for the day and will wait for you outside the various temples. *Song thaew* are also available for 20–50B. Just wave them down when you see them, but unlike in other cities, the *song thaew* are more like *song thaew*–motorcycle hybrids and do not seem to ply set routes. If you're looking for self-powered transport, consider renting a bicycle from a guesthouse (even if you're not a guest) for 40–50B per day. **Motorcycles** are also available at rental agencies around town for about 150B per day.

If you are arriving by train, there are plenty of **taxis** at the station willing to take you around for the day, and in the station, there is also a list of set prices for destinations. Expect to pay around 1,000B for a half-day with a car and driver.

LOPBURI
จังหวัดลพบุรี

Lopburi Province is directly north of Ayutthaya, and like the former Thai capital, it has a storied past. The city of Lopburi, formerly known as Lawo, is one of the kingdom's oldest settlements. It has been inhabited since the sixth century, and it was part of the Khmer Empire, based in Cambodia, during the 10th–12th centuries. Lopburi was eventually subsumed by Ayutthaya and the Ayutthayan King Narai, who ruled 1656–1688 and built a second palace in the city. Though it was ostensibly just a summer retreat, Lopburi became a de facto second capital of the Ayutthaya Kingdom because Narai spent so much time here, returning to Ayutthaya only during the rainy season.

Today, the city of Lopburi is a small provincial capital known more for its annual monkey festival than any role it may have played in the kingdom's history. Most of the city has developed just like the rest of Thailand's small cities—there's plenty of concrete and not much personality. But there are some ancient ruins in the old town, just west of the railroad tracks. This area is quite appealing, with its many temples and its sedate feel.

Lopburi is best visited on a day trip from Bangkok or as a stopover on your way from Ayutthaya. Unless you are an archeology or architecture buff, you can see everything the city has to offer in just a few hours. Realistically, the city doesn't have enough historical or cultural attractions to hold most visitors' attention for more than that.

The temple ruins are open year-round, but the best time to visit is during the last weekend in November, when the city puts on its annual monkey festival. Locals put out a lavish spread of food for the city's hundreds of monkey residents who have overtaken Lopburi's temples and just about everything else in the city. It's Lopburi's high season, though, so the city will be crowded.

Note for those with a fear of simians: While often entertaining, monkeys are wild animals and deserve respect and distance, even if it seems they won't afford you the same. Some of Lopburi's monkeys can get quite aggressive, so be sure to keep a close eye on your bags and personal belongings, not to mention any food you might have on your person. These monkeys are used to humans and they won't hesitate to jump on or grab visitors, threatening minor injury in their never-ending search for snacks.

Sights

The King Narai Palace and National Museum (พิพิธภัณฑสถานแหงชาติ สมเด็จพระ นารายณ, Sorasak Rd., tel. 03/641-1458, palace 7 A.M.–5:30 P.M. daily, gallery 9 A.M.–4:30 P.M. Wed.–Sun., 30B) was built in 1677 and is the former second residence of King Narai from Ayutthaya. Although the palace is now in ruins, the sheer size and architectural details that remain are a good clue as to the importance of the structures—the palace was a de facto second administrative center for Narai's Kingdom, much like a second capital.

The once-opulent palace, with enormous gateways around a central courtyard and high walls, was where Narai received guests. The palace incorporates Khmer and European styles. It was designed with input from French architects, and parts of the building are said to have contained mirrors imported from France. The palace fell into disrepair following the king's death, and it was refurbished by King Rama IV in the mid-19th century. Despite Rama IV's efforts, today it is little more than crumbling brick and stone ruins with a few structures still standing.

The museum's exhibits are housed in a modern building on the palace grounds and contain an excellent collection of Lopburi Buddha images and other art. Depictions of the Buddha that were common during the Lopburi Empire are unique in that they display Khmer influences. Buddha faces done during this time often have wide mouths that appear to be slightly smiling.

The **Phra Prang Sam Yot** shrine (พระปรางค์- สามยอด, Wichayen Rd., 8 A.M.–6 P.M. daily, 30B), built during the 13th century, is one of Lopburi's monuments that is particularly overrun with monkeys. It is a Hindu-Buddhist temple with three towers, or *prang*. The laterite towers, which resemble large ears of corn, were once embellished with stucco engravings.

Prang Khaek (เทวสถานปรางค์แขก, Wichayen Rd.) is thought to have been built in the eighth century. It has three brick towers,

and its monument is believed to represent the Hindu god Shiva.

In the center of **Wat Phra Si Mahathat** (วัดพระศรีมหาธาตุ, Na Wat Rd.) is a 12th-century stucco-encrusted *prang* (ปรางค์, tower) done in Khmer style. Built when Lopburi was a Khmer outpost, the *wat* fell into disrepair, but King Narai oversaw its rehabilitation. It also contains a large *wihan* (Buddhist assembly hall) that was created by Narai. This *wihan* contains arched windows that bear Persian influences.

Food

White House Restaurant (Phraya Kamchat, tel. 03/641-3085, 11 A.M.–11:30 P.M. daily, 50–150B) specializes in Thai-Chinese dishes. There's little in the way of upscale dining in Lopburi, but this is among the most pleasant places to eat in town. The manager is an expert on happenings in the area.

The **central market** (between Wichayen Rd. and Ratchadamnoen Rd., 8 A.M.–2 P.M. daily, 20–100B) is a great place for tasty chicken—both fried and roasted—as well as various fruits. The fried bananas are a favorite.

Getting There and Around

Lopburi is two hours from Ayutthaya by bus. The trip costs 47B. Buses leave every 20 minutes. The train from Ayutthaya to Lopburi—a popular means of transport—takes 20–30 minutes and costs 13–140B, depending on whether it's making local or express stops. Trains make the trip hourly from the morning through the night.

If you're driving from Bangkok, take Highway 1 to Lopburi via Saraburi. It takes two hours or less to drive the 153 kilometers. Lopburi is two hours away from Ayutthaya by car. Starting in Ayutthaya, take Route 32 north to Route 347, which will take you into Lopburi.

Lopburi is a little too big to get around by foot, but there are *song thaew* and *samlor* in the city. *Samlor* rides will cost 20B and up, depending on the distance. *Song thaew* commonly run an east–west route on Phra Narai Maharat and cost 5B per ride within the city.

Kanchanaburi Town and Province

Kanchanaburi Province (จังหวัดกาญจนบุรีและตัวเมือง), situated to the west of Bangkok, has surprisingly rugged terrain considering its close proximity to the metropolitan Thai capital. Kanchanaburi is Thailand's third-largest province, after Nakhon Ratchasima and Chiang Mai, and it contains a plethora of sights that include waterfalls and natural parks. Most visitors head to Kanchanaburi Town, at the eastern edge of the province, which is just 130 kilometers from the Thai capital.

At under three hours by car or bus (and just a four-hour train ride away), Kanchanaburi is a popular destination for visitors who find Bangkok too chaotic or who simply want to experience a more rural part of the country without having to go too far. This sleepy, picturesque river town is exceedingly tranquil, with the slow-moving River Kwai snaking its way through limestone hills.

© SUZANNE NAM

waterfalls in Kanchanaburi Province

This is where you'll find the infamous River Kwai Bridge—or as it's better known, thanks to the 1957 film, the **Bridge on the River Kwai.** During World War II, the Japanese forced Asian laborers and Allied POWs to construct a railroad between Thailand and Burma. Approximately 115,000 men perished due to inhumane working conditions and disease. Today the bridge stands as a grim tourist attraction.

Farther to the west are **Sai Yok National Park** and the town of **Sangkhla Buri,** which stretch to the edge of Burma.

SIGHTS
Kanchanaburi War Cemetery
สุสานทหารสัมพันธมิตร
The Kanchanaburi War Cemetery (Saeng Chuto Rd., 8 A.M.–6 P.M. daily), also known as the Don-Rak War Cemetery, contains the remains of nearly 7,000 British, Dutch, and Australian POWs who perished at the hands of the Japanese during the World War II–era construction of the Thailand–Burma railway. The grounds are maintained beautifully, and plaques at the entrance provide information about the railway and the men memorialized in the cemetery.

◖ Thailand-Burma Railway Centre
พิพิธภัณฑ์ทางรถไฟ ไทย-พม่า
The excellent Thailand–Burma Railway Centre (73 Jaokunnen Rd., tel. 03/451-2721, www.tbrconline.com, 9 A.M.–5 P.M. daily, 80B adults, 30B children) is just 100 meters from the cemetery on the western side of the grounds. This expertly constructed museum clearly conveys the brutality inflicted on the Asian laborers and Allied POWs. There are moving illustrations, informative videos, and detailed exhibits highlighting not only the technical aspects of the railway but also the human toll that its construction exacted. Particularly moving are the personal effects—wallets, pouches of tobacco, letters—of the dead soldiers that are on display.

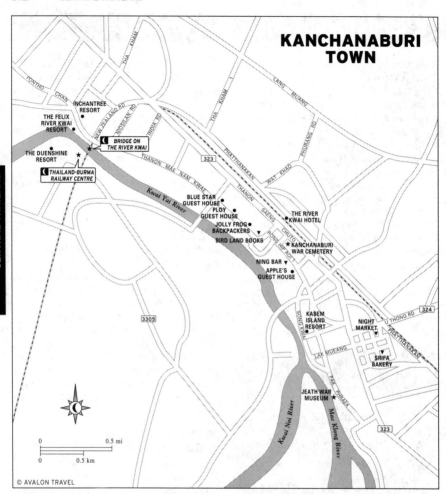

© AVALON TRAVEL

Visit this museum before you go to the River Kwai Bridge and you'll have a well-informed understanding of the dark history surrounding the railway.

JEATH War Museum
พิพิธภัณฑ์อักษะเชลยศึก
The JEATH War Museum (inside Wat Chai Chumphon, Saeng Chuto Rd., 8:30 A.M.–6 P.M., daily, 30B) commemorates the suffering that the Allied POWs and Asian laborers faced in building the Thailand–Burma railway. The initials JEATH stand for Japan, England, America, Australia, Thailand, and Holland. The museum resembles the bamboo huts used to imprison the workers. There are photos of soldiers and newspaper clippings from the era on display.

☪ Bridge on the River Kwai
สะพานข้ามแม่น้ำแคว
Officially called the **Death Railway Bridge** (Mae Nam Khwae Rd., north of Kanchanaburi

THE BRIDGE ON THE RIVER KWAI

First-time visitors are often surprised to find that the notorious River Kwai Bridge is not much to look at. Far from having a dramatic appearance befitting its worldwide reputation, it's a simple steel construction that spans the slow-moving river below. It's supported by a series of pillars and has curved black steel railings on its sides. Seen from a distance, the bridge looms low on the horizon, with verdant trees near the shore and Kanchanaburi's limestone hills poking up behind it. Visitors are allowed to walk the length of the bridge. There are several restaurants along the banks of river. Small boats ply the water, and there's a buzz in nearby markets.

While this everyday scene surrounding the bridge is quiet and understated, the history of its construction is grim. During World War II, the Japanese Imperial Army occupied Thailand. In 1942, they wanted to extend their reach west and conquer India as well but were hamstrung when their supply routes were choked by an Allied sea blockade. So they decided to build the Thailand–Burma railway – what's now called the "Death Railway."

Due to the mountainous terrain along the 415-kilometer route, engineers with the Japanese Imperial Army projected it would take five years to build under normal circumstances. But by using massive amounts of forced labor – and unending brutality – they completed the task in a mere 16 months. The human cost was staggering: Approximately 115,000 Asian laborers and Allied POWs were worked to death, with 18-hour shifts commonplace. Many men died from diseases like cholera and malaria. It is said that, ultimately, one man perished for every single railway tie that was laid.

Thanks to the Academy Award-winning 1957 film *The Bridge on the River Kwai*, many Westerners are familiar with the sacrifices that Allied troops made during this time. But what's not as frequently discussed is the toll that was exacted on local laborers. Of the approximately 61,000 Allied troops – British, Dutch, Australian, and American – who worked on the railway, it's believed that about 16,000 died. Meanwhile, some 200,000 local laborers, many of them Thai, were pressed into service, with about 80,000 losing their lives.

Why were the POWs and laborers treated so badly? Part of the reason may be that Japanese Imperial Army troops adhered to the samurai code, which held that surrender was intolerable – worse even than death. Thus, Allied POWs were thought by many Japanese soldiers to be subhuman and undeserving of any human dignity.

A particularly good time to come to Kanchanaburi is during the annual River Kwai Bridge week, which runs from the end of November through early December. There are light and sound shows and even nightly re-creations of the Allied bombing runs that destroyed part of the bridge as the war came to a close.

© SUZANNE NAM

CENTRAL THAILAND

© SUZANNE NAM

floating *salas* (pavilions) on the River Kwai

Town), this construction was immortalized in the 1957 film *The Bridge on the River Kwai.* The bridge stands as the most notorious feature of the grisly 413-kilometer-long "Death Railway" that was built between Thailand and Burma. The Japanese Imperial Army was forced to engineer this rail link during World War II after the Allied forces blockaded their sea routes. The Japanese did so between 1942 and 1943 using forced labor and unending brutality. The result: Approximately 115,000 local laborers and Allied POWs lost their lives due to 18-hour work shifts, cholera, malaria, malnutrition, and inadequate medical care.

Today, the bridge is a tourist attraction, with museums of varying quality in Kanchanaburi town and even occasional festivities during late November and early December, when there are fireworks and light shows. Much of the original bridge was destroyed by Allied bombing runs, but it was reconstructed by Japanese war reparations.

The bridge is 2.5 kilometers north of town. To get there, you can rent a bicycle or motorcycle in the downtown area. Or if you're up for a long walk, it's a pleasant stroll. Just follow Mae Nam Kwai Road north from central Kanchanaburi.

Ancient Kanchanaburi
โบราณสถานในเขตเมืองกาญจนบุรีเก่า
The remnants of ancient Kanchanaburi, an Ayutthaya-era town that was believed to have prospered in the 13th century, are in Tambon Lad Ya (Lad Ya subdistrict), 20 kilometers from Kanchanaburi Town in neighboring Suphan Buri Province, on Highway 3199. There are few remnants of the once-great border town; the most notable attraction here is a deserted temple called **Wat Pa Lelai.** The 800-year-old structure contains a large sitting Buddha.

Ban Kao National Museum
พิพิธภัณฑสถานแห่งชาติ บ้านเก่า
The Ban Kao National Museum (Ban Kao subdistrict, tel. 03/465-4058, 9 A.M.–4 P.M. Wed.–Sun., 30B) is 34 kilometers west of Kanchanaburi Town. It's built near a

Neolithic burial site that was unearthed by a Dutch POW who was forced to work on the Thailand–Burma railway during World War II. The Ban Kao (which means "old village") museum houses various items that were found in the area, where people lived beside a river 4,000 years ago. The remnants include human bones, jewelry, tools, and more. Check with travel agencies in Kanchanaburi Town regarding transportation via minibuses or taxis.

ENTERTAINMENT AND EVENTS
Bars

Given that Kanchanaburi attracts quite a few backpackers, there is no dearth of cheap beer bars to visit. **Ning Bar** (southern end of Mae Nam Kwai Rd., tel. 08/2403-1492, 6 P.M.–1 A.M. daily, drinks from 60B) has multicolored lights, a plethora of photos of the Thai king and queen, and loud music. It's a popular place on the southern end of the strip.

Bird Land Books (central Mae Nam Kwai Rd., tel. 08/6801-6738, 10 A.M.–1 A.M. daily, large beer from 60B) is a bookshop and local watering hole that consists of little more than 4–5 stools and a small bar on the sidewalk right in the center of the Mae Nam Kwai Road strip. The place is worth visiting if only to have a chat with the gregarious, eccentric owner, Jimmy, a San Francisco native who has lived in Kanchanaburi Province for decades. You'll know you've reached the place when you see a sign that says "Cowboys, Rednecks, Backpackers, Old Hippies, Vikings, and Dutch Welcome." You can find all of the following here: books, music (Jimmy's always open to requests), beer, liquor, jewelry, and cheese-and-sausage appetizers.

SPORTS AND RECREATION
Tours

Kanchanaburi Town has a multitude of tour agencies through which you can book expeditions farther afield in the province. Most agencies offer 8 A.M.–5 P.M. trips to see Hellfire Pass, a rugged passage of the Thailand–Burma railway, or Erawan National Park, famous for its seven-tier waterfall. A visit to the River

Kwai Bridge and perhaps some elephant rides are often thrown in as well. Other tours focus on bamboo rafting or a trip to the Tiger Temple. These one-day tours typically cost 500–1,100B.

Two travel agencies in town are **Kanchanaburi Travel Center** (99–101 Mae Nam Kwai Rd., tel. 08/6396-7349, www.tourkanchanaburi.com, 10 A.M.–6 P.M. daily), on the main strip near Jolly Frog Backpackers, and **Good Times Travel** (63/1 Mae Nam Kwai Rd., tel. 03/462-4441, 10 A.M.–6 P.M. daily), just north of Ploy Guest House.

Kayaking

A well-established outfit that runs river kayaking trips is **Safarine** (4 Taiwan Rd., tel. 03/462-4140, www.safarine.com), near the River Kwai Bridge. There are package and custom tours available. Prices run from 400B for a couple of hours on the River Kwai to 2,000B for a multiday trip with camping. All supplies and equipment are provided, and no previous kayaking experience is necessary.

ACCOMMODATIONS

Kanchanaburi tends to have a larger concentration of inexpensive guesthouses catering to backpackers than it does of any other accommodations option. You'll find a cluster of them along Mae Nam Kwai Road. If you cross the river or head slightly out of town, you'll find larger resorts along the river that often cater to large groups of local travelers. These are a great option if you want to relax and enjoy the river scenery, but if you do not have your own transport, they can be very difficult to use as a base since you'll be reliant on sometimes expensive hotel transfers and tours to get you from one place to another.

Under 1,500B

◀ **Jolly Frog Backpackers** (28 Soi China, Mae Nam Kwai Rd., tel. 03/451-4579, www.jollyfrog.net, 400B) is at the heart of Kanchanaburi's budget traveler scene. Its large open-air restaurant, reception area, and book shop, surrounded by dense plants and trees, is where many guests congregate to chat, or simply to read and drink beer. The grassy central courtyard overlooking the river has several hammocks, big lounge chairs, and a bunch of chilled-out visitors listening to tunes and hanging out in the sun. Über cost-conscious visitors will be interested in the tiny fan-cooled single rooms that go for the astonishingly low price of 70B. Slightly more expensive are the fan-cooled and air-conditioned double rooms (200–400B). These guest rooms are small, and their mismatched furnishings could stand to be refurbished—there's a bed, a desk, a bath (with cold water), and little else. Guests flock to the Jolly Frog, however, for its friendly vibe. This is the place to go if you'd like to socialize, meet new friends, and save your money for beer or treks outside of Kanchanaburi.

Blue Star Guest House (241 Mae Nam Kwai Rd., tel. 03/451-2161, bluestar_guesthouse@yahoo.com, 500B) is a good low-cost choice for those looking for the added amenities of hot water, cable TV, and more space to stretch out. The private wooden bungalows have big beds and patios with wooden deck furniture that look out toward the river. All of the bungalows are accessible via a wooden walkway elevated above a marsh.

The extremely tidy family-run **Apple's Guest House** and **Apple's Retreat** (tel. 03/451-2017, www.applenoi-kanchanaburi.com, 490–690B) are two other excellent options for budget-conscious travelers. The very popular Apple's Guest House has split into two separate new properties and continues to impress backpackers. The guest rooms aren't fancy, but they're clean: The beds have crisp sheets, and there are Thai-style decorations on the walls. A variety of services are available at Apple's. In addition to the highly rated restaurant, there's an Internet café in the reception area, Thai massage, and a popular cooking school. There's no online booking, but you can contact them through the website, and they will confirm your booking (if available) within a day or two.

Ploy Guest House (79/2 Mae Nam Kwai Rd., tel. 03/451-5804, www.ploygh.com, 600B)

is an upscale guesthouse, and what you get here would easily cost twice as much in Bangkok or Chiang Mai. The place is well designed, with white buildings covered in palm fronds and a large grassy courtyard shaded by palm trees. The guest rooms—all of which have air-conditioning, hot water, and cable TV—have white walls and incorporate driftwood and tree stumps into their design. The large soft beds are situated on raised platforms and come decked out with a slew of soft pillows. Some of the guest rooms have open-air baths leading to small gardens with plants and rocks. (This is a nice touch, but be sure to keep the bathroom door closed lest you let in mosquitoes.) The large restaurant looks out over the river and makes for an excellent place to unwind as you eat breakfast. Plus, there's even a swimming pool. Ploy's is what a good mid-range hotel should be: peaceful, stylish, economical, and comfortable.

Kasem Island Resort (44–48 Chaichumpol Rd., Ban Tai, tel. 03/451-3359, www.kasemisland.com, 1,400B) is located on an island in the middle of the River Kwai. The guest rooms have fans and air-conditioning, and while some of the buildings could use some repainting, there are good views of the river and the surrounding hills. There's a pool, and you can catch a free shuttle to the place from Chukkadon Road, at the south end of Kanchanaburi Town. Kasem Island Resort also has floating rafts on the river that you can rent and sleep in.

The Duenshine Resort (Thamakham Rd., tel. 03/465-3369, www.duenshine.com, 1,200B) is located across the river from the River Kwai Bridge. The guest rooms are somewhat sparsely appointed, with simple wooden furniture and old-fashioned bedspreads, but many have large patios and good views of the river. The grounds are quite tranquil, with an abundance of thick trees. There's also a swimming pool.

1,500–3,000B

The River Kwai Hotel (284/15–16 Saeng Chuto Rd., tel. 03/451-3348, www.riverkwai.

co.th, 1,800B), between the train station and the bus station, will interest travelers looking for a more conventional hotel that's in Kanchanaburi Town and is removed from the cluster of guesthouses along Mae Nam Kwai Road. All guest rooms have standard offerings like air-conditioning, cable TV, and hot water. What differentiates the River Kwai Hotel from other spots in town are items like minibars, room service, and currency exchange. The guest rooms feel impersonal, with their rather run-of-the-mill Thai-style decorations and bed coverings, but the accommodations are large and in good condition. Note that there's a popular bar and disco on the premises.

The Balinese-style **Inchantree Resort** (Mae Nam Kwai Rd., tel. 03/462-4914, www.uhotelsresorts.com/inchantree/, 2,000B), near the River Kwai Bridge, has sloped roofs and dark-wood buildings. Its 30 guest rooms all have air-conditioning, TVs, and open-air hot showers. A riverside terrace makes for a peaceful spot to unwind. Inchantree opened in 2006.

Pung Wan Resort (72/1 Mu 2, Thamakham, tel. 03/451-4792, www.pungwaanriverkwai.com, 2,500B) is a large high-end resort on the banks of the River Kwai about 30 minutes by car from the center of town. The large grounds are nicely kept and expansive. The guest rooms are comfortable, clean, and modestly furnished; river-view rooms are the best, although they are a bit of a walk from the main part of the resort. The coolest place to sleep is on one of the small floating huts on the river, but these are much less luxurious than the ones on dry land. This is a typical large resort catering to local tour groups, so you'll find some nice amenities, including restaurants on the grounds and organized tours arranged by the hotel.

3,000-4,500B

The Felix River Kwai Resort (across the river from the River Kwai Bridge, tel. 03/455-1000, www.felixriverkwai.co.th, 3,000B) is one of the town's most popular upscale hotels. Its enormous and well-tended grounds encompass a large swimming pool with a bar, and various creeks course through the resort. The reception

area and restaurant are gigantic. Felix River Kwai is popular with package travelers who want to be close to the bridge and are looking for an extra bit of luxury. The standard guest rooms have up-to-date furnishings and are clean with spacious baths. The more expensive guest rooms have views of the river and inviting patios. This is the place to stay if you want luxurious lodgings within sight of the bridge.

FOOD

Kanchanaburi Town's dining options are somewhat limited—they're mostly centered on guesthouses and resorts. But there are one or two gems to be found outside the stretch of budget lodgings on Mae Nam Kwai Road.

The restaurants at **Apple's Guest House** and **Apple's Retreat** (www.applenoi-kanchanaburi.com, 7 A.M.–2:30 P.M. and 6–10:30 P.M. daily, 100B) serve excellent Thai food. The owners, Apple and Noi, specialize in curries, with the Massaman curry—typically beef with coconut milk and spices—a particularly popular choice. Highly rated one-day cooking classes are also available at Apple's. Classes run 10 A.M.–2:30 P.M. and costs 1,250B. Participants learn to cook five dishes.

The restaurant at **Jolly Frog Backpackers** (28 Soi China, Mae Nam Kwai Rd., tel. 03/451-4579, 7 A.M.–10:30 P.M. daily, 50–200B) has a wide-ranging menu encompassing Western and Thai breakfast foods, coffee drinks, fresh-baked bread, sandwiches, burgers, pasta, pizzas, steak, ice cream, various fruit shakes and *lassis,* and beer and wine. The Thai dishes to choose from are equally diverse. And unlike the Thai fare at other restaurants that cater to foreigners, the local dishes aren't under-seasoned for more sensitive Western taste buds. Just be sure to specify if you want your food spicy.

The tiny **Daily Club Restaurant** (Mae Nam Kwai Rd., no phone, 8 A.M.–8 P.M. daily, 50–200B) has Western and Thai-style breakfasts—eggs, bacon, toast, fruit, rice porridge, and more. There are also sandwiches, fruit shakes, and various Thai dishes.

Srifa Bakery (just east of the bus station, tel. 03/461-3074, www.srifabakery.co.th, 7 A.M.–5 P.M. daily) has a variety of cakes, breads, cookies, pastries, and more. This is a good option if you're in need of a carb fix.

The nighttime **food market** (Lak Meuang Rd., just north of the bus station, 5–10 P.M. daily, 20–80B) is a place to escape the traveler-oriented restaurants downtown. The market has numerous vendors selling steaming-hot juicy *hoi thot* (mussels fried in egg batter). This dish can be oily if not done right, but here it's light and crispy. There are also multiple pad thai vendors as well as stalls serving fried chicken, noodle soups, and other items. And while there are various Thai desserts on offer, such as cakes and custards, you can't go wrong with the mango sticky rice. Just do what the locals do: Order some food, sit down at one of the metal tables, and watch the Thai soap operas blaring from the TVs set up nearby. Foreigners rarely come here, so expect to attract some attention from curious Thais.

INFORMATION AND SERVICES

Kanchanaburi Town has a small **Tourism Authority of Thailand** office (TAT, Saeng Chuto Rd., tel. 03/451-1200, 8:30 A.M.–4:30 P.M. daily) that offers maps and basic information about attractions in the region.

GETTING THERE AND AROUND
Bus

From Bangkok's Southern Bus Terminal (which Thais call *sai tai mai,* สายใต้ใหม่), the journey on a standard air-conditioned bus will cost you approximately 90B. Buses leave Bangkok for Kanchanaburi every 30 or 60 minutes throughout the day, and the trip might take as long as 3.5 hours. In Kanchanaburi the bus station is located near the corner of Saeng Chuto Road and Wisutharangsi Road, just around the corner from the TAT office.

A better idea, though slightly more expensive, is to contact a travel agency in Bangkok, on Khao San Road or anywhere along Sukhumvit Road, to arrange transport to Kanchanaburi in an air-conditioned minivan. It might be a tight squeeze along with nine or 10 other passengers, but you'll make it to Kanchanaburi in about two hours. This typically costs 150B.

Train

You can take the train from Bangkok's Noi station (not the central Hua Lamphong station) in Thonburi. The trip takes about four hours and costs 100B. The cars, however, don't have air-conditioning. In Kanchanaburi the train station is located in the center of town, within walking distance of the downtown stretch of guesthouses along Mae Nam Kwai Road. For an additional 100B, you can also take the train from Kanchanaburi farther north, along a historic part of the line that continues over the River Kwai Bridge and stops at the Namtok station, farther west, near Erawan National Park.

Trains leave Bangkok Noi train station in Thonburi at 7:45 A.M. and 1:30 P.M. You can catch the train from Kanchanaburi back to Bangkok at 7:15 A.M., 2:45 P.M., and 5:40 P.M. The two-hour trip from Kanchanaburi to Namtok station costs 100B and takes approximately two hours. These trains leave Kanchanaburi at 5:50 A.M., 10:20 A.M., and 4:20 P.M. Trains from Namtok back to Kanchanaburi leave at 5:20 A.M., 12:50 P.M., and 3:15 P.M.

Once you arrive in Kanchanaburi, you can take a taxi from the bus or train station to your guesthouse or hotel. A nice option, if you're coming from the bus station, which is farther from the center of town, is a cyclo-taxi. Expect to pay about 50B and to move slowly, but this mode of transportation affords a good chance to see what the town looks like as you make the trip from outside town into the central area.

Car

Cars can be rented from various agencies in Bangkok for about 2,000B per day. Unless you're traveling in a large group, taking the train or bus is much easier, likely less expensive,

© SUZANNE NAM

getting lost in central Thailand

and will probably afford you the chance to make the journey with local people. If you do drive, Kanchanaburi is only three hours away by car, as long as there's no traffic leaving Bangkok. Take Route 338 out of Bangkok heading west, then switch to Highway 4 to Kanchanaburi.

Getting Around

Kanchanaburi Town is too large to see on foot, and it's impossible to walk to farther-flung sights such as Three Pagodas Pass. For getting around within town, there are motorcycles and bicycles available for rent in the guesthouse area. *Samlor* and *song thaew* are also available. A short *samlor* ride will cost 20B and up; *song thaew* run along Saeng Chuto Road northwest toward the bridge and cost only 10B per ride.

Although some hotels and guesthouses may be able to arrange a car rental, there are no large car rental companies in the area, and most people who plan on driving to explore the area pick up a car in Bangkok before heading here.

SAI YOK
ไทรโยค

Sai Yok, the area to the west of Kanchanaburi Town, has a wealth of natural beauty and several interesting sights worth checking out. About 100 kilometers from Kanchanaburi, this area can be visited as part of a day trip from Kanchanaburi. There are public buses from Kanchanaburi that leave every half hour 6 A.M.–5 P.M. heading for either Sai Yok Yai or Sai Yok Noi. The trip will take under two hours by bus and costs around 40B, depending on where you're going. If you are returning by bus, before you get off make sure to ask the driver when the last return bus heading for Kanchanaburi leaves; it's usually around 4 P.M.

Hellfire Pass Memorial Museum
ช่องเขาขาดพิพิธภัณฑ์แห่งความทรงจำ

The Hellfire Pass Memorial Museum (www. dva.gov.au/commem/oawg/thailand.htm, 9 A.M.–4 P.M. daily, free) commemorates a particularly arduous passage of the Thailand–Burma railway that POWs and other laborers were forced to cut through a mountain using rudimentary tools in a mere six weeks. The swath is about 500 meters long and 26 meters deep. The workers also constructed a walking trail. The museum was constructed by the Australian government to memorialize the Australians and other laborers who perished here. The museum has models, illustrations, and photos. To get to the facility, which is in the rainforest just south of Sai Yok National Park, 80 kilometers northwest of Kanchanaburi, take the bus heading toward Sangkhla Buri and get off at Hellfire Pass (it's not a standard stop, so tell the driver you're getting off there). The ride costs 45B and takes 1.5 hours. Buses leave Kanchanaburi for Sangkhla Buri throughout the day, with the last bus to Kanchanaburi coming by at approximately 4 P.M. By car, take Route 323 northwest until kilometer marker 66.

Prasat Muang Sing Historical Park
อุทยานประวัติศาสตร์ปราสาทเมืองสิงห์

The Prasat Muang Sing Historical Park (tel. 03/452-8456, 7:30 A.M.–5 P.M. daily, 40B), 43 kilometers west of Kanchanaburi Town, contains the remnants of what's believed to be the Khmer Empire's westernmost outpost, which was centered in Muang Sing Town. There are various ruins and shrines, and artifacts include carvings, shards of pottery, and other items dating to the 16th century. To get here, take the train from Kanchanaburi to the Tha Kilen station. Trains leave daily at 6:07 A.M., 10:30 A.M., and 4:30 P.M. The journey takes about an hour. Returning trains leave Tha Kilen at 6:14 A.M., 1:51 P.M., and 4:27 P.M. You can also check with tour agencies in Kanchanaburi Town to see about tours or minivans going to the park. By car, take Route 3305, which follows the same route as the train tracks.

Sai Yok National Park
อุทยานแห่งชาติไทรโยค

The 500-square-kilometer Sai Yok National Park (tel. 03/451-6163, www.dnp.go.th, 7 A.M.–4:30 P.M. daily, 200B adults, 100B children) is a good place to check out caves, waterfalls, and various streams. (The park is famous in cinematic circles as the location where parts of the 1978 film *The Deer Hunter* were filmed.) Wildlife here includes wild elephants, barking deer, and gibbons, among other creatures. If you want to stay overnight, there are bungalows (tel. 02/662-0760, 800–2,100B) within the park that sleep up to six people, along with raft guesthouses and food stalls. Maps of the park are available at the park's visitors center, although they often run out, in which case you'll have to rely on the posted trail map instead.

The park is 98 kilometers west of Kanchanaburi Town. To get here, take the bus from Kanchanaburi Town bound for Sangkhla Buri. Tell the driver you're going to the park. Buses depart from Kanchanaburi regularly; the ride costs 50B and takes four hours. If you're returning to Kanchanaburi, look for the last bus around 3:30 P.M. Another option is to check with travel agencies in Kanchanaburi to see about booking a tour or catching a ride in a minivan. Minivans can be arranged by your guesthouse or any travel agent in town; expect to pay about 200B round-trip. The park is easily reached by car from Kanchanaburi by taking Route 323 northwest until you see signs for the park's entrance.

Wat Pa Luangta Bua Yanasampanno (Tiger Temple)
วัดป่าหลวงตาบัว ญาณสัมปันโน

Visitors who want to see live tigers up close have been heading to Wat Pa Luangta Bua Yanasampanno (Sai Yok district, tel. 03/453-1557, www.tigertemple.org/Eng, tiger viewing usually 3:30–5 P.M. daily, 300B)—better known simply as the Tiger Temple-for years, where monks in a forest monastery have been purportedly rehabilitating and taming orphaned tigers since 1999. The temple, however, has come under increased scrutiny and criticism, and many believe that the treatment the tigers receive is neither humane nor designed to further the cause of wild tigers. Care for the Wild, a UK-based animal conservation group, released a scathing report of the temple's practices in 2008, providing evidence that the temple had been engaged in the illegal breeding and trade of tigers, that tigers on the temple grounds lacked appropriate medical care and physical facilities, that they were deliberately abused to make them compliant, and that the temple was doing nothing to further the cause of tiger conservation.

Erawan National Park
อุทยานแห่งชาติเอราวัณ

An especially popular day trip from Kanchanaburi Town is the seven-tiered waterfall in Erawan National Park (tel. 03/457-4222, www.dnp.go.th, 8:30 A.M.–6 P.M. daily, 200B adults, 100B children). The waterfall has several good pools for swimming, and you can take the two-kilometer hike to the top, provided you have proper footwear. To get to the national park, you can book a tour with an agency in town or take a bus from Kanchanaburi for 40B. Buses run every hour 8 A.M.–5:20 P.M., and the journey takes 1.5 hours. Buses returning to Kanchanaburi stop running at 5 P.M. To get here by car, take Route 3199 from Kanchanaburi heading northwest; the park's entrance is right off the main road and is well signed.

SANGKHLA BURI
สังขละบุรี

The quiet town of Sangkhla Buri has a population of just over 10,000 and is ethnically diverse, with Karen, Mon, Burmese, and Thai residents. The town is 225 kilometers northwest of Kanchanaburi Town and just inside the Thailand–Burma border. Few foreigners make it this far outside of Kanchanaburi Town because it's such a long drive. For those who do, Three Pagodas Pass offers a rare opportunity to visit Burma easily.

Sights

Khao Laem National Park (อุทยานแห่ง ชาติเขาแหลม, tel. 03/453-2099, www.dnp. go.th, 8:30 A.M.–6 P.M. daily, 200B) contains limestone mountains and the Khao Laem reservoir. Boats and canoes can be rented. There are also some caves, waterfalls, and viewpoints. Bungalows that sleep up to six people are available for 900–1,800B, and there's a restaurant within the park. It's best to travel by car; take Highway 323 from Kanchanaburi. The park is located right off the highway, with signs pointing the way.

On the eastern side of Sangkhla Buri is **Three Pagodas Pass** (ด่านเจดีย์สามองค์), which straddles the Thailand–Burma border. The three small pagodas signify a route taken by invading forces—one of the few passable routes in this mountainous region—from Burma from the 14th to the 18th centuries. Visitors are allowed to go from this area over to Burma for the day, where there are shops, a market, and Burmese teahouses in the town of Payathonzu.

Although it's hard to get more than a cursory look at Burma at this border town, those who make the trip into Burma are struck by the relative lack of development. Just on the other side of the border, Thailand is a country of paved roads, air-conditioned buildings, ATMs, and convenience stores while Burma has dirt roads, hastily constructed structures, and simple markets.

No visas are necessary, but travelers must leave their passports and a passport photo with Thai immigration. On the other side, you have to give the Burmese immigration office US$10 or 500B along with a copy of your passport photo page and another photo. You get your passport back when you return to Thailand. Note that visa extensions are not available here. You are not allowed to go any farther than the border town, and attempts to continue traveling through Burma will be stopped.

Three Pagodas Pass is right off of Route 323 if you are driving. You can also take *song thaew* from Sangkhla Buri, which leave about every hour 6 A.M.–6 P.M.; the ride will cost around 30B.

Accommodations and Food

There are very limited accommodations available in Sangkhla Buri, and the best of this very small group of lodging option is

P. Guest House (8/1 Mu 1, Tambon Nong Lu, tel. 03/459-5061, 200B), which has stone bungalows overlooking the reservoir. The guest rooms are no-frills—the walls are made of rocks, after all—but some have air-conditioning and hot water, and they're all very clean.

On the Burma side, if you decide to cross over into Payathonzu, there are some typical Burmese teashops serving strong tea with sweetened condensed milk and pastries. Typically, you'll be brought out half a dozen plates of snacks when you order a drink. Don't worry about the cost—you are only charged for what you actually eat.

Getting There
Buses to and from Kanchanaburi Town

make the 230-kilometer trek along the rough road six times a day, leaving from the main bus terminal starting at 6 A.M. The last bus is at 1:30 P.M. The trip takes about six hours and costs 90–160B, depending on whether you take an air-conditioned or normal bus. Although the journey is bumpy, the scenery is spectacular.

If you're **driving,** Route 323 connects Kanchanaburi and Sangkhla Buri. The drive takes about four hours.

Getting Around
No **cars** are available for rental in this area; if you want your own vehicle, you'll have to rent it in Bangkok. You can rent a **motorcycle** for 150–200B per day.

Phitsanulok Province   จังหวัดพิษณุโลก

Phitsanulok is located in the northern part of the central plains, and the provincial capital is often used as a jumping-off point for visits to the ancient ruins of Sukhothai. Phitsanulok Town—or, as it's often abbreviated by Thais, "Philok" (พิโลก)—is notable for having been the de facto Thai capital between 1463 and 1487, when Ayutthaya's King Borom Trailokanat resided here. The area has just a few sights, but like many towns in Thailand that are farther removed from the tourist trail, it's interesting in its own right.

PHITSANULOK TOWN
เมืองพิษณุโลก
Phitsanulok Town is located on the banks of the Nam River. Much of the city is newly built in a modern style, as a fire destroyed much of its older area in 1955. Phitsanulok Town has been a community since the 11th century, when it was an outpost of the Khmer Empire. The town also has some traditional houseboats on the Nam River, some of which have been converted to restaurants.

Sights
The **old city walls** (แนวกำแพงโบราณ) were once made of clay but have now largely deteriorated; what remains can be seen to the east and north of town. The 12-meter-wide city moats, however, are still intact.

Wat Phra Si Mahathat (วัดพระศรีมหาธาตุวรมหาวิหาร, near Singhawat Rd., 10B), on the northern end of town, is also known as Wat Yai (วัดใหญ่, big temple) or Wat Mahatha. It was built in the 14th century and contains one of Thailand's most remarkable and well-known Buddha statues, the bronze **Phra Phutthachinarat** (พระพุทธชินราช). The statue depicts a Buddha with a halo that is indicative of the Sukhothai style.

Wat Chula Mani (วัดจุฬามณี, Borom Trailokanat Rd.), five kilometers south of town, is the province's oldest temple. It was built during the Sukhothai period (mid-13th–mid-14th centuries). Borom Trailokanat, an Ayutthayan king, was the first Siamese king to be ordained. He became a monk here in 1416. The *wat* has a *prang* (pagoda) built in the Khmer style. It

PHITSANULOK TOWN

was constructed of laterite—reddish soil—and is decorated with swans.

If you're into history and you've got a green thumb, you won't want to miss the **Giant Tamarind Tree** (Ban Kok subdistrict)—it's said to be 700 years old and counting.

Accommodations

At the popular **LiThai Guesthouse** (73/1–5 Phayalithai Rd., tel. 05/521-9626, 300B), a short walk from the railroad station, all of the spacious guest rooms have air-conditioning and TVs, and breakfast is included. Beds are big and comfortable, and the staff is congenial.

Amarin Lagoon Hotel and Convention Center (52/299 Praongkhao Rd., tel. 05/522-0999, www.amarinlagoonhotel.com, 1,100B) is an excellent mid-range option (really the only large mid-range option in town). The guest rooms at this large hotel are modern and have cushy furniture. There's a pool, a fitness center, a spa, and even an 18-hole golf course.

The **Pattara Resort & Spa** (349/40 Chaiyanupap Rd., tel. 05/528-2966, www.pattararesort.com, 2,400B) is a good choice for more upscale lodgings. The spacious resort has pool villas and traditional hotel rooms, all designed and furnished in a modern Asian style. Guest rooms have five-star amenities, including DVD players and rain showerheads, but the property is not quite up to par with international chain hotels. The nicely maintained grounds are very impressive, including the massive swimming pool.

Food

Fah-Herah (786 Phra Ong Dam Rd., 6 A.M.–2 P.M. daily, 20–40B), near the mosque, serves excellent Thai-Muslim food. In addition to the signature curries, there's fresh yogurt and roti.

Rin Coffee (Salreuthai Rd., tel. 05/525-2848, 9 A.M.–9 P.M. Mon.–Fri., 7:30 A.M.–9 P.M. Sat.–Sun., 20–60B) is an expansive café where you can get a wide variety of coffees and teas. There are also Western staples such as sandwiches and waffles along with other breakfast foods.

The **night market** (next to the river, 5 P.M.–3 A.M. daily, 40–80B) is a great place to eat a local specialty, *phakbung loifa* (ผักบุ้งลอยฟ้า)—stir-fried morning glory with garlic.

Getting There

Trains make the seven-hour trip from Bangkok's Hua Lamphong station to Phitsanulok daily at 5:50 A.M., 7 A.M., 2:30 P.M., 7:50 P.M., and 8:10 P.M. Second-class tickets are 309B. Better yet, there are faster trains that make the journey in just five hours. These daily second-class express trains leave at 8:30 A.M., 10:50 P.M., and 7:20 P.M. and cost 449B. And finally, if you prefer to take a red-eye, first- and second-class overnight trains leave Bangkok at 7:35 P.M. daily. These take six hours and cost 1,064 (first class) and 629–699B (second class).

Buses to and from Bangkok's Northern Bus Terminal run more or less hourly 6 A.M.–10 P.M. The trip takes about six hours and should cost 300B or less.

There are two ways to get from Bangkok to Phitsanulok by **car.** You can take Highways 1 and 32 to Nakhon Sawan, and then take Highway 117 to Phitsanulok. Or you can take Highway 1 to Ayutthaya, followed by Highways 32 to In Buri, 11 to Wang Thong, and 12 to Phitsanulok. The journey will take about five hours.

The easiest—though most expensive—way to travel between Phitsanulok and Bangkok is via **Thai Airways.** There are daily flights that take just 55 minutes and cost 2,185B one-way.

Getting Around

Phitsanulok is small enough that you can cover the city on foot if you're willing to walk a few kilometers. There are also plenty of *tuk tuks* to take you around; expect to pay 30B for a short trip.

There are two car-rental outlets at the Phitsanulok airport that charge rates starting at 1,350B per day: **Avis** (tel. 05/524-2060, www.avisthailand.com) and **Budget** (tel. 05/525-8556, www.budget.co.th).

Small 125-cc motorcycles can be rented at **PN Motorbike** (Mittraphap Rd., tel. 05/530-3222) for 200B per day.

THUNG SALAENG LUANG NATIONAL PARK

อุทยานแหงชาติทุงแสลงหลวง

Thung Salaeng Luang National Park (tel. 05/526-8019, salaengluang_np@hotmail.com, www.dnp.go.th, 8:30 A.M.–6 P.M. daily, 400B) was once a foreboding place. Until the 1980s, the area was not only malaria-ridden, it was used as a base by communist guerrillas who were part of the banned Communist Party of Thailand (CPT). Today, however, the 1,262-square-kilometer park is much more welcoming. There are forests, meadows, and waterfalls. The area's mountain streams feed the Nam River. Thung Non Son meadow, in the center of the park, is known for its many wildflowers, visible October–December. And the striking Kaeng Sopha waterfall—which some call the "Niagara Falls of Thailand"—resembles a cascading staircase. The waterfall is at the 68-kilometer mark of the Phitsanulok–Lomsak Highway. There are restrooms, food vendors, and an information center here as well.

Getting There

The park is approximately 150 kilometers due east of Phitsanulok Town. Take Highway 12 directly to the park entrance. Park headquarters are at kilometer marker 80. There is an hourly bus that runs from Phitsanulok Town to Nakhon Thai, which is about 30 kilometers from the park and about a two-hour ride from Phitsanulok. From the town, you have to find a *song thaew* (which only run every hour 9:30 A.M.–3 P.M., or when full) the rest of the way.

NAMTOK CHAT TRAKAN NATIONAL PARK
อุทยานแห่งชาติน้ำตกชาตการ

The mountainous Namtok Chat Trakan National Park (tel. 05/523-7028, reserve@ dnp.go.th, www.dnp.go.th, 8:30 A.M.–6 P.M. daily, 400B), located 145 kilometers northeast of Phitsanulok Town, is best known for its namesake Chat Trakan waterfall. The falls are surrounded by sheer cliff walls and empty into a large pool. The remnants of what are believed to be prehistoric carvings are on some of the cliffs. There is an information center for the park located off Route 1237, a few kilometers from the waterfall. Camping can be arranged by contacting park officials prior to arriving.

Getting There

To get to the park via car, take Highway 12 and turn left after 68 kilometers onto Highway 2013 to Nakhon Thai. Then take Highway 1143 to Chat Trakan. The drive takes about two hours from Phitsanulok Town.

PHU SOI DAO NATIONAL PARK
อุทยานแห่งชาติภูสอยดาว

Situated in the Chat Trakan district along the Thailand–Laos border is Phu Soi Dao National Park (tel. 05/543-6001, phusoidao07@hotmail.com, www.dnp.go.th, 8:30 A.M.–6 P.M. daily, 400B). The park, 199 kilometers from Phitsanulok Town, has a 2,102-meter-high peak, various hills, and cool weather. The area is renowned for its many wildflowers. The Phu Soi Dao and Sai Thip waterfalls have five and seven tiers, respectively.

The park is closed January 15–June 31 every year to provide protection for the forested areas. In addition, when the park is open, visitors must bring their own camping equipment to stay overnight, as there are no bungalows. Restaurants or food vendors may or may not be available, so visitors are advised to bring their own provisions just in case.

Getting There

From Phitsanulok Town, take Highway 11 to Highway 1246. At Ban Pae, pick up Highway 1143. After you get to the Chattrakarn district, take Highway 1237 to Highway 1268 to the park entrance. The drive is about 200 kilometers and takes about four hours.

Sukhothai and Vicinity   สุโขทัย

In the north of Thailand, the sleepy, charming, and now-abandoned ancient city of Sukhothai was the first capital of Siam. Formerly an outpost of the Cambodia-centered Khmer Empire, Sukhothai was taken over and established by Tais in 1238. It is important in that it was the first truly independent Tai kingdom. It was here that the great King Ramkhamhaeng united the Tais, established the royal code of law, and formulated the first written Thai scripts. Sukhothai was prominent until the 14th century, when it was abandoned and the Ayutthaya Empire came to the fore.

The ancient city's small but well-preserved ruins, contained within the larger historical park, are popular with foreign and Thai visitors today. The park is in excellent condition and well maintained as a crucial part of Thailand's cultural heritage. The old city (Old Sukhothai), where all the cultural attractions are, is on the west side of town, while the new city (New Sukhothai) is to the east.

Bicycles are the preferred mode of transportation here, and the guesthouses and restaurants surrounding the central part of the historical park all rent them very cheaply by the day.

Do you need to visit modern Sukhothai? Probably not, unless you're really desperate for a place to stay or have a particular interest in generic midsize Thai cities.

Apart from visiting Sukhothai, usually accessed via Phitsanulok or on one of Bangkok Airways' flights, few foreigners venture to this section of north-central Thailand. This is partially due to its location: It's too far from Bangkok for day trips, and most visitors who come this far north tend to skip over it in favor of Chiang Mai.

◖ SUKHOTHAI HISTORICAL PARK
อุทยานประวัติศาสตร์สุโขทัย

Sukhothai Historical Park (tel. 05/569-7310, 8:30 A.M.–4:30 P.M. daily, 30–50B per section, 150B for all areas, small surcharge for cars,

Sukhothai Historical Park

© SUZANNE NAM

motorcycles, and bicycles) is a large park that covers an area of 45 square kilometers and encompasses approximately 40 temple complexes. The most interesting temples can be found in the central part of the park, which is easily accessed by bicycle or on foot and has a large concentration of ruins.

The park as a whole, a UNESCO World Heritage Site, contains architectural styles that are recognized as being quintessentially Thai, with various *chedi*—bell-shaped stupas—on display. Khmer-style *prang* (towers) are also visible here due to the area's Khmer roots. Within the park are ruins of the royal palace, moats, canals, and the old city gates and walls. These have been restored by the Thai government and UNESCO and are very well maintained, but bear in mind that Sukhothai's ruins are just that—ruins, and some of them, especially outside the inner historical park, are hard to identify.

The larger park is broken up into five geographic sections—central, north, south, east, and west. The sections aren't marked, but if you start at the inner park, which is set off by moats and gates, and think of it as the center, the handful of other sites in the larger park that are worth visiting are north and east of it. There are scattered ruins to the south and west as well, although most are small and dilapidated.

One slightly confusing fact to bear in mind: The historic park encompasses parts of Old Sukhothai that are now just normal parts of the town, including shops, restaurants, and guesthouses.

Inner Park (Central)
เนินปราสาทพระร่วงหรือเขตพระราชวัง

This area, surrounded by moats and the old city walls as well as a gate on each side, is the heart of Old Sukhothai and the first place to visit. It was here that essentially all of the city's (and kingdom's) administrative business was transacted, where the king's palace was located, and where Sukhothai's most significant temples were.

A stone inscription found by King Mongkut while touring Sukhothai in 1833 says that King Ramkhamhaeng put a bell at one of the Royal Palace's gates and told his subjects that if they had a dispute, they should ring it and he would come to mediate. The stone is now on display in Bangkok's National Museum and, unfortunately, little remains of the palace itself. The site where it is believed to have been located, in the center of the inner park, is marked off.

Just across from the Royal Palace grounds and southwest of the center of the park is Sukhothai's most impressive ruin, **Wat Mahathat** (วัดมหาธาตุ). This large *wat* complex is partially surrounded by a moat and contains nearly 200 small *chedi* within the old brick walls. Some of them are in good enough condition that you can still see the intricate carvings that once adorned the whole complex. There are also scores of Buddha figures throughout the complex, many in excellent condition. The grounds of the complex are very well maintained and a beautiful place for a stroll if the weather is not too hot.

South of Wat Mahathat is **Wat Si Sawai** (วัดศรีสวาย), which was originally built as a Hindu temple. It has three Hindu-style *prang* (towers) and is surrounded by a laterite wall. Part of the structure contained a Hindu sculpture, but the *wat* was later made into a Buddhist monastery. Some of the *prang* here still have their original stucco embellishments.

Wat Sra Si (วัดสระศรี), in the northwestern part of the center of the park, is another temple surrounded by water. It sits on an artificially constructed island in the center of a large pond. The *wat*'s architecture is simple, with one large bell-shaped *chedi*, in the Sri Lankan style, dominating the complex.

◀ Ramkhamhaeng National Museum
พิพิธภัณฑสถานแห่งชาติรามคำแหง

Just east of the palace grounds is the small Ramkhamhaeng National Museum (tel. 05/561-2167, 9 A.M.–4 P.M. daily, 30B). The museum has a variety of artifacts from the Sukhothai period that serve as a good introduction to the period's arts and crafts. Don't miss the bronze Walking Buddha, which is part of the collection of Sukhothai-style Buddha representations. Just east of the museum is **Wat Traphang Thong,** a picturesque temple in the middle of a lake. The wat has a Sri Lankan–style *chedi* that resembles a lotus bud and dates from the 14th century, and its outer walls contain intricate carved figures.

North of the Inner Park
If you exit via the north gate of the inner park, head up the main road (either by car or by bicycle) to **Wat Phra Pai Luang,** one of the largest temple complexes in Sukhothai and possibly the oldest. The structures, mostly foundational elements, the remains of a Buddha, and a large *mondop* (square pavilion), are believed to have been built sometime in the 12th century during the Khmer period. There are large lakes on either side of the complex, and if it's not too hot and sunny, it is a very nice place to explore on foot.

Wat Si Chum (วัดศรีชุม) is just east of Wat Phra Pai Luang. The magnificent temple is well-known for its *mondop* and brick Buddha image covered by stucco known as Phra Achana. The 15-meter-tall, 11-meter-wide Buddha is seated and is famous for its long fingers. It's also notable because it's one of the best-preserved Buddha figures in Sukhothai. The inside of the wall contains a passageway, above which are many engraved slate slabs that depict Jataka scenes, stories about the Buddha's previous lives.

Farther north on the main road are the **Celadon Kilns** (เตาเผาสังคโลก), the location of an old Sukhothai celadon factory. This is an archeological excavation site, and there are few structures to see.

East of the Inner Park
A few hundred meters from the east gate along the main road is **Wat Chang Lom,** a remarkably well-preserved temple consisting of a bell-shaped *chedi* on a base surrounded by large carvings of elephants.

OTHER SIGHTS
Sangkhalok Museum
พิพิธภัณฑ์สังคโลกสุโขทัย
The Sangkhalok Museum (Mu 3, Muangkao Rd., tel. 05/561-4333, 8 A.M.–5 P.M. daily,

100B adults, 50B children), one kilometer outside town on the way to Phitsanulok, has a wide selection of Sukhothai-style pottery and ceramic wares. The term *sangkhalok* refers to the type of pottery created during this time. Glazes were often dark in color, and stoneware sometimes featured fish motifs.

SPORTS AND RECREATION
Bicycle Tours
Various bicycle tours are available at **Ban Thai Guest House** (38 Prawet Nakhot Rd., tel. 05/561-0163, banthai_guesthouse@yahoo.com), including one-hour, half-day, or full-day tours (100–700B) and evening tours (250B). Tour guides can accommodate riders of varying skill and fitness levels. A typical tour of the park's ruins includes commentary and explanation of each *wat*'s architectural and historical significance.

ACCOMMODATIONS
Sukhothai does not have a huge selection of places to sleep, but there are good options whether you are looking for an inexpensive guesthouse, a mid-range hotel, or a high-end resort. For convenience, the best accommodations are either right near the inner historic park or just a few kilometers away in less-developed parts of Sukhothai. There are also resorts and guesthouses closer to and in the new city of Sukhothai, which is about 13 kilometers from the historic park and 20 minutes away by car. If you stay in that part of Sukhothai, you will need to find transportation to the sights. Most hotels and resorts offer some form of shuttle service for a fee.

Under 1,500B
Vitoon Guest House (49/3 Jarot Withithong Rd., tel. 05/563-3397, www.vitoonguesthouse.com, 400B) is about as basic as it gets, but it has the best location in Sukhothai, right across the street from the city's most important sights. Guest rooms are clean and basic but have their own TVs and baths.

Thai Thai Sukhothai Guest House (407/4 Napho-Khirimas Rd., tel. 08/4932-1006, www.thaithaisukhothai.com, 1,200B) is great value for those who want a convenient location very close to the historic park and more privacy and comfort than a typical guesthouse. Guest rooms at this basic resort are filled with teak and Thai art and have a rustic, cabin-like quality, although the baths are very modern.

1,500-3,000B

Le Charm Sukhothai Resort (9/9 Napho-Khirimas Rd., tel. 08/4932-1006, www. lecharmesukhothai.com, 2,500B) is very conveniently located 800 meters from the entrance to the inner historic park and offers nearly every amenity one would expect at a full-service resort, despite its relatively small size (45 guest rooms). Even basic guest rooms are nicely decorated with some modern Thai furnishings, but the high-end rooms and villas, in brightly colored stand-alone bungalows scattered across the grounds, are very charming. There is swimming pool and a restaurant.

Visitors looking for some stylish pampering should consider the exceptional 【 **Tharaburi Resort** (113 Srisomboon Rd., tel. 05/569-7132, www.tharaburiresort.com, 3,000B). This boutique hotel, which opened in the mid-2000s, has just 12 guest rooms and suites. All of the guest rooms are sumptuously decorated in a contemporary Asian style, with various prints and hangings on the walls and airy, well-lit designs. Even the most basic guest rooms have plush beds, balconies, rain showerheads, and flat-screen TVs. The suites are essentially apartments unto themselves and have their own private pavilions. There is a very small swimming pool and a restaurant on the grounds. This resort is just a few kilometers from the inner historic park in an otherwise undeveloped part of Sukhothai.

FOOD

Within Old Sukhothai, there are very limited eating options aside from a couple of noodle shops and stalls. **Ran Jay Hae** (Jarot Withithong Rd., no phone, 11 A.M.–9 P.M. daily, 40B) is a basic noodle shop, but it's also one of the most popular spots in the city to

try the famous eponymous Sukhothai noodles. The *guay teow* is much like what you'll find in Bangkok or anywhere else in the country, except that it's a little spicier and has more generous meat and vegetable portions. Look for the sign that reads "Sukhothai Noodles."

The Coffee Cup (Jarot Withithong Rd., tel. 05/563-3480, 7 A.M.–9 P.M. daily, 100B) is the perfect spot if you're looking for basic backpacker fare—iced coffee, pad thai, and smoothies. The café also has nice Western breakfast dishes if that's what you're craving.

The new city has more food options. **Sukhothai Suki-Coca** (Sawatdiphong Hotel, Singhawat Rd., Amphoe Muang, tel. 05/561-1567, 10 A.M.–9:30 P.M. daily, 40–100B) offers one-pot meals that are cooked by diners themselves. This is part of a small chain of restaurants throughout the country, so expect unexciting decor and lots of Formica.

The **night market** (near Nikhon Kasem Rd., 6–10 P.M. daily, 40–80B) has standard Thai fare such as noodles and rice dishes. You can also try *kai ping*—roasted eggs.

Dream Cafe (86/1 Singhawat Rd., tel. 05/561-2081, 10 A.M.–10 P.M. daily, 60–250B) is the place to go in the new city for a nice meal. The extensive menu has both Thai and Western food (the former is better than the latter), but it's the unique atmosphere that's the draw: You'll dine amid 19th-century Thai antiques. You can also try the herbal liquors, which come in medicine vials.

GETTING THERE
Air
Bangkok Airways has two daily flights from Bangkok to Sukhothai. The 80-minute flight into the charming little Sukhothai airport usually costs around 3,500B each way. This is the most convenient way to get here from Bangkok, but definitely not the cheapest.

Bus
Buses from Phitsanulok to Sukhothai depart every 30 minutes 7 A.M.–11 P.M. and cost 30–54B, depending on the class. The trip takes one hour. From Bangkok, the ride is seven

hours and costs around 350B. The bus station in Sukhothai is just outside the new city off Route 101. It's about a 20-minute walk to the center of town, or there are *song thaew* for 20B.

Car
Driving from Bangkok takes about five hours. Once you get to Phitsanulok, follow Route 12 heading east to Sukhothai.

GETTING AROUND
If you are staying in the new part of Sukhothai, you'll need some form of transportation, as the old city is about 11 kilometers away. There are frequent *song thaew* on Jarot Withithong Road that go between the historical park and the new city during the day; expect to pay 15B or less. Within the new part of the city, it's easy to walk from place to place as the central area is quite small, but there are also *samlor* and *tuk tuks* available for longer rides.

Within the historic park, it's probably best to rent a bicycle either from one of the many bike rental shops and touts surrounding the entrance to the city or from your guesthouse. Day rates for bicycles are under 50B.

SI SATCHANALAI HISTORICAL PARK
อุทยานประวัติศาสตร์ศรีสัชนาลัย

Si Satchanalai Historical Park (40B, waived if you purchased the 150B multiple-section ticket from Sukhothai), 50 kilometers north of Sukhothai, isn't visited as frequently as the Sukhothai Historical Park, but many who have visited both prefer these ruins. They're no less impressive—the remains are from a 13th-century Sukhothai satellite city called Si Satchanalai and what is believed to be a Khmer settlement called Chalieng that predated it. Here, farther away from Sukhothai proper, the mood is more sedate, and the view overlooking the Tom River is pleasant.

The best way to visit the ruins at Si Satchanalai is on a day trip from your base in Sukhothai. Since Si Satchanalai is north of Sukhothai, if you are heading to Chiang Mai,

you could visit on your way from Sukhothai, but to do so you'll need to forgo the larger, flatter Highway 1 for a smaller road for much of the trip.

Sights
The grounds comprise seven square kilometers, and a 12-meter-wide moat encircles the area. At the heart of the complex is the 13th-century **Wat Chang Lom,** which has an enormous *chedi* constructed in Sri Lankan style and containing relics from King Ramkhamhaeng. Thirty-nine elephant statues are built into the *chedi*'s base. Don't confuse this temple with the Sukhothai temple of the same name. Though they are both surrounded by elephants, they are in different places.

Near Wat Chang Lom is **Wat Chedi Chet Thaew,** which contains seven rows of *chedi* and a sanctuary with crumbling ancient murals; one *chedi* contains the stucco image of a Buddha with an overarching *naga* (sacred snake).

Wat Nang Phaya is dominated by a Sri Lankan–style *chedi* probably built around 500 years ago. Although the *wat* is not in very good condition, there are remains of some ornate stucco carvings of lotus flowers and other images in the complex that make it a popular destination. The carvings are in the former *wihan* and are protected by a useful but unsightly roof.

Information
There is a small visitors center (9 A.M.–5 P.M. daily) just outside the old city walls on the southern part of the park that has maps of the ruins. The center is about a 10-minute walk from the park's entrance on the eastern side of the old city.

Getting There
King Rama VI was such a big fan of the historical park that he had a special railroad extension built to Sawankhalok so that he could more easily access the ruins. Service is still active: There's a daily train that leaves from Bangkok (7 hours, 482B) at 10:50 A.M., stops in Phitsanulok at 4 P.M., and arrives in

Sawankhalok at 5:50 P.M. A train makes the return journey at 7:40 P.M. daily and arrives in Bangkok at 3:30 A.M. It's possible to take this train from Sawankhalok to Phitsanulok for just 50B.

To get from New Sukhothai to the historical park, hop on the **bus** heading for Si Satchanalai. The two-hour trip costs 38B. Tell the driver that you want to get off on Highway 101, outside the park entrance. The last bus back to New Sukhothai departs at 4:30 P.M.

Note: When you get off the bus for the park, be aware that that you'll need to cross the Yom River via a footbridge. If arriving by **car,** from Sukhothai take Route 101 heading north. After about 55 kilometers, you'll see a sign for Si Satchanalai, just off the main road.

Getting Around

The park is too large to cover on foot, especially in the heat. There are bicycles available for rent outside the park for about 20B per day.

CHIANG MAI AND NORTHERN THAILAND

Distant mists, birdsong, and a distinct chill greet most mornings in the mountains and valleys of northern Thailand. Among the region's soaring peaks, lush rainforests, and fertile plains you will find a patchwork of lifestyles still largely steeped in tradition. Agriculture, and more recently tourism, is the bread and butter here, and with everyone eventually congregating in the region's string of provincial towns, there is a rich palette of culture, history, and adventure to experience. While modern first-class amenities can usually be found, the pace is relatively slow and the atmosphere relaxed, with the Thai word *sabai* (happy) often on the lips of the local people and visitors.

With the exception of Chiang Mai itself (which is far quieter than Bangkok), even the largest towns in northern Thailand are comparatively peaceful places, with smaller crowds and less traffic than other parts of the country. You will find a colorful array of mom-and-pop establishments, including little bars and restaurants, boutique hotels, and art shops, dotting the streets and keeping close company with produce markets, traditional medicine shops, and the hawker stands of the hill tribe people who come to sell their art, often dressed in their vibrant and elaborate ancestral costumes. Elegant spas, isolated resorts, sparkling waterfalls, and Buddhist temples spanning seven centuries add to the verdant tranquility on offer. Although you will find the various pit stops in this region woven together with a common thread of lifestyle, cuisine, and history, each locale has managed to retain its own unique character.

© SUZANNE NAM

HIGHLIGHTS

Wat Chiang Man: Chiang Mai's oldest *wat* is also one of the best examples of Lanna-style architecture in the city (page 340).

The Saturday Market: Excellent handmade goods, street snacks, and a relaxed vibe make for a perfect weekend afternoon in Chiang Mai (page 353).

Mae Sa Loop: Starting just outside of the city of Chiang Mai, this loop drive takes you to enchanted botanical gardens, small handicraft villages, and elephant camps, all set amid rolling mountain scenery (page 380).

Doi Mae Salong: Settled by fleeing Chinese soldiers, this town is a bit of China in Chiang Rai Province, with tea shops and Chinese temples (page 400).

Mae Hong Son: This small border town, surrounded by mountains and rainforest, offers plenty of opportunities to trek and explore without the crowds you'll find in Chiang Mai (page 403).

LOOK FOR **C** TO FIND RECOMMENDED SIGHTS, ACTIVITIES, DINING, AND LODGING.

CHIANG MAI

For travelers on a budget, the region can be a refreshing change from Bangkok and the islands, where the hordes of tourists seem to drive prices for accommodations, food, and transport higher every year. Northern Thailand is extremely popular with both international visitors and Thais on vacation, but it remains an exceptional-value destination.

PLANNING YOUR TIME

It's possible to experience Chiang Mai in just a few days, and if you don't mind limiting what you take in, you could distill all of northern Thailand into a week. Of course, you could also spend a month relaxing, trying your hand at any number of exotic and quirky activities, getting back to nature in steamy green rainforests, luxuriating at gorgeously appointed spas, taking in the rich mix of culture both in the

villages and up on the mountains with the hill tribes—the list is almost endless, and in fact, some people never go home. In other words, it's up to you. If you only have a few days, you can easily fly into the town of your choice (for most people, this is Chiang Mai), sign up for a quick rainforest trek, visit the hill tribes, a museum, and a few other key sights, and fly back out having sampled the best of the north and enjoyed a few exciting dining experiences to boot. It's also entirely reasonable simply to come out to enjoy the fresh mountain air and relative peace and quiet, doing nothing other than indulging in the good life at great prices.

If you are ambitious and on a tight time budget, Chiang Mai makes a good base to sample the best that the north has to offer. You can combine getting back to nature in the mountain rainforests with visiting one of the

CHIANG MAI AND NORTHERN THAILAND

MYANMAR (BURMA)

LAOS

Mae Sai

DOI MAE SALONG

Chiang Saen

Mae Chan

CHIANG RAI

Tha Ton

Mae Fa Luang

Fang

Chiang Rai

Mekong River

Doi Ang Khang

Mae Lao

Khun Tan

THAILAND

Mae Suai

Thoeng

Chiangkham

MAE HONG SON

Pai

Phayao

PHAYAO

NAN

Mae Taeng

Samoeng

MAE SA LOOP

Chiang Mai

THE SATURDAY MARKET

WAT CHIANG MAN

Nan

CHIANG MAI

Doi Inthanon National Park

Ngao

LAMPANG

Lamphun

Chom Thong

LAMPHUN

MAE HONG SON

Mae Sariang

Lampang

Yom River

Nan River

Den Chai

PHRAE

UTTARADIT

Thoen

Uttaradit

TAK

Ban Tak

SUKHOTHAI

PHITSANULOK

Mae Ramat

Sukhothai

Tak

MYANMAR (BURMA)

Mae Sot

KAMPHAENG PHET

Phitsanulok

Kamphaeng Phet

Phichit

0   25 mi
0   25 km

© AVALON TRAVEL

most important temples in the region, Wat Doi Suthep, which is best seen at sunrise or sunset. Many who have gone before you would argue that if you skip the Elephant Nature Park, you've made a big mistake, so along with Doi Suthep, head out to Mae Taeng and wash and feed elephants for the day.

The hill tribes, particularly the "long neck" Karen or Padaung, are not to be missed—their future is uncertain, and you might not get another chance, so plan for at least a half-day visit, but select your tour guide carefully. The more rural, authentic villages are seen from Mae Hong Son, as the tours out of Chiang Mai are often to villages that no longer function as hill tribe mainstays now that there is so much tourism. A half-day trek could be combined with a quick visit to some of the shopping areas located outside of town, with their unique handicrafts and some of the best prices for souvenirs and local art in the country. Add to that a day starting with an early-morning foray to the beautiful Chedi Luang or Suan Dok temples at dawn, a leisurely lunch, a quick trip to the National Museum, and an evening stroll to take in a few of the city's liveliest and most absorbing streets, ending with a cruise through the spirited Night Bazaar and a well-earned Thai beer of your choice. Of course, since the region is famous for elephants, you should probably order the Chang. But one too many and you'll end up with what is referred to as a "Changover."

For those who become restless with too much relaxation, northern Thailand offers many exhilarating adventures set in the surrounding rainforest; somewhere among the bungee jumping, trekking, mountain biking, and even light plane rentals, you are sure to find something to get your adrenaline up. Of course, if that's not your scene, there is also plenty to keep history hunters, culture bugs, and shopping aficionados wide-eyed and open-mouthed for days on end.

Mercifully falling somewhere between a rural backwater and a world-class tourist zone, northern Thailand has all of the transportation benefits of a well-traveled resort area with none of the big-city urban sprawl and traffic congestion. Networks of bus routes spread out from Chiang Mai to almost every northern town; many locales have airports, and flights are short and generally inexpensive; dozens of organized tours cover the full gamut of local destinations; and reasonably well-maintained and intuitive road systems combine with cheap car rentals to make the north about as accessible as one could hope for. Most towns in the region are so small that walking to your destination is frequently a viable option, and when it's not, taxis, *tuk tuks,* and *song thaew* (สองแถว) can usually be found nearby.

If you are seeking a more in-depth experience and have the time, consider enrolling in one of the surprising assortment of courses designed to provide you with a uniquely Thai experience and a one-of-a-kind souvenir: a new skill. Courses on offer last from a single day up to a week or more and cover such exotic subjects as *muay Thai* boxing, Thai cooking, traditional dance, meditation, yoga teacher training, massage, and traditional arts. Prices are generally very reasonable by Western standards, and some include room and board.

HISTORY

To visit northern Thailand is to step into the ancient kingdom of Lannathai, "the land of a million rice fields." For centuries the Lanna Kingdom was the northern counterpart to the Siamese Kingdom of Sukhothai, to the south. While a cultural and territorial tug-of-war between Siam and Burma gripped the kingdom for centuries, Lannathai eventually became the loyal and integrated part of modern Thailand that you see today. However, the northern Thais still see themselves as distinctly different from their southern compatriots, and indeed they have a history, language, and ancestry all their own.

While there is evidence that the mountains and valleys of northern Thailand have been inhabited for at least 2,000 years, the cultural roots of the current residents began in the sixth century A.D. when the Mon people made their way through the forests from what is now Burma (also called Myanmar). Drawn by trade to the fertile valleys and rivers, they created their capital at Hariphunchai, the city now known as Lamphun. Spreading insatiably across Thailand, Laos, and into Cambodia over the following 400 years, they brought cultural and artistic influences that are still in evidence today. Most importantly, it is believed that they introduced Buddhism to the region, a thread that is deeply entwined with the daily lives of residents even now, 1,500 years later.

The Lanna Kingdom was the creation of the young King Mengrai, 13th-century ruler of the people living in what is now the southern Chinese province of Yunnan and the northern sections of Burma, Laos, and Thailand. Born in Chiang Saen, he set about unifying the people scattered throughout the region under his banner and in 1262 founded Chiang Rai, the capital of his new kingdom, which he named after himself. Ambitious and charismatic, he did not stop there. Pushing south, he expanded his territory through conquest and persuasion all the way through the intervening Mon settlements to the borders of the Sukhothai Kingdom of southern Thailand. After annexing Hariphunchai, King Mengrai felt that his kingdom needed a strong city in its new territories. After inviting his friends the kings of the Sukhothai and Payao Kingdoms to inspect a verdant plain near the Ping River and to help him build a city there, in 1296 Nopburi Sri Nakorn Ping Chiang Mai was founded. Each of the three kings made a small cut in his wrist and spilled blood into a silver chalice; each then drank from the cup and vowed everlasting support to one another. Whether the consumption of blood played a role or not, there were no wars between the three kingdoms during the reigns of these men. A statue was erected for the three kings and can still be found in the city (Intawarorot Rd. at Phra Pokklao Rd.), whose name was later shortened to Chiang Mai, which means simply "new city." Near the three kings statue in the center of the old city is a shrine to King Mengrai. According to legend, it stands at the spot where he was struck by lightning and killed in his

© SUZANNE NAM

brick *chedi* (pagoda) in Chiang Mai's old city

80th year, concluding his life with a ferocity that seemed to match the passion with which he had lived it.

Strategically positioned on the trade route between Yunnan Province and the ports of Burma, the Lanna Kingdom flourished and experienced a golden age of prosperity through the 15th century, expanding its territory to include most of northern Thailand, large tracts of Burma and Laos, and a small part of southern China. Chiang Mai became the capital in 1345 and in 1477 was the site of the Seventh World Buddhist Conference. Unfortunately, finding itself surrounded by hostile neighbors in Burma, Laos, and the Ayutthaya Kingdom that had replaced the Sukhothai Kingdom to the south, the Lanna Kingdom was weakened by conflict in the 16th century and swayed between independent control and foreign occupation. In 1558 Chiang Mai fell to Burmese forces and for the following two centuries was exploited as a key military base in their campaign against Ayutthaya. Finally the Lanna people allied themselves with the Siamese forces and drove out the Burmese, but the city was left in such a state of devastation that it was completely abandoned in 1776 for 15 years, with the capital shifting back to Lamphun, the original Mon center.

It was King Rama I of the current Chakri Dynasty who resurrected Chiang Mai; he reestablished leadership for the region in the form of the title of prince awarded to a former military leader. The new prince then went on to encourage repopulation by the people who had spread out and become disorganized during the years of conflict. This firmly established the northern provinces as the loyal part of Siam that they are today. Finally, the addition of the railroad, built in 1921, opened the north to the rest of the country, providing access both to natural resources such as teak and farmland as well as to the villages for migration and tourism. The last 20 years have seen enormous growth in these mountain towns, whose relative isolation was so complete until so recently that the imprint of isolation continues to be felt, at least for now.

Chiang Mai เชียงใหม่

Despite its status as one of the country's largest cities and its population of 1 million people, Chiang Mai has managed to hang onto its small-town feel even as it developed into a modern center. Even though it boasts the biggest hotels, flashiest night spots, and the bulk of tourism services in northern Thailand, as you cruise the city's ancient streets and wander through its wealth of temples, you may find yourself wondering where the 1 million people are. In fact, the population is spread out around the city's periphery, but after spending a few days in the area, you might think the right answer is "at the markets." Shopping draws Thais and travelers alike to Chiang Mai, and its markets are the heart of local activity. This, of course, means more foreigners and slightly higher prices than you'll find elsewhere in the north, but even at these elevated levels, both remain very reasonable. Seven hundred years of history has left a perceptible footprint here that can be felt in the *wats,* religious icons, antiques shops, and ancient structures, such as the remains of the old city walls that still serve, along with the original moat, as the border of the town's heart.

SIGHTS

Chiang Mai, the regional urban center and the largest city in the north, abounds with international flavor, modern conveniences, respectable infrastructure, and well-developed visitor attractions. While these are certainly a comfort to travelers, what makes the city so special is the subtlety with which these have been blended with the rich cultural history, natural beauty, and agrarian way of life that preceded them by so many centuries. Here you can visit mysterious ancient temples, trek through mountainous rainforests, hunt among antiques and a wealth of local products for that perfect memento, indulge in world-class pampering in one of the lavish spas, and then settle in for a sumptuous dinner and fancy cocktails with live music by the river, all in the space of one day. Of course, no one will blame you for setting a more relaxed pace, if you prefer.

Wats

Even the most modest of after-lunch strolls in the streets of Chiang Mai is bound to find you skirting past monks and shielding your eyes as the sun glints off mirrored tiles adorning one of the 300 incredible *wats,* at least as many as sprawling Bangkok claims, that garnish every corner of this city. Cool green meditation gardens, shining pagodas, exotic statues, and Buddha images of every size and description await your exploration with a welcoming vibe unique to the houses of Buddhism. Although you are clearly spoiled for choice, don't assume that sheer volume means these temples are more

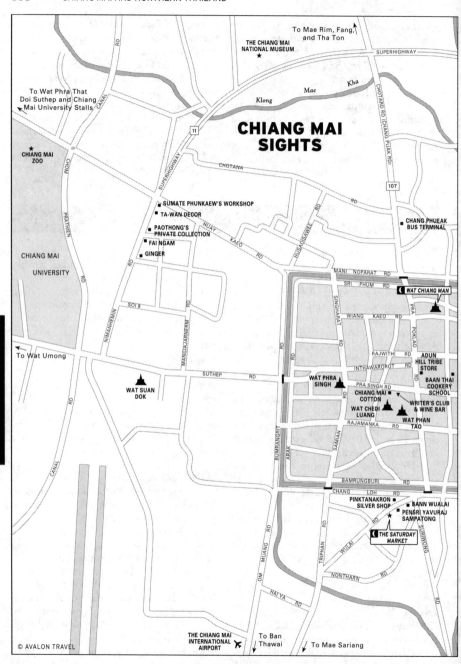

CHIANG MAI

CHIANG MAI SIGHTS

To Mae Rim, Fang, and Tha Ton

THE CHIANG MAI NATIONAL MUSEUM ★

SUPERHIGHWAY

To Wat Phra That Doi Suthep and Chiang Mai University Stalls

Mae   Kha

Klong

RD

CANAL

CHOM

11

SUPERHIGHWAY

CHOTANA

107

★ CHIANG MAI ZOO

PRATHIEN

RD

■ SUMATE PHUNKAEW'S WORKSHOP
■ TA-WAN DECOR
■ PAOTHONG'S PRIVATE COLLECTION
■ FAI NGAM
■ GINGER

HUAY   KAEO   RD

THUSADISAWEE   RD

CHANG PHUEAK BUS TERMINAL ■

CHIANG MAI UNIVERSITY

NIMANHEMIN   RD

SOI 9

MANGKLAJARNERM   RD

RD

MANI NOPARAT   RD
SRI PHUM   RD

SINGHARAT   RD

WIANG   KAEO   RD

♨ WAT CHIANG MAN ▲

PRA

POKLAO

To Wat Umong

SUTHEP   RD

WAT SUAN DOK ▲

RAJWITHI   RD

INTHAWAROROT   RD

RD

WAT PHRA SINGH ▲

PRA SINGH RD

CHIANG MAI COTTON ■
WAT CHEDI LUANG ▲▲
WRITER'S CLUB & WINE BAR
WAT PHAN TAO

ADUN HILL TRIBE STORE ■

BAAN THAI COOKERY SCHOOL ■

RAJAMANKA   RD

BUMRANGRIT   RD

ARAK   RD

SAMIAN   RD

BAMRUNGBURI   RD

CHANG   LOH   RD

PINKTANAKRON SILVER SHOP ■
★ BANN WUALAI
■ PENSRI YAVURAJ SAMPATONG

♨ THE SATURDAY MARKET

OM   RD

MUANG   RD

TRIPHAN   RD

WUTLAI   RD

SURIWONG   RD

NONTHARN   RD

HAIYA   RD

CANAL

THE CHIANG MAI INTERNATIONAL AIRPORT ✈

To Ban Thawai

To Mae Sariang

CHOTARD RD (CHANG PUAK RD)

© AVALON TRAVEL

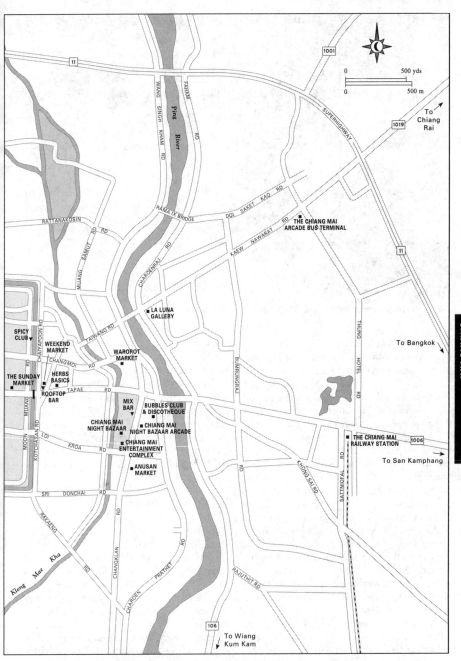

CHIANG MAI

Detailed reliefs adorn many of Chiang Mai's *wats* (temples).

© SUZANNE NAM

or less clones of one another. There is a surprising variety on offer, with some featuring vivid murals, others mysterious relics, and a few even have small museums of Chiang Mai history. Far from being shrouded with indecipherable dharma (rules of Buddhism) guarded by stern, tight-lipped priests, these gleaming compounds often employ displays that seem almost designed to speak to those with no knowledge of the teachings or of the language that they are written in. There are a few that are particularly notable, but wandering into any one that you come across might reveal an arcane tidbit or rewarding cultural experience and leave you feeling just a little bit more enlightened. In addition, Chiang Mai's role as the culture capital of Thailand means that thousands of novice monks from around the country are sent here to serve at the city's *wats,* dotting the streets with their fluorescent orange "learning" robes and shy, bright smiles.

If you want to spend a bit of time checking out the temples, you can cover a few of the best by following a simple route starting at Chiang Mai's oldest temple, **Wat Chiang Man** in the northeast section of the old city, then heading south to **Wat Chedi Luang,** and after that striking out east to hit **Wat Phra Singh, Wat Suan Dok,** and finally **Wat Umong.** While you won't really be able to claim that you've seen all there is to see of Chiang Mai's temples, you will get a nice overview touching on a few things that are really unique and important, and have a pleasant half-day excursion in the process.

◖ WAT CHIANG MAN
วัดเชียงมั่น

Wat Chiang Man (171 Ratchaphakhinai Rd., near Chang Phueak Gate, Si Phum subdistrict) was built in 1297 and is Chiang Mai's first and oldest temple; it is believed that King Mengrai lived here while he was planning and building the city. In fact, a stone tablet found at this site tells the story of the city's founding and was used by historians to place the date of the city's construction. The tablet can still be seen on the outer wall of the ordination hall at the northeast corner of the compound. Chiang Man is an excellent example of a *wat* decorated in the Lanna style, as seen in its red roofs, abundance of red lacquer, liberal use of gold leaf, and multicolored tiles of mirrored glass. One of the best-loved features of this temple is its unusual elephant pagoda, consisting of a bell-shaped *chedi* drenched in gold leaf and supported on a base of plaster elephants facing outward on all sides, which is the oldest structure in the compound. Even more venerable, however, is the *wihan* at the north end of the compound, easily recognized by the particularly beautiful *nagas* (mythical snakes) adorning the stairs and roof and sparkling in mirrored finery. This building houses two very ancient and sacred Buddha images; one is the marble Buddha bas-relief that it's believed was created in Sri Lanka about 2,000 years ago. It has a reputation as having the power to bring rain, and so is paraded around the city during Songkran to protect against drought. The other is the 1,800-year-old crystal Buddha that was relocated from Lopburi and is believed to protect the city against disaster.

WAT CHEDI LUANG
วัดเจดีย์หลวง

South on Phra Pokklao Road at the intersection with Ratchamanka Road is the 600-year-old Wat Chedi Luang (tel. 05/327-8595), also called the Royal Pagoda, as well as a more modern temple in front of it. The ancient *chedi*, with its surrounding elephant statues and *nagas*, looks very old and mysterious, due in part to the fact that it is only partially restored. Built in the 1440s, it was probably the tallest and most impressive of the city's *wats* at one time; no one is quite sure how it was destroyed. Some theories include earthquakes or cannon fire, but since there is no consensus on what it originally looked like, work on putting it back together has never been completed—which only adds to its charm. Chedi Luang is also famous for having once housed the Emerald Buddha that is now on the must-see list of attractions in Bangkok. A jade Buddha now sits in its place here.

A novice monk cleans the steps at one of Chaing Mai's golden *chedis* (pagodas).

© SUZANNE NAM

WAT PHAN TAO
วัดพันเตา

Adjacent to Chedi Luang is a gorgeous old teak building that was once the gilded hall of Chiang Mai's king, Chao Mahawong, who ruled from 1846 to 1854. The *wat* remains one of the more beautiful legacies of the old city. Built entirely of dark wood, supported by pillars and gilded in gold and mirrors, it is tiny but a lovely treasure to explore. Unlike most Lanna temples, where the roof reaches close to the ground, Phan Tao's roof is much taller and steeper, with its inlaid carvings taking the form of water dragons, peacocks, and even a dog. While the 28 large wooden pillars within the temple wholly supported the original building, a stronger foundation has been added to ensure the temple stays standing as it ages. Next to the temple is a huge tree, towering over both Chedi Luang and Phan Tao. Visit at dusk and watch the branches change color in the setting sun, as the temple's lights come on for the evening.

a mural at Wat Chedi Luang

WAT PHRA SINGH
วัดพระสิงห์

On your short trip east to Wat Phra Singh (Singharat Rd. at Ratchadamnoen Rd., tel. 05/381-4164), you'll see many little cafés where you can get iced coffee and snacks or stop for a beer. Visiting the temples requires a fair amount of walking, and it can be uncomfortably hot and sunny in some parts of the compounds, so if you need a pit stop, this area is a good choice. Once you arrive at the *wat,* it's a good idea to take your time, as Phra Singh is one of the more enjoyable temple grounds to stroll around.

What makes this one of the most important of Chiang Mai's 300 temples is the Phra Singh Buddha image for which the *wat* is named. It is located in the *wihan* behind and to the left of the main temple building, although even without the relic, this *wihan* would be enough to put Phra Singh on the map. Its three-tiered roof is a wonderful example of Lanna architecture, and the beautifully detailed gold tracery and carvings found in its gables and veranda

are worth closer inspection. When you head inside you will see the bronze cast **Phra Singh relic,** whose name means "Lion Buddha." This image is the most sacred of all of Chiang Mai's Buddhas and is important because it is a very rare combination of elements from Indian religious art styles with the usual Sukhothai style common for this period. It's thought that Lanna artisans must have seen examples of the Indian style carried by travelers and set about incorporating it into their own works. Looking at the image, you can see that the Buddha is a little plumper than most you'll see, and that he sports a lotus on the top of his head (meant to be a flame). There are only a handful of examples in this genre remaining, and no one is sure which, if any of them, may be the original that inspired the brief Lion Buddha trend. Before you leave the *wihan,* take a moment to enjoy the murals depicting scenes from the Lanna court as it was in the early 1800s, when the paintings were done.

Although completely lacking any historical significance, one fun and quirky feature of Wat

Phra Singh is its rather unique meditation garden, which commands a large section at the rear of the compound. Not only are the shade and an opportunity to sit and relax for a moment a very welcoming prospect, but a stroll along its path yields the tranquil garden backdrop that you might expect, and a little something extra. As you walk around you will notice that a variety of wise sayings have been posted on the trees, and they're even in English. You will find a few that may put a smile on your face, such as "There is no glory for a lazy person, no matter how good-looking" and a few that might leave non-Buddhists a little puzzled, such as "The best revenge is to end revenge." Walking among the trees bearing lessons in this quiet natural setting creates a pleasant vibe that is not difficult to pick up on.

Wat Phra Singh is one of the Chiang Mai temples that supports Monk Chat (another is Wat Suan Dok), a free program designed to provide visitors a chance to better understand what goes on at the *wats,* while giving the monks an opportunity to practice their English. You can ask them any questions that you want, from what it's like to live in a monastery to what the meaning of life is, although they are still working on their English, so they might stumble a little with their answers. For an outsider, it's a great way to see the human side of the saffron-robed monks that we unconsciously tend to give a wide berth; for the most part you will find them to be open and friendly, and by no means above occasionally dissolving into the giggles. If you are a woman, it is important not to touch or offer to shake hands with the monks, even after a chat.

Given its importance to the city, the *wat* is also a focal point for any Buddhist festival in Chiang Mai. Be it Thai new year, Loi Krathong, or the lesser known Magha Puja Day in February, Phra Singh will be filled with Thais, piles of incense, and—of course—food vendors aplenty.

WAT SUAN DOK AND WAT UMONG
วัดสวนดอกและวัดอุโมงค์

If you haven't had your fill of temples by this point, you might want to hire a taxi to get to Wat Suan Dok and Wat Umong, which are both outside the old city walls. **Suan Dok** (tel. 05/327-8967) or Wat Buppharam (วัดบุปผาราม) is located on Suthep Road, west of Suan Dok Gate, and while it does have some interesting history, its claim to a much more eerie feature is what sets it apart. Before Wat Phra That Doi Suthep was built, this temple was home to a very important Buddha relic and was the location of the apparent miracle that inspired the monarchy to build a special *wat* to honor and house the relic (Wat Doi Suthep). The "eerie" attraction here is the unusual aboveground cemetery that is home to the cremated remains of members of Chiang Mai's royal family, a feature found in very few locations around the country. Although this collection of whitewashed monuments might strike you as something you'd expect to see in an old mausoleum back home, walking among them, you see that the style is clearly Thai. The monuments are mostly miniature *chedi* of various sizes and descriptions, and you will notice that people still actively come to the site to pay their respects by laying lotus flowers and other offerings at the markers. Suan Dok is one of the bigger temples in town and currently houses a fairly significant population of novice monks and students. There is also a popular vegetarian restaurant just behind the temple, a favorite with locals and tourists alike.

Wat Umong (Soi Wat Umong, Tambon Suthep, tel. 05/327-3990), or "Tunnel Temple," is a forest temple located near the base of Suthep Mountain, a little off the beaten path. Despite requiring a trip outside the city, it has a well-deserved reputation for being the most unusual temple in Chiang Mai and is well worth the effort to visit. To get here, follow Suthep Road west over the Chonlaprathan Canal, and then pass through a rabbit warren of small roads that make up a small local community. There are signs, but unfortunately not always where you need them, although driving through this community with its tiny shops and houses is interesting in itself. If you're taking a *song thaew,* be sure to ask for Wat Umong Thera Jan—there is another Wat Umong inside the old city. Once you have arrived, you might think that you are in the wrong place because the compound looks nothing like a typical *wat;* what you are looking for is the raised mound with a *chedi* on top, which you will find heading left from the parking area. Wat Umong is basically an artificial mound of dirt crisscrossed with a small network of interconnected tunnels. Legend suggests that the *wat* was built in the late 14th century to accommodate Thera Jan, a monk that was so in touch with the Buddha that he was a bit out of touch with the world around him. The monk was highly revered but had an unfortunate tendency to wander off, so they built the tunnels to make it difficult for him to find his way out, though no one today knows how well it worked.

Wat Umong was abandoned for many years and only came back into use in the 1940s; as a result much of the sprawling grounds are overgrown and well forested, which adds a lot of charm to the site. Simply walking along the tranquil paths and down to its lake while gazing at the flowers and butterflies is quite a treat. People come here to meditate in peace and quiet, and you will probably see the odd acolyte in yoga gear sitting under a tree. After you have explored the tunnels and climbed to the top of the mound to visit the *chedi* and take a few photos, walk around the base of the mound and investigate the outbuildings. As you go, you will see the broken Buddha repository where people leave their old and broken icons and offerings to honor them; the rows of damaged statues create quite an effect. Among the modern buildings next to the mound is a spiritual theater of paintings where local artists have decorated every available surface with murals depicting their contemporary take on Buddhism. Most of these murals are as different as night and day from the usual temple art, and you will see interestingly rendered scenes attempting to portray everything from the peace of meditation to philosophies on race relations in a variety of styles.

OTHER *WATS*

If you have time to take in a few additional *wats* while in Chiang Mai, you're in luck—there

detailing on a *wat* (temple) in Chiang Mai

© SUZANNE NAM

are hundreds of them to choose from. Though they may not be as historically or architecturally relevant as those listed above, if you are in the area, they are worth at least a few minutes of your time.

Wat Jed Yot (วัดเจ็ดยอด, Chiang Mai–Lamphun Rd. at Huay Kaew Rd., between Rte. 1004 and Rte. 107), a few kilometers northwest of the city, is one of the oldest and most historically significant *wats* in Chiang Mai. Built in the 15th century for the World Buddhist Council, the *wat* is loosely based on the Mahabodhi Temple in India, where the Buddha embraced the "middle way," the heart of Buddhist philosophy. The temple is named for its seven peaks, but unfortunately these spires and the rest of the stone structures have not been restored and remain in a state of disrepair. Despite their age and condition, there are still some beautiful sculpted human figures on the buildings worth close inspection.

Just off Tha Phae Road between the moat and the river, at the end of a narrow alley, is one of the city's loveliest unsung *wats*, **Wat Saen**

Fang (Tha Phae Rd., just before Chang Moi Tat Mai Rd., no phone). The Burmese-style *wat* is worth a visit for its elaborately decorated *chedi*, a multileveled white stepped *chedi* leading up to a golden spire. The center of the *chedi* is covered in multicolored tiling, and the three-tiered effect of the combination of white stone, colored tiles, and gold is unique in Chiang Mai. The *wihan* and *ubosot* are both red wooden structures with elaborate painted gold panels.

On the east bank of the Ping River is **Wat Ket Garam** (between Charoenrat Rd. and Na Wat Ket Rd., no phone, museum 9 A.M.–5 P.M. daily, donation), a fascinating *wat* with some interesting features. The most striking, and rarest, is the five-gabled *wihan*. The five-stepped roofs give the illusion that there are five prayer halls in succession instead of just one; this is not something you'll see in any other *wat* in the city or perhaps even in the country. The white *chedi* itself is not particularly interesting, but the small museum in the *wat* complex is worth visiting. There is some Buddhist paraphernalia, but the collection of old photos of Chiang Mai, with subjects both secular and sectarian spanning more than a century, is a real find.

One of the quirkiest *wats* in Chiang Mai is **Wat Wela Wanaram** (Chotana Rd. at Ku Tao Rd., tel. 05/321-1842). Most of the buildings that make up this 17th century complex are not extraordinary, but the *chedi* is a series of five balls that diminish in size as the *chedi* climbs to the sky, representing five Buddhist alms bowls. The *wat* is also known as Wat Ku Tao, which means watermelon *wat,* although many visitors find it looks more like a series of gourds or balls than watermelons. Historians are not sure who built Wat Wela Wanaram or why the *chedi* looks the way it does, as there are no others like it in the country. Some speculate that it was built by Yunnan Chinese, others by Burmese.

The Chiang Mai National Museum
พิพิธภัณฑสถานแห่งชาติเชียงใหม่

The Chiang Mai National Museum (Chiang Mai–Lamphun Rd., tel. 05/322-1308, www.thailandmuseum.com/thaimuseum_eng/chiangmai/main.htm, 9 A.M.–4 P.M. Wed.–Sun., 30B) is the best bet for getting a little bit of background to put your visit to northern Thailand in context. Home to a wonderful collection of ancient jewelry, 14th-century kilns, ancient art and Buddha images, and traditional weaponry, this stylish and well-organized attraction will lead you through the basics of Lanna culture and allow you to see past the modernized towns into the long history of development in the region. On a hot or rainy afternoon, in particular, the museum provides a few very comfortable hours of sightseeing and education. It's not advisable to walk along the superhighway, so get a taxi or *tuk tuk* from the center of town; there should also be a few waiting nearby once you are ready to return.

The museum's facilities were renovated and upgraded for the city's septcentennial in 1996, and you can see this reflected in the well-designed exhibits and displays. As you approach, take a moment to appreciate the architecture of the main building, which is a grandiose reproduction of a traditional Lanna-style house, including a very elaborate example of the classic roof. There are six themes or topics meant to be followed in chronological order, and navigating the museum is made very easy by the visitor-friendly signs and English-language information plaques associated with the displays. Each topic is well organized into its own wing of the building, and as you set out you will pass through the area dedicated to the region's natural and cultural background and earliest history. After that, continue to the period from Chiang Mai's establishment to its capture by the Burmese, and then to the period where Lanna became a part of Siam.

The second floor deals with art and modernization and offers an interesting assortment of ancient farming equipment along with an excellent collection of photographs. The first exhibit is in the north wing and focuses on a brief history of the Lanna Kingdom's trade and economy from the late 1700s to the early 1900s, which marked the beginning of the end for many traditional systems. You will then pass through the section dedicated to the modern way of life along with information on contemporary social, agricultural, and economic management. The final exhibit is one of the best and covers the development of the Lanna art style and the history of art in Thailand. The collection boasts some very ancient and beautiful pieces, such as 14th-century San Kamphaeng ceramics and 15th-century Lanna Buddha images that have made their way here from religious sites and private treasure vaults throughout the region.

ENTERTAINMENT AND EVENTS
Bars

A very popular nightspot among locals and visitors is the atmospheric **Riverside Bar and Restaurant** (9–11 Charoenrat Rd., tel. 05/324-6323, www.theriversidechiangmai.com, 6 p.m.–1 a.m. daily). Scoring big points for ambience, this three-level open-air establishment is all teakwood and lanterns with live music and fairy-tale views overlooking the river and the old city on the other side. On the main level the band, the bar, and the majority of the crowd sets the stage, but you can choose the lower level, right next to the river, or the upper level, with the best view, for a quieter, more intimate setting. The transition from restaurant to bar begins when candlelight and soft instrumental music gives way to up-tempo acoustic and eventually live Western rock and pop all the way until closing time at 1 a.m., with the generally large and welcoming crowd laughing and singing along right until the end. You can order the usual beer and highballs, but a nice selection of wine and cocktails is also available at reasonable prices and can be ordered in small, medium, and large carafes that are perfect for sharing.

Just a short way up the same street is **The Brasserie** (37 Charoenrat Rd., tel. 05/324-1665, 6 p.m.–1 a.m. daily, 150B), which distinguishes itself with live jazz and unique decor. Less crowded and a bit quieter than the Riverside Bar and Restaurant, The Brasserie is also located on the river and has a look all its

own. Gauzy lanterns, lush greenery, and rugged woodwork give this place a funky tropical feel, keeping things fun without sacrificing sophistication. Drinks are a little more expensive here than at the Riverside, but getting to drink them in the soft light cast by paper lanterns shaped like giant mushrooms has a transporting effect that offsets the slight price difference.

For a break from exploring the streets at the night market, the **Chiang Mai Night Bazaar Arcade** (just off of Chang Khlan Rd., north of Loi Khro Rd., 6 p.m.–1 a.m. daily) is a good bet for a quick drink. It's a small section in the heart of the night market where you can choose from a number of little bars that spill out onto the sidewalks and run together, creating a big open area that hums with activity for your casual drink under the stars. There are quite a number of these little places standing side by side on the arcade, and they usually draw a lot of people without being too crowded. There isn't a whole lot of variation between them, so just pick the one that seems to have the best crowd and that is playing music you like.

While it isn't the most trendy for an evening drink, you can relax on the loftlike floor of the **THC Rooftop Bar** (19/4–5 Kotchasarn Rd., tel. 05/320-6886), near Tha Phae Gate. Even though it's a reggae bar, "THC" in this case doesn't stand for the active component in marijuana but rather "Tribal Heritage Conservation." You will find an often-unstaffed hemp shop on the main level as you go in, and after that you start up a steep, narrow staircase on your way to the rooftop bar. About halfway up, you have to take off your shoes; take care not to toss them into what becomes a giant pile of footwear as the night heats up—place them somewhere you can find them, and be careful not to drink so much that finding them and making your way down these slightly scary stairs will be a problem. When you make it to the top, you will find yourself on a rooftop filled with triangle pillows and sitting mats, and packed with character. A popular place for travelers and expats, it is rare to find Thais grabbing a drink here. But the decor—mellow multicolored lanterns and strings of lights, street art done in Day-Glo paint sprawling over the walls, and not a chair in sight—makes for a fun (if not bizarre) experience. With open beams instead of windows, you can gaze out at Suthep Mountain, with Wat Doi Suthep shining over the city during the day, and the golden electric glow of Tha Phae Gate in the evening. The atmosphere is friendly, and with tables placed so close to each other, it's a good place to meet people. There is no cover charge, and drinks are fairly inexpensive; you can order cocktails by the bucket if you're up to it.

More refined options include the generally subdued and inexpensive **Writer's Club & Wine Bar** (141/3 Ratchadamnoen Rd., tel. 05/381-4187, noon–midnight Sun.–Fri.), where you can order basic cocktails, exotic imported beers, and carafes of wine with your cheap but tasty plate of traditional Thai snacks. The name sounds a bit pretentious, but in reality the mood is friendly and the venue quieter and calmer than most places in its price range, although the decor is fairly plain except for the small outdoor seating area.

Cocktail and wine bars can be found at some of the upscale hotels, including The Dusit D2, a very plush hotel under the Dusit Hotels and Resorts umbrella, which boasts one of Chiang Mai's trendiest nightspots. The **Mix Bar** (DusitD2 Hotel, 100 Chan Klan Rd., tel. 05/399-9999, 6 P.M.–1 A.M. daily), located in its lobby, mixes cocktails and some very creative martinis, which are served alongside light snacks. Billing itself as "defying all style genres," the mood is sort of ultramodern lounge with an open floor plan, soft imaginative lighting, and an eclectic mix of furniture. It's the place to sip a lemongrass-and-ginger martini while breaking in any chic new fashion pieces you've picked up in the city's high-end boutiques.

For a laid-back feel in a modern, comfortable setting, look no farther than **The 2nd Floor Gallery & Cafe** (43 Ratwithi Rd. at Ratchaphakhinai Rd., tel. 08/9167-6798, 8 P.M.–midnight daily). With plenty of couches, an outdoor terrace, and strong cocktails, the newly opened bar is becoming a popular place with expats for a drink or two. The bar also offers free salsa lessons starting at 8 P.M. on Thursday, drawing quite a diverse and lively crowd. True to its name, the top floor also houses a gallery with a rotating set of various photography or art exhibitions.

Almost every town has an Irish pub, and Chiang Mai is no exception. Popular with the expat crowd for its Guinness beer, football matches, and Thursday Quiz nights (they turn off the Wi-Fi so no one can cheat), **The UN Irish Pub** (24/1 Ratwithi Rd., tel. 05/321-4554) is an option for those wanting a low-key evening to catch up on sports with a pint of beer.

A sleek new bar in the Nimmanhemin area, **The Y Bar Wine Bar** (44/1 Nimmanhemin Rd., tel. 05/328-9313) has a lengthy wine list and a loyal customer base among Thais from Chiang Mai and Bangkok alike. With modern tables and booths and a lounge-like atmosphere, this wine bar feels like a slice of New York City in the middle of Chiang Mai.

Nightclubs

Though not as lively as Bangkok's club scene, Chiang Mai does have its share of fun nightclubs to choose from. One of the best is **The North Gate Jazz Co-op** (9–95/1–2, Sri Phum Rd., tel. 08/1765-5246, 10 P.M.–1 A.M. daily), popular with locals and expats alike. The North Gate has a wide variety of live performances and impromptu jam session and is often so busy that the crowd spills onto the street. A thorough drink menu with wine and cocktails is on offer; show up on the early side to snag a seat before the music takes over.

Warm Up (40 Nimmanhemin Rd., tel. 05/340-0676), a crowded dance floor lined with different DJs to choose from, is a favorite on trendy Nimmanhemin Road that has something for everyone. Many young Thais come to see live bands or their current DJ faves, while expats who want to get away from the backpacking crowd have no trouble dancing their night away. It is open quite late, and is usually the second stop in a club-hopping evening.

Hugely popular with the backpacking and expat crowd is nighttime hotspot **Zoe in Yellow** (48/4–5 Ratwithi Rd., tel. 08/3762-0446, 7 P.M.–late). Cut off from traffic and set away from the street, Zoe's two cheery, yellow-painted bars face each other, one enclosed and boasting a nightly DJ spinning jazz, blues, and hip-hop, the other spinning music from an open-air table-filled lawn, replete with a fire-thrower and buckets by the dozen. It is certainly not a quiet evening in Chiang Mai, but well worth taking a look if you are interested in an entirely different vibe in the old city.

If it's after 1 A.M. and you're just not ready to stumble back to your hotel, you can head over to **Spicy Club** (82 Chaiyaphum Rd., tel. 05/323-4860, 7 P.M.–late daily, no cover), alongside the moat and opposite Somport Market. Somewhere between a bar and a nightclub, it does have a bit of dancing and not a whole lot else to recommend it. It is however where everybody in Chiang Mai goes for a late-night, or early-morning, drink, and it's the only place that is open after 1 A.M. It's dark and usually crowded; most people arrive here already intoxicated, and young locals dominate the scene. Drinks are cheap, and the music runs a fairly broad spectrum, so if you feel like the night is still young and everything seems to be closed, do what everyone else does and head to Spicy.

Festivals and Events

Chiang Mai is home to a handful of fun and festive events throughout the year, the most popular being the celebration of the national New Year holiday, Songkran. Timing for all of these events varies from year to year; make sure to check with the Tourism Authority of Thailand (www.tourismthailand.org) for specific dates.

Coinciding with the tourism high season, in late December–early January the city hosts a **Cool Season Fair** in the area surrounding the Tha Phae Gate. During this time the year-round market atmosphere becomes even more intense, and the number of food and handicraft vendors grows exponentially.

The **Flower Festival,** held in early February, is a three-day event with a flower show and a parade where you'll see elaborately and colorfully decorated floats making their way through the city. In addition to the flowers, there are live-music performances, dance performances, and plenty of eating and shopping.

Songkran, the celebration of Thai New Year in mid-April, gets particularly intense in Chiang Mai. Here, instead of the normal three days, the city has stretched it out to five days of water-soaked celebrations. Thais line the city's moat on both sides, dousing passersby with buckets of water if they dare slow down, taken from the moat itself by lowering the bucket down to the water with a strong piece of twine. And inside the old city's walls, wide streets come to a standstill, bottlenecked by hundreds of people with water guns and ice water ready for attack.

Loi Krathong, celebrated in late October or early November, is perhaps the country's most beautiful holiday, made even more visually stunning in Chiang Mai. On Loi Krathong everyone buys or makes a *krathong*—a small float made from deep green banana leaves and covered with flowers and candles—and sets it free onto the river in the evening, resulting in thousands of lighted floats on the water. In Chiang Mai, they also launch large translucent-paper hot-air balloons that light up the skies. The festival, with roots in Hinduism and Buddhism, has taken on additional meaning in modern times. The release of the *krathong* symbolizes letting go of anger, grudges, and bad luck, and the atmosphere during this holiday is particularly cheerful and friendly. Tradition dictates that you put a lock of your hair into the moat and think of all the anger and negativity you want to let go before setting your *krathong* into the water and watching it float away.

SHOPPING

It has been said that visitors to Thailand should wait until they get to Chiang Mai to do their shopping, and with good reason. Considered one of the major traditional art centers of Asia and well known for its enticing bargains,

Chiang Mai is a favorite shopping destination for Thais, travelers, and even international dealers. From street stalls to upscale art and antiques dealers, you'll find silks, silver, ceramics, lacquerware, clothing, interior decor, art, rattan, and, of course, all of those little souvenir knickknacks for the people back home. Many high-quality items are available, but cheaply made goods and fakes are also easy to find, so examine the products carefully. Shoppers looking just to take home some handcrafted housewares and accessories are really in luck, as prices for these items are generally very reasonable and the quality high. If you've bought too much, don't worry. You'll also have no trouble finding extra suitcases and even shipping services to help you get that meter-tall wooden elephant carving home. For some guidance, also pick up the latest copy of *Art & Culture–Lanna,* a free magazine distributed to some of the more popular shops in town (including Black Canyon Coffee and WaWee Coffee on Ratchadamnoen Rd.) and at the Thai Airways kiosk at the airport. Updated monthly, the magazine has great up-to-date information about specialty shops, antiques, and handicrafts.

Shopping Malls

For basic Western amenities, department stores, and export stores (for people who are too tall for standard Thai sizes), two main malls will provide the needed retail therapy. **Kad Suan Kaew** (21 Huay Kaew Rd., tel. 05/322-44441 10 A.M.–9 P.M. daily) has a Western-style supermarket and bakery, a large department store, and plenty of mobile and electronics kiosks. Thursday–Saturday nights, a small market, *Kad Sum Murd* ("Midnight Market"), sets up on the stairs to the mall, offering scarves, clothes, and accessories as well as some quick bites to eat until midnight. A sister mall, **Central Airport Plaza** (2 Mahidol Rd., tel. 05/399-9199, 11 A.M.–10 P.M. Mon.–Fri., 9:30 A.M.–10 P.M. Sat.–Sun.), has a large Robinsons department store, smaller cosmetic stores, and hair salons along with all the usual electronics kiosks expected in a mall of that size.

Clothing and Fabrics

For stunning silk and cotton togs, don't miss world-class designer Sumate Phunkaew's workshop **Classic Model** (95/2 Nimmanhemin Rd., tel. 05/321-6810, 10 A.M.–6 P.M. daily). Although his fashions are displayed in Bangkok, Chiang Mai is his home, and Sumate's work is avant-garde, imaginative, and quite Thai in flavor, allowing you to find something that's both chic and totally unavailable back home.

A wonderful collection in an exciting array of fabrics can be found at Ajarn Paothong's breathtaking shop named, quite simply, **Paothong's Private Collection** (4 Nimmanhemin Soi 1, tel. 05/321-7715, 10 A.M.–5 P.M. Tues.–Sun.). As well as showcasing Paothong's exceptional designs, this three-story Chinese-style house also displays a variety of interesting artifacts and pieces from his collection of vintage fabrics, all of which inspire his work.

An incredible array of clothing, textiles, and other works from Chiang Mai and beyond can be found in **Northern Village** (2 Mahidol Rd., tel. 05/399-9199, northern_village@centraplaza.co.th, 10 A.M.–8 P.M. daily), taking up several floors at the large Airport Plaza mall. Featuring small boutique shops within the larger store, including shops by well-known designers such as Classic Model, the store is a good place to find all the gifts or handiwork you've missed if you're about to leave Chiang Mai.

For beautiful ecofriendly textiles, visit **Studio Naenna** (22 Soi 1 Nimmanhemin Rd., tel. 05/389-5136, www.studio-naenna.com), owned and operated by art historian Patricia Cheeseman, an expert on Thai and Lao art. Open daily, her studio uses 100 percent natural dyes, and all of the cotton, silk, ikat, and ecotextiles are dyed by hand.

Chiang Mai Cotton (141/6 Ratchadamnoen Rd., tel. 05/381-4413, www.chiangmaicotton.com) is a chic boutique selling goods made from exquisite cotton in many styles of tops, pants, skirts, and dresses. They also carry accessories and jewelry. If you want to order large quantities wholesale, they are equipped to export, and you can create your own styles. There are also locations at the Kalare Night Bazaar

SONGKRAN FESTIVAL IN CHIANG MAI

If you are lucky enough to be visiting Chiang Mai in mid-April, you will find yourself in the best location in Thailand to enjoy the raucous fun of the ancient festival Songkran. Originally the new year's celebration of the Tai people, Songkran is older than Thailand itself and is considered a time to honor family, community, and religion, and to show respect for water, the most important element in the agricultural lifestyle of so many people of the region.

Despite such a noble pedigree, the festival is probably most famous for its reputation as a giant three-day nationwide water fight. Visitors can expect to find themselves right in the middle of three full days of ritual merrymaking and celebration. The spectacle of people participating in the antiquated Songkran rituals is not to be missed, but do not get your hair done in the days leading up to the festival – simply leaving your hotel room guarantees that you are going to get very wet. The water fight is a sort of natural extension of the bathing ceremonies at the heart of the Songkran meritmaking rituals, and you will see this theme on all three days of the festivities.

The first day, Maha Songkran, symbolizes the end of the old year and usually falls on April 13; if you sleep late, don't be alarmed by the crack of explosions beginning early in morning – it is simply the local people lighting firecrackers in an attempt to chase off the bad luck of the previous year. In Chiang Mai there is a procession of floats and Buddha images beginning at Naowarat Bridge and winding its way to Wat Phra Singh. People will usually also clean their homes, bathe, and wear new clothes on this day.

Wan Nao or Wan Da is Preparation Day, the second day of the festival. People will set to work preparing a variety of offerings to honor Lord Buddha. Head to the Ping River in the afternoon to see people gathering sand to be used to build sand stupas, which will be richly decorated with colorful flags and flowers and presented to Lord Buddha at the temples later that day.

Day three, Wan Phaya Wan or Wan Taleung Sok, is the actual first day of the new year. Go to the temples to see offerings of food and other gifts made to the monks, and the Tan Kan Kao, the honoring of elders and late ancestors with offerings of food and good wishes. This is followed by the unusual ritual of using sticks and branches to prop up Sri Maha Bodhi trees, made famous for their reputation as the tree that Buddha was sitting under at

(Room D146) and the new Northern Village at the airport (Room 012A, 1st Fl.).

Antique and contemporary textiles, including beautiful, rich textiles from local ethnic groups, can be found at the delightful **Pa Ker Yaw** (180/184 Loi Kroh Rd., tel. 05/327-5491, Mon.–Sat.), owned by Ms. Thongdeelert and her sister. Close to the night bazaar, it provides an ideal place to pick up souvenirs if the stalls at the markets have been disappointing.

The **Hilltribe Products Promotion Center** (21/17 Suthep Rd., beside Wat Suan Dok, tel. 05/327-7743) cobbles together the best of crafts from royally sponsored projects throughout northern Thailand, including products from Akha, Karen, Yao, Lisu, and Hmong communities. Profits are dedicated to funding art and handicraft courses within these communities, and the center has a cross-section of fabrics and household products made using textiles from the region.

Arts and Handicrafts

If it's art you're looking for, **La Luna Gallery** (190 Charoenrat Rd., tel. 05/330-6678, www.lalunagallery.com) has two floors of Thai, Burmese, and Malaysian contemporary works available for purchase. Not limited to paintings, they also sell an abundance of furniture and ceramics in a wide range of styles and prices. With the size of this collection, it's handy that their website includes a the moment he became enlightened. Weave your way through the crowds and simply take in the kaleidoscope of activity as people continue to make merit by setting captive birds and fish free and by bathing Buddha images with sweetly scented water. The young will also bathe the hands of their elders and ask forgiveness for past misdeeds in the Rot Nam Dam Hua ritual. There will be a procession of dancers in traditional costume and beautifully arranged flowers in which water is poured on respected monks and high-ranking government officials. Unique to the northern provinces, the stupas containing the ashes of ancestors will also be bathed in order to pay respect and receive forgiveness.

The festival is set in April as a result of a meeting of the Tais' rich agricultural identity with the importance of rice sowing and harvesting cycles to their daily lives, and the strong astrological associations that Buddhism inherited from Brahman India. The Tais originally placed Songkran in late November, a time of harvest in southern China where they lived. As they migrated south into what is now Thailand, these cycles were adapted to the warmer, more tropical climate, although there are a handful of rural people who keep with tradition and still celebrate Songkran in November. As Buddhism captured the hearts of the Tai people, auspicious movements of the heavenly bodies that coincided with the April harvest were discovered and also played a role in setting the date. In fact, the term *songkran* means "a move or change in the position of the sun from Aries to Taurus." Even today the position of the sun and the phase of the moon still give the last word on what exact date Songkran falls; it may occur anywhere between April 10 and 18, although the buzz of excitement precedes the event for days.

If you're in Chiang Mai or any part of Thailand during this period, stores and shops will be closed, and at the height of the festival it may appear that order has completely broken down. The streets will be teeming with people of all ages toting high-pressure water guns and buckets of water. You'll even see kids piled into pickup trucks acting as mobile watering units complete with 40-liter drums of sometimes icy water. And no one will shy away from dousing you just because you are a foreigner. Locals take precautions such as stashing their mobile phones in ziplock bags, and you probably should too.

comprehensive catalog of what's available for those can't afford to spend hours wandering around the large gallery.

For fun, funky jewelry design and unique T-shirts and clothing (including Western sizes), look no farther than **Nok 'Em Ded Designs** (162/5 Phra Pokklao Rd., opposite Wat Chedi Luang, tel. 08/7034-4067, www.nokemded. com).

Recently moved to an expanded space on Loi Kroh Road opposite the Yeti Tibetan and Nepali Arts gallery,, **Rare-Earth Tribal Art** (35 Loi Kroh Rd., tel. 08/7179-2880, rarearth-art@gmail.com), has a thorough collection of old textiles, ethnic costumes, ancient beads, silver ornaments, and other sundry objects of beauty, each handpicked by Rare-Earth's owner, Chris.

Centrally located on Tha Phae Road, **Kesorn Arts** (154/156 Tha Phae Rd., tel. 05/387-4325, hilltribeasia@hotmail.com) specializes in arts, beads and textiles from local ethnic groups and has a large selection of fabrics and weavings from local communities in northern Thailand and abroad. The shop is packed from floor to ceiling, so beware: You might lose a good part of your day poring over the many beautiful handicrafts Kesorn has on offer.

Ta-Wan Decor (1 Nimmanhemin Rd., tel. 05/389-4941, tawan76@hotmail.com, 10 A.M.–9 P.M. daily) features an interesting assortment of unique home-design items made

© SUZANNE NAM

Chiang Mai abounds with handmade goods.

from mango wood that is smoked and then dyed; pieces are accented with threads of native fibers in stylish designs. This one-of-a-kind technique won't be found in the markets or in any of your favorite shops back home. There are plenty of photo frames, gift boxes, and wooden handicrafts to choose from in this fun shop.

For a sustainable project to benefit the Pwo Karen people in the Sop Moei district of Mae Hong Son Province, visit **Sop Moei Arts** (150/10 Charoenrat Rd., tel. 05/321-2935, www.sopmoeiarts.com). The store has English-speaking staff and carries a variety of handicrafts, including large baskets, wall hangings, and beautiful textiles. Beginning as a public health project financed by the Swedish International Development Agency in 1977, Sop Moei Arts now operates income-generating initiatives such as textile-weaving and basket-making in several villages in the Chiang Mai area.

Loi Khro Road, which leads up to the night market, has a string of woodcarving, sculpture, "antiques," and textile shops. Many do

wholesale as well. Alongside them are street-side massage parlors, if you want to take a break, and a couple of shops worth noting. Newcomer **Sangdee Gallery** (5 Sirimankalajan Soi 5, tel. 05/389-4955, www.sangdee.org) is a nonprofit gallery devoted to showcasing up-and-coming Thai artists as well as hosting international talent. The gallery often has a variety of film screenings (*sangdee* is Thai for "good light") and also hosts filmmaking and design workshops on weekends. Check their website for an updated calendar of events.

Beauty Products

Herbs Basics (172 Phra Pokklao Rd. at Ratchadamnoen Rd., tel. 05/341-8289, www.herbbasicschiangmai.com, 9 A.M.–6 P.M. Mon.–Sat., 2–9 P.M. Sun.) offers chic high-end toiletries and spa-beauty products at surprisingly reasonable prices. The number of scents is practically endless, and you can cut your own soap bar for 0.50B per gram. They also sell things in multiple sizes, which is great for traveling; many products are priced at 50B or 100B. Don't miss their peppermint herbal body scrub, and for those with sensitive skin, their glycerin soap (the vanilla is a particularly nice one). They have many accessories as well and will make up a gift package for you—wrapping is free.

Markets

Market shopping in Chiang Mai is like no other part of the country. If you decide to hit all the markets in the area, you'll need at least a few solid days to see everything on offer.

CHIANG MAI NIGHT BAZAAR
เชียงใหม่ไนท์บาซาร์

The best known of Chiang Mai's markets, the Night Bazaar is a kaleidoscope of color, activity, and bargains. Located right in the heart of the city on Chang Khlan Road, hemmed in by Chiang Mai Road to the north and Loi Khro Road on the south, the market begins to stir in the early evening and hums until midnight daily. You can go into the actual three-story Night Bazaar building, or simply prowl the little shops that pour out all over the road. A must-see for most visitors, shoppers will delight in the sheer number of heavily laden street stalls displaying all kinds of woodcrafts, paintings, textiles, jewelry, clothing, ceramics, and much, much more. Even nonshoppers will enjoy the amazing congregation of people from all over Thailand and the rest of the world, not to mention the many little spots to stop for a snack or a beer, perfect for watching the commotion in relative comfort. If you're a discerning shopper, you will find lots of cheap crafts and knockoffs. Better to continue on to the pleasant and spacious **Anusan Market,** or the pavilion housing **Galare Bazaar-Food and Shopping Center** in the center of the bazaar, where you can find higher-quality goods, or do as the trendy visiting Thais do and schedule your visit around the weekend markets.

THE SUNDAY WALKING STREET MARKET
ถนนคนเดิน

The Sunday Market (Ratchadamnoen Rd., 2–10 P.M. Sun.) is one of the bazaars that has made Chiang Mai famous among travelers, and this is definitely a gaze-and-saunter experience. While the main market stretches the length of Ratchadamnoen Road, it has expanded onto all of the surrounding side streets. Many come here from around the region to sell their goods, which include everything from cute silk-screened T-shirts to handwoven baskets, key chains, elaborate jewelry, and wrought-iron sculptures. You will also see shops around town with stands, and there is original artwork as well. It's a great place for small gifts, although it can be difficult to make decisions, as there is so much to choose from. Massage stands offer hour-long foot or back massages for 120B, and each of the *wats* lining Ratchadamnoen are filled with food vendors selling grilled pork, noodles and soups, and even roasted crickets. It is hugely popular with travelers from within the country, and many weekenders from Bangkok pack the streets, hoping for a bargain. Bring your wallet as well as your appetite—there is enticing street food all around.

◖ THE SATURDAY MARKET
ถนนคนเดิน

More relaxed and less spread out than the Sunday market but gaining popularity by the week is the Saturday Market (Wualai Rd., 5:30–10:30 P.M. or later Sat.). It has many small producers selling their wares, including sandals made from local plants, silk scarves, and wood carvings, most of whom will bring their wares to the walking street the next day. Although there's plenty of inexpensive stuff to lug back home, some of the pieces are definitely of higher quality. Bargaining is expected, but the prices are already very reasonable because of the competition. This market is often the favorite of the repeat visitors to Chiang Mai, and locals will typically recommend it as the best of its kind in the city.

WEEKEND MARKET
ตลาดนัด

Selling similar goods, but a bit quieter and more relaxed, is the Weekend Market (3 P.M.–midnight Sun.) just outside the Tha Phae Gate.

Prices here are often better than at the Night Bazaar, and although there is less to choose from, the market is a bit more open and less claustrophobic. Often vendors are easier to bargain with toward the end of the evening. And, of course, you will find local food, cafés, and places to refresh yourself with an icy beer should the shopping become too much, in addition to the Sunday Walking Street's many temples, filled with cheap Thai food and fresh juice.

WAROROT MARKET
ตลาดวโรรส

If you want to have a day out for your senses rather than for your pocketbook, consider spending some time in one of the more traditional markets. Warorot Market (7 A.M.–4 P.M. daily), between Chang Moi Tat Mai Road and the Ping River, offers a feast of brightly colored fabrics, flowers, fresh food, and traditional medicines; stroll among the vendors and simply take in the sounds, sights, and aromas of a traditional Thai market. Many of the shops lining the old city buy their wares in bulk at Warorot, so if you have found an item you want to take home as a souvenir, you're best bargaining for it here. Don't forget to keep an eye out for things you've never seen before and for that perfect photograph. The market takes up several chaotic buildings near the Ping River, with the flower market facing the river itself and fruit and vegetable sellers in the tiny snaking alleyways between Chang Moi and Praisani Roads. The flower market is a separate beast altogether, with multicolored blooms lining the entire edge of the Ping River's near Warorot. Inside the buildings, lower floors sell housewares, kitchen accessories, and in the center of the floor, piles of northern Thai sausage, dried fruit and nuts, and bamboo filled with sweet sticky rice. Upper floors house textiles and *longyi* from Burma, northern Thai weavings, and practicalities like jeans, everyday clothes, and backpacks or bags.

Antiques

With 700 years of history and an entire kingdom gone to dust under its feet, it's no surprise that Chiang Mai is considered an antiquing hot spot. You can find everything from ancient Buddha images and other religious relics to timeworn opium paraphernalia and antique jewelry laid out for you in high-class shops and portable street stalls. While it is possible to pick up something truly special for a song, you need a practiced eye to avoid the fakes and illegal items that are sometimes sold at the markets. Genuine pieces should come with a certificate from the National Fine Arts Department, but it's important to note that no sacred Buddha images (as opposed to reproductions), new or antique, can be legally removed from Thailand without obtaining permission. All images created for a specific religious purpose fall under this category, despite what dealers may tell you.

There are a handful of dealers along Tha Phae Road, and there are some reputable shops on the upper level of the Night Bazaar, but by far the best selection and best prices will be found at Ban Thawai. Even window-shoppers will enjoy gazing at the broad selection of antique pieces and simply wondering at their past. There's furniture, farm tools, glass, stone and wood carvings, and statues in bronze, brass, copper, pewter, and porcelain—even if you are not a collector, there is a good chance that you will find something to capture your imagination.

Another good option for antique finds is **Vila Cini** (30/34 Charoenrat E Rd., tel. 05/324-6246, enquiries@vilacini.com), set in an old teak house on the Ping River. In addition to beautiful old teak pieces, the store has a sophisticated collection of silks, which can be purchased by the meter.

Chilli Antiques & Arts (Night Bazaar, 2nd Fl., Rooms 25–28, tel. 05/381-8475, 7–11 P.M. daily) has been in business for over two decades, and with four branches in Thailand (including one at the Mandarin Oriental Hotel) it is a reliable choice for authentic antiques of superior quality—with a price point to match. They also manufacture replicas to order, including bronze figures or wooden statues from current collections. It is not for those on a budget. A larger store is accessible from Hang Dong; call 05/343-2281 for more information.

RECREATION
Thai Cooking Schools

The popularity of Thai culinary classes is well earned not only because they can be a lot of fun and are a great place to meet people but because of the undeniable appeal of being able to go home and create savory mementos to remind you of your trip and wow your friends. Chiang Mai has an impressive concentration of cooking courses available both inside the city and in outlying areas, and although not all are created equal, many of them are very well put together. The best classes offer not only cooking instruction but also a trip to a local wet market to select ingredients. It's almost worth the tuition simply to go to a market with a local person and have them finally explain some of that strange-looking Thai produce to you, as well as how to go about choosing the best specimens among them. Fees also generally include all the menu expenses, a lift to and

from your hotel, a Thai cookbook that you can keep, and, of course, lunch—once you are finished stirring, chopping, and simmering, you'll be able to sit down and judge your creations for yourself. Since many of the schools offer small classes, it's important to book your lesson at least a couple of days in advance.

With its handy location right in town near the Tha Phae Gate, **Baan Thai Cookery School** (11 Ratchadamnoen Soi 5, tel. 05/335-7339, www.baanthaicookery.com, morning class 900B, evening class 700B) runs classes each day of the week, keeping them to intimate groups of 6–10 students and setting a friendly and casual atmosphere. The classes each take up most of the day and teach a variety of menus featuring classic Thai favorites. As of this year, evening classes are available as well, running four hours instead of seven. The classes include basics like making the different curry pastes and important Thai sauces, and a highly enlightening trip to the local market to pick up the ingredients for the day's cooking. And if, two months later, you find yourself

© SUZANNE NAM

khao soi, the region's signature dish

stuck trying to remember the correct method for crushing coriander or braising bamboo shoots, you can take advantage of their offer of free lifetime Thai cooking support by email; of course you'll need to give them a couple of days to get back to you, so if necessary, make sure to contact them well before that fancy Thai dinner party.

Newcomer **Basil Cookery School** (22/4 Soi 5 Siri Mangkalajarn Rd., tel. 08/9557-9992, www.basilcookery.com, 1,000B) also brings you to the local markets for preclass shopping but has received rave reviews for its smaller class size of 1–6 students. Choose from morning or evening classes, each led by the lively Boom and teaching a full seven dishes—and be sure to leave room for all of the delicious food.

Chiang Mai Thai Cookery School (47/2 Moon Muang Rd., tel. 05/320-6388, www.thaicookeryschool.com, one-day course 1,450B) is one of the most popular cooking schools in the region and offers 1–5-day group courses in traditional Thai cuisine as well as individual training for more accomplished chefs and a homestay option if you prefer to intensify your experience. If you take the full week of classes, you'll learn everything from making your own curry paste to traditional fruit-carving techniques in addition to instruction on how to create Thai dishes such as pad thai and *tom yam kung.*

If you prefer organic ingredients, the **Thai Farm Cooking School** (2/2 Ratchadamnoen Rd. Soi 5, tel. 07/174-9285, www.thaifarmcooking.net, one-day course 900B) offers lessons on their organic farm just outside the city. Although you'll select some of your ingredients from the local market, you'll also get to tour the farm and see how local vegetables and herbs are grown. The full-day course will have you preparing at least four dishes, and all of the instruction is hands-on. The price includes transportation to and from the farm.

Spas

Chiang Mai has scores of day spas and massage parlors if you're looking to relax sore muscles after some hiking or just indulge after some shopping. You'll find a good selection across price ranges, and except for the absolute top end, you'll find services in general to be less expensive than in Bangkok. If you're just looking for a basic massage at one of the many small massage parlors, expect to pay 200–400B for an hour. If you want a real spa, a 60–90-minute massage will cost 600B and up. Hours vary; call for an appointment at the following establishments.

Cheeva Spa (4/2 Hussadhisawee Rd., tel. 05/340-5129 or 08/1961-0578, www.cheevaspa.com), is on the higher end of the spa spectrum (600B for an hour of Thai massage) but offers a true Lanna spa experience, with carefully decorated teak rooms and thoughtful service. Certified by Chiang Mai Province and a recipient of the Thai Lanna Award for their expertise, they offer body massages, treatments, or spa packages (from 1,300B). While the spa might be set away from the old city, it is worth the trip out, and they offer free transportation from inside the moat's walls if you call ahead of time for an appointment.

Spa Mantra (30/11 Chareun Suk Rd., tel. 05/322-6655, www.spamantra.com) is another good mid-price day spa. Treatments get creative and often seem to involve food products—there are yogurt, wine, coffee, sesame, and rice treatments—but if you're not up for a scrubbing or a detox treatment, the basic massages are good too. The exterior of this spa is not particularly stunning, but the treatment rooms themselves are nicely decorated.

Sinativa Spa Club (22/1 Nimmanhemin Soi 9, tel. 05/321-7928, www.sinativaspaclub.com) is in a wooden house off of Nimmanhemin Road and offers plenty of typical spa treatments, including facials, scrubs, wraps, and, of course, massage. Although the spa is not amazingly fancy, the setting is relaxing and tranquil, and the treatments are reasonably priced. They also offer pickup and drop-off from your hotel if it's too far on foot.

For a slightly more medical approach, the **RarinJinda Wellness Spa and Resort** (14 Charoenrat Rd., tel. 05/324-7000) offers treatments in their modern spa-resort near the river. The focus here is on wellness, but if you just want a massage or scrub, they will happily oblige. The spa has received awards for Best Day Spa in Thailand (2009 Asia Spa and Wellness Festival) and Best Destination Spa (2009 Thailand Tourism Awards), and it has received rave reviews from travelers and expats alike.

Mungkala Traditional Medicine Clinic (21 Ratchamanka Rd., tel. 05/327-8494, http://mungkala.com) uses Eastern medicine to focus on wellness and balance. With acupuncture, massage, or traditional Chinese medicine consultations, the clinic is set in a quiet garden off of Ratchamanka Road and is certified by the Thai government for its treatments. Dr. Rungrat's acupuncture sessions (at only 500B each) have helped many an injured expat in town.

At the top end are the **Four Seasons Spa** (Mae Rim–Samoeng Rd., tel. 05/329-8181, www.fourseasons.com) and the **Dheva Spa** (51/4 Chiang Mai–San Kamphaeng Rd., tel. 05/388-8888, www.mandarinoriental.com/chiangmai/spa) at the Dhara Dhevi Mandarin Oriental. The Dheva is particularly striking—the spa grounds are on a recreated temple, and all of the private treatment rooms are large and luxurious. Both have won international recognition for their services and decor and are priced accordingly.

If you'd like to learn massage instead of getting one, the **Thai Massage School of Chiang Mai** (203/6 Mae Jo Rd., Mu 6, T. Fa Ham, tel. 05/385-4330, www.tmcschool.com) and the **Thai Massage School** (238/8 Wualai Rd., tel. 05/320-1663, www.thaimassageschool.ac.th) offer one-week and longer courses. Although these are very well priced (less than 10,000B for a full two-week course), both are professionally run programs with classroom and hands-on components. They are designed for local and foreign massage therapists and those just interested in learning Thai massage techniques. In addition, the new **Chiang Mai Spa Academy** (68 Chiang Mai–Lamphun Rd., tel. 05/324-1074, www.cmspaacademy.com), on the Ping River, offers government-certified courses in Thai and Swedish massage, hot stone massage, foot reflexology, and beauty treatments.

Hiking and Climbing

As Chiang Mai attracts more expats, its climbing and hiking scene becomes more diverse. A quick climb of Doi Suthep will get those leg muscles warmed up, but other options exist in the surrounding area. For starters, the **Chiang Mai Hiking Club** (chiangmaihiking@gmail.com) organizes occasional hikes in the nearby foothills. If you enjoy rock climbing, Chiang Mai has become a new hub for climbing with the success of the **Chiang Mai Rock Climbing Adventures and Bouldering Club** (55/3 Ratchaphakhinai Rd., tel. 05/320-7102, www.thailandclimbing.com), cofounded by the 2002 winner of the Thai National Rock Climbing championships. Climbing enthusiasts, companies, and schools have all done day trips with great success. Their website provides thorough background to the club and its offerings as well as options for day trips or lessons. The club also offers free climbing for beginners 5–8 P.M. the first Tuesday of each month. In addition, kids under 12 can climb free 1–5 P.M. the third Saturday of each month, and Ladies Night free climbing for women is 5–8 P.M. the second Thursday of each month.

ACCOMMODATIONS

A hugely popular tourist town for both local and international visitors, Chiang Mai is full of places to sleep. Inexpensive guesthouses geared toward backpackers and large, sterile hotels once dominated the scene, but increasingly there are excellent small mid-range hotels available for those who want to enjoy some of the charms of the city without having to rough it, as well as some amazing resorts just outside the city. If you're picky about where you stay and don't want to be bothered by touts or have to carry your bags around as you hunt for a place to stay, book ahead. Even the most inexpensive guesthouses usually have websites, making it simple to inquire about availability and make a reservation before you arrive. If you are coming during high season in December–January,

CHIANG MAI

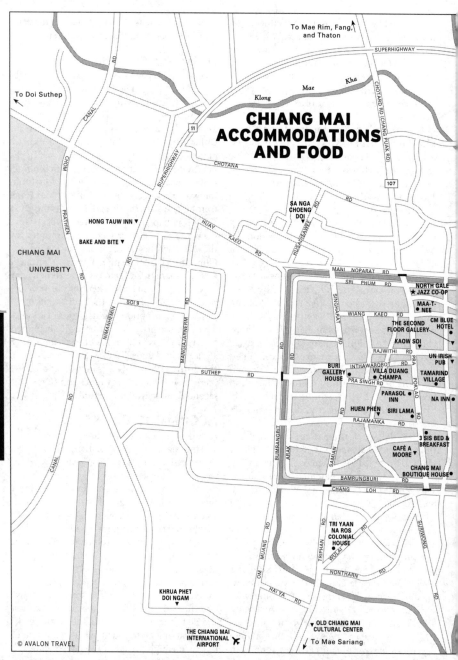

To Mae Rim, Fang, and Thaton

SUPERHIGHWAY

CHO TAOD RD (CHANG PUAK RD)

Mae Kha Klong

To Doi Suthep

CANAL RD

CHOM

PRATHIEN

11

SUPERHIGHWAY

CHOTANA

107

SA NGA CHOENG DOI

HONG TAUW INN ▼

BAKE AND BITE ▼

HUAY KAEO RD

HUA NGISAWEE

CHIANG MAI UNIVERSITY

NIMANHEMIN

SOI 9

MANGJAJARNERM

SINGHARAT RD

MANI NOPARAT RD

SRI PHUM RD

WIANG KAEO RD

RAJWITHI RD

INTHAWAROROT

PRA SINGH RD

NORTH GALE ★ JAZZ CO-OP

MAA-T-NEE ▼

THE SECOND FLOOR GALLERY

CM BLUE HOTEL ▼

KAOW SOI ▼

KAOW SOI

UN IRISH PUB ▼

BURI GALLERY HOUSE ●

VILLA DUANG ● CHAMPA

TAMARIND VILLAGE ●

PARASOL INN ●

NA INN ●

SUTHEP RD

HUEN PHEN ▼

SIRI LAMA ●

POKLAO RD

RAJAMANKA RD

3 SIS BED & BREAKFAST ●

CAFÉ A MOORE ▼

CHANG MAI BOUTIQUE HOUSE ●

BAMRUNGBURI RD

BUMRANGRIT

ARAK

SAMLAN

CHANG LOH RD

TRI YAAN NA ROS COLONIAL HOUSE ●

TRIPHAN

WULAI

SURIWONG

OM MUANG RD

CANAL RD

NONTHARN RD

KHRUA PHET DOI NGAM ▼

HAI YA RD

THE CHIANG MAI INTERNATIONAL AIRPORT ✈

OLD CHIANG MAI CULTURAL CENTER

To Mae Sariang

© AVALON TRAVEL

CHIANG MAI ACCOMMODATIONS AND FOOD

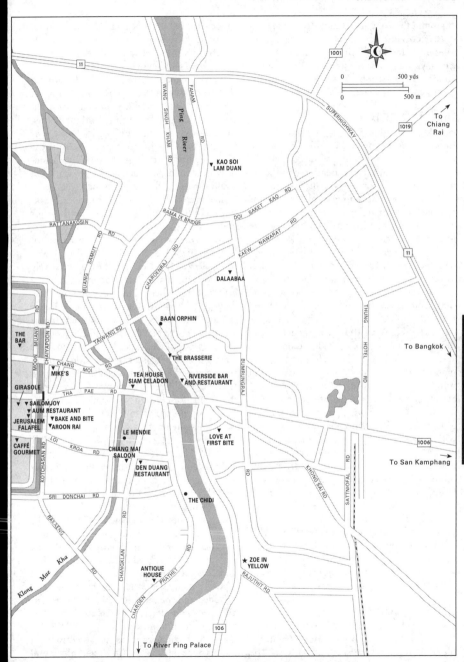

or around the Songkran and Loi Krathong festivals, you must book ahead. If you are planning on doing any hiking or visiting the hill tribes, your hotel or guesthouse will be able to arrange the excursion for you; many even have tour agencies attached.

Under 1,500B

For those on a budget, the bright **CM Blue House** (30/1 Moon Muang Rd., Soi 6, tel. 05/341-8512, www.cmbluehouse.com, 400B) is a cheap, clean, accommodating guesthouse in the heart of Chiang Mai. Guest rooms are large and (true to its name) bright blue; baths all have hot water and have recently been renovated. One of the nicest perks of staying here is a leafy garden area where you can enjoy a meal, sit and relax with a book, or grab a drink with the friendly French owner and his staff. A Western breakfast is available (from 60B).

Another nice inexpensive guesthouse inside the old city is **Na Inn** (136/7 Ratchaphakhinai Rd., tel. 05/327-6823, www.lannacondo.com/nainn, 650B). With 10 stylish, modern guest rooms each housing a large fridge, roomy bath, and king bed, the guesthouse feels much more high-end than its rates would imply. Located minutes from the bustling Sunday Walking Street market and in the center of town, it is an ideal base from which to explore Chiang Mai, and its friendly English-speaking owner will be happy to help with your plans.

West of the moat in the Nimmanhemin area is **Baan Say-La** (Nimmanhemin Rd. Soi 5, tel. 08/6911-1184, www.baansaylaguesthouse.com, 950B), a small, stylish boutique guesthouse with well-furnished guest rooms in a white colonial-style wooden house. The decor is a blend of traditional colonial and Thai styles, but the photography and modern art on the walls give the property a modern edge. There is a comfortable common sitting area and kitchen if you'd like to prepare your own meals.

1,500-3,000B

In a prime location, **Parasol Inn** (105/1 Phra Pokklao Rd., Klang Wiang Intersection, tel. 05/381-4011, www.parasolinn.com, 1,590B) is a modern hotel with breakfast included. Guest rooms are very well kept and have cable TV and fridges or minibars. Only the top-floor rooms have windows.

Newly opened in April 2011 is the **Chiang Mai Boutique House** (2 Ratchaphakhinai Rd., tel. 05/328-4295, chanaratw@gmail.com, 1,000–1,700B). Painted bright orange from the outside, this quirky guesthouse near Chiang Mai Gate is hard to miss. Despite the bright exterior, its 32 guest rooms are tastefully decorated, its spacious baths each boast a rain showerhead, and out front a small pool is shaded from passersby. Rates include breakfast and Wi-Fi, and discounts are available for longer stays.

Buri Gallery House (102 Ratchadamnoen Rd., tel. 05/341-6500 to 05/341-6504, www.burigallery.com, 1,600–2,000B) is a relatively new hotel in an amazing location: right in the center of the old city. Housed in a beautifully made Thai-style wooden house made into a small modern hotel, some of the guest rooms are very small, but the service is excellent. Breakfast is included, and they have an outside seating area. There is a massage parlor right in the lobby, and Internet access is free if you need to check email. Free roundtrip transportation to the airport for hotel guests is a nice bonus.

The top-notch charming service and beautiful open lobby send many visitors home happy after staying at **(3 Sis Bed & Breakfast** (1 Phra Pokklao Soi 8, tel. 05/327-3243, www.the3sis.com, 1,500B); it makes for a pleasant stay right in the old city, a block away from Wat Chedi Luang. Downstairs is a very chic café serving Thai and Western dishes with ingredients from the organic farm run by the three sisters' father. Guest rooms are very comfortable, the baths particularly lavish for the price, and there's free Wi-Fi throughout. The hotel has garnered passionate reviews and loyal repeat customers. Considering that breakfast is included and the place is run very professionally, with completely modern amenities, the rates are more than worth it.

Off Ratchamanka Road, set away from the bustle of the moat, is the **De Naga Chiang Mai**

(21 Soi 2 Ratchamanka, Moon Muang Rd., tel. 05/320-9030, www.denagahotel.com, 2,300B), a modern hotel decorated in traditional Lanna style, with old teakwood furniture and plenty of Thai silk. Standard guest rooms are stylish and open, with dark wood floors and a warm red theme. A full breakfast is included, and it's not to be missed. The Naga Suite includes a huge dragon, the namesake of the hotel, etched into the headboard.

Just outside of the city on the east side of the Ping River, **(** **Baan Orphin** (150 Charoenrat Rd., tel. 08/1616-4016, www.baanorapin.com, 2,100B) is a lovely little family-owned hotel with guest rooms and private bungalows, all done in teakwood with traditional Thai decorations throughout. The grounds are luxuriant, and there's even a swimming pool. Four-poster beds and airy verandas make Baan Orphin a great place for couples looking for a tranquil romantic getaway, but the larger suites are good for small families too.

A must for the upscale bohemian traveler, **Villa Duang Champa** (82 Ratchadamnoen Rd., www.villaduangchampa.com, 2,200B) is a newer addition, right behind the Three Kings' Monument. In an exquisite top-notch refurbish of a breezy antique building, each guest room is unique and simply a pleasure to enter. Style is tasteful and plush yet simple. All guest rooms have flat-screen TVs, and some have bathtubs. Original artwork is on display in the sun-filled interior where you take your breakfast, which is included. There's also Wi-Fi.

All of the individually designed, comfortable guest rooms at **Tea Vana** (75 Chiang Mai–Lamphun Rd., tel. 05/330-2805, www.tea-vana.com, 2,500B) have a slightly Chinese feel to them, but the real theme here is tea. Each guest room is named after a kind of tea; there are even tea-based treatments at the adjacent spa. This small, chic boutique hotel is located on the Ping River, and there's also a swimming pool and a restaurant-café.

3,000–4,500B
Tri Yaan Na Ros Colonial House (156

Wualai Rd., tel. 05/327-3174, www.triyaann-aros.com, 3,675B) is a truly different kind of hotel that takes great pride in its traditional blend of architecture that captures the "proud history of Chiang Mai." Tri Yaan Na Ros has a bit of a homey bed-and-breakfast feel, as it is small, but the guest rooms are still totally luxurious, and the setting is a blissfully secluded, quiet interior. Breakfast is included in the rates and is best taken by the tranquil pool. Besides a small dining room, they have an interesting gallery of many arts and antiques from northern Thailand and the region; ask to be shown. Service is impeccable. It was the 2004 winner of the Best Conserved Structure Award by the Lanna Architect Association and is conveniently located on the Saturday Night market street, just outside the old city.

Newly opened **Le Meridien Chiang Mai** (108 Chang Klan Rd., tel. 05/325-3666, www.lemeridienhotelchiangmai.com, from 3,500B) is part of the Starwood Hotels chain and is conveniently located right next to the Chiang Mai night bazaar. Its 384 large guest rooms, each with a glass and marble bath with massaging rain showers and uncluttered views of Doi Suthep, are fast becoming a popular option for those looking for luxury outside the old city. The hotel also houses a fully-equipped state-of-the-art gym and sizeable swimming pool as well as a top-end Italian restaurant and the Latitude 18 bar.

Over 4,500B
(**Tamarind Village** (50/1 Ratchadamnoen Rd., tel. 05/341-8896, www.tamarindvillage.com, 6,000B) is an oasis in the middle of the old city, a boutique hotel set in a large walled-in green space that somehow manages to create an aura of true peace and quiet right in the middle of backpackers and *tuk tuks*. Guest rooms are rustic in that they have more classic than modern design elements, but they're also spacious, clean, and luxuriously appointed. Tamarind Village is often booked months in advance, especially around holidays.

Built in 2008, the **Sirilanna Hotel** (89/3

Ratchaphakhinai Rd., tel. 05/327-9107, www.sirilanna.com, 6,000B) is another luxury compound in the heart of Chiang Mai's old city. Its 15 large guest rooms are richly decorated with Victorian-style Lanna furnishings (including antique-style furniture and huge, ornate wooden doors), and a large pool fills the inside of the hotel courtyard. Deluxe guest rooms include a four-poster bed and a jetted tub, and the Sirilanna Suite has its own private pool and library.

If you are looking for absolute luxury, the **Four Seasons Chiang Mai** (Mae Rim–Samoeng Rd., tel. 05/329-8181, www.fourseasons.com/chiangmai, 18,000B) has enormous stand-alone villas set on a green paddy field. Although the property is outside the city, there is a daily shuttle to the center and plenty of activities such as cooking classes and even a rice-harvesting class to keep you busy if you stay here.

The **Mandarin Oriental Dhara Dhevi** (51/4 Chiang Mai–San Kamphaeng Rd., tel. 05/388-8888, www.mandarinoriental.com/chiangmai, from 15,750B) is a resort that has been designed to make you feel as though you've stepped back a few centuries into a Lanna Kingdom palace. The architecture of all of the structures interwoven among the property's paddy fields is northern Thai, Shan, or Burmese, and the effect is stunning. This is the most beautiful resort in northern Thailand. Guest rooms and villas are very spacious and have individual outdoor lounge areas. There is also an expansive (and expensive) spa on the premises.

With its minimalist decor and discreet style, housed in what was once the British Embassy, **The Chedi** (123 Charoen Prathet Rd., tel. 05/325-3333, www.ghmhotels.com, from 14,000B) is an expensive but unique option for high-end lodging in Chiang Mai. Centrally located and with impeccable design and service, the hotel sits next to the Ping River and also houses an excellent restaurant on the premises. Its 84 guest rooms have large balconies and private courtyard entrances, each with an outstanding view. The hotel grounds include a large pool and a fitness center as well as a full business facility with conference rooms and video equipment. The hotel also made the *Condé Nast Traveler* 2009 and 2010 Gold List.

FOOD

Chiang Mai has scores of restaurants to choose from, and the variety of options available is second only to Bangkok. Here you'll find typical guesthouse fare, restaurants geared toward Western travelers, traditional Thai street stalls and restaurants, and a lot of vegetarian options. Because Chiang Mai is such a well-visited town, it's hard to find places to eat that don't attract other travelers, so don't be dismayed if you're eating with visitors from around the world. It usually doesn't mean the food isn't authentic, but rather that it's good.

Markets and Food Stalls

At any of the shopping markets in the city there will also be plenty to eat, from mango sticky rice to fruit shakes to *khai nok kratha* (fried quail eggs served in little banana-leaf baskets). Most of what you'll find is meant to be eaten on the go to keep you energized while you shop, but there is also more substantial fare available. The **Chiang Mai Night Bazaar** has food stalls interwoven with the crafts and trinkets, including lots of *satay* and even *khao mok kai* (chicken and yellow rice), but to go where locals go for a quick dinner, head to **Chiang Mai Gate's** dozens of food stalls and smoothies. **Anusan Market,** on the corner of Sri Dornchai and Chang Klan, has plenty of local Thai and Chinese food stalls that offer excellent inexpensive food, as do the **Sunday Market** and **Warorot Market.** Expect to spend 15–30B per dish or item.

Between Chang Phueak Road and Hussadhisawee Road is a daytime wet market and prepared-food market. Although you probably won't be carrying any raw meats or vegetables back to your hotel, the prepared food area is very accommodating to travelers. There is a coffee shop as well as a sit-down area with pictures of the dishes offered. These visuals are perfect if your Thai isn't quite up to speed.

Try one of the many Thai desserts or, if you're braver, one of the many varieties of crunchy insects. Another location that is worth checking out if you happen to be on a day trip to Doi Suthep or around Nimmanhemin Road is the food stalls surrounding Chiang Mai University.

Newly opened in early 2011 across the street from Chiang Mai University gates, **Malin Market** (Huay Kaew Rd.) is packed with locals and specializes in Japanese food of all varieties. Sushi, Peking-style duck with fluffy pancakes, hotpot, sushi, and *takoyaki* all can be found here for a bargain. Hugely popular with the hip, young Thai crowd, it's worth a visit if you want a change from the old city. And if you're in the mood for something sweet after your meal, ice cream and bubble tea stalls abound.

Local Cuisine

Khao soi—soft noodles in sweet, savory, rich yellow curry, covered with crispy fried noodles, and usually served with chicken or beef—is one of Chiang Mai's best-known dishes. The provenance of the dish is not clear. Some maintain it is an interpretation of a Shan dish, others that it is a Thai Muslim dish, and others that it's a hybrid of both. Wherever it comes from, to really know Chiang Mai you'll have to try a dish yourself. Though nearly every restaurant serves it, you'll find the best renditions in an area locally referred to as **Fa Ham.** The neighborhood is on the east bank of the Ping River, across the Naowarat Bridge in the area surrounding Charoenrat Road. Here you'll find a bunch of open-air *khao soi* restaurants, but **Lamduan Kao Soi** (352/22 Fa Ham Rd., tel. 05/324-3519, 8 A.M.–4 P.M. daily, 40B), just north of the Rama IX Bridge, is considered by most to be the best in the neighborhood, and the owner used to prepare dishes for the King when he would visit Chiang Mai.

If you're not in the neighborhood of Lamduan, head for the nameless restaurant with the green sign in English reading **Kaow Soi** (Inawarorot Rd. at Jhaban Rd., tel. 05/321-0944, 6 A.M.–3 P.M. daily, 30B), near the Three Kings monument. This is a very casual, local

place serving *khao soi,* soups, and garlic rice, a great accompaniment to the traditional dish. This may not be the most beautiful restaurant in the city, but the *khao soi* is among the best. For those in the mood for something other than soup, they also make a great *khao man kai,* tender boiled chicken over rice, served with a special ginger and chili sauce.

Nearby on the popular Walking Street is a stylish alfresco restaurant, **Hot Chili** (27/32 Ratchadamnoen Rd., tel. 05/327-8814, 11 A.M.–11 P.M. daily, 100B). Richly decorated in colorful silks and adorned with handcrafted masks, rice paper lanterns, and a rainbow of cushions and tablecloths, the restaurant packs quite a punch for its small size. With no windows, you can people-watch to your heart's content, and two coveted swings hanging from the rafters make for an ideal place to do so. While the decor speaks louder than the food, presentation of each dish is excellent, and the beverage list is extensive and generous.

Sa Nga Choeng Doi (7/1 Soi Santitam, off Chanoensuk Rd., tel. 05/335-7301, 40B) is worth the adventure it takes to find it. From the northwest corner of the moat, head down Hussadhisawee Road (there is a little police box on the corner). About five blocks down, Chanoensuk Road, on your left, will be the first noticeable signage. Head down this street, and on your left, across from the School of Massage for Health—Chiang Mai, you'll see the red-and-white tablecloths, which means you've arrived. With no Roman script and a garage-like atmosphere, this place offers some of the best southern Thai and Muslim food in town. The *roti mataba* (curry in a roti shell) with accompanying cucumber salad is delicious, and the *khao mok kai* (roasted chicken with saffron rice) topped with crispy fried shallots and cilantro garnish is not to be missed. Chances are you will be the only visitor in sight.

Thai-fusion restaurant **Dalaabaa** (113 Bumrungraj Rd., tel. 05/324-2491, www.dalaabaa.com) has been around for several years but still draws in the crowds with its elegant presentation and delicious food. Large glass windows and a mishmash of furniture contribute to its modern feel, and the restaurant draws a very diverse crowd. Try the deep-fried crab spring rolls or the spicy herbal young-coconut milk soup with chicken, both excellent bets.

Set in an old Thai house, lunchtime hot spot ◖ **Huan Phen** (112 Ratchamanka Rd., tel. 05/327-7103, 8 A.M.–3 P.M. daily, 30B) offers the usual suspects for northern Thai food, including excellent *khao soi,* northern Thai sausage, and chicken and pork grilled to perfection. At night, Huan Phen becomes a proper sit-down restaurant. The food is as good as the lunch offerings, but it's presented in a less casual way.

Newly opened **Café de Moore** (63/65 Phra Pokklao at Phra Pokklao Soi 4, tel. 08/9433-7688, 9 A.M.–6 P.M. daily), right in the heart of downtown, is a fun outdoor dining option with a creative twist on traditional Thai dishes and an adjacent café, Drink de Moore, with free Wi-Fi. Try their lychee panang curry with rice (50B) or the green curry with dragon fruit (60B). The owner speaks excellent English and cooks all the meals herself. If you're wandering near Chiang Mai Gate, this is a great place to stop for a quick, delicious bite.

For charming, lively atmosphere, head to the popular **Riverside Bar and Restaurant** (9–11 Charoenrat Rd., tel. 05/324-3239, www.theriversidechiangmai.com, 11 A.M.–1 A.M. daily, 250B). The large, well-established restaurant on the Ping River serves an expansive Thai menu of everything from pad thai to *khao soi,* but the darker curries, such as the Burmese and the Massaman, are particularly tasty, and the panang curry has a bite that can stay with you all evening. There are also burgers and pizza if your dining companions are looking for something a little more familiar, along with vegetarian fare for noncarnivores. There is also a nightly dinner cruise at 8 P.M.; be sure to make reservations if you want to dine on the water. After dinner the restaurant often has live music, and it stays open until 1 A.M.

Just across from Nimmanhemin Soi 1 is the **Hong Tauw Inn** (95/16–17 Nimmanhemin Rd., tel. 05/321-8333, 11 A.M.–midnight daily, 150B), which translates as "shophouse." Full of quirky

decorations and funky clocks, this restaurant offers a wide range of classic Thai dishes. There are also quite a few set-menu options for two or four people, which is perfect if you're new to Thai food or if you like to share (sharing is Thai tradition; the formal northern meal in which food is shared and hands are used is called *khan toke*). The real winners include the green curry and the northern sausage, and don't be afraid to try the whole fish or a spicy salad. Another helpful feature of the menu is the phonetically written Thai coupled with English descriptions; this way you can order your favorites at a later date *and* practice your Thai.

Although **Aroon Rai** (43 Kotchasam Rd., Tha Phae Gate, tel. 05/327-6947, 9:30 A.M.–10 P.M. daily, 60B) often has a decent number of foreigners in attendance, this shouldn't take away from the absolute "Thai-ness" of the place. With very little ornamentation, this place is only concerned with the food. The *som tam* (spicy papaya salad), *khao soi,* and *kaeng hong lay* (a popular dark northern curry with pork) are all quite good. If you're feeling adventurous, try the *rot duan* (caterpillar), *meng muan* (termite), or *ging gong* (cricket).

Fitting right into the Nimmanhemin neighborhood, **Khun Nai Teun Sai** (Nimmanhemin Soi 11, tel. 05/322-2208, 5:30 P.M.–midnight daily, 150B) is a casual but elegant place with a colorful garden. Translated to English, its name means "the boss wakes late," explaining its unusual dinner-only service time. The modern restaurant, decorated with modern art, offers well-prepared typical Thai dishes such as spring rolls and *satay,* but it's more about atmosphere. This is a great place for couples or groups of adults; children may feel a little less comfortable.

Khrua Phet Doi Ngam (267/1 Mahidol Rd., tel. 05/320-4517, 11 A.M.–9 P.M. daily, 100B) is another adventure in itself. It is a ways out of the city toward the southwest; if you are traveling by taxi or *tuk tuk,* you can show this to the driver: ครัวเพชรดอยงาม. They have authentic soups such as *kaeng pak siang da khai mot* (vegetable curry with ant eggs). They also offer *kop* (frog) and *sai ua* (a northern sausage).

Don't be afraid to ask the waiter what's good, or simply say *arai godai* (which basically means "whatever") and hope for the best.

Khan Toke
ขันโตก

Khan toke is a special Thai dinner, indigenous to Chiang Mai, in which various dishes are served on a large tray, either made of teak (*yuan khan toke*) or woven bamboo and rattan (*lao khan toke*). The presentation is lovely, but the real attraction is the variety of foods you'll get to sample. Your meal will be an assortment of dishes, including *namphrik* dips and curries, sticky rice or plain rice, and dessert. There are many places in the city that offer this meal, most with a traditional dance show included in the price. A few worth visiting are **Old Chiang Mai Cultural Center** (185/3 Wualai Rd., tel. 05/320-2993, www.oldchiangmai.com, 7–9:30 P.M. daily, 420B), **Antique House** (1 Charoen Prathet Rd., tel. 05/327-6810, 11 A.M.–midnight daily, 400B), and **The Khantoke Palace** (288/19 Chiang Klan Rd., tel. 05/327-2757, www.kantokepalace.com, 7–9:30 P.M. daily, 350B). All of these venues also have classical dance and music shows and nice settings in old teak houses. It's all a little touristy and contrived, but the performances are well executed and the food is good. Antique House also gets great reviews as a regular à la carte restaurant, but if you want to catch a show and have the full dinner at any of these places, make sure to call ahead for reservations.

Vegetarian
In the last few years, the traditional vegetarian options have expanded many times over, and there is now a wide variety of great vegetarian food in town. Over and above the plentiful vegetarian offerings at **Pun Pun** (Suthep Rd., west of Suan Dok Gate, tel. 08/6101-8508, 150B), in a courtyard next to Wat Suan Dok, restaurants from laid-back to trendy pepper the city's streets.

For those who have tired of noodles and rice, **The Salad Concept** (49/9 Nimmanhemin Rd. Soi 13, tel. 05/389-4455, 11 A.M.–10 P.M. daily, 30–100B), newly opened on Nimmanhemin Road, will provide a welcome respite. With large portions of crisp, hydroponic lettuce, a huge amount of toppings and dressings (favorites include Thai mint and tamarind sesame) to choose from, and reasonable prices, Salad Concept is fast becoming a popular place to eat. If you have meat eaters in your group, the choice of toppings includes grilled chicken and beef in addition to the tofu. The restaurant also serves coffee, juices, and dessert, as well as providing Wi-Fi.

Another great vegetarian place, set in an airy covered garden with modern white furniture, is the excellent **Khun Churn** (4 Nimmanhemin Soi 17, tel. 05/322-4124, 8 A.M.–10 P.M. daily, lunch buffet 11 A.M.–3 P.M. daily, 100B). Hugely popular for its impressive buffet lunch (with hot and cold options, salads, and a plethora of colorful teas like the blue butterfly pea or the red rosella), the dinner menu is also varied, and their tofu–cashew nut dish served over rice is not to be missed. They also make a mean pumpkin curry.

Located inside Tha Phae Gate next to Black Canyon Coffee, **Aum Restaurant** (65 Moon Muang Rd., tel. 05/327-8315, 8 A.M.–2 P.M. and 5–9 P.M. daily, 70B) offers an extensive vegetarian menu. Also a great used bookshop, this charming spot captures the essence of Chiang Mai in one small hole-in-the-wall restaurant. The extremely tasty *khao soi* comes with tofu and potatoes instead of chicken or beef, and there are plenty of other vegetarian options to choose from.

Taiwanese-style vegetarian restaurants **Tien Sieng** (54/56 Phra Pokklao Rd., tel. 03/320-6056, 8 A.M.–3 P.M. Mon.–Sat., 2 dishes over rice 25B) and newly opened **Ming Kuan** (98/4 Ratchadamnoen Rd., tel. 05/322-1069, 8 A.M.–8 P.M. daily, 25B) each offer delicious *khao soi* and noodle soups, but they really shine with their rich and flavorful green and red curries and bright vegetable dishes cooked to perfection. At both, 25B will buy you a heaping plate of red rice and two dishes of your choice; the same price will also get you a steaming bowl of noodle soup. Using seitan and mushrooms, they also offer a version of the popular pork or chicken balls on a skewer that you see around town.

International Cuisine

With a locally well-known Mediterranean chef, **Girasole** (71 Ratchadamnoen Rd., tel. 05/327-6388, 11 A.M.–11 P.M. daily, 300B) is most decidedly Italian and not an Asian impersonation (except a baby corn in the soup here or there), and the food is downright delicious. They have a plethora of pasta dishes and a lot of different pastas to choose from, including a spinach and spirulina fettuccini that is enjoyable even if you're not very health conscious. Besides pizzas out of a brick oven (open to spectators), they also have meat and seafood dishes, and Italian appetizers as well such as minestrone soup and carpaccio. Don't forget to end with a gelato or something from the dessert menu. The service is very good (albeit a bit surly), and even better if the kind manager-chef is there. It won't break your wallet either; the prices are the same as any other Italian place around. The best time to go is for dinner, especially if you get a table in the courtyard.

For more upscale Italian eats, the **Beccofino Trattoria Chiang Mai** (20/2 Soi 7, Nimmanhemin Rd., tel. 05/322-6590, www.beccofino.co.th/chiangmai.html, 250–400B) offers pillowy handmade pastas in rich sauces, thin pizzas baked in a wood oven, and a variety of mouthwatering appetizers. Although it isn't for the budget-conscious, if you want to treat yourself to an Italian meal, this Nimmanhemin Road establishment is a great place to do so. Try the baby penne with eggplant, fresh tomatoes, ricotta cheese, and basil (250B).

For a quick bite, drop into **Jerusalem Falafel** (35/3 Moon Muang Rd., tel. 05/327-0208, 9 A.M.–11 P.M. Sat.–Thurs., 80B). The tried-and-true place for Israeli food, this is your place if it's is hummus or tabbouleh that you're missing. Jerusalem Falafel also has a bakery as well as soups and baguettes. It is a bit gruff on the service side, but if you want Middle Eastern food, this is the place to get it.

Mike's Original (Chaiyaphum Rd.; Tha Phae Gate outer moat road; Anusan Market at the Night Bazaar, 6 P.M.–3 A.M. daily, www.mikesoriginal.com, 100B) has a loyal following among the local expat community and has been "converting vegetarians" since 1979 (depending on when you arrive, it may seem more like they are "serving the drunk after-hours crowd"). Open until 3 A.M. and now with locations outside the city center, Mike's has burgers, chili dogs, and onion rings, along with milkshakes—malted, even. Their options also include chicken burgers and breakfast deals (bacon and eggs), chili, and garlic bread—sure to satisfy any nostalgia for American cuisine.

Easily the most popular and authentic Mexican food in town, **Miguel's** (106/1 Chaiyaphum Rd., tel. 05/387-4148, 10 A.M.–11 P.M. daily, www.miguels-cafe.com, from 60B), near the Sriphum corner of the moat, has a thorough menu at reasonable prices. With outdoor seating, all the Mexican dishes you'd expect, and crispy nachos for all, it has spawned a second location on Chiang Mai–Lamphun Road near the airport.

Japanese food is becoming increasingly trendier with local Thais in and around Chiang Mai, as evidenced by the popularity of the newly opened Malin Market. Nimmanhemin Road boasts several reliable Japanese eats, serving a typical menu of *gyoza* dumplings, *bento* boxes piled high with tempura and versions of teriyaki fish, meat, and tofu, and appetizers aplenty. But for some special options, try **Rico de Rica** (5/3 Nimmanhemin Soi 5, tel. 05/321-3121, 6 A.M.–11 P.M. daily, 150B), a Spanish-inspired Japanese tapas joint, or eat well and do good by dining at newcomer **Saitong** (21 Sirimangkalajan Soi 11, tel. 05/322-2379, lunch and dinner Thurs.–Mon., 100B), with proceeds going to the Ban Rom Sai orphanage. Be sure to try Saitong's delicious signature five-appetizer taster.

While there are several Burmese restaurants in town, the most authentic and delicious is easily **D-Lo** (16/1 Huay Kaew Rd., tel. 05/322-1969 or 08/0316-5248, 11 A.M.–10 P.M. daily), in a quiet soi off Huay Khaew near Chiang

Mai University. It's in the same alley as the Holiday Garden hotel; look for the signs. A favorite among the Burmese community in Chiang Mai, you'll often find an impromptu acoustic guitar jam session in the corner of their dining room. With basic wooden tables and a smiling, attentive staff, it's a pleasure. If you're new to Burmese food, great choices include the tea leaf salad made with fermented tea leaves and topped with dried nuts and tomatoes, the pork curry, and the roasted eggplant salad, each delicious and very different in taste from Thai food.

Cafés

Since so much coffee is grown in the mountains of northern Thailand, it's not surprising that it seems like everyone in Chiang Mai is obsessed with coffee and café culture. In addition to large international chains (the largest Starbucks in the country is in Chiang Mai) and multiple Black Canyon Coffee outlets, there are plenty of smaller cafés brewing locally harvested coffee and tea and serving cakes and pastries.

◖ **Tea House Siam Celadon** (158 Tha Phae Rd., tel. 05/323-4518, www.ramingtea.com/eng_tea_house.php, 9:30 A.M.–6 P.M. daily, 100B) is in an elegant, renovated colonial-style building and serves tea, coffee, and light meals in an airy, gorgeous, but relaxed setting. You'll get to sample teas grown around the region as well as sandwiches, pastas, and ice cream. If you find yourself coveting the plate your club sandwich is on, you can buy it: The teahouse is also a celadon shop and many of the pieces you see are for sale.

Set in a wooden house with a large, shady garden **Fern Forest Cafe** (2/2 Soi 4, Singharat Rd., tel. 05/341-6204, 9 A.M.–8 P.M. daily) is a perfect place to relax for a few hours. With a variety of cakes on offer and free Wi-Fi, it's a tiny oasis in the middle of old Chiang Mai.

Located outside the city's moat, **Akha Ama Coffee** (9/1 Hussadhisawee Rd., Soi 3, tel. 08/6915-8600, www.akhaama.com, 8 A.M.–9 P.M. Mon.–Sat., 8 A.M.–6 P.M. Sun., from 35B) is a fair-trade coffee shop with

coffee from Maejantai, an Akha village in the north of Thailand. Run by a young Akha man named Lee and his family, freshly picked coffee is driven in daily and shucked on the premises, making it some of the best-tasting coffee in town. You'll also be supporting a movement toward fair trade and organic coffee, and you'll be able to relax on wooden benches away from the chaos of downtown. If you're interested in a closer look at the Akha people and how the coffee is grown, Lee offers fascinating "coffee journeys" November–February (when coffee is harvested) to his tiny village. See the Akha Ama website for more details.

Newly opened **Café Shong** (2 Singharat Rd., tel. 08/1716-8037, 8 A.M.–6 P.M. daily, 30B) makes strong coffees and a killer Thai iced tea at incredible prices. Air-conditioning and Wi-Fi make it an ideal place to stop—it's just across the street from Wat Phra Singh. They also serve a Western-style breakfast and assorted sandwiches, cookies, and cakes.

Across the Naowarat Bridge, away from the old city just off Tha Phae Road, is **Love at First Bite** (28 Chiang Mai–Lamphun Rd. Soi 1, tel. 05/324-2731, 7 A.M.–4 P.M. Tues.–Sun., www.loveatfirstbite.co.th, 100B). If you are in need of a few moments of peace and quiet and you have a sweet tooth, this is an ideal stop. The lush garden and glass enclosure allows air-conditioning appreciators also to embrace the surroundings. The menu is extremely colorful, and although it features desserts, it also has some hearty staples such as macaroni and cheese and chicken pot pie. Some particularly explosive choices include the volcano cheesecake and the love cup. There are quite a few varieties of cheesecake, including a green-tea slice. With corny classical adaptations of Broadway musicals playing in the background, Love at First Bite is an ideal dessert destination.

GETTING THERE
Air

The **Chiang Mai International Airport** (CNX, 60 Mahidol Rd., Suthep, tel. 05/327-0222, www.airportthai.co.th/chiang_mai/en/home.php), located 10 minutes southwest of

Chiang Mai city, is a relatively small and quiet airport, but you can still expect all the usual modern conveniences such as ATMs, foreign-exchange services, tour and taxi agents, and a few small shops and cafés. Recent air-route deregulation has lured a lot of budget carriers out this way, including **Nok Air** (www.nokair.com) and **Air Asia** (www.airasia.com), and the increased competition has reduced fares to the point that even budget travelers often abandon the more traditional overland routes. A one-way fare from Bangkok will typically set you back 1,500–2,000B, but you can sometimes find one for as little as 600B. Daily domestic flights come and go to most of the country's major airports, and a few international routes per week run to nearby countries, although most travelers arriving from outside Thailand will be routed through Bangkok.

There is a taxi-service counter on the main floor where you can arrange a lift to the city; the standard fare to most parts of the city is 120B. It's a good idea to check with your hotel before you arrive because many of them offer a free transfer service. From the city center back to the airport, red *song thaew* will take you for 40–80B, depending on the number of people. Budget a bit more time in this case, as the *song thaew* will stop along its regular route before making its way to the airport.

Train
Rumbling along on a cross-country train trip is probably the most flavorful way to get to Chiang Mai, especially if you haven't had the chance to ride the rails this way before. It's also one of the most economical, and unfortunately one of the slowest, options, taking up to 14 hours from Bangkok and costing under 900B for a second-class overnight sleeper.

The **Chiang Mai railroad station** (27 Charoen Muang Rd.) is the country's northernmost train station and is positioned just east of town on the far side of the Ping River; it's not much more than a platform, but there are a few kiosks selling drinks, snacks, maps, and souvenirs. Taxis and *tuk tuks* are usually waiting to take passengers into town; some hotels will also arrange a pickup for you.

Bus
Chiang Mai's two bus stations see dozens of coaches rolling in and out every day, providing fairly respectable access to southern Thailand and to most northern towns. The **Chiang Mai Arcade Bus Terminal** (tel. 05/324-4664) is northeast of the city center and handles the Bangkok, Chiang Rai, and Pai routes; while the **Chang Phueak Bus Terminal** (tel. 05/321-1586) is just north of the Chang Phueak Gate and handles destinations that are closer to Chiang Mai.

Car
With the white-knuckle insanity of Bangkok traffic, it's surprising that so many visitors to the Kingdom opt to rent a car in the capital for their trip to Chiang Mai, but in reality it's a fairly popular option. Of course, if you really want to experience the trek north, with the freedom to explore whatever captures your interest, it's definitely your best choice, and once you're outside of the urban area the drive becomes rather pleasant and the roads are well marked. On the eight-hour drive from Bangkok you are bound to see a lot of Thailand, much of it beautiful and fascinating, and there are a number of interesting spots where you can stop along the way. There are two possible routes for this trip; the first is to take Highway 1 (Phahonyothin Road) and then turn onto Highway 32 (Asia Highway), passing Ayutthaya, Ang Thong, and Nakhon Sawan, then switch to Highway 117 until Phitsanulok, and finally Highway 11 from Lampang to Chiang Mai. Alternately you can stay on Highway 1 from Nakhon Sawan, passing Kamphaeng Phet, Tak, and Lampang, to Chiang Mai. They both take about the same amount of time, so choose based on what you want to see along the way.

GETTING AROUND
The old city, within the bounds of the moat, is less than three square kilometers in

area, making it easily walkable if you want to explore the *wats* and markets on foot. Depending on where you are in relation to the Tha Phae Gate, it's also an easy walk to the Night Market just east of the old city. If you're heading farther outside the old city, to the Nimmanhemin area, for example, you'll probably need to use motorized transportation. Just outside the moat is a multilane roadway that circles the old city, with fast-moving cars and motorcycles at nearly all hours of the day. Once you cross that road, traffic slows down again and is more manageable.

Bicycles
Many guesthouses and resorts have bikes available for rent by the day, and this can be a nice way to get around. Chiang Mai is not a big city, but even inside the moat area there are plenty of cars and motorcycles, making it difficult to cross streets or even change lanes with a slow-moving bicycle. Only those who are confident on two wheels find biking beyond the moat pleasant.

Motorcycles
There are a handful of rental shops in the old city and on the road surrounding the moat renting motorcycles and scooters by the day. Rates vary, but expect to pay 200–300B per day. Many guesthouses and hotels also offer scooter rental or can arrange to have a bike brought to you; make sure to ask as you may be able to avoid an unnecessary trip. Also make sure that the rental company has insured the motorcycle prior to renting it. You will usually be required to leave your passport with the rental company as collateral for bringing back the motorcycle.

Song Thaew
These modified pickup trucks with two benches in the back are very popular in Chiang Mai and offer a convenient, inexpensive, and slightly adventurous means of getting around. They run about 7 A.M.–7 P.M., depending on the route; many of the trucks running routes heading out of the city stop and start at Warorot Market and are color

CHIANG MAI

© SUZANNE NAM

song thaew rates and routes

coded. If you're going somewhere within the city (even outside the old city), you'll probably be taking one of the ubiquitous red *song thaew*, which run on fixed routes and can also be used as taxis if there are no other passengers. Typically you stand on the sidewalk and flag one down; some of the fixed-route *song thaew* have signs in English indicating where they are going. Tell the driver where you're going, he'll let you know if he's going there or not, and then you clamber up into the back, and you're on your way. When you want to get off, press the button on the bars above you, and he'll pull over; then go around to his window and pay him (maximum 20B inside town, unless he takes you to a custom destination). While red *song thaew* ply the routes within Chiang Mai, yellow ones are destined for Mae Rim, white *song thaew* travel the eastern route to San Kamphaeng, and blue ones go to Sarapee and Lamphun to the south. Occasionally you'll see a green *song thaew*, headed northeast to Mae Jo.

Although there is no posted schedule in English for *song thaew*, almost every resident of the city will know the schedules and general routes, so do not be afraid to ask where you can pick one up to take you wherever you are going.

Tuk Tuks

Tuk tuks are available throughout the city and travel both to city destinations and places a few kilometers out. Fares are entirely up to negotiation, but expect to pay 40–80B for a short ride.

samlor driver in Chiang Mai

© SUZANNE NAM

Samlor

Chiang Mai is one of the few cities in the country where rickshaw bicycles still ply the streets, although there are very few of them. It's not the fastest way to get around, and you can't fit more than a couple of people and a few bags into one, but they tend to be popular with visitors anyway. *Samlor* are generally slightly more expensive than *tuk tuks*, and fares are also subject to negotiation with the driver. The *samlor* drivers usually congregate around Warorot Market during the day.

Excursions from Chiang Mai

For many travelers, the real appeal of a visit to Chiang Mai lies in the greater Chiang Mai Province or just beyond, outside of the city. If you like adventure or are athletically inclined, you will probably find yourself among this group. Apart from the obvious rainforest trekking and hiking, there is an impressive selection of outdoor activities available through local tour agencies and guesthouses, including the regular complement of mountain biking and horseback riding as well as some more exotic options such as bungee-jumping, rock climbing, and even glider rentals. However if that's not your idea of a good time, you can explore craft villages, visit with the hill tribe people, lose yourself in flower gardens, and take in the Chiang Mai Zoo or one of the famous elephant camps. Chiang Mai is a day-tripper's paradise, and unless you've got a lot of time, it's likely that you won't get a chance to do it all; it's a good idea to short-list some of the things that you really don't want to miss.

Tour Operators

If you're planning on making a trip to one of the outlying villages, there are plenty of tour companies in the city of Chiang Mai who can set up either a group or individual tour, and many people schedule hiking and other tours (even multiday tours involving camping) as little as one day before they'd like to depart. Many guesthouses function as tour sales agents or even lead tours themselves, so it's not necessary to worry too much about planning ahead. Although there are scores of tour agencies, the tours themselves are usually quite similar to one another, and the tours on offer will include day tours to Doi Suthep, Doi Inthanon, the Handicraft Highway, and elephant camps. Multiday hiking tours will almost always be group tours and are structured to include a visit to an elephant camp, hiking, bamboo rafting on a river, and accommodations in a hill tribe village. However, the longer day treks are a little canned; many of the more authentic,

off-the-beaten-path treks can be taken from Mae Hong Son Province or Doi Mae Salong in Chiang Rai Province.

If you want something different from Chiang Mai, you'll need to negotiate that in advance and expect to pay substantially more if you're asking a guide to get off the beaten path—otherwise, it does feel a bit like a zoo with both the long-neck villages and the elephants. Ethical concerns with trekking, specifically exploitation and overtourism, have not detracted from its popularity, and most guesthouses will offer to arrange treks for you. In general, guides should be officially licensed by the Tourism Authority of Thailand (TAT) and have a TAT license to show you if asked. Because of the constant turnover of guesthouses, tour companies, and guides, tour operators have only been mentioned here if they have a solid reputation for responsible tours and are well-reviewed. Keep in mind that because there is often an intermediary involved in selling these excursions, prices are subject to negotiation, and sometimes travelers will find that they paid more or less than other travelers for the same trip. If you are on a budget, shop around and compare prices before spending your baht.

WAT PHRA THAT DOI SUTHEP
วัดพระธาตุดอยสุเทพ

One of the more renowned *wats* in Chiang Mai and an important footprint of the Lanna Kingdom, the 600-year-old mountaintop monastery Wat Phra That Doi Suthep (Huay Kaew Rd., 6 A.M.–8 P.M. daily, 30B, 50B with tram ride) has a number of features that make it worth the 16-kilometer journey outside the city, and this half-day excursion is a must for any visitor to Chiang Mai. A prime example of the lavish grandeur of the Lanna Kingdom, Doi Suthep remains one of the holiest sites in the kingdom and is a major pilgrimage site for faithful Buddhists. Even if you take the trip only for the stunning view, you will be rewarded with a postcard vista of Chiang Mai city, especially at sunrise and sunset. During the dry-season months, the view is often obscured by fog, but it is ideal November–January. If the view alone is not enough to draw you, there is still the mysterious Buddha relic, with its reputation for performing miracles, buried beneath the pagoda, and the many free daily programs offered by the International Buddhism Center housed here. Try to visit on a weekday—the weekend crowds can be oppressive—and if at all possible, in time for sunrise or sunset when the view is at its most exhilarating.

Once you get to the temple, have a look at the giant *nagas* that line the sides of the more than 300 stairs leading to the top, and as you ascend, keep a sharp eye out for some of the tropical birds that live on the mountain. (For those who don't want a cardio workout, opt for the tram). Once at the top, pause outside the walls to check out the many temple bells. Don't be shy about ringing them (softly) for good luck. You will also find a small snack bar to refresh you after the hike. At the back of the outer area are a small museum and a good spot to take in the view of Chiang Mai on a clear day. As soon as you enter the inner compound, you will notice the giant gold-colored Lanna-style *chedi* that houses the Buddha relic; the four elaborate umbrellas that surround the *chedi* are also interesting. Don't forget to head around the back of the compound, where the most impressive *wihan* (outbuilding containing images of Lord Buddha) sits. You will see a number of Buddha images around the compound, but the white marble Buddha near this *wihan* stands apart from those made of more common materials. As you wander through the complex, watch among the usual images and statuary for the unique and strangely lifelike monks cast in metal, gaze at the abundant murals with vibrant depictions of Buddha's life, and wonder at the strange rituals of merit-making that you will see all around you. Beyond just the typical sticks of incense and lotus flowers, you will see flags tied to sacred trees, gold leaf scratched onto many surfaces, flags made

of banknotes, and even coins pressed into tablets of wax. There is also a beautiful museum building with a small collection of Buddhas and Thai currency.

According to legend, the relic lurking beneath the pagoda is a shoulder bone from Buddha himself (*phra that* means relic of the Buddha), found after an old priest had a dream telling him where to look for it. Once dug up, the relic reportedly performed occasional miracles, such as glowing brightly with a mysterious internal light, and at one point even replicating itself. The priest later came to Lanna to teach Buddhism, bringing the bone with him, and after it spontaneously doubled, plans were made to build a pagoda in honor of the powerful relic. The only trouble was finding the right place for the tribute, and so an appropriately elaborate scheme was devised. The relic was put on the back of an elephant, which was then turned loose to roam at will, the idea being that wherever the elephant decided to stop to rest was where the pagoda would be built. The elephant headed up the hill, passing up very convenient locations for construction along the way, and eventually stopped way up the mountainside at the *wat*'s current location. The elephant died shortly thereafter, and a monument still stands on the temple grounds to honor his contribution; you can see it standing along the wall at the corner to your left from the top of the stairs.

Before you make your way back down to earth, you might want to spend a few moments in the bookstore where you can find English literature on Buddhism and a selection of Thai and northern Thai music. If you have questions or are interested in learning more about Buddhism, you can visit the International Buddhist Center and talk to one of the monks, who can answer your questions, and in English, no less. At the center you can also find out about the courses and programs that they offer, including some longer-term meditation retreats.

The *wat* and Doi Suthep are only part of what makes up the several hundred-square-kilometer Doi Suthep–Doi Pui National Park, which includes **Doi Pui,** slightly taller than

Suthep. If you have a motorcycle, a side trip from Doi Suthep includes the Hmong village of Ban Doi Pui, where you can purchase a variety of Hmong handicrafts and weavings. There is also a tiny museum in the village (10B), where you can learn more about the hill tribe's history and their handicrafts.

Getting There

To get to the mountain, you can take a red *song thaew* from Chiang Mai University, Chang Phueak Gate on Suthep Road, or Chiang Mai Zoo for around 100B round-trip (or flag one down anywhere along the route). If you need a snack before jumping on your ride, directly across from Chiang Mai University is a row of cheap northern Thai restaurants with fresh grilled chicken, papaya salad, and soups. The *song thaew* run multiple times per hour during the day. From the parking area at the base of Doi Suthep mountain, you can enjoy the leisurely tram ride up to Wat Phra That Doi Suthep, or you can brave the 300-plus steps that will take you to where the temple sits, halfway up the mountain.

THE RUINS OF WIANG KUM KAM
เวียงกุมกาม

For an interesting cultural half-day trip from Chiang Mai, consider the ruins of the town of Wiang Kum Kam, located between the Ping River and the Lamphun highway. This city was originally a Mon settlement and existed as a satellite in the Hariphunchai Kingdom, based in Lamphun, until the 12th century. It then was claimed by the Lannathai when they toppled the Mon Empire; it's believed that King Mengrai lived here for a few years before Chiang Mai was built. Abandoned for 300 years because of flooding, Wiang Kum Kam became a town in legend only until it was rediscovered in 1984 after local people found a number of artifacts in the area. Rumors of valuable relics began to circulate, attracting would-be treasure hunters, and the national government's Fine Arts Department finally stepped in to preserve the site. There are now

42 historical monuments spread over the nine-square-kilometer site; most are simply ruined platforms and *chedi,* but there are two *wats* still in operation, and the peaceful country scenery is enjoyable in itself. Start out at **Wat Chedi Si Liem** (วัดเจดีย์เหลี่ยม), or Wiang Kum Kam (วัดกู่คำหลวง), where you will find an information center orienting you to the site and describing the historical significance of the town and the lifestyle of the people who lived there as well as food and drink stalls during peak hours. You can also see a good example of Lanna architecture if you look at the *wat*'s main assembly hall, which was built entirely without nails, supported on huge pillars of teak. Since Wiang Kum Kam is too big to cover on foot, you can also rent a bicycle, hire a pony carriage from Wat Chedi Si Liem (200B for 45 minutes), or join a tour around the site from this *wat.* The other still-functioning temple, **Wat Kan Thom** (วัดกานโถม), is another noteworthy visit. Khan Tom has a Cultural and Local Wisdom Learning Center where you can see a replica of a traditional Lanna house and other objects. There is also a Lanna market selling food and local clothing, though it's really a re-creation for visitors and not authentic.

Getting There

There is no regular bus or *song thaew* service out to Wiang Kum Kam (เวียงกุมกาม), so you'll either need to hire a ride for the 10-kilometer trip or make the drive yourself. If you hire a ride, you'll have to negotiate with the driver, but expect to pay about 100B if you are going one-way. It might be a good idea to have the driver wait, though, since you may not find a ride back easily. If you're driving, take Route 106 (Chiang Mai–Lamphun Rd.) south for five kilometers and look for the Wiang Kum Kam sign, which is in Thai: เวียงกุมกาม. From here it's another two kilometers until the right turn into the park. Alternately, veer right onto Ko Klang Road (just after the Holiday Inn) from Route 106 and head south, hugging the river for about 500 meters before turning right into the park; this will put you on the road to Wat Chedi Liem.

CHIANG MAI

CHIANG MAI ZOO
สวนสัตว์เชียงใหม่

The Chiang Mai Zoo (100 Huay Kaew Rd., tel. 05/322-1179, chiangmaizoomail@gmail.com, http://chiangmaizoo.com, 8 A.M.–9 P.M. daily, entry 100B adults, 50B children), renovated in 2004, has over 7,000 avian, reptilian, and mammalian residents on 80 hectares of habitat. Now the home to a new baby panda, with rumors of a polar bear for the recently built "snow dome," the zoo remains a popular attraction, though not the most ideal place for animals accustomed to colder climes. Positioned at the foot of Doi Suthep, the facility has been around since 1974 but was fairly unremarkable until 2004 when a black-and-white pair of new arrivals sparked enough "panda-monium" to attract a huge injection of cash (and a baby panda in 2009), which funded the spiffy layout you see today.

The animals tend to be more restful during midday, so if possible, start out early so you can see them going about their morning activities, and in some cases munching on their breakfasts. Once you're ready to start exploring, take a moment to look at the big map near the entrance and plan which displays you really want to take in so that you don't end up backtracking in the mazelike zoo. There's a lot to see, but try to include the regal white tigers and, of course, the star attraction, the much-loved giant pandas. The zoo is arranged around a very long loop road with smaller trails leading off to and from the different exhibit areas; you'll find food and drink kiosks along with restrooms throughout the park, so once you know what you want to see, you are ready to start exploring. Besides basic admission, there are additional à la carte fees for many of the attractions, including the adventure park (20B adults, 10B children) and the monorail (150B adults, 50B children). The biggest attractions are listed below, roughly in order from the northern part of the zoo (near the Huay Kaew Road entrance, on the road to Doi Suthep), to the southern part.

Nakornping Aviary

With about one hectare of rambling forest and 800 free-flying inhabitants, the Nakornping Aviary is one attraction definitely worth a visit. As you walk along the shady green forest floor, searching for the feathered denizens and enjoying the flowers, one thing you won't notice is the enclosing netting cleverly concealed high above the treetops so as not to break the mood. Perhaps the most interesting aspect of the aviary, though, is the walkways that ascend upward through the trees, taking you all the way to leaf-level, where you can get a unique "bird's-eye" perspective on life in the rainforest canopy.

Open Zoo

Another open-concept exhibit is the "Open Zoo" area that is home to over 200 mingling critters, including the zoo's ever-increasing collection of deer. Raised walkways through this 16-hectare enclosure keep you on track and aid you in getting a good view of the wildlife. From time to time you can also find vendors selling snacks so that you can try out hand-feeding some of the animals; the giraffes are especially gracious diners.

Freshwater Aquarium

If you've gazed into the murky waters of one of Thailand's many rivers and wondered what might be lurking beneath, or if you engage in the occasional angling trip back home, you might want to check out the zoo's freshwater aquarium (450B adults, 350B children), just west of the aviary. At a cost of almost 600 million baht to build, the aquarium's Sea Tube Tunnel allows freshwater and saltwater creatures to coexist under one roof for your viewing pleasure. Animals include 60 species of Southeast Asia's tropical freshwater fish, including the giant Mekong catfish, the Siamese giant carp, and the *ture* eel as well as stingrays, starfish, and clownfish.

Snow Dome

The zoo's latest attraction is a covered snow dome (150B adults, 100B children), allowing tropical Thais to discover what it's like to build a snowman, start a big snowball fight, or make snow angels for the first time. The entry fee includes a warm jacket and snow-appropriate shoes.

Giant Pandas
The zoo's beloved pair of giant pandas (100B adults, 50B children) were presented to the Thai government as "friendship ambassadors" by the government of China in honor of Queen Sirikit's birthday in 2004; they were placed in the care of the Zoological Park Organization of Thailand, who chose the Chiang Mai Zoo as their home. Because there are so few opportunities to see giant pandas outside China, the gift instantly put Chiang Mai's zoo on the map, drawing thousands of Thais to peer at the rare and elusive giants. In May 2009 a baby panda was born in the Chiang Mai Zoo and has since drawn even more excitable visitors to get a glimpse of her as she grows. A public competition to name the female cub drew more than half a million entries, with Limping eking out the rest as the new panda's name. The pandas get their breakfast at 9 A.M. and are usually pretty active at this time of day; if you turn up in the afternoon, you're less likely to see panda antics, but then they're still pretty adorable even when they're just relaxing.

Children's Zoo
Naturally, the zoo is an ideal spot to visit if you have kids among your traveling companions. Apart from the usual appeal of animals, open spaces, and sunshine, the park also has a separate area designated as the Children's Zoo. This section is a big grassy area up on top of a small hill in the southern part of the zoo, were you'll find several playgrounds along with a bunch of kid-friendly games and exhibits. They can also get a bit of hands-on time with some of the animals at the smallish petting zoo, and occasionally donkey rides are available.

Getting There and Around
The zoo is located at the base of Doi Suthep, right after Chiang Mai University on Huay Kaew Road. A short *tuk tuk* ride (about 100B) will get you to the zoo from the city center,

or if you like, any of the *song thaew* headed for Wat Doi Suthep can also drop you at the entrance to the park for the customary 20B if you're in a group; traveling solo or in twos will raise the price slightly. You can find these *song thaew* at Chang Phueak Gate on the north edge of the old city, but if you're already on the main road, you can either flag one down or board at Chiang Mai University. You'll have no trouble picking one up in the return direction because there are always a few drivers hanging around the exit waiting for a fare. The park's huge grounds and hillside location mean that if you decide to go on foot, you're in for a lot of walking, much of it uphill; but if that turns you off, take one of the open-air trams running between exhibits (20B for an all-day tram ticket), or you can even take your rental vehicle in with you for a small fee.

BAN THAWAI
บ้านถวาย
Dedicated shoppers should consider making the short trip to Ban Thawai (90 Mu 2 Ban Thawai, Khun Khong, Hang Dong, tel. 08/1882-4882, www.ban-tawai.com, 9 A.M.–5:30 P.M. daily), a small village 16 kilometers south of town off Hang Dong Road. Sponsored by One Tambon One Product (OTOP), a government program designed to encourage villages to make and sell handicrafts, Ban Thawai is akin to an outlet center for any kind of specialty Thai and hill tribe art. Everything is sold wholesale, and you can't beat the prices—if you have already spent time around the Sunday Market in Chiang Mai, you will notice the difference. Ban Thawai is mainly known as a woodcarving village, but now it is also a center for traditional rattan work, bamboo goods and crafts, furniture, lamps, pottery, and all sorts of other artwork and handicrafts. It supports a traditional industry by bringing handmade original goods to consumers. There is a lot of original design and styles—you will see many "no photos please" signs. The sheer number of places and the amount of handmade goods is astonishing. The quality is very good all around; you may find items to be more

"polished" at the more upscale showrooms and boutiques in Ban Thawai, although the prices will reflect this.

Allow yourself a trip here to gaze around, and then to buy. The village and different "zones" are very well marked, which makes it only slightly less overwhelming.

Many visitors, Thai and foreign alike, come with the purpose to buy furniture or large-scale items. Rest assured that most places are equipped for shipping.

Getting There

The best way to get to Ban Thawai market, if you're not driving yourself, is to hire a taxi or *tuk tuk* for a few hours (expect to pay a few hundred baht round-trip). You'll probably need the space to carry everything you've bought, and on the way to Ban Thawai there are many producers, manufacturers, and exporters of wooden goods and locally made crafts—although you'll really want to check out Ban Thawai before buying anything else.

BO SANG AND SAN KAMPHAENG
บ่อสร้างและสันกำแพง

Every year thousands of faithful shoppers make a pilgrimage to the handicrafts mecca that is San Kamphaeng Road, a.k.a. the **Handicrafts Highway,** which, along with the charming Umbrella Village of Bo Sang, makes up a little shopping district where you can peruse some surprisingly unique goods and get a firsthand look at how these traditional arts are created. Along this stretch of highway is a hot springs and a sacred cave to add a little variety to your day trip; you should plan to spend from four hours to a whole day out here.

Bo Sang
บ่อสร้าง

Bo Sang is located eight kilometers east of Chiang Mai on Route 1006; once here you will quickly see that the title of "Umbrella Village" was not randomly assigned to this little community, whose inhabitants specialize in the manufacture of natural papers and crafts made from the paper. *Sa* paper is made from the bark of the *sa* tree, which is native to the region and is a relative of the mulberry. Its use in paper-making has been understood and practiced by locals for many generations. The families of this town have been dedicated to the art of making parasols for over 200 years and have long been famous for their delicate and colorful creations. The process begins with some tree bark and sticks of bamboo and ends with a filmy hand-painted parasol. It's a fascinating example of a traditional handicraft, and at Bo Sang you are able to view each step of the process. Historically, families would each have a particular specialty, with one making and cutting the paper, one constructing the frame, another putting them together, and the final family hand-painting them with traditional images. The easiest way to see the whole process from bark to bumbershoot is to visit either the **Umbrella Making Center** (corner of Rte. 1006 and Rte. 1014, tel. 05/333-8324, www.handmade-umbrella.com, 8 A.M.–5 P.M. daily) or **The Sa Paper and Umbrella Handicraft Center** (Rte. 1006 Km. 8, 99/16 Ban Nongkong, San Kamphaeng Rd., tel. 05/333-8414, www.saa-handicraft.com/new, 8 A.M.–5 P.M. daily).

Bo Sang parasols have won awards for being one of the best travel souvenirs available worldwide, and the only trouble with taking one home with you will be choosing from the hundreds of designs available in sizes ranging from 10 centimeters to two meters across. Another fun option is to ask the local painters to paint a traditional Bo Sa design on a piece of clothing, on your bag, or on just about anything else that you want, although you will need to provide them with the item to be painted. You can have them paint any design you want, from the usual floral subject matter to a 100 percent custom image of your own creation.

In late January, Bo Sang puts on its annual **Umbrella Festival;** if you are in Chiang Mai at the time, you should not miss it. The whole town is dolled up from head to toe with these umbrellas in a remarkable feat of color. There is an exotic procession in the streets featuring traditional costumes and, of course, a lot of umbrellas—including a citywide Umbrella Beauty Pageant, where contestants in the pageant ride bicycles with their parasols—and every effort is made to keep the decor and events as close as possible to a traditional Lannathai festival.

San Kamphaeng
สันกำแพง

San Kamphaeng is a weaving and silk village located just five kilometers farther east of Bo Sang on Route 1006. It is traditionally famous for its exquisite textiles and is the major production center for Thai silk and cotton. The town's main street, San Kamphaeng Road, is a virtual gauntlet of shops not only fronted by the sidewalk but spilling out onto it, and it is a major stop for tour buses, so arrive prepared to brave a crowd. While weaving is done in the side *sois,* shops on the main road sell only the finish product.

Muang On Cave
ถ้ำเมืองออน

San Kamphaeng is an easy jumping-off point for the spooky and mysterious Muang On Cave site and the privately owned San Kamphaeng Hot Springs, which lie about 19 kilometers east of town on Route 1317. They can be a much-needed diversion from the crowded shops and markets. Muang On Cave scores top points for atmosphere, and it's not for the faint of heart or the claustrophobic, but it has a few features that make the trip from Chiang Mai more than worth the effort. From the parking area, you climb a 90-meter *naga* staircase to the cave's entrance. There you will find a small whitewashed *chedi,* built to house the earthly remains of the monk Phrakhru Ba Si Wichai, who spent much of his time meditating at the site and whose ghost some claim to have seen in the cave. At the entrance, you pay the attendants the 10B fee, which is used for maintenance of the site, and head downward into the gloomy heart of the cavern.

About a dozen steps or so down the concrete stairs that lead into the vault, you have to stoop to squeeze through a narrow passageway for a short distance before continuing downward on the other side. Once through the passage,

electric fixtures light your way; stop frequently to look at the interesting features around you, such as the wear patterns on the walls, the embedded minerals, and the occasional stalactite. As you continue downward, keep an eye out for Buddhist icons occasionally tucked into the niches and natural ledges of the walls, including images of old men and a strange statue of a man with a cow's head. Farther down you'll come to a very strange site and one that is the subject of some controversy. Announced only by a small and unimpressive sign is the large and very impressive imprint of a prehistoric monster, which some claim is what's left of a dinosaur skeleton embedded in the 245-million-year-old cave wall. Although the validity of that claim remains untested, a careful look of the image is enough to spark debate. Creating an incredibly eerie effect, the nine-meter-long Phra Garoona Sai Yars reclining Buddha reposes languidly beneath the looming monster.

The stairs lead ultimately into a large open grotto that clearly shows the religious importance of the site to local Buddhists; strewn about in the niches and ledges of the cavern are Buddha images of all shapes and sizes left by followers who clearly felt a sense of spiritual awe in the presence of this incredible cavern. Presiding over the assembly is a large Buddha statue sitting high atop a natural ledge that perches above a natural basin of water. And just in case this isn't your first cave and you're not easily impressed, the vault's centerpiece, the multihued nine-meter-tall, three-meter-wide **Jedee Mae Nomm Fah stalagmite** should be enough to tip the scales.

After the cavern—or instead of it, if the idea of descending into the bowels of the earth leaves you a feeling a little green—you can take a path leading from the cave's entrance farther up the hill, where you can take in a Buddhist shrine and take some really idyllic photos of Muang On Town and the valley below.

San Kamphaeng Hot Springs
น้ำพุร้อนสันกำแพง

One kilometer east of Muang On Cave on Route 1317 is the turnoff for the hot springs, indicated by a large blue sign; three kilometers down a small road are the relaxing San Kamphaeng Hot Springs (10B) and adjacent **Roong Aroon Resort** (Ging Amphur Mae-On, tel. 05/393-9128, www.chiangmaihotspring.com, springs 40B). Here you will find natural geysers and steaming therapeutic mineral baths whose high sulfur content will quickly blacken your silver, so consider leaving your jewelry at the water's edge with your clothing. You can have a soak, take advantage of the handful of spa facilities that have sprung up, or stroll through the gardens nearby; both the San Kamphaeng Hot Springs and the Roong Aroon Resort offer accommodation (1,200B) if you take a liking to the spot.

Getting There

You have a few options for getting out to Bo Sang and San Kamphaeng. There are many daily buses that ply the route leaving Chiang Mai from Charoen Muang Road across from San Pa Khoi market; you can get off at Bo Sang or stay on until San Kamphaeng. There are also *song thaew* leaving frequently from Chang Phueak bus terminal that will drop you at either location; both of these options will cost 15B. Bo Sang is only nine kilometers from Chiang Mai, and San Kamphaeng is about 16 kilometers, so you don't have to worry about sweating it out for ages on less-than-five-star local transportation, making this option reasonable if you want the experience and if you aren't planning to pack a lot of new acquisitions back with you. A good way to do the trip is to rent a motorcycle or scooter in Chiang Mai, which gives you a lot more freedom of movement for as cheap as 300B; it's probably the option that is the most fun. However, if you are expecting to do a fair amount of shopping, renting a car or hiring a taxi for the day is next to essential for convenience and comfort. This can be arranged at one of many agents in Chiang Mai, or you can try to negotiate with a taxi driver on the street. You shouldn't have to pay more than 600B for the taxi service unless you are planning to travel farther than San Kamphaeng, but as always, ask around to see

what price you can get. Alternately, many of the tour agencies will be offering this route as part of an organized day trip, which can be a fun and easy option.

MAE KAMPONG

With a homestay program and an ecovillage in the hills of Doi Mon Lam, Mae Kampong has recently become a popular option for a side trip in northern Thailand. The village, Ban Mae Kampong, is situated on a hill about 50 kilometers from downtown Chiang Mai and recently won a Gold Award from the Pacific Asia Travel Association for its emphasis on culture and preservation. Nearby is the beautiful **Chae Son National Park** with waterfalls aplenty. The village's homestay (contact Mr. Phrommintr Phuangmala, tel. 08/5675-4598, basic lodging 1,500B per night) is run as a cooperative, a project that began in December 2000 when some 20 families renovated their homes and opened them up to visiting travelers. In addition to the national park, villagers grow and pickle tea leaves, which are sold at markets in and around northern Thailand. Another option is the more upscale **Tharnthong Lodge** (99/1 Mu 8, Huay Kaew subdistrict, tel. 08/6420-5354, www.tharnthonglodges.com), with hot showers, bathrobes, and complimentary tea parcels to take home, located near Mae Kampong village and set in the quiet hills. To get here, take Route 1317 toward San Kamphaeng and bear right at the Ban Huay Kaew junction.

DOI INTHANON
ดอยอินทนนท์

At 2,565 meters above sea level, the cool, misty summit of Doi Inthanon is the highest point in all of Thailand, presiding over one of Chiang Mai Province's most popular national parks. Thick forest clings protectively to bogs, valleys, and hillsides, sheltering more than 350 species of tropical birds as well as Hmong and Karen hill tribe settlements. It is a 97-kilometer excursion west along Highway 108 from Chiang Mai to the top of Doi Inthanon, which has a smattering of artisanal villages, dramatic mountain vistas, and waterfalls to break up the drive, but the round-trip can be done in a day if you start out early enough. This day trip is a good one to do by organized tour because they will ferry you to all of the best spots, and you can sit back and enjoy the route's gorgeous scenery without worrying about navigating winding mountain passes and hairpin turns with steep vertical sides. If you do strike out on your own, it's best not to take an automatic motorcycle or scooter because they may struggle getting up some of the hills. Whatever you do, be sure to bring a jacket—the temperature at the top can be as low as 0°C during the winter, when the humidity is high.

Muang Kung Earthenware Village
บ้านเหมืองกุง

The first point of interest along the way is about 10 kilometers from Chiang Mai on Route 108. The Muang Kung Earthenware Village, as the name suggests, is home to many artisans who specialize in pottery and earthenware in all shapes and styles, from traditional Lanna designs to more modern pieces. If you visit during the day, you'll be able to find people working, see the huge kilns fired up and the pieces drying in the sun, and pick up some souvenirs.

Chom Thong
จอมทอง

The next stop is Chom Thong Town, at kilometer 58 on Route 108, where you can stop for some refreshment and to collect your energy before heading into the national park; it also claims that some believe to be the most beautiful temple in northern Thailand, **Wat Phra That Si Chom Thong,** for which Chom Thong District is named. The site dates back to the 14th century, although the current *wihan* was built in 1817. As you approach you are presented with an exquisite example of Lanna-Burmese woodcarving in the wonderfully rich gilt portico. Part of the beauty of this building is the wonderful flow of the design: Far from being stark and out of place, the carvings on the outside fit perfectly with the interior and its beautiful Burmese-style altar and

bronze Buddha images. Legend has it that part of the Buddha's skull was found on this spot in 749 and that it is still enshrined at the altar in this *wihan,* for once residing aboveground rather than buried underneath a *chedi,* as is the usual custom for Buddha relics. Before you leave, stop to look at the delicately carved elephant tusks and the glass case near the altar that holds an interesting assortment of ancient Thai weaponry. The Burmese-style *chedi* near the *wihan* is the oldest part of the temple and was part of the original 1451 construction. Chom Thong is also an ideal place to stock up on snacks for the trip into Doi Inthanon; its daily market has a good selection of grilled skewers, sticky rice, and freshly cut fruit for a picnic atop Thailand's tallest mountain.

Ban Rai Phai Ngam Cotton Weaving Village
บ้านไร่ไผ่งาม

At this point, you could continue 16 kilometers farther south on Route 108 to visit the Ban Rai Phai Ngam Cotton Weaving Village, where the villagers weave cotton cloth in the old style with traditional looms. The **Pa Da Cotton Textile Museum** (108 Chiang Mai–Hod Rd., 8:30 A.M.–5 P.M. daily, factory Fri.–Wed.), and its associated textile factory, located in an old teak house, offer some well-done textile weaving displays. The museum also houses a loving tribute to its founder, Khun Saeng-da Bunsiddhi, born in 1919. Like many women of northern Thailand, she learned weaving skills from her own grandmother and added additional weaving techniques from surrounding hill tribes. She wove fabrics for her family and village, including her husband's uniforms in World War II. After the war, she began to grow native cotton plants and reenable some of the old weaving looms. Together with other local women, she started the Housewives Union to increase income and employment opportunities, to preserve traditional dyeing and weaving techniques, and to promote handicraft production. The left turnoff to Ban Rai Phai Ngam is just after kilometer 68; a three-kilometer road will take you to the village.

Doi Inthanon National Park
อุทยานแห่งชาติดอยอินทนนท์

You can head straight down the road to Doi Inthanon National Park (119 Ban-Luang, Chom Thong, tel. 05/328-6728, www.dnp. go.th/parkreserve/asp/style1/default.asp, 200B), which you passed just as you were heading into Chom Thong. From the north end of town, turn west onto Route 1009, which will take you past the toll booth where you can pay the 200B entry fee and get a brochure, and then through the park leading up to the summit.

The park covers 482 square kilometers of forest and includes the whole of Doi Inthanon mountain. As you travel toward the peak, watch for the terraced rice fields of the hill tribes along its slopes among the misty greenery, which make for great photos. This park is on the short list for naturalists who visit Thailand, and if you are very lucky, you may spot some rare and exotic animals, including swinging gibbons, the Indian civet, barking deer, giant flying squirrels, and the Asiatic black bear, which counts this mountain as one of its last remaining habitats. There are numerous dirt tracks branching off from the main road that lead to walking paths, meditation and prayer sanctuaries, hill tribe villages, caves, and several waterfalls. The smaller ones should not be attempted without a 4WD vehicle, especially during the rainy season. The first important spot to check out is the **Mae Ya waterfall,** which crashes to the earth in a tiered cascade from over 300 meters above. Another popular waterfall is the **Mae Klang waterfall.** You can drive most of the way to the falls, but you have to leave the car near the Buddhist College. After you park, cross the bridge leading to the gardens of the college and walk along a short footpath to the base of the falls. Nearby is **Birichinda Cave,** where you can see some remarkable stalagmites and stalactites along with an interior stream. It's worth stopping to walk around and take in the **Vachiratararn Falls,** one of the finest on the route. You can stay in the bungalows here if you book ahead, or inquire about camping.

The summit of Doi Inthanon is misty, mossy, and comfortably flat; check out the visitors center for information on the ecology of the park, and look for the *chedi* above the center that holds the remains of Chao Inthawichayanon, the last ruler of the Lanna Kingdom before it merged with Siam. Most people get here by car using the 48-kilometer Summit Road in the park, but there is one trail that will take you to the top on foot. From the base, the hike will take a moderately fit hiker about four hours. There is also a trail called Kew Mae Pan (closed June–Oct.) halfway up the summit at kilometer 42. This is a beautiful though somewhat strenuous three-kilometer trail and is a good option for those who do not want to spend the whole day hiking but prefer not to drive all the way to the top. Moderately fit hikers can complete the trail in about two hours. There are a few walking paths at the summit, but most are restricted to reduce the impact on local plants and animals; across the road from the visitors center, however, the unrestricted Aangka Trail follows a boardwalk through a small sphagnum bog that is worth a look; wildlife is frequently spotted along this trail.

◀ MAE SA LOOP

Another option for a day trip from Chiang Mai is to wind your way along the scenic Mae Sa Loop (sometimes called the Samoeng Loop), following Routes 1096, 1269, and 107 into the beautiful Mae Sa Valley, where you will find quiet roads, breathtaking scenery, and some rather well-done attractions to spice up the drive. You could conceivably spend 2–3 days seeing everything there is to see on this route, and accommodations are available at Samoeng and Mae Rim Towns as well as at various spots along the Mae Rim–Samoeng Road, but one full day is enough to experience the best stuff. This strip of highway comes complete with world-class gardens, elephant camps, doggie talent shows, snake farms, pony rides for kids, and a variety of ATV tours and bungee-jumping centers, to name a few of the options.

There are organized tours doing this loop, but you might have more fun renting a car or motorcycle and setting your own pace, especially because this route is considered one of the most scenic circuits in northern Thailand. Although public buses are available, they are infrequent and aren't a very realistic option for this stretch of highway. If you plan on driving, you have to decide whether to head north toward the town of Mae Rim and then loop back around west and south; or to leave Chiang Mai from the southeast and travel north to Samoeng, looping around east and back south on the return. Either way, you'll have about 56 kilometers and a lot of stops to cover, especially if you take your camera. There are a number of picture-perfect viewpoints along the way, and parts of the trip are very secluded and luxuriant. Give yourself at least a full day so that you can get the most out of it. You can also do it in two or more days by staying overnight in Mae Rim. There are some severely winding stretches of road, and in places there are steep ravines next to the road, so if you decide to do your own driving, take it slow and watch out for the tour buses. The sights are listed in clockwise order, although you can do the route in the opposite direction too. The **GT Rider** website (www.gt-rider.com) has frequently updated maps, photo galleries, and suggested routes for those looking to do the loop on two wheels.

Tiger Kingdom Mae Rim

If the tigers at the Chiang Mai Zoo don't suffice, Tiger Kingdom Mae Rim (51/1 moo 7 Rimtai, Mae Rim, tel. 05/329-9363, www.tigerkingdom.com) is another option for your big cat viewing pleasure. Unlike the Tiger Temple farther south, this animal park has a reputation for treating its tigers well and allows you to spend time with the small, medium, or one-year-old tigers. In doing so, you can get the requisite photo of you lying next to one of the big cats or trying to keep your camera strap away from the baby tigers, who want to play (watch out, they bite). On your arrival you have to sign a waiver indicating you understand the risks of playing with big cats, and prices are à la carte depending on how many tigers you choose (420–520B per tiger age group), and

you can also watch feedings and bathing. A restaurant on the premises serves up delicious Thai food at reasonable prices. To get here, take the Chiang Mai–Fang Road, and at kilometer 10 there's a traffic light clearly marked with a sign toward Tiger Kingdom, where you make a left. Alternately, you can arrange private transportation with a *tuk tuk* for approximately 300B round-trip from Chiang Mai.

Samoeng Town
เมืองสะเมิง

Once you get to Samoeng Town, you will have to connect to Route 1096, but if you're hungry or want to rest your glutei maximi, this is a good place to stop. Samoeng is a small village where dense rainforest crowds the margins, seemingly waiting for its chance to reclaim the site. It has one main street with a few shops and restaurants where you can stretch your legs.

Afterward, head back to the loop road and continue onto Route 1096; this is the Mae Rim–Samoeng Road, and it's where you'll find the best attractions in the loop. If you just want to visit Samoeng and aren't too concerned about seeing the surrounding area, you can get one of a few daily unair-conditioned buses from Chang Phueak Bus Station in Chiang Mai.

Queen Sirikit Botanic Garden
สวนพฤกษศาสตร์สมเด็จพระนางเจ้าสิริกิติ์

Nesting high in its mountain niche, the ambrosial Queen Sirikit Botanic Garden (100 Mu 9, Km. 12, Mae Rim, www.qsbg.org/index_E. asp, 8:30 A.M.–4:30 P.M. daily, 40B adults, 10B children, 100B vehicles) is an attraction that always rates highly with visitors to Chiang Mai. Nature lovers, horticultural hobbyists, children, and those who simply relish fresh air and beautiful surroundings are likely to enjoy poking among the exotic and sometimes bizarre plant species and investigating the botanical projects being carried on by the scientists doing research here. The best time to visit is November–March, when you'll find the most flowers in bloom.

The gardens are located just a few minutes from Route 1096, heading from Samoeng, on your right. As you approach it, you'll see Doi Suthep–Doi Pui National Park on your left. Originally named Mae Sa Botanical Gardens, the site opened to the public in 1992 and was renamed in 1994 to honor the current queen; it was the first project of its kind in Thailand. Many pursuits aimed at preserving and propagating rare and valuable plant species are carried out at the facility, along with some insect studies such as a firefly conservation effort. No motorcycles are allowed inside the garden grounds or on its many winding trails.

Elephant Camps
ปางช้างแมสา

There are a handful of so-called elephant camps along the Mae Sa Loop, but the Elephant Nature Park in the Mae Taeng District is widely considered the most responsible of them all.

Mae Sa Elephant Camp (ปางช้างแมสา, Rte. 1096, Chiang Mai office 119/9 Tapae Rd., tel. 05/320-6247, www.maesaelephant-camp.com, 7 A.M.–4 P.M. daily, elephant shows 8 A.M., 9:40 A.M., 1:30 P.M. daily), about 8 kilometers from Route 107 heading west, is an alternative, and while not a conservation park, the elephants do appear to be treated well. On March 13, National Thai Elephant Day, the park puts on the world's largest elephant buffet, Lanna *khan toke* style, and all 70 of their elephants are invited. The camp's founder, Choochart Kalmapijit, established the park in 1976 by purchasing elephants that had no commercial value from across the country. He later launched a successful breeding program to battle the animal's rapidly dwindling numbers and to help ensure a future for the Asian elephant in Thailand. If you leave Chiang Mai no later than 9 A.M., and save Samoeng and the botanic garden for afterward, you should be in time to catch the morning elephant show, with a bathing session for the stars, who aren't above shooting a playful jet of water at anyone within range. There are usually a couple of brave baby elephants who will come over to see if they can get a few pieces of banana or sugar cane from their love-struck audience; don't worry, vendors will be on hand to provide the willing with these goodies. After the bathing, the animals assemble in the arena, where they perform acts designed to showcase their strength and coordination; you will see them moving large logs as their ancestors would have done hundreds of years ago for the Lanna Kingdom, dancing and playing music, and demonstrating their uncanny painting skills, but the best part is the elephant soccer game, where the participants will amaze you with their coordination and usually provide a few laughs to boot.

Before you leave the camp, swing by the gallery and exhibition hall, where you'll see some great photographs of newborn elephants, a collection of traditional elephant hunting weapons, and most wonderfully, art created by the facility's remarkably skilled painting elephants—it will definitely give you something to think about. You might expect that a painting pachyderm would create at best a colorful yet abstract work, "splash of red there and a streak of black over here" sort of stuff, but these very clever elephants not only casually produce obvious landscapes, they do a better job of it than a lot of humans could, with true-to-life color schemes and deliberate dimension and depth. In fact, Mae Sa's artists earned a Guinness World Record award and Ripley's Believe It or Not distinction in 2005 when they produced the world's largest and most expensive painting ever created by elephants. Titled *Cool Wind, Swirling Mist, Charming Lanna,* the astonishing eight-panel, 12-meter-long modern impressionist work depicting the northern Thai countryside was painted in six hours by eight elephants working side by side, contributing a panel each. Incredibly, the artists all seemed to have been on the same wavelength about what they were painting because the transitions between one elephant's section and the next are virtually seamless. The painting sold for 1.5 million baht and was then donated back to Thailand in two parts, one as a gift to the Thai government, and one to be displayed in Mae Sa Camp's gallery, where it can still be seen.

If you only manage to visit the Queen Sirikit

Botanic Garden and the elephant camp, you will have covered two impressive attractions, but there are a lot of other options on the route between Samoeng and Mae Rim. If you want to stay out in the mountains rather than in Chiang Mai, this area is a good choice; you will have no trouble finding something to suit you among the bungalows, guesthouses, hotels, and resorts located both on Mae Rim–Samoeng Road and in Mae Rim Town. A quiet, opulent option in Mae Rim Valley is the **Away Suansawan Resort** (43/1 Mu 6, tel. 05/304-4095, www.awayresorts.com, 1,500–2,500B), with its lushly decorated guest rooms, swimming pools, and on-site restaurants. With large hotel grounds hosting fishponds and quiet gardens, it's a chance to rest for a night away from Chiang Mai city but in the heart of the nearby valley.

Twelve kilometers along from Mae Rim is the **Mae Sa Valley Crafts Village and Resort** (86/2 Mu 2, Pongyang, tel. 05/329-0052, maesa1@ksc.th.com, 9:30 A.M.–9:30 P.M. daily), a fairyland of succulent greenery dripping with impossible quantities of colorful flowers. You can stroll around the grounds, check out the working farm, and visit the artisans who make *sa* paper, fashion umbrellas, paint ceramics, and practice traditional culinary arts in the Mae Sa Valley. If you want to try your hand at their trades, half-day courses are available for 800–2,000B with all materials provided; you can, of course, take your creations home with you. Cooking classes are available on the premises if you missed out on trying your hand at Thai cooking in Chiang Mai.

Mae Taeng District
แม่แตง

Mae Taeng District is on the rise as a popular trekking area, and its thick rainforests, towering mountains, and magnificent rivers are beginning to draw their fair share of adventure tourists. A number of organized tours have begun to come out this way, and there are lots of interesting options for checking out this relatively pristine part of Chiang Mai Province. Regular mountain biking, hiking, and white-

water rafting tours leave from Chiang Mai city, as well as daily private and group tours offering an air-conditioned vehicle and driver; one of the most-loved of these is the elephant trek, hill tribe, bamboo river rafting, and oxcart ride combination offered by many tour agents. If your time budget is small, this is a good option for experiencing the best excursions in the quickest way possible. For those with a love for adrenaline, consider **Crank Adventures** (3/2 Ratchaphakhinai Rd., tel. 08/1952-7699, www.crankadventures.com), who run day-long and multiday mountain biking trips and multisport expeditions (including white-water rafting) through the Mae Taeng Valley and surrounding areas.

This can be an interesting drive, and taking a rental vehicle up this way isn't difficult, although some of the roads leading to the hill tribe villages are in rough condition and require a 4WD vehicle or a motorcycle to traverse. No matter how you go about it, you'll either start out on Route 107 from the north, as you would going to Mae Rim, or leave town from the south on Route 108, taking the path to Samoeng and then joining Route 107 via the Mae Rim–Samoeng Road. If you go via Samoeng, you'll be taking the slightly longer scenic route, but if you haven't done this day trip already and have the time, it's easy to add the key sights located on Mae Rim–Samoeng Road to your venture north, staying overnight in Mae Rim or Mae Taeng before continuing north. Accommodations and basic amenities are available in most of the towns on the road to Fang, but selection dwindles as you get farther from the Chiang Mai tourism belt, and it's a good idea to get your cash before leaving the city as some of the smaller towns don't have ATMs or 7-Elevens, and many have only one, leaving you few options if anything goes wrong. Also remember to fill up on gas whenever you leave a town site because there are very few gas stations on the highway.

A short 23 kilometers north of Mae Rim (39 kilometers from Chiang Mai) lies the town of Mae Taeng, whose primary claim to fame is its convenient location close to many of the popular trekking routes; it's also the last major town before Chiang Dao, 32 kilometers farther north. This is a good place to stop for a bite to eat and to pick up any necessities before hitting the attractions strung out along the highway just north of the town.

Wat Tung Luang (วัดทุ่งหลวง) presents a rather unusual spectacle that may not be to all tastes, but it has managed to bring the otherwise unremarkable temple some notoriety. This was the home of the much venerated monk Khru Ba Thammachai, who died in 1988 at age 73. The buildings of this *wat* have been brightly decorated in his honor, and there is a very lifelike wax model of him in the *wihan*. The unusual and slightly macabre feature, however, is the view of his body available through the glass top of his coffin, still standing to the right of the wax effigy. The *wat*'s grounds are also lined with a series of golden Buddhas, unremarkable one by one but together painting a fluid, pretty picture.

Heading north again, you'll come to an east turnoff at kilometer 43 that signals the beginning of a stretch of elephant camps, some of them offering a range of trekking options. Although several of the camps do treat their elephants well, the **Elephant Nature Park** (in the Mae Taeng Valley, main booking office in Chiang Mai, 209/2 Sridom Chai Rd., tel. 05/381-8754, www.elephantnaturepark. org, one-day trip 2,500B, weeklong packages available) is the best and most responsible of them and serves as a sanctuary for abused and mistreated Asian elephants rescued from a wide variety of situations. Some were overworked while logging or trekking, others were street elephants, begging with their mahouts for change. A large number of the elephants have serious mental and physical handicaps as a result of their mistreatment. Founder Sangduen Chailert, known affectionately as Khun Lek, has won her nature park numerous well-deserved awards since its inception in the early 1990s. Not only does it house elephants, but the sprawling grounds also serve as a sanctuary for endangered species and for rainforest preservation. Located 1.5 hours from Chiang Mai,

the Elephant Nature Park is in a verdant valley, and a one-day package will include bathing and feeding the elephants, educational talks and videos, and a delicious buffet lunch.

For those looking to spend more than one day with the elephants, weeklong packages for small groups of volunteers allow for even more up-close and personal interaction. Shadowing the mahouts as they lead the elephants into the rainforest for the night and back to the Nature Park during the day, volunteers will be able to sleep in tree houses in the rainforest, drifting to sleep to the sound of elephants foraging below. Other volunteer opportunities include working with Antoinette van de Water, author of *The Great Elephant Escape,* at the Elephant Jungle, a newly purchased tract of land where elephants are able to roam freely during the day. Volunteers will help to build facilities and reforest land that was previously used for farming.

While prices exceed those for the other elephant camps, the money goes to feeding the elephants (they eat several tons of food each day) and running the nature park. If you only have time for one elephant activity in Thailand, this is the best option available. Transportation to and from Chiang Mai is included in the package prices.

Chiang Dao
เชียงดาว

Just before Route 107 splits off to Route 1178, halfway to Fang, is Chiang Dao, a small market town that serves the local Lisu, Hmong, Akha, and Padaung hill tribe villagers. This is about as far as you would want to come if you are planning to return to Chiang Mai the same day, and it makes for a great motorcycle ride if you're comfortable on two wheels. The Chiang Dao daily market starts at dawn and is unremarkable, but on Tuesday the hill tribes descend from the surrounding hills, and the market is a boisterous, bright, and pungent affair, a 100 percent Thai agrarian market. You won't find much in the way of goods for visitors here, which is part of its charm—the market is truly for the surrounding villages, and it's a fascinating glimpse into a wholly different life. The earlier you arrive, the better. The town's **Wat Tham Pha Plong** is also worth a visit; it sits halfway up the side of Doi Chiang Dao in a small cave surrounded by trees, with more than 500 steps leading to the top. Given its height, it affords some great views and is often visited by Lisu tribeswomen in full costume, paying their respects to the *chedi*. The temple was also the last teaching place of revered monk Looang Boo Sim Buddhacaro.

If you go east from Chiang Dao, past Wat Indra, you can check out some traditional lowland villages, and if you have a 4WD vehicle, you can continue up to the plateau beyond, where there are a number of hill tribe villages. The leafy dips and peaks of Doi Chiang Dao are considered to be one of the most beautiful vistas in Chiang Mai Province, and you'll get a number of viewpoints on your way into town; it's worth taking a moment here and there to stop and breathe it all in.

What really draw travelers, however, are the **Chiang Dao Caves** (Tham Chiang Dao, 20B), a vast maze of five interconnected caves extending as far as 16 kilometers into Doi Chiang Dao. Getting to the cave complex is fairly simple: Follow the main road through town until you see a sign for the caves, and then bear left and continue on for another seven kilometers. Alternately, ask anyone in town for a point in the right direction. The site is viewed as sacred to local Buddhists and is an active site of worship; along with a trove of spectacular natural formations, many Buddha images repose in silent meditation. The legend of the Chiang Dao Caves centers around a hermit-sage who lived on Doi Chiang Dao for 1,000 years, eventually becoming so intimate with the realm of the deities that he was able to convince some mythical beings to endow the caverns with seven magical wonders: a solid-gold Buddha with a stream flowing from its pedestal, a cache of divine textiles, a mystical lake, a *naga* citadel, an immortal elephant, and the tomb of the hermit himself. According to the locals, these arcane treasures are hidden so deep within the cave system that, other than the hermit, no one

has ever seen them. Of course, it wouldn't do you or Indiana Jones any good even if you did find them because, as you might expect, they're protected by a powerful curse: Apparently anyone attempting to remove so much as a pebble from the caverns is doomed to become hopelessly lost in the warren of tunnels and wander for eternity.

This is not the place to wander away from the well-lit pathways without a guide—there are many kilometers of inky-black tunnels twisted into a confusing labyrinth that even a very good flashlight can't help you navigate, not to mention the occasional unmarked sudden drop-off. But not to worry; the five caves that are open to the public are safe and well maintained, some with electric lighting, and guides are waiting with oil lamps to take you through for 100B per group. At the main entrance, just five kilometers west of town, you will find the stairs ascending to the caves and a pool of spring water sporting some rather large overfed fish; you can purchase some fish food and add to their obviously ample diet, if you like, before paying your 20B admission fee and carrying on to the caves. Exploring two of the caves, **Tham Phra Non** (360 meters) and **Tham Seua Dao** (540 meters), on your own is easy with electric lighting provided by the city to accompany you, but **Tham Ma** (7365 meters), **Tham Kaeo** (477 meters), and **Tham Nam** (660 meters) are unlit, so pick up one of the waiting guides, who can tell you a little bit about the different formations you'll see as you clamber around sweeping caverns, squeeze through a few tight spaces, and even crawl from time to time. Obviously, anyone suffering from claustrophobia should probably sit this one out, but if you can stomach the occasionally uncomfortable conditions, you'll be rewarded with some very weird and wonderful geology naturally sculpted into over 100 strange and beautiful formations.

In recent years, Chiang Dao's popularity has increased, and like Mae Hong Son it is now regarded as an alternative to escape the weekend crowds of Chiang Mai and Pai. As a result, accommodation options—fairly sparse until now—have multiplied, with some lovely guest-houses sitting in the shadow of Doi Chiang Dao. **Malee's Nature Lovers Bungalows** (144/2 Mu, tel. 08/1961-8387, maleenature@hotmail.com, www.maleenature.com, 650–1,550B, 7th night free) is a family-run guesthouse with guest rooms nestled next to the mountain. Spacious bungalows are built in solid wood with mosquito nets, en suite hot-water showers and toilets, and all are set around a beautiful garden; there is free Wi-Fi on the premises. The **Chiang Dao Nest** (144/4 Mu 5, tel. 08/6017-1985, http://nest.chiangdao.com, from 500B) is another option for a few days in Chiang Dao, with 20 clean and well-maintained bungalows next to the mountain. It also has free Wi-Fi, a small swimming pool, and a critically acclaimed restaurant on the premises that, while more expensive than the usual backpacker fare, is not to be missed. The popularity of the Nest (book ahead if you're heading to Chiang Dao in high season) led to an expansion and the creation of another guest-house, **Chiang Dao Nest 2** (tel. 05/345-6242, from 700B), one kilometer away. The Nest 2 has supplemented the original Nest's European fusion restaurant with a very good mid-range Thai restaurant and has six quaint bunga-lows, each with impressive mountain views. **Marisa Boutique Resort and Spa** (304 Mu 4, Muang-Ngai, Chiang Dao, tel. 05/337-5517, www.marisaresort.com, 1,500–2,000B), a col-lection of wooden bungalows and guest rooms in a lush, green setting overlooking a small river with nice mountain views from most of the rooms. Guest rooms and baths are all comfortable, clean, and modern, although not quite up to urban boutique-hotel standards. The stand-alone villas, which can accommo-date small families or groups traveling together, are a bargain for their size and may persuade you to use the resort as a base for exploring the rest of the region.

After Chiang Dao, you'll have a green ex-panse of rice fields, rainforest, and towering mountains for company as you press on to Fang, but at this point you're out of the tour-ist zone, and the last 80 kilometers don't offer much to stop for. There is, however, an oppor-tunity to check out a natural Thai teakwood forest 10 kilometers north of Chiang Dao at the junction of Route 1150. Head east down Route 1150 for a pleasant few minutes to see these trees, which have played a key role in Thai art and culture from the times of Lanna until today.

Chiang Dao is almost 75 kilometers north of Chiang Mai along Route 107. To get here with-out transportation of your own, buses leave hourly until the early evening from Chiang Mai's Chang Phueak Terminal and cost 50B—the bus will be headed toward Tha Ton; just ask the driver to let you off at Chiang Dao. From Chiang Dao's bus terminal, *song thaew* will charge 100–150B to bring you directly to your guesthouse.

DOI ANG KHANG
ดอยอ่างขาง

Route 107 continues north from Chiang Dao, past farms and small villages and a few of the more rugged sightseeing venues such as rain-forest trekking, river rafting, and spelunking in some rather impressive caves. It will eventually take you to the town of Fang, 151 kilometers from Chiang Mai and very close to the north-ernmost part of Thailand and its border with Burma. From here you can take the smaller Route 1089 a little farther to the border town of Ban Tha Ton. If city life isn't your scene and you want to get away from the tourist trail and into something 100 percent Thai, you might consider sojourning up this route. This is also the best direction to head if you want to visit the hill tribe villages of the Lahu, Lisu, Karen, and Hmong people, which can be done in a single day or with overnight stays either nearby or right in the villages with the local people. A very worthy trip on the route to Fang and the border is Mae Fang National Park's Doi Ang Khang.

Easily one of Thailand's most beautiful mountains, Doi Ang Khang sits at 585 meters above sea level. It has an unusually temperate climate year-round, which local farmers have traditionally made use of for growing crops that are unsuited to the warmer environment found everywhere else. The apricots, peaches, and plums grown on its slopes are considered rather exotic among Thais, and carrots, herbs, and salad greens thrive here along with flower farms turning out carnations, roses, asters, and chrysanthemums. The unique conditions have resulted in Doi Ang Khang being used as something of an agricultural petri dish, with all kinds of crops brought to the mountain to see if they will grow. There is a **Royal Agricultural Project** station (Ban Khum, Mae Ngon, tel. 05/345-0107, 30B pp, 50B vehicle) at the summit where research into various substitute crops for the hill farmers to replace opium is ongoing. The station has public gardens and sells produce, literally showcasing the fruits of their labors; there are also restaurants and even a guesthouse (800–900B) to receive visitors. Unfortunately, the mountain's ability to produce exotic flora has prompted overcultivation and deforestation, although regulations have been put in place, and the damaged areas are beginning to come back. An interesting side effect of all these ventures and projects has been remarkably diverse forests, with leafy escapees growing among the original complement of plants on the mountain. This in turn has attracted a huge variety of birds that come to the mountain to feast on the array of fruits—in fact, Doi Ang Khang is generally considered to be one of the best spots for bird-watching in northern Thailand, and it's also pretty good for wildflowers.

The mountain is home to a number of **Lahu, Lisu,** and **Hmong** hill tribe villages, and there are even a few **Yunnanese settlements** transplanted from China. If you pack along a decent map, you can visit them and even hike a few of the trekking trails without needing a guide. Maps are available in Fang and at the military checkpoint on Route 1249, which takes you into Mae Fang National Park. For those with more time and a budget to match, an overnight option exists at the upscale **Angkhang Nature Resort** (1/1 Mu 5 Ban Koom Tambon Mae Ngon, tel. 05/345-0110, www.oamhotels. com/angkhang, from 2,000B), developed as part of the Royal Angkhang Research Station. You'll see signs for the turnoff on Route 107. With over 70 guest rooms and a Swiss-style lobby with fireplaces and a huge high ceiling, you'll feel as though you've temporarily left Thailand. Guest rooms are fully decked out in modernity; each has a minibar, TV, and telephone with its large en suite bath. Half of the resort's staff come from hill tribes in the surrounding villages, and the Nature Resort's restaurant uses only organic locally sourced foodstuffs from the Royal Project.

Most people make for the summit of Doi Ang Khan by turning east off Route 107 at kilometer 137, which is 16 kilometers before Fang, and driving the steep, rainforest-hemmed 24 kilometers to the top. Adventurists, however, might be interested in braving the more scenic and more rugged back road. Route 1178 departs Route 107 just north of Chiang Dao, right after the Chiang Dao Caves, and winds its way north past archaic mountain villages and agrarian vistas, meandering along a ridge for 48 kilometers to the top of Doi Ang Khang. This is not a good place to get stuck or have a breakdown, so if you go this way, use common sense, pack along the things you might need, including a full tank of gas and a flashlight, and be extra careful after wet weather. Despite (or possibly because of) its rustic quality, it's an exciting route to take to get to Fang. Make sure to connect to Route 1340 (keep heading north) at its junction with Route 1178, then depart the mountaintop via Route 1249 to return to Route 107 and the last short northward hop to Fang Town.

Fang
ฝาง

All the way at the north terminus of Route 107, for most people Fang village is only a brief stop on their way to bigger destinations, but it has a few interesting elements of its own if you have a bit of time on your hands. You will find most of the basic amenities, including a few banks, some currency-exchange services, restaurants, and accommodations, and you can wander around exploring the back streets, where odd local shops wait with their dusty wares crammed into the recesses of the wooden buildings. Nearby expanses of Mae Fang National Park shelter a few Karen and Mien hill tribe villages, and the Fang Hot Springs that simmer sulfurously just eight kilometers northwest of town. Apart from the apparatus of the geothermal energy station, an Israeli-built sustainable-power project, the four-hectare forested hot springs area is an attractive and pristine location for an outing; many locals come here on weekends to picnic and enjoy some quality time with their families. The park is literally bursting with springs, and there are over 50 spots where hot water escapes to the surface in temperatures ranging 40–100°C. Many of the fonts shoot from the earth either continuously or at intervals, sending steaming jets of water meters into the air and shedding the pungent aroma of sulfur.

While many people opt to breeze through Fang on the way to Tha Ton, the morning market is a worthy reason to stay for the night. Leave some room for sampling the myriad of stalls that dot the market's street, from delicious Yunnan food to traditional northern Thai soups and Chinese-style steamed *bao* buns stuffed with barbequed pork. For lodging, an excellent option is the warm and inviting **Phumanee Home Hotel** (122/1 Mu 4, tel. 05/345-2875 or 05/345-2876, www.phumanee-hotel.com, 600B, breakfast included), owned by a Lahu couple. The hotel's guest rooms are simple, with white tiled floors, Lahu textiles, and hot-water showers, and they include free Wi-Fi and TV. Head to the second floor for a small Lahu textile and history exhibit, and be sure to ask the helpful owners for any information about Fang or Lahu communities. A small restaurant on the premises serves Lahu, Chinese, Thai, and Western food.

Numerous daily local buses depart Chiang Mai's Chang Phueak Bus Station for the three-hour trip to Fang (80B).

Tha Ton
ท่าตอน

Only 32 kilometers north of Fang on Route 1089, tiny Tha Ton is actually surprisingly well set up to handle travelers, and given the choice, most people prefer to stay in this charming, colorful little town rather than in Fang. Nestled in its valley and clinging to the banks of the Mae Kok River, this rainforest-clad hamlet manages to attract travelers mainly because of its daily 3–6 hour (depending on river conditions) **longtail boat rides** to Chiang Rai (12:30 P.M., 450B) that take you past hill tribe villages, soaring green mountains, and steamy lowland rainforest so tranquil and beautiful that it almost makes your heart ache. With the number of people passing through on their way to and from Chiang Mai and Chiang Rai, it was only a matter of time before guesthouses, restaurants, and even full-fledged resorts sprang up to serve them. You often see hill tribe people around town, and the surrounding area is full of their villages. This is a great place to plan a do-it-yourself visit; most people rent a bicycle or motorcycle, but you can even simply hoof it right from town and hike to some of the closest ones.

There are a number of tour agents operating in town, and all kinds of organized and informal trekking, biking, and rafting adventures set out daily to take in the surrounding countryside. There are a handful of small tour outfitters (available by phone only) in the town of Tha Ton, including **Thaton Tours** (tel. 05/337-3143). All can arrange half-day to multiday tours that include hill tribe visits, hiking, and river rafting. Expect to pay around 2,000B per day for a private boat, which will include basic accommodations in the rainforest as well as food and drink.

Wat Tha Ton (www.wat-thaton.org/index-english.html) is the local monastery and is reached by a staircase that takes you up to its perch on the mountainside, with impressive ornamental gardens and wonderful views of the valley. The temple takes up a large swath of land—more than 65 hectares—and houses nine levels or hills, each with a stupa or Buddha to visit. The trip from the base level to level 9 will involve at least 30 minutes of walking time. Level 4 has a meditation cave, which can be used to sit and meditate for a few hours along the way. The temple also houses a school for monks, novices, and youths as well as a drug rehabilitation center and a hill tribe support unit. The giant bell at the monastery is loud enough to be heard all through the valley, and it's rung once at 4 A.M. to wake the monks and once at 6 A.M. to signal the period of alms-collecting.

One very popular, if fairly rugged, excursion is the river route to Chiang Rai, spread out over three days, during which you cruise aboard a bamboo "house" raft, consisting of a lashed bamboo platform with a small bamboo hut erected on one end of it. During your journey, you sleep and dine on board or at hill tribe villages; your raft comes with a captain and cook, so all you have to do is take it easy and take it in. The trip will cost a few thousand baht pp, and there are usually at least four passengers to a boat. Though not for the faint of heart or sensitive of rump, the excursion scores pretty big points for excitement while failing in basic comforts, and it promises a pretty unforgettable experience for those who dare. You can book a raft through one of the tour agents, or simply go down to the dock and see if you can work out a deal with one of the boat owners.

If you're planning on making the trip from Chiang Mai a multiday affair, which is recommended if you can afford the time, there are several reliable accommodations in or near Tha Ton. **Old Tree's House** (323 Ban Rumthai, M. 14, tel. 08/5722-9002, www.oldtreeshouse.net/en, from 1,200B, breakfast included), owned by French-Thai husband and wife team Paulo and Nid, is a slice of paradise in the forests of northern Thailand. The bungalows are set around a garden and tiny pool, each with a king

bed, a DVD player, and an en suite tiled bath. The hotel also offers free laundry service, so if you've been on the go for quite a few days, you can take advantage of it. Perched at the edge of the Mae Kok River with a stunning mountain backdrop and flower-filled bungalows is the charming **Apple River Villa** (555 M. 14, Mae Ai, Tha Ton, tel. 05/337-3144, applethatton@yahoo.com, 800B). Bungalows each have air-conditioning, hot water, and cable TV and are newly built with clean en suite baths. Chairs and tables set up along the villa's tiny river boardwalk provide an ideal place to sit and watch the sunset. A more upscale option is the popular **Maekok River Village Resort** (P.O. Box 3, Mae Ai, tel. 05/305-3628, www.maekok-river-village-resort.com, reservations room@maekok-river-village-resort.com, 3,250B d, 4,950B family room), with 36 spacious guest rooms set at the river's edge and meticulously manicured grounds full of ponds, trees, and flowers. The resort is fairly new, and each guest room has built-in furniture and an airy, open feel; with large windows and private terraces, it feels like a home away from home. The resort can organize regional treks and also offers cooking classes or mountain biking, or you can relax in its small swimming pool. The restaurant on the premises will satisfy your food needs, but a smattering of riverside restaurants adjoins the resorts at the river's edge for some variety, and the boat dock also houses several local food stalls.

There are six unair-conditioned buses running daily from Chiang Mai's Chang Phueak Bus Station (4 hours, 150B)—not the most comfortable option, but currently no air-conditioned buses or minivans make their way to Tha Ton.

CHIANG MAI

Chiang Rai Province จังหวัดเชียงราย

While the town of Chiang Rai doesn't have enough attractions to hold your attention for too long, the surrounding area is beautiful and far less traveled than Chiang Mai Province, making it a good choice if you want to enjoy the scenery and meet people from the surrounding hill tribes. If you're interested in hiking or trekking, there plenty of options based at Doi Mae Salong and Chiang Rai for every level of experience.

Chiang Rai is the country's northernmost province, barely beating Chiang Mai by about 32 kilometers, a generally mountainous area bordered on the north by Burma on one side and Laos on another. This border region was once notorious for its drug trade but now is better known for its cooler mountain weather, hill tribe communities, and beautifully crafted goods as well as good regional agricultural products such as coffee and tea. It is a region not to be missed, especially for those who like the outdoors and are curious about the incredibly diverse ethnic groups living in the region.

Even if you only have a few days, the scenery and sights around Chiang Rai are an important addition to your trip. The most beautiful thing about Chiang Rai is the surrounding area; the city is small, and it's easy to get a feel for it and then hit the main roads. Do not hesitate to rent a motorcycle or even a bicycle; many of the surrounding sights are less than 20 kilometers from town, and the roads are in good condition and far from busy.

CHIANG RAI TOWN
เมืองเชียงราย

Less developed than its sister to the south, Chiang Rai is smaller and more intimate than Chiang Mai, and if you were disappointed to find so much traffic and commotion in Chiang Mai, you may find Chiang Rai more to your liking. Most of the town can be covered on foot, and there are many refreshing little sidewalk cafés to fortify you as you stroll its pleasant streets and explore its curious *sois*.

Although the atmosphere is distinctly Thai, fellow travelers, tour agencies, guesthouses, and a handful of international restaurants are still easily found. You can enjoy the benefits of being a bit farther off the well-beaten tourist track without sacrificing key comforts and conveniences. Many travelers base themselves in the town and set off on single or multiday treks through the mountains.

The city was founded by King Mengrai in 1262 and was an important city to the Mengrai Dynasty until it fell to Burma. Under Burmese rule from 1558 to 1774, Chiang Rai was annexed to Siam in the late 1800s and only became a province of Thailand in 1933.

Sights

If you're spending a day or two in Chiang Rai, make sure to check out a few of the town's *wats* and museums. The most important historically is **Wat Phra Kaeo** (Trairat Rd., near Reuang Nakhon Rd., sunrise–sunset), which has a small museum inside displaying artifacts and texts. It is also where the revered Emerald Buddha that now resides in Bangkok's own Wat Phra Kaeo was found in the 15th century. The little green Buddha, which has been replaced by a replica, is one of the most important Buddha images in Thailand and perhaps the most important for the ruling Chakri Dynasty; it is said to have been made more than 2,000 years ago in Sri Lanka and then moved to present-day Burma and Cambodia, then Ayutthaya, and finally Chiang Rai, where it was hidden away under plaster. Legend has it that the Emerald Buddha was only discovered after a fortuitous bolt of lightning struck the *chedi* in 1434, cracking it open and revealing the green jade beneath the plaster. Soon after its discovery, the Buddha was moved to Lampang, then Chiang Mai, then Laos, and finally to Bangkok in 1778. In its place, a smaller replica has been installed, carved out of Canadian jadeite donated to Chiang Rai. The large bronze Buddha inside Wat Phra Kaeo differs from

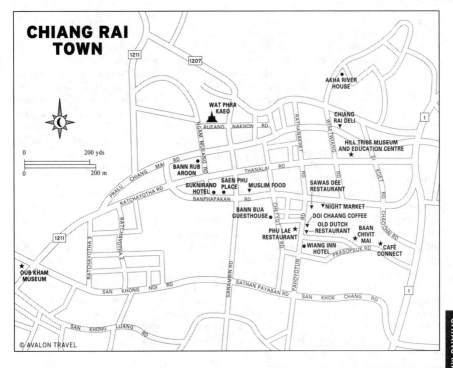

most Buddhas in that it remains ungilded; it is enormous, however, and considered one of most beautiful in Thailand. Originally outside of Chiang Rai proper, the Buddha dates back to the 1300s and was moved to Wat Phra Kaeo in 1961. The temple complex itself has been renovated over the centuries but remains a largely wooden structure, decorated with red and ornate gold details. It was originally called Wat Pa Yia, "yellow bamboo forest," after the bamboo that grew in the formerly rural area. Several bamboo copses still surround the *wat* today, a monument to its past.

The **Hill Tribe Museum and Education Centre** (620/25 Thanalai Rd., 3rd Fl., tel. 05/371-9167, www.pda.or.th/chiangrai/hill-tribe_museum.htm, 9 A.M.–6 P.M. Mon.–Fri., 10 A.M.–6 P.M. Sat.–Sun., 50B) is a must-stop if you are going to be doing any trekking to hill tribe communities in the region. Run by the Population and Community Development Association (PDA), the small museum offers a wealth of information about the cultures of the different ethnic groups living in the region as well as some interesting exhibits on the cultivation of opium. The PDA also runs nonprofit tours to surrounding villages, all of which are designed to reduce the negative impact of tourism on these small communities while bringing as much of the monetary profit from them directly to the villagers. If scheduling permits, this is probably the most responsible way to see the hill tribes. If not, supporting the PDA's community development projects is a piece of cake—the shop at the center has a great selection of goods at more than reasonable prices. There is a particularly good variety of different woven goods—bags, pouches, wallets, even bottle holders, representing different hill tribe styles. They also have a wide selection of gifts, including nutcrackers and garlic presses made from forest wood.

CHIANG MAI

Dazzling in the high sun and a superb work of intricate, dizzyingly complicated craftsmanship is Chiang Rai's "White Temple," **Wat Rong Khun** (วัดร่องขุ่น, Tambon Pa-Or Donchai, tel. 05/367-3579, 7 A.M.–6 P.M. daily, free). The temple is one of the strangest you'll see, and that alone makes for a worthy visit, but the effort and story that went into its creation as well as its undeniable beauty make Wat Rong Khun a must-see for any trip to Chiang Rai. Just 13 kilometers south of town, it has been visited by over 5 million people (only 200,000 of which were foreigners) since construction began in 1997. Still unfinished, the temple is the work of famous Thai painter Chalermchai Kositpipat, who has funded construction of the temple himself. The temple gleams from afar, constructed with shards of glass and whitewashed between the glitter. The profuse whiteness is meant to symbolize the purity of the Buddha, while the mosaic of mirrors represents the Buddha's wisdom, shining from afar. Every statue and carving was carefully chosen to weave Kositpipat's broader philosophical point; the grounds are full of strange artwork, riddles, and Buddhist messages. The temple is surrounded by a pond brimming with black and white fish and guarded by a panoply of statues and dragons; it is reached via a bridge. Hundreds of finely sculpted hands reach out to you as you walk the bridge to the *wat,* reminding you that happiness can only be obtained by overcoming earthly desires. Inside the wat, walls are adorned with a curious mix of Buddhist and modern scenes, with paintings that include a plane crashing into the twin towers, and many movie and comic characters such as Neo, Batman, Superman, and even *Star Wars* droids. While photography inside the temple is discouraged, the outside provides plenty of photographic wonder. Don't miss the "golden" restroom. A small souvenir store is on the premises too, with earnings going toward further construction of the temple.

Also slightly out of town to the west of Chiang Rai is **Mae Fa Luang Art and Cultural Park** (313 Mu 7, Ban Pa Ngiew, tel. 05/371-6605, 9 A.M.–5 P.M. Tues.–Sun., www. maefahluang.org/mfl_art_cultural_park.php, 200B). The art center, a project of the king's late mother to preserve Lanna culture, contains displays of devotional and secular art and artifacts from the Lanna Kingdom. Objects include 19th-century murals, Buddha images, and household objects, and there are also some very large carved wood pieces within the park. The collection is housed on the grounds of a 26-hectare botanical garden speckled with lily ponds and *salas.* This is a lovely place to spend an afternoon strolling the grounds and enjoying the collection of art.

If you're interested in Lanna Kingdom art, stop into the private **Oub Kham Museum** (พิพิธภัณฑ์อูบคำ, 81/1 Thanon Na Khai, Rop Wiang district, tel. 05/371-3349, 10 A.M.–9 P.M. daily, www.oubkhammuseum.com, 200B), just outside town. Set in a beautiful garden, the museum houses a private collection of art from the Lanna Kingdom, including jewelry, devotional art, and housewares. Guided tours are included in the entry fee, and the museum's grounds are replete with gilded statues and fountains aplenty.

Food

The **Night Market** (Phahonyothin Rd. and Prasobsuk Rd., 6–10 P.M. daily), next to the bus station, is a great bet for a large selection of inexpensive food, and you'll find dishes from all over the country for sale. As an added bonus, there always seems to be something going on at the market, be it a local dance performance or even an outdoor movie.

If you want to sit down and eat, try the food court in the **Center Point Night Bazaar** (tel. 05/374-0122, 6–11 P.M. daily, 100B) right in the middle of the night market. It may seem a little touristy, but the Thai dishes are exceptionally well prepared. Their Thai menu is massive and includes all sorts of specialties, such as northern and Isan food. Local vegetables are often featured, as is fish. There is an especially good selection of Thai spicy salads, including some less common ones such as pineapple salad and fish *maw,* or Kraphopla (กระเพาะปลา) salad. There are also some

© SUZANNE NAM

hill tribe children and hikers at a village rest stop

Western options if you have the urge for some spaghetti or a tuna sandwich.

Known as Rot Prasoet in Thai, the only name on the English sign is **Muslim Food** (407/1 Isaraparb Rd., 7 A.M.–8 P.M. daily, 50B). This Thai-Muslim restaurant next to the mosque on Isaraparb Road serves freshly prepared halal meals, including an absolutely delicious Thai-style chicken *biryani, khao mok kai*. It's best to go in a group so you can eat family style and sample several dishes in one sitting.

Air-conditioned, brightly lit, and centrally-located **Phu Lae Restaurant** (612/6 Phaholyothin Rd., Tambon Wiang, tel. 05/360-0500, 11 A.M.–11 P.M. daily, www.phulaerestaurant.com, 100B) is popular among Thai travelers and locals alike. With wooden furniture and a bright, easy-to-spot red logo, the menu spans the globe from Western food to Thai specialties, curries, and steaks. It is a very informal eatery with a solid selection of foods to try.

Near the night bazaar is old favorite **Sawadee Restaurant** (112/29, Mu 18, 2nd Fl., tel. 08/4483-1689, 6–11 P.M. daily, www.

thaisawaddee.net, 50–150B) offering just about any Thai dish, north or south, that you could want. Try their fiery *kaeng pa kai,* a thick red curry with chicken, vegetables, and generous amounts of Thai basil.

For a cup of coffee and some free Wi-Fi, head to **Café Connect** (70-171 Mu 18, Prasobsuk Rd., tel. 05/375-4181, http://connectcafe-chiangrai.blogspot.com, 9 A.M.–8 P.M. daily, 50–100B), near the old Chiang Rai bus station. With bright striped walls and funky furniture, it's a great place to hang out and catch up on email or relax and meet new people in town. Besides fresh coffee made from locally grown beans, they offer an extensive menu of Thai and Western food at very reasonable prices (including sandwiches and soups, for those craving some Western snacks) as well as a smoothie and coffee concoctions. A delicious array of baked goods from their own bakery rounds out their offerings.

If you're looking for a quick meal and a good cause, consider stopping in at **Baan Chivit Mai** (Prasobsuk Rd., tel. 05/371-2357, 8 A.M.–9 P.M.

Mon.–Sat., 100B), opposite the old bus terminal. The name means "home for new life," and this tiny café and bakery's profits go toward training hill tribe children in new vocations, and hopefully providing them with a life away from the unfortunate reality of human trafficking. The bakery offers cakes, cookies, and pastries as well as breakfast sets and a small selection of Western and Thai dishes.

Set in a tiny teak house just north of the King Mengrai monument, **Salung Kham** (Phahonyothin Rd., tel. 05/371-7192, 10 A.M.–10 P.M. daily, 250B) is a terrific spot to try northern Thai delicacies in a quiet setting. The owner is a native of Chiang Mai and recipes are from her family's exploration with Thai cooking. The food here is carefully prepared and delicious; recommended dishes include Burmese-style curry, green chili paste *namphrik num,* and anything made with northern-style sausage. A comfortable garden provides an alternative if the dining room is full.

If you're tired of Thai food and need a little Western food fix, **Old Dutch** (541 Phahonyothin Rd., tel. 05/371-4282, 10 A.M.–10 P.M., 200–1,000B) is a comfortable and friendly restaurant that, with its mirrored, ornate bar and rounded tables, seems like it has been imported directly from Europe. Owned by a Dutch chef, the restaurant's menu is incredibly vast—if you're craving something specific, you can probably find it here. A long drink list matches the food selection, including a large array of beers, whiskey, and wine.

Accommodations

A popular place for the budget-conscious, ❰ **Baan Rub Aroon Guesthouse** (65 Ngammuang Rd., tel. 05/371-1827, www. baanrubaroon.net, 550–750B, breakfast included) has five bright and airy guest rooms with high ceilings and fresh white linens. On-site cooking classes, free Wi-Fi, a helpful owner with plenty of information on the surrounding area, and the uniqueness of a tiny hotel set in a white colonial house makes this an excellent option for lodging in Chiang Rai. Hammocks and plenty of relaxing nooks and crannies for

guests will make you loath to leave the house and explore. Dorm rooms are also available for those on a serious budget.

On a hill 10 kilometers outside Chiang Rai, **Naga Hill Resort** (Mu 8, Ban Pha-oo, Tambon Bandu, tel. 08/1818-9684, www.nagahill.com, 1,200–1,800B, breakfast included) offers beautifully crafted wooden bungalows in a dense tropical garden, each with a mosquito net, a fan, and an outdoor en suite bath with a ceramic tiled tub. Bungalows come in three sizes (small, medium, or large) and guests can take advantage of the large pool on the premises. It is not the place for late-night parties or nightlife-seekers, but if you are looking for peace and quiet, this might be your place.

The ❰ **Akha River House** (423/25 Mu 21 Soi 1, Kholoy Rd., tel. 08/9997-5505, www. akha.info, 250–900B) guesthouse, owned by the same Akha people who run tours to neighboring hill tribe communities, is a great inexpensive option, offering comfortable, well-designed guest rooms and bungalows set right on the river in a very scenic, verdant area of Chiang Rai. Recently renovated guest rooms are not luxurious but extremely well kept and decorated in log furniture with a retiled private bath. Nearly everyone who stays here books one of the tours, which may account for the relatively low rates. A far more rustic alternative, also arranged through Apae, the owner of the Akha River House, is a night at the **Akha Hill House,** 23 kilometers outside Chiang Rai (97/7 Doi Hang, apaehouse@hotmail.com, www.akhahill.com, 200B). While not for those who want the comforts of home, a night in the surrounding rainforest is a fun and different way to discover Chiang Rai. They also offer free pickup or drop-off anywhere in Chiang Rai town.

Suknirand Hotel (424/1 Banphaprakarn Rd., tel. 05/371-1055, 600B) is small and charming guesthouse, set back from the road. Rooms are comfortable and clean and up to Western standards, though not particularly luxurious. There are also fan-only guest rooms here that are about 30 percent less expensive than those with air-conditioning. This hotel is very well located for seeing the town's sights.

Baan Bua Guesthouse (879/2 Jet Yot Rd., tel. 05/371-8880, www.baanbuaguesthouse. com, 300–500B) has 17 clean, quiet guest rooms a short hop from Chiang Rai's old bus station. Opened in 1995, the guesthouse still attracts a loyal following. Wi-Fi is free for guests, and the guesthouse is set around a quiet garden, perfect for reading and relaxing after a long day of exploring. Opt for the 500B guest rooms if they are available.

Opulent **Le Meridien Chiang Rai** (221/2 Mu 20 Kwaewai Rd., tel. 05/360-3333, www.starwoodhotels.com/lemeridien, 4,500–7,500B), set directly on the banks of the Mae Kok River, opened in 2009 and has received rave reviews. The resort grounds include sprawling landscaped gardens complete with a tranquil artificial lake and a large pool and fitness area. Guest rooms are spacious, most with a river view and a roomy balcony. A copious plate of fruit and brownies to welcome new guests is a nice touch. If you do not have a car or motorcycle, the resort offers a free shuttle service from the hotel into Chiang Mai town, which takes approximately 10–15 minutes. Free use of the business center is included for all guests.

Walk into the lobby of the **Wiang Inn Hotel** (893 Phaholyothin Rd., tel. 05/371-1533, www. wianginn.com, from 2,800B) and you'll forget you are in Chiang Rai, or even Thailand, for that matter. This is probably the most Western place in town; the 260-room behemoth of a hotel even has a bar right in the lobby. This is a good choice if you want large, clean guest rooms and the ease of staying at a big hotel and don't mind going without the charm of smaller properties.

◖ **The Legend** (124/15 Mu 21, Kholoy Rd., tel. 05/391-0400, www.thelegend-chiangrai. com, 3,900–5,900B, breakfast included) is a beautiful boutique hotel just 1.5 kilometers from the center of town. All the guest rooms are done in a Thai-tropical style. Baths have showers separate from the toilets, all done in plenty of natural stone and natural light. The villas are particularly lovely with their own whirlpool tubs. The hotel has everything you would expect—a spa, two restaurants, and impeccable service—and it also offers a free shuttle to the Night Bazaar as well as bikes for rent and tricycle taxis.

Getting There

With daily direct flights from Bangkok on Thai Airways, Orient Thai Airways, Bangkok Airways, and Air Asia, it's easy to visit Chiang Rai. The **Chiang Rai Airport** (CEI) is just a few kilometers out of town; if your hotel or guesthouse isn't picking you up, there are taxis waiting.

If you are coming from Chiang Mai, you can take a three-hour bus; there are more than a dozen official government buses and private buses departing throughout the day, and an air-conditioned bus will cost under 200B, with VIP buses making the trip for 360B. Buses from Chiang Mai will drop you at the new bus station ("Bus Station 2") and from there you can pile into a *song thaew* (15B) for a shuttle to the old bus station ("Bus Station 1"). Only buses from within Chiang Rai Province depart and arrive at Bus Station 1; from elsewhere in Thailand you'll be dropped off outside the city at the newer station.

Driving is a great option for those who want to tour the area and enjoy the scenery. The drive from Chiang Mai takes under three hours, but there's a lot to do along the way, so if you are planning to use a car, make sure to allow time for stops. The route to take is the **Mae Sa Loop** from Chiang Mai. You'll only get to do half of it, and whether you choose the top or bottom, you'll have to turn onto Route 118 heading east, then Highway 1 heading north, to get to Chiang Rai.

Getting Around

The city itself is easily walkable, and there's no need for motorized transport if you're just going from your guesthouse to a restaurant or one of the city's sights. Many guesthouses offer bikes for rent or to borrow; it's a great way to get the full run of town without being too exhausted at the end of the day. If you're staying outside the city or want to visit something farther away, you'll need to hire a *tuk tuk* or taxi.

© SUZANNE NAM

mountain village in Northern Thailand

Outside the city, you'll need to either hire a taxi or get your own transport to enjoy all of the sights and scenery. There are numerous shops renting motorcycles, and in the airport are **Avis** (tel. 05/379-3827, www.avisthailand. com), **Budget Car** (tel. 05/374-0442), and **National Car Rental** (tel. 05/379-3683).

DAY TRIPS FROM CHIANG RAI TOWN

There are many day trips to be taken from Chiang Rai, and dozens of tour companies and guesthouses in the city to arrange them. The most common itinerary for a multiday trek starting in Chiang Rai involves trekking out to one of the nearby Lahu, Akha, Karen, or Hmong villages, spending a couple of hours visiting an elephant camp and riding elephants, and some rafting on a nearby river. Longer treks may even take you as far as the Mekong River on the border with Laos. As these are group tours, it is not possible to customize them, but if you are interested in just doing some rafting or hiking, you can arrange a one-day tour to do

so. Nonprofit tours run by the **Population and Community Development Association** (PDA, 620/25 Thanalai Rd., tel. 05/371-9167, www. pda.or.th/chiangrai) are a great choice for their promise of responsible tourism, with options of 1–3-day trips in the surrounding hills. Profits are reinvested in sustainable projects to improve HIV/AIDS education and institute scholarship programs for children of the surrounding hill tribes. Tours can be organized during a trip to the PDA Museum. Another trekking option is **Akha Hill House** (423/25 Mu 21, Soi 1, Kholoy Rd., tel. 08/9997-5505, www.akhahill.com or www.akha.info), also a good choice for local, sustainable trips. The Akha group runs one-day and multiday treks from the Akha River House to their base near the Akha Hill House, 23 kilometers from the city.

CHIANG SAEN AND THE GOLDEN TRIANGLE
เชียงแสนและสามเหลี่ยมทองคำ

After reading about the wild past of the Golden Triangle, you may be surprised to find that

THE GOLDEN TRIANGLE AND OPIUM TRADE

The rosy-hued blossoms of *Papaver somniferum*, or opium poppy, have been swaying in the mountain breezes of the Golden Triangle region for over 1,000 years. Originally mixed into tonics, it was a common ingredient in traditional medicine among locals and was grown and consumed in a remarkably responsible fashion for centuries before trade interests and methods for increasing its potency created the movie-like drama of smugglers, addicts in dark urban rooms, crime lords, and the exotic subculture glamour that some associate with the flower's cultivation today.

Known for much longer in Europe and the Middle East, opium was brought to East Asia by Arab traders around the seventh century. The controversy and excitement really began in the 1700s when the Dutch introduced the practice of smoking opium in tobacco pipes, vastly increasing its potency and hallucinogenic and addictive properties. Abuse of the drug quickly spread through China and the Golden Triangle region, and in 1729 the Chinese emperor placed a ban on its recreational use. About this time, European trading companies, most notably the famous British East India Company, recognized the new demand among the addicted Chinese for illegal opium. This solved the growing problem created by low demand for European products in the East, which had forced them to trade silver for expensive commodities such as tea, silk, and porcelain. With vast holdings in India, they began to smuggle Indian opium into China in enormous quantities. The level of addiction mushroomed in China and spread through Southeast Asia, and the demand for it became almost bottomless, with the British East India Company alone unloading an incredible 75 tons of the resin in 1773. The Chinese government's attempts to seize illegal cargo sparked the Opium Wars with England and ended with the ceding of Hong Kong and eventually the legalizing of opium sales. Import of the drug skyrocketed to 4,810 tons by 1858. With so many addicts and hugely inflated prices created by British attempts to monopolize the industry, secret poppy fields became a cash crop for the farmers of the Golden Triangle, with smugglers and drug barons popping up to aid in the distribution of the product.

Medical advances in the 1800s saw opium refined into morphine and then heroin and popularized the practice of administering it by hypodermic injection. It was mixed into all kinds of medicines, such as laudanum, which were distributed legally worldwide with devastating effect. Drug lords soon began to manufacture heroin in hill stations along the Thai-Burmese border, and it made its way in boats and caravans to the northern villages and eventually to Bangkok. In 1914 the India-China opium trade was finally abandoned, increasing the profits of the farmers and hill tribes growing it in the Golden Triangle. Rising addiction and social fallout threw opium and heroin into disfavor in most markets worldwide beginning in the 1920s, and in Thailand it was declared illegal in 1959. Unfortunately this created a black market that sparked the rise of crime syndicates in Bangkok dedicated to smuggling heroin internationally for illegal distribution. With an export market, the farmers of the Golden Triangle became the world's largest producers of opium, contributing 70 percent of the world's supply in the 1970s. Efforts by the Thai government, under the patronage of the monarchy, have since driven poppy farms almost to extinction. Programs to help farmers switch to other profitable crops, campaigns to rehabilitate addicts, and the destruction of illicit fields with charges being brought against their growers have nipped the problem in the proverbial bud. Still, there are a few fields that have not yet been wiped out, finding mostly Burmese customers and netting over 26,000B – nearly US$900 – per kilogram for those who are willing to risk it. As for the black market mafiosi, it appears that many of them have unfortunately switched to moving amphetamines, but heroin at least is no longer lining their pockets, concluding a dramatic and tragic era that has now dispersed like smoke on the wind.

Chiang Saen is a quiet, normal-looking town with a nice little museum and some interesting ruins. Set on the banks of the Mekong River, it lies farther south of the more heavily visited towns and has been populated on and off for thousands of years. Once an important city in the Lanna Kingdom, the sleepy town, formerly known as Wiang Hiran Nakhon Ngoen Yang, served as King Mengrai's capital before he moved it to Chiang Rai in the mid-1200s. During the 14th century, under the command of King Saen Pu, it was a small double-walled town with more than 70 temples within its boundaries and many more outside the wall. Like much of the northern Thai empire, the town was captured by the Burmese, but it hasn't been truly revived since. As a result of its long history, the town has had a series of archeological finds—tiny *chedi* here, small stupas there—that indicate its former glory. Despite its proximity to the Golden Triangle, if you walk around, you're more likely to see scattered ruins from the past than poppies.

Sights

Most people pass through Chiang Saen on their way north to the touristy heart of the Golden Triangle, but if you're in the city, stop into the **Chiang Saen National Museum** (702 Phahonyothin Rd., tel. 05/377-7102, 9 A.M.–4 P.M. Wed.–Sun., www.national-museums.finearts.go.th/thaimuseum_eng/chiangsaen/main.htm, 30B), housed next to **Wat Chedi Luang.** The museum houses mostly Lanna art from the 14th–16th centuries, including some excellent replicas of the era's style of Buddha statuary. In addition, rotating exhibitions of indigenous art from the surrounding hill tribes, such as opium accessories, sculptures, musical instruments, and more, make the museum a worthy stopover for an hour or two.

About eight kilometers outside the city is the **Hall of Opium** in **Golden Triangle Park** (Mu 1, Ban Sop Ruak, Wiang, tel. 05/378-4444, www.doitung.org/tourism_other_hall_opium.php, 8:30 A.M.–4 P.M. Tues.–Sun., free), a large museum run by the national government and

chronicling the history of opium in the region. In its own words, the museum seeks to target teens and young people susceptible to opium to "help reduce demand through education." The exhibits are entertaining and educational, yielding some fascinating information about the economic role of poppy cultivation in the region, the political role opium has played in East-West relations, as well as the drug trade in general. Updated often, the current exhibit addresses the growth of opium and subsequent eradication programs in Afghanistan. The museum and 16-hectare park surrounding it are part of Thailand's efforts to reclaim the region from illegal drug trafficking and give indigenous people other opportunities to earn money.

Be careful not to confuse the Hall of Opium with the more modest, privately run **House of Opium** (221 Mu 1, Tambon Wiang, tel. 05/378-4060, www.houseofopium.com, 7 A.M.–7 P.M. daily, 50B adults, free children under 120 centimeters), which conveys roughly the same information but with much less swish. They use conventional displays, mostly in Thai, and have an interesting selection of opium artifacts, many collected from southern China, and a unique gift shop. The House of Opium focuses specifically on the drug's effect on the local region and communities rather than on Asia as a whole, lending an intimate atmosphere to the small museum.

Accommodations

The lodging choices within Chiang Saen are fairly bleak, but outside town the options improve considerably. The **Viang Yonok** (201 Mu 3, Yonok, Chiang Saen Lake, tel. 05/365-0444, www.viangyonok.com, 2,200B) is a tiny family-run resort with rustic, comfortable bungalows and nice grounds that include a swimming pool. Popular with travelers passing through town but unwilling to drop serious amounts of money on the five-star resorts, it's a charming mid-range place to stay for a couple of days as you explore the area.

Another mid- to upper-range lodging option is the newly built **Serene at ChiangRai Hotel** (569 Mu 1, Tambon, tel. 05/378-4500, www.sereneatchiangrai.com, from 4,000B), on the edge of the Mekong River outside Chiang Saen proper. With free transport to Chiang Saen and complementary mountain bikes for hotel guests, the staff can also help plan out a few days in the surrounding hills. Guest rooms are clean and modern, with Wi-Fi, air-conditioning, and newly furbished en suite baths. While lacking the attention to detail present in the luxury resorts, this is a good spot to base yourself for exploring the Golden Triangle.

If you really want to splurge, there are two main luxury options in the heart of the Golden Triangle. The first is the **Four Seasons Tented Camp** (Chiang Saen, tel. 05/391-0200, www.fourseasons.com/goldentriangle, 45,000B inclusive), an extreme luxury experience and perhaps the most expensive place to stay in all of Thailand. The camp, set in the middle of the rainforest, has just 15 tents set on a river. Of course, these are not just any tents; they're the size of small homes and are surrounded by their own private decks. Accommodations include all meals and drinks as well as excursions and spa treatments, and breakfast time for guests also means feeding the baby elephants on the premises. As expected in this price range, the service is incredibly attentive, and amenities abound. Alternately, the **Anantara Golden Triangle Resort & Spa** (229 Mu 1, Tambon Wiang, tel. 05/378-4084, http://goldentriangle.anantara.com, 12,000–16,000B), one kilometer past Golden Triangle Park and opposite the Hall of Opium, is one of the more beautiful resorts in Thailand. Perched on the hills of the Golden Triangle, the 77 guest rooms are beautifully decorated with Lanna-style furniture, hill tribe textiles, and huge oversize bathtubs, and they boast some seriously jaw-dropping views. There are multiple pools, cooking classes, and a fitness center, but the real attraction is the on-site **elephant camp**. The camp's director scouts out at-risk elephants and their mahouts, particularly those who've been panhandling on the streets of Bangkok, and brings them to the Anantara's camp and mahout village. If you're interested in learning how to work with an elephant, they offer a

three-day mahout training program, but otherwise you can just visit the village and watch the elephants. Although this is a great place for a romantic getaway, most children will really enjoy the elephants.

Getting There

There are **buses** every 15–30 minutes during the day from Chiang Rai to Chiang Saen. The journey will take about 90 minutes and costs 50B. From Chiang Rai, you can catch a Chiang Mai–bound bus (an additional three hours). Blue *song thaew* also ply the route between Chiang Saen and Mai Sai via the Golden Triangle (every 30 minutes, 50B). If you are **driving**, follow Highway 1 from Chiang Rai to Mae Chan, then turn east onto Route 1016.

MAE SAI AND MAE FA LUANG DISTRICTS
แมสายและแมฟาหลวง
Mae Sai
แมสาย

As the northernmost town in the kingdom, Mae Sai attracts a fair number of travelers, many curious about the border with Burma (also called Myanmar). But although this tiny town is colorful and bustling, there isn't a whole lot to recommend. Swirling markets spontaneously materialize in the street on the approach to the border crossing, and it can sometimes be difficult to turn around in this area, especially with hundreds of pedestrians and vehicles trying to move between countries. Somewhat more formal shops are folded into the buildings lining this street, and there is a hodgepodge of Thai, Lao, and Burmese goods for sale.

You can cross the border yourself if you want—you will be stamped out of Thailand, negating the balance of any single-entry visas or 30-day visa exemptions, and stamped into Burma (US$10 at the time of writing). The Burmese authorities will keep your passport until you exit the country the same day. Tours deeper within Shan State, to Kentung, can be arranged at the Myanmar Travel and Tours office just next to the immigration booth. No travel to Kentung is permitted without an official MTT guide. In such case, you will be permitted to stay up to 14 days in Burma, and the authorities at the Tachileik border post will keep your passport the entire time, providing you with a temporary ID card instead, which will be stamped at checkpoints along the way to Kentung. Regardless of your visa, you must **provide only new (post-2003) U.S. banknotes, with no visible tears or creases.** The Burmese authorities at Tachileik will likely reject any damaged U.S. currency.

You'll find a very similar constellation of shops, markets, and vendors on the Burmese side, but more interesting is watching the legions of local people coming and going between countries. If you're looking to buy cheaper tobacco on the Burmese side, keep in mind that reports of Burmese tobacco repackaged with Western packaging are quite common. On the return to Thailand, you'll be stamped back into the country with only a 15-day visa exemption.

While there isn't much to see or do in Mae Sai, there is good food to be had at the night market in town, much of it delicious Shan food from Burma. Try fermented tea leaf salad and yellow Shan tofu salad with cabbage, chilies, and chopped peanuts. If you see *khao soi* on the menu, this is different from the coconut-filled northern Thai–style soups; Shan *khao soi* involves noodles, a thick meat broth, and delicious spicy tomato and chicken toppings. A tiny Muslim restaurant serves up reliable favorites such as *biryani* and roti; it's also on Phahonyothin Road. And if you're stuck and need to spend the night, the **Khanthongkham Hotel** (40 Mu 7 Phahonyothin Rd., tel. 05/373-4222, www.ktkhotel.com/eng/home. htm, from 800B) has 45 guest rooms to choose from, right near the border with Burma. It's a fairly new hotel, and while lacking in charm, it's a good place to stay for the night if you want to get an early start to Tachileik.

Given the sporadic (and occasionally violent) border clashes between Shan State armies and the Burmese national army, or between Burma and Thailand, it is important to check on the border situation from Chiang Rai or Chiang Mai, as the border can be closed without notice. When the border is open, regular buses run to Mae Sai from Chiang Saen (usually a blue *song thaew,* 50B), Chiang Rai (1.5 hours, 40B), and Chiang Mai (2 hours, 250B).

Doi Mae Salong
ดอยแม่สะลอง

Mae Fa Luang district is in a sense a memorial to the late Princess Mother Srinagarindra, mother of Thailand's current king. She took a special interest in the welfare of the people of this region, from the hill tribes and their struggle with opium to the border police and their families, and in fact, "Mae Fa Luang" was the affectionate nickname given to her by the locals. It means "mother sky royal" in reference to her habit of arriving in the area by helicopter. The Mae Fa Luang Foundation was begun under her patronage and direction, and it has been involved in reforestation projects, opium substitution farming initiatives, cottage-industry preservation and promotion, and education and health care programs, having a huge impact on the people in this region. Signs of these efforts are easily found as you travel to the summit of Doi Tung; much of the forest that you see was planted through the efforts of this foundation, and a zoo and arboretum are among the local projects.

A favorite place to visit for people traveling to Mae Fa Luang is the hamlet of Doi Mae Salong, unique in both culture and history. The villagers here are not ethnic Thais; they are Yunnan Chinese, and their way of life has drifted very little from their native traditions. They have a strange and vibrant past full of political struggles, war, and opium, recent enough to be recalled firsthand by the town's elders. This small town is integrated into the hills, on top of the world at 548 meters elevation, and enchanting landscapes combine with a simplistic agricultural existence to define the mountain sanctuary.

In the 1940s the Kuomintang were a political group opposed to the communist takeover of China, fighting bitterly against them from

Yunnan Province in the south. They were eventually forced to flee, escaping to Taiwan and into hidden locations deep within the Burmese rainforest, where they established camps and regrouped to continue their resistance effort. After 12 years of brutal struggle, engaged in opium-funded guerrilla warfare against both the Burmese and Chinese armies, in the 1960s the weary community eventually retreated to neighboring Thailand to regroup. Rainforest-savvy, they trekked deep into remote and inaccessible tracts of Chiang Rai's forests, eventually settling in their current location of Mae Salong, precariously close to the territories controlled by the opium warlords of the Golden Triangle. Before long, the Yunnanese settlers began their own tidy trade in illegal opium, further isolating them from mainstream Thai society and sparking violent clashes with the private armies of the local crime barons, including the infamous Khun Sa.

Eventually the Thai government initiated its crackdown on the region's drug trade, instituted crop-substitution programs en masse, and paved the roads up to the village's doorstep, effectively ending the seclusion that had virtually stopped time in this community for decades. Doi Mae Salong finally settled into a quiet agrarian existence, enjoying real peace for the first time in many years and earning the Thai government's symbolic renaming of their village to Santikhiri (Hill of Peace).

Despite the sudden increase in accessibility, however, the villagers still keep to their ethnic roots, making this little town seem like a lost piece from a Chinese jigsaw puzzle. In fact, many of its citizens are more recent immigrants from China, who both help to maintain the cultural authenticity of this community and ultimately somewhat erode its unique qualities. The elevation and temperate climate are ideal for the villagers' orchards, tea, and traditional herbs, and their produce is very highly regarded. The villagers have even imported cherry trees from Yunnan, and the fluttering pink finery of these trees in bloom during December–January is a particular visual delight. The influence of their homeland is also seen in the local cuisine, language, architecture, and sect of Buddhism, and it's interesting simply to stroll around exploring this town. Try not to miss the marketplace, where you can see some unusual items for sale, including piles of elaborately named loose tea and even dried insects hawked by the kilo.

ACCOMMODATIONS AND FOOD

Although many visit this area on a day trip from Chiang Rai, there are a few good guesthouses in the region. The choices are quirky and tend to exploit the connection to China quite aggressively, but they are generally comfortable and charming too. **Maesalong Mountain Home** (9 Mu 12, Mae Salong Nok, tel. 08/4611-9508, http://maesalongmountainhome.com, from 900B) has mountain or tea plantation views from each of its nine chalets, built with traditional thatched roofs and bamboo furnishings. Each bungalow has a private balcony and a hot-water bath, and the guesthouse grounds include a large open-air restaurant and free Wi-Fi.

Mae Salong Little Home (31 Mu 1, Mae Salong Nok, tel. 05/376-5389, www.maesalonglittlehome.com, bungalow 800B, guesthouse room 300B) is clean, well-kept, and central. More a cluster than a single house, Little Home is right in the middle of Doi Mae Salong but on a small hill, affording a great view. Bungalows are decorated with Thai silk bed skirts and pillows, with an en suite bath and a large porch. A small Yunnan and Sichuan menu provides a change from the usual Thai fare elsewhere in the country. Don't miss the steamed buns and braised pork leg.

Shin Sane Guesthouse (119/1 Mu 1, Mae Salong Nok, tel. 05/376-5026, 100B for basic room with shared bathroom, 300B for ensuite bungalows) was the first hotel to open in Mae Salong over 40 years ago. For another Yunnan option, visit the **Mae Salong Villa** (2 kilometers east of town, tel. 05/376-5114, 100B), for delicious tea leaf salad and pork leg on the bone. For coffee and an impressive menu of snacks and baked goods, stop in at **Sweet Maesalong Bakery** (41/3 Mu 1, Mae Salong Nok, tel. 08/1855-4000, 60B).

GETTING THERE

A big part of the charm of a trip up to Mae Salong is the picturesque drive itself, with its captivating panoramas, and there are even a few opportunities to stop along the way. Akha, Hmong, Lisu, and Mien hill tribe villages, some of which are unfortunately pretty touristy, are located on this route, along with Kuomintang tea plantations and a few small waterfalls; if you go with an organized tour from Chiang Rai, they will usually include these in their itinerary. It's possible to do your own driving; if you do, it's a good idea to pick up a visitors map in the city so that you can do a bit of exploring, but stick to the main roads and attractions because some of the smaller trails lead off into unsafe territory. You can also pick up a thorough GT Rider map in Chiang Rai or Chiang Mai with detailed information about the routes and side routes in the mountainous north.

From Chiang Rai, drive 20 kilometers north along the divided highway (Route 110) to Mae Chan; once there, turn left onto Route 1089, which will take you through the mountains and forests to the turnoff at Route 1234, leading directly to Mae Salong on some of the most nauseating mountain turns you'll experience in northern Thailand. If you plan to detour to see any of the hill tribe villages, you should rent a 4WD vehicle, but if you stick to Route 1089, it isn't necessary. Alternately, you can continue on Route 110 from Chiang Rai and turn off at Route 1130, following it until you hit Mae Salong.

Using public transportation, there are two options. From Chiang Rai, take a Mai Sai–bound bus to Ban Pasang (30 minutes, 25B), then catch a blue *song thaew* from Ban Pasang to the mountaintop for under 60B each way. Be sure to ask for the Ban Pasang that is on the way to Mae Salong; there's another Pasang in exactly the other direction. From Tha Ton there are yellow *song thaew* that run directly to Mae Salong. Leaving Mae Salong, both yellow and blue *song thaew* trucks wait near the 7-Eleven in the center of town, leaving when full.

Doi Tung

The other adventure popular with day-trippers to Mae Fa Luang is wandering up the lush and winding road that ascends the heights of Doi Tung ("Flag Mountain"), whose forested limestone peaks stretch to a height of 1,800 meters in places and where captivating vistas often steal the show from the handful of local attractions. Route 1149 snakes along from the divided highway to the peak of Doi Tung, and other than the copious hairpin turns, it's a fairly easy drive; the west turnoff to Route 1149 is 40 kilometers north of Chiang Rai and 20 kilometers south of Mae Sai. Doi Tung is very close to Burma, and an alternate route from Mae Sai is to take Route 1334, but given the sporadic fighting between Thailand and Burma, this road is often closed and can be a risky choice regardless. If you do go this way, inquire about recent threats at the army checkpoint en route, then drive through without stopping. If you're coming from Doi Mae Salong, Route 1338 will take you on a roller coaster of hills and valleys, climbing to meet Route 1149 and delivering you at Doi Tung. Most people, however, visit Doi Tung on an organized tour, although a rental car or motorcycle is also an option if you don't mind focusing on the road rather than the scenery.

The Princess Mother Srinagarindra lived in Switzerland for a number of years while her children were attending school, and she remembered the Swiss countryside fondly after her return to Thailand. Therefore, when she decided to build a home on Doi Tung where she could live while working on her social projects, she chose a fusion of Thai and Swiss styles for its design. After her death in 1995, the **Mae Fa Luang Garden and Royal Villa** (Rte. 1149, 7:30 A.M.–5 P.M. daily, garden and villa 150B) were opened to visitors and have become the key attractions on this tour. The villa has been converted to a museum and preserves everything almost exactly as it was when she lived here, but the royal gardens get most people's attention. Again in keeping with the princess's love of the Alps, this garden overflows with flowers that may strike Thais as incredibly exotic, but Westerners will already be familiar with the snapdragons, delphiniums, and begonias on display. Despite this, visitors often count this garden among the most beautiful they've seen anywhere in the world, and the delightfully ornate landscaping is very cleverly planned for aesthetic impact. It's worth taking an hour to stroll around, snapping photos and enjoying the pretty grounds and wonderful vistas of the surrounding mountains, and then relaxing with a tea or coffee on the open-air terrace of the cafeteria.

After the Royal Villa, the road continues up to the summit and **Wat Doi Tung,** passing breathtaking views of Burmese mountains and landscapes that until recently were crowded with poppy fields, but have now been supplanted with macadamia trees, coffee plants, and a variety of fruit. At the top you will find the twin pagodas of **Wat Phra That Doi Tung,** which are small but ancient, at 1,000 years old, and reputed to contain a relic in the form of a bone from the Buddha's body. This is a very

sacred temple for Thais as well as for local Shan and Chinese Buddhists, and every year many of the faithful make pilgrimages here to the highest point in the province, ritually ringing the row of large bells along the walkway. There are magnificent views of the countryside from up here, and you get a sense that the temple's builders once stood where you are standing and admired it themselves long ago.

If you've got the time to spare, rooms are available at the **Doi Tung Lodge** (Doi Tung Development Project, Doi Tung Royal Villa, Mae Fah Luang District, tel. 05/376-7015, www.doitung.org/tourism_accommodation_doitung_lodge.php, 1,600–2,500B), developed by the Princess Mother. Although the views are exquisite, the guest rooms are exciting more for their genesis than their current splendor, and are much more popular with Thai travelers than those from farther afield. The grounds include botanical gardens and temples, and the restaurant on the premises serves organic vegetables and fruit from the Royal gardens in the area.

Mae Hong Son Province   จังหวัดแม่ฮ่องสอน

To the west of Chiang Mai Province and bordered by Burma to the east, Mae Hong Son Province, surrounding by forest and nauseatingly winding mountain roads, still feels like a bit of a frontier region. Although it's not filled with specific sights to see, it's a wonderful place to go hiking into the mountains for a few days or to visit some local hill tribe communities. Although the province is welcoming more visitors every year, compared to Chiang Mai and even Chiang Rai it will probably feel much less visited—that is, until you get to Pai.

◖ MAE HONG SON
แม่ฮ่องสอน

The City of Three Mists, as Mae Hong Son is nicknamed, has a large population of Shan people who have migrated from the Shan Province of Burma. Tucked away in a misty valley whose mountains shelter it from Burma

to the west and Chiang Mai Province to the east, the people of this region lived for centuries as loosely organized forest farmers with no central government. Only the cacophony of wild elephants and the occasional passage of the Burmese army on their way to attack northern Siam or Ayutthaya interrupted the sleepy populace and their deeply traditional lives. The city itself was founded in the 1800s when Lord Kaeo, a Lanna military chief, was sent to capture and train wild elephants for use in labor. As he traveled he unified the scattered settlers into villages and collected armies of elephants. Finally stopping at a suitable site, he established an elephant training camp and village, naming it Ban Mae Rong Son, or "Village of the Elephant Training Camp." The town flourished, attracting Shan hill farmers from the surrounding forests and an influx of Shan fleeing fighting in Burma in the mid-1800s.

© SUZANNE NAM

mountains of Mae Hong Son Province

Until recently the area had dense rainforest and no modern infrastructure, with the town serving as a base for logging and occasionally involved in the more lurid opium activities of the Golden Triangle. As a result, Mae Hong Son has only been accessible to travelers for two decades, and it shows. The tiny town is only a few kilometers across, and as you wander through its bustling produce markets and Burmese-style temples, you might feel as though you have stepped back in time, if not for the shiny new hotels and ATMs that have sprung up like daisies in recent years. Still, the town only has a paltry three 7-Elevens, quite a low number for towns in Thailand. While Mae Hong Son itself has very little to see other than a few scattered *wats,* its relaxed atmosphere and interesting day trips make it an ideal place to stop for a few days.

Day Trips from Mae Hong Son
BAN RAK TAI
บ้านรักไทย
Follow the Communist Party's takeover of China in 1949, Kuomintang (KMT) soldiers who refused to surrender to the new government fled to Burma's Shan State, where they set up their own infrastructure in the rugged hills near Kentung. Chased out by Burma in the early 1960s, many were sent to Taiwan while some made the push toward Thailand, crossing the porous border and settling near the Golden Triangle and in Ban Rak Tai (also known as Mae Aw), 44 kilometers north of Mae Hong Son. Save for a tiny KMT museum in a peeling mud hut, little of Ban Rak Tai's chaotic history can be felt today. Instead, the town is known for its tea, growing impressive amounts of oolong, jasmine, and *tieguanyin.* Day trips can be organized with **Friend Tours** (21 Praditjongkham Rd., Mae Hong Son, tel. 05/361-1647, 7 a.m.–6 p.m. daily) offering tea tastings and a Yunnan-style lunch. Those making the trip by motorcycle can stop at **Lee Wine Ruk Thai Resort** (3 Mu 6, Ban Rak Tai, tel. 08/9950-0955 or 08/1999-1889, www.leewinerukthai.com, family-style dishes 90–120B) for braised pork, tea salads, and, of course, generous servings of tea.

HILL TRIBE TREKS, LONG-NECK VILLAGES, AND RAFTING

If you've come to Mae Hong Son and you're not planning on enjoying the surrounding rainforests, you're probably in the wrong place. But if that's what you're looking for, you'll find plenty of agencies organizing multiday hiking trips that include visits to hill tribe villages, waterfalls, and rafting trips on the Pai River. Expect to pay around 1,000B per day for hiking (which includes accommodations and basic food) and a little more per day for a rafting trip. When they need a driver, many of Mae Hong Son's nongovernmental organizations use **Friend Tours** (21 Praditjongkham Rd., tel. 05/361-1647, 7 A.M.–6 P.M. daily) to guide them, and they're a good bet for à la carte daylong and multiday trips out of Mae Hong Son.

Wats

While not as grandiose as those in Chiang Rai or Chiang Mai, Mae Hong Son's *wats* merit a visit. The twin *wats* of **Wat Jong Klang** and **Wat Jong Kham** sit at the edge of Lake Jong Kham and remain a popular attraction. During the day, their silver and white *chedi* gleam in the sun, and a tiny museum (8 A.M.–6 P.M. daily) houses antique wooden sculptures and dolls from Burma. Lit up at night, their reflections shimmer against the lake and make for the perfect Mae Hong Son photo opportunity. Climbing Doi Kong Mu to **Wat Phra That Doi Kong Mu** offers a solid view of the surrounding hills, and the effort to get here at dawn will be rewarded with a carpet of fog over Mae Hong Son, drifting away once the sun rises. You can reach the *wat* by climbing the zigzagging staircase at the base of Doi Kong Mu or by taking a motorcycle to the summit via the road.

Accommodations

Mae Hong Son is one of the few popular tourist spots left in Thailand where you can still find a reasonable place to sleep for less than 200B per night. In fact, many of the city's accommodations seem geared toward travelers with tighter budgets, and finding plusher places to rest can be a little bit challenging.

Though there is nothing extravagant in the city (the more expensive options are outside town), there are some nice mid-range options that are great values. Most of the accommodations here can book trekking tours—either they are re-selling them or offering them—and have small restaurants on the premises.

Newish **Jongkham Place** (4/2 Udom Chao Ni-Thet Rd., tel. 05/361-4294, 800–1,200B), not to be confused with Jongkham House at the other end of the street, offers four sturdy wooden bungalows, each with air-conditioning, a fridge, and a private balcony. Wi-Fi is free on the premises. A stone's throw from Jong Kham Lake, it is an attractive mid-range option in the middle of town.

A few steps down from the twin *wats* on Jong Kham Lake is **Romtai House** (22 Cham Nan Sathit Rd., tel. 05/361-2437, 500–900B), offering a wide variety of options, from simple clean guest rooms to well-kept bungalows facing a small lily pond. In early 2011, the Thai government awarded Romtai a Green Certificate for sustainable environmental practices.

《 The Residence (41/4 Nivespisarn Rd., tel. 05/361-4100 or 08/1562-6552, www.theresidence-mhs.com, 900B d, 1,200B t, 1,400B quadruple) is located within walking distance of the airport and offers a clean and modern two-story guesthouse with free Wi-Fi and bright, uncluttered guest rooms. Newly built with a welcoming lobby and shared picnic tables, the hotel also provides its guest with free bicycles to explore Mae Hong Son. Those concerned about noise needn't worry: The tiny airport only has a few flights per day.

Near the center of town but a quick walk from Jong Kham Lake is the **Mountain Inn Hotel & Resort** (112/2 Khunlumprapas Rd., tel. 05/361-1803, www.mhsmountaininn.com, 2,400–4,500B), which offers significant discounts if when you book directly on their website. Guest rooms are simple but well-stocked with a fridge, a TV, air-conditioning, and hot water, and they are built around a small pool and garden. The resort has its own restaurant on the premises and offers free transfers to and from the airport.

CHIANG MAI

A few kilometers outside of the city is the luxuriant and comfortable **Rim Nam Klang Doi Resort** (108 Ban Huai Deau, tel. 05/361-2142, 500–900B). Set on the river, with guest rooms and stand-alone wooden bungalows, this is a great spot to pick if you're more interested in getting out into nature than anything the small town of Mae Hong Son has to offer. For those on a budget, the resort also offers a longhouse with cold-water, fan-cooled rooms. Shuttle service to town does not run like clockwork, so don't make this your base if you want to spend most of your time in the city proper.

Piya Guest House (1/1 KhunLumphrapat Soi 3, tel. 05/361-1260, 600B) isn't as modern as The Residence, but it's conveniently located at the edge of Jong Kham Lake in the heart of Mae Hong Son. With a slightly overgrown garden on the premises buffering the bungalows from the main road, it has the amenities of a larger hotel in an intimate setting.

About 1.5 kilometers outside the center of town are the **Sang Tong Huts** (Mu 11, Makasanti Rd., tel. 05/362-0680, www.sangtonghuts.com, 700–1,600B), a small group of bamboo bungalows run by friendly, interesting staff. The guest rooms are clean, the beds comfortable, and the baths well kept up. There are also outdoor balconies to lounge on and even a small shared swimming pool on the premises. The cheapest guest rooms here have shared baths, but the larger bungalows have their own baths and are considerably more plush—a great value in the middle of the price spectrum. There is a small restaurant on the premises serving Thai dishes and freshly baked bread, plus fresh-brewed hill tribe coffee in the morning. If you arrange to have dinner prepared for you in advance, you'll be able to help with preparations and take an impromptu cooking class too.

If you're looking for clean, rustic, and charming but don't want to do without a little luxury, pick (**Fern Resort** (64 Mu Bo, Pha Bong, tel. 05/368-6110, www.fernresort.info, 2,500–3,500B, breakfast included). There are no compromises here, just large, nicely furnished bungalows with sprawling beds, private terraces, and a great view of the surrounding rainforest and mountains. The resort, a few kilometers out of town, also has a swimming pool and an open-air restaurant with food good enough that you probably won't feel the need to venture out for any of your meals. The staff is very knowledgeable about hiking in the area and there are even some short two-hour trails right around the resort that you can venture onto without needing to hire a guide. There is a shuttle to and from town, and the resort will arrange free pickup from the airport or bus station.

At the high end of the hotel spectrum is the opulent **Tara Hotel Imperial** (149 Mu 8, Pang Mu, tel. 05/368-4444, www.imperialhotels.com/imperialtaramaehongson, 4,000–5,500B, breakfast included), located outside town. With high ceilings, chandeliers, and a fully equipped fitness room, pool, and sauna, it feels slightly out of place in quiet, unobtrusive Mae Hong Son. Its Lanna-style guest rooms are spacious and include all the amenities you would expect from a hotel chain of this caliber, and its Golden Teak restaurant boasts terrific views.

Food

The first place to find food is the **Morning Market** (Singhanat Bamrung Rd., next to Wat Klang Muang, 5–9 A.M. daily), a colorful and bustling market in the center of town frequented by Mae Hong Son's local population and those from the surrounding hill tribe villages. With stalls boasting pots of curry, noodle soups, or piles of fresh fruit and snacks, it is an ideal place to grab food if you are an early riser.

Newly opened **Pi Nik Bakery** (53 Singhanat Bamrung Rd., tel. 05/361-2973, 7:30 A.M.–9 P.M., daily, 5–20B) has fluffy donuts, fresh-baked bread, and homemade yogurt, making it a perfect place to snack if you've had more than your share of Thai food. Although bakeries from Chiang Mai have come calling, the owner has resisted franchising for the moment; it's better for Mae Hong Son as she can focus on her delicious treats. A small table and chairs adjacent to the bakery allows you to eat and run.

❰❰ Salween River Restaurant (23 Praditjongkham Rd., tel. 05/361-3421, 7 A.M.–1 A.M. daily, 60–120B) is a favorite of the nonprofit workers stationed in Mae Hong Son and has a broad menu, with fiery Burmese tea leaf salad and Shan curries as well as several popular vegetarian options. Boasting one of the heartier breakfast menus (with bacon and cheese, no less), it is located right in the heart of Mae Hong Son, next to Jong Kham Lake. There is also a one-for-one book exchange if you are in need of something new to read.

Also popular with the town's nonprofit workers, **Thai-Yai Restaurant** (51 Singharat Bamrung Rd., tel. 05/362-2471, 7:30 A.M.–3 P.M. daily, 30B) serves traditional northern Thai curries over rice as well as soups and a smattering of other dishes, including their specialty, a succulent sweet pork belly.

A lakeside staple, **Sunflower Café** (7 Singhana Thoumrung Rd., tel. 05/362-0549, 7:30 A.M.–9 P.M. daily, 50–120B) is an ideal spot to people-watch and indulge in some pizza or Thai staple dishes. For dessert, enjoy a cappuccino made with hill tribe coffee and a slice of cheesecake. The café also has a tour agency that organizes multiday hiking tours in the area.

❰❰ Bai Fern Restaurant (Khunlum Phrapat Rd., tel. 05/368-6110, 10:30 A.M.– midnight daily, 200B) is part of the same group that owns the Fern Resort, and the restaurant likewise does not disappoint. The menu includes Thai, Shan, and Western dishes, and all is served in an open-air wooden dining room. A cozy coffee shop adjacent to the restaurant serves up strong hill tribe coffee and sweets.

If you're tired of walking and want to rest your weary feet, **Baan Tua Lek** (59 Chong Kham, tel. 05/362-0688, baantualek.mhs@ gmail.com, 60B) provides a quiet respite in the center of town. The tiny café serves strong coffee, smoothies, and juices and has several trays of cakes and cookies to choose from.

The only formal bar in town, **Crossroads** (16 Khunlum Phrapat Rd., tel. 08/1020-6776, 9 A.M.–11 P.M. daily), also serves up Western-style food and basic Thai dishes and, of course, plenty of beer.

Getting There

Mae Hong Son is not the easiest place to get to, as you generally have to pass through Chiang Mai on your way farther north. The city is served by daily **flights** from Chiang Mai on Nok Air (www.nokair.com).

There are five daily **buses** from Chiang Mai making the 7–9-hour journey for 150B, and the same trip can be done with a more comfortable **minivan** for 250B, stopping in Pai along the way. If you get carsick, stick to the front seat: There are 2,626 curves in the road from Chiang Mai to Mae Hong Son.

From Bangkok, there is one scheduled bus from the Northern (Mo Chit II) Bus Terminal per day for 600B, leaving at 6 P.M. for the 17-hour overnight ride.

If you're **driving** from Chiang Mai, take Route 108 through Mae Sariang or Route 1095 through Pai. Although the roads are well maintained and the scenery beautiful, you'll encounter a lot of mountains and switchbacks on the way. The drive takes around three hours from Chiang Mai to Pai, and an additional three to Mae Hong Song in a car, longer if you are on a motorcycle. Be sure to fill up with gas if you are looping from Chiang Mai to Pai—there are very few places to fuel up once you start up the steep mountain roads.

Getting Around

Within the town of Mae Hong Son, the best way to get around is on foot, and the town is small enough that almost anyone will feel comfortable walking from place to place. You can rent a motorcycle for the day from **PA Motors** (21 Pradit Jong Kham Rd., no phone), who share a building with Friend Tours.

PAI
ปาย

Time doesn't stand still in Pai, but it certainly slows down a lot, so reset your mental clock— if it's still on city time, you might feel a little alarmed here. On the other hand, if you need some help getting out of work mode but still want to be sociable, this might be just the place to do it. In recent years, Pai has gone from a humble and idyllic little town to a more crowded and popular destination, but nonetheless it offers a slightly bohemian feel for travelers. A sprinkling of souvenir art shops, open-air bars, and street vendors attempting to "go international" set the stage. Keep an eye out for these seemingly incongruous Thai incarnations designed to catch the traveler's attention; notable among them is KFG, unofficially "Kentucky Fried Gai," *kai* being the Thai word for chicken. Another odd local favorite is "Mama's Falafel," whose recipes, perfected over the years with helpful advice from Israeli visitors, have been so successful that she's been able to upgrade from a street stall to a permanent indoor location. Pai seems to have a sand-in-the-eyes effect on those who visit, almost as though some sort of magic saps any desire they have to leave. This is reflected in the smorgasbord of people you will find here. Although there is a bit of hippie subculture in most of the towns in the north, it reaches its zenith in Pai, drawing the most interesting assortment of people as well as the not-so-occasional scent of marijuana wafting through the mountain air. Most of the travelers have come to enjoy some "R&R&R"—rest, relaxation, and rejuvenation—and you will find many escapists and sojourners who have fallen under the town's spell; for some, a few weeks' holiday becomes a many-year, semiresident affair. In recent years, Pai has become extremely popular with wealthier Thais from Bangkok, many of whom have purchased a second home in Pai. During high season (Nov.–Jan.), the streets will be packed with Thai visitors as well as foreign backpackers and travelers, and a quiet corner within the tiny town is hard to find.

Despite the hippie overtones, in recent years there seems to be an increased tendency of visitors to Pai and locals going "off the rails." Though you may only see this in the form of general drunken and disorderly conduct in the late evening (watch for out-of-control scooter drivers), there have also been incidents of bar fights resulting in serious injury. Although Pai is generally safe, this is something to keep in mind.

Notwithstanding the rowdy downtown core, the area around Pai remains peaceful and beautiful, set in a green valley surrounded by mountains in the distance and flanked by a small river. Several quiet accommodations options exist just outside the center that serve as a perfect base for exploring the area. Aside from the landscape and appeal to the hippie traveler (and despite Pai's popularity), there really is not much to see in Pai itself, with most activities requiring a day trip or more from town.

Hiking, Rafting, and Waterfalls

Although it's tempting to spend your time in Pai just hanging out and enjoying the natural scenery and the people-watching, the valley is ripe for exploration, and there are plenty of hiking and rafting trips on offer, be it for a day or a week. Hiking trips are generally 1–3-day affairs and usually include some elephant-camp visits and tours of local hill tribe villages, though many travelers, usually women, remain sensitive to treating hill tribes like they are in a zoo. For an adventurous trekking option, **Mr. Chart's Jungle Adventures** (tel. 08/4484-9063, info@trekpai.com, www.trekpai.com) offers off-the-beaten-path "roughing it" treks to surrounding villages with the very colorful owner, Mr. Chart.

More socially conscious is a white-water rafting trip on the Pai River, usually a two-day trip that involves camping. Although any tour agency can arrange this trip, **Thai Adventure Rafting** (tel. 05/369-9111, www.thairafting.com, 1,500B pp per day) is extremely professional and has considerable experience on the river.

Good day trips from Pai and an excellent way to escape the heat are visits to **Mo Paeng,** nine kilometers West of Pai, past Satichon, and **Pam Bok,** on the road to Chiang Mai near Pai Canyon. Any of the tour operators in Pai can arrange for a waterfall excursion, or motorcycle rental spots can provide a map and a rough itinerary. Another day-trip option is the **Tha Pai Hot Springs** (8 A.M.–6 P.M. daily, 200B),

30 minutes out of town by motorcycle past Pai Canyon on the road to Chiang Mai.

Cooking Classes

There are a dizzying number of cooking classes to choose from as many Pai hotels, much like those in Chiang Mai, offer classes of their own. **Pai Cookery School** (Soi Wanchaloem, tel. 08/1706-3799, www.paicookeryschool. com, 750B per day) is a solid choice, offering 1–3-day cooking classes with a recipe book to take home.

Nightlife

Pai is full of bars that cater both to Western travelers and the increasing number of Thai travelers, along with some that feature live music. As there's not much else to do at night, regardless of the crowd, having a few drinks after dark is a popular pastime in the town. During high season, Chaisongkran Road turns into a connect-the-dots series of bar trucks offering cheap libations for the visiting hordes. For a less casual drinking hour, try one of the following.

(Bebop (188 Mu 8, Rangsiyanon Rd., 7 P.M.–1 A.M. daily), a casual live-music venue, is one of Pai's longest-standing watering holes. The two-story wooden structure is much larger than most of the shophouse-style bars in the center of town. There are nightly live performances of rock, blues, and jazz music, and the crowd is generally mixed and relaxed. Bebop is about a 10-minute walk outside the center of town but worth the short journey.

Another option is **Park@Pai** (75 Mu 3, Vieng Tai, tel. 08/5090-0945, salin_sidang@ live.com, www.parkatpai.tk, 7 P.M.–midnight daily), with live music nightly and quirky, off-beat decor and a solid live-music lineup, this sister bar to Bangkok's trendy and popular Parking Toys is a good bet for a fun night out.

The stylish but unassuming **Phu Pai Art Café** (22 Mu 4, Rangsiyanon Rd., tel. 08/4209-8169, 7 P.M.–1 A.M. daily), housed in an old Lanna-style teakwood building, features live music most nights. Sometimes it's folk, other times it's open mike—be prepared for anything

when you arrive. The crowd is lively but doesn't get out of hand, making it a nice place to have a few drinks and relax.

Accommodations

Quiet Pai used to be a place to find scores of budget guesthouses, but with its recent popularity and need to rebuild after floods destroyed much of the infrastructure in 2005, prices are now considerably higher. Unless you're just looking for a cheap room to stumble into after some late-night drinking at one of the town's many little bars, your best bet is to head to one of the guesthouses just outside town. In low season (mid-Mar.–Sept.), prices will be considerably lower, often half the rack rates. During high season, it's extremely wise to book ahead, as the town is now a go-to place for both foreign and Thai travelers alike.

If budget accommodations are what you're after, **Breeze of Pai** (131 Mu 3, Vieng Tai, tel. 08/1998-4597, www.breezeofpai.com, 500–800B) between Chaisongkran Road and the Pai River, is a popular guesthouse by the river offering A-frame bungalows, each with an en suite bath and hammocks to watch the river stream by. There is free Wi-Fi on the premises and a friendly English owner who can help plan the rest of your stay in town.

Another option for the budget traveler is newly opened, quirky **(Bueng Pai Farm** (85 Mu 5, Tambon Mae Hee, tel. 08/9265-4768, www.paifarm.com, 500–1,200B), by the former owners of the popular Sun Huts. With sturdy, individually decorated bungalows set around a quiet lake, Bueng Pai offers free Wi-Fi, mosquito nets, and en suite baths with hot water. The on-site restaurant serves organic vegetarian food grow by welcoming owners Orn and Run. Set a short motorcycle drive away from Pai proper, it's a perfect place to spend a few days.

Baan Pai Village (88 Mu 3, Vieng Tai, tel. 05/369-8152, reservation@baanpaivillage.com, www.baanpaivillage.com, 700–2,000B) has basic bungalows just one minute on foot outside the center of town. Although not as lavish as the more expensive choices, the location is convenient, and the guest rooms themselves comfortable and well maintained, if a little sparse. This property is a great value, but if you're looking for something a little farther away from the center, they also have 60 bungalows available during high season at the **Baan Pai Riverside,** a few minutes out of town.

On the edge of the Pai River, **Rim Pai Cottage** (99/1 Mu 3, Viang Tai, tel. 05/369-9133, www.rimpaicottage.com, 1,000–3,500B, breakfast included Oct.–Feb.) is considerably cheaper in low season and has a dizzying variety of bungalows to choose from, some with a garden view, some with a river view, and all well kept with mosquito nets and clean, fresh linens. Most bungalows offer air-conditioning and an attached bath, but those on a tighter budget can opt for the Thai-Yai traditional guest room with twin beds and a fan.

At the higher end of the accommodations spectrum, **Baan Krating Pai Resort** (119 Mu 2, Wiangnua, tel. 05/369-8255, http://baankrating.com/Pai, 1,300–2,100B, breakfast included) has individual luxury bungalows set in a picturesque paddy field next to the river. While the bungalows look rustic from the outside, appearances are deceiving; they are modern and clean with crisp white sheets and renovated baths. The resort grounds boast a large pool, jetted tub, and northern Thai restaurant and bar. Book directly through their website for a discounted rate.

◖ **Belle Villa Resort** (113 Mu 6, Wiangnua, tel. 05/369-8226, www.bellevillaresort.com/pai, 2,500–3,500B) is just a 10-minute walk to town but feels worlds away. The individual wooden bungalows in a green paddy field are as well-equipped as modern hotel rooms but far more charming. Each comes with its own small deck and hammock, and there is a small swimming pool and a very nice casual restaurant on the premises. The property is exceptionally well kept and clean.

For those traveling with families, **Pai Treehouse** (90 Mu 2, Tambon Maehee, tel. 08/1373-1820, www.paitreehouse.com/eng, 3,000–4,000B, tents 500B) will provide some wide-eyed, wondrous nights if you book in advance and manage to reserve one of the tree houses tucked into a huge tree on the premises. If those are full, Pai Treehouse offers several other accommodations options, including modern thatched wooden bungalows with mosquito nets, cheerful villas, and tents. The sprawling hotel grounds have three restaurants and a rustic outdoor coffee shop. The hotel is located approximately five kilometers from Pai on the road to Mae Yen, near the hot springs.

Slight farther out of town is **Pripta Resort** (99 Mu 3, Tambon Maehee, tel. 05/306-5750, www.pripta.com, 4,500–6,000B), its name meaning "out of sight" from Pai. The resort, which opened in 2008, has eight thatched bungalows carefully decorated in simple antiques and quality linens, each with a teak bed, high-speed Internet access, open-air hot-spring bathtub, and the usual amenities such as a fridge, a hairdryer, and a safe.

Food

Pai is filled with things to eat, although if you're looking for quality Western food, you may need to look elsewhere. Upscale restaurants just don't fit in with the town's culture, but if you want something a little nicer, the Belle Villa Resort has a nice restaurant serving typical Thai food, as does Baan Krating Pai Resort.

For inexpensive, delicious Thai food, look no farther than **Na's Kitchen** (Ratchadamnoen Rd. near Rangsiyanon Rd., tel. 01/387-0234, 30–80B). One of the most popular Thai restaurants in town with Thai and foreign travelers alike, Na's Kitchen is an excellent choice for a reasonably priced well-cooked meal. Try the Massaman curry if you're looking to branch out from the usual Thai staples.

Another Thai food option set away from the town center is **Baan Ben Jarong** (Rangsiyanon Rd., tel. 05/369-8010, 11 A.M.–11 P.M. daily, 200B), near the Bebop bar. With a wide menu to choose from and an outside terrace, the more upscale restaurant serves delicious coconut stews as well as central and southern Thai food. Try the salted fish and herbs in coconut milk (*lon pla insee*), and choose from the restaurant's large wine selection for a drink to accompany your meal.

Angie's Kitchen (Rangsiyanon Rd., tel. 05/369-9093, 60–90B) is another casual Thai restaurant with a bit of atmosphere. Set in an old wooden house, it's not luxurious, but the meals are good and the environment relaxed, even by Pai standards.

If you are craving Western food and don't mind a little meat, the popular **Burger House** (Rangsiyanon Rd., tel. 05/369-9093, 80–200B) is a reliable option. Serving a wide variety of juicy patties, the restaurant has some of the best burgers in Thailand.

For a healthier option, consider **Charlie and Lek's Restaurant** (Rangsiyanon Rd., just south of Ratchadamnoen Rd., tel. 08/1733-9055, 10 A.M.–2 P.M. and 6–10 P.M. daily, 60–100B). Much of the vegetarian menu is cooked with food from a local organic farm, and with a garden seating area and healthy sides like steamed vegetables or brown rice, the restaurant is a change from the usual stir-fried fare.

You can't come to Pai without considering **Coffee in Love** (Rte. 1095, tel. 08/7175-8180), on the road from Chiang Mai, just before the turnoff to Mae Hong Song. Impossible to miss with a large heart and cursive lettering, it is an extraordinarily popular coffee spot perched on a tiny hill above Pai. It does offer great views of the valley and a strong cup of coffee, but be prepared for a huge influx of weekenders from Bangkok.

Getting There

From Chiang Mai there are five daily **buses** making the four-hour journey for around 120B. If you have a propensity for motion sickness, be warned that this may be an unpleasant ride. There are also five daily buses between Mae Hong Son and Pai. The journey takes around four hours and cost 80B for an unair-conditioned bus, 100B with air-conditioning. Minivans also ply the same routes, taking three hours from Chiang Mai's Arcade Bus station and costing 150B; a front seat is a must if you tend toward nausea.

Driving to Pai from Chiang Mai takes you through some beautiful mountain areas and is a great drive if you're comfortable on that terrain. Take Route 107 north from Chiang Mai until you get to Route 1095, which you follow all the way to town. As with Mae Hong Son, be sure you leave the city limits with a full tank of gas—there won't be many places to fill up along the way.

CHIANG MAI

ISAN

Isan (อีสาน) is the country's agricultural heart, and here's where you'll find endless, sweeping green plains, rice fields, dirt roads, and water buffalo as well as impressive mountain ranges and the meandering Mekong River. Aside from some beautiful landscapes, Isan is also home to scores of impressive ruins from the Khmer Empire, some of the most important archaeological sites in the country, and even a few wineries.

Perhaps it's a lack of effort by the region's PR folks, or that the Andaman coast and Chiang Mai are so much more popular. Whatever the reason, few foreign travelers ever make it to Isan. Those who do, however, routinely rave about the region's charms and cuisine and wonder why it took them so long to get here. If you have a few extra days in the country or are looking for an experience that will take you far from well-worn tourist trails, head for the northeast.

Poorer and less developed than most of the rest of Thailand, Isan is often looked at by city folks as a backwater. It's true that life on the plateaus of northeast Thailand is a lot slower, but the people generally have an open friendliness not always seen in the more visited parts of the country. None of the common gripes about the rest of the country apply here—there's no overcrowding, very little sex tourism (except in major cities), and no sense that everything around you has been created to cater to travelers. Isan is sincere and true to its own identity. Although high-end tourist accommodations are few and far between, there are many opportunities to spend a few days with people in

© SUZANNE NAM

HIGHLIGHTS

◖ **Prasat Hin Phimai:** These well-preserved Khmer ruins have the largest sandstone temple in Thailand (page 426).

◖ **Phanom Rung Historical Park:** Sometimes called Thailand's Angkor Wat, the ruins of this 1,000-year-old city are amazingly well preserved and sit dramatically atop a hill overlooking the rest of the region (page 429).

◖ **Khao Phra Wihan:** Although these Khmer ruins have not been completely restored, the sheer size of the complex is worth taking the day trip into Cambodia to see (page 432).

◖ **Ban Chiang Archaeological Site and National Museum:** A little glimpse of what life must have looked like during the Bronze Age can be found at this well-preserved and easily accessible site (page 441).

◖ **Phu Luang Wildlife Reserve:** Home to more than 50 wild elephants, this mountainous wildlife reserve can only be visited on a ranger-guided tour (page 446).

LOOK FOR ◖ TO FIND RECOMMENDED SIGHTS, ACTIVITIES, DINING, AND LODGING.

their homes, tour local farms, and learn about active cottage industries. Many homestays and small tour companies are family- or village-run, and much of the money you spend stays in the communities you visit.

Bordered by Cambodia to the south and Laos to the north and east, the region seems more influenced by its neighbors than by Thai culture. To some extent this is true—Isan dialect shares many similarities with Lao, and Isan food is very close to Lao cuisine. Food is the region's most successful export, and throughout the rest of the country you'll find *som tam* or sticky rice, both distinct Isan specialties.

PLANNING YOUR TIME

Isan is the largest region in the country, and unless you've got months to spare, it's probably unrealistic to hope to see everything, especially if you're seeing the region in addition to the coast or the Chiang Mai area. Part of Isan's appeal is the slow pace that seems to pervade the region, and rushing around to relax would make no sense here. It's better to pick a few places to visit and get the most out of them.

Though Isan's cities are well served by trains and buses (either from Bangkok or within the region), there are also a number of airports in the region, in Udon Thani, Loei, Khon Kaen, Ubon Ratchathani, and Nakhon Ratchasima. If this is your first time in Isan, head to Buriram and visit the stunning **Phanom Rung** Khmer ruins, then spend a few days exploring the other temples in the area, including **Phimai.** If you have more time, head up north and enjoy the mountains of Loei, or to Khao

ISAN

ISAN

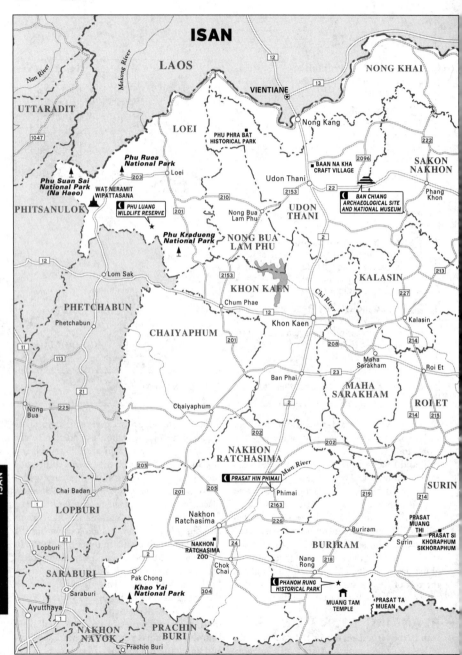

Yai National Park, one of the country's largest and only a couple of hours by car from Bangkok.

Hiring a Guide

Independent travelers will get by in the region just fine, but if you really want to get the most out of it, consider hiring a local guide. Finding temples and other sights can be tricky, and a local guide will generally not only help you use your time efficiently but give you a chance to see things you wouldn't on your own. Although the phrase *tour guide* might bring to mind large air-conditioned buses and slick folks carrying clipboards and shuttling groups around on impersonal tours, this is not generally what you'll find here. Most guides in the region are small-business owners or even teachers or other professionals who work as guides on the side and generally take only one group at a time, often for very reasonable prices (500–1,500B per day, depending on how long you are with them and how far you are driving). Through friend and family networks, they will bring you to smaller villages, even to people's homes, where you can see how life is really lived in Isan, and if you're lucky, sample some home-cooked meals. Unless you already have friends living in Isan, you won't get these types of experiences on your own. The best way to arrange a guide is to ask the resort, hotel, or guesthouse you are staying at for a recommendation. They can generally set something up for you on as little as one day's notice, though you will be better off if you send an email a couple of weeks in advance and follow up to confirm before you arrive.

Getting from one place to another in the region can be difficult. English is less likely to be spoken here than almost any other part of the country, and while there are buses and sometimes trains connecting all of the major areas, few will take you to exactly the spot you'll need to be in (you'll need a combination of local *song thaew,* taxis, and motorcycles for that), and figuring out schedules without speaking the language can be tricky. Renting a car or hiring a guide may be the best way to explore in a reasonable amount of time. You'll have to spend a

ISAN

OVERLAND TO LAOS

If you're heading to Laos after Thailand, or want to spend a day or two in Vientiane, the capital city, or even just renew a 30-day Thai tourist visa, there are four places in Isan where you can get a visa on arrival in Laos to enter the country.

Crossing into Laos requires a little bit of time, as you need to deal with both countries' immigration procedures, so be prepared to spend at least an hour on just that. The immigration offices' hours vary depending on the location. Nong Khai is open 6 A.M.-10 P.M. daily, but others have more limited hours. You cannot cross the border if you arrive too late.

When you arrive at the border on the Thai side, you must process your departure paperwork. This just amounts to handing your passport to the immigration official, but make sure you've filled out the departure card that's stapled into your passport. Then either walk or take a *tuk tuk* or shuttle bus to the Laos immigration office. Depending on the border crossing, this is usually across a bridge. Lao officials will process your entry paperwork. If you are entering from Thailand, you'll pay 1,400B for the Lao tourist visa, which you can usually pay either in U.S. dollars or in baht. There is no need to have Lao currency (kip), but note that the exchange rate applied by immigration officials is never favorable to you.

FROM NONG KHAI
The Thai-Laos Friendship Bridge in Nong Khai near Udon Thani is by far the most popular place to cross between Thailand and Laos because the crossing is just half an hour from Laos's capital city, Vientiane. Since so many people do it every day, things tend to move efficiently.

Nong Khai is the closest town to the border in Thailand but is actually about 11 kilometers from the bridge. Once you cross over into Laos, Vientiane is about 19 kilometers from the bridge. In each instance, you have to get local transport, but there are plenty of *tuk tuks* and taxis available in both Thailand and Laos.

If you are arriving at the Udon Thani airport, there are minibuses that make the one-hour journey to Nong Khai for around 200B pp. You can pick one up at the limousine counter at the arrivals terminal.

If you are coming from Bangkok by bus, there is currently an overnight bus that leaves from the Bangkok's Northern Bus Terminal at 10 P.M. nightly. The bus has air-conditioning and reclining seats; the fare is under 500B for the 10-hour ride.

There are also three overnight trains to Nong Khai, leaving Bangkok at 6:30 P.M., 6:40 P.M., and 8:45 P.M., that take 11-12 hours. A first-class sleeper will cost just over 1,200B, and a second-class sleeper will cost just over 700B. Sleeper seats sell out quickly, so make sure to book as far ahead as you can.

If you are taking a train or government bus, you'll arrive in Nong Khai and have to take a *tuk tuk* or taxi to the border. There are scores of *tuk tuks* and taxis at the train and bus station waiting to pick up passengers. Expect to pay 30-100B for the ride.

After you obtain a tourist visa in Laos, you'll need to get to Vientiane either by taxi, *tuk tuk*, or bus. Taxi prices are usually around 200B for the half-hour ride; the cost of other

little more money, but you'll also have a chance to get off the backpacker trail, as gently worn as it is in this region. In no part of the country is it a wiser move.

WEATHER
The northeast region experiences a three-season weather pattern similar to the rest of the country. The best time of year to visit is during the cool, dry season (Nov.–Feb.). Evenings and early mornings can be cool, especially if you are in the northern part of the country or in the mountains, though the average high temperatures will be in the high 20s Celsius, and there will be little, if any, rain. During the hot season (Mar.–May), high temperatures are

transport is negotiable but should be cheaper than a taxi.

From the Khao San Road area in Bangkok, it is also possible to take a bus that goes to Vientiane, although you will have to get off the bus at the border and reboard once you have dealt with immigration. These buses are staffed with people who will give you all the necessary paperwork in advance, and they will even help hasten the journey by having the paperwork processed en masse and take care of all of the necessary transport. These buses cost 700–1,000B. Be warned that they almost never leave on time.

You can also take a bus from Nong Khai to Vientiane, and staff will also help with paperwork to hasten the process. The bus will wait for passengers to deal with the bureaucracy, and it takes about 90 minutes total.

FROM MUKDAHAN
Head to the quiet and otherwise unremarkable town of Mukdahan in central eastern Isan to cross over the Mekong River into Laos's second-largest city, the former French trading center Savannakhet.

The center of Mukdahan is a little over three kilometers from the bridge crossing over the Mekong into Laos. The cheapest way to get to the bridge is to take a local bus from the Mukdahan bus station. If you don't have your own transportation, this may be the best option, as there are very few taxis in the town. You can also buy a minibus ticket in Mukdahan that will take you all the way to Savannakhet, allowing you to disembark to go through immigration formalities in Thailand, reboard to cross the bridge, and do the same on the Lao side.

FROM NAKHON PHANOM
About 80 kilometers north of Mukdahan along the Mekong River is Nakhon Phanom, a scenic rural town on the Mekong. From there you can cross into Tha Khaek, Laos, by boat.

The immigration offices here have much more limited hours, closing by early afternoon, so make sure to get to Nakhon Phanom by midday at the latest. Ferry boats will only shuttle passengers across when they are full, so be prepared to wait a while to cross over.

Once you cross, you won't need transport to get to Tha Khaek, as the town is right on the banks of the river and there are food and accommodations options a short walk from the ferry stop.

FROM CHONG MEK
Just outside of Ubon Ratchathani, about 24 kilometers south of Khong Jiam, is this busy land crossing between Thailand and Laos. The town of Chong Mek has a market filled with mostly local goods. Across the border is Vang Tao, around an hour from the popular Lao city of Pakxe.

Most people who cross here come from Ubon, and there are frequent air-conditioned buses leaving from the Ubon bus station that go to Chong Mek. Once you arrive and go through immigration on the Thai side, you can walk a short distance to the Lao side to get a visa and enter the country.

Although you may want to stay in the small town of Chong Mek once you get your paperwork in order, most people head straight for Pakxe. There are *song thaew* and taxis that make the journey regularly, they will be lined up and waiting as you leave Lao immigration.

often in the mid-30s and sometimes approach 40°C. It's generally pretty dry during this season, although by May there can be significant rainfall. June–October is hot and humid and can be very wet.

Loei Province, in the northern part of the region, is often described as having the most extreme weather conditions in the country,

and people will even tell you temperatures can reach freezing. But if you're heading here, don't necessarily pack the down parka. On the coldest days of the year in December–January, it may dip below freezing at the tops of the highest mountains, but in most of the area lows will be in the low teens and highs around 30°C. If you plan on camping at one of Loei's beautiful national parks, however, make sure you bring some warmer clothes.

HISTORY

Isan is home to one of the earliest Bronze Age civilizations in Asia, discovered in the 1950s just 50 kilometers from Udon Thani. The Ban Chiang excavation site caused something of an uproar when the bronze tools, pottery, and skeletal remains were first unearthed. Archaeologists originally dated the Ban Chiang items as far back as 4000 B.C., which would have made the little village the oldest Bronze Age civilization ever discovered. Later analysis put the age at around 2000 B.C., which still makes Ban Chiang the oldest Bronze Age civilization in Southeast Asia and the site of the most significant archaeological find in Thailand.

The first ancient culture to flourish on the Isan plateaus was the Dvaravati, originally Hindus but later Buddhists, starting sometime around the sixth century A.D. Later it was the Khmers. Although their power base was in Angkor (present-day Siem Reap in Cambodia), the expansionist empire left the region strewn with magnificent temples, only to retreat eastward beginning around the 13th century with the rise of the Kingdom of Sukhothai.

Isan, however, was not part of the Sukhothai Empire, and although the Khmer Empire left, many Khmers stayed in the region, adding to the ethnic mix.

The Lan Xang Kingdom, whose power base was Luang Phrabang, also significantly influenced Isan between the 14th and 17th centuries. The Lao presence continues to this day, and Isan was not officially or fully incorporated into modern-day Thailand until the beginning of the 20th century, when the Kingdom of Siam gave up claims to Laos and in exchange took Isan.

Nakhon Ratchasima Province จังหวัดนคร ราชสีมา

If you don't have the time to commit to a full-blown tour of Isan but want to see some of the best the region has to offer, you're in luck, because Nakhon Ratchasima is not only the closest province to Bangkok but also has some of the most dramatic and best-restored temple ruins and the largest national park in the country. You'll also find opportunities to sample traditional Isan food at every roadside stop and restaurant, check out a thriving cottage industry of silk weaving, and enjoy plenty of the friendly charm the people of the region are known for. If that's not enough of a draw, consider the province's gorgeous mountains, rustic resorts, and local wineries.

NAKHON RATCHASIMA (KHORAT) CITY
เมืองนครราชสีมา (โคราช)

The city of Khorat can be a convenient place to base yourself if you're exploring the region, as transport will be easier to find and there are more guesthouses and other accommodations available for international visitors. The small, relatively quiet city isn't particularly scenic or reflective of Isan's distinct identity or long history, however; rather, it's a testament to generic, concrete urbanization, and most visitors will probably find it less interesting than the smaller towns and rural areas that surround it.

Sights

If you decide to base yourself in the city or are passing through on your way to somewhere else, spend a few hours at the small **Maha Wirawong National Museum** (Ratchadamnoen Rd. at Jomsurangyat Rd., tel. 04/414-2958, 9 A.M.–4:30 P.M. Wed.–Sun., 10B), housing artifacts collected by a Buddhist abbot and later acquired by Thailand's Fine Arts Department. There are plenty of excellent examples of Buddhist devotional art from the Dvaravati, Khmer, and Ayutthaya periods. The abbot also collected prehistoric artifacts including

THAI SILK IN ISAN

Many of the exquisite jewel-colored silk fabrics you'll see in shops throughout the country started life in Isan. Here, silk weaving is a true cottage industry, and many women support their families by growing silkworms, harvesting silk, and dyeing and weaving it in their homes. The resulting product is often sold to larger silk companies, who take the material and manufacture it into scarves, pillows, dresses, and other products.

Silk weaving can be found throughout the region but is centered in Pak Thong Chai, about 32 kilometers outside Khorat City. It's here that many companies have set up shop, either employing locals to work in their factories or buying pieces from women who work at home.

There are seldom organized tours of the area, but if you're interested in seeing how the material is dyed and woven, it's easy to wander around the village. On any weekday you will see silk drying out on racks, women sitting at looms, and normal village life. Be respectful, but don't be shy; many of the crafters will be happy to show you what they are doing and even offer an impromptu lesson in silk weaving.

If you want to bring home some silk, in the center of town are numerous shops selling an unbelievable amount of silk in hundreds of colors. Most is a solid color, but there are some traditional and not-so-traditional prints available too. Prices here are generally very reasonable, and Bangkok residents have been known to make special day trips in search of material.

If you happen to be in the area in late December-early January, visit the **Jim Thompson Mulberry Farm** (555 Mu 1, Tambon Takob, Pak Thong Chai District, Nakhon Ratchasima, tel. 04/437-3116, www.jimthompson.com/JT_Farm), where you'll not only get to see what silkworms eat but watch the whole process from start to finish. Unfortunately, the company only does the tours a few weeks of the year.

---

pottery, tools, and other household items found both around Khorat and in other parts of the country. The museum is housed in a one-story home on the grounds of **Wat Sutthachinda,** a beautiful little temple with intricate carvings adorning the exterior.

Built in the 17th century, the **Chumphon Gate** (Chumphon Rd.), in the central part of the city, is one of the few hints that Khorat is actually not a modern city. The brick, plaster, and wooden gate was originally one of four that surrounded the city and is the only one that has survived.

Right in front of the gate is the city's most famous landmark, the "Kunying Mo" or **Thao Suranari Statue,** built to commemorate the area's most famous heroine. According to the legend, during an invasion by Lao forces from Vientiane in the 19th century, Thao Suranari, the wife of a local government official, tricked the invaders into celebrating prematurely. After she'd got them all drunk, she led a successful resistance effort, ensuring freedom for the people of Isan. The statue was constructed in 1934 and since then has become a very popular spot for worship. There's also an annual festival during the last week of March to celebrate Thao Suranari's bravery.

The modern 81-hectare **Nakhon Ratchasima Zoo** (111 Mu 1, Nakhon Ratchasima–Pak Thong Chai Hwy., tel. 04/435-7355, 8:30 A.M.–4:30 P.M. daily, 30B adults, 10B children), about 16 kilometers outside of Khorat City, is the largest in the region and a great break if you're visiting with children. The animals in the zoo are not all indigenous to Southeast Asia—in fact, among the more than 1,000 animals on display are African elephants, rhinos, cheetahs, and even penguins. For many, the main attraction is the gibbons, however, especially when there are new babies. The park is large, and though you

ISAN

can walk it, there's also a tram, and you can rent bicycles. If you get hungry while you're there, don't worry; there's plenty to eat, including casual Thai food at outdoor canteens and ice cream.

To drive to the zoo from town, take Route 304 heading south until you see the signs for the zoo. By public transportation, there is a city bus, no. 1415, that goes directly to the zoo and costs less than 50B.

Accommodations

Although there are better places to stay in the area, including laid-back Phimai or at one of the lodges around Khao Yai National Park, if you are going to stay in Khorat, you'll find hotels significantly less expensive than in bigger cities or on the coast. The quality of accommodations isn't stellar, though, and within the city most of what you'll find are inexpensive, basic guesthouses without much charm.

If you just want a cheap, clean place to rest, **San Sabai** (335 Suranari Rd., tel. 04/425-5144 or 08/1547-3066, 350B) is all you need. The small guesthouse is within walking distance of all the city sights and has air-conditioning and TVs in every guest room. The decor leaves much to be desired, and the guest rooms are not spacious, but in this price category it's as good as it gets.

The Doctor's House (78 Serbsiri Soi 4, tel. 04/425-5846, 400B) is a quirky, friendly, run-down guesthouse with basic guest rooms with en suite baths and lots of charm. If you're more interested in friendly proprietors and personality than high-end comforts, you may just love this place.

Bussarakam (68 Pimpasut Rd., tel. 04/333-3666, www.bussarakamhotel.com, 1,000B) is a large, modern hotel that caters to local businesspeople and tourists. This is a solid choice for those looking for clean, comfortable guest rooms and reliable service. Although it does not have much exotic character, you will still feel like you are staying in Thailand, given the other guests and the staff.

The (C) **Dusit Princess** (1137 Suranari Rd., tel. 02/636-3333, www.dusit.com, 1,700B),

just outside of the center of the city, is an excellent value. Part of the luxury Dusit chain (though less than half the price you'd pay in Bangkok), the hotel has beautiful grounds and well-furnished spacious guest rooms with cable TV, Internet access, and other modern amenities. It's not up to the level of Bangkok's five-star hotels but is nevertheless the nicest option in the area. There are also two restaurants on the property as well as a fitness center, a large swimming pool, a tennis court, and a spa.

Just one step below the Dusit is the **Sima Thani Hotel** (2112/2 Mittraphap Rd., tel. 04/421-3100, www.simathani.com, 1,600B), offering most of the same amenities, including plenty of restaurants to choose from, a nice pool, and modern guest rooms. It's not quite five-star either, and furnishings might feel a little more run-down than at the Dusit, but the property still stands head and shoulders above most other options.

Food

The best food in Isan is found in casual restaurants and in markets where vendors sell *som tam* and *kai yang* from makeshift street stalls. Finding small restaurants can be a little tricky in Khorat, as few of the best local joints have English menus, phone numbers, or even names you'll be able to identify. Luckily, Khorat has two different night markets right in the center of town to choose from if you're looking for some regional cuisine for dinner. The **Night Bazaar** (Manat Rd. between Chumphon Rd. and Mahathai Rd., 6–10 P.M. daily, 30B) has food stalls selling quick, cheap meals as well as lots of low-end T-shirts, sneakers, and other clothing. If you're feeling really brave, try some *menda thot* (fried water bugs), sold by one of the many fried-bug sellers you'll see at the market. The smaller **Wat Boon Market** (Chumphon Rd. near Kudan Rd., 6–10 P.M. daily, 30B), across from Wat Boon, has fewer shopping stalls but more food, including non-Isan dishes such as pad thai and noodle soups.

Khorat also has a good selection of midrange sit-down restaurants. Although you will

ISAN

encounter inevitable language-barrier challenges, don't be discouraged—people are generally patient and friendly even in the city.

Baan Lan Look Mai (309 Soi Savai Lieng, Mukkhamontri Rd., tel. 04/425-3281, 11 A.M.–11 P.M. daily, 200B) offers excellent Thai dishes in a charming old-fashioned house and garden setting, a great place to take a date. Dishes here range from traditional and reliable Isan regulars to innovative and unexpected flavors. For a bit of the latter, try the duck curry with grapes.

The Population and Community Development Association of Thailand, a local nongovernmental organization dedicated to community health and population control, opened **Cabbages and Condoms** (86/1 Serbsiri Rd., tel. 04/425-8100, 150B) to support the organization's mission. The extensive menu covers Thai regional dishes from across the country in addition to Isan specialties. The restaurant is brightly decorated (with, of course, a condom motif) and is a step above most basic restaurants in the area, though still a comfortable place if you're looking for something relaxed and casual. All profits from the restaurant, as in the other locations throughout the country, help fund the organization.

Kai yang is one of the most popular dishes in the city, and you can't miss the plentiful small shops and stalls selling the grilled chickens. **Kai Yang Wat Pa Salawan** (Soi 3, Serbsiri Rd., no phone, 10 A.M.–7 P.M. daily, 100B), near Wat Pa Salawan, is a very casual canteen-style sit-down chicken shop that also serves Isan favorites such as *larb mu* and sticky rice.

Getting There and Around

Nakhon Ratchasima is easy to get to whether you're driving on your own or taking public transportation. There are multiple trains daily from Bangkok's Hua Lamphong Station to Nakhon Ratchasima, with a travel time of 4.5–6 hours and a cost around 200B. There are currently 11 trains daily from Bangkok, departing 5:45 A.M.–11:40 P.M. The slightly faster option is to take a bus from Bangkok's Northern Bus Terminal (Mo Chit), which will

take about three hours, depending on traffic, and cost around 200B. Buses leave Bangkok every half hour 5:30 A.M.–10 P.M. daily. If you are driving, Nakhon Ratchasima is on Highway 2. You can rent a car from **Khorat Car Rental** (136 Phonsaen Rd., tel. 04/439-3730, www.koratcarrental.com).

The city itself is too big to cover on foot. The best way to get around is either to use the city's public buses or *tuk tuks*.

BAN PRASAT ARCHAEOLOGICAL SITE
แหล่งโบราณคดีบ้านปราสาท

Even visitors with the tiniest interest or curiosity about archaeology and ancient people should visit Ban Prasat Archaeological Site (Mu 7, Tambon Than Prasat, Amphoe Non Sang, 8:30 A.M.–4 P.M. daily, donation), about 16 kilometers from Phimai and 40 kilometers north of Nakhon Ratchasima. The remnants of a 3,000-year-old agricultural community, including evidence of rice cultivation, animal domestication, weapons, and ornamental objects, are displayed in the attached museum, but many of the artifacts of this civilization remain in the excavation pits where they were found, and those are open to the public.

Homestays

Ban Prasat Homestay is perhaps one of the best ways to experience life in Thailand and know that your money is going to the people around you. The villagers of Ban Prasat have been hosting visitors since 1993, shortly after exploration of the pits was completed. The project started with just Thai and foreign archaeology students but was quickly expanded, with the help of the Tourism Authority of Thailand (TAT), to travelers. To arrange a visit, call the village head (tel. 04/436-7075) or the regional TAT office (tel. 04/421-3666). You'll be matched with a family who will invite you into their home, feed you, and bring you to see things such as silk weaving, basket making, and traditional food preparation. For around 400B per night, this is an amazing bargain.

ISAN

EATING IN ISAN

Although foreigners generally don't have the opportunity to try Isan food until they arrive, once they do, many people consider it to be the best in the country. To get the most out of northeastern Thai cuisine, seek out the markets and street vendors in any city or town in the region. The best Isan food is unpretentious, freshly prepared, inexpensive, and casually eaten. Often the small, nameless street-side stands selling dishes for 20B are better than any air-conditioned sit-down restaurant in the area.

Isan food differs significantly from central Thai, northern Thai, and southern Thai cuisines. Many use similar ingredients, such as cilantro and lime juice, but Isan fare tends to use a combination of sweet, sour, and savory flavors and relies heavily on fresh vegetables. Many of the dishes and flavors can also be found in Laos, which is not surprising considering its proximity and the historical relationship between northeast Thailand and Laos.

As you are tasting everything Isan has to offer, remember that people in the region usually prefer their food spicy. Locals know that not everyone has the same courage under fire as they do, but sometimes even the phrase *mai phet* ("not spicy") isn't enough – for someone from Isan, it may translate into too spicy for everyone else. Instead, take advantage of the fact that nearly everything is made to order, and request that the chef cut down on the number of chilies he or she is using. For most people who can handle a little spice, one chili is plenty in any dish, so when you're ordering, say *prik nung met* so they'll know to prepare it with just one chili. If it's not spicy enough, next time ask for it *prik song met*, and you'll get two chilies instead.

COMMON ISAN FOODS

· **Khao neo:** Sticky rice that accompanies almost any Isan dish, served either in small plastic bags or bamboo baskets. It is impossible to eat with a fork, so just pinch off a bite with your fingers.

· **Som tam:** Perhaps Thailand's most popular dish, the basic version is made of shredded green papaya, fresh long beans, tomatoes, dried shrimp, peanuts, lime juice, fish sauce, garlic, palm sugar, and chilies. The ingredients are mixed together with a mortar and large pestle, and you'll know if a particular stand is serving *som tam* if you see the mortar or a pile of shredded papaya waiting to

Getting There

Buses going from Khorat to Phimai stop at Ban Prasat Archaeological Site along the way. There are frequent buses from Khorat during the day—at least every hour 6 A.M.–6 P.M.—and the ride is about one hour. If you are driving, follow Route 2 northeast for about 40 kilometers.

WINERIES

Nakhon Ratchasima Province is home to some small wineries producing local wines. In addition to selling wine, some offer tours and tastings as well as wonderful restaurants. These are family-run operations, so it's best to call and confirm a tour instead of just showing up.

PB Valley Vineyard

ไร่ พีบี แวลเลย์

PB Valley Vineyard (102 Mu 5, Phaya Yen, Pak Chong, tel. 02/262-0030 or 03/622-6415, www.khaoyaiwinery.com, 8:30 A.M.–4:30 P.M. daily, free) produces nearly 1 million bottles of shiraz, tempranillo, and chenin blanc each year and offers tours of the property. The **Great Hornbill Grill** (10 A.M.–8 P.M. Sun.–Thurs., 10 A.M.–10 P.M. Fri.–Sat.), set on the winery's lovely grounds, has Thai and European offerings, including pizza to go with your tempranillo. Stop by for a tour and for 700B (350B for kids) you'll get a set meal at the restaurant.

If you are traveling by car from Khorat,

be mixed. Nearly every visitor who tries it wants to eat it every day. A popular version in Isan is *som tam pu,* made with raw salted river crab. *Som tam* is often served with a small side order of cabbage, long beans, and herbs.

- **Larb:** A marinated meat salad made from ground beef or pork, fish sauce, dried chilies, cilantro, mint, shallots, lime juice, and toasted rice. The salad is usually served at room temperature accompanied by extra mint leaves.

- **Namtok:** Another marinated meat salad, with similar ingredients to *larb* except that it's made with sliced grilled beef or pork instead of ground meat. If you've ever tried a dish called Thai Beef Salad outside Thailand, it's a version of *namtok nua,* which literally means "waterfall beef." Why it is called "waterfall" is anyone's guess. Some say it's because of the sound the meat makes when it's grilled, others because the spiciness can make tears flow. If you don't want to shed any tears, make sure to try it *mai phet* first to appreciate the flavors.

- **Kai yang:** Translated, it means "grilled chicken," but it's not just roaster pieces thrown on a charcoal grill. Properly prepared *kai yang* involves flattening the chicken and then grilling it whole. The result is a juicy, perfectly cooked bird. *Kai yang* is often served with sweet and spicy sauce to accompany it.

- **Sai crock Isan:** Sometimes it's better not to know what you're eating, and this Isan sausage is one example. The small, round sausages are stuffed with rice and fermented pork, and as a result they have a tangy flavor that is surprisingly satisfying, especially with a cold Chang beer.

- **Sato:** Although you can sometimes find commercial versions of this alcoholic beverage in convenience stores across the country, the best is the homemade stuff, which you'll sometimes see vendors selling in small plastic bags. *Sato* is made from rice, sugar, yeast, and water, and the result is a lightly alcoholic, slightly sweet, slightly bubbly rice "wine." Many people in Isan make *sato* at home, and although it is technically illegal to sell it, if you can find the homemade version, take the opportunity to try it.

take Highway 2 heading west (toward Bangkok, or east if you are coming from Bangkok), and turn off heading south at kilometer marker 144 and follow signs about 16 kilometers to the vineyard. If you are without a car, the vineyard will arrange a driver service for you from either Khorat or Bangkok.

Granmonte Asoke Valley
ไร่องุ่นกรานมอนเต
Granmonte Asoke Valley (52 Mu 9, Phayayen, Pak Chong, tel. 03/622-7334, www.granmonte.com, 8 A.M.–4 P.M. daily, free) also offers tastings and tours of their small family vineyard producing syrah and chenin blanc.

The property is set in a scenic valley and is also home to █ **Vincotto** (11 A.M.–8 P.M. Thurs.–Tues., 1,200B), an intimate, personal restaurant serving indulgent dishes such as foie gras and duck filet salad. Make sure to visit the gift shop too: It's stocked not only with wine but also lots of yummy homemade jams, sauces, and snacks.

If you are traveling by car from Khorat, take Highway 2 heading west (toward Bangkok, or east if you are coming from Bangkok), and turn off heading south at kilometer marker 144 and follow signs about 16 kilometers to the vineyard. If you are without a car, the vineyard will arrange a driver service for you from either Khorat or Bangkok.

ISAN

KHAO YAI NATIONAL PARK
อุทยานแห่งชาติเขาใหญ่

Khao Yai National Park (Pak Chong, tel. 08/1877-3127, 08/6092-6531, or 08/1063-9241, www.dnp.go.th, 400B adults, 100B children) was the country's first national park and covers over 2,000 square kilometers of parts of four provinces—Nakhon Ratchasima, Saraburi, Nakhon Nayok, and Prachinburi. Inside you'll find waterfalls, mountains, evergreen forest, tropical forest, grasslands, and rivers populated by over 300 species of birds, gibbons, macaques, deer, and even elephants and tigers. You can hike, white-water raft, swim in the waterfalls, observe animals, and even do a night safari. In fact, it's possible to spend a week at Khao Yai and not feel like you've seen and done everything available.

There are 20 major waterfalls in the park, including Haew Narok, the largest, and Haew Suwat, the most famous (it was used in the movie *The Beach*). At Haew Suwat, the waterfall ends with an 18-meter drop into a small reservoir, and visitors can swim under the falls.

The main visitors center (or your hotel or guesthouse, if you're staying outside of the park) can also arrange wildlife tours.

The park is vast, and either unfortunately or conveniently, depending on how you look at it, there is a main road that cuts through the park, providing well-paved and maintained access to all of the larger sights. The main visitors center, right in the center of the park and on the main road, has some ecology and wildlife exhibits as well as park rangers available who can answer questions. Be warned that the rangers have occasionally tried to dissuade visitors from hiking the trails with warnings about the difficulty and length of them. If you are even a novice hiker and in good physical condition, do not worry. Most of the trails are fairly well marked, and none are very long; in fact, you won't be able to find a trail longer than about 9.5 kilometers. If you're starting from the main visitors center, the trail to the Haew Suwat waterfall, at about eight kilometers, is a nice intermediate hike. There are a

---

HOWDY THAI COWBOYS

Just off Highway 2 on the way from Bangkok to Khao Yai National Park is **Farm Chockchai** (tel. 04/432-8485, www.farmchokchai.com, tour reservations farmtour@farmchokchai.com), an impressive Thai dude ranch and working cattle and dairy farm. Come for a day and spend some time riding horses, watching a cowboy show, visiting the petting zoo, or learning how to milk a cow.

Although much of Thailand is rural, there are plenty of young Thais who've never set foot on a farm, and watching how other tour guests respond to the cowboys and animals is as fun as the tour itself. This is much more of a cultural experience than you'd expect, and it's a lot of fun.

Tours start every 20 minutes on Saturday-Sunday but only twice a day during the week. If you don't have time for a tour, stop into one of the many restaurants and cafeterias at Farm Chockchai. They have everything from a high-end steakhouse to a burger joint plus a few kiosks where you can buy the farm's homemade ice cream. On weekends it seems like every family in Bangkok along with innumerable tour buses are here, so be prepared for crowds.

---

total of about 48 kilometers of hiking trails in the park, most of which begin at the main headquarters.

Accommodations and Camping

If you are planning on camping in Khao Yai, you must register at the campground before 6 P.M. Especially over a weekend, be prepared for crowds of fellow campers and tents lined up just a few meters from each other. The campsites (50B) all have tents and sleeping bags for rent (they can run out of these on very busy weekends), small food shops, canteens serving homey, inexpensive Thai meals, and clean coldwater showers and restroom facilities. One even has a small espresso cafe, but no alcohol is sold in the park, so if you want a beer, make sure to bring it in with you.

There are also accommodations available for rent, and they run the gamut from dormitory rooms with bunk beds to spacious bungalows with hot water, modern tiled baths, and wicker furniture from which you can sip the espresso being sold at the café. These tend to book up quickly, as the park is a popular destination for students and other groups. Bungalows start at 800B, and bungalows and houses that can comfortably sleep as many as eight people cost 2,400B per night. As with all of the national parks in the country, you must reserve your spot by emailing reserve@dnp.go.th and dnp_tourist@yahoo.com and then transferring payment to the parks department before arrival.

If you're visiting Khao Yai but don't want to camp, the area is filled with some medium-sized properties and a lot of small resorts taking advantage of the beautiful landscapes in the area; you'll see signs literally lining the road on the drive up to the park. The range runs from basic to high-end, and there are even some wineries that rent out bungalows or cabins on their grounds. If you're comparing what you'll get for the money versus a very touristy and popular spot such as Phuket, Khao Yai is an unbelievable bargain. Wherever you stay, hotel staff can arrange day tours of the park.

Eco Valley Lodge Khao Yai (199/16 Mu 8, Nongnamdaeng, Pak Chong, tel. 04/424-9661, www.ecovalleylodge.com, 1,400B) has small bungalows and villas for rent and is located a few kilometers off the main road to the park if you're coming from Khorat. The furnishings aren't very chic, but the bungalows are large and well maintained and even have TVs and Internet access. The grounds are also large and very green, and there are two swimming pools and a restaurant on the premises. Look past the mismatched bedspreads and wicker furniture, as this is a great-value resort.

If you consider yourself a rustic outdoorsy type but enjoy a little pampering too, try the **Village Farm and Winery** (103 Mu 7, Thaisamakkee, Wang Nam Keow, tel. 04/422-

8407, www.villagefarm.co.th, 2,200B). The least-expensive lodgings are in an old converted barn, though you'll still enjoy good beds and hot water. The nicest guest rooms have minibars, music players, and satellite TV. All are decorated with lots of exposed wood and surrounded by farmland. The property is also a working winery, and you can tour the vineyard or, if you feel like relaxing instead, just drink a glass of wine or visit the spa. The restaurant, **Village Cuisine** (8 A.M.–9 P.M. Sun.–Fri., 8 A.M.–10 P.M. Sat., 400B) serves European and Thai dishes and is worth a visit even if you're not staying here.

Although the **Juldis Khao Yai** (54 Mu 4, Thanarat Rd., Pak Chong, tel. 04/429-7297, www.khaoyai.com, 1,900B) is a little too close to the main road to be considered in the woods, and a little too large to be considered a resort, it is a good choice if you want hotel-style amenities and proximity to the park. There is a main hotel with guest rooms that have airy balconies, clean comfortable beds, and modern baths. The suites in the smaller satellite buildings are more spacious and have more modern decor. All enjoy the property's surrounding gardens and swimming pool, tennis courts, and spa. The hotel is not really a luxury property, but it is much nicer than a guesthouse.

The **Greenery Resort** (188/1 Thanarat Rd., Pak Chong, tel. 04/429-7224, 2,200B) is a nice blend of rustic and polished—the grounds of the hotel are lush and green. Some of the guest rooms have a little modern flair to them, and not just because of the minibars, coffeemakers, and TVs but because of the Thai decor. On the grounds you'll find swimming pools, a spa, and a restaurant.

Perhaps the nicest property in the area is the **Kirimaya Resort** (1/3 Mu 6, Thanarat Rd., Pak Chong, tel. 04/442-6099, www.kirimaya.com, 9,000B). Set on the plains and surrounded by mountains, the resort has amazing scenery. The guest rooms have modern lines and modular furniture, subdued by neutral colors. If you're willing to spend some extra cash, the tented villas are designed as standalone camping tents, except that they are the

ISAN

size of small homes and include luxuries such as soaking tubs.

Getting There and Around

The best way to see the park is with your own transportation or on a guided tour. It's not really feasible to tour Khao Yai without a car as the park is too big and there are not enough marked trails to get you from one place to another on foot. Some visitors choose to hitchhike, and considering that many of the other guests are families with their kids, it might just be a safer place to engage in an otherwise risky behavior. Still, you're better off on a tour or in your own car.

If you are driving from Bangkok, it's less than three hours. Take Route 305 to Route 33 at Naresuan, and then turn onto Route 3077, which will take you directly to the park's entrance about 40 kilometers from the turnoff.

If you are arriving by public transportation, you can take a bus from Bangkok to **Pak Chong.** That's still more than 16 kilometers from the closest entrance to the park, so you'll need to either hire a taxi or motorcycle, or take a *song thaew.*

PHIMAI
พิมาย

Phimai, less than 64 kilometers from Khorat, is home to Thailand's best Khmer ruins, followed closely by Phanom Rung in Buriram. It's a must-see spot if you are in the area. Centered around the old temple, the ancient city was built about 1,000 years ago, and most of the modern town is now found within the old boundaries (much of the ancient city wall is gone, but many traces of it remain). Phimai itself is very quiet and laid-back, with few things to distract from the main attraction. Although many folks see the ruins as part of a day trip, it's worth staying one night in Phimai so you can catch the temple at dusk or sunrise and not feel rushed viewing the collection at the Phimai National Museum. The town is definitely tourist-friendly, although there is not a lot of tourist development aside from a handful of moderate guesthouses and casual places to eat.

◖ Prasat Hin Phimai
ปราสาทหินพิมาย

Right in the center of the town is Prasat Hin Phimai (tel. 04/447-1568, 7:30 A.M.–6 P.M. daily, 40B), built in the 11th century by a Khmer king soon after the Dvaravati Kingdom was conquered by the Khmer Empire. The impressive stone structure, with a central tower reaching nearly 30 meters into the sky, has been carefully restored and is the best example of Khmer architecture in the country. There is some disagreement as to whether the structure was originally started as a Hindu temple. Whether it was or not, Prasat Hin Phimai has both Hindu and Buddhist carvings but became a Mahayana Buddhist temple before it was completed, reflecting either the diversity of religions or the tolerance of the Khmer during the period. The Hindu carvings weren't removed, rather Buddhist artwork added, giving visitors an excellent opportunity to see both.

The ancient city plan was a rectangle surrounded by a city wall and an exterior moat, the remnants of which still exist, along with various scattered ruins interwoven with the modern town of Phimai.

Although similar in style to Cambodia's Angkor Wat, Prasat Hin Phimai was built a century earlier, and unlike other Khmer temples that face east toward the rising sun, this one faces Angkor, the former capital city of the Khmer Empire. Subsumed by the rainforest for centuries, an ancient road to Angkor, a **Khmer highway** of sorts, begins in Phimai and was only fully mapped in 2005 by the **Living Angkor Road Project** (http://larp. crma.ac.th). The road is littered with sculptures, building remains, and other artifacts of the lost empire.

Phimai National Museum
พิพิธภัณฑสถานแหงชาติพิมาย

The Phimai National Museum (Tha Songkran Rd., tel. 04/447-1167, 9 A.M.–4 P.M. daily, 30B) was originally created to house artifacts from Phimai and has a collection of lintels, sculptures, and other objects from the temple. It has since also become Isan's main regional museum and now has an extensive, excellent collection of regional art and artifacts from prehistory onward. If you're visiting the Maha Wirawong National Museum in Khorat as well as the Phimai National Museum, you can buy a combined ticket for 100B that entitles you to visit both for a month.

Tours and Homestays

What Phimai lacks in upscale accommodations it more than makes up for in small, excellent tour companies. If you're looking for a chance to engage with the people around you and fall in love with Isan, skip the guesthouses and group tours and arrange to spend a few days with one of these operations.

Lamai Homestay (tel. 08/6258-5894 or 08/6246-5813, www.thailandhomestay.com), an ecofriendly, community-friendly, family-run company, offers short and multiday tours of cultural sights in the region, including Phimai and Phanom Rung in neighboring Buriram. The British Husband–Thai wife team are dedicated to ensuring that visitors experience the people of Isan as well as its sights, and if you tour with them, you'll get a chance to spend time talking to villagers, visiting local schools, and even learning how rice is planted and harvested. The multiday tours—including accommodations at the family's homestay with comfortable air-conditioned rooms and modern facilities, meals, and transport—are a great value at around 6,000B pp for five days if you book a group.

Toy's Tours (tel. 08/6267-5518, toystours@ hotmail.com) is another small family-run operation offering very reasonably priced personalized tours of the Phimai area, including the temple itself, the national museum, and the surrounding rural area, starting at around 2,000B per day. They can also arrange homestays with local village families if you are interested in a truly Thai experience while you see the area. Toy's also offers cycling and motorcycle tours.

Accommodations

There are no high-end hotels in Phimai, just a handful of adequate hostels and small two-star hotels to choose from.

Old Phimai Guest House (124 Mu 1, Chomsuda Sadej Rd., tel. 04/447-1918, 450B) is really a youth hostel with clean, comfortable dormitory-style rooms and reasonable modern baths. There are some private guest rooms available.

The **Phimai Hotel** (305/1-2 Haruthairom Rd., tel. 04/447-1306, 300B) has clean, comfortable guest rooms, and some come with private baths, air-conditioning, and TVs.

The nicest hotel in the area is the **Phimai Inn** (33/1 Bypass Rd., tel. 04/447-1175, 400B), about a 20-minute walk from town. Slightly reminiscent of an economy lodge off a major highway, the guest rooms are nonetheless clean and reasonably furnished, and there's even a swimming pool and a restaurant on the premises.

Food

As in the rest of the country, the quality and taste of food generally really matter to the people of Isan, and even in small Phimai you'll get differing opinions about where to get the best meal of one type or another. Most of the best places to eat are street stalls and small hole-in-the-wall restaurants with no signs, phone numbers, or even names that you'll be able to recognize. During lunch and dinner, find one of these places, or if you're feeling adventurous, just go to the shops and stalls that seem to have the biggest crowds. Remember that the beauty of the surroundings and the price you pay for a meal often have no correlation to how well it was prepared or, for that matter, how memorable it will be.

The **Phimai Night Market** (Anantajinda Rd., 4–9:30 P.M. daily, 35B) has many food stalls serving a variety of dishes, including regional favorites such as *som tam,* fried chicken, and grilled meats, making it the best choice if you're not sure what you want to eat and you don't mind the casual atmosphere. You'll also find dumplings and other snacks. For dessert, try some *kanom Thai*—coconut puddings scented with jasmine and other unexpected

ISAN

© SUZANNE NAM

food stall at one of Isan's night markets

flavors—or sweet purple sticky rice traditionally packed inside bamboo.

On the edge of the market in the southern part of the city is a noodle shop referred to as **Guay Teow Rua** (10 A.M.–2 P.M. daily, 25B) serving up just about every noodle-soup combination you can imagine, from wide, flat rice noodles with meatballs and broth to egg noodles with vegetables. You'll probably encounter a little confusion if you don't have any Thai language skills, but don't be put off. The best way to get what you want here is to go up to the counter and just point to the type of noodles and extras you want. If in doubt, order *bah mee mai sai nam tan, sai mu, mai sai luk chin*—a bowl of egg noodles barely moistened with a little broth and served with pork.

Jay Jar Cafe (no phone, breakfast–late evening, 30B) serves *khao man kai,* a simple, flavorful dish of sliced chicken served on top of rice. You'll find a similar chicken-and-rice dish throughout the region up to southern China, where it probably originated, and there's a

reason it's so popular: Although rice and chicken may seem basic, the chicken is always tender, and the rice is prepared with chicken stock and other flavors, making it far more tasty than a normal bowl of grains. The dish is served with a spicy ginger-infused soy dipping sauce that can transform the meal from comfort food to exciting with a few teaspoons. There are also other dishes available here.

If you aren't up for the challenge of finding or ordering from one of the casual local places listed above, there are a couple of traveler-oriented restaurants complete with English-language menus. The **Phimai Inn** (33/1 Bypass Rd., tel. 04/447-1175, 8 A.M.–10 P.M. daily, 150B) has a pleasant restaurant attached to the main hotel with a large selection of Thai food from across the country as well as a Western breakfast. There is indoor and outdoor seating and live music some nights.

Getting There and Around
The good news is that once you arrive in

Phimai, you'll be able to walk the main ruins without needing any transportation. To get to Phimai, there are frequent buses from Nakhon Ratchasima that take under two hours and cost about 50B. If you are driving from Nakhon Ratchasima, take Highway 2 heading northeast until you get to Route 206. From there, head eastward for about eight kilometers to Phimai.

Buriram Province
จังหวัดบุรีรัมย์

This province is home to one of the best archaeological sites in the country, Phanom Rung, and some smaller temples, but otherwise it doesn't usually grab the attention of foreign visitors, who usually choose to see the sights as part of a day trip from Khorat. The province feels more rural than Khorat, largely because there's no big main urban area in the province. Buriram Town is quite small for anyone who has lived in a big city. Don't be put off, however; the region is laid-back, authentic, and unjaded by the commerce of tourism. This makes it a great opportunity to see life in Thailand and to find ways to bring your tourism dollars directly to the people who live in the area.

SIGHTS
Ⓒ Phanom Rung Historical Park
ปราสาทหินพนมรุ้ง
Set in the middle of a quiet rural area on top of an extinct volcano mound is the awe-inspiring **Phanom Rung temple** (tel. 04/478-2715, 6 A.M.–6 P.M. daily, 50B). Begun during the 10th century by the Khmer king Rajendravarman as a Hindu shrine, it was completed in the 13th century by King Jayavarman VII, whose final additions incorporated Buddhist elements.

You enter the complex by way of a laterite path more than 120 meters long and lined with posts topped with carved lotuses. At the top of a massive set of stone stairs lies the six-building complex, with a main *prang* rising into the sky.

In the overall architecture, you'll see multi-tiered roofs and indenting, repeating patterns. The ruins also have intricate detailed carvings throughout, depicting the gods Shiva and Vishnu as well as representations of religious ceremonies and plenty of *nagas.*

Phanom Rung is best visited 14 days before and after the equinoxes, when you'll be able to ponder the astronomical knowledge the Khmers must have possessed. The complex's 15 doorways offer a straight view from east to west throughout the year, but at these times of year they line up precisely with the sun's path, allowing for spectacular views of the rising and setting sun, illuminating the stone lingam within the complex and spilling through all of the doorways. There is still much speculation as to why the temple (and other, though not all, Khmer temples) were built to showcase the sunrise and sunset during these four times of the year instead of just twice a year during the equinoxes themselves. These solar events at Phanom Rung are the most popular time to visit the temple. To find the dates, just add or subtract fourteen days from the date of the vernal or autumnal equinox, which are around March 20 and September 23 every year.

If you can, visit this temple in conjunction with a tour of **Phimai,** as they are the two best preserved and most impressive Khmer ruins in the country and a testament to the power and glory of the Khmers nearly 1,000 years ago.

Phanom Rung is about 64 kilometers south of Buriram Town. If you're driving, take Route 219 south to Highway 24 and follow it west for about 19 kilometers until you turn off (heading south) onto a smaller road that will lead you to the temple park.

Public transportation is frankly not great, but if you're without your own wheels, you can take a bus from Nakhon Ratchasima (Khorat) heading toward Surin. Get off at Ban Tako,

ISAN

about 120 kilometers away, and from there, hire a motorcycle for the rest of the journey. You'll need to have the motorcycle wait for you, as there's generally no transportation back from the temple. Alternately, you can hire one of the **tour guides** listed in the *Phimai* section, inquire at any travel agency in Khorat, or ask your hotel or guesthouse. Any of them will be able to arrange transportation for you.

Muang Tam Temple (Prasat Muang Tam)
ปราสาทเมืองต่ำ

Although Muang Tam (tel. 04/478-2715, 30B) is less impressive than Phimai or Phanom Rung, it is definitely worth visiting if you are already in the area, and it is just eight kilometers south of Phanom Rung. This Khmer temple complex is set on a large rectangle surrounded by walls. Once inside the first courtyard, there are L-shaped ponds at every corner. The inner courtyard contains the main buildings, with five large brick *prang*. Although small, the temple is adorned with intricate Hindu sculptures and carvings.

ACCOMMODATIONS

Choices within the town of Buriram are very limited, but there's really no reason to stay in the small center anyway. It's better to look for places outside of town or in neighboring Nang Rong, just to the south.

Cabbages & Condoms (81 Mu 6, Chokchai-Dej Udom Rd., Nang Rong, tel. 04/465-7145, 700B) has a laid-back little resort and restaurant whose proceeds go toward the work of the Population and Community Development Association. There are some hostel-like accommodations here, but the basic double guest rooms with private baths are comfortably furnished and spacious, and the grounds surrounding the resort are nice. There's also a branch of the restaurant on the premises, a great place for Thai food from around the country.

About 48 kilometers from Buriram Town, the **Ruan Nang Rong Resort** (Sri Kallaya Rd., Nang Rong, tel. 04/462-2385, www.ruannan-grong.com, 600B) in Nang Rong has some very modern, comfortable little cottage-style guest rooms set in a well-maintained complex. Guest rooms are simple and a little underdecorated, but considering the price of the accommodations, it's a minor drawback. There are few foreigners here, so you may have a bit of trouble communicating.

GETTING THERE
Train

There are multiple trains daily from Bangkok to Buriram, including an overnight train, which take six hours or longer, costing from 250B to over 1,000B, depending on the level of service. From Khorat, the trip is about 90 minutes, with trains leaving 10 A.M.–5:30 P.M.

Bus

The Northern Bus Terminal in Bangkok has frequent buses to Buriram; the trip takes about six hours and costs just over 200B. Khorat and Buriram are on the same bus line from Bangkok. If you are leaving from Khorat, the ride is about two hours.

Car

If you are driving, Buriram is served by Route 24, which splits off Highway 2 before Nakhon Ratchasima (if you are coming from Bangkok). Buriram is about 100 kilometers east of Khorat; follow Route 226 east to Buriram.

Surin and Sisaket   สุรินทร์และศรีสะเกษ

East of Buriram Province are Surin and then Sisaket, primarily agricultural provinces bordering Cambodia to the south. Although the provinces have few international attractions aside from their amazing Khmer ruins, Surin has become known throughout the world for its elephants and mahouts, or elephant trainers. If you're interested in either, make sure to visit in November, when the annual Elephant Roundup takes place.

There are dozens of Khmer ruins scattered around the two provinces. Most are crumbling, individual structures, and none match Phimai or Phanom Rung in size or majesty, but they are worth visiting, especially if you've got wheels and you can see them in succession. Seen together, they illustrate how much the Khmer Empire must have built in the region to have so many structures remaining nearly 1,000 years later. The best—or at least the most interesting—is Khao Phra Wihan, which is actually in Cambodia (where it's called Preah Vihear). Although the border crossing is well worn and easy to do in a day, Cambodia and Thailand have been fighting over ownership of some of the land for decades, and since 2008 the mostly diplomatic battle has at times escalated to armed conflict, and access has been severely limited.

KHMER RUINS
Prasat Sikhoraphum
ปราสาทศรีขรภูมิ

Prasat Sikhoraphum, a small group of ruins that include five squat brick stupas surrounded by a pond, has been restored in recent years and is a beautiful site. Much of the detailing, including the statues and other art that must have adorned the buildings, is long gone, but there are still magnificent carvings, especially surrounding and above the doorways. From Surin Town, head east on Route 226 for about 32 kilometers; turn off for the ruins at kilometer marker 34.

Prasat Muang Thi
ปราสาทเมืองที

Prasat Muang Thi was once five large stupas and has been reduced to just three, all of which are styled with indented corners diminishing in size as the stupas get higher, in addition to the crumbling remains of the outer wall of this temple. The site is now also home to a modern

ELEPHANT ROUNDUP

Elephants are a significant part of the kingdom's history and culture. Thailand's first digital animation film, *Khan Kluay*, which told the story of an Ayutthaya-era elephant who was separated from his parents and went on to save the kingdom from the Burmese, was the country's highest-grossing film to date when it was released in 2006.

In real life, elephants still play a meaningful role in everyday life in some parts of the country. The Gai or Suay people, a small ethnic group based around Ban Ta Klang village in Surin, have become known through the centuries for their ability to keep and train elephants. Many of the mahouts in the country come from this region.

Once a year, in November, Surin puts together an annual elephant roundup, where elephants and their mahouts make the trip to Surin to demonstrate their skills, engage in some friendly competitions, and have a lot of fun. There are scores of elephants and thousands of people from around the world who come to watch. Activities include an elephant talent show, football games, and a parade. Call the Tourism Authority of Thailand's northeastern regional office (tel. 04/421-3666 or 04/421-3030) to check dates for upcoming roundups.

ISAN

Buddhist temple, **Wat Chom Suthawat,** which was built just adjacent to the three stupas. These ruins and the modern *wat* are 16 kilometers east of Surin on Route 226.

The **Prasat Ta Muean** group of sandstone ruins is thought to be the remains of one of the 17 rest stops along the **Khmer highway** linking Phimai with Angkor Wat. It's right near the Cambodian border in a verdant forest area but easy to access by car and really worth a detour, as it's one of the largest ruins in the area. This former rest area has not been restored but was once a grouping of buildings that included multiple stupas, pools, and a main sanctuary. Many of the stupas are still standing, and you may be able to discern a hint of the buildings' former glory in the remaining lintels and other pieces with intricate carvings. To get here, you can pick up Route 2407, a small road heading south toward Cambodia, from Route 24, which runs along the southern part of the region from east to west. If you are coming from Surin, head south on Route 214 until you get to Route 24, then head west.

◖ Khao Phra Wihan
เขาพระวิหาร

Khao Phra Wihan is one of the most impressive Khmer sights in the area. Although it is not as restored or complete as either Phimai or Phanom Rung, the immense scale and location are enough to warrant making the journey to see it. The temple ruins are situated on the edge of the Dangkrek Mountains, more than 457 meters high, overlooking the surrounding Thai and Cambodian countryside. The complex, referred to in Cambodia as **Prasat Preah Vihear,** was most likely built over the course of 300 years by Khmer kings, beginning in the 11th century. When completed, Khao Phra Wihan consisted of grand stairs leading to numerous stone buildings covered with intricate carvings and surrounded by magnificent sculptures of *nagas* and other figures. Set atop a mountain, it must have been an awe-inspiring sight. What's left now are mostly pillars, doorways, some walls, and incomplete structures covering more than 30 hectares. Some

of the amazing detailing remains even after 1,000 years.

The site has been the subject of much debate, and even international legal action between Thailand and Cambodia, who both claimed the land. In 1962 the World Court agreed that it belonged to Cambodia, but it was not until 2003 that visitors from Thailand could tour the ruins. The wrangling between the countries continues to this day and is often the subject of discussions among their leaders. In 2008 the issue once again bubbled to the surface, and the two countries have since intermittently engaged in small-scale armed conflict around the border. When you visit, this may or may not be resolved, so make sure to check as to whether access is even possible.

Getting to the site is an adventure in itself. You'll need to travel to the **Khao Phra Wihan National Park** (Kantharalak, Sisaket, tel. 04/581-6071 or 04/581-6000, reserve@dnp. go.th and dnp_tourist@yahoo.com, 400B), since the only way to cross into Prasat Preah Vihear, Cambodia, is inside the park. If you are heading to the park from Surin Town, head south on Route 214 until you pick up Route 24, then head east until you get to the junction with Route 221. Take Route 221 south until you see the entrance to the park. The road to the border crossing starts at the main visitors center; you can drive most of the way there (although you have to walk the last few minutes). There is no public transportation available. You will leave Thailand and enter Cambodia, but you don't need a visa. Instead, hand your passport over to Thai immigration officials, who'll give you a ticket for 5B, which you will then need to show to the Cambodian immigration officials. You have to pay a 200B fee to enter Cambodia. Once inside Cambodia, the journey has not ended, as you'll need to climb numerous steps and paths to get to the top. Before you reach the main structure, there are a couple of landings and paths punctuated with five entry towers, called *gopuras,* in various states of decay. The third *gopura* is among the best preserved, and after you pass through it, you'll enter a small courtyard followed by another tower, another courtyard, the final tower, and then the main structures.

Although it's tempting to head right to the ruins, the national park has some scenic landscape, waterfalls, and a couple of smaller ruins to visit. The **Pha Mor I Daeng Cliffs** offer a good spot from which to view the ruins at a distance and also have some fascinating cliff carvings.

There are only two bungalows available for rent in the park, and they are often reserved months in advance. They sleep 4–6 and cost 1,000–2,000B. If you can get one, you'll be staying in relative luxury. Reserve by calling or emailing the national park. There is also a small campground with tents available for rent and restrooms.

ACCOMMODATIONS

There are some larger hotels, local resorts, and a handful of inexpensive guesthouses in the town of Surin, but otherwise the region is lacking in lots of accommodations choices for foreign visitors. If you're touring the region, you will probably be best off staying in Surin, from where you'll easily be able to travel to see the ruins. Keep in mind that most of the accommodations in Surin and vicinity are geared toward Thai visitors, not foreigners, so you may find limited resources in English, and staff may not speak much English either. If you are staying in Surin during the Elephant Roundup in November, prices may double or even triple, and you should make reservations well in advance to guarantee you get a room.

Surin

The **Pirom-Aree Guest House** (Soi Arunee, Thungpo Rd., tel. 04/451-5140, 200B) seems to be everyone's favorite place in Surin. The simple guesthouse set in an old wooden Thai home is worth the 20-minute walk from the center of Surin. Guest rooms are clean and basic, and baths are shared, but you might want to consider it even if you were hoping for something a little more luxurious. The lovely Thai couple that own the guesthouse are an excellent source of knowledge of the area and cook up a great meal. Even if you're not staying

here, you can arrange to spend a day or two touring the region with owner Khun Pirom.

Le Bien Resort (45 Mu 7, Surin–Buriram Rd., tel. 04/472-5559 or 08/1732-4615, www.lebienresort.com, 800B), about eight kilometers outside town, offers a dozen charming little cottages with clean, comfortable rooms with air-conditioning, TVs, and even a bit of style (which is hard to come by in this price range). The ecofriendly owners of the resort also have fish farms, paddy fields, and fruit gardens surrounding the property. The adjacent **Ra Bieng Nam Restaurant** is beautifully set on a body of water and serves excellent local cuisine, including fresh fish from their farm.

Thonkoon Resort (417 Mu 6, Surin–Sangkha Rd., tel. 04/453-0077, www.thonkoonresort.com, 800B), just a couple of kilometers outside of town, is a small hotel, built in 2009, with massive, spotless guest rooms and pleasant grounds. There isn't much in the neighborhood in the way of restaurants or entertainment, but for guests with their own transportation, it makes an excellent base from which to explore Surin and beyond.

About 24 kilometers outside of Surin Town is the **Surin Country Lodge** (47 Ban Huay Ravee Mu 10, Khwaosinarin, tel. 04/265-67507, 1,000B), with spotless guest rooms and comfortable beds in their leafy little compound. Guest rooms, all situated in small cabins, have TVs and air-conditioning, and there is a restaurant on the premises. Staff can arrange tours of the area if you request it in advance.

If you want to stay in Surin Town, the **Surin Majestic** (99 Jit Bamrung Rd., tel. 04/471-3980, 800B) is a large, well-located property with lots of amenities you won't find in smaller guesthouses. The property opened in 2006, and the guest rooms are large and modern, if a little generic. There's a swimming pool, a fitness center, free Internet in the lobby, and a decent buffet breakfast.

FOOD

Around the bus station in downtown Surin are a handful of basic local eateries as well as a few restaurants opened by expat Westerners that serve both Thai and Western dishes. **Farang Connection** (257 Jitbumroong Rd., 7:30 A.M.–midnight daily, 250B) looks sort of like a Thai-shophouse restaurant but has an extensive Western menu that includes an English breakfast, so those craving English-speaking company and familiar food will find it comforting and foreign at the same time. Farang Connection also offers some tour services.

Markets

The **Surin Night Market** (Krusiri Nai Rd., 4:30–9:30 P.M. daily, 30B) is compact but has all the best Isan dishes available, including *som tam,* sticky rice, and grilled chicken. Make sure to try the *sai crock Isan,* grilled Isan sausage. The slightly tangy flavor of fermented pork mixed with sticky rice might sound unappetizing, but the result is both unexpected and comforting, especially if you're looking for a snack after you've tried some of the local liquors.

Local Restaurants

Like any other downtown area in Thailand, you can't throw a rock without hitting a place to eat. There are countless basic eateries in the town of Surin, especially surrounding the bus station and near the train station, but many shophouses close early, and it's hard to find something to eat after 9 P.M.

If you are looking for something a little nicer than the average shophouse, there are a handful of outdoor Thai restaurants near the stadium that serve mostly Isan food. **Nga Chang Restaurant** (Khochasan Rd., 4–11 P.M. daily, 200B) is one that's set in a large, pretty garden with little fish ponds. Servers do not speak a lot of English but are very friendly, and the extensive Isan menu has some options in English. Everything is fresh and homey, but make it clear that you don't want your food spicy because the default chili factor will blow your socks off.

GETTING THERE

Surin and Sisaket are both east of Nakhon Ratchasima and Buriram, following a line from west to east.

Bus

From Bangkok, there are frequent buses stopping in Surin and then Sisaket; they take 8–10 hours or more and cost 350–450B. There are also buses available from the large neighboring cities.

Train

Trains heading for Ubon Ratchathani stop in both towns, taking about 8–10 hours from Bangkok and costing under 400B.

Car

If you're driving, both Surin and Sisaket are on Route 226 on a west–east line. The best way to get to Route 226 from Bangkok is to take Route 2 to Route 24, south of Nakhon Ratchasima, and then head north to Route 226

Ubon Ratchathani Province   จังหวัดอุบลราชธานี

From a prehistoric settlement of people living off the area's fertile plains to part of the Khmer Empire to the staging ground for U.S. air strikes, Ubon Ratchathani has had quite a history for a province tucked into a corner of Thailand on the Cambodian and Lao borders. But while the region's past is interesting, it's what's going on now that makes it a great place to visit. Ubon Ratchathani is the commercial center of southern Isan. There's plenty of hustle and bustle to be found in the city—albeit on a much smaller scale than Bangkok, considering that the whole province has less than 100,000 residents.

At the province's eastern border, you'll find Khong Jiam, where the Mun River, which starts in the mountains of Nakhon Ratchasima Province, flows into the Mekong River, flanked by a valley and surrounded by lush greenery. While the scene may not be as dramatic as the

FOREST *WATS* OF UBON RATCHATHANI

Most visitors to Thailand will see scores of *wats* during their time here. The art and architecture of some are certainly stunning, but looking at *ubosots* and murals may not shed much light on the teachings of the Buddha or how to incorporate them into your life if you are so inclined. As in the rest of Thailand, you'll find plenty of *wats* to tour in Ubon Ratchathani. But the region also attracts foreigners wishing to study Buddhism and meditation, and there are a number of *wats* you can visit and stay at. These *wats* are intended for those who have a sincere interest, not just a visitor's curiosity.

Wat Pah Nanachat (Ban Bung Wai, Warin Chamrap, www.watpahnanachat.org) is a forest *wat* located about 16 kilometers from Ubon. It was established as a monastic community for foreigners and has an easily accessible program for English speakers. If you visit, you can participate in meditations; if you stay, you'll be expected to abide by the community's guidelines – segregated by gender, rising at 3 A.M., and eating one meal per day. If you stay for longer than three days, you'll be required to

shave your head, as all novice monks do. If you want to study at Wat Pah Nanachat, you must write in advance to ask for permission. Even if you're not intent on visiting or staying, the *wat*'s website has an excellent explanation of the daily life of a monk that's worth reading.

Wat Nong Pa Phong (Ubon Ratchathani, tel. 04/532-2729) shares the same founder as Wat Pah Nanachat, and you can walk from one to the other in less than two hours. Like its sister temple, this *wat* offers meditation instruction to foreigners, although it does not have accommodations for people who want to stay for only a few nights.

Wat Pah Ban That (Udon Thani, webluangta@gmail.com), about 16 kilometers southeast of Udon Thani, offers meditation instruction in Thai, English, and sometimes German. It is possible to stay at the *wat* for a couple of days if you are interested in studying, but note that during Phansa (Vassa, or Buddhist Lent) you may not be able to get a place to sleep. Phansa starts on the first day of the waning moon of the eighth lunar month (usually in July) and lasts for three lunar months.

towering mountains or azure waters you'll see in other parts of the country, the calm beauty of the landscape will leave a lasting impression on all but the most jaded travelers.

UBON RATCHATHANI
อุบลราชธานี

If you want to experience Isan urban life, spend a couple of days in Ubon Ratchathani. On the surface it may look like just another small modern city, but Ubon, as it's sometimes referred to, has a distinct Isan identity that sets it apart. This thriving little city is home to only a few interesting sights, but it's worth wandering around in, if only to sample the delicious Isan fare sold by the city's many street vendors. The Mun River flows just south of the city and, though it may not hold your attention for days, is worth a bit of your time. If you'd like to stay on the river, there are some charming resorts

outside of the city, and this could be a great place to base yourself for regional touring if you feel like doing a little relaxing as well.

Sights and Events
The city used to be known as the Royal City of the Lotus Flower, a rough translation of its name. Nowadays, however, the city's most popular icon is the candle. Candles play an important role in marking Asaraha Bucha, the beginning of **Phansa** (Vassa, or Buddhist Lent), an annual three-month period where monks retreat back into temples and avoid unnecessary travel. The start of the retreat, said to protect young plants from being crushed underfoot, is marked by celebrations across the country, and many laymen choose to start their novice monk training on this day. Traditionally, followers bring candles to the monks, since they'll need them while they wait out the Phansa period in

their temples. While the whole country celebrates the start of Phansa, Ubon Ratchathani has taken it even further, with an annual **Candle Festival,** where artists from Thailand and around the world create enormous intricately designed candles out of wax. These candles, oftentimes representing a particular event in Buddhist or Thai history or mythology, are paraded through the city amid music, dancing, and other celebrations. The festival, which is held on the first full moon of the eighth lunar month, usually falls in July, but the regional Tourism Authority of Thailand office (tel. 04/524-3770) can provide specific dates.

Even if you are not visiting during Asaraha Bucha, you can still get a sense of the amount of work that goes into each of the scores of candles displayed in the festival by visiting the permanently displayed 18-meter-high golden candle replica, which sits on an elegantly carved boat surrounded by *garudas* and *nagas* in **Thung Si Mueng Park** (Uparat Rd. at Si Narong Rd.).

The **Ubon Ratchathani National Museum** (Kheuan Thani Rd., tel. 04/525-5071, 9 A.M.–4 P.M. Wed.–Sun., 30B), housed in the city's former city hall just south of the gigantic candle, now holds a collection of art and artifacts from around the region, spanning prehistory to the present. The museum is laid out in chronological order, and the earliest works include pottery and tools found dating back more than 1,500 years. The collection of Dvaravati pieces from as far back as the seventh century includes Buddha images and Hindu art, most notably a statute of Ardhanarishvara—Shiva and Shakti merged into one god. There are also some excellent pieces of Khmer work in the form of building fragments. The museum houses more contemporary craftworks such as regional textiles and instruments. If you're visiting the museum around lunchtime, head for the vendors just in the back for a good selection of casual food.

Wat Phra That Nong Bua (no posted hours, free), as everyone will tell you, stands out as the only temple with square *chedi* in the region. That distinction may not seem significant until you visit the *wat* and view the interesting architecture. From a distance the two *chedi,* more like elongated pyramids than any of the more typical designs, seem plain and unadorned, but as you approach you'll begin to see the amazingly detailed bas-relief covering the surface of each. Sometimes the *wat* is referred to simply as Wat Nong Bua, the *phra that* means "bone of the Buddha," although you'll hear conflicting information as to whether there are any relics inside. The *wat's* distinctive design is said to be a copy of the Mahabodhi Temple at Bodh Gaya, where the Buddha was said to have reached enlightenment. Although there's some resemblance, the Indian version is significantly less austere. The *wat* is about 11 kilometers outside Ubon Ratchathani off Route 212.

Accommodations

The **Sri Isan Hotel** (62 Ratchabut Rd., tel. 04/526-1011, www.sriisanhotel.com, 500B) isn't quite the boutique hotel it markets itself as; still, it is modern, clean, and even a little bit charming. Guest rooms are simple but have TVs, minibars, and air-conditioning; the lobby and other common areas feel almost like an old Chinese shophouse, but not quite, as the building is a bit too modern.

The **Ratchathani Hotel** (297 Keunthani Rd., tel. 04/524-4388, www.theratchathani. com, 750B) is another almost-boutique hotel in Ubon. Things like white duvet covers, minimalist furniture, and a slick lobby make you feel like you're in Bangkok. Like Sri Isan, it's not perfect, but it's so well priced that you can't complain.

The urban-chic trend seems to be everywhere, including small towns in Isan, by the looks of **Tohsang City Hotel** (251 Palochai Rd., tel. 04/524-5531, www.tohsang.com, 1,200B). Just outside the center of town (which, in a town like this, means a 15-minute walk), this new hotel has very modern, spacious guest rooms and nice baths. It might be trying a little too hard, but if you want to stay close to the center of Ubon but still feel like you're away from it all, this should be your choice.

Food

Ubon Ratchathani is full of restaurants. Many serve traditional Isan food, but you'll also find lots serving Thai food from around the country and even quite a few serving up casual (and often mediocre) Western fare, should you have an urge for something a little different.

Boonniyon Uthayan (73 Srinarong Rd., tel. 04/524-0950, 9 A.M.–2 P.M. Tues.–Sun., 30B) is run by a Buddhist sect and offers a vegetarian buffet made from wheat-gluten protein and locally produced organic vegetables. The sect's beliefs are quite austere, but they are friendly and welcoming to outsiders. This is very basic, open-air, cafeteria-style dining— no dishes made to order—but vegetarians will find the food a welcome change.

Smile Pub & Restaurant (200/1 Srinarong Rd., tel. 04/526-2407, 5–11 P.M. daily, 150B) is a slightly more upscale and trendy casual restaurant serving mostly Thai food and a few Western meals. You'll find a good selection of Isan and other Thai favorites, and if the weather is nice, you can forgo the air-conditioned main room and sit out on the deck. There's also live music at this dinner-only spot, so it's a nice place to get a little nightlife in without going off the rails.

Jampahom Restaurant (49/3 Pichitlangsan Rd., tel. 04/526-0398, 5–11 P.M. daily, 150B) is another great choice if you want a bit of atmosphere, some good food, and a selection of Thai and Western dishes. If you don't want to eat inside, there's a little garden area, and you can get fresh bread from the bakery next door. You'll get live music here too, and they are only open for dinner.

You'll know you've arrived at **Samchai Gai Yang** (282/1 Palochai Rd., tel. 04/520-9118, 200B) if you see a couple of three-meter-tall chicken statues. That, and the name, which means "Samchai's grilled chicken," should give you a good idea of what you can eat here for lunch or dinner. Make sure to order some *som tam* and *khao neo* (sticky rice) to go with your *kai yang*, and you've got the quintessential Isan meal.

Kai Yang is a big deal in this part of the

© SUZANNE NAM

Traditional Isan cuisine is considered to be some of the best in the country.

ISAN

country, and **Somtam Pornthip** (136 Sunpasit Rd., tel. 08/9720-8101, 9 A.M.–6 P.M. daily, 60B) is another contender for Ubon's best grilled chicken and *som tam* restaurant, or at least for everyone's favorite.

If you head south of the city to the Mun River, you'll find two great options for eating. The first is the **River Night Market**, where you'll likely find lots of families and couples. The market isn't massive but there's enough typical Isan food for around 25B to fill you up, and it's a cool location to see the river from. There are also a bunch of **floating restaurants** on tethered rafts on the river where you can eat and take in the view.

Getting There

Ubon Ratchathani has a small airport, and Air Asia, Nok Air, and Thai Airways all have daily flights from Bangkok to the city. If you can get an inexpensive ticket from Nok Air or Air Asia, flying into Ubon is a great option, as overland travel will take you at least eight hours. Once you land, the airport is just a few kilometers outside the city. You can actually walk into town from the airport, although you can also pick up a taxi heading into town for about 250B. If you want to pick up a car at the airport, there are rental agencies open during normal business hours with rentals running 1,000–2,000B per day.

Ubon Ratchathani is the last major city on Route 226, which connects all the urban areas in lower Isan with each other. If you are driving from any of the other destinations, beginning with Nakhon Ratchasima, head east on Route 226 and continue until you get to Ubon.

If you take the train, you'll be arriving in neighboring Warin Chamrap, but it's easy enough to grab either a taxi or a local *song thaew*. There are seven trains daily from Bangkok; most take about 10 hours, and the overnight train will get you into the city in the early morning. The fare from Bangkok starts at 500B; first-class sleepers are around 1,200B. All trains that stop in Ubon Ratchathani also stop in Nakhon Ratchasima, Buriram, Surin,

and Sisaket, so it is easy to connect to any of the cities by train.

If you are going by bus, there are frequent buses throughout the day that follow Route 226 both east and west to and from Bangkok. The ride from Bangkok is about eight hours and costs a little over 400B for a comfortable air-conditioned ride. There are also buses to and from neighboring cites. If you are taking a bus from Nakhon Ratchasima, the fare for an air-conditioned coach is around 275B, and the ride is about five hours.

Getting Around

If you're just in the immediate area, most of the places you'll want to visit are accessible on foot, and there are numerous city *song thaew* that run up and down the avenues, arranged in a grid. Ubon is also one of the few places left in Thailand that still has *samlor,* three-wheeled rickshaw-like bicycles. If you don't have any problems being moved around on someone else's pedal power, short trips start at 30B, and the *samlor* can usually fit two people.

OUTSIDE UBON RATCHATHANI
Ubon Ratchathani Cultural Centre
ศูนย์วัฒนธรรม จังหวัดอุบลราชธานี
Visit the Ubon Ratchathani Cultural Centre (2 Ratchathani Rd., tel. 04/535-2000) on the Rajabhat University campus a few kilometers out of town, if only to see the architecture—the building looks like a cross between a Disney fantasy castle and a traditional Thai *wat*, with plenty of repeating roof lines, *chofas* rising high in the sky, and terraces throughout. Inside there are some exhibits chronicling the area's history, including dioramas and re-creations of local crafts. Some of the explanations are only available in Thai, however. You can also stay at the cultural center if you call to reserve a guest room in advance (800B). Accommodations are clean, modern, and spacious, most have their own small terraces, and it might be the area's nicest building to stay in.

Ban Pa Ao Village
พิพิธภัณฑ์ชุมชนบ้านปะอาว

Ban Pa Ao Village is about 16 kilometers outside Ubon and is one of the oldest continuously populated villages in the region. For two centuries the families here have been crafting brass, silver, and silk. The metalwork is cast using beeswax and clay, and you can watch the process if you arrive during the day.

You can get to the village by driving on Route 23 west for approximately 16 kilometers. Otherwise, you can hire a taxi in town to take you. You may want to negotiate a round-trip fare, as it's difficult to find transport from the village; expect to pay anywhere from 500B.

Khong Jiam
โขงเจียม

About 56 kilometers east of Ubon and just west of the confluence of the Mekong and Mun Rivers sits the little town of Khong Jiam (sometimes spelled Khong Chiam), with tranquil views of the water and neighboring Laos. There's not a lot to do here, but that's the point; it is a wonderful stop if you want to relax and refresh or, if you are driving, a great base to visit other sights in the region if you're content to move at a slow pace. Make sure to take a look at the spot where the Mun River and Mekong River meet. It's called **Two-color River,** and depending on the water level, you really will notice the blue of the Mun and the red of the Mekong flowing into each other. The best time to see it is during rainy season.

You can also stay in Khong Jiam; there are a handful of guesthouses and even small resorts. If you're just looking for an inexpensive place to sleep, the **Mankhon Guest House** (Khong Jiam Town, tel. 08/1312-0249, komanee@yahoo.com, 400B) has clean guest rooms in an old wooden building in the center of town. Some rooms are air-conditioned, and fan-cooled rooms are about half the listed price.

The 🄲 **Tohsang Khongjiam Resort** (68 Mu 7, Ban Huay-Mak-Tay, tel. 04/535-1174, www.tohsang.com, 2,200B) is a posh midsize resort with luxuriously appointed guest rooms decorated with Thai and Khmer-style furniture and accents. All guest rooms have views of the Mekong River. There is a large swimming pool with plenty of room to lounge around as well as a spa on the premises. The resort's restaurant serves local cuisine and is set on a lovely spot overlooking the river.

Khong Jiam is almost directly east of Ubon Ratchathani. If you are driving, follow Route 217 out of the city until it becomes Route 222, which will lead you to Khong Jiam. There are a few buses each day leaving Ubon for Khong Jiam. The trip can take as much as two hours, since it stops at various points along the way, and it costs less than 40B for the journey.

Khon Kaen Province
จังหวัดขอนแก่น

Khon Kaen is Thailand's fourth-largest city, but it is rarely a destination on its own for vacationers. The city is Isan's business hub: It has an airport with frequent daily flights from Bangkok, lots of restaurants, hotels, and banks, and even a Tourism Authority of Thailand office. The only thing it really lacks is a big attraction for visitors. It's also not particularly convenient as a transit hub to other parts of the northeast. Depending on your travel plans, Khorat, Ubon Ratchathani, and Udon Thani are better places to use as a base. Still, if you find yourself in the city for a day or two, it can at least be a nice break from the small towns and countryside should you be craving a bit more of an urban experience in Isan.

SIGHTS
The Khon Kaen National Museum
พิพิธภัณฑสถานแห่งชาติขอนแก่น

The Khon Kaen National Museum (Lang Sunratchakan Rd., tel. 04/324-6170,

9 A.M.–4 P.M. Wed.–Sun., 30B) is one of the Fine Arts Department's national museums and has a good collection of art and artifacts from the region. There is plenty of Buddhist devotional art to view, but there are also many prehistoric housewares and tools on display, some Khmer artifacts that include carved lintels, and Hindu objects. The Buddhist works on display include an extensive collection of Dvaravati period items.

Wat Nong Waeng
วัดหนองแวง

This modern *wat* is not historically significant, but its dramatic design makes it worth a visit. The square-based, nine-level stupa looks like a cross between a Thai Buddhist temple and an office building from the 1970s. Most find the combination surprisingly aesthetically pleasing, and if not, the grounds, a few minutes out of the city, offer a panoramic view of Khon Kaen. The *wat* is on the southern end of Kaen Nakhon Lake, less than two kilometers from the city center. The easiest way to get there is just to walk south from Kasikorn Samron Road, skirting the lake. Otherwise, there are public buses heading south from the city center; you can hop on one for under 10B—just make sure to tell the driver you are going to the *wat*.

ACCOMMODATIONS

Though not a huge tourist destination, the city has quite a few business and other travelers passing through, so finding a place to sleep is not a problem, and there is a good selection, from inexpensive to international, to choose from.

Under 1,500B

You can't beat the **Amarin Plaza Hotel** (181/1 Rop Muang Rd., tel. 04/332-1660, 400B) if you want an inexpensive room but don't want to stay in a guesthouse. The guest rooms are unremarkable and could definitely use some refurbishing, but for the price, they are adequate.

Chaipat Hotel (106/3 Na Muang Rd., tel.

04/333-3055, 600B) is similar to Amarin Plaza—inexpensive but unremarkable. The guest rooms are a little more nicely decorated, but you may feel like you've entered a time warp. The hotel has a restaurant on the ground floor serving basic Thai food.

1,500–3,000B

The **Charoen Thani Princess** (260 Si Chan Rd., tel. 04/322-0400, www.charoenthanikhonkaen.com, 2,000B) hasn't quite been brought up to the standards of the other luxury chain hotels, but it's nevertheless one of the nicest business hotels in Khon Kaen. Guest rooms are large, comfortable, and very clean, although the property in general feels rundown and shopworn. It does have all the necessary amenities for a business trip, along with a swimming pool.

Pullman Khon Kaen Raja Orchid (9/9 Prachasamran Rd., tel. 04/332-2155, www.accorhotels.com/Pullman-Thailand.com, 2,500B) is hands down the best hotel in the city. The large hotel is modern but has some Thai design elements in the outside architecture and the guest rooms, which are spacious, comfortable, and clean. There is a spa, a gym, and multiple restaurants on the premises. Baker's Basket, the hotel's bakery, is a very popular spot for brunch or coffee.

FOOD

The first place to stop for food in Khon Kaen is the **Night Market** (Ruen Rom Rd., between Klang Meung Rd. and Na Meung Rd., 6–11 P.M. daily, 35B). Here you'll find plenty of Isan specialties freshly prepared and served in a very casual open-air setting.

If you're looking for something more formal, head south just a few minutes toward the lake, where there are a few restaurants, the most popular being **Suan Ahan Bua Luang** (Robbueng Rd., tel. 04/322-2504, 11 A.M.–10 P.M. daily, 200B). This restaurant, which serves Thai, Chinese Thai, and seafood dishes, is on a small island in the lake. It may not be a five-star restaurant, but it has a great view and a very comfortable family atmosphere.

A great choice for both atmosphere and the menu is **Ahan Namai** (42/14 Ammart Rd., tel. 04/323-9958, 11:30 A.M.–10 P.M. daily, 250B). The restaurant is set in a restored wooden house, and the extensive menu covers everything from typical Isan fare to *namphrik* and plenty of seafood dishes.

The Lighthouse Pub (260/10 Srichan Rd., tel. 04/322-0400, 8 A.M.–10 P.M. daily, 100B) is a good compromise if you want Thai food but prefer a more familiar setting. The pub seems to attract more English speakers than most spots, and there are plenty of typical Thai choices on the menu (think fried rice and noodles). All are well prepared and inexpensive.

GETTING THERE

Thai Airways has multiple daily flights from Bangkok to Khon Kaen. The flight is just under an hour, and tickets booked in advance are generally around 3,000B one-way. If you're coming by train, there are four trains daily—three overnight and one during the day—from Bangkok's Hua Lamphong Station that stop in Khon Kaen

before terminating in either Udon Thani or Nong Khai. The ride is about eight hours and costs 400B for a second-class seat or 1,200B for a first-class sleeper. If you are coming to Khon Kaen by bus, there are buses leaving from Bangkok's Northern Bus Terminal (Mo Chit) at least every hour 7:30 A.M.–9:30 P.M. daily for the eight-hour ride. Tickets on air-conditioned buses cost under 350B. There are also hourly buses leaving from Nakhon Ratchasima to Khon Kaen. The trip is about three hours and costs under 100B.

GETTING AROUND

Khon Kaen is a relatively large city, making getting around on foot difficult. There are plenty of *tuk tuks* in the city, and a short ride in town should cost under 50B—expect to pay more if you're going out of the city. There are more than a dozen routes served by *song thaew* during the day—just make sure to ask at your hotel which *song thaew* number you should take to get to a particular destination. The price for a ride in town is 5–15B.

Udon Thani Province   จังหวัดอุดรธานี

While the city of Udon Thani, or Udon as it's known for short, may not blow you away, the province is a great place to visit if you are interested in archaeology. Don't kick yourself if you don't spend too much time in this area other than to see the impressive archaeological sight at **Ban Chiang** or to catch a flight from the airport. It's not that the area is unpleasant, it's just that there's not much for visitors to see. If your time is limited in Isan, there are other places in the region worth a visit first. The area does tend to get a lot of visitors, but it's mostly because Udon Thani is a transit point on a well-beaten backpacker path to Laos. Many travelers will stop in Udon Thani on their way to Nong Khai north of Udon on the border, where you can cross into Laos and continue northward.

SIGHTS

Udon's best sights aren't all clustered together, but are easily accessible by a short drive from the city, which is located in the center of the province. The city, although not that interesting in itself, is a good base for a day or two to take in the rest of the region. There are also plenty of travel agents and tour operators in the city who can arrange day trips or transport.

◖ Ban Chiang Archaeological Site and National Museum
พิพิธภัณฑสถานแห่งชาติบ้านเชียง

This is the star attraction of the region and you really should not miss it if you're anywhere nearby, as it is one of the most significant archaeological sights in Southeast Asia. After an American student's fortuitous stumble led him to the discovery of ancient

ISAN

LOOTED ART

In February 2008, after a five-year undercover investigation centered around two Los Angeles antiques dealers, federal agents in the United States raided four museums in California in search of artifacts taken from Ban Chiang. Although the investigation centered on possible tax fraud by the dealers, who had arranged for some Ban Chiang pieces to be donated to museums in exchange for inflated tax deductions, investigators asserted that nearly all of the Ban Chiang pottery in the United States was stolen from Thailand.

The Thai government has backed that claim. According to Thai officials, the government has never given anyone permission to take items found at the site out of the country, and independent experts believe that most of the pieces from Ban Chiang were probably looted. The problem is, Ban Chiang pottery is on display in countless museums in the United States, including the Freer and Sackler Galleries, which are part of the Smithsonian Institution in Washington, D.C.; the Museum of Fine Arts in Boston; and the Metropolitan Museum of Art in New York. In most cases, the pieces were either purchased by the museum from collectors or donated, and as of the printing of this book, the fate of the objects has not yet been made clear.

pottery buried in the small village of Ban Chiang, a joint team of Thai and University of Pennsylvania researchers began an excavation that revealed the remains of an ancient Bronze Age culture. Initially, archaeologists believed the origin of the culture dated back as far as 4000 B.C.; later dating methods would reveal the artifacts were around 4,000 years old, still putting Ban Chiang comfortably into the category of the oldest Bronze Age civilization in Southeast Asia. You can read about the history and findings in more detail at the University of Pennsylvania Museum website (www.museum.upenn.edu/new/research/ Exp_Rese_Disc/Asia/banchiang/banchiang.shtml).

You can tour the museum, the archaeological site, which has been preserved with many objects still in situ, as well as the small village, whose main focus now seems to be the excavation site. What you'll find in addition to comprehensive descriptions of each item on display is some exceptionally well-preserved pottery, intricately designed jewelry, tools, and household items dating back thousands of years as well as skeletal remains of the people who inhabited this village during prehistoric times. In fact, the collection spans millennia, as there is evidence that the village may have been nearly continuously populated from before the Bronze Age. Many will find the distinct artistic style of Ban Chiang pottery, with its bold, sometimes swirling geometric designs, impressive and surprising, and swear to themselves that it had to have been manufactured more recently than the archaeologists' research would suggest.

Ban Chiang is about 56 kilometers east of Udon Thani, just off Route 22. You can arrange a round-trip taxi; expect to pay at least 400B, depending on how long you stay at the museum. If you are traveling by public transportation, you can take a public bus from Udon Thani to the town of Ban Pulu, and from there pick up a *tuk tuk* to the museum. The bus will cost under 30B, and the *tuk tuk* ride should cost the same. Buses run at least every hour throughout the day.

Phu Phra Bat Historical Park
อุทยานประวัติศาสตร์ภูพระบาท

In the northwest part of the province is Phu Phra Bat Historical Park, where you'll find a fascinating collection of natural rock formations that seem to defy gravity. While these were made by nature (specifically, by glaciers), what's even more interesting here is the human interaction over thousands of years. From the prehistoric period there are cave and rock paintings and later Dvaravati and then Buddhist shrines, indicating that many must have considered the area sacred or holy ground. Although grown-ups will no doubt find the park interesting, this is a great place to take children, who can run around and explore the rock formations.

To drive to Phu Phra Bat Historical Park from Udon Thani, follow Highway 2 about 13 kilometers north toward Nong Kai, then turn west onto Route 2021. From there, follow the road till it becomes Route 2346, and from there watch for signs for the park's entrance.

Ban Na Kha Craft Village
บ้านนาข่า

If you want to get a little shopping in while you're in the area, stop at this little village on the route to Nong Khai. Sure, it's a little commercialized, but you'll be able to see decorative handwoven cloth being made and bring home some one-of-a-kind souvenirs knowing your money is going directly to the craftsperson (or at most through one or two intermediaries). The cloth you'll find—*pha kit*—is generally a sturdy material made from vibrant colored yarns and has bands of geometric patterns separated by smaller stripes.

The village is just 16 kilometers north of Udon, heading toward Nong Kai on Highway 2. There is a sign in English for the turnoff from the main road.

ACCOMMODATIONS
Under 1,500B

Overlooking a lagoon amid rice fields, **Tanita Lagoon Resort** (113 Ban Nong Huaw Mue, Nadee, Muang, tel. 05/481-8846 or 08/6654-6334, www.tanitaresort.com/lagoon.htm, 1,200B) is an interesting place to stay outside the city (about 15 minutes by car to the center of Udon). There's a restaurant on the premises, all of the accommodations are in old teak houses, and there's a swimming pool. It's not quite a resort, but you're certainly not paying resort prices either. Guest rooms and attached baths are spotless, and although not exceptionally well decorated, white duvet covers and little extras such as slippers make them a step above basic.

If you want to stay in a big hotel in the city, the recently rebranded **Centara Hotel and Convention Center** (277/1 Prajak Rd., Mak Khaeng, tel. 04/234-3555, www.charoensrigrand.com, 1,300B) is a very popular choice. The large hotel has spacious, comfortable guest rooms that are generally up to international standards, though some may be a little more worn than others (ask to see your room before you check in). The location is great if you are looking for some city life—a large shopping complex is right next door with a Robinsons and all sorts of other places to spend your baht (though if you are looking for high-end shopping, you probably wont' find any).

The colorful **Silver Reef Bed & Breakfast** (338/8 Prajak Rd., Mak Khaeng, tel. 04/234-4081, www.silverreefudon.com, 750B) is well located just a few minutes away from the bus station and shopping areas. Most would not consider it the boutique hotel it markets itself as, but if you forgive the overreaching, you'll find it a nice small hotel with lots of quirky personality. Guest rooms and common areas are colorfully decorated, giving the place almost the feel of a nursery school, but in a good way. Baths are modern and clean (the property opened in 2007) and guest rooms, though a little on the small side, have sitting areas and plenty of beds.

Bamboo Guest House (542 Soi 10 Mu 2, Nongsung Village, tel. 04/229-5229, 450B) is a friendly, laid-back little guesthouse about 16 kilometers outside the city. Guest rooms are basic, clean, and comfortable, and they even have TVs; the small grounds are well maintained, and there's even a small swimming pool and a little restaurant with inexpensive casual food. For the money and proximity to the city, this is a great place to pick; you can even take a public bus from Udon to the property in less than 30 minutes.

Over 4,500B

About 24 kilometers south of Udon Thani is ◖ **Gecko Villa** (126 Mu 13, Ban Um Jaan, Prajak Sinlapakom, tel. 08/1918-0500, www.geckovilla.com, 5,500B), an exceptional little retreat that stands head and shoulders above everything else in the region. The

ISAN

accommodations are set in a traditional wooden home, with modern amenities, a lovely swimming pool, and luxuriant green grounds surrounded by paddy fields. Guest rooms are all nicely furnished with traditional and modern Thai elements, and you'll feel like you're a guest in someone's very nice home in Isan. The house has a full modern kitchen, but you don't have to worry about using it if you don't want to, as staff are happy to prepare anything you ask for. They will also give impromptu cooking lessons if you're interested in learning how to make traditional Isan fare or other Thai dishes (meals and cooking lessons are included in the cost of your stay). If you're interested in touring the area, the manager will make any arrangements; if you just want to relax and have some privacy, they'll also make sure to leave you alone. The villa has up to three bedrooms available, so it's a great place to stay if you're with a group, although it tends to be a favorite among couples too. It's a small property and has quite a following, so book ahead if you are interested.

GETTING THERE AND AROUND
Air
There are daily direct flights from Bangkok to Udon Thani on Nok Air, Air Asia, and Thai Airways; flying time is one hour. Round-trip flights from Bangkok run 2,500–6,000B, depending on the airline and the schedule. Udon Thani's airport is just outside the city, and a taxi to the center will run less than 100B. Many accommodations both in the city and in surrounding areas offer transportation to and from the airport. **Udon Thani Car Rental** (tel. 04/224-4770, 8 A.M.–8 P.M. daily) is located in the airport.

Train
There are four trains daily on the Northeast Line from Bangkok to Udon Thani, but these do not stop in Buriram, Surin, Sisaket, and Ubon Ratchathani along the way; trains will take around 10 hours and cost under 400B. If you're taking an overnight train, you can get a sleeper for around 1,200B.

Bus and Car
A bus trip from Bangkok takes around eight hours and costs under 500B. There are frequent buses—at least once every two hours—every day between Udon Thani and Nakhon Ratchasima. The trip takes around five hours and costs under 160B. If you're driving into the area, Udon Thani is on Highway 2.

Loei Province   จังหวัดเลย

If you're approaching Loei by air and happen to look out the window on descent, you'll be stunned by the beauty of the region's landscape: small undulating mountain ranges and lush green valleys as far as the eye can see, and very little development other than well-maintained major roads. From the air, you may feel like you've gone back in time to an era before urbanization, when green, instead of concrete gray, was the predominant color. Of course, the region does have plenty of modern amenities, but maybe because it's so far north, on the border with Laos, it feels more rural and more natural than most parts of the country. When you land, at an airport so small it's only open a few days a week, you'll realize you're in a place like nowhere else in the country. A pleasant mix of the north's mountains and temperate weather with the *sabai* attitude of Isan, Loei is a province that is best enjoyed by those looking to take in the beauty of the area and relax a little too. In fact, aside from the annual **Pi Ta Khan festival,** when things get a little crazy in the small town of Dan Sai, there's not much to do here aside from touring the national parks and trying the local wines.

Choose the town of Loei as your base if you're planning to make frequent day trips and

© SUZANNE NAM

Isan's Pi Ta Khan festival

don't want to lug your stuff around with you. The town is not really remarkable, however, and you're better off taking advantage of the lodgings in one of the national parks or resorts in the mountains instead.

When planning your trip in Loei, bear in mind that it can be a challenging place to navigate using public transportation. You can probably get to the town of Loei easily enough, but once here, you'll have to rely on the local bus and *song thaew* system. While this works well in dense high-traffic parts of the country, in Loei you may find yourself waiting hours for the next ride to the destination you have in mind. Loei, and the whole region, is better enjoyed if you have access to your own wheels or hire a driver. You'll pay for it, but if you haven't got the luxury of time, there's really no other way.

SIGHTS
Wat Neramit Wipattasana
วัดเนรมิตรวิปัสสนา
Even if you're tired of seeing temples, stop in

here. Surrounded by a manicured garden and set on a hill in Dan Sai, this is a beautiful, fanciful *wat* complex. Characterizing the architectural style of the mostly brick structures is impossible. Part modern, part traditional, with little details reminiscent of the Moorish style more regularly found in Spain, it gets even more interesting when you look around and see the funky topiaries. Still, this isn't just a mishmash of crazy designs; the end result is aesthetically pleasing, if unexpected. The more conventional ordination hall is stunning—surrounded by colorfully painted murals, with intricately painted columns lining the way to three large golden Buddhas. The *wat* is just outside Dan Sai. To get here from Loei Town, about 73 kilometers away, take Route 203 west to the junction with Route 2013, then continue west until you hit Dan Sai.

Phu Kradueng National Park
อุทยานแห่งชาติภูกระดึง
One of the oldest national parks in the country, Phu Kradueng is technically one large

ISAN

mountain, about 1,200 meters above sea level at its highest point, with a large plateau and plenty of waterfalls, cliffs, and a variety of habitats to explore on your way up, along with surrounding hills. There are about 48 kilometers of marked trails at Phu Kradueng, the most well-worn being the nearly five-kilometer trek to the top. Some of the most notable sights at the park are the **Lomsak Cliff,** a rock outcropping perched over a drop. This is a very popular place for people to stop and have their pictures taken, but the view minus all the people is even more spectacular. Try to be there during sunset if you can. The **Tat Hong Waterfall,** a steep, rocky waterfall that seems to tuck itself into a corner, is another impressive sight, and you'll be able to hear the roaring water well before you see it.

The weather in the park is usually very mild, and at the top it can even reach freezing, so if you are planning on hiking or camping here, make sure you bring appropriate clothing. The park is closed to visitors June–September due to frequent flash floods.

There are campsites at the peak of the mountain as well as many bungalows you can rent from the national park service if you make arrangements in advance. Don't worry too much about food, as there are vendors and a few canteens at the camping and bungalow sites to keep you fed.

The national park is about 65 kilometers south of Loei Town on Route 201. The park's headquarters is just past the main entrance to the park. At the headquarters are restrooms and a small canteen. You'll also be able to pick up a trail map, but the most recent one was only available in Thai.

◖ Phu Luang Wildlife Reserve
เขตรักษาพันธุ์สัตว์ป่าภูหลวง

This amazing reserve, home to more than 50 wild elephants, tigers, and gibbons as well as other wildlife and fossil remains, is set on mountainous terrain with a large flat plateau. Aside from the animals, the reserve is known for its colorful array of wildflowers and orchids.

The reserve was closed to the general public in 1974 but can sometimes be visited if you plan in advance with National Parks officials (tel. 04/284-1566). Usually these visits are escorted tours with a ranger over 2–3 days and require camping at the reserve. There are no operators offering casual day tours of this reserve, but if you are interested in learning about the flora and fauna here, you can't beat the opportunity to spend a few days in one of the country's few remaining pristine wildlife areas. The Bangkok-based nonprofit **Siam Society** (contact Khun Prasert, info@siam-society. org, www.siam-society.org) offers occasional multiday study trips to the reserve, and if one is planned while you are in the area, you can try to get a spot with them. The tours, which include flights from Bangkok, land transportation, camping, meals, and expert guides (a recent tour was lead by the director of the Queen Sirikit Botanic Garden in Chiang Mai), are very reasonably priced, although you'll have to join the society to take part in any of their events.

Phu Ruea National Park
อุทยานแห่งชาติภูเรือ

This national park isn't as big as Phu Kradueng and has fewer amazing sights within it, but it does offer some spectacular views of the surroundings if you decide to summit the 1,200-meter mountain. The well-marked trail to the summit is not too challenging for most; try to come in the early morning when the mist has yet to burn off and the surrounding mountains look ethereal and magical. The mountain is also home to various colorful wild orchids, and if you happen to be here when they are in bloom, the varieties are beautiful and interesting. There are campsites and bungalows for rent here too, as well as basic cafeteria-style canteens serving up meals daily.

The Phu Ruea National Park is about 40 kilometers east of the town of Loei off Route 203. The park's headquarters is about five kilometers from the main entrance to the park, and there is a visitors center here with small exhibits of the park's wildlife and posted maps. There are also restrooms and a small canteen.

Phu Suan Sai National Park (Na Haeo)
อุทยานแห่งชาติภูสวนทราย (นาแห้ว)

This park, also commonly called Na Haeo National Park, is a forest park over mountainous terrain, and is a great park to visit if you want to just enjoy some beautiful views in the middle of nature. There are plenty of small waterfalls to visit, and none of the trails are particularly strenuous.

ACCOMMODATIONS AND FOOD
Under 1,500B
Take the name of **Loei Palace** (167/4 Charoenrat Rd., Loei, tel. 04/281-5668, www.oamhotels.com/loeipalace, 1,200B) with a grain of salt, because it's not a luxury resort. It is a nice hotel in the middle of Loei, though, with comfortable guest rooms and amenities. The property is large and attracts local tour groups, so breakfast time can be a little hectic.

Baan Fadow Family Resort (141 Mu 8, Ban Nongmapang, tel. 08/1871-9371 or 04/283-4663, www.baanfadow.com, 1,400B) is a medium-sized resort just outside Loei, with well-furnished contemporary rooms and villas set on well-manicured grounds. The property also has a swimming pool, a restaurant, and some nice *salas* as well as other spots for relaxing and taking in the scenery.

1,500-3,000B
Set on a large plot of land, the **Loei Leelawadee Resort** (159 Mu 6, Pongsoong, Dansai, tel. 04/280-1277 or 08/1914-7898, www.loeileelawadee.com, 2,000B) is an interesting mix of rustic cabins and traditional Thai hospitality. The guest rooms are comfortable, clean, and modern, although the decor is characterized by exposed wood and other outdoorsy themes. There's a swimming pool and a small spa on the premises, although it may not be the best place to go for peace and quiet, as it can be a popular location for office and other group retreats. It is a good place for families, as guest rooms are on the large side and there's plenty of room for small kids to run around.

GETTING THERE
Buses from Bangkok make the 10-hour, 350B trip on a daily basis. Loei is about nine hours from Bangkok by car on Route 201.

GETTING AROUND
You'll really need a car, motorcycle, or driver to get around the region unless you have a lot of time on your hands; the province is large and mountainous, and public transportation is more difficult to access if you do not speak Thai. Your hotel or guesthouse can arrange to rent a motorcycle or hire a driver. There are local buses running from Loei to Dan Sai, leaving approximately every 90 minutes 6 A.M.–6 P.M. daily. The ride is nearly two hours, and the fare is under 60B.

ISAN

THE SOUTHERNMOST PROVINCES

At the southern tip of Thailand at the Malaysian border lie the three provinces that make up the Pattani region: Pattani, Narathiwat, and Yala. Roughly three-quarters of its residents are ethnic Malay Muslims, so the region provides a taste of a completely different side of Thailand. Beautiful mosques and temples, quiet fishing villages, and long ribbons of uncrowded beaches abound, and the mixture of Malay, Thai, and Chinese culture will make you feel that you've traveled to a different country altogether.

The local muezzin starts the day with a predawn call to prayer that you'll hear from anywhere in town. During the day you'll taste richly spiced foods often more reminiscent of Indian cooking than Thai. The spoken and written Thai you mastered up north here gives way to Yawi, the Malay language that the majority speaks on the streets and writes in a modified form of Arabic. You can visit local tea shops and mosques, villages and beaches, perhaps catch a bit of the old Portuguese architecture during an evening walk in town, and by the time the muezzin calls prayer again at nightfall, you will have seen a side of Thailand that most other visitors miss.

There are many worthwhile attractions if you venture to the Pattani region. In the center of Pattani Province you will find the Pattani Central Mosque, the largest in Thailand, and the region is also home to some of Thailand's other beautiful mosques, including Krue Se Mosque in Pattani and the Yala Central Mosque. The coastline in the eastern part of the region is filled with beaches and fishing

© SUZANNE NAM

HIGHLIGHTS

(**Wat Khuhaphimuk:** A 1,200-year-old Buddha reclines in a secluded cliff-side cave (page 460).

(**Hala-Bala Wildlife Sanctuary:** This nature reserve is home to some of Thailand's densest rainforest and rarest species (page 463).

(**Narathat Beach:** At this locals' hang-out, you can relax, walk in pine groves, and rest your feet at your choice of dozens of food stalls (page 463).

(**Wadil-Hussein Mosque:** This wooden mosque is a must-see for its incorporation of Thai, Chinese, and Malay styles and impressive carved panels (page 465).

LOOK FOR (TO FIND RECOMMENDED SIGHTS, ACTIVITIES, DINING, AND LODGING.

towns quieter than you will find on most of Thailand's islands, and archaeological sites in Yarang, just outside Pattani Town, provide an interesting glimpse into Thai life in the 12th–14th centuries. Add ancient cave temples, dozens of waterfalls, and untouched national parks, and you have a full agenda.

HISTORY

The three provinces of Pattani were originally part of Langkasuka, an ancient Hindu-Malay kingdom believed to have been founded in the second century A.D. either in Kedah, the Malaysian state just west of Pattani, or in Pattani itself. Scholars regard Langkasuka as the earliest kingdom on the Malay Peninsula, and it is frequently mentioned in Chinese, Javanese, and Tamil chronicles of the first millennium.

By the seventh century A.D., when much of the southern region of the Malay Peninsula was still covered in rainforest, the areas of Langkasuka had become part of the Srivijayan Kingdom, a Sumatra-based maritime confederation that began to dominate much of the northern Malay Peninsula as well as trade along the Straits of Malacca. A Javanese epic refers to Langkasuka for the last time in the 14th century, and soon after it is replaced in the records by the Kingdom of Patani (spelled with one t in Patani Malay, or Yawi, the primary language of the region).

Historians disagree on when Islam first came to the Kingdom of Patani. Many suggest that Islam spread to the region as early as the 10th or 11th centuries, brought by missionaries from Langkasuka, but the court did not convert to Islam until 1457 when King Paya Tunaqpa,

THE SOUTHERN PROVINCES

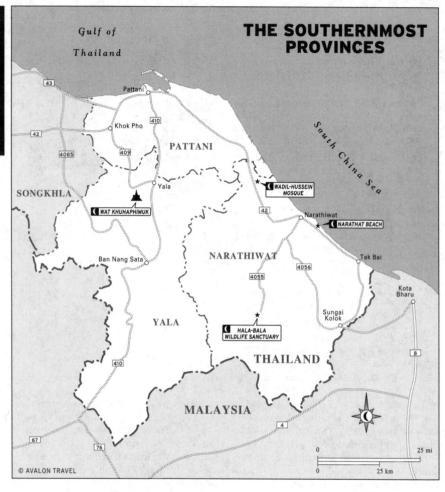

suffering from an incurable disease, had the good fortune to meet a Muslim preacher in town. The preacher agreed to rid the king of the disease on the condition that the king converted to Islam. The cure worked. The king changed his name to Sultan Ismail Shah, and the region has been Islamic ever since.

The kingdom prospered through increased trading with Chinese, Dutch, Portuguese, and English merchants and reached its zenith under the leadership of its four great queens, known by their colors: the Green, Blue, Purple, and Yellow Queens. But then, with the inevitable passing of the Yellow Queen in the 17th century, the kingdom started to decline and fell fully under the control of Siam by the latter 18th century under the reign of Rama I, the first in the line of monarchs who still rule Thailand today.

The region was officially annexed by Thailand in 1902. Five years later Thailand and Britain signed the Anglo-Siamese Treaty,

IS THE SOUTH SAFE FOR TRAVELERS?

The short answer is no. Most organizations and government officials have been discouraging travel to the Pattani region since 2004 due to an ongoing and violent separatist campaign. Although the violence has not been directed at tourists in particular, some bombings have targeted tourist hotels and several tourists have been killed. The violence, which escalated sharply in 2004, has continued unabated despite attempts to stanch the bloodshed by former prime minister Thaksin Shinawatra, the military junta that followed him, and the newly elected governments that followed them. Nothing has worked.

Although there has been a history of separatist violence in the region since the 1960s, a strong reemergence of separatist guerrilla groups began in 2001. Most striking about these groups is the anonymity of their leaders and the absence of any concrete demands from them, although their apparent aim is to form an independent Islamic state from the three provinces. It is generally assumed that the attacks stem from a long-standing resentment of Thai culture and imperialism in the area, although the region's economic difficulties are said to play a part as well, and some authorities believe that the guerrilla groups are now connected to drug traffickers or even global terrorist groups such as al-Qaeda (this is not a mainstream belief).

In 2004 martial law was declared in the area, and in 2005 Prime Minister Thaksin assumed extraordinary powers to address southern violence, but his aggressive tactics were ineffective and stoked further resentment. Locals generally supported the military junta that replaced Thaksin. The junta adopted a more conciliatory approach to the region, but the violence continued, with 1,300 more deaths after the junta took power in September 2006. Since 2004, over 4,000 people have been killed and 7,000 injured. The violence has also spilled out of the region, with bomb attacks in the Songkhla region as well.

While the attacks have generally occurred in more rural areas, insurgents have targeted schools, hotels, restaurants, discos, and train stations in the main cities and towns, and it is impossible to predict if any location is safe. Given the situation, whether to visit or not is a tough decision. You can argue that tourists have generally not been victims, although that might be because so few are there in the first place. You might also say that with deaths from violence averaging more than one a day, you're pretty safe for a two- or three-day trip – but the counterargument is that more than 11,000 people have been killed or injured here since 2004, and that's out of a population of 1.6 million people in an area not much bigger than Connecticut.

The south has a lot to offer, and the absence of visitors is a tempting draw for the adventurous traveler looking to see a different side of Thailand, but there is no doubt that you are taking a risk in a country that is otherwise quite safe. We made a trip to have a look for ourselves, but just after we left, the hotel we had been having coffee in was bombed.

Note that the situation could change quickly. If you are considering a trip to the region, check first with the local tourist authority and your embassy to get the most current information. Then, as with any risky endeavor, you need to weigh the risks and benefits to determine what's best for you. If you're just looking to get away from the rest of the travelers, here's a safer alternative: Get a good map, point to a village or town that is not in this guidebook or any other, and then go. In no time you'll find yourself the only foreigner among Thais.

DRIVING THE DEEP SOUTH

You'll know when you've arrived. Even if you overlooked the welcome sign, you won't miss the roadblock and the bunker. You zigzag through an obstacle course of sandbags and fences set up to slow you down as you approach. Three armed soldiers stop the car and ask where you're going while other soldiers with heavier artillery stay covered behind the sandbags. They are puzzled when you answer *bai tiew* (out for pleasure), but this being Thailand, they smile and wave you through, convinced you're not a terrorist even if they think you are a bit psycho. Welcome to the south.

We had picked up a rental car in Hat Yai earlier in the day. There are official rental car agencies near the airport, but they were closed when we arrived, so our taxi driver stopped on the side of the road and dialed a friend. Ten minutes later a man named Arsan stepped out of a small Toyota with his child in hand, asked for a passport as collateral, and then handed over the car for 100 bucks for three days. Arsan might have gotten in trouble for the deal – his wife's purse was still in the glove compartment, and it's hard to believe she was happy with the news that he lent the family car to two foreigners heading south.

The roadblock set the tone: anxiety. Suddenly every covered pickup truck looked like a bomb threat, and I was suspicious of anyone carrying a large parcel, even when it was obviously just a birdcage. In downtown Pattani, 10-year-olds with blue shorts and schoolbags could send me ducking for cover into a shop with no intention to make a purchase. Eating lunch in the outdoor coffee shop of the C. S. Pattani Hotel, we eyed the cars pulling up out front. More bunkers and military vehicles sprang up between towns on the way to Narathiwat, and suddenly I forgot what I learned in driver education about riding behind a Humvee with a mounted weapon. Should I pass? Maybe not. I tailgated instead – wrong idea. Afraid that the rented Toyota was planning an ambush, the Humvee lumbered to the side of the road and the gunner turned from his weapon to wave us past.

After a few hours of driving through rubber plantations, past beaches, and through quiet small towns, we arrived in Narathiwat, where a vendor told us to avoid the beach. He used the word *antarai* – danger – and I assumed he meant terrorist danger until I realized he was just talking about currents that were dangerous for swimming. By 10 P.M. the streets of Narathiwat were empty, so we double-locked our door and lay in bed listening for noises.

The next day we adopted some of the locals' complacency. Narathiwat is relaxed and beautiful, and despite the obvious threats the crowds still gather in markets, the vendors of the morning sell *nasi dagae* and fruit while the vendors of the evening sell roti and curry. Not to say the people are unaffected by the danger, but rather that the local style of life has a way of persisting despite the most adverse conditions. We say *local* life – by day two, the only foreign travelers we saw were two cyclists on a cross-country ride. We walked the town, the beach, and the pine forests of the national park and enjoyed being alone among the residents.

which gave Thailand sovereignty over Pattani while granting control of Kelantan, just to the south, to Britain. With the exception of a brief Japanese invasion during World War II, Thailand has maintained continuous control over the region.

During World War II, the Malays demanded Pattani's independence in return for helping the British fend off the Japanese, but their requests were unheeded after the war. Resistance groups sprouted soon after and have fought with varying intensity for Pattani independence ever since. Since 2001, the Pattani United Liberation Organization (PULO) and similar groups have stepped up the violence, which has claimed approximately 2,700 lives and continues to this day. Indeed, the contest for this area, started centuries ago, is far from over.

Having seen two cities, Pattani and Nara-thiwat, we decided to try our luck driving to Yala through the mountains that form the spine of the peninsula. Our maps were poor, but we had a compass and a vague sense that we needed to go west and then north. Report-edly more dangerous than the cities, the small towns between Narathiwat and Yala reminded us of the region's real hazards. Soldiers at these checkpoints asked more questions and wanted to know exactly which towns we were going to. Many vehicles were subjected to full searches, and in town the locals parked their motorcycles with the seats up to show there were no bombs inside. Driving was more dif-ficult too. The roads were often in poor condi-tion, and in several places landslides blocked most of the way. Twice our road degenerated into a remote dirt mountain path and we had to backtrack past isolated families who eyed us for the second time without expression. At one derelict checkpoint in the mountains, order had broken down, and soldiers in un-dershirts smoked cigarettes and listened to music in the sun with their M16s while two oth-ers with shotguns rode around on a scooter as if in a smaller version of *Apocalypse Now.* The only thing more unsettling than military order is military disorder. We were happy to be waved past.

In Yala we stayed at the Yala Rama Hotel, a reasonably priced, comfortable hotel by the train station in the center of town, but we avoided the karaoke bar that had been bombed in 2006. We ate wonderful seafood for dinner and the following day drove to Wat Khuhaphimuk outside town, with its 700-year-old reclining Buddha resting in a cave on the face of a cliff. It's one of the most beautiful temples in Thailand, and it's utterly empty. A lone monk chanted prayers in front while a group of children fed Ritz crackers to mon-keys and a Humvee rolled lazily around the vacant parking lot. Inside the cave, there was no sound except the occasional bat in the darkness overhead.

And then we drove back north. We shook hands with each other when we crossed the last checkpoint, relieved to be safely out of the south, and drove into Hat Yai past tourists and fast-food chains declaring in loud neon that we had returned to Thailand as most people know it. In the airport parking lot we shut the door of the rental car, Arsan appeared from nowhere and handed me my passport, and we flew home to Bangkok. It is sad how leav-ing a whole region can feel like nothing more than closing a closet door, packing the whole experience into a corner of the mind as if it were something beautiful and yet remote and forgotten, as these places often are.

But the experience wasn't packed away for long. Two days later came the news of a bomb-ing at the C. S. Pattani Hotel. First, a small bomb went off in the lobby restroom to chase people outside, and then a more powerful one went off outside to target the people who had just fled from indoors. Fifteen injured, two dead. Thankfully the two of us had safely fin-ished our meal there a few days earlier. But it was another reminder of the tone of a trip to the south: anxiety. As it should be.

PLANNING YOUR TIME

Ongoing separatist violence has escalated sharply since 2004 and has continued de-spite different approaches that various politi-cal parties in Bangkok have taken to stem the violence. More than 4,000 people have been killed since 2004 and thousands more injured. Foreign travelers have not been targeted, al-though that might be due to the fact that there are so few travelers here in the first place. Whatever the case, several travelers have died as a result of bombings in previous years, and for years the Tourism Authority of Thailand has not been promoting the region as a desti-nation for tourists. Before planning a trip, it is critical to check on the current situation.

If you are passing through the region on your way to or from Malaysia, you can get a quick impression of Thailand's Islamic side by spending just a day here. The train to Malaysia stops in Yala, making it the likely destination for the day-tripper or single-night visitor. You'll have time to have a few local meals, take in a mosque and a temple, walk the back streets, and then continue on your way.

A more thorough exploration of the area requires at least 2–3 days—or more, depending on how much time you want to spend on the beach and in the national parks. Getting from one town to the next can take you a half a day by the time you arrange for transportation, complete your journey, and settle into the next place. Two or three days will be enough to see a few towns and mosques and perhaps a national park, especially if you have your own transportation. But if you are looking to relax seaside or go deeper into the mountains, you may want to lengthen your stay to 4–5 days. A good itinerary is to start in Hat Yai, which is relatively safe and easy to get to, and from there travel south to Pattani and Narathiwat, if you are looking for the sea, or head toward Yala and then south to explore the mountains.

Temperatures in the far south are more constant than in other parts of Thailand, hovering around the high 20s Celsius, but the best time to visit is during the drier season, November–mid-March.

GETTING THERE AND AROUND

Because the region is over 960 kilometers from Bangkok, you're probably not coming here as an afterthought unless you're passing through on your way to Malaysia. Many people travel first to the hub of Hat Yai, 96 kilometers north of Pattani Town and the closest of the three major towns in the region. You can generally take buses and trains from Bangkok directly to the major towns as well. There are no direct flights from Bangkok to anywhere in the region. The fastest way to get here by plane is to fly to Hat Yai, the main Thai gateway to this region. The ever-friendly Nok Air runs five flights each day for about 2,000B one-way from Bangkok's Don Muang Airport. There are also flights available on Thai Airways and Thai Air Asia. Trains run from Bangkok to Hat Yai several times each day. The Bangkok–Hat Yai fare for second class is 350B, and the trip takes about 16 hours, depending on what kind of train you get.

Once you are in the region, getting around is cheap and easy. There are trains running to Pattani, Narathiwat, and Yala as well as many buses running daily between all the major towns. Although buses aren't always the most comfortable means of transport, most trips cost less than 100B. For shorter journeys around the towns or to destinations nearby, there are also motorcycle taxis and *song thaew* for hire.

Cars are available for rent from **Avis** (Hat Yai Airport, tel. 07/425-0321) in Hat Yai. The main roads in the south, as in all of Thailand, are generally quite good, although you should use caution driving at night or in the rain, as the poor street lighting leads to poor visibility. You might be able to find rental cars elsewhere in the region, but they are usually arranged by negotiating with individuals. Of course, you can drive all the way from Bangkok, but you'd better pack a case of Red Bull before you start.

Pattani Province   จังหวัด ปัตตานี

In the old days, Pattani was famous for powerful queens and big cannons. The queens' reign ended in the middle of the 17th century, and the largest of all Thai cannons, the Phaya Tani, moved to Bangkok, where it stands today by the Ministry of Defense. Fortunately there are still other things to see in Pattani. The province is home to two of Thailand's most significant mosques, the Central Mosque and the Krue Se Mosque, and also features waterfalls, fascinating fishing villages, and over 160 kilometers of coastline with many quiet, isolated beaches.

PATTANI
ปัตตานี

The town of Pattani has a rich past, having been a trading center for international merchants, including Chinese, Dutch, British, and Portuguese, 400 years ago. Although you will see little of that past today, you can still spot traces of the old Chinese-Portuguese architecture near the Pattani River, and the city still has a substantial Chinese population. On the streets you will certainly hear Yawi spoken more often than Thai. The C. S. Pattani hotel just outside town is the nicest hotel in the region, a good place for a final splurge before heading farther south or as a last hurrah on the way back. As regional capitol, Pattani can feel quite crowded, and you will have to brave some traffic and hunt around a bit to find the best beds, meals, and sights.

Sights

The **Pattani Central Mosque** (Yarang Rd., 9 A.M.–3:30 P.M. Sat.–Thurs.), less than one kilometer south of town, also known as Matsayit Klang, is the religious heart of the region and the center for major religious celebrations. The

© SUZANNE NAM

ruins at Yarang Ancient City in Pattani

© JOHN BROWN

Krue Se Mosque

mosque was completed in 1963 after nine years of construction and is the biggest mosque in the area. With its red facade and green-capped minarets, it's worth a visit if you are in town, although there is nothing written in English to guide you around the building. It is on Yarang Road just south of the center of Pattani Town. Keep an eye out for it on the right side when you're heading out of town.

They say if it weren't for the curse of Lim Ko Niao, the **Krue Se Mosque** (Hwy. 42), 6.5 kilometers from Pattani Town on the road to Narathiwat, would be completed by now—but they've been saying that for 400 years. The mosque was started in 1578 by a Chinese man named Lim To Kieng, whose sister came from China to persuade him to give up and come home. The rumor is that the sister cursed the mosque to remain unfinished, but the fact is that she finished herself with a noose hung from a nearby cashew tree. Lim To Kieng then gave up on the mosque and built her a grave instead. You can still see the mosque and a shrine at Ban Krue Se, on the left side of Highway

42 on the way to Narathiwat. Though unfinished, the mosque was restored in 1982 and is well-maintained by the locals, although it was the scene of a standoff between militants and Thai Special Forces in 2004 that resulted in 34 deaths. As for the cashew tree, it has been enshrined, and Lim Ko Niao is worshipped as a goddess.

While **Yarang Ancient City** (Rte. 4061, Yarang, tel. 07/343-9093), 16 kilometers from Pattani Town, might have been an ancient city some time ago, today it looks pretty much like any other modern Thai town: concrete shops, motorcycles, and street vendors. However, there are a few reminders of the grand old days. The most significant is called Ban Jalae Monument, a crumbling brick structure believed to be an ancient religious site. The structure sits under an open pavilion, and there are some picnic tables nearby in case you brought lunch. It's not big, so don't get your hopes up for something like Ayutthaya. Following the road from Pattani to Narathiwat, you will see signs for Yarang 16 kilometers out of town. Once here, watch for the blue overhead sign pointing left. About 1.5 kilometers down the road you'll see a sign for Ban Jalae, which is 90 meters in on the left. It is possible to call ahead and have someone guide you through several of the region's ruins.

Kallayaniwatthana Institute of Arts and Culture (Songkhla Nakarin University, Pattani Campus, Amphoe Muang, tel. 07/331-3930, 9–11:30 A.M. and 1–4 P.M. Mon.–Fri., free) is divided into two sections, the Phra Thepyanmoli Museum, devoted to Buddha images, pottery, and coins, and the Khatichon Witthaya Museum, which depicts local Muslim households, utensils, and arts.

Beaches

There are a number of beaches just to the north and the east of Pattani, and many others along the main road toward Hat Yai and in the other direction, toward Narathiwat. These are great places to stop, get your feet wet, and perhaps go for a swim, but they are day beaches. The facilities are basic, and the conservative locals haven't cultivated a beach-vacation culture. If you're looking for a savage tan and piña coladas, stay north on the islands, but if a basic small beach with adequate sea is your thing, then the south may be appealing.

Events

Once a year the **Chao Mae Lim Ko Niao Festival** is held in honor of Lim Ko Niao, enshrined at Krue Se Mosque. The event usually takes place in late February or early March and includes processions, Chinese opera, and various vendors selling local products.

Accommodations

Pattani has a handful of hotels scattered around the city. If you are looking for something upscale, go to the C. S. Pattani; for cheaper and more central accommodations, look around on Phiphit Road by the river, where you will find a few basic guesthouses.

You won't break the bank at the **Palace Hotel** (10–12 Soi Thepwiwat Phiphit Rd., A No Ru, tel. 07/334-9711, 200B). It's basic, but

the guest rooms are clean, and they have attached baths. The lobby is small, but there are a few big old wooden chairs and even a few mounted animal heads in the hallway that may impress the big-game lover in you. The staff is friendly and speaks basic English. There are a few decent restaurants and a karaoke place outside the door, and the night market is just 90 meters down the road.

The top-end choice is the (**C. S. Pattani** (299 Mu 4, Hnongjik Rd., tel. 07/333-5093, www.cspattanihotel.com, 1,200B). It's a few kilometers outside the center of town on the road toward Hat Yai, but it has a great lobby and open-air restaurant, large and modern guest rooms, and two great pools. It's a bargain for the price. If you want a final night of luxury before easing your way farther south, this is the place. Government and military-sponsored events are frequently held at this hotel, which can make it a target for violence. Two people died and 15 were injured when a bomb went off in the front of the C. S. Pattani in early 2008.

Food

Pattani is filled with small basic concrete-box restaurants, many of which have surprisingly good food. You will find a higher concentration of restaurants in the square block between Phiphit and Prida Roads by the river, especially along Soi Thepwiwat, where the **Night Market** is. The best bet is to start there, and then pick your way onward.

For a great place to watch the sunset over the river, try (**Janpen Restaurant** (Pattanipirom Rd., tel. 07/334-9644, less than 100B), the first shop on the right after you make a left from Prida Road. Serving mainly Chinese and Thai food, it is very well priced, with a plate of local food and a beer running under 100B.

The **C. S. Pattani** hotel (299 M.4 Hnongjik Rd., tel. 07/333-5093, cspatani@cscoms.com, 150B) also has a breezy restaurant on the ground floor looking out onto the courtyard (which is mainly a parking lot) where they make fresh roti with your choice of a variety

SOUTHERN STYLE – FUSION FOOD AT ITS BEST

Ranging from heavy, rich, and spicy, sometimes salty, and other times sour, to delicate herbs and fruits, the food of southern Thailand frequently resembles Indian cuisine as a result of the influence from the subcontinent that Muslims have introduced over the centuries.

Geography, religion, and national cultures are the three great ingredients. Given the region's long coastline, it is no surprise that the local tables offer seafood in hundreds of shapes, colors, and tastes. You first notice fish grilling everywhere, then the dozens of fish and shrimp curries and rice dishes, and finally you uncover the hidden seafood such as shrimp paste and the omnipresent fermented-fish condiment known as nam budu. Coconuts are a major local crop, turning up in curries, rice, vegetable dishes, and even as fuel for the grills. Of course, you will find less pork in the Muslim south than elsewhere in Thailand, but more than enough beef and fish to make up for it. Mixing with the traditional Thai staples are satay from Malaysia, roti from India, and a healthy measure of dry roasted spices, all heartily attesting to the great fusion that marks southern Thai cooking.

Your best bet is to follow your senses and eat whatever your eyes, nose, or tongue tell you to, but there are a few local specialties you shouldn't go home without. Breakfasts are big in the south. Locals often start with nasi dagae, a mixture of three types of rice (white, sticky, and brown) tossed with coconut milk and topped with tuna curry, half a hard-boiled egg, and a sprinkling of banana peppers. Get it early – by lunchtime this dish is generally unavailable. Also popular is khao yum, a salad of rice, shredded herbs, and nam budu.

Also don't miss the popular yellow rice with chicken, a turmeric-and-rice dish that will remind you of a biryani, or Massaman curry, the mild yellow curry often made with beef, onions, and potatoes. Adventurous eaters should try kaeng tai pla, one of the south's hottest curries, made from salted fish kidneys. Like many first-timers, you might find the dish more fun to blog about than to eat, but it's worth a small taste just to say you did.

All these specialty dishes are common, but don't expect to find them everywhere. Most of the more noticeable restaurants in the south are typical Thai-Chinese restaurants, which will not offer them. If you see Chinese characters, brightly painted facades, or beer signs, you might well get great food, but it will be similar to the food you get in Bangkok. The local Muslim restaurants tend to be understated – a small sign with Arabic script, simple tables, great food. Note that female travelers are usually welcome in these establishments, although sometimes there is separate seating for men and women. Keep your eyes open and take cues from the locals. Both men and women should also dress modestly – avoid shorts and tank tops.

of curries. There is also an extensive menu of other foods.

Getting There

Trains run from Bangkok to Pattani several times a day, and the trip takes about 17 hours, depending on what kind of train you get. Pattani's Khok Pho Station is 32 kilometers outside of town, so you will have to take a 20B bus ride into town. There are buses to Pattani from Bangkok's Southern Bus Terminal, and tickets cost approximately 400B for an air-conditioned bus.

PANARE
ปะนาเระ

As with most of the small towns in the south, you will find Panare to be very basic. There is always food, but accommodations are generally not available in these towns. Consider Panare more of a stopping-off point for hitting the nearby beaches.

Beaches

Khae Khae Beach (Rte. 4157, Tambon Nam Bo), 9.5 kilometers southeast of Panare, evidently gets its name from a local word meaning "loud noise," but you'll more likely find peace and quiet here, just as you will at the other beaches in the area. Large granite rocks along the beach distinguish Khae Khae from the other beaches in Panare. Popular with both locals and Asian visitors, the beach is about 1.5 kilometers past Hat Ratcharak.

There are many great beaches easily accessible from town by motorcycle taxi. Not all of them are well marked, and many have only basic food and beverage service, but relative solitude will compensate for what lacks in convenience. All of them are just off Route 4157, which runs along the coast.

Panare Beach is located just to the east of Panare. This long, clean beach is a favorite for locals on day trips, although with the fishing boats docked along the shore, it is not great for swimming. You will find some basic food and beverages here. It is a great choice for a quick morning swim or an afternoon in the sun.

Cha La Lai Beach is located three kilometers southeast of Panare. Cha La Lai is known for nearby marshlands, long rows of pine trees, and its relaxed atmosphere.

Farther south of Cha La Lai by 1.5 kilometers, **Ma Ruat Beach** is distinguished by its small rocky mountain and long sidewalk.

Another 1.5 kilometers from Ma Ruat Beach, **Ratcharak Beach** offers only the most basic food and drink, but in the off-season you might find you have the beach to yourself.

Getting There

Panare is about 42 kilometers east of Pattani. There are public buses that run between the two towns during the day.

SAI BURI
สายบุรี

About 48 kilometers down the coast from the town of Pattani is the small quiet town of Sai Buri. Although the town consists primarily of concrete architecture today, there are some brilliant old wooden houses as well as some old-fashioned Chinese shophouses. Most of the sights for visitors are on the beaches to the east.

Sights

Ban Paseyawo (Rte. 4157 N.), five kilometers from Sai Buri, is a small village outside Sai Buri that is famous for the production of indigenous *korlae* fishing boats, the pointed and colorful boats you see in the fishing villages and along many of the beaches. You can purchase much smaller models for decoration or use in the bathtub, and while you are at it you can also pick up a bottle or two of the south's popular *budu* sauce, if that floats your boat.

A quick ride from Sai Buri, **Wasukri Beach** (Rte. 4157 N.), 6.5 kilometers from Sai Buri in Patatimo Village, is a simple pine-lined beach where you will find basic bungalows for rent and quite a good stretch of sea for swimming.

Events

In May there is an annual **fishing competition** on Wasukri Beach in Sai Buri. In addition to seeing the local anglers showing off, you'll be treated to a variety of local foods and might finally have the chance to see some traditional lamb fighting.

Getting There

Sai Buri is approximately 48 kilometers from Pattani town and is easily accessible either by bus or taxi.

THE SOUTHERN PROVINCES

Yala Province   จังหวัด ยะลา

The largest and southernmost of the three southern provinces, Yala takes its name from the local word for fishing net, an odd fact given that Yala is the only one of the region's provinces to be landlocked. Many visitors see the province as nothing more than a pit stop, yet this mountainous, rainforest-covered province holds many attractions, both fascinating and unique. You will find the Namtok Tan To Forest Park with its nine-level waterfall in the middle of dense forest. Malaysian and Thai travelers visit Betong in the south for its mist-covered mountain, well-regarded local foods, and its massive mailbox. In Tambon Ban Hae you will find the Sakai, an ancient aboriginal tribe different in culture and appearance than any other in Thailand. If you have only a few weeks in Thailand, Yala might not be your first choice, but if you have more time and are passing through anyway on your way to Malaysia, a day or two in the area won't go to waste.

YALA
ยะลา

With about 100,000 residents, the town of Yala is twice as big as the two other provincial capitals in the region. The city feels bigger, and yet it is clean and quite orderly at the same time. You'll be surprised to see how many green park areas there are near the administrative buildings just outside of town. There isn't a lot to see in the city itself, although there are certainly a few good places to eat, and it serves as a good base for exploring the rest of the region.

Sights
YALA CENTRAL MOSQUE
มัสยิดกลางยะลา

The primary mosque of Yala, Yala Central Mosque (Rte. 410 N.), 2.5 kilometers from the town center, was completed in 1984, and its white-and-aqua frame sits high atop 30 central steps. There have been several mosques on this site over the last century, one of which

was destroyed by the Japanese during their brief foray into Thailand during World War II. Like many modern mosques in the region, the Central Mosque is more significant from a cultural and religious point of view than from an architectural one. Driving north from town on Route 410, you will see the mosque just past the train tracks on the left.

◖ WAT KHUHAPHIMUK
วัดคูหาพิมุข

On the road to Amphoe Yaha, 6.5 kilometers west of Yala, is the ancient cave temple of Wat Khuhaphimuk (Yala–Hat Yai Rd.), or Wat Na Tham, as it is often called by locals. It's a regional gem that you shouldn't miss. The reclining Buddha inside the cave has found a cool and secluded place to rest, and the experts' best guess is that he has been here since A.D. 757. There are dozens of other impressive Buddhas in the cave as well, and you will probably have the place nearly to yourself. When you climb down from the main cave, be sure to follow the path to the left to another small cave around the corner that is worth seeing. There is also a crowd of monkeys around here who accept donations in the form of food.

MU BAN SAKAI
หมู่บ้านซาไก

Almost vanished today from Thailand, the Sakai are believed to be the original inhabitants of the Malay Peninsula, having settled here in the Stone Age, and they are part of the same race who populate the Andaman and Nicobar Islands in the Indian Ocean. There is still a small Sakai settlement in Yala Province known as Mu Ban Sakai (Mu 3, Tambon Ban Rae), 80 kilometers south of Yala toward Betong. Today, the Sakai have adopted many Thai customs and earn their living through rice and rubber cultivation, but you can still see a bit of their traditional way of life here. Note that although most Thais will call them by the name Sakai, that word takes its roots from a Malay word meaning "savage"—certainly not fair; they call themselves the Mani people.

Events

Every year in the first week of March, Yala hosts the **ASEAN Barred Ground Dove Cooing Festival.** The name says it all. It attracts dove lovers from all over the region, including Malaysia and Singapore, and features over 1,400 competitors. An assortment of local products is also on sale, and you can even buy your own dove at prices up to 1 million baht, depending, presumably, on the bird's musical abilities.

Accommodations

There are plenty of hotels in Yala, ranging from the very cheap to the middle of the road, and most cater to either local travelers or visitors from neighboring Malaysia. Although there are hotels scattered all over town, you are better off staying in one near the train station, which is where most of the "action" is in town, if that is the right word for the small collection of restaurants near the front of the station.

Near the station, a good budget option is the **Thepwimarn Hotel** (Sribamrung Rd., tel. 07/321-2400, 200B s, no a/c). It's simple, but it's just down the street from the train station. To get here, walk straight out from the train station one block, turn left at Thara Seafood, which you will see on the corner on the left, and go two blocks down to the hotel.

A good choice in the mid-range is the **Yala Rama Hotel** (15–21 Sribamrung Rd., tel. 07/321-2563, 420B), just two blocks away from the train station. You'll see it a block before you get to the Thepwimarn Hotel, above. Although this might just be the nicest hotel in the area, guest rooms are basic but clean, quiet, and theoretically air-conditioned. In some rooms the air-conditioning gets to lukewarm at best, so don't be afraid to request a room change if needed. There is a karaoke bar on the premises (good or bad news, depending on your taste) but note that it was bombed in 2006.

Food

The typical first food stop in Yala is ◖ **Thara Seafood** (35–39 Pipet Pakdee Rd., tel. 07/321-2356, 200B with drinks). Walk straight out of the central train station, and you will see Thara Seafood on the corner one block down on the left. The grills outside will give it away. Their English is spotty; the food is not. Get the grilled fish in banana leaf for sure—you'll see everyone else around you eating it too. Then go for clams, mussels, squid, crab omelets—you name it—depending on your mood. Discreetly looking at what others are eating and then ordering what looks good is always a smart move.

If you walk around the block where Thara Seafood is, you will find a number of other Chinese, Thai, and Muslim places to eat. All of them are even cheaper than Thara. Note that Yala is an early city, no doubt partly due to the fact that curfews are periodically imposed as a counterterrorism measure. By 9 P.M. the restaurants are clearing out, and by 10 P.M. the streets are empty and soldiers come out to keep watch over the train station.

Getting There

Trains run from Bangkok to Yala several times a day, and the trip takes about 18 hours depending on what kind of train you get. The station is right in the center of town. There are buses from Bangkok's Southern Bus Terminal, and tickets cost approximately 400B for an air-conditioned bus.

BETONG
เบตง

Tucked into the far southwest of the Pattani region lies the Betong District, the very south of the south. The whole area is largely mountainous, covered in dark green forest and often with a beautiful layer of fog in the early morning. Although it is out of the way, it makes a good base camp for trekking into the nearby forests and parks.

Sights

If, after your travel in the rest of Thailand,

you are suffering from a skin disease or muscle pain, you'd benefit from a trip to the **Betong Hot Springs** (Ban Charo Parai Village, Tambon Tano Mae Ro) about 13 kilometers outside of Betong Town. The spa's natural mineral-water springs are also good just for relaxing and for cooking eggs—in seven minutes, at the hottest part of the spring. Go 4.8 kilometers north of Betong Town on Highway 410, then turn off and go eight more kilometers to the village.

If you've already seen the world's largest ball of yarn and the largest fire hydrant, then you won't want to miss the **world's largest mailbox** (Clock Tower Intersection, Betong). We have little means to verify this claim, but standing over three meters tall, this letter-eating giant will redefine your conception of postal magnitude. It is still in regular use, so do have some postcards ready to go.

Getting There

Betong is about 145 kilometers south of Yala. It is a scenic mountain drive in one of the cars or vans that depart hourly from just opposite the Yala Railroad Station.

Narathiwat Province   จังหวัด นราธิวาส

The name Narathiwat derives from Sanskrit and means "the residence of wise people," so you would guess that the locals have a smart reason to live here. The gold mines are one reason, but there are many other attractions for visitors too, including long stretches of beaches lined with pine trees, expansive peat swamp forests, Ban Yakang Village, where you can still find authentic batik cloth, and numerous waterfalls, mountains, and cliffs.

NARATHIWAT
นราธิวาส

If it weren't for the terrorism, you could easily see Narathiwat Town becoming a regional hub for visitors exploring the region, much like Chang Mai is for the north. With its 1.5-kilometer-long strip along the Bang Nara River, the Narathat Beach and park complex to the north, the other-worldly Ao Manao National Park just to the south, and plenty of great Thai and Muslim food, there is plenty to keep you here for a few days. Consisting primarily of two long streets running parallel to the river, Narathiwat is quieter and more relaxed than Pattani or Yala and is just beginning to blossom with some new restaurants and hotels that might yet make it a destination.

Sights

Built in 1981, the **New Central Mosque** (Ban Bang Nara, Narathiwat) is said to be modeled in the Arabian style, although it looks a bit like the 1970s style too. It is, however, an important religious site for Thai Muslims. There is a convention hall on the first floor and prayer rooms on the second and third floors. You'll find it in Ban Bang Nara, north of town. Make a left just before Narathat Beach and you will see it.

Ban Yakang Village (Hwy. 4055), 3.2 kilometers south of town toward Amphoe Rangae, is an old community known for its production of batik fabrics—perfect for showing off when you get back to Khao San Road. The village is just over three kilometers from the Provincial Hall on Highway 4055.

Generally used as the royal family's summer palace, the **Taksin Ratchaniwet Palace** (Rte. 4084), eight kilometers from Narathiwat on the road to Tak Bai, is a pleasant place to have a look around—if you're allowed in. Like most royal palaces in the country, this one is open on paper but closed on arrival. Try your luck, though; it's just another 3.2 kilometers past Ao Manao. Reportedly, the grounds provide a great view of the beach and water, and there is an aviary as well. If you manage to get in, maybe you're part of the family.

© SUZANNE NAM

life by the water in Narathiwat

Hala-Bala Wildlife Sanctuary
เขตรักษาพันธุ์สัตว์ป่าฮาลา-บาลา

Established in 1996, Hala-Bala Wildlife Sanctuary is one of Thailand's most recent conservation areas and is home to some of Thailand's greenest, densest rainforest and various endangered animals, including large black gibbons, the Asian two-horned rhinoceros, and an impressive variety of rare birds that make it a great spot for bird-watchers. Hala and Bala are actually two separate forests but part of the same reserve. Hala is the one in Betong, while Bala is in Narathiwat. From Narathiwat Town, follow signs for Sungai Kolok, and then continue on toward Waeng. From there you will see signs toward the sanctuary.

Beaches
NARATHAT BEACH
หาดนราทัศน์

Certainly worth visiting, Narathat Beach is just 1.5 kilometers north of town and easily accessible by minibus, motorcycle, or on foot.

Go straight north on Pinchet Bamrung Road, cross the small bridge, and you are there. The sand is quite nice, and thick rows of pine trees provide shade if the heat gets to be too much. There are also dozens of simple restaurants with seating on mats and benches that serve pretty good food. The area is bigger than it might first appear, so make sure you walk the land, because the area bends around several hundred meters to the right after you cross the bridge, looping back down into the mouth of the Bang Nara River.

AO MANAO
อ่าวมะนาว

The beach at Ao Manao (Mu 1, Kaluwo Nuea subdistrict, Narathiwat, reserve@dnp.go.th) is actually part of the Ao Manao–Khao Tanyong National Park complex, 4.8 kilometers south of Narathiwat Town. From the clock tower, head south and follow the sign for Route 4084. You will soon see signs for Ao Manao on the left. The beach is rugged, with rough surf and a

local girls waiting for the bus after school

number of downed trees from beach erosion, but this adds to the natural charm. Don't swim here—there are short-tempered currents and floating trees. Instead, a few hundred meters from the beach are shady forests where a thick gray bed of pine needles, small bands of goats hunting for grass, and the sound of the sea in the distance keep you on the lookout for the elves that seem likely to appear any minute. There are a few basic food vendors here, and camping in the park is permitted.

Events

Every September, Narathiwat puts on its **Khong Dee Muang Nara** festival at roughly the same time the royal family comes to visit the local summer palace. The weeklong festival features *korlae* boat racing and a cooing dove competition as well as an assortment of local foods and crafts.

Accommodations

Narathiwat has a number of decent choices in various price ranges, although you won't find anything particularly nice. They all tend to cluster around the few blocks between the clock tower and the river.

A cheap and basic choice, the **Pacific Hotel** (Worakham Phipet Rd., tel. 07/351-1076, 500B) offers TV, air-conditioning, and clean guest rooms and baths, with refrigerators in the guest rooms to keep things cool. The guest rooms have balconies, so you can watch the quiet streets at night. It's not the best value for the money, and it's a bit loud, but it will do.

Right on the river is the **Ocean Blue Mansion** (Phuphaphakdee Rd., tel. 07/351-1109, 450B). It sits just off the road; you'll see the large blue sign and then the Florida Keys–style blue pastel building. Don't expect Florida comparisons to go farther than that, however. If you're lucky, the manager might be a bit more talkative than the assortment of dogs sleeping in the lobby. But whatever happens in the lobby, the river view from your guest room is great, especially at sunrise.

The **Imperial Narathiwat** (228 Pichitbumrung Rd., tel. 07/351-5041, www. imperialhotels.com, 1,000B) is the pick of traveling Thai businesspeople. For the price it's a pretty good deal, although at the official price in their brochure at the front desk (2,000B) it's less of a deal. It's just north of the clock tower on the left. If you're in the mood for a nicer place in town, stop in and try to get the better rate.

Food

Like anywhere in Thailand, there's food everywhere in Narathiwat. For a good concentration of options, start from the clock tower and head east to the river. In the blocks just north and south, you'll find dozens of restaurants with both Thai and Muslim food. Don't expect to find anything in English, but with a combination of smiles and discreet gesturing toward appetizing foods that others are eating, you ought to emerge back into the sun happy and satisfied.

One new and more modern place on road by the river is ◖ **Mantra** (353 Phuphaphakdee Rd., tel. 07/351-6747, 100B). You'll spot it from its tan painted wood exterior and then be guided a surprisingly long way through to seats right on the river. Start with the excellent *pat prik nua gap khao* (fried beef and peppers with rice), and move on from there. The breeze on the river will make you forget how hot it is outside, and with dishes at 30–40B and cheap cold beer, you might stay longer than you expected.

Getting There

Trains run from Bangkok to Narathiwat several times each day, and the trip to Tanyongmat Station takes about 19 hours, depending on what kind of train you get. The station is 32 kilometers outside of town, so you will have to take a 20B bus ride into town. There are buses from Bangkok's Southern Bus Terminal, and tickets cost approximately 400B for an air-conditioned bus.

BACHO
บาเจาะ

◖ Wadil-Hussein Mosque
มัสยิดวาดีอัลฮูเซ็น

If you make it to Bacho, the Wadil-Hussein Mosque (Ban Talo Mano, Tambon Subo Sawo), just off Hwy. 42, also known as the Talomanoh Mosque, the 300-Year-Old Mosque, and Telok Menok Mosque, is a must-see. The mosque was most likely constructed in 1769 and combines Thai, Chinese, and Malay styles. Made entirely of wood, the mosque also features impressive carved wooden panels in a variety of styles. You usually have to get permission from the local imam (prayer leader) in order to go inside the mosque.

Getting There

Bacho is about 24 kilometers northwest of Narathiwat. There are plenty of *song thaew* and taxis from Narathiwat to Bacho.

BACKGROUND

The Land

Located in the center of the Southeast Asian Peninsula, Thailand's irregular shape defies any easy analog in nature, but it has loosely been compared to the shape of an elephant's head, with the northern part of the country the animal's face and ears and the thinner southern part down the Malay Peninsula its trunk. The country is bordered by Burma to much of its western boundary, with the lower western boundary facing the Indian Ocean; by Burma and Laos in the north; and by Laos and Cambodia in the east. The Gulf of Thailand cuts a horseshoe shape into the lower central part of the country, and the far southern border is shared with Malaysia.

GEOGRAPHY

Thailand covers 514 square kilometers of land over four geographical regions. The central region, home to the country's capital, is the southern part of the river basin of the Chao Phraya River. The northernmost region is mountainous and forested, with four major rivers flowing north to south. The northeast region is mostly flat plateau lands, and the southern region the Malay Peninsula, with coastline on both sides and hundreds of small islands flanking the land mass.

The North

Mountains cover much of the northern part of

© SUZANNE NAM

the country, in ranges that continue on from neighboring Burma and Laos into Thailand. The highest point in Thailand, 2,565 meters, is at Doi Inthanon in Chiang Mai. The four major rivers—the Nan, the Yom, the Wang, and the Ping—running from north to south and flowing down into the central basin, follow roughly parallel tracks through four major river valleys, and it's in these valleys that most of the population of this region lives.

The Central Basin
The Chao Phraya River Basin, fed by the four rivers that begin in the north plus three other major rivers, is conspicuously lacking any significant elevations, something you'll notice in Bangkok and the surrounding areas. This area is characterized by flat, green expanses as far as the eye can see. This is the country's most fertile land, particularly well suited for growing the region's staple grain, hence the nickname the "Rice Bowl of Thailand." At the south of this region is the top of the Gulf of Thailand.

The Khorat Plateau
This flat, level land covers most of the country's northeast region, Isan, and makes up one-third of Thailand's land mass. The plateau, bordered on the north and northeast by the Mekong River, has an average elevation of 180 meters but slopes down from the highest point in the north part of the region, where it borders Laos, to the lowest in the south, where it borders Cambodia. With surrounding lands dropping off around it and less ability to retain water, the Isan Plateau contains the country's least fertile lands, although the population in this part of Thailand is mostly agricultural.

Southern Region and Islands
Thailand's peninsula stretches from the bottom of the central basin around Phitsanulok Province all the way to the Malay Peninsula. At its thinnest point, the narrow strip of land between the Gulf of Thailand and the Indian Ocean is known as the Kra Isthmus. Home to smaller mountain ranges that cut down the center of the peninsula and dramatic karst

landscapes as well as the Indian Ocean, the region is one of the most beautiful in the country. It is in this region, primarily on the west coast, that you'll see many mangrove forests, where trees flourish in the muddy, salty water on the edge of the coast.

CLIMATE
With the exception of the southern region, Thailand has three seasons—cool, rainy, and hot. To someone used to a temperate climate, it may be difficult to feel any difference between them, as regardless of the time of year or part of the country, most of the days are as hot or hotter than a typical North American summer. The cool season, November–February, is generally mild, with temperatures in the 20s to mid-30s Celsius. Although there may be occasional showers, during this time of year there is usually little rainfall and less humidity. In the north and mountains, weather patterns are similar, although temperatures can drop to around 15°C at night. At the highest elevations these temperatures can be even lower.

The hot season spans March–May; it's during this time of year that temperatures in Bangkok will soar above 35°C during the day, sometimes approaching 40°C. Chiang Mai won't feel much better—in fact, in the city, temperatures can climb slightly higher than in the capital. Though not yet the rainy season, rains begin to pick up in April, and May is sometimes one of the wettest months of the year. The rainy season spans June–October, generally peaking in September across the country, when average rainfall in Bangkok is 330 millimeters. This is a season of frequent flooding, even in major cities.

The southern part of the country is essentially a tropical rainforest climate, with average temperatures around 30°C throughout the year. Rainfall follows a similar pattern as in the rest of the country, although on a slightly different schedule. December–May are the region's driest months, with little or no rainfall. Beginning in April, rainfall picks up, and the wet weather continues through November.

ENVIRONMENTAL ISSUES

Thailand's biggest environmental challenge not caused by humans is the availability of water in the northeast (Isan) region. The slight elevation of the Khorat Plateau (essentially all of Isan) means there are frequent droughts despite monsoon downpours during rainy season. The region is primarily agrarian, and most small farmers rely on rainwater instead of irrigation, so the impact of drought on the production of food, income, and quality of life is profound. Isan is Thailand's poorest region, and many economists, development specialists, and policy makers point to the lack of water as the primary cause.

Thailand's many islands also routinely face water shortages. Popular and heavily visited islands have experimented with pipelines, desalination plants, and other methods to ensure an adequate water supply, but none have been without drawbacks. Pipelines are expensive and untenable for islands far from the mainland. Desalination is energy-intensive, and the by-product, water with a high saline content, may have an impact on sealife when it is discharged into the ocean. The islands are a huge tourist draw, and local and national governments are reluctant to place limits on the number of people who can visit, so water supply will continue to be a challenge.

The rapid economic growth that has propelled Thailand from a developing country to a middle-income country in the past few decades has also created air-quality issues. Air pollution in large cities has been one of the country's major challenges, and you cannot help but notice some city residents going about daily life wearing surgical masks to avoid inhaling particulate matter from car and motorcycle exhaust and industrial activity. As bad as it may look, the Thai government has done an amazing job cleaning up the air. Since air quality hit an all-time low in the 1980s, policies such as higher emissions standards for gas-powered vehicles and incentives to switch to natural gas–powered cars have been put in place to reduce pollution. The surgical masks are still popular, but the air quality in Bangkok and other major cities in Thailand is now within acceptable limits when measured by U.S. Environmental Protection Agency standards, and nearly acceptable limits when measured by European Union standards.

Other environmental issues include solid waste management, deforestation, erosion, and rising sea levels.

Flora and Fauna

Because Thailand is a tropical country stretching more than 1,900 kilometers over an area of over 823,000 square kilometers from north to south, it has an incredibly diverse range of flora and fauna in varied habitats. Tthe country's terrain starts from the high mountains in the northwestern hill tracts along the Tanasserim Range to the hill plateaus of the northeastern region, moving down through the Central Plain into the eastern corner adjacent to Cambodia and into the peninsular region south of the Kra Isthmus to the Malaysian border.

Sadly, due to human ills such as poaching and deforestation, Thailand has a less diverse range of vegetation and animal life than it once did, although the government has taken steps in recent years to prevent further erosion of its natural environments. There are now over 100 protected national parks in Thailand, which provide endless opportunities for visitors to get an up-close look at the country's natural beauty. The largest of the bunch is Khao Yai, a 2,000-square-kilometer sanctuary that contains more than 70 species of mammals, including tigers and elephants, as well as 320 varieties of birds, not to mention hundreds of types of vegetation.

© SUZANNE NAM

typical jungle vegetation

FLORA
Trees

It is estimated that about 25 percent of Thailand's land mass is covered with forest, with the UN's World Development Report ranking the country 44th in the world in terms of natural forest cover. Thailand's forests can be classified into two main types—evergreen and deciduous—with two basic types of deciduous forest: monsoon forest (with a dry season of three months or more) and rainforest (where rain falls at least nine months of the year). The mixed deciduous forest in the northern region is considered the most commercially valuable forest of Thailand.

Northern, eastern, and central Thailand mainly consists of monsoon forests, while southern Thailand is predominantly a rainforest zone. To complicate things further, many of these forests overlap, with some zones featuring a mix of monsoon and rainforest vegetation. Meanwhile, one-quarter of the country's forests consist of freshwater swamps in the delta regions, forested crags (found everywhere), and pine forests at higher altitudes in the north.

There are hundreds of tree species native to Thailand, with some of the best known including an array of fruit-producing varieties such as the widely popular rambutan and durian. Then there are rubber trees (*Hevea brasiliensis*), the lovely floral frangipani (*Plumeria rubra*), the durable rattan—a climbing palm found deep in Thai rainforests used for furniture—and the much-utilized bamboo (*Bambusa vulgaris*). In fact, Thailand is believed to have more species of bamboo than any country outside China, and its wood has been used for centuries in everything from buildings and tools to weapons and cooking utensils. You might even find yourself cruising down the river on a bamboo raft if you're touring in the north. Two other highly sought-after trees are the rosewood (*Dalbergia cochinchinensis*) and teak (*Tectona grandis*), popular for use in fine furniture due to their durability and beauty, much to the detriment of the forests. In the past, Thailand

© SUZANNE NAM

wildflowers in bloom

was a center of teak logging; now it is banned in all but controlled plantations in response to severely depleted resources. Today, the government has a policy to protect 15 percent of Thailand's land area as forest.

Other Vegetation

Flowers have long played an important role in Thai society, used as offerings at temples or spirit houses, in festivals such as the annual Loi Krathong celebration, and even as food in certain dishes. It's not surprising then that the country has over 25,000 species of flowers; the best-known variety is the orchid, Thailand's national floral symbol. Botanists have found there are 17,500 species of orchid in the world, and 1,150 of those species originated in Thailand's forests. Today there are a number of orchid farms throughout the country, dedicated to the breeding and export of this highly coveted flower.

Given the diversity of Thai cuisine, it's only natural the country is also home to a wide range of herbs and plants. Among the most

common are several varieties of basil, Kaffir lime, mint, pepper, chili, cumin, garlic, lemongrass, and ginger, many of which grow wild throughout the country, particularly in the mountainous north.

FAUNA
Mammals

Thailand is home to approximately 300 species of indigenous mammals, but most can be found in the country's national parks or wildlife sanctuaries, since poaching and development have drastically depleted their numbers in many areas of the country. These include tigers, leopards, elephants, bears, gaur (Indian bison), banteng (wild cattle), serow (an Asiatic goat-antelope), deer, pangolins, gibbons, macaques, tapirs, dolphins, and dugongs (sea cows). Forty of Thailand's 300 mammal species, including the clouded leopard, Malayan tapir, tiger, Irrawaddy dolphin, *goral,* jungle cat, dusky langur, and pileated gibbon, are on a number of international endangered-species lists.

Although once highly revered, elephants today are treated with far less respect in Thailand. Few travelers will escape a trip to the country without witnessing an elephant walking down a city street, mahout (trainer) perched atop ready to accept a few baht from those who would like to feed the exhausted animal. Many domesticated Asian elephants have been born and raised in captivity, put to work in the logging industry in rural villages. Using elephants for jobs like this is now illegal in Thailand, so their owners have found work in the many tourist camps that offer rides to foreign visitors. A small number of wild elephants do remain, however—mostly in national parks now that their native habitat is dwindling. Ironically, for centuries elephants were highly valued creatures in Thailand, used in battle to fight the Burmese on many occasions. A white elephant even features on the flag of the Royal Thai navy, and the Order of the White Elephant is one of the country's highest honors, bestowed by the king. Contrary to popular belief, white elephants are very rarely completely white, although the skin has to be very pale in certain areas for it to qualify as a genuine white elephant and thus a prized commodity.

Chances are that visitors will also encounter more than a few primates in Thailand, as there is no shortage of the crafty little fellows, whether they are hanging off the telephone lines in Lopburi, looking for handouts at temples, or stealing cameras from bewildered travelers. Species include white-handed *lar* and pileated gibbons, as well as different varieties of long- and short-tailed macaques and langurs.

On the other hand, traditional hunting and poaching for medicine have devastated Thailand's wild cat populations. The tiger is the largest and best-known of all Thailand's wildcats, with populations kept and bred in captivity by private collectors. The country's Western Forest Complex, which features 17,800 square kilometers of protected rainforest habitat, is currently home to 720 tigers, according to a study by Thailand's Department of National Parks, Wildlife, and Plant Conservation released in 2007. But Thailand's parks and wildlife reserves could hold up to 2,000 wild tigers, about three times their current level, if the government steps up efforts to control poaching. Using survey data from camera traps in the Huai Kha Khaeng Wildlife Sanctuary in 2004, researchers determined that the density of tigers in the rugged, hilly reserve about 300 kilometers west of Bangkok was three times lower than in comparable but better-protected tiger reserves in India. Many say the problem is that Thai law is too soft on tiger traffickers, imposing small fines rather than jail time on offenders. Tigers are mostly under threat due to habitat loss and poachers who sell their skins and body parts to medicinal and souvenir markets, mostly in China.

Bears in Thailand don't fare much better. There are two species found in the country, the Asiatic black bear and the Malayan sun bear. The black bear is bigger, recognized by the white V on its neck, and found all over the country. The sun bear is smaller and more aggressive, commonly found in Thailand's southern region. Although prohibited by law, bear cubs are often taken from the wild as

one of hundreds of amphibian species in Thailand

pets, while older bears are known to have been poached for their gallbladders and paws to be used in traditional Asian medicines.

Reptiles and Amphibians

Thailand features around 313 reptiles and 107 amphibians, a population that includes 163 species of snakes, 85 of which are venomous. Among these are the common cobra (of which there are six subspecies), king cobra (hamadryad), banded krait (three species), Malayan viper, green viper, and Russell's pit viper. Thailand's largest snake is the reticulated python, which can grow to a length of 15 meters and is found in the rainforests of northern Thailand. There are also many lizards throughout the country, including geckos and black jungle monitors.

Birds

Bird-watchers will be kept busy in Thailand, given that the country is home to over 1,000 recorded resident and migrating species. Distribution varies according to geography and climate. Among the more predominant species are various types of partridge, quail, pheasant, fireback, duck, goose, woodpecker, barbet, hornbill, trogon, kingfisher, bee-eater, cuckoo, *malkoha,* parrot, parakeet, swiftlet, needletail, owl, frogmouth, dove, nightjar, pigeon, crane, crank, sand piper, jacana, plover, gull, tern, kite, eagle, vulture, falcon, cormorant, broadbill, oriole, flycatcher, fantail, robin, forktail, starling, bulbul, warbler, babbler, laughing thrush, sunbird, and spiderhunter, to name a few. One of the best ways to go bird-watching is by heading to one of Thailand's national parks.

Hornbills and kingfishers are two of the most popular species due to their unique features. Thailand has 15 species of kingfishers, and most of them have bright plumage. Kingfishers typically perch in trees in an upright exposed posture, plunging into the water for food. Some species, such as the white-throated kingfisher, inhabit inland areas. They're commonly seen around rice fields looking for lizards, frogs, and insects, and they will amaze even the most jaded of nature lovers, providing an absolutely stunning sight when the sunlight hits their shiny blue feathers. Hornbills, meanwhile, make their nests in holes in trees and are easily recognizable by their hooked beaks. Of the 54 species of hornbill worldwide, Thailand is home to 13 varieties. Hornbills are primarily frugivorous (fruit eaters), although they will take small reptiles, insects, and even other smaller birds when they are molting or rearing young.

Loss of habitat due to human development is the greatest threat to Thailand's birds. For instance, shrimp farms along the coast are robbing waterfowl of their intertidal diets, while the popularity of bird's nest soup has led to the overharvesting of swiftlet nests in the south. Of the country's roughly 1,000 bird species, about 30 are listed as being critically endangered, which means they face possible extinction within 50 years.

Serious bird-watchers will want to check with the Bird Conservation Society of Thailand (www.bcst.or.th), an excellent source of information on the latest sightings, tours, and data.

History

Thailand has long been a cosmopolitan kingdom that played an important role in international trade and worked to defend its existence against its neighbors. It should come as no surprise that they were able to use their well-practiced diplomatic skills to maintain their sovereignty even as most of their neighbors became de facto European colonies. Thailand's greatest challenge has not been maintaining its identity or becoming a major economic player; rather, it has struggled for almost 100 years with different interpretations of "progress," and particularly what that means for politics and governance.

WHO ARE THE THAI?

There is evidence of human activity in the mainland of Southeast Asia dating back 180,000 years. There are signs of civilization dating back at least 6,000 years, but the area did not see significant growth until the development of rice agriculture and bronze tools circa 2500 B.C.

Some people believe that the Thai people were originally from southwestern China and migrated to Southeast Asia. Some people believe that they originated in Vietnam and spread north and west to China, India, and Burma, and then southwest to Laos and Thailand. Although the question is not entirely settled, it is known that they were influenced by the Chinese, both genetically and culturally. There were also significant Indian influences. By the eighth century A.D., there were a number of related peoples who shared similar languages and cultures on the mainland of Southeast

Asia. They were distinct from other groups on the mainland, particularly the Khmer, the Mon, and the Burmese. While many of them lived in what we now call Thailand, there were also settlements in Vietnam and the Malay Peninsula as well.

THAILAND? SIAM? IT'S COMPLICATED . . .

The larger discussion about the differences between ethnicity and nationality and how they are influenced by language is beyond the scope of this book. However, because of the way those ideas shaped Thailand's later history, some explanation is provided.

Tai is the language of many of the peoples who resided in Thailand, Vietnam, and Malaysia. The word itself means "free." The Tai written language is based on Mon and Khmer, but the spoken language is based on the Indian languages Sanskrit and Pali. We will refer to the language for the rest of this section as "Thai" in keeping with the modern convention.

The word *syam* is of Khmer origin and is first recorded in the 12th century in the temple complex at Angkor Wat. It means "dark brown" and refers to the Thai peoples who were vassals of the Khmer at that point. Even after the Thai peoples won their independence, that word endured as a descriptor for the people. Hence, "Siam" eventually became the name of the country in the 19th century.

However, like many modern nations, Thailand's borders have changed through the centuries. Further, multiple Thai kingdoms co-existed with each other at certain points. We will refer to the kingdoms by their names but the people of those kingdoms as "the Thai."

It should also be noted that for much of Thailand's modern history, there was significant migration from southern China, particularly during the 19th century. Although many eventually returned to China, a large population stayed, most of whom became assimilated into Siam's population. Thus, while the majority of Siam's population was indeed Thai-speaking, Chinese was a significant minority language.

EARLY KINGDOMS AND INFLUENCES
Ban Chiang

There are signs of a well-established stable civilization on the Khorat Plateau in Northeast Thailand near Laos. It's believed that it was settled by 4000 B.C. Although it is widely held that the Bronze Age did not begin until 3500–3000 B.C. and was confined to the civilizations in China and Mesopotamia, bronze and iron tools and utensils have been found at Ban Chiang dating back before that time. Elaborately decorated ceramic vessels, silk, stone, and glass beads as well as printed textiles dating to the same period have also been found here. Scholars are not in agreement about whether this indicates migration of an established civilization into Ban Chiang or whether the inhabitants developed these skills while in Southeast Asia. However, it can be reasonably asserted that this provides evidence that these early inhabitants were involved in some trade. It has been theorized that Ban Chiang may have suffered from overfarming by 2000 B.C., a development which might have necessitated the migration to the Chao Phraya River Valley.

Dvaravati

The Dvaravati period lasted from approximately the 1st century B.C. to the 11th century A.D. During this time, the Mon people migrated from India through Burma into an area from northern Siam to the west half of the Chao Phraya River Valley. Most probably the area had already been exposed to Indian culture, particularly the idea of the divinity of kings, styles of art and architecture, political structures, and Hinduism, including Hindu literature.

Although little is known about this period, we do know that Buddhism came to Siam at this point. In addition to the Mon migration, there was also movement from the inhabitants of Tibet, Burma and China into central and northern Thailand.

The Dvaravati kingdom disappears from history by the 11th century, possibly as a result of conflict with the powerful Khmer empire.

The Mon were assimilated into the larger Thai civilization, but they persist in modern times as an independent influence in Burma.

Srivijaya

Srivijaya was a Buddhist trading empire that arose in the seventh century. It controlled the Strait of Malacca and the Sunda Strait. Because these two points were essential connections in the spice route, Srivijaya's dominion over them made them a powerful force in the region. It overlapped in time with the Dvaravati but was centered in the Malay Peninsula and southern Thailand.

Sources on Srivijaya's origins are limited, but it is believed that their first centers were Palembang and Jambi in Suvarnadvipa, otherwise known as the "gold land" in central-south Sumatra. By the end of the seventh century, Kedah and Perak on the Malay Peninsula and Perlis on the Kra Isthmus were key vassal states.

The wealth from their trade activities facilitated their patronage of Buddhist learning, and Srivijaya became known as a center of Buddhist scholarship. In 671, the Chinese Buddhist traveler I-Ching reported that he had spent six months in Srivijaya, studying Sanskrit in a "walled city inhabited with a thousand monks." According to him, the Mulasarvastivada Nikaya, the Hinayana canon in Sanskrit, was popular, but Mahayana Buddhism was new to the empire.

Mahayana Buddhism grew in importance in the empire during the next century, particularly after Srivijaya was visited by Vajrabodhi, abbot of the famous Mahayana Buddhist cloister of Nalanda in Bihar, India, and founder of the Yogacara sect. Atisa, a reformer of Tibetan Buddhism, also studied in Srivijaya between 1011 and 1023.

As trade between China and India grew in the 11th century, so did the power of the Srivijayan trade networks. Not surprisingly, other kingdoms coveted their control of key positions, particularly the kingdoms of East Java and the Cholas of south India. The Cholas attacked in 1025 and captured Srivijaya's

maharaja. Srivijaya never recovered, and by 1286 what remained of it was conquered by the East-Javanese Singhasari king Kertanagara.

Khmer

The Khmer Empire was a Hindu kingdom established in the early ninth century in what is now northern Cambodia by Jayavarman II. It was the primary rival of the Thai kingdoms for centuries. During its primacy, it was the power center of Southeast Asia.

The Khmer city of Angkor Thom arose after 900. Filled with temples, palaces, and towers and protected by walls and moats, all decorated with details of Hindu deities, it rivaled both contemporary London and, more importantly, Paris—all the more impressive when it is considered that the Khmer built it in the middle of a rainforest.

Construction on the more famous Angkor Wat temple complex began in 879 but was completed under the patronage of Suryavarman II in the early 12th century. In addition, Suryavarman II also increased the holdings of the empire, extending it into Thailand, Burma, Malaysia, and Vietnam. He also established diplomatic relations with China in 1119.

Conflict with Vietnam in the late 12th century weakened the Khmer. Jayavarman VII repulsed them in 1181, and under his rule there was a brief revival of Angkor Wat and renewed conquest, but after his death the empire began to lose its holdings again. In 1431 they were sacked by Ayutthaya and were never again a regional force.

Lanna Thai

Lanna Thai was the dominant kingdom in northern Thailand 1259–1558. It was established during the reign of King Mengrai (1259–1317). The phrase *lan na* means "land of a million rice paddies." It made its capital first at Chiang Rai and then at Chiang Mai. A successful alliance with the southern kingdom of Sukhothai helped fend off both the Mongols in 1301 and then Ayutthaya in 1372.

Until the 15th century, Lanna was characterized by alternating periods of stability and unrest. The kingdom peaked under Tilokaracha (1441–1487), but soon after his death it was under constant threat from Burma until it finally fell to them in 1558.

Sukhothai

The word *sukhothai* literally means "dawn of happiness." The Sukhothai Kingdom was founded in 1238 by King Indraditya and affiliated princes to defend against the Khmer empire. The kingdom was defined by Indraditya and his son Ramkhamhaeng. The latter ruled 1275–1317 and was not only a skilled military leader but also a savvy diplomat who established relations with Chiang Mai and Chiang Sen as well as China, Burma, India, and Ceylon (now Sri Lanka). At the time, Ceylon was the seat of the influential school of Theravada Buddhism, and this came to be the dominant religion of the Sukhothai Kingdom. The Thai alphabet was also created under Ramkhamhaeng's auspices in 1283. Sukhothai was known for its great works of art and architecture, including temples, palaces, and statues, many of which are revered to this day.

Ramkhamhaeng continues to be held as a model Thai ruler who embodies the Buddhist ideals of kindness, mercy, and fairness. However, his heirs lacked his talents, and the kingdom declined after his death. By 1365, it came under the control of Ayutthaya.

Ayutthaya

Ayutthaya was founded by U Thong, later known as Ramathibodi I, in 1350. It was under Ayutthaya that much of modern Thailand was first united. The kings were held to be *devaraja*, or god-kings, according to the Hindu tradition.

Politically, the kingdom utilized a system of ministers, including ones for local government, finance, agriculture, and the royal household. Additionally, laws were codified to discourage revenge and move toward rational justice.

Within its first century, Ayutthaya established itself as a key player in Southeast Asia, first conquering Sukhothai, then Chiang Mai, and finally the Khmer empire itself. For close

to a century, they enjoyed a period of relative peace and great prosperity.

It was during this period that the kingdom first made contact with European powers. Shortly after its conquest of Malacca, Portugal established relations with Ayutthaya in 1512. Portugal knew that Ayutthaya was already an important trading power in Southeast Asia, and they saw the kingdom as an opportunity to further their interests in Asia. Ayutthaya saw the benefit of increased trade as well but did not limit themselves to one European nation. Relations were subsequently established with the Dutch in 1605, Great Britain in 1612, Denmark in 1621, and France in 1662. These diverse relationships would be a political asset to the Thai two centuries later.

The vacuum created by the defeat of the Khmer was filled by the Burmese. Ayutthaya battled with Burma in 1538, 1549, 1563, and 1569. During the last conflict, the Ayutthaya prince Naresuan was taken as a long-term hostage of the Burmese and raised with their crown prince. By all accounts, the relationship between the two combined the worst of sibling and political rivalry. Nevertheless, Naresuan was asked to lead a mission into Ayutthaya territory for the Burmese. He surprised everyone by turning against Burma and later killing the Burmese crown prince in hand-to-hand combat. Naresuan reigned over Ayutthaya from 1590 to 1605, and the Burmese threat was lifted for the time being.

By the 18th century, Ayutthaya was a key participant in a robust trade network and was held to be one of the most cosmopolitan cities in the world. When Japan opened for trade, Thai animal hides were in great demand. Rice, spices, sappanwood, eaglewood, lac, and benzoin were also popular items. Ayutthaya also imported Indian cloth, luxury goods, firearms, and metals, in particular silver.

Trade was not an official or royal enterprise. The Siamese merchants were able to independently manage trade, but they frequently used royal commissioned ships. This was a sophisticated trading scheme that utilized Chinese and Sino-Siamese crews and networks of Chinese,

Sino-Siamese, and Muslim traders. Siamese merchants recognized early on that including European nations into their networks would increase demand, prices, and profits.

It is during this period that the strange episode with "Phaulkon the Greek" took place. Not only did non-Thais work extensively in commerce, they also worked in government. There was even some preference to give certain jobs to certain nationals, particularly the royal guards, who were usually Japanese. Constantine Phaulkon, a Greek with connections to France and later Japan, made his way into the court of Ayutthaya through a series of fortunate encounters and manipulation. He rose to become the leading minister (some accounts say prime minister) under King Narai (1656–1688). During this time, some conservative elements of the court were concerned about the growing European and Asian influences that were diluting both their power and income. When Phaulkon went so far as to promise the French court of Louis XIV that he would convince Narai to convert to Catholicism, he was accused of treason and later executed in 1688.

The conservatives hardened into reactionaries and used this episode as an excuse to significantly limit non-Thai activity in the kingdom and, to a lesser extent, in their trading networks. It should be noted that even during this period, Chinese immigrants were still allowed to participate, probably more fully than other non-Thai groups, both as laborers and in administration.

The internal conflicts at the court and in the realm overall engrossed the government, and they missed the signs of the resurgent Burmese threat. As such, they were unable to respond in time to stop the Burmese attack in 1767. The result was that Ayutthaya was utterly destroyed. Thousands were killed, and many priceless artifacts and examples of architecture were lost forever.

Taksin and Thonburi

Taksin, a Sino-Siamese governor from Western Siam who rose to power through the military ranks, defended Ayutthaya against the Burmese, but when it was evident that Ayutthaya was going to fall, he gathered his followers and established a base near the Cambodian border. After the Burmese troops retreated, he retook the Thai plain. In addition to setting up an orderly government, he also distributed food to the starving, devastated population. He led an attack against the Burmese and defeated them in battle. While the Burmese may eventually have been able to successfully fend off Taksin's forces, Burma was subsequently invaded by China. Taksin and his followers exploited that distraction and decisively defeated the Burmese. Later, he and his generals expanded the territory of the kingdom into what is now Cambodia and Laos.

Because of the devastation Ayutthaya suffered, it was no longer suitable as the capital of the kingdom. Taksin made the decision that it would be easier to build a new city at Thonburi than to rebuild Ayutthaya.

What Happened to Taksin?

Taksin was revered for his salvation of the Thai people, but he is not the ancestor of the subsequent (and current) ruling dynasty. His fall from power, and the rise of his general, Buddha Yodfa Chulaloke, also known as Chao Phraya Chakri, is a subject of controversy. The simplest explanation may be, as one writer put it, that military success often leads to political strife.

Although Taksin was sponsored at the Ayutthaya court at a young age and grew to achieve a military rank and a post as governor, he was not from the royal line or any of the aristocratic houses that sometimes supplied successors to the throne. We can only speculate, but it is probably fair to say that under normal circumstances he would not have become the ruler of Ayutthaya. These, however, were not normal times.

Within 15 years of his ascension to the throne, Taksin is said to have demanded to be worshipped as a Buddha and to have meted out cruel and arbitrary punishments, including executions, for what we might today consider minor offenses. He was perhaps suffering from a prolonged mental breakdown, or he might have grown megalomaniacal.

A few historians have suggested that Taksin's breakdown may have been caused by his awareness that he was an outsider and that the conservative factions of his court distrusted him, particularly because his father was Chinese. There are almost always traditionalists in any court or government, but this explanation is more appropriate for the nation-building 19th century and the nationalist early 20th century. Further, many wealthy Chinese had married into well-connected Thai families during this period, including that of Chao Phraya Chakri.

According to most accounts, Chao Phraya Chakri was in the middle of a campaign in Cambodia when relations in Thonburi broke down and Taksin was overthrown. He returned to Thonburi, put the coup down, and then took power himself, eventually naming himself king. By all accounts, he ordered the execution of Taksin in 1782. According to some, Taksin was beheaded; according to others, he was put in a velvet sack and beaten to death. Yet another version states that a double was beaten to death in his place and that Taksin was spirited away to the mountains, where he lived until 1825.

If we are not certain about Taksin's fate, what can we say about Chao Phraya Chakri's motivations? Many popular histories have posited that he made himself king because it was his duty to the Thai people. There are two legends that suggest that he was fated to be king. The most popular is that the king of Burma declared that to him during a personal meeting on the battlefield. Another legend states that as children, both Taksin and Chao Phraya Chakri were told that they would grow up to be kings.

Chao Phraya Chakri could not have taken the throne without the support of powerful interests at the court and in the military, so it is fair to say that he was "made" king, after a fashion. Also, he was perhaps one of a handful of men who held positions of power and influence in both the military and government that would make him appropriate for the throne.

Despite these dynamics, it would be naive to assert that he was acting without any personal ambition. This insight shouldn't detract from the achievements of either his reign or his dynasty's, but it should highlight that they were the work of people, not fate.

The Chakri Dynasty and Bangkok

Chao Phraya Chakri, later renamed Rama I, moved the capitol to Bangkok, in part because Thonburi was still not completed and in part perhaps as a way of separating his reign from Taksin's. He repulsed another Burmese attack in 1785. From this point on, although there would be later hostilities with Burma, they would never again present a serious threat to the Thai. Once the Burmese were neutralized, Bangkok began to expand its borders. By the end of the First Reign, the kingdom included all of modern Laos and Cambodia and parts of Burma, Vietnam, Malaysia, and China.

Bangkok was consciously styled after Ayutthaya and became a worldly city at the center of a sophisticated culture. During this period there was an intentional effort to "Siamize" other works of art and literature. While they may have subsumed elements of an Indian storyline in verse and paintings, the characters are clearly Siamese.

The Bangkok court also consciously cultivated what might be termed a "Buddhist" style of rule, inviting open discussion and attempting to deliver judgments based on dispassionate Buddhist ideals as opposed to human passions. At the same time, there was a tolerance for the other non-Buddhist religions and cultures represented by the inhabitants of the city. At this time, classics from other Asian countries were translated into Thai, particularly the Chinese *Romance of the Three Kingdoms,* the Mon *Ratchathirat,* the Javan *Dalang* and *Inao,* the Indian *Unarut,* the Persian *Duodecagon,* and the Pali–Sri Lankan *Mahavamsa.* The translations were not only in prose but in less elaborate language than that of the Ayutthaya period and thus more accessible to more readers.

The trade that was interrupted by the Burmese wars was purposefully revived in the

First Reign, particularly with China. During the Second Reign (1809–1824), under Buddha Loetla Nabhalai, Rama I's eldest son, who ruled as Rama II, Bangkok maintained diplomatic relations with China, Vietnam, Burma, and Malaysia. It also received representatives from both Portugal and the East India Company.

A Problem with Succession

Although there was some bias in the Thai court to keep the succession of monarchs within the current king's family and to favor the sons of the king's official queens, the succession to the throne did not follow the hard-and-fast rule of primogeniture; there was an election of sorts by the king's advisors and court. Rama II's older son Phra Maha Jessadarajachao, although not born to a queen, had a good claim on the throne, was experienced in state affairs, and was popular with some of the more traditional elements in the court. Another son, Mongkut, was Rama II's oldest son by his queen but much younger than Nang Klao. Mongkut was seen to have the intellect and character that a monarch required even at an early age. However, although he may have had a better technical claim, he was too young to have established the supporters at court his older brother had. Many historians believe that Rama II strongly encouraged Mongkut to enter a monastic order so that he would be shielded from the machinations and dangers usually attendant to a succession fight. Whatever the motivations, Mongkut was in a monastery when his brother, now known as Rama III, became king. Mongkut used his time wisely, not only studying Buddhism in depth but also mastering Western languages, politics, and science. His thorough understanding of the Western world would prove to be of great value.

While the First and Second Reigns saw the expansion and solidification of the Thai kingdom, the Third Reign (1824–1851) saw rebellion from within and new opportunities from without. Both Vientiane (1827–1828) and Malay (1831–1832, 1838–1839) rebelled against Thai authority. More uprisings occurred in Cambodia (1833–1834, 1841–1842, and 1845–1847). Most of these rebellions were put down, but they were a frequent characteristic of the Third Reign.

During this period, Bangkok strengthened relations both with the Chinese and the Chinese government. Trade became even more important to the Thai economy, as did Chinese immigrant labor. The new immigrants were hired both as tax farmers and paid laborers.

Perhaps in light of the military rebellions, Bangkok began to increase contacts with the Western world, signing treaties with the British East India Company in 1826 and the United States in 1833. While this was done with an eye to affirming Bangkok's trading positions, conservative elements in the court frowned on these changes.

Relations with Europe

Although the Thai had always interacted with European nations and traders, things became more complicated in the late 18th and early 19th centuries. After the founding of Singapore in 1819, the British believed that developing trade relations with the Malay Peninsula and Bangkok were vital to Singapore's success. However, most Europeans saw the trade in Bangkok as byzantine and corrupt. The Thai were aware of this and realized how such a viewpoint could be used to justify military action against it.

When relations between Kedah and Bangkok broke down, the Sultan of Kedah sought protection from the British at Penang. This matter complicated British and Singaporean efforts to begin diplomatic and trade relations with the Thai in 1821. In the end, Bangkok agreed only to recognize the British acquisition of Penang—which had been completed four decades earlier.

By the middle of the 19th century, Western nations demanded more open trade, diplomatic relations, and extraterritorial legal protections for their nationals in Bangkok. In 1850 the American John Balestier and the Briton Sir James Brooke tried unsuccessfully to negotiate terms with Siam. They were both angered and offended that the Thai refused to, as they saw it, negotiate in good faith.

statue of King Rama IV in Bangkok

Why might the Thai, well-known for their shrewd diplomacy, suddenly become so hard to work with? Because Rama III's health was failing and his court knew that a succession fight was looming. In light of the colonial incursions by Western powers in neighboring lands, they did not want to enter into any negotiations that might compromise a new monarch. Although the Thai negotiators were publicly obstructionist, they sent word to their contacts abroad that they should be patient until the succession was settled.

By the time Mongkut assumed the throne as Rama IV, European powers were willing to use force to obtain the terms they wanted. In 1855, Bangkok signed the Bowring Treaty. Although Siam felt that they could not change the terms being forced on them to reduce trade duties, they made the calculation that the increased traffic would make up for those losses. They were also able to continue to control opium, gambling, alcohol, and the lottery, activities that were not within the purview of the treaty. It should be noted that while the Thai on the whole benefitted, it did hurt the livelihoods of the Chinese minority that dominated trade. Although they were powerful and influential, it was believed that it was better to alienate them than to risk conflict with Europe.

Having seen the influence of the British in Burma and the French in Vietnam, Bangkok sought to limit the influence of any one party by opening itself to multiple countries. The Thai not only played countries off each other but also exploited competing entities in the same country, particularly in Britain, France, and their colonial offshoots.

MODERN TIMES
Mongkut, Chulalongkorn, and Modernization

When people think of Thai history, they think of Mongkut, and not only because he was immortalized in *The King and I* (a sore subject for many modern Thais). His knowledge of Western methods and thought and his ability to meet European nations on their terms was invaluable at this moment in history. When Europe called Bangkok corrupt or backward, it was understood why. More to the point, the Thai court understood that this perceived corruption and the potentially negative impact it would have on international business was the reason Europe demanded changes and why Siam (and other countries) agreed in principle to open themselves to Western suggestions.

What did Europe find so objectionable? First, official government business was conducted in the homes of the nobles in office. Europeans characterized this as at best unproductive and at worst inhumane. Justice, as in so many other places, could be biased and influenced by money and power sometimes more than by written law. Civil administration was influenced by nepotism, and, even worse, officials received a cut of the business they helped facilitate and transact.

It might also be fair to say that the government was neither transparent nor efficient. Branches of government (Mahatthai in the north, Kalahom in the south and Phrakhlang along the coast) performed multiple duties, including governance, taxation, raising troops, administering law, and sometimes most importantly, organizing labor for public works. Not surprisingly, families in the higher offices of these branches did their best to make sure power and position stayed within the family.

Had it simply been a monarch and his court in charge, Mongkut may have made all of the sweeping changes immediately demanded by Europe. However, even an absolute monarchy has its limitations. At this point, there were enough vested interests in Bangkok's bureaucratic aristocracy that Mongkut could not simply declare change. He knew that Western reforms would be felt and resisted most keenly by them. His strategy was to move gradually toward them. Unfortunately, he died before he could complete those reforms.

Mongkut was succeeded by his son Chulalongkorn, who ruled as Rama V. He was educated by Western instructors (Anna Leonowens perhaps being the most famous), and continued his father's reforms. Despite his training and the groundwork laid by Mongkut's administration, Chulalongkorn's reign is punctuated by a humiliating loss made palatable only because Siam's neighbors were faring much worse in the evolving new world order.

In 1893, Siam was maneuvered out of Laos east of the Mekong by both French manipulation and British inaction. Although the Siamese were rightfully indignant that they lost so much of their kingdom (especially in light of the fact that they were lured into a conflict that required them to defend themselves, and that their allies allowed it to happen to maintain a "balance of power" in Southeast Asia), Siam has also been hailed for its work during this period. As embarrassing as it was to lose parts of their kingdom, it was a better fate than many in Asia, who were being colonized wholesale.

Chulalongkorn toured Europe in 1897 and saw for himself how uneven the process of modernization had proceeded there, particularly in the East End of London. This, perhaps, enabled him to begin his own Thai modernization campaign in earnest. As part of the modernization initiative, much of Siam's landscape was changed to meet demands for rice production to feed other Asian countries, particularly India and China. In less than 50 years, from the late 1850s to the turn of the 20th century, the volume of rice exported increased by a factor of 11, and the price of rice doubled. During that period, the area that was cultivated for rice production grew from 928,000 hectares to 1.44 million hectares. Thousands of households contributed to this by expanding the land they cultivated, clearing and planting new land, and utilizing more intensive farming methods. This was possible because debt-bondage and slavery were restricted, and corvée labor abolished by 1905.

As a result, the rural population increased, spread out, and became more mobile. While they were less controlled than before by their local nobility, they were more vulnerable to government intrusion. At this time, land also became more valuable, although probably not yet more valuable than labor, and there was more economic variation in rural villages as some farmers prospered more than others.

During this period, public education and particularly village schools were promoted. While the idea of public education was not unique to Siam, it was more successfully implemented here than it was in many other countries during this time because the royal family made it a visible part of their domestic policy. By end of the Fifth Reign, the kingdom was committed to universal compulsory education, but this goal was not fully realized for several decades.

Although there was a genuine desire to improve the education of all, the goal was not to improve prospects equally. Instead of importing a foreign tutor for his children as his father had, Rama V instead began the tradition of sending his children abroad to be educated. His four oldest sons were sent overseas in 1885. This was emulated by the elite families of Thailand. There were also special private schools and academies established during this period. The King's School was founded in 1897 to help prepare students for studies overseas. While other schools (the Suan Kulap School, the Civil Service School, and the Military School, in particular) had special mandates to train students for civil or military service, many of them were explicitly intended for noble or royal relatives. When some commoners did enroll, the fees were increased to a level that only the elite could afford.

Chinese immigration grew during this period because of unrest in southern China. The new immigrants found work with established Sino-Siamese residents and as substitutes for Siamese corvée labor. Generally, this new population stayed in urban areas and found work in trade and government. Assimilation was easier when only Chinese men immigrated and later took Siamese wives and fathered Sino-Siamese children. There was more hostility when Chinese women accompanied the men later because this allowed the immigrant population to marry among itself.

Ironically, the dependence on Chinese immigrants for labor, combined with their large numbers, may have led to some of the beginnings of later mistrust. While earlier waves of migration could be controlled by co-opting leaders into their system of bureaucracy and delegating responsibility for those populations to them, the numbers and diversity of this new wave of immigrants made that strategy unworkable. Thus when trouble broke out, the government used force. The sugar tracts east of Bangkok were particularly vulnerable, and in 1870 Chinese miners almost won control of the town of Ranong during a riot. Further, in 1889, Chinese gangs battled each other in the center of Bangkok for three days. These episodes and others like them made the government fear that Chinese laborers could bring Bangkok to a standstill. After such a strike did in fact stop business in Bangkok for three days in June 1910, Rama V himself warned that "[the Chinese] influence is tremendous."

Despite the upheavals this population would experience, they were major contributors to the creation of both modern Bangkok and Siam. In addition to their contributions in commerce and government, it has also been suggested that the farming expertise of the Chinese immigrants was responsible for the transformation of the Chao Phraya delta in the 19th century. This transformation of the landscape increased the area that rice could be farmed on and positioned Siam to take advantage of the boom in demand for food in Asia as colonial cities and plantations were built and populations grew.

Nascent Nationalism

Vajiravudh succeeded his father as Rama VI. Like many of his brothers, he had been educated in Europe. It is not surprising, then, that his reign is remembered for taking the first steps toward defining the Thai "nation." But as so many other countries experienced during the early 20th century, the elite classes were beginning to embrace not only the idea of nationalism but also democratic or republican reforms. It can be said that the monarchy wanted to have it both ways: continued emphasis on hierarchy with limited reforms to serve the "national" interests. What Vajiravudh and his successors were to find was that Siam was progressively less willing to accept change in everything but its political institutions.

What was the Sixth Reign's idea of the nation? Ideally, it was the triumvirate of nation, religion, and monarch (*chat-satsana-phrama-hakasat*). The nation could be seen as composed of similar people who were unified in their desire for the good of the many. It was something that its members should be willing to defend even with their lives. Not surprisingly, during this period the issue of ethnicity assumed greater importance, as it did around the world.

Another worldwide phenomenon that touched the Thais at this time was xenophobia. If it is a common identity that is the primary unifier of those within the nation, those who are different can be a threat. Although Thailand was long home to different ethnic and language groups, the Chinese, by virtue of their numbers and importance in trade and bureaucracy, attracted the most negative attention. Rama VI himself wrote an infamous pamphlet called "The Jews of the East." In it he accused the Chinese of being disloyal, entitled, and overly reverential of wealth while clinging to their ethnic identity. Their relationship to Siam's economy was compared to "so many vampires who steadily suck dry an unfortunate victim's life blood."

This was one of the low points in Thai history. However, it's useful to examine it not only to understand internal Thai relations but also Siam's role in the larger world. As repugnant as it is to modern readers, anti-Semitism was a popular political and social orientation in early 20th-century Europe, particularly among the aristocratic elite. Further, the British and other European nations saw the Chinese as a commercial threat. By the 19th century, Europe had made so many breakthroughs in technology and conquest that they perceived themselves to be the ascendant leader into the future and China as the decadent symbol of a failed past. Many of the Thai nobility and royal family, including the king, would have been educated with these people from a young age, and it follows that many of them adapted this world view to their special circumstances.

If his father and grandfather in many ways were the right monarchs for their times, Vajiravudh may have been the wrong one for his. His extravagance, suspected homosexuality, and Western style made him seem in some ways too foreign to many of the people he governed, which is ironic given his promotion of national unity. He also seemed at times more interested in the arts than affairs of state. Further, he appointed some of his favorites, many of whom came from the common class, to positions of importance in his cabinet. This was a break with the precedent his father had established in which his well-educated uncles and brothers would normally have filled the majority of the top posts. Although many questioned the motivations behind these appointments, they helped to establish an example that was later used in subsequent reigns to allow commoners access to government positions.

The country was still smarting over its 1893 territorial losses when World War I broke out. Many of Vajiravudh's advisors opposed his decision to declare war on Germany and send a token force to fight for the Allies (which included Great Britain and France) in 1917. However, this ended up yielding important rewards. Not only was Siam able to alter its treaties with Britain and France to its advantage, it also earned a seat at the Treaty of Versailles and became a founding member of the League of Nations.

Those achievements are best appreciated in hindsight. Post–World War I contemporaries found Vajiravudh increasingly more a burden than an asset to Thailand. He was not the first extravagant ruler, but in light of the post–World War I economic depression, his continued lavish expenditures did nothing to endear him to a populace that was already beginning to question the utility of an absolute monarchy.

After the war, the demand for rice and silver, two of Bangkok's primary exports, declined. The steps taken to address the falloff led to deficits and borrowing. In addition, some of the promises the royal family had made in the years before the war were beginning to look thin. Although education was a stated priority, it took only 3 percent of the budget; 23 percent went to military spending and more than 10 percent to royal expenditures under the auspices of the Privy Purse and the Ministry of the Palace.

Political tensions were rising, and nationalism began to take hold in Southeast Asia. While the Malay and Lao populations in Bangkok were easily controlled, the larger and more influential Chinese were not. They were angered over Japanese activities in China and staged anti-Japanese boycotts and protests. Bangkok also became a focus of Vietnamese, Lao, Cambodian, and Burmese nationalist activity against their European colonizers. The Thai government was sympathetic, but they were leery about alienating the European nations.

Thai students who returned from abroad—particularly France—were increasingly dissatisfied with Bangkok's progress toward modernization. Two such student leaders, Pridi Phanomyong and Plaek Phibun Songkhram, were to play important roles later in Thai history.

The End of Absolute Rule

Vajiravudh died in 1925 only days after his queen gave birth to a girl. He was succeeded by his youngest brother, Prajadhipok. Prajadhipok was the youngest of Chulalongkorn's sons and the second-youngest of all of Chulalongkorn's children. Because of his birth order, it had been unlikely that he would inherit the throne. He chose a military career and earned commissions in both the British and Thai armies. By 1925, however, many of his older brothers had died, and he was the logical successor.

Before his death, King Vajiravudh had realized that the government needed to be ready for democracy, but he advised caution and a slow course. The Advisory Committee of the Privy Council was established in 1927. That experiment ended as the economic situation improved and criticism of the government subsided. However, nascent activity among students and "resident aliens" continued.

Prajadhipok was initially heralded as a reformer who would finally bring the political reforms for which the Thais had been agitating. Initially, he removed Vajiravudh's favorites from office and announced that his government was considering economic and political reforms with the express purpose of gaining the population's favor. However, the only concrete actions he took were toward uniting the court and trying to create a check against an imprudent monarch. He created both a Supreme Council of State and a Privy Council, but he filled both bodies with members of the royal family. As a contemporary Thai journalist observed, these bodies were more likely to create legislation that would benefit the upper classes from which they drew their members rather than the population at large.

Prajadhipok had only been on the throne for seven years when the bloodless coup replaced an absolutist with a constitutional monarchy. While he has been accused of being too incremental and not sensitive to the needs of the overall population, the coup clearly reflects forces that had been building for decades. The immediate instigators were a group of young students who met in 1927 in Paris and agreed to the principles of moving to a constitutional monarchy and using the state as an instrument to initiate economic and social progress for all. Among this group of idealistic young students was Plaek Phibun Songkhram, a student in one of the military colleges, and Pridi Phanomyong, a gifted law student. These two would later be archrivals, but for now they were unified in their desire to bring Thailand into the future.

There were two primary forces in this group. The first studied the political philosophy popular in Europe. Their central belief was that the state could be a positive force for change. The other group was disgruntled by the growing feeling that the Thai government was, for all its lip service to progress, still more concerned with the upper class than the majority of the country.

The press, both popular and underground, was critical of the absolutist monarchy. By the early 1920s their position had evolved from criticism to advocacy for reforms: independence, public safety, economic planning, equal rights, and universal education.

Finally, even the business community saw the current system of government as a hindrance to the economy, especially as the country suffered through the Great Depression. When business leaders petitioned for the government to take measures to improve the economy, they were met with skepticism. While modern-day readers may find that surprising, in the 1920s and 1930s such economic planning was seen as dangerously reminiscent of the communist Soviet Union's central economic planning.

While the coup may have been inevitable, Prajadhipok's government's reaction to the economic conditions exacerbated frustration with the status quo. The government chose to balance the budget by cutting the funds of officials, reducing spending on education, and raising taxes. When corruption was discovered in several parts of the government, penalties were limited to the lower ranks. When even the upper ranks of the government began to take exception to official policies, the response became reactionary. Criticism was firmly discouraged, and some transgressions were punishable by death or deportation. The regime also closed certain newspapers and threatened critical journalists.

In 1932 the People's Party had attracted about 100 members, many of whom were in the military. By the morning on June 24, 1932, the party had arrested the commander of the royal guard and members of the royal family and declared that the era of absolute monarchy was over. There was one shooting episode, but no one was killed. People from all walks of life throughout Thailand welcomed the announcement. For his part, Prajadhipok had decided against resistance in favor of cooperating with the People's Party.

Both Prajadhipok and the People's Party decided that they would be more successful working together, at least publicly. The People's Party took some of the king's former senior officials into their Assembly, and the constitution was drafted to include a greater role for the king than they had originally planned. Most importantly, it was arranged that the king would present the constitution as if he and his advisors had drafted it themselves.

Most popular histories assert that the reason Prajadhipok ultimately abdicated in 1935 was that he felt he was powerless to effect changes to the constitution that would counter some of the autocratic tendencies of the new government. In reality, the king and the rest of the royal family were deeply concerned that the new government was going to heed popular calls to confiscate royal property and use it to revive the economy. Because of these concerns, he encouraged a coup in May 1933. The reaction was a countercoup in June 1933. When it was clear the royalists had lost the struggle, the king called for amnesty, despite implications that he had funded and helped to organize the initial coup and the following response. By the end of 1933, there were 230 people who had been arrested, 23 had been killed, two members of the military had been executed, and one prince had been sentenced to life in prison.

By 1935 the king had left Thailand for Europe, ostensibly to receive medical treatment. Once away, he refused to sign legislation that would reduce the spending power of the king as well as the royal prerogative. In reply to appeals for his return, he demanded changes to augment the king's power and role, including the power to veto legislation and appoint members of the Assembly. By March 1935, Prajadhipok abdicated, leaving Thailand without a monarch.

Militarism Versus Reform

The designated heir was Prince Ananda Mahidol, a nephew of Prajadhipok. As the young prince was only 10 years old and studying abroad, he would not be a factor in Siam's politics for at least a decade. The power vacuum this created was filled both by the military and intellectuals, led by Phibun and Pridi, respectively. Phibun took control and at this point changed the name of the country to Thailand.

Phibun and his supporters were openly enamored with the strength of the militant nationalism espoused by Italy, Germany, and Japan. Further, the Thai felt a kinship with the Japanese as their two countries were the only ones in Asia that had escaped European colonization during the 19th century. Despite this, he did not have any desire to enter a war between the Allied and Axis powers and strove to keep balance between the two interests in Thailand. However, once France capitulated to Germany in 1941, Phibun took the opportunity to snatch back the parts of French Cambodia that had been lost in 1893. Japan sweetened the deal with Thailand by giving them territory to the north and east of their borders.

Thailand's entry into World War II on the side of the Japanese was complicated. On one hand, Phibun was hopeful that if Japan could use Thailand as a base, they would be able to gain back more "lost" territory. Indeed, they did gain territory from Burma and Malaya in 1943. On the other hand, resisting the Japanese would have been disastrous. After Japan's initial request to use Thailand as a base in December 1941, Phibun's aides attempted to delay giving an answer for a day. When Thailand was invaded at nine different points on the same day that the Japanese infamously struck at Pearl Harbor, however, the Thais felt they had no choice but to comply with the Japanese terms.

Initially, Phibun imagined that Thailand could be a partner with Japan that would throw off the hated European colonialists. However, it quickly became apparent that the Japanese saw Thailand as an occupied country and not an ally. They forced the Thai government to make "loans" to them and used their supplies for their war effort.

The war alienated the civil leaders, such as Pridi, from the militaristic followers of Phibun. Nevertheless, when it was apparent by 1943 that Japan would not be victorious, both factions began to make contacts with the Allies to undermine the Japanese. They were joined by Seni Pramoj, a member of the royal family who was serving as the ambassador to the United States and had refused to serve the notice of war to the U.S. government. These efforts came together in the Seri Thai (Free Thai) movement.

By 1944, Pridi's civilian group took power from Phibun, in part to improve their chances with the Allies after the foreseeable Axis loss. This maneuver did in fact help the Thais when the British and French, indignant over the manner in which the Thais had taken advantage of their weaknesses during the war, demanded retribution. The United States, which had never officially been at war with Thailand, instead insisted that it be treated as an enemy-occupied state. After Pramoj was invited to return to Thailand as prime minister, the British were convinced to settle for a compensation of rice and the return to prewar boundaries. These negotiations were the beginning of the strong ties between the United States and Thailand.

Progress, Stability, and the Cold War

Although most scholars now agree that Thailand could have suffered far worse at the end of World War II, contemporary Thais were unsatisfied with both the reparations and the loss of territory. Inflation and the disorganized new government contributed to their discontent.

Nonetheless, Pridi's government was able to craft a constitution in May 1946 that created a bicameral legislature. The House of Representatives was elected by popular vote, and the Senate was elected by the House of Representatives. In the 1946 election, Pridi's party, the Constitutional Front, and the Cooperation Party won a majority of the seats in the lower house and thus were able to fill the upper house. Thailand seemed to be well on its way toward political stability.

The mysterious death of King Ananda, who ruled as Rama VIII, forced another change in power. Ananda was found dead of a gunshot wound in his bedroom in 1946. To this day, a definitive ruling on whether Ananda was murdered, committed suicide, or accidentally shot himself has not been made. Rumors began to circulate that Pridi had been responsible for his death, perhaps in order to turn Thailand into a republic. Although most now agree that this was not what happened, Pridi resigned, and Phibun returned to power through two coups in 1947 and 1948. The throne went to Bhumibol Adulyadej as Rama IX, the current king.

The militaristic Phibun was well-positioned to take advantage of the burgeoning Cold War and the genuine rise of communism in Asia. His government became a valuable asset to the United States. Thailand became the recipient of millions of dollars in U.S. aid, both to the economy and to the military.

Phibun's second period of control was marked by instability as elements within the military attempted to push him out of power. Several attempted coups were followed by mass arrests as Phibun attempted to purge dissident elements within the military that seemed to threaten his power base the most. The constitution was altered in 1949 and then suspended in 1951. Thailand returned to the 1932 version that stipulated only one legislative house and allowed the government to appoint half its members. Not surprisingly, the majority of the appointed members were from the military.

The government validated the suspension of the 1949 constitution with the fear of communist assault. The Phibun government returned to the anti-Chinese policies it had employed in the 1930s and married them to the anticommunist sentiment of the 1950s. The harassment of the Chinese included arrests, closing Chinese schools, and banning Chinese organizations. As crackdowns on suspected communists became more aggressive, the United States was impressed and rewarded Thailand with increasing amounts of economic and military aid.

As of 1951, Phibun was sharing power with two other military strongmen. General Phao Siyanon was the director of the police, and General Sarit Thanarat was the commander of the Bangkok battalion. It was an uneasy triumvirate, and Phibun knew he was vulnerable, especially to the younger and more ruthless Sarit. He was able to maintain his power, however, in part because Phao and Sarit were locked in a struggle with each other and individually too weak to remove Phibun.

By 1955 it was clear that Sarit had more support among the military leadership than Phibun or Phao. In desperation, Phibun attempted to engender allegiance from the people. He stated that he wanted to make a present of *prachathipatai,* or democracy, to the Thai people. He encouraged open criticism of the government both in public forums and in the press. He also ended many of his anti-Chinese policies and promised to give municipal governments more power.

The 1957 election disappointed most interested parties in Thailand. The party Phibun and Phao founded, the Seri Manangkhasila, just barely won a majority. Even those results were called into question, particularly by Sarit. Many students were outraged at the outcome as well and protested the fraudulent results. At this point, Phibun called a state of emergency and effectively ended the experiment with democracy.

Phibun's Thailand could hardly be called a democracy. Even if the 1957 election and his later reforms had been above reproach, a true democracy requires more than attempted reforms and a questionable election. Further, many of his reforms were undone by his successors after he was forced from power in a bloodless 1957 coup. Thailand needed to maintain a semblance of a democratic state, however, for the sake of their American patrons.

On assuming power, Sarit dissolved parliament. The ouster of Phibun was approved by the royal family, who had disapproved of Phibun's policies since the 1930s. Sarit briefly relinquished control to his deputy Thanom Kittikachorn so he could receive medical treatment, but when he returned to Thailand in 1958, he began to rule in earnest. He suspended the constitution, citing the "experiments" up to that point a failure that had not improved the lives of the Thai people. He also shut down over a dozen newspapers and jailed those who were critical of the government, including academics, students, labor leaders, journalists, and legislators.

The strategy Sarit used to validate his regime was a return to the proto-nationalist policy of nation-religion-king. If Sarit embodied the nation, he needed to ensure that the other two mechanisms were visible and beloved. Sarit encouraged the king and queen to tour Thailand and serve as unofficial ambassadors of Thailand abroad. He also moved the administration of the monasteries to a body friendly to his government and employed the monks to advocate for government programs. This was a controversial tactic. Many felt that it disgraced and even corrupted the religious orders.

In spite of these criticisms, many remember the 1960s as a period of political stability and economic development. The staunchly anticommunist Sarit nonetheless instituted a series of economic plans with the objective of increasing employment and modernizing the country. Spending on education was increased, and irrigation, electrification, and sanitation projects were initiated, some of which was partially funded by the United States.

The Vietnam War and escalating communist activities in Southeast Asia provided the justification for Thailand's continued anticommunist policies. When the Americans stationed troops in Thailand in 1962, the government claimed it was a sign of their commitment to protecting Thailand from communism. U.S. aid continued to grow, as did U.S. tourism. This continued presence exposed Thais not only to American culture but also to American values.

There was a peaceful transition of power in 1963 when Sarit died and his deputy Thanom succeeded him. He continued Sarit's domestic and international policies. His priorities were maintaining the political stability that had been established under Sarit, continuing economic development and using that to help raise the standard of living for all Thais, and protecting the country from both domestic and regional communist threats.

Thanom's primary departure from his predecessor was his acceleration toward a democratic government. In addition to directing the newly appointed Constituent Assembly to draft a constitution, he also relaxed restrictions on the media. Reaction within the government was mixed; some saw this as an opportunity to increase popular support, but others worried that party politics would create openings that communists could exploit.

The constitution was decreed in 1968, the same year political parties were legalized. However, Thailand remained under martial law. Not surprisingly, the general election in February 1969 gave Thanom's United Thai People's Party the majority of the seats in the parliament.

The Thai economy grew at an unprecedented rate of 8 percent per year during the 1960s and 1970s. Much of that can be directly traced to military aid from the United States. Loans as well as foreign investment from the United States, Japan, and Taiwan also increased the foreign-exchange rate during this period.

Thailand was increasingly preoccupied with Laos. Thanom's government worried that a victory by the Pathet Lao would make Thailand vulnerable to a communist attack. Part of their strategy to address Laos was to strengthen their ties with the United States and allow it to use Thailand as a base of operations against North Vietnam. By 1968, more than 45,000 American troops and 500 fighter planes were stationed in Thailand. This was in addition to a contingent of Thai soldiers who were sent to South Vietnam.

When the Johnson administration made the decision in 1968 to stop bombing Vietnam and included no plans for Laos, Thanom's government was deeply concerned that this would allow the Pathet Lao to achieve victory. While they continued to maintain a close relationship with the United States, they also remained involved in South Vietnam and Laos.

Activities in and near Malaysia were also a cause for concern. There were communist and Muslim insurgents on both sides of the Thai-Malaysian border, some of whom were agitating for separation from Thailand. Further, while Thanom's government had begun a campaign to improve the standard of living, conditions in the northeast lagged behind the rest of the country. Opposition groups exploited these complaints to advocate for a change in government. Thanom's reaction was to conflate most dissent with communism, thus demeaning legitimate criticism.

By 1971, Thanom decided that the experiment with parliamentary democracy had been a failure and launched a coup against his own government. Once again, the constitution was suspended and Thailand was ruled by martial law. Power was now held by the National Executive Council, which included Thanom as prime minister and Field Marshal Praphat Charusathian as his deputy prime minister. Narong Kittikachorn, Thanom's son and Praphat's son-in-law, rounded out the council.

Between martial law, dependence on the United States, increased Japanese investment, and the obvious corruption of the military leaders, many groups were disenchanted with Thanom. They were particularly nervous about Narong's appointment. In light of the cooling relations between Thanom and the king, many were genuinely concerned that Thanom was making a move to overthrow the king and replace the monarchy with a "republican" dynasty. Dissenters included students, labor, civilian bureaucrats, and even rival factions in the military.

When Thanom published a new constitution in December 1972 that created a fully appointed legislative body that drew two-thirds of its membership from the military and the police, the opposition movement grew. By June 1973, labor and students were holding public protests against Thanom's government and demanded a democratic constitution and parliamentary elections. After eleven students were arrested for handing out opposition pamphlets, demonstrators took to the streets in increasing numbers. On October 13, more than 250,000 people, many of them students, gathered at the Bangkok Democracy Memorial to demand a more democratic government. Troops opened fire on the crowd the next day, killing at least 75 people, and then occupied Thammasat University.

The king, who had been increasingly dissatisfied with Thanom, summoned him and his council and compelled them to resign. The king allowed them to leave rather than forcing them to stand trial. After consulting with the student leaders, he appointed Sanya Dharmasakti, the rector of Thammasat University and someone known to be sympathetic to the student demands, as interim prime minister.

The constitution of 1974 created a fully elected lower house and required an election to be held within 120 days. During this period, no overwhelmingly favored party or leader appeared. Instead, 42 officially sanctioned political parties ran for the 269 seats, and most did not have a well-organized platform, ideology, or reform package to offer. Further, only 47 percent of the eligible population participated in the election held in January 1975. These problems were not the result of corruption but rather inexperience.

If the student groups had expected a left-leaning government, they were disappointed. The vast majority of the seats went to center and right-of-center parties. Of those, no one held a clear majority. Seni Pramoj of the Democrat Party was able to put together a weak coalition, but his government only lasted one month. His brother Kukrit Pramoj, the leader of the more conservative Social Action Party, created a more secure coalition. While Kukrit's government proposed reforms to give municipalities more power in financial planning, he was unable to overcome the status quo, and those measures failed.

The change in internal affairs, combined with the shift in regional politics, increased the criticism of U.S. presence and influence. Many were concerned that the United States was responsible for an increase in the severity of crackdowns on communists and other government critics. Further, they felt the relationship with the United States was alienating them from their neighbors. The government, for its part, did not want to do anything that would discourage the flow of international aid and investment.

Between 1975 and 1976, a total of 27,000 American troops left Thailand. When the United States used the Ban U Tapao base for a rescue operation in Cambodia, however, without first obtaining permission, the Thais saw it as an insult to their sovereignty, and anti-American demonstrations were held in Bangkok.

Thailand's diplomacy with the new communist regimes in South Vietnam, Laos, and Cambodia were initially unproductive. In 1975, however, they were able to both reestablish diplomatic ties with the Chinese as well as become an active participant in the Association of Southeast Asian Nations (ASEAN) in technical and economic regional planning.

Growing Unrest

While Thai politicians of this period did not always make the best choices, it is not entirely fair to blame them for the unrest of the 1970s. Population growth and economic changes also contributed to the instability.

Although the United States continued to invest in the Thai economy, the end of the Vietnam War meant a sharp decrease in the amount. Further, although the Thai economy continued to grow at an impressive rate, the population grew more quickly. In 1960 there were 26 million Thais; by 1970 there were 34 million. In addition, agricultural gains, particularly in rice, were made not through increased productivity but increased land use. By the mid-1970s, there was little uncultivated arable land. As farming became a less attractive option for the population, migration to the urban areas exploded in the 1960s and 1970s, in some cities by as much as 250 percent. By 1980 the population of Bangkok-Thonburi reached 4.5 million.

Conditions in Thailand were already more favorable to business than labor. The large youthful population meant a large labor pool. Many recent university graduates found themselves without jobs, and many of those with jobs found themselves working for lower wages and longer hours.

The fear of communism persisted, and as frustrated opposition groups increased the volume and frequency of their complaints, they found themselves more vulnerable to accusations of communism, even in more moderate circles. As those groups grew more radicalized, right-wing support and paramilitary groups arose, including the Nawa Phon (New Force), the Red Gaurs (Red Bulls), and the Luk Sua Chaoban (Village Tiger Cubs/Scouts). By the mid-1970s, membership in those groups totaled close to 100,000. As right- and left-wing groups clashed, political arrests and assassinations became more commonplace.

In this atmosphere, it followed that many media outlets became sensationalized. Many of the organizations that arose after a relaxation of the censorship laws were known more for circulating rumors than accurately reporting or analyzing current events. While there were also reputable news agencies, it was very easy to find publications that reinforced what one already believed.

After attempting to curb the corruption of the military, Kukrit was pushed out of power. He was replaced by his brother Seni as the head of a right-wing government after bloodshed during the 1976 election season left 30 dead.

With so many tempers running high, it may only have been a matter of time before an event pushed Thailand to a breaking point.

In August 1976, Praphat briefly returned from Taiwan. As angry as many leftist groups were, they were outraged when Thanom himself returned in September. Some say he snuck in disguised as a monk, others that he was expressing his desire to join a monastery.

By the first days of October, factional discontent was at the highest point it had ever been. When a right-wing newspaper altered a picture to make it appear that students were burning a member of the royal family in effigy, right-wing radio stations called for the death of students and communists. On October 6, paramilitary groups and the police attacked student activists at Thammasat University. Over 400 students were brutally murdered, hundreds wounded, and thousands were arrested.

The military assumed power once again and established the National Administrative Reform Council. The council chose Thanin Kraivichien to lead the new government. A staunchly anticommunist former judge, he quickly earned a reputation for being harsher and more reactionary than his military predecessors. The government reinstated martial law, censored the media, and purged the universities of dissidents. Many felt he went too far, and by October 1977 he was replaced by Kriangsak Chomanan. Kriangsak, in comparison to his predecessor, was more moderate. He gave amnesty to the students who had been tried after the October 1976 riots and gave the press more freedom. He also showed openness to labor and increased the minimum wage in 1978 and 1979.

Perhaps most importantly, he published a constitution at the end of 1978 and allowed for an election in 1979. The House of Representatives would be popularly elected but the Senate would be appointed. The Senate had the power to block any House of Representatives legislation that affected national security and financial and economic matters. Further, neither the prime minister nor the cabinet was required to be popularly elected.

In 1979, the Thai government supported remnants of the Khmer Rouge, perceiving them as a necessary counterweight to the communist elements in Southeast Asia, particularly Vietnam. This support continued in spite of the regime's well-publicized atrocities in part because the numbers of Cambodian and Lao refugees only added to the destabilization the government had been working to keep under control.

"Premocracy"

The unforeseen oil crisis in the late 1970s forced the most dramatic changes. Inflation reduced the standard of living in Bangkok, and government inaction delayed the implementation of policies that were meant to help farmers. The announcement of a rise in energy prices generated protests on a scale similar to what had been seen in 1973. Kriangsak resigned, and in March 1980 General Prem Tinsulanonda became prime minister.

Prem lent credibility to his term by resigning from the military and appointing civilians to his cabinet. In addition, he cultivated the support of the royal family. Such support was critical to his ability to put down an attempted coup in 1981 by younger military officers.

Although Prem was able to remain in power, unrest persisted within the government, the military, and the economy. Although not as radical as they were in the 1970s, students remained both dissatisfied and politically active. Civilian political parties were also gaining strength, in large part because the population was disenchanted with the failures of previous military regimes. These challenges were overcome within the first three years of Prem's term in power, and the rest of his tenure was seen by many as a model of stability and prosperity.

Prem's control of Thailand (1981–1988) marked a period of partial democracy referred to sometimes as "Premocracy." While the defense, interior, finance, and foreign ministries were held by men from the military and trusted technocrats, less-important ministries were held by elected parliamentarians. Elections were held during this period, and the parliament was a functional body. Some other generals followed Prem's example and resigned their commissions to legitimize their own service in the parliament.

Although dissent was less dramatic in the 1980s than it had been in the previous decade, political persecution continued, particularly in rural areas. The Internal Security Operations Command, in conjunction with the Village Scouts and the Red Gaurs, dealt ruthlessly with rural activists, quietly executing many.

Part of the Prem government's relative longevity can be explained through its strategic investments in alleviating poverty. The poorest villages, most of which were concentrated in the northeast, benefitted from programs to improve water supplies, irrigation, electricity and soil quality as well as to build schools and roads. (It should be noted that there was another reason to create roads for the poorer villages: It allowed the army easier access to areas that were known centers of dissident activity.) While these programs improved the quality of life for the poorest citizens, overall inequality persisted.

The new infrastructure made it possible for the rural population to connect to the cities, both physically and culturally. The roads made possible the growth of bus and motorcycle manufacture. By the mid-1990s over 60 percent of all households owned a motorcycle. The motorcycle was used by everyone, whether it was going to market, taking children to faraway schools, or getting farmers to work.

Electricity in rural areas led the way for another important acquisition: the television. By 1990, almost every Thai household, rural and urban, owned a television set. This was a boon not only for the consumer but for the government. In comparison to print media, censorship of television and radio was much simpler: all television and radio stations were controlled by government or military figures. Not only could they control what news would be broadcast, they could also set the terms for the cultural messages. A popular theme in many of the programs was the middle class family, prospering and maintaining their values despite the temptations of an outside world that included nepotism, violence, and corruption.

Under Prem's government, Thailand began to export more finished products than raw materials. In the 1980s, agriculture accounted for close to half its exports, but by the 1990s those products accounted for about 10 percent. As an example, in 1978 the top export was tapioca, followed by rice. In 2001 the top export was computer parts, followed by garments and motor cars; rice was seventh on the list.

Although internal and international groups had been calling for a change to export manufacturing since the mid-1970s, it wasn't until the early 1980s that business could force the shift. As U.S. investments tapered down and the price of oil increased again, the economy suffered. By 1984 a banking crisis developed, and the business community and economic reformers used this as an opportunity to facilitate the shift to manufacturing. Tariffs and taxes were revised to encourage investment in the manufacturing sector.

Between 1984 and 1989, the annual increase in exports was 24 percent. Because Japan had allowed the yen to rise against the U.S. dollar and dollar-backed currencies such as the baht, the value of exports to Japan tripled in worth at the same time. Japan, along with Korea, Taiwan, and Hong Kong, found it less expensive to operate in Thailand and began opening factories at an unprecedented rate. By the mid-1990s a new Japanese factory was opening in Thailand every three days.

Tourism grew in the same years. Between the mid-1970s and 2000, annual tourism grew from the hundreds of thousands to 12 million. The sex industry, which had grown during the Vietnam War, was now marketed to tourists.

Unsteady Footing

In 1988, Prem bowed to public pressure and moved to the Privy Council. The election of 1988 brought to power General Chatichai Choonhavan. Chatichai's power base came not from the military but from regional businesspeople, particularly those in the northeast. He alienated both the military and established bureaucrats by moving important cabinet functions to elected legislators and reducing the military budget. By this time, aid from the United States had ended, and the military elite perceived this as a direct threat to their livelihood.

When stories of bribes connected to infrastructure projects surfaced in 1989, the press criticized Chatichai's government and called them the "buffet cabinet." The middle class soured on Chatichai, and by 1991 he was removed from power by the military.

Anand Panyarachun, a foreign-service official and later businessman, was picked to be the interim prime minister. Anand's cabinet consisted of technocrats who drew up liberal business reforms that were eagerly received by the middle class and urban businesspeople.

The warm relations were short-lived. The faction that came to power as a solution to the retail politics of its predecessor did nothing to curb their own excesses in public. When lucrative telecommunications contracts were called into question (including one awarded to Thaksin Shinawatra, a future prime minister), even Anand could not support them. As international governments began to discourage tourism to Thailand because of its new leadership, the business community was eager for an alternative.

The publication of the military junta's constitution sparked a prodemocracy movement reminiscent of the 1973–1976 period. The king's attempts to soothe the divisions were successful for a short time. Despite earlier promises, General Suchinda Kraprayun assumed power after the 1992 election and filled his cabinet with military leaders and well-known money politicians.

By May, the middle class had had enough and supported the prodemocracy demonstrations. On May 17, about 200,000 people protested in Bangkok, including many from the middle class. Though jokingly called the "mobile phone mob," protestors also included migrants, workers, and students. Similar demonstrations were held throughout the provinces.

Suchinda declared that the demonstrations were an attack against "nation, religion, and king," and he unleashed fully armed soldiers onto the crowds. The violence continued for three days, and the government was unable to stop domestic and international news outlets from broadcasting images from the crackdown. Estimates of the death toll are between 40 and hundreds. On May 20 the king intervened and demanded a halt to the violence. Suchinda resigned.

Immediately after the crisis, a career in the military was seen as a liability for the first time in Thai history. Some were publicly harassed or even refused medical treatment. Thousands lost their positions in government and business. However, they refused to give up the idea that they were not only entitled but required to participate in politics, if only to ensure national security.

Anand returned to power until the election of September 1992. The election was won by the "Angels" (civilian political parties) only after the "Devils" (supporters of the military and money politicians) threw their support to the Democrat Party's candidate, Chuan Leekpai.

Those who hoped for reforms were disappointed. Momentum for reform faded after the end of the violence and assurances that middle class and business prosperity was no longer threatened. The government failed to take substantive action on education reform, decentralizing government functions, or loosening controls on the media.

Rural areas felt increasingly compromised. The Forestry Department announced the creation of new national parks where hill tribes and peasants traditionally lived. Businesspeople and politicians used their connections to obtain land for commercial development. The people who lost access to the land launched protests. In 1994, almost 1,000 individual protests were held over land rights.

Banharn Silpa-archa was elected in 1995. The majority of his support came from the provinces. His government ignored signs that the economic boom was ending and instead focused on repaying political favors with cabinet positions. After his government fell in 1996, he was succeeded by Chavalit Yongchaiyudh. Chavalit promised to stop the impending financial collapse, but lacked both the people and the political power to do so. By 1997 the value of the baht fell from 25 to the U.S. dollar to 56.

Most agreed that the economic failure was the result of political failure, and many protested to demand the constitution drafted in 1995–1996 be passed. The constitution curbed military power, liberalized the press, reduced the power of the Senate, and attempted to control corruption at the voting booth and in office.

Chavalit was forced to resign in 1997, and Chuan returned to replace him. By 1998, his government concluded an agreement with the International Monetary Fund (IMF) to bail out the economy. The US$17.2 billion aid package included the provision that revenues exceed expenditures by 60 million baht. It also required high taxes and interest rates.

The effects of the collapse were devastating. Between 1996 and 1998, the rate of suicides increased 40 percent, and the number of abandoned children grew. The use of child labor remained stable; because that number had been decreasing in recent years, this was a negative indicator of the finances of the citizenry.

The IMF program was condemned in Thailand. The baht stabilized at 40 to the U.S. dollar, but the austerity program was politically and financially ineffective. Confronted with business collapse, social misery, and international criticism, the IMF backed away from the austerity program in 1998. The Thai government launched a stimulus program, and by 2002 the economy began to recover.

Big Money Politics

Thaksin Shinawatra, the wealthy telecommunications businessman, formed the Thai Rak Thai (TRT, "Thai Love Thai") political party. In 2001 the TRT was the overwhelming victor and won 300 of the 500 seats in the House of Representatives.

In many ways, the Thaksin administration combined the nationalism of the 1930s with the adoration of international finance of the 1990s and 2000s. Instead of a military strongman, Thaksin strove to be the "CEO premier." His first priority was the economy. His government's goal was not to return Thailand to 1997 levels but to earn First World economic standing. He methodically identified which sectors of the economy required intervention and at what levels.

Thaksin centralized power not by force but by corporate-style intimidation. By routinely emptying and then reappointing governmental bodies, he made clear the need to remain loyal. Additionally, he set up consultative bodies that effectively substituted his ministries.

Thaksin was not above force and intimidation, however. His campaign against the methamphetamine drug trade, although touted as a success, cost 2,700 lives and was criticized by the king. Once again, media content was censored, whether through official decree or unofficial favors and intimidation. Individual critics, nongovernmental organizations, and regional groups were harshly attacked, but now the term "anarchist" replaced "communist."

Whereas Phibun wanted to define "Thai," Thaksin wanted to prepare the Thais to take their place on the world stage. He increased the usage of the Thai flag, going so far as to use Phibun's phrase "unite the Thai blood-flesh-lineage-race" underneath the flag on every bus in Thailand.

While Thaksin weakened corrupt tit-for-tat politics, he replaced it with a big-party model that required big money and, by extension, big business.

Thaksin's Demise

Thaksin, though undeniably popular among the electorate, especially the rural working class, was not as popular among those in the existing power structure of Thailand, which included royalists, some members of the military, and some big business interests. Much of the so-called Bangkok elite were not supporters, either.

Citizens decorated tanks with flowers after the 2006 coup.

The catalyst for broader anti-Thaksin sentiment came when Thaksin's family sold their interest in Shincorp, the country's largest mobile phone company, to Singapore's investment arm for US$1.9 billion. Thaksin's detractors saw it as a slap in the face to Thailand's sovereignty and just another way that Thaksin was squeezing money out of Thailand for his own gain. Demonstrations in Bangkok, which had begun in small numbers by a group calling itself the People's Alliance for Democracy (PAD), ballooned into protests involving thousands of people. In protest of Thaksin's actions, two of his cabinet members resigned from their positions, and in February 2006 Thaksin responded by dissolving parliament and calling a snap election.

The Democrat Party boycotted the election and Thai Rak Thai won a majority of seats in parliament. Thaksin said that he would not accept the position of prime minister, but would continue as caretaker prime minister until new elections were held. The election was invalidated in May following an investigation into vote-rigging allegations, and this effectively returned Thaksin and his TRT party to the seat of power.

In September 2006, while Thaksin was out of the country, General Sonthi Boonyaratglin, then Commander-in-Chief of the Royal Thai Army, deposed Thaksin in a bloodless coup and martial law was declared again. The constitution was once again abolished and a retired general, Surayud Chulanon, was installed as a temporary prime minister.

Since the Coup

On September 22, 2006, Chamlong Srimuang, a core member of the PAD, who had also helped bring down General Suchinda in 1992, said "not once in Thai history have Thais been so divided. Nothing but a coup could have remedied such a situation."

But the country has remained divided since 2006, and although the coup was bloodless, the numerous events of civil unrest since have not been without loss of life.

Thailand's first democratic elections since the military coup were held in December 2007. Although Thaksin's Thai Rak Thai party had been banned from participating in the elections, a new party, Phak Palang Prachachon (the People's Power Party), allied with Thaksin Shinawatra and probably financially supported by him, too, won a majority of seats in parliament. The new prime minister, Samak Sundaravej, was largely regarded as a Thaksin proxy. In January of 2008, Thaksin returned to Thailand after 17 months and it looked as though the coup might be forgotten and Thailand might pick up where it left off in 2006.

But the PAD and Thailand's Democratic party, long the opposition party to TRT, were not satisfied with the results and over the course of the next nine months, thousands of protesters took to the streets once again, breaking into Government House and intermittently closing down government offices across the country.

A court decision in September of 2008, which kicked Samak out of office for conflict of interest stemming from his paid participation in a cooking show, seemed to quiet things down for a while but his replacement, Somchai Wongsawat, Thaksin's brother-in-law, was perhaps even more controversial and incendiary. He was removed from office less than two months later. During his short tenure, the PAD managed to take over Bangkok's international airport, halting flights for more than a week, stranding passengers from all over the world and disrupting trade in and out of Thailand.

When the dust had settled, the PPP and affiliated parties were dissolved by the Constitutional Court, leaving the once minority Democratic party in power for the first time in history.

Having been disenfranchised during the 2006 coup and then again after the 2007 elections did not sit well with thousands of mostly rural, less affluent Thais who had supported Thaksin and the parties later affiliated with him. They took to the streets after the Democrats came into power in 2008 and while the PAD had worn yellow shirts, this group wore red and thus became known to the world as the red shirts.

In 2009, anti-government protesters stormed a meeting of regional leaders in Pattaya, resulting in Songkran festivities effectively being cancelled in Bangkok till the following week.

By March 2010, things had gotten much worse as red shirts began gathering in central Bangkok. Numbers of red shirts in the Rajaprasong area continued to grow for weeks with little military or police intervention. Protesters, who demanded that the current prime minister step down and new elections be called immediately, shut down roads, burned tires, and forced businesses to close. Bombs in central Bangkok killed bystanders, and sporadic clashes between military and protesters resulted in more deaths of innocent people.

On April 10, 2010, conflicts exploded out on the streets, including on typically tourist-filled Khao San Road, where protesters clashed with army/police resulting in deaths and injuries (including to tourists). The escalating conflict finally came to a head on May 19, when security forces stormed areas where red shirts had gathered, resulting in more bloodshed. According to Human Rights Watch, between March and May of 2010, at least 90 people were killed and at least 2,000 injured in clashes between security forces and anti-government protesters.

Thaksin's Return?

When democratic elections were held in 2011, the Pheu Thai Party, the successor to Thaksin's Thai Rak Thai party, fronted Yingluck Shinawatra, Thaksin's younger sister, as their party head. Pheu Thai won a majority of seats in parliament and she became Thailand's 28th prime minister and first female prime minister on August 5, 2011.

During the campaign, Yingluck made no secret of the fact that she continued to take counsel from her older brother, and many of her populist policies, including support for the country's rural poor, can be seen as a continuation of where Thaksin left off. Yet she has proven to be popular in her own right. One of her platforms during the campaign was reconciliation after years of political upheaval. Whether she, or the country itself, is able to pull that off, remains to be seen.

Government

In 1932 Thailand was changed from an absolute monarchy to a constitutional monarchy, allowing the king to remain as head of state but stripping him of his absolute governing powers. Although the king has had some executive legislative powers in the successive constitutions that have followed since the end of the absolute monarchy, he holds tremendous moral sway over the population. Generally the king has remained quiet on political matters, though after more than 60 years on the throne, he is perceived as a moral leader by the people. It could be said that his opinions can affect the direction that his country takes, and there is a certain degree of reassurance present when major governmental changes are made with royal assent. The king's silence during the 2008 political turmoil has been variously interpreted, but there has frankly been little vigorous discussion of it outside of a few international publications. Lèse-majesté, which makes it a crime to criticize the king, has been used as a political weapon by various parties and has had the (perhaps) unintended consequence of stifling debate and conversation.

The country has only recently returned to a democratically elected government following the military coup in September 2006. After more than a year of military rule, a new constitution was approved in 2007, shortly after which a parliamentary election was held. When democratic elections were held in 2011, the Pheu Thai Party, the successor to Thaksin's Thai Rak Thai party, fronted Yingluck Shinawatra, Thaksin's younger sister, as their party head. Pheu Thai won a majority of seats

© SUZANNE NAM

Government House in Bangkok, where the country's parliament meets

in parliament and she became Thailand's 28th prime minister and first female prime minister on August 5, 2011.

ORGANIZATION

The executive branch essentially consists of the king, the prime minister, and the other ministers, who do not necessarily have to be elected members of parliament. The Council of Ministers, or cabinet, is in day-to-day control of the government and all of its activities, except those of parliament itself and the separate entity of the courts and judicial system, and they meet regularly to establish government policy and prepare budgets for due consideration by parliament. Along with their deputies, the ministers head their respective departments and give policy direction to the permanent agency officials who supervise the actual work done by regular employees of the agency.

The legislative branch, otherwise known as parliament or the National Assembly, has the primary responsibility of adopting laws to regulate Thai society, although all bills must

be signed into law by the king. It consists of two bodies, the Senate and the House of Representatives, each with its own secondary responsibilities and duties.

The Senate consists of 150 members, 74 of whom are appointed by a sub-committee of the Electoral Commission from around 500 applicants across all professions, and 76 of whom are democratically elected to represent the 76 provinces of Thailand. They consider laws and bills previously approved in the lower House of Representatives, inspect and control the administration of state affairs, as well as approve or remove people in higher positions of power.

The House of Representatives contains 480 seats, with 400 of these occupied by members of parliament democratically elected from electoral constituencies, and 80 on the basis of proportional party-list from groupings of votes in the provinces. One party will sit in sole majority, or in coalition with other parties, with opposition coming from any parties not elected to power. The House selects a prime minister from its members to administer state affairs and have the general duties of approving legislation to be brought in front of the Senate, inspecting and controlling the administration of state affairs and expenditure, and to be a representative of the people.

The direct administration of Bangkok and Pattaya comes under elected governors, while appointed governors administer the other 74 provinces, with these being broken down into districts, subdistricts, and villages for purposes of local management. At the village level, a mayor (*pu yai ban*) will be elected by the people subject to approval by the central government, and often the mayor is the first contact for settlement of minor disputes within the community before the matter is brought to the attention of the higher authorities.

POLITICAL PARTIES

As of 2011, the dominant political party in Thailand is Pheu Thai, the third iteration of Thaksin Shinawatra's Thai Rak Thai party. The People's Power Party, which was formed after Thai Rak Thai was dissolved, was itself dissolved in late 2008 by Thailand's Constitutional Court after it found electoral fraud and other misdeeds by members. Despite questions about Thaksin's administration, Thai Rak Thai attracted a great deal of support among the people due to its populist policies, including debt suspension and universal health care for the poor and low-cost housing for those with low incomes, as well as the prospering economy under his leadership. As demonstrated during subsequent elections, its successor parties continued to retain that support.

The People's Power Party won a considerable amount of support from fans of Thaksin in the 2007 election, though this was still insufficient for them to take an outright majority. Their coalition partners were smaller parties receiving between 2 percent and 10 percent of total votes each, and most of them had similar election platforms of populist policies, with conservative and royalist ideals at heart. The Royalist People's Party, Thais United National Development Party, and Neutral Democrats Party were formed mostly by former allies of Thaksin, which is reflected in them having very similar standpoints to the People's Power Party. The For the Motherland Party was formed by a mixture of Thaksin's opponents and supporters and had a much more central manifesto of policies, with a slogan of "Bring happiness and well-being to the people." Thai Nation Party has more history than the other parties and had previously joined a coalition with Thai Rak Thai in 2001, but fiercely opposed them in later years. There had been talk of mergers between some of these parties prior to the election, so the coalition was not too surprising in some ways, but the Thai Nation Party in particular found themselves heavily criticized by their voters when they joined the coalition in apparent defiance of their stated position against Thaksin and his cohorts.

The Democrat Party, once the sole party in opposition to the PPP, became the ruling party in the wake of the 2008 airport siege. Though they shared the common populist policies and royalist conservative ideologies of many other parties, they have remained steadfast in opposing much of what Thaksin stands for, and what he has been accused of. In doing so they have won the support of areas of the country that did not directly benefit from Thaksin's policies, such as Bangkok and the south, but have alienated voters in the poorer north and northeast.

In the July 2011 elections, Pheu Thai won a decisive victory, taking 265 of the House of Representatives' 500 seats, even more than their predecessor party took in 2007. Party head, Yingluck Shinawatra, Thaksin Shinawatra's younger sister, became Prime Minister in August 2011.

POLITICAL ISSUES

Though there were clearly problems within the political processes at work in Thailand prior to the September 2006 coup, the army's action was met with mixed responses from within Thailand and some condemnation from the international community. As democracy had been upheld in Thailand since the events of

Black May in 1992, it was felt that a step backward had been taken.

The United Nations raised concerns over human rights, and the United States, United Kingdom, European Union, Australia, Malaysia, and New Zealand all voiced their misgivings. Others, such as Japan and South Korea, looked more to a successful resolution and a return to democracy, and China seemed almost unconcerned.

With the return to a democratically elected government in 2007, Thailand had once again become a part of the international community, with previously suspended aid being recommenced and diplomatic relations being reestablished. However, the People's Alliance for Democracy's seizure of the airport, the implicit support the Democrat Party took from them in taking power, and the continued sometimes violent civil unrest have once again caused people to question the country's ability to govern itself in a democratic manner.

Whether the 2011 elections, which took place as this book was going to press, mark an end to political unrest or just another chapter, is impossible to say. Yingluck's main platform during her campaign was reconciliation, and there is no arguing that her party enjoys far more popular support than the opposition. However, in the weeks since Pheu Thai took power, there have already been indications that they will seek to have Thaksin's conviction set aside and attempt to bring him back to Thailand. Were they to be successful at either or both, it would most likely be a catalyst for further strife.

Internal problems also remain, most notably in the deep south, where thousands have died in the past five years. Political measures taken by previous governments have been considered ineffective, and military actions have sometimes been considered brutal, but the conflict is no closer to being resolved.

JUDICIAL AND PENAL SYSTEMS

The Courts of First Instance deal with all legal matters in Thailand, with civil, criminal, and provincial courts adjudicating on general matters, issues involving juveniles and family concerns, and specialized areas such as bankruptcy and tax. Bangkok has many district courts dealing with criminal cases and three main civil courts, including municipal courts that handle only minor cases that can be dealt with quickly. All other provinces have at least one provincial court that will exercise unlimited jurisdiction, and all cases in the province are considered there. At least one judge will sit on a case with no supporting jury, though in some matters a quorum of up to four judges may be established depending on the severity and complexity of the case.

Each region also has a Court of Appeal, and a quorum of three judges including one chief justice will hear every case. The next and last step is for a case to be referred to the Supreme Court, where again a quorum of three judges will sit, with the president of the Supreme Court playing a personal role in some judicial matters.

It is widely accepted that any custodial sentence in Thailand is a very unpleasant experience, and the bookshelves of airports will usually have a few first-hand accounts of the treatment that can be expected. The notorious Bang Kwang jail, or Bangkok Hilton, houses a number of long-term foreign prisoners who often came to be there as a result of drug offenses, sometimes with sentences of over 50 years. In a typical jail they would live alongside Thai murderers and drug dealers who have avoided the death sentence, which is often meted out but usually commuted except in severe or high-profile cases.

Policing at the local level varies. Thailand has recently been at the center of some internationally coordinated arrests, and there is no doubt that the very highest standards of policing can be seen in the country. It also should be recognized that the average salary for a local police officer is relatively low, and that stories of on-the-spot fines or outright bribes being offered and taken are common. Consequently it can seem that crimes of almost any level can be paid off with a substantial donation to the police or, where appropriate, even to the victim's family themselves.

Though this does little to encourage a sense of justice being done, it does mean that it is possible to pay for minor misdemeanors to be overlooked. Police officers in tourist areas have understood this for many years, and travelers faced with the official 50,000B fine and deportation or even a jail sentence for a small drug bust might prefer to take the option of a large cash fine. However, unsuccessfully attempting to bribe a police officer would probably have very dire consequences, and this course of action is not recommended.

People and Culture

Current estimates place the population of Thailand at around 65 million people, with 31 percent of those living in urban areas and the remainder in poorer, rural areas around the country. The area around Bangkok officially contains some 10 million residents, and the city itself claims to be home to around 6 million, making it by far the most populous place in Thailand and well ahead of Chiang Mai, which has around 250,000 city inhabitants and 1.3 million in the surrounding province.

The population is split almost evenly between men and women, though the spread widens in the older population, with 55 percent of over-65s being female. This is reflected in mean life expectancies. Men live an average 70.2 years; women generally outlive them by nearly half a decade to 75.0 years. During their lives, average women will give birth to 1.64 children, providing for a rate of population growth of just 0.663 percent. This has declined dramatically from 3.1 percent in 1960, particularly in the last few years. For now, nearly 25 percent of the population is under age 15, but decreasing birthrates will age the population in due course.

Though the average annual wage is officially quoted as 250,000B, the legal minimum wage can be as low as 55,000B per year. In addition, the fact that the minimum legal wage is not always paid results in unskilled workers in impoverished regions working full days of heavy labor for as little as 100B per day. Officially, 10 percent of the population lives in poverty and just 2 percent are classed as unemployed, and there are currently no standard government subsidies to help them.

IMMIGRATION

Since Thailand became a country in its own right as Siam in the 13th century, the almost-constant battles over borders with its neighbors and easy integration of the vanquished has resulted in a healthy ethnic mix. At present, 75 percent of the population consider themselves to be of Thai descent, 14 percent of Chinese heritage, and 11 percent as the "others" who have come to live here for reasons of profession or trade, choice or lifestyle, or as refugees from war.

The Indians were the first visitors from distant countries who settled here in the first century A.D. as merchants and to spread the word of the Buddhist religion, and the next major influx was in the 13th century when Chinese from Yunnan fled the danger of the Mongol Empire and settled under the protection of the Siamese king. But these migrations were nothing compared to the numbers of Chinese who started to arrive in ever larger numbers in the 18th century, until by the 1920s over 100,000 were settling each year, and stricter immigration laws had to be introduced. Nowadays, migrant workers come from Burma, China, Cambodia, and Laos to work in factories, agriculture, and domestically with around 1.3 million working legally and up to 700,000 working without permits.

The wars in Southeast Asia from the 1960s led to large-scale issues with refugees, with 600,000 Cambodians, 320,000 Lao, and 158,000 Vietnamese being displaced and seeking asylum in Thailand. Nearly all of these people were eventually repatriated or settled in other countries, but a small number still

WHO ARE THE HILL TRIBE PEOPLE?

Thailand is home to a number of minority ethnic groups living in the hills and mountains of northern Thailand as well as in Burma and Laos. There are seven major groups – the Karen, Hmong, Yao, Lisu, Lahu, Lawa, and Akha – as well as smaller groups and subgroups of the major groups.

Although the term *hill tribe* is commonly used, it is somewhat misleading. Individuals within each ethnic group share a common history and language, and often a distinct dress and tradition, but there is no real tribal organization within each group, and populations are generally dispersed throughout the region.

Within Thailand, the population of these groups is as high as 500,000, with the Karen making up more than half that number (not counting the many refugees from neighboring countries who come from the same ethnic groups). Many of these people have lived in the region for generations but do not identify strictly with the national boundaries that have been created around them, nor are they always recognized as belonging to the country they live in.

In fact, many hill tribe people are stateless, holding no citizenship, no passport, and no right to vote or receive the basic benefits of citizenship. These ethnic minorities are among the poorest in Thailand, and many continue to live as their parents and grandparents before them – off the land, in basic wooden bungalows in small communities in the mountains. Income sources are generally limited to small-scale agriculture and cottage-industry handicrafts.

These poor minority groups are a major tourist draw in northern Thailand, thanks no doubt to their often colorful traditional dress and craft production and the desire of travelers to catch a last glimpse of traditional people before they are swept away by modernization. The long-neck Karen or Padaung (mostly in the Mae Hong Son area) are particularly sought after by travelers, as the women wear vivid colors and a series of tight brass chokers that elongate their necks, creating a striking visual effect. You can't see these women walking down the street in a typical Thai town; they mostly live in refugee camps that can be visited if you're willing to pay a few hundred baht entrance fee. Where that money goes is up for debate. Some goes to the Karenni National Progressive Party, a Burmese Karen separatist group that has been both specifically recognized by the United States as not a terrorist group and criticized by the United Nations for recruiting child soldiers. Some money may go to tour operators. Little goes to the Padaung themselves.

The circumstances of these ethnic minorities differ substantially from one group to another, and whether you should visit them and who you should visit is not a question to be taken lightly. If you do decide to visit, keep in mind that most of the income made by these groups from tourism generally comes from the handicrafts that they sell and not from the money you pay tour guides or for admission fees.

To learn more about the hill tribe people, check out the **Virtual Hill Tribe Museum** (www.hilltribe.org), a website created by hill tribe people in Thailand to document their culture as they see it.

---

remain in Thailand. More recently, the refugees from persecution have been arriving from Burma, with nearly 150,000 of the Karen people currently living long-term in refugee camps near the Burmese border. These people are part of a larger group of ethnic minorities that live in Thailand, including the various hill tribes in the north of the country whose somewhat nomadic lifestyle has been restricted by both tighter border controls and an unwelcoming attitude from some of Thailand's neighboring countries.

Thais do choose to migrate from Thailand; this practice essentially started in the 1970s when professionals could earn much higher salaries in more developed countries such as the United States, continuing through the 1980s when skilled workers were attracted by the opportunities available in the oil regions of the Middle East. More recently the draw has been for Thai people at all levels to work in the prospering industrialized countries in Southeast Asia, with Taiwan particularly attracting professionals, semiskilled workers in fields such as transport, and even unskilled workers as domestic help. Large Thai communities have developed outside Thailand, most notably in Los Angeles, which has a Thai population of around 200,000 and is jokingly referred to as "the 77th province of Thailand."

YOUNG THAIS

All Thais now receive free education for 12 years, with nine years' attendance being compulsory, and this has resulted in literacy levels of 15-year-olds improving from 71 percent in 1960 to 92 percent today. University education is not individually subsidized apart from some scholarships that are offered, and it remains prohibitively expensive for many, with associated costs of 150,000B each year. Nevertheless, around 12 percent of students go on to complete the four years minimum for a graduate degree, which is almost an essential requirement for any progressive career in the social sciences or business. These lines of work account for some 37 percent of usual employment, with industry accounting for around 14 percent and the remaining 49 percent associated with agriculture.

Income levels depend greatly on qualifications, so young unskilled workers can expect to receive as little as 3,500B per month, skilled workers maybe up to 5,000B; police and teachers start at 6,500B, whereas a new graduate could realistically earn 8,000B, or more in Bangkok. However, employment in the capital brings the problem of higher living costs—the minimum apartment rental is around 5,000B per month, compared to less than 2,000B in the rural towns. Alternatively, nearly every Thai male has the chance to enter the armed forces either as a volunteer or as a conscript to make up the numbers, although this is only really a viable long-term career path for commissioned officers.

Young people are particularly at risk from untimely deaths in inopportune ways, as motorcycle accidents account for over 30 deaths and 400 injuries every day, with most of these being young males; 1.3 percent of the population has HIV or AIDS and is under the age of 25, resulting in around 50,000 deaths every year. These figures have reduced greatly following government campaigns in the past, and now the government is looking at other problems that may affect youth. Alcohol advertising has essentially been banned, and sales are becoming more restricted, which has also been the case with cigarettes. Additionally, the war on drugs has recently been resurrected, with the main target being the cheap methamphetamine from Burma and Cambodia called *yah bah*, which is becoming increasingly available and popular.

THE CHANGE OF PEOPLE

Since the years after World War II, Thailand has seen a rapid increase in economic development and a corresponding decline in the "traditional" way of life. Financial aid from the United States started in the 1950s and helped to accelerate economic development, but this led to an increase in people leaving their home villages and migrating to the urban areas to work. An eventual effect of the rapid economic growth was a greater reliance on money and not on the produce of the land, and a corresponding increase in personal debt.

Tourism started to bring different influences in the 1960s, which also saw the heightened presence of American troops in certain parts of the country, further shaping the development of the country. They both generated income in different ways and amounts than ever before, with tourism becoming a vital part of Thailand's economy over the next 30 years.

This had a profound effect on the seaside villages that had lived on fishing the waters for hundreds of years and were now finding their homes being quickly transformed. People who had led very simple lives and were deeply reserved in many ways were suddenly exposed to the money and behavior of a significantly different group of people: foreign tourists.

RELIGION

Buddhism has played a significant role in Thailand since the sixth century and pervades the history and culture of the country. Today, Theravada Buddhism, which came into Thailand through Sri Lanka during the Sukhothai period, is by far the dominant religion, and more than 90 percent of the population of Thailand call themselves Buddhists. Although Thailand considers itself a pluralistic society and there are large numbers of Thai Muslims as well as citizens of other religions, Buddhism still plays a major role in everyday life. The Thai calendar begins at the time of the Buddha's life, 543 years before the Western calendar (i.e., the year 2011 is 2554 by the Thai calendar). Although Thais move seamlessly between the two systems, all official documents are dated using the Buddhist calendar. Monks are allowed free passage on public transportation, and there are even seats reserved on most buses, trains, and boats for them. In Bangkok, you'll notice many people, from executive to laborer, wearing Buddhist amulets. No matter where you are in Thailand, you're never far from a Buddhist temple, called a *wat* in Thai. There are thousands, ranging from simple structures to ornately decorated compounds, and *wats* serve not only as places of devotion or worship but also to house the particular order's resident monks. In fact, most Thai Buddhist men will ordain as monks at some point in their lives and spend a month or more living as a monk.

Monks rely on the community to care for them. Walk the streets any morning before 6 A.M. and you're likely to see orange-robed monks walking barefoot, carrying their alms bowls. You'll also see residents going to their doors to offer food, water, and other necessities to the monks. This concept of "merit-making" through good deeds, be it feeding a monk or contributing to a *wat* or helping a stranger, is a very important concept in Thai Buddhism.

But Thailand isn't an entirely Buddhist country, and the second largest religious group, representing about 5 percent of the population, are Muslims. Though Thai Muslims live all over the country, the four southernmost provinces have the highest concentration, with more than 70 percent of the population. Most Thai Muslims are Sunni and are originally Malay, with their own language and cultural identity. The southernmost provinces were once known as the Kingdom of Pattani, and this part of the Thai population, known to some as Yawi, was historically more connected with neighboring Malaysia than with Thailand. Over the past 500 years, the region has alternately been under the control of Thailand (then Siam) and revolting against it.

After a period of calm, violence in the deep south of Thailand has continued for more than a decade. Although the violence is often connected to Muslim separatist groups, it is still not clear who is leading them and what the specific aims are. Thailand's seemingly monolithic and inflexible Buddhist identity and the central government's seeming inability to grapple with difficult cultural, religious, and social issues that this large minority population presents have only exacerbated the problem, according to some pundits.

Art and Architecture

Throughout Thailand's long and diverse history, art has always played a key role in society, providing outlets for worship, educating the masses on Buddhist values, or glorifying national achievements. By looking at the country's varied artistic and architectural forms, one can trace Thai history back through the ages, with two major sources of inspiration playing a continuous role—religion and monarchy—while a diverse mix of foreign influences have also slipped in. Even the tiniest temple in a rural village is often home to a wealth of artistic treasures, such as priceless Buddhist sculptures and murals depicting deeply entrenched religious beliefs.

Indeed, temples were the main source of art in Thailand for about 800 years, as every royal court made it a priority to build these ubiquitous religious structures to enshrine Buddha statues. The walls were decorated with murals, intricate wood carvings, and lacquer works, reflecting the complex court culture with its heavy Indian influences. Today, the nucleus of Thai art is Bangkok, where several quality museums feature classic and contemporary art from Thailand and abroad, while Chiang Mai is becoming a major center for the arts in its own right, highlighted by collections of Lanna pieces from past and present depicting the unique culture of the region.

MAJOR ART EPOCHS
Mon Dvaravati Period

The Mon Dvaravati period is particularly notable as it planted the first artistic seed in Thailand, influencing the various styles that would later emerge. Dvaravati art was the product of the Mon communities that ruled Thailand from the 7th to 11th centuries, prior to the arrival of the Khmers. Most art forms produced during this period were sculptures made of stone, terra-cotta, bronze, and stucco, influenced by Hinayana and Mahayana Buddhist and Hindu religious subjects. Perhaps the most distinctive Dvaravati sculpture is the Wheel of Law, a symbol of the Buddha's first sermon erected on high pillars that is still today placed in temple compounds. Fine examples of Dvaravati art can be found in Bangkok's National Museum and the Jim Thompson Museum.

Sukhothai Period

One of the most prominent Thai kingdoms was Sukhothai, established in 1238. Its art was heavily influenced by Theravada Buddhism, merging human form with the spiritual. Buddha images and ceramics were the most popular art forms, and sculptures were characterized by elegant bodies and slender, oval faces. Emphasizing the spiritual aspect of Buddha by leaving out anatomical details, the effect was enhanced by casting images in metal, as opposed to carving them. Brick and stucco Buddha images can still be found in the ruins of the Sukhothai Historical Park, while many examples of art from this period were moved to the National Museum in Bangkok.

Ayutthaya Period

An era spanning 400 years, 1351–1767, the Ayutthaya Kingdom spawned a wide variety of art forms, influenced by everyone from the Khmers and Chinese to the Japanese and Europeans, a byproduct of mid-16th-century trade and diplomacy. The early Ayutthaya period reflects Dvaravati and Lopburi influences, featuring Buddha images carved primarily of stone, while paintings featured only red, black, and white coloring, with rows of juxtaposed Buddhas. Due to the destruction and pilfering of the Ayutthaya Kingdom by the Burmese, few artifacts of this period remain, but some examples of Ayutthaya art can be found at the National Museum in Bangkok as well as Wat Rajaburana in Ayutthaya.

Lanna Period

In the 15th century, the northern region of Thailand began to flourish, referred to as the

Lanna era. This was the golden age of Chiang Mai, when King Tilokaraja ruled and great emphasis was placed on the arts. The word *lanna* translates as "land of one million rice fields," and its art is characterized by Burmese, Lao, and Sukhothai influences but boasts a distinct identity all its own. Lanna people were considered a gentle and sweet group—a stereotype that remains today. Many works are based on the artists' natural surroundings, featuring paintings of flowers, leaves, and outdoor scenes. Lanna murals depict cultural traditions, including ceremonies, festivals, and regular activities in the village, as well as religious dharma images. Local artisans are today keeping the Lanna tradition alive by creating reproductions; workshops and retailers can be found throughout Chiang Mai.

Rattanakosin Period

The Rattanakosin period—also referred to as the Bangkok era—was born with the Chakri Dynasty that still rules today, founded after the collapse of Ayutthaya in 1767. Art from this era is characterized by two themes, the promotion of the classical Siamese traditions under the reigns of three kings—Ramas I, II, and III—followed by the rule of Rama IV, when Western elements found their way into Thai art. Initially the art scene during the Bangkok era was focused on salvaging what was left from the pillaged war-ravaged areas, and new pieces of art continued in this vein. Later, however, ornamentation became a dominating factor, and images became more realistic. Murals began to flourish, as did the ornamentation of temples with gilded colorful images, statues, and intricate designs. For the best examples of art from the early Rattanakosin period, visit Wat Phra Kaew and the Grand Palace in Bangkok.

Contemporary Art

Interestingly, the father of modern Thai art is actually a foreigner, an Italian sculptor named Corrado Feroci who was invited to Thailand by Rama VI in 1924. Feroci created bronze statues of Thailand's past heroes and in 1933 was asked to establish an institute of fine arts to instruct a new generation of artists in modern art. The school eventually became a university and was called the Silpakorn (Fine Arts) University, and Feroci's own name was changed to Silpa Bhirasri. He remained in Thailand until his death in 1962. With the introduction of modern art, painters began experimenting with impressionism and a bit of cubism. Today, Thailand's contemporary art scene is centered in Bangkok, with an increasing variety of works available on the market. Although many younger artists have departed from the religious themes of the past, there are still some who remain influenced by traditional Buddhist values, hence they tend to be more popular among the general public. Much to the dismay of the traditionalists there are some Thai artists breaking away from these norms by addressing more controversial issues in their work, often stirring up public controversy in the process.

FAMOUS THAI ARTISTS

While few Thai artists have made a name for themselves on the international stage, there are several notable individuals who led the Thai art scene into uncharted territory, such as Angkarn Kalayanapongsa (born 1926) and Misiem Yipintsoi (1906–1988). Chakrabhand Posayakrit (born 1943) was also a groundbreaking artist, painting portraits that interpret classical themes in soft colors. Montien Boonma (1953–2000) was one of the only Thai artists to create a buzz overseas, his works appearing in many international exhibitions. Works by Montien reflect sections of Thai life that have undergone rapid change, using local materials and motifs in an incredibly unique style. Most Thais will also recognize the name Chalermchai Kositpipat (born 1955), Thailand's most successful painter today. The Chiang Rai native's works have been exhibited worldwide, and he is known for his innovative use of Buddha images in his art that often raise eyebrows. Some say he has lost his confrontational edge, but nonetheless he is still admired by many high-profile clients, including King Bhumibol Adulyadej.

ARCHITECTURE

Fabulous teak mansions built high on stilts, golden palaces, colorful *wats,* and even quaint rows of shophouses built by Chinese immigrants are all major hues on Thailand's architectural palette. The country's history is heavily imprinted on its wide-ranging architectural gems, allowing for a developmental history of Thai society to be traced back in time. Because Thailand's capital kept changing locations throughout the ages, there are several key areas that are home to some of the country's key architectural highlights; however, contemporary architecture is mainly found in forward-thinking Bangkok.

Sukhothai

The Sukhothai period (13th–14th centuries) is regarded as the apex of Thai culture, advancing major achievements in architecture. During this period the mainstays of Thai temples were developed, including the *phra chedi* (stupa), *bot* (where Buddha image is enshrined), and *prasat* (castle). Khmer elements abound, while the Mons—dominant from the sixth to ninth centuries—also provided Theravada Buddhist influences. Sukhothai-era houses and palaces built of wood have long since vanished, but ruins of stone and brick temples in the Sukhothai Historical Park—a UNESCO World Heritage Site—remain to provide evidence of the period's distinctive architecture.

Ayutthaya

Architecture of the Ayutthaya period (14th–18th centuries) was largely an extension of the Sukhothai style, but while Sukhothai laid the groundwork, Ayutthaya was the golden age. In a rich and powerful city renowned for its military might, buildings erected during this period took on a royal grandeur of sorts, with golden temples and glittering palaces becoming a mainstay. During the Ayutthaya period there was also a Khmer revival, when kings built a number of neo-Khmer-style temples and edifices. During the 13th–15th centuries the influence of the Chinese appeared in the form of kilned ceramic roof tiles and mother-of-pearl inlay, while in the 16th–17th centuries European styles slipped in with the arrival of foreign diplomats and high-ranking officials. Much of the ancient city's architecture was destroyed in 1767 when Ayutthaya was sacked by the Burmese; however, ruins of the ancient city remain and have been designated a UNESCO World Heritage Site.

Rattanakosin

For most travelers to Bangkok, their first views of historical Thai architecture come courtesy of Wat Phra Kaew and the Grand Palace, two attractions that have shaped the architectural image of the country in the world's eye. Indeed, the Rattanakosin period is the most diverse of all Thailand's eras in terms of architecture, given that it began with the founding of Bangkok in 1782 and continues today. Much like the earlier art of this era, architecture was designed to mirror the dominant styles of the former capital Ayutthaya in the wake of its destruction. This meant incorporating Khmer (such as Wat Arun), Chinese, and a few Western elements into temples and palaces.

Traditional Thai styles began to decline around 1900, when buildings increasingly took on European forms. For craftspeople to be considered masters of their trade they were required to learn Western techniques, hence the concepts of Frank Lloyd Wright and Mies van der Rohe were embraced by local architects. Neoclassical elements were incorporated, a fine example of this being Wat Benchamabophit (Marble Temple) in Bangkok, which was erected for King Chulalongkorn in 1900 and designed by his half brother, Prince Naris. A few decades later, art deco became a key style, evident in buildings such as the Hua Lamphong Train Station and those along Ratchadamnoen Avenue.

Starting a few decades ago, when Bangkok's urban center really began to grow, a feeling of "anything goes" appears to have emerged, with elements of modernism, Greek revival, Bauhaus, sophisticated Chinese, and native Thai styles all mashed together into eclectic designs that are often quite eye-catching but occasionally quite garish. Today's urban architecture has few features to distinguish it from that of any other major international city, with glassy high-rises, ritzy condominiums, and flashy shopping malls becoming the norm. That said, many government buildings and universities have been built combining Thai styles with sensible contemporary design for a pleasing effect.

Traditional Thai structures can still be found throughout the country, and even the simplest building with uniquely Thai elements can be a great source of beauty. There are elegant classic wooden houses on stilts with curved roofs, Malay-inspired buildings in the south, "raft" homes over the river, Chinese shophouses, and Sino-Portuguese buildings in areas such as Phuket. It is in this diversity that Thailand's architectural beauty can be found, a stark contrast to the glittering high-rises that are becoming the mainstay in the capital.

ESSENTIALS

Getting There

AIR

Thailand is served by two large international airports: **Suvarnabhumi Airport,** just outside of Bangkok, and **Phuket International Airport,** on the island of Phuket on the Andaman coast. There are also four other smaller airports in the country that have limited international flights. If you are flying from North America or Europe, you'll most likely land in Suvarnabhumi first regardless of your destination, as the Phuket airport and other smaller international airports only serve direct international flights from parts of Asia as well as limited seasonal charter flights from Europe. Once you've landed in Bangkok, you can transfer to a flight going to one of more than a dozen regional airports around the country, including in Chiang Mai, Chiang Rai, Krabi, Ko Samui, and Surat Thani.

The **Airports of Thailand Public Company Limited** (AOT, www2.airportthai.co.th) runs most of the airports, and their website has information about the larger ones. Click "ENG" in the upper-right-hand corner of the welcome page to navigate the website. Some airports, such as the Samui Airport, are not part of AOT. To access information about the Samui Airport, visit the website for **Bangkok Airways** (www.bangkokair.com), as they are owned by the same company. Other smaller

COURTESY OF NOK AIR

airports, such as the **Loei Airport,** are so small they don't have any Web presence.

Carriers

If you are coming from the United States, the only direct flight to Bangkok is the Thai Airways flight from LAX, which takes about 18 hours coming to Thailand and 15 hours going back. If you're not flying on Thai Airways from Los Angeles, you'll have to change planes either in Europe or another Asian city before making your way to Bangkok. In that case, the shortest flight combination is about 20 hours. If you're not flying from a major hub in the United States, add an additional flight and at least another couple of hours.

Bangkok's airport is a major hub for long-haul flights, so if you are visiting Thailand from another part of Asia, from Europe, or from Australia, there are plentiful options. All major regional carriers, including **Singapore Airlines** (www.singaporeair.com) and **Cathay Pacific** (www.cathaypacific.com), have multiple daily flights to Bangkok.

Don't forget to check the regional budget carriers too. **Air Asia** (www.airasia.com) has many daily flights to Bangkok from Singapore, Malaysia, Indonesia, Hong Kong, Macao, India, Cambodia, Vietnam, Taiwan, Burma, and some cities in China. Their long-haul budget airline, **Air Asia X,** offers flights from Australia, New Zealand, and Europe through Malaysia. Check **Nok Air** (www.nokair.com) for flights from Vietnam, **Jet Airways** (www.jetairways.com) from major Indian cities, **Jetstar** (www.jetstar.com) from Australia, and **Tiger Airways** (www.tigerairways.com) from Singapore.

Costs and Booking

A round-trip ticket from North America to Bangkok costs US$900–1,500, as of early 2011, but prices can vary wildly depending on the route and time of year you are traveling, and how far in advance you book your flight. Although all of the major travel websites will show you flights to Bangkok, remember that you can sometimes find better prices and schedules by visiting the websites of individual airlines directly, and that even the major websites such as **Orbitz** (www.orbitz.com), **Travelocity** (www.travelocity.com), and **Expedia** (www.expedia.com) cannot book flights for all of the airlines you may want to travel on. Deals such as **Cathay Pacific's All Asia Pass,** which allows you to fly to Hong Kong then add an additional four destinations, including Bangkok, for a fixed fee, are a great bargain, especially if you are combining a trip to Thailand with some regional travel, but it won't show up on the travel websites. This is a very popular product, and it has some time restrictions and is only offered during some parts of the year, so you have to book it through Cathay Pacific's website or through a travel agent well in advance of your trip.

Since you'll probably have a stopover anyway, another option is to consider flying into Singapore, Malaysia, Korea, Japan, or another destination in Asia, then purchasing a separate ticket to Thailand. This involves a little more planning but can sometimes result in a cheaper overall price, especially if you are flying into one of the cities served by the regional budget airlines. For example, flights from cities such as Singapore and Kuala Lumpur can routinely be found for under $100 on Air Asia.

Checking In

For international flights, make sure to reconfirm your flight a few days in advance. In addition, sign up for notifications by email or mobile phone so you'll find out immediately if there have been any changes to your schedule. Especially if you are flying from a busy U.S. airport, make sure to give yourself plenty of time to check in. With stringent security protocols and the requirement at some airports that you bring your checked baggage through the security screening process after check-in, allowing three hours is not excessive. You may end up hanging around in the terminal for a while, but it's better than risking missing a flight for your vacation.

Passengers on international carriers have not been subject to the greatly reduced baggage allowances we've seen for domestic flights in the United States and are typically allowed two checked bags on flights from North America to Asian destinations, but make sure you check with your airline before you pack. That same rule applies to carry-on baggage, although for now you'll find that regional carriers are more generous with their rules on how many bags you can bring in the cabin. Regional budget airlines, however, will charge a modest fee per checked bag. Restrictions on liquids are essentially uniform across the globe at this point, so know what you are allowed to bring onboard with you by checking the Federal Aviation Administration's website (www.faa.gov). You can use their rules as a guide for the rules airports in other countries will apply, but always check with individual carriers for additional regulations.

Insurance

There are many types of travel insurance, covering everything from unforeseen events that result in missed flights to medical treatment when you are abroad to lump-sum payments to designees should you be killed or maimed while traveling. Flight insurance will cover you for accidents and flight cancellations, meaning that you will be repaid the amount of money you've spent on your vacation if your flight is canceled or if you miss it due to sickness or injury. While this can come in handy if you are flying with a charter company or taking a cruise, for many people it is just a waste of money. Most international carriers will allow you to reschedule even non-refundable tickets, and generally you won't be required to put down a deposit for accommodations in Thailand (though you may be charged a one-night cancellation fee). Agents will try to persuade you that the policy is worth the $50 or more for the peace of mind, but it's probably better to save that extra cash unless you absolutely cannot afford the costs of canceling a trip.

LAND

If you are already in Southeast Asia, you can enter Thailand by bus or train at one of the border crossings with Malaysia, Cambodia, and Laos (currently you cannot enter Thailand through Burma). There are no buses that cross from one border to another; instead, you'll have to get to a border stop, such as Poi Pet for Cambodia or Nong Khai for Laos, cross the border on foot, and board another domestic bus. This can be time-consuming and cumbersome, but thousands of backpackers and other travelers have worn these paths smooth and flat before you. If you are doubtful about whether a crossing is possible, check the Internet for information, but always contact the embassy of the country you are trying to enter to confirm whatever you read.

If you are traveling from Singapore or Malaysia, there is train service linking these countries to Thailand. From Singapore, you'll have to change trains twice, but you can buy one ticket that will take you all the way. **The Man in Seat 61** (www.seat61.com/Thailand. htm) has the best description of the process as well as up-to-date information on schedules and prices.

SEA

There aren't many opportunities to enter Thailand by sea, however you can do it if you are coming from Langkawi Island in Malaysia. There are frequent ferries (www.langkawi-ferry. com) from this island that will deposit you in the town of Satun in southern Thailand, from where you can continue your travels.

Getting Around

AIR

Thailand has many regional airports served by national airlines and competing low-cost carriers. If you are short on time and don't mind the extra expense, this is the best way to travel around the country. **Thai Airways** (www.thai-airways.com), the country's flagship carrier, has flights to the Andaman coast, Isan, and the north. **Bangkok Airways** (www.bangkokair.com) serves Ko Samui, Sukhothai, Krabi, and other traditionally tourist destinations. But do not forget the budget airlines. Small ones seem to pop up all the time, but two are reliable and popular. **Nok Air** (www.nokair.com) is partially owned by Thai Airways, and **Air Asia** (www.airasia.com) is one of the largest budget carriers in Asia. Both have extensive schedules to popular destinations such as Phuket (between the two there are more than a dozen daily flights) and limited flights to less-popular places. None of the budget airlines show up on any of the travel websites, so you have to book through their websites, by phone, or at the airport. Luckily both have very user-friendly websites. Nok Air even lets you book by phone (call 1318 or 02/900-9955) and then pay for and pick up your ticket at a 7-Eleven. This will only work for flights scheduled more than 24 hours in advance, but it will really come in handy if you are having trouble using a credit card on the Internet.

TRAIN

Thailand has an extensive railroad system serving all parts of the country. The train system is run by the **State Railway of Thailand** (www.railway.co.th/home/) and you'll find schedules and fares on the website. Seats are available in first through third class, depending on the route, and range anywhere from plush and comfortable air-conditioned cars with snacks and beverages served to your seat to wooden benches, open windows, and café cars serving local beer and inexpensive Thai dishes. Sleepers likewise run the gamut, but even the second-

Train station vendors hawk food to travelers.

class sleepers are quite comfortable (you'll even get freshly laundered sheets and blankets). This is a great way to get to see the country and meet people, but it's definitely not the fastest way to travel (buses are routinely faster).

Note that you cannot book train tickets on the Internet; you'll need to go either to the train station in person or stop in at any travel agent (you will pay a small fee for this service). If you are planning on traveling on a weekend or around a national holiday, you must book well in advance (especially if you are taking an overnight train and want a sleeper). Tickets will often sell out days or even weeks in advance of popular travel dates.

BUS

Thailand is covered by an extensive network of interregional, regional, and local buses, and it is possible to get almost anywhere in the country via bus if you're willing to spend the time navigating the system. From Bangkok and other major cities, there are frequent air-conditioned buses (sometimes referred to as **VIP buses**) where you'll be guaranteed a comfortable reclining seat on an express route. If you are traveling to a popular destination, it may be as easy as that. To get to more far-flung areas, you'll generally need to take a bus to the closest big city and then switch to a local or interregional bus for the rest of your journey. A ticket on a standard bus, which may be the only option, depending on where you are going, does not guarantee you a seat, and they can get packed. You may find yourself standing for hours or smashed up against the windshield as the bus speeds along a highway.

Unfortunately there is no central repository for bus schedules and routes, and they can change. Although there is plenty of information available on the Internet, the best bet is to contact someone at your final destination who will be able to advise you on the best route possible.

The main bus company, with routes from Bangkok to all parts of the country and back, is **The Transport Co.** (www.transport.co.th). The website lists all of the routes, fares, and schedules to and from Bangkok.

TAXI

You will find taxis in most of the major cities and popular destinations in the country, though you most likely will not find them in rural areas or less affluent places. In Bangkok, taxis are generally reasonable and easy to find. A trip anywhere in the city should run less than 150B (sometimes significantly less, as the meter starts at 35B). In places such as Phuket, finding a metered taxi is nearly impossible, and local taxis charge exorbitant rates to take you from one part of the island to another.

SONG THAEW

For short trips between neighboring villages (or even between neighborhoods in Bangkok), these vehicles—essentially pickup trucks with seats in the back and roofs overhead—are a common and easy option. They usually run specific routes and will stop to pick up and discharge passengers along the way for anywhere from 5B, depending on the length of the journey. Schedules aren't posted, nor are prices or routes, or even stops. They may seem totally inaccessible, but any local person will know the route and be able to direct you. When in doubt you can just say *song thaew bai [destination]* and, after a couple of tries, someone will point you in the right direction.

CAR

Thailand's major road system is exceptionally well maintained and relatively easy to navigate. Driving in Bangkok is probably not a good idea unless you're really comfortable navigating confusing streets, dealing with informal rules that often seem completely at odds with what you learned in driving school, and sitting in traffic for hours. But once you are outside the city, driving is perhaps the best way to cover a lot of ground and see the country at the same time (you'll beat the buses and the trains). If you are traveling with small children, it is unfortunately also the only way to guarantee that you are even going to get a seat belt. For very small children, bring a car seat with you or buy one at one of the high-end department stores before you hit the road. The larger **Central Department Stores** will have them in stock, as will the department stores in **Siam Paragon, Central World Plaza,** and **Emporium** in Bangkok. Outside Bangkok you may not be able to find one easily, and their availability at car rental agencies is limited. If you are coming from North America, remember that in Thailand, your steering wheel is on the right and you must drive on the left.

Rental Agencies

All of the major agencies, including **Avis** (www.avis.com), **National** (www.nationalcar.com), and **Hertz** (www.hertz.com), have locations in Thailand, although generally in places such as Phuket and Bangkok. Prices are typically $50–100 per day, with a slight discount if you rent by the week. Most international agencies will require that renters be at least 25 years old. There are also local rental-car companies, and prices may be significantly cheaper if you choose one of these. Make sure you understand the insurance you are getting, however, as you may be liable for any damage to the vehicle.

Legal Requirements

You must hold a valid driver's license from your home country to drive in Thailand. An international driver's license is not required unless you are going to be in the country for an extended period of time. Make sure you carry your passport or a copy of it if you are driving. If you get pulled over, the officer will require it, and you'll save yourself a trip to the police station if you have it with you.

Road Rules

Speed limits are expressed in kilometers, as are speedometers. On the highway the speed limit is generally 80 kilometers per hour (just under 50 mph) to 120 kilometers per hour (about 75 mph). On nonhighway roads outside of cities and towns it's 80 kilometers per hour. In cities and towns it is usually 60 kilometers per hour (35 mph). Seat belts are required for both the driver and the front-seat passenger. Although this law is routinely broken, it's best to stay within the bounds of the law if you are driving in a foreign country (not to mention the safety issues). **Drunk driving** is a serious offense in Thailand, and a blood alcohol level of 0.05 percent is all that is required to land you in jail. Remember that local beer is significantly stronger than the average North American brew. At 6.4 percent, one Chang Beer, especially if it's a large one, is probably enough to keep you off the road for an hour or two at least.

Remember that you **pass on the right** and slower vehicles stay in the left lane.

Though most of the signs and rules of the road are technically the same as the rest of the world, the **informal rules of the road** are probably a lot different than you are used to and might not make sense if you didn't grow up driving in Thailand. Suffice it to say that other drivers may (and probably will) do things you are not expecting, such as changing into your lane with less than a meter to spare or turning without signaling. The best way to handle this is to drive cautiously, watch out for other drivers, and keep a *sabai* attitude.

Gas Stations

On major roads and on highways there are plenty of gas stations, some open 24 hours (especially on highways). In smaller village areas, gas stations may close as early as 7 P.M., so keep an eye on your tank if you are driving to more remote areas. You can get diesel, leaded, and unleaded gas, but most of the newer cars run on unleaded. If you are in doubt, the gas station attendant will know the right mix. Gas is relatively inexpensive in Thailand. It is sold by the liter and recently has run around 33B per liter, which equals around US$2.25 per gallon.

Parking

Street parking in Bangkok is nearly impossible

Gas is relatively inexpensive in Thailand.

and not advised unless you can read the infrequent street signs in Thai to discern the rules, but it is relatively easy to find an inexpensive parking lot wherever you are headed. All major malls, hospitals, hotels, and many larger restaurants offer parking, often with valet service. If you are parking your car in a lot, do not be surprised to see other cars lining the drive and blocking each other. This is normal and drivers are expected to leave their cars in neutral without engaging the emergency brake (obviously this does not apply on any sort of grade) so they can be pushed out of the way if necessary.

In less densely populated areas, parking is considerably easier, and there are generally parking lots at larger hotels and restaurants if street parking is unavailable.

Motorcycles

Motorcycles are very common in Thailand. If you are driving or even a passenger in a car, it is your responsibility to watch out for them. Motorcycle drivers will often straddle lanes, pass between cars, cross highways, and do all sorts of unanticipated (for other cars, at least) things. Be aware that there are always motorcycles on the road, and sometimes they are difficult to see in your side and rearview mirrors. If you are on a major highway, it is not unheard-of to see someone on a bike attempting to cross perpendicularly in front of you, and there are plenty of motorcycle fatalities every year. If you are opening the door of a car or a taxi, look behind you beforehand. Motorcycles have been known to snake in and out of parked cars, and a quickly opened door can lead to disaster.

Renting a motorcycle outside Bangkok is probably easier than buying a can of soda. You will need your passport and cash; it's almost unheard-of to be asked for a license. Sometimes rental agencies will hold your passport as collateral, and other times they will ask for a deposit of 500–1,000B (if you are asked to leave your passport, make sure you keep a copy of it as well as the rental receipt in case you are pulled over). Expect to pay 200–300B per day. In smaller areas, the rental shops have even

been known to lend out a bike without asking for anything in return. You are required by law to wear a **helmet,** and the police are generally quick to pull over foreigners without them.

The helmets you get with a rental bike are sometimes little more than plastic hats with chin straps. Ask for the best helmet available, and if no good ones are forthcoming, consider heading to the nearest **Tesco, Carrefour,** or **Big C** to buy one.

Most of the bikes available are 100–125 cc semiautomatic scooters, which means that you have to shift gears with your foot but do not need to engage a clutch to do so. That part is easy enough, but do not consider riding a bike unless you know what you are doing. Motorcycles are often the cheapest, easiest, and most fun way to get around, but there are accidents and even deaths every year by foreigners who are overconfident and think that just because everyone in the country is doing it, they can too. Yes, it's true that in any small village you'll probably see 12-year-old girls in their school uniforms piled three on a bike, sipping sodas, talking on mobile phones, and navigating these machines in their bare feet. That doesn't make it safe or easy. Motorcycles are a part of daily life, especially in rural areas, and the kids you see riding them probably literally grew up doing so. Even they are not immune— hundreds of Thais are involved in serious motorcycle accidents every year.

Maps and GPS

Detailed road maps of Thailand are available at bookstores in Bangkok, but it can be difficult to find ones that have place names translated into English. **Nelles Maps** and **Michelin** have maps that are generally available at **Bookazine** and **Kinokuniya** in Bangkok, but you won't be able to find them at local gas stations.

You can get a GPS system in a rental car if you are renting from one of the larger agencies. If you have a smart phone with GPS, you can also use that for navigation, but be aware that outside of major cities, connection times can be slow, so maps will not load quickly (this is separate from the satellite navigation).

Traffic in Bangkok is a real nightmare.

Roads and Highways

Thailand has a highway system running all the way north from the edge of Malaysia and linking nearly all major cities. Multilane major highways and tollways are generally in excellent condition, well signed, and fast. These are noted as "Highway" and almost always have a single-digit identifier (such as Highway 4). Secondary roadways are usually identified with a two-digit number or a four-digit number and are referred to here as "Route." Usually these branch off larger roads and are usually in good condition, although they can be considerably smaller than the 4–5 lanes drivers on the largest highways enjoy. When the secondary roads pass through urban areas, they will also function as large Main Streets, with plenty of commerce lining them and plenty of traffic during normal rush hours. Roads denoted with three-digit numbers are of varying quality, including dirt or country roads. These can be particularly difficult to navigate in rain in areas prone to flooding, and even in the best conditions, it's very slow going.

Traffic

Unless you are a Los Angeles native, Bangkok's traffic will probably shock you. Then it will frustrate you, and finally, after you realize you've gone just over one kilometer in the past twenty minutes, you'll come to an understanding with it. There's just no beating it. Outside the capital city, traffic eases up significantly but is still significant in major cities throughout the country, as well as in Phuket and other very popular areas. Just like home, it tends to be worse on Friday afternoons before long weekends, and on the last Friday of the month, which is payday for many folks.

If you are driving somewhere on a schedule, make sure to ask a local person how long it will take. Between traffic and secondary roads, the drive might take a lot longer than you've estimated.

Visas and Officialdom

Thailand has an easy tourist visa process if you hold a passport from one of the 71 countries the kingdom has deemed eligible for a **visa on arrival.** Countries include the United States, Canada, most European countries, many countries in Asia and the Middle East, and some countries in South America (check www.thaiembdc.org for the complete list). If you are entering from one of these countries, you technically still need a visa but you do not have to pay any fees for it, and you can get it at the airport when you arrive.

After you pick up your bags at the airport, you'll stand in line at the immigration counters, where you will be asked to hand over your passport and arrival card and have your photo taken. Fill out your **arrival card** before you reach the counter. Immigration officials are generally patient, but if there is a long line or someone has had a bad day, you may be sent all the way to the back of the line if you show up empty-handed. If you did not get an arrival card on the plane, there are desks stocked full of the white-and-blue sheets. After your passport has been scanned and you've been photographed, you'll be given an automatic 15–30-day tourist visa (depending on your passport—visitors from most countries, including the United States, Canada, and EU countries, get 30-day visas) and part of the arrival card will be stapled inside your passport. Do not lose it—you need it to leave the country, and if you don't have it when exiting, at the very least you will have to fill out forms and paperwork, which can take upward of an hour.

If you are staying in the country for longer than the visa on arrival permits, you can get an automatic **30-day extension** by visiting one of the Immigration offices in the country and paying a 1,900B fee. Do not overstay your visa. If you happen to be picked up by the police or even stopped for a minor traffic infraction, you will be thrown in jail until you are deported. That scenario may be unlikely, but when you leave the country you will be fined heavily by immigration. Under current rules, the first day of an overstay is free, but each day after that results in a 500B fine, up to 20,000B. You will be required to pay this fine at the airport or other border before you can leave.

If you are planning on staying in Thailand for more than a couple of months, you must contact the Thai consulate or embassy in your home country. Thailand used to have a very permissive system whereby you could just leave the country at one of the many land border crossings for a few minutes and return in order to refresh your tourist visa for another 30 days. But in recent years the government has cracked down on these border runs. The rules continue to change, so be sure to check for the most recent policies.

STUDENT AND WORK VISAS

Students wishing to do study-abroad programs in Thailand must obtain a **student visa.** Although the process is straightforward, you must make arrangements with an accredited school in the country first, as they will need to provide documentation to the Thai consulate or embassy in order to obtain the visa. In addition to the major universities, which all offer foreign exchange or other study-abroad programs (both degree and nondegree), there are some language schools that are accredited and can support an application for a student visa.

Obtaining a **work visa** if you are planning on teaching English in Thailand is also relatively easy. You must have a job before you can apply for the visa, and your employer will generally walk you through the process and paperwork (although not all schools will pay the visa costs for you). Many people wishing to work as teachers in Thailand arrive in the country on tourist visas and proceed with their job search once in the country. There are many teaching opportunities in the country, for varying levels of pay, in rural and urban areas, and for teachers of various skills. There are scores of websites that cater to teachers in Thailand; it's wise to do some research first.

THAI EMBASSIES AND CONSULATES

In the United States, the Royal Thai Embassy (www.thaiembdc.org) is located in Washington, D.C. There are three main consulates, in Los Angeles, New York, and Chicago, and an additional 13 offices of honorary consuls in Montgomery, AL, Denver, CO, Coral Gables, FL, Atlanta, GA, Honolulu, HI, Leakwood, KS, New Orleans, LA, Boston, MA, Broken Arrow, OK, Portland, OR, Dallas, TX, El Paso, TX, Houston, TX. The main consulates can process all visa applications, but if you are closer to an honorary consul, call the office to see whether they might be able to help you. The honorary consuls are generally far less busy than the full consulate offices and you may have a faster turnaround.

FOREIGN EMBASSIES IN THAILAND

You should know the location and contact information of the embassy of your home country in Thailand, as this is where you will be able to find information about voting as a citizen abroad, register the birth of a citizen in Thailand, replace a lost or stolen passport, seek legal advice if you've been arrested, help arrange a medevac if necessary, or, in worst-case scenarios, notify families of deaths of citizens abroad. Remember that while your embassy is there to help you and can assist you or refer you to assistance, they are not able to get citizens released from police custody, pay medical bills, or help you return home. All embassies are located in Bangkok, though some countries have smaller offices in other parts of the country too. To contact your embassy or consulate in Thailand, visit the following: **U.S. Embassy** (American Citizen Services, 95 Wireless Rd., Bangkok, tel. 02/205-4049, www.bangkok.usembassy.gov); **Australian Embassy** (37 S. Sathorn Rd., Bangkok, tel. 02/344-6300, www.thailand.embassy.gov.au); **British Embassy** (14 Wireless Rd., Bangkok, tel. 02/305-8333, www.britishembassy.gov.uk);

Canadian Embassy (15th Fl., Abdulrahim Pl., 990 Rama IV Rd., tel. 02/636-0540, http://geo.international.gc.ca/asia/bangkok).

CUSTOMS

Customs regulations in Thailand limit the amount of goods you may bring into the country. If you stopped at a duty-free shop before entering the country, remember that you are limited to two cartons of cigarettes and one liter of alcohol. Generally you can bring in personal electronics, including laptops, cameras, and video cameras, but customs may charge you duties on anything over 80,000B. This rule does not seem to be applied to travelers who are not bringing in loads of equipment (click on "Travelers" in the English version of www.customs.go.th). You are generally not permitted to bring plants or animals into the country, but there are some exceptions that change over time. If you have any doubts, call the Agricultural Regulatory Division (tel. 02/579-1581).

When you are leaving the country, remember that you must report cash that you have in baht over 50,000B. You can also be stopped if you are exporting counterfeit goods or any art or artifacts of questionable provenance. There is still a significant trade in sculptures, carvings, and other artwork that is considered the property of the nation and rightfully belongs inside the country. Do not attempt to leave the country with anything that you have been told is an authentic piece from a ruin, temple, or other cultural heritage site.

BORDER CROSSINGS

There are numerous land border crossings between Thailand and Cambodia, Laos, and Malaysia. If you are planning on leaving the country by land, you must check with both the Thai Immigration office and the immigration office of your destination country to make sure the border location where you intend to cross has the necessary officials to process your paperwork. For example, you can get a day pass to visit Tachileik, Burma, from Mae Sai, but you may not be able to get a tourist visa into the country. Rules change quickly and are best found by calling embassies and checking on the Internet.

POLICE

Thailand is generally a very safe place for tourists but (comparatively) wealthy tourists are sometimes targets for property crimes. Dial **1155** from any phone in Thailand if you need assistance. This is a special **tourist police** number set up with the Tourism Authority of Thailand to help visitors; they will be able to assist you in English. In certain heavily touristed areas, including **Pattaya,** the tourist police have set up kiosks where you can walk up and ask for help.

There are scores of anecdotal stories about minor corruption among police officers in Thailand. Generally these stories revolve around the payment of 100–200B to avoid a traffic ticket; rarely are there "shakedowns" of foreigners, especially those who are otherwise avoiding any trouble.

The **Thai Royal Police** wear dark-brown uniforms and mostly patrol on motorcycles. If you are approached by a police officer, be respectful and courteous and provide any information and documentation you are asked for. You are required by law to carry your passport with you at all times and you may be asked to produce this.

Accommodations

Accommodations in Thailand run the gamut from guesthouses with shared baths for as little as 100–200B per night to amazingly posh and spacious five-star resorts. If you are not traveling during high season, you generally do not need to book ahead unless you have your heart set on a particular property in a particular location. Unless otherwise noted, the prices listed in this book are based on high-season rates for a double-occupancy room.

During high season, especially in late December–early January, it can be very difficult to find a place to sleep in heavily touristed beach areas. The same is true if you happen to be visiting Surin during the Elephant Festival in November, or any town during a festival or popular event. There is really no low season for tourism in Thailand, but you can expect rates to be substantially lower than those noted in this book if you are not traveling during high season.

Unfortunately, there is no universal rating system for accommodations in Thailand, and the use of any amount of stars by a property is an arbitrary distinction that may have no relation to your expectations. Purported three- and four-star properties seem to be the worst offenders. Make sure to understand what you are getting for your money.

GUESTHOUSES

Guesthouse is the common term for small locally owned and operated accommodations. These are the cheapest lodgings you'll find in the country, and there is no rating system for them. At a minimum, you'll get a bed and a fan with a shared bath, although some guesthouses have private facilities and air-conditioning. Many also have attached cafés or small restaurants, but you should call in advance if you have any doubts about the level of amenities available. Generally, guesthouses do not have dormitory-style lodgings; these are commonly referred to as hostels.

BUNGALOWS AND CABINS

Bungalow is perhaps the most widely used term in the hospitality industry in Thailand, and the word can mean nearly anything. Generally bungalows are freestanding accommodations and are almost always at or near a beach. Other than that, anything goes. Some bungalows are literally four walls tacked together with a corrugated roof and a squat toilet. You'll also find bungalows as large as small apartments, with air-conditioning, cable or satellite TV, minibars, luxurious baths, and charming thatched roofs.

Occasionally you'll see **cabins** offered for rent, especially in or near national parks. These are also generally freestanding and also follow the same rules (or lack thereof) as bungalows.

HOTELS

Hotels are found in almost all price ranges, from 300B in small urban areas to upward of 6,000B in Bangkok. All hotels offer private baths, and most have minibars, TVs, air-conditioning, and some sort of food available on the premises. More expensive hotels have swimming pools, room service, and concierge services.

RESORTS

Any property calling itself a resort will have a swimming pool and some amount of property surrounding the accommodations. Resorts also generally have restaurants or bars on the premises. More expensive resorts, and those run by international chains, almost always have sports facilities such as tennis courts or fitness centers, organized activities, and plenty of space to wander and relax.

SERVICED APARTMENTS

Serviced apartments typically have rooms and suites larger than the average hotel room, sometimes with multiple bedrooms plus a living room, and a small kitchen. Service can be more limited than in a hotel, so for example housekeeping may clean three times per week instead of every day. These are usually intended for long-staying guests or families and can be a great value depending on the size of your party and your needs.

Food

Walk down any main street in any city or town in the country and you'll notice that there is food everywhere. From little street-side vendors selling all sorts of snacks to sit-down restaurants, you cannot go hungry in Thailand. Food is very important here—the average citizen of the kingdom eats out 13 times per week. That's almost two meals per day. Fortunately there is a lot to choose from.

Although Thai food is far more complex and varied than you may be used to if you've eaten at a Thai restaurant in your home country, there are some predominant flavors. First, you'll probably notice that food in the kingdom can be really spicy, and the liberal use of chili peppers is common. But it's not just the heat that distinguishes the cuisine but rather a subtle mix of flavors such as cilantro, galangal (similar to ginger), lemongrass, lime juice, fish sauce, coconut milk, and, oftentimes, peanuts.

Thailand has four regional cuisines—northern, northeastern, central, and southern—and each has its own specific flavors and specialties in addition to the common themes throughout.

The country has also integrated many Western foods into its daily menu, albeit with a slight twist. In larger cities you'll find plenty of hot dogs and sausages being served by street vendors alongside *mu ping* and *sai crock Isan*. There's also Thai pizza, which is a little sweeter than the food by the same name in Italy. It's also served with toppings such as corn and spicy shrimp.

THE FOUR REGIONS

Northern Thailand is where you'll find lots of soups, a predominance of sour and bitter flavors, and generally richer dishes such as *khao soi*—flat egg noodles served with rich, meat-based curry soup—as well as sticky rice, which is eaten by rolling it into balls in your hand, instead of the fluffier version.

Northeast Thailand is known for its *som tam,* the spicy papaya salad that has made its way from the humble plains of Isan to virtually every corner of the country. In this region you will find a predominance of spicy food, many salads (called *som*), grilled meats, and, of course, sticky rice.

RESTAURANTS

Thailand is full of places to eat, from restaurants to street stalls, and you'll easily find meals and snacks in any urban area or tourist destination. Be aware that your expectations of what constitutes a restaurant may be different than those here. In smaller towns, the fanciest restaurant you'll find will usually be a fan-cooled shophouse with plastic chairs for seats and limited restroom facilities. These shops, which probably make up the majority of food places in the country (including in major cities and many tourist areas), aren't always spotlessly clean by Western standards, and some visitors may be put off by the way they look. Many of the suggestions in this book are just those types of local restaurants, but we've tried our best to adjust expectations by indicating what you'll expect inside. If you come across a restaurant falling into this category, don't dismiss it. This really is where you'll find the freshest and best-prepared food in the country. It also happens to be the cheapest food (apart from street food), and meals will usually cost around 50B with a soda.

In Bangkok, Phuket, Ko Samui, and Chiang Mai, you will be able to find a good selection of air-conditioned sit-down restaurants that probably look a lot like what you're used to at home. When warranted by quality of food or convenience, we've included these places, and if you can't tell from the description, you should be able to tell from the prices listed; these types of restaurants are usually at least twice as expensive as the shophouses.

one of thousands of street markets in Thailand

you'll see dishes influenced by Indian cuisine, including the use of turmeric and the delicious pancake-like roti, served plain, sweet, or with savory curries. Curry dishes can be quite hot here, and you'll often see platters and plates of raw vegetables and herbs served at the table to complement the spice. You'll also see a dish called *khao yum* unlike anything you'll find anywhere else. This is essentially a rice salad served with numerous chopped and shredded vegetables as well as ground spices.

THE MOST TYPICAL THAI FOODS

One dish you'll find everywhere is *guay teow*, noodle soup, which probably originated in China but has become a staple in Thailand. While noodle soup may sound boring, you can find it prepared in infinite ways, from a simple bowl of beef broth and large, flat rice noodles to a sweet and spicy bowl of *guay teow tom yum*. Other common foods you'll find nearly everywhere in the country include *khao phad*, which is a fried rice dish, and many regional

Central Thailand is known for its fragrant *hom mali* rice, similar in flavor and texture to jasmine rice, often eaten with spicy coconut milk–based curry. You'll also find coconut milk in dishes such as *tom kar gai* and even in the *tom yam kung*.

In the south, you'll find a cuisine less like that of the rest of the country. Here's where

© SUZANNE NAM

a plate of pad thai

dishes such as *som tam, tom yam kung,* and many curries.

MEALS

Thailand's love affair with food ensures that you can generally eat whenever you want without worrying about offending anyone. **Breakfast** is available anytime from 7 A.M. onward. For locals, this may consist of a bowl of *jok* with crispy fried cruller slices, a soft-boiled egg, cilantro, and slivers of ginger or some noodles, although lots of people will take a more Western-style coffee and baked item instead, and you'll find plenty of street vendors in big cities selling sweet waffles and other more familiar breakfast treats. A Thai breakfast meal will cost 20–40B, but you may pay more for Western fare. If you are in the mood for a substantial Western breakfast, you'll have to hit one of the larger hotels or Irish or English pubs (if you are in Bangkok or Phuket), where you should be able to find what you are looking for.

Lunch is generally eaten 11 A.M.–2 P.M. If it's a workday and you happen to be in a city around this time, you'll notice throngs of people coming out of their offices for their afternoon meal—it's almost unheard-of to pack a lunch. And why would you? Chances are there's plenty to choose from. During the week, lunch is often a social event, and casual restaurants and the tables of street vendors will be full of work colleagues or groups of college students taking a break and enjoying a meal together. If you're eating from a street vendor (and everyone does, from CEOs to domestic workers), expect to pay around 35–40B per dish. You may pay double, triple, or quadruple that if you're in an air-conditioned sit-down spot.

Dinner is as important as lunch, and you'll also find popular street-food areas packed full of families and friends from around 7 P.M. onward. In larger cities you'll be able to find a meal in a restaurant anywhere from 6 P.M. to midnight, but places in more rural or less populated areas will probably close earlier.

Snacking is nearly a national pastime. If you drop into anyone's office, you'll probably see a little corner set aside just for snacks, which can range from grilled fish balls to cookies to traditional *khanom thai.* You'll also find food vendors around throughout the day, in case the mood strikes you.

Conduct and Customs

SOCIAL BEHAVIOR
The *Wai*

You can't go more than 10 minutes in Thailand without noticing people putting their hands together in a prayer-like motion and bowing their heads at each other. Though this isn't a totally casual greeting, it is a sign of respect and will almost always be used to greet elders, teachers, bosses, and even hotel guests. The *wai* is an important social gesture and, for a Thai person, the absence of a *wai* when otherwise called for can be taken as a serious breach of norms. As a foreigner you won't necessarily be expected to use it in business situations where it would otherwise be appropriate (a handshake is fine), but if you are visiting someone's home and meet their parents, or are talking to a monk, or engaged in some other activity of that nature, make sure to *wai* as a greeting.

Daily Conduct

Another thing you'll notice immediately upon arriving (well, maybe once you leave the airport) is the general level of politeness in the country. The use of polite particles *ka* and *kap* is near universal: People will greet you when you walk into a restaurant or step into a taxi, and when someone bumps into you on a crowded street or even in a nightclub, chances are they'll say "excuse me" or apologize with a smile. A *mai pen rai* attitude, which loosely translates as "no worries," pervades casual social interactions, and acting aggressive and impatient will generally get you nowhere fast.

Although it's difficult to make generalizations, and exceptions always occur, the Thais are extremely friendly, social, and curious people, especially when it comes to foreigners. Don't be surprised if the taxi driver you just met wants to know whether you're married, how many children you have, and even your salary. There's no offense meant; this is just friendly banter, and you should take the opportunity to ask questions about the other person's life too.

Although it might seem counterintuitive if you've ever seen a Thai go-go bar, people in the country are usually reserved and conservative in their behavior in public. "Conformist" may be too strong a word, but there is a propensity to behave in a manner that does not rock the boat. Very strange behavior or dress can make people very uncomfortable, although they may be too polite to express that discomfort to you.

Etiquette

There are few etiquette rules you'll need to remember when visiting, other than general politeness and respect. There are a couple of important ones, however. Do not criticize the monarchy. Although in small circles of close friends you will be able to have such a discussion, most people will take great offense. The king is generally revered, and in any case it is illegal to speak out against him. Twice a day, at 8 A.M. and 6 P.M., the national anthem is played on loudspeakers in all cities. Do as those around you do and stop where you are until the music is finished. If you are

---

VISITING *WATS*

Most of the *wats* listed in this book are active Buddhist temples (an exception is Wat Phra Kaew in Bangkok). Part of each temple's income is from visitor donations, but their purpose isn't to be a tourist attraction but rather a place for meditation and devotion. Generally there are no posted hours, but you can visit any time there's someone there to let you in. Most of the time you can just walk into the complex at any hour and wander around, although some of the buildings might be locked. Since Buddhist monks are supposed to abstain from unnecessary worldly items, there are usually no telephones in temples.

seeing a movie in a cinema, you are required to stand when the brief show about the king is played.

Also refrain from pointing your feet at anyone, especially at a Buddha in a temple, and don't touch anyone except little children on the head. Finally, you are expected to give your seat up to a monk if you are riding on public transportation, and there are even some specially reserved seats for them in trains and boats. Women are not allowed to touch monks, or vice versa, but the onus will fall on you to get out of the way if contact seems imminent.

Public Displays of Affection
In general, Thais are very affectionate in public but not in a sexual manner. It's quite common to see two girls, even in their teens, holding hands, parents hugging and kissing kids, and friends with their arms around each other. What is not common is seeing people hugging and kissing in a nonplatonic way.

Tips for Travelers

WHAT TO TAKE
You can find nearly everything you need in Thailand at a reasonable price, including international health and beauty products, so don't waste space in your luggage for shampoo or other toiletries. In general, pack as lightly as you can; your ability to explore the country will be limited if you're weighed down by baggage.

Thailand is a casual country, but people are generally quite style-conscious. If you don't want to stand out too much, don't disregard fashion sense just because you're on vacation. When **visiting temples** you will be expected to dress more modestly. That means no shorts for men and women, and no sleeveless tops for women. If you haven't planned ahead, most temples offer one-size-fits-all cloaks for rent. In some **Bangkok restaurants and nightclubs,** you'll be refused entry if you're wearing anything that looks too casual. If you're traveling during the **rainy season,** consider bringing a lightweight rain jacket with a hood.

Thailand is on a **220-volt system,** so if you're traveling from North America, you'll need to bring a voltage converter for any appliances. Most mobile phones, laptop computers, and cameras can be charged on any voltage between 110 and 220.

TRAVELERS WITH PHYSICAL DISABILITIES
Thailand is unfortunately an extremely difficult place to get around if you have difficulty walking. Although some (not all) of the high-end accommodations are wheelchair-accessible, sidewalks in major cities are often torn up or uneven and lack curb cuts, and using public transportation or even crossing major streets requires that you climb stairs. Likewise, museums and *wats* will often require some climbing of stairs. In rural areas you may not even find sidewalks, making navigating a wheelchair almost impossible.

There are several organizations that promote and facilitate accessible travel. Although there is no specific information about travel in Thailand available through any of these organizations, they can offer general tips and strategies. The most well known is **The Society for Accessible Travel and Hospitality** (www. sath.org).

TRAVELING WITH CHILDREN
Thailand is a great place to take your kids, thanks to plenty of outdoor activities, friendly people, and of course, the elephants. Thais are very friendly toward children and, except as noted in the entries for a couple of resorts, most places you'll want to go are appropriate

TIPS ON VISITING NATIONAL PARKS IN THAILAND

Thailand has more than its share of national parks, many of which cover not only mainland nature areas but also swaths of sea and some of the islands off the coast.

ACCOMMODATIONS AND FOOD

Many parks provide camping and bungalow facilities. The campsites often offer tent rentals, baths with cold-water showers, and even small canteen restaurants serving up more than decent local Thai food at reasonable prices.

The national parks also rent out simple bungalows that have baths with cold-water showers, and some even have air-conditioning. Beds are provided but generally not linens, so you'll have to bring your own sheets.

If your priorities are exploring the natural wonders of Thailand, or you even just want to enjoy a beautiful beach or island without the feeling of too much development around you, staying in one of the parks is an excellent option. It's also very budget-friendly. Pitching a tent will cost around 100B per night, and renting one of the bungalows often costs less than 1,000B per night.

During low season, it's possible to walk out to one of the park stations and ask if there are bungalows available, but even then there are times when the bungalows are booked solid for weeks. If you're interested in staying at one of the national parks, make sure to book a bungalow as far in advance as possible. You can book up to 60 days in advance, and in order to reserve a spot, the national parks department requires that you pay in full before you arrive. To do that from abroad, you'll have to make a wire transfer to the National Park, Wildlife and Plant Conservation Department. Although the process can seem a little daunting, they've laid out the bank codes you'll need to use at www.dnp.go.th/parkreserve/howtoreservation_4.asp?lg=2. Once you've confirmed that there's an available bungalow and transferred the funds, you must email reserve@dnp.go.th and dnp_tourist@yahoo.com with the confirmation information.

HOURS AND ADMISSION FEES

All national parks are open 8:30 A.M.–6 P.M. daily. Nearly all of the parks used to charge a 200B entry fee for foreigners, but many have raised the fee to 400B.

GETTING THERE AND AROUND

You may find that the mainland parks lack many well-marked hiking trails, and when they are marked, they are often only a couple of kilometers long. Since there are so few trails, it's also seemingly impossible to get around the parks without wheels of your own. It is not advisable to arrive at a national park without transportation. There is generally no public transportation within a park, sights are kilometers apart, and it's difficult even to get a trail map once you arrive. Many parks have large main roads cutting through them, making driving a convenient, if not very environmentally friendly, way to cover a lot of ground. But once away from the roads, you'll find the parks peppered with amazing waterfalls, beautiful scenery, and wildlife.

Thais who visit national parks (and this is the vast majority of visitors) are usually not hikers. Most visitors drive from parking lot to parking lot to see waterfalls and viewpoints, and that's really how the parks are designed to be used. Information centers rarely have trail maps available, and when they do, they are usually not in English.

for children. Challenges for parents, though, include getting around and keeping kids cool in the hot weather.

Sightseeing

All sightseeing and other activities listed in this book are open to people of all ages, the only exception being the diving sights. Particularly child-appealing sights are noted, but bear in mind that kids can have shorter attention spans than grown-ups, of course, and four-hour museum tours may be difficult for them (and as a consequence, for you) to bear. Depending on your child's age, take advantage of the inexpensive child-care options available in the country if there are some sights you can't miss but don't want to take them along.

Restaurants

Especially in more casual restaurants and eating spots, children are more than welcome, and you may even find the proprietors making a fuss about them, in a positive way. You may also notice that kids in the country are less restricted than you may be used to. It's not uncommon for a parent to let their child wander around a bit in a restaurant. Other guests and waitstaff will general keep an eye out, though obviously you are responsible for your kids.

You won't find special meals or menus for children except in some of the more upscale resorts. But if your child wants something particular, or can't tolerate spicy food at all, the chef will generally be more than happy to whip up something special. They may even suggest it or just bring it to the table. A great dish for kids is pad thai, since it's soft, mild, and not spicy. If your kids are really picky, there's always international chain food as a last resort. All major cities and resort areas have at least a McDonald's in the area.

Transport, Accommodations, and Supplies

Although Thailand is very child friendly, it's not necessarily child safe, and you should bear that in mind as you are traveling from place to

place. Many taxis do not have seat belts in the back, and it can be difficult to find a car seat. If you are traveling with a small child, try to bring your own car seat so that you know your child will be secure when you leave the airport. If you're traveling by airplane, even on budget carriers, your child will probably get some extra attention and a coloring book or some other toy to keep them occupied. The national trains will probably be the object of much fascination and have plenty of places to explore, though you should keep a careful eye on them as they can be dangerous too.

Children under 12 almost always stay free if they are sleeping in their parents' room. If you need a cot or crib, you may be charged an extra fee, however. Almost all larger hotels have babysitting services. Generally, the more you are paying for the room, the more likely you are to get a babysitter who speaks English.

You should be able to find baby formula at almost any 7-Eleven, but it may not be the brand you're used to, so stock up before leaving. The same goes for baby food, as most Thai babies don't grow up on canned or bottled food. Diapers can be a little more difficult to find, but any major hypermarket or large supermarket will stock them.

Nightlife

There are certain areas of the country, including Phat Phong in Bangkok and Walking Street in Pattaya, that are notoriously known for go-go bars and prostitution. Even walking through those places during the day will probably expose your children to things you don't want them to see. If you have kids old enough to understand what's going on, bear this in mind when planning your trip. Skip Pattaya altogether, and avoid the Phat Phong area in Bangkok and the Patong area in Phuket. There are plenty of family-friendly spots where you won't see sexpats or prostitutes.

WOMEN TRAVELING ALONE

Thailand is generally an easy and safe place to travel if you are a lone woman. You may get a bit of unwanted attention from both locals and other travelers, but it usually stops at attempts at small talk and offers of drinks. The good news is that it's really easy to meet other travelers if you want to find other people to tour around with. Once people get to Thailand, they tend to pick up the local vibe and get friendlier and more open.

Common Sense and Safety

If you are traveling alone, whether male or female, you must use common sense. Just because everyone in Thailand is friendly and laid-back doesn't mean you are always safe. Make sure you aren't in areas where no one else is around, especially late at night. Do not go for walks on the beach alone at night. In Bangkok, make sure you know where you are going if you're out late. Getting lost after clubbing can be a nightmare, worse so if you are worried about your physical safety.

Property crimes occur all over the world, and purse snatchings and muggings, though rare, can happen. Do not keep a lot of money on your person (better to take only what you need for the day from one of the thousands of ATMs in the country). If you have to hit an ATM late at night, find a 7-Eleven. Most have ATMs right outside and, since they are open all night, you can be assured that someone will be around. Also make sure to keep your bag close to your body, especially if you are walking in areas with lots of pedestrian and motorcycle traffic. This isn't just to safeguard you from getting your purse snatched; motorcycle drivers weave in and out of foot traffic too, and getting your bag snagged on a passing bike can lead to serious injury for you or the driver.

In 2010, violent civil unrest spread to some of the most touristed areas of Bangkok, including Khao San Road. Though there was ample warning that protesters would be in these neighborhoods, many travelers did not change their plans, and some were caught up in the melee (some were seriously injured). Take any warning seriously, and avoid any area where there may be civil unrest. Outbreaks of violence can occur without warning.

Staying in Touch

Make sure to give your itinerary and the contact information at your hotel to someone back home, and check in frequently. There are Internet cafés in all but the most remote parts of the country. They are cheap and easy to find; use them. Also consider buying a mobile phone if you don't have a tri-band or quad-band phone with a removable SIM card already. If you are arriving in Bangkok, you can pick up a used one for as cheap as $25 at MBK, then purchase a SIM card either there or at a 7-Eleven. These are prepaid phones, so all you have to do is buy a refill card for as little as 30B. Text messages to the United States are very inexpensive, and calls can be as little as 6B per minute.

Harassment and Violence

Thai culture does not really condone or encourage aggressive behavior toward strangers, but some do not feel that normal social rules apply to travelers. Usually it's as innocent as a catcall or a comment about your body. Once in a while it can be a little more offensive. If someone says something to you, just ignore it and walk away. If you are in a crowded area, you have nothing to worry about.

Rape and violence are rare, but there have been attacks on female travelers in the past. You must exercise normal precautions, the same ones you'd exercise at home. If you feel like someone is following you, immediately find other people. You may not be able to communicate the problem, but you can either just say "police" or stay with them until you are safe. Don't brush off an uncomfortable feeling out of embarrassment.

GAY AND LESBIAN TRAVELERS

Whether because of the large population of out gays and transsexuals or because of the generally permissive culture, Thailand is a very comfortable place for people of any sexual orientation to travel. There are numerous clubs and neighborhoods in all major cities that are either completely gay or mixed, and in general, no one at any "straight" club will bat an eye if a same-sex couple enters.

Remember, however, that public displays of affection of a sexual nature are not appropriate regardless of sexual orientation.

Health and Safety

In major urban areas and popular tourist destinations on the coast, you'll find easy access to medical treatment and other emergency services, but in more rural areas, services can vary widely. Currently there is no nationwide EMS system in Thailand. If you are involved in an accident in Bangkok, the **Narenthorn Center,** a division of the Ministry of Public Health, has a **hotline number, 1699,** and is connected to a network of hospitals and ambulances and can dispatch emergency medical services quickly. The national number for the **police is 191,** but you probably will not get someone on the phone who speaks English. To ensure you get someone on the phone you can communicate with, call **1155, the tourist police hotline.** For nonurgent care, ask to be taken to a hospital, called a *rung paya ban* in Thai. There are also numerous privately run small clinics set up in urban and tourist areas that you can visit for minor health problems.

By Western standards, the cost of health care in Thailand is exceptionally inexpensive, and the quality of care at private hospitals in big cities is on par with what you will find at home. Many of the larger private hospitals in Bangkok have excellent, clean, modern facilities. Doctors are routinely fluent in multiple languages, and many have studied at top universities across the country and around the world. An emergency room visit, even at one of these hospitals, will cost as little as 5,000B. Scheduled appointments with specialists are generally under 1,000B, meaning the complete cost of treatment will oftentimes be even less than the co-payment or deductible on your insurance back home. In fact, scores of patients from counties with national insurance programs travel specifically to Thailand for treatment they might otherwise have to wait months for back home, and each year perhaps thousands of people from around the globe come for cosmetic and other elective procedures; there are numerous websites dedicated to this topic.

BEFORE YOU GO

Before arriving in Thailand, as in any foreign country, make sure your medical information is current and you have sufficient supplies of any necessary prescription drugs. Carry a copy of your prescription with any drugs you are carrying in case you need a refill or to prove that the substance was legally obtained. Pharmacies and hospitals will normally have most common prescription drugs, but they are often named differently in different countries. If there is a chance you'll need something while you are here, make sure you know not only the brand name of your medication but the generic name as well.

Health Insurance

Check with your health insurance provider at home to determine whether you are covered in foreign countries and, if so, the extent of your coverage. There are numerous companies that provide health insurance for travelers and expatriates, including **Bupa** (www.bupa-intl. com) and **Travel Guard** (www.travelguard. com). If disaster strikes and you need to be transported home for treatment, not all policies will cover the cost, which can run in the tens of thousands of dollars, so look at the fine print on the policies.

If your health insurance policy already covers you for medevac and emergencies abroad,

RESTROOMS

Restrooms in Thailand can present a challenge for those who are only used to Western-style sit-down toilets. Though sit-down toilets are very common, squat toilets are also quite common. For many Western travelers these present some particular challenges, and you may have to face them if you need to use a restroom at a public park, roadside gas station, or even perhaps a small restaurant. There are no tried-and-true tricks to get you through this if you're not used to using one; just be aware that at one point in your trip, you'll probably have to. Often these toilets do not have a flush handle. Instead, there will be a bucket of water and a smaller pail – you have to pour a few cups of water directly into the bowl to wash everything down.

Sit-down or squat toilet aside, you may notice a couple of additional confusing things about the restrooms you encounter in Thailand. The first thing you'll see is a water sprayer, and that's used exactly as you'd expect. The second is a waste bin next to the toilet. That's for toilet paper, as the plumbing infrastructure can't handle paper waste (except in most Western-oriented high-end hotels and restaurants). Make sure not to flush your paper. Also, it's wise to carry a small pack of tissues with you, as many public restrooms will not have toilet paper available.

In the women's room, if you encounter a line, people usually line up in front of individual toilet stalls instead of in one line. It's confusing and doesn't seem to be very fair, but that's what everyone does.

In the men's rooms of some nightclubs, you may come across something even stranger – the urinal neck rub. There are men working in the restrooms whose job it is to give massages. The first time you saddle up to a urinal and feel someone rubbing your neck, it will probably come as a total shock, and you can ask politely that they stop. Don't worry, though, it's all on the up-and-up, and the most you'll be asked for is a small tip.

---

you are probably wasting your money buying any additional coverage. Even if there is a high deductible, remember that medical care is very inexpensive in Thailand.

Vaccinations

Check with your doctor, but most advise that the only vaccination you'll need for Thailand (assuming you are traveling in developed areas for a short period of time and not working in the health profession) is **hepatitis A,** a viral liver disease that is easily transmissible but also easily preventable. **The Centers for Disease Control and Prevention** (CDC) in the United States recommends that travelers to most countries outside North American and Europe get this vaccine. The vaccine is a series of two shots and should ideally be started about a month before you travel.

Malaria

Malaria is a very serious, sometimes fatal, disease transmitted by mosquitoes. Although it is extremely rare in most parts of the country, there is some malaria risk if you are traveling in rural, remote areas on the borders of Burma, Laos, and Cambodia. The CDC is currently recommending that you take prophylactic antimalarial drugs if you are going to be traveling in these areas and also recommends that you purchase them at home instead of abroad. Antimalarial drugs are strong drugs with difficult side effects and should be handled accordingly, despite the fact that you may be able to buy them over the counter in some parts of Southeast Asia. Know where you are traveling and determine whether there is a risk of malaria before you arrive, and talk to your doctor about which antimalarial you should take. Side effects of even the most commonly prescribed drugs can be harsh and include not only stomachaches and nausea but vivid dreams, anxiety, and in rare cases, seizures or even fatal heart disturbances.

If you haven't seen a doctor in your home country but are considering traveling to a possible malaria zone when you are here, all of the major hospitals in Bangkok that cater to tourists (B&H, Bumrungrad, and Samitivej) have travel specialists who will advise you whether an antimalarial is appropriate and, if so, prescribe it to you. Do not take matters into your own hands by doing research on the Internet and stopping in at a local pharmacy. Also, check the CDC website (wwwn.cdc.gov/travel/destinationThailand.aspx) for any changes in recommendations.

HEALTH MAINTENANCE

Most minor health issues can be addressed at a local pharmacy, and pharmacists in Thailand can dispense drugs that are often prescription-only back home, including antibiotics and antiviral medications. **Boots** (www.bootsthai.com) has many English-speaking pharmacists and a 24-hour hotline (tel. 800/200-444) that you can call if you want to find the closest location. In smaller towns, most pharmacists do not speak English.

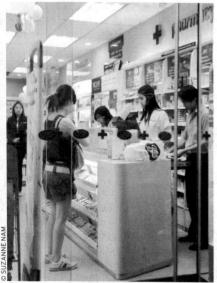

Pharmacies are available in all major cities.

If you are arriving in any populated area, don't worry too much about bringing common first aid items with you. Any drug store or pharmacy will have bandage strips, antiseptic cream, antidiarrheal treatments, and acetaminophen—the generic form of Tylenol, called paracetamol in Thailand. It will probably be cheaper than if you bought it back home. If you just need some pain reliever, every 7-Eleven and mom-and-pop shop will carry paracetamol, often in tear-off strips costing just a few baht per pill.

HEALTH ISSUES
Allergies

People with allergies to peanuts and shellfish may encounter serious difficulties in Thailand. Those are very common ingredients and, although most food preparation is hygienic, there is no guaranteeing that cross-contamination will not occur or that you will adequately be able to communicate the importance of avoiding such ingredients. Also, many prepared foods have warnings that they may contain traces of peanuts.

Bug Bites

Insects, especially mosquitoes, are common in Thailand, and aside from the inconvenience, they can pose a serious health threat. Aside from malaria, certain types of mosquitoes also carry **dengue fever,** a flu-like, debilitating, rarely fatal disease found in many parts of the world where mosquitoes are common. While malaria is almost never seen outside of rural areas, dengue outbreaks seem to occur annually even in Bangkok, and everyone who lives in the city knows someone who's had the disease. There is currently no vaccine for dengue; the only way to prevent the disease is to avoid mosquito bites. Despite questions about the long-term safety of using a DEET-based bug repellent, this is probably your best bet, and you can find plenty of options at drug stores in the country. Apply bug repellent liberally on both your skin and your clothing and re-apply as directed according to the brand you are using. You can further reduce the risk of getting bitten by wearing long pants and sleeves, although this may be difficult to pull off if you are going to the beach. Although dengue-carrying mosquitoes generally bite during the day (just after sunrise and before dusk seem to be the most common times), you should make sure wherever you are sleeping has been mosquito-proofed or that you have a mosquito net. Dengue symptoms include fever, headaches, and muscle pains and should be treated immediately.

Heat Stroke and Dehydration

If you are coming from North America, the temperature in Thailand, even during the cool season, may be hotter than the summers you're used to. Many travelers make the mistake of thinking they are immune to the effects of heat and sun and end up dehydrated, uncomfortable, or worse. Children and those over age 60 are even more susceptible. It may seem like common sense, but know your limits and pay attention to signals your body is sending you, as well as the condition of the people you are traveling with. If you aren't particularly physically active or used to the heat, walking around for hours on end in the hot sun will wear you down quickly, leaving you exhausted and cranky—not a great way to vacation. Make sure you drink lots of water. Bottled water is sold in virtually every corner of the country for little money; take advantage of the convenience and don't worry about lugging it around with you unless you will be in parts of the country that don't have any commerce.

Avoid heat exhaustion by avoiding strenuous activity during the hottest parts of the day and taking frequent breaks. It's probably not wise to go on a walking tour of Bangkok at 1 P.M., so plan your daily itineraries with temperature and sun patterns in mind. Outside activities are best done in the early part of the day and the later afternoon. Visiting museums and shopping malls and doing other indoor activities are great at midday, when the air-conditioning will be most appreciated. Also, take a cue from the locals: You'll probably notice that most people waiting to cross the street will find a shady spot, even if it's three meters from the curb, or walk slowly during the hottest parts of the day. There's a reason for that.

If you feel dizzy, get yourself to a cool place immediately and drink some water. If you begin to feel disoriented or confused, or have a rapid heartbeat or shortness of breath, you may be suffering from heat stroke and should seek immediate medical treatment. If you are traveling with children, pay especially close attention to how they are feeling and make sure they drink a lot of water. They may not be able to express that they are feeling the effects of the sun, but crankiness, short tempers, and fatigue are good clues that some rest and cooling down are in order.

Sexually Transmitted Diseases

Thailand did a laudable job in the 1990s of increasing public awareness and reducing the incidences of sexually transmitted diseases, including HIV/AIDS. But the 2006 UNAIDS Report noted that prevention awareness, specifically regarding HIV/AIDS, had "dropped off the radar screen," leaving a whole generation of Thais uninformed and unable to protect themselves. Although there are conflicting statistics, HIV/AIDS may once again be on the rise. If you are engaging in sexual activity while you are here, you must protect yourself. Condoms are commonly available everywhere in supermarkets and convenience stores and are inexpensive and prominently displayed.

In Thailand it is sometimes difficult to tell whether someone is a commercial sex worker. If you meet someone in a bar, especially if that person approached you first, odds are higher that this is not the first time he or she has ever done that. It is best to avoid pickups or one-night stands entirely.

Skin Care

Depending on where you are coming from, the sun in Thailand may be considerably stronger than what you're used to. That, amplified by the fact that you will probably be spending more time outside on vacation than you would during a normal day at work or home, means you have to use sunscreen even if you're not hanging out by the pool or on the beach. Larger chain drug stores, including **Watsons** and **Boots,** carry a range of sunscreen products for face and body. At these stores you are likely to find products that use the same SPF rating system used in the United States, so unless you have a particular favorite brand, skip packing the big bottle from back home. For your face, you will find international brands such as L'Oréal and Garnier with SPF 50, using Mexoryl as the active ingredient, for significantly cheaper than you will find anywhere else.

Traveler's Diarrhea

This is the most common traveler's ailment and is usually caused by contaminated food or drink. Conservative guidelines insist that travelers not buy food or beverages from street vendors, but the cost of that precaution is high. Thailand's food culture is difficult to access without eating food that has been prepared on the street or in places that may not seem as clean as you are used to back home. It is a shame to miss out on the experience, although if your immune system or health is already compromised and the consequences of getting a stomach bug could be severe for you, you should. If you decide to eat street food nonetheless, do not throw precaution completely to the wind. Fresh ingredients that have been prepared to order at high temperatures are the safest bets. Look for vendors who are busy, so you know the ingredients aren't sitting around for too long. Order foods that must be boiled, stir-fried, or deep-fried, and avoid any of the outdoor buffets where large pots of various foods are sitting out for extended periods of time.

Although some people will argue that the tap water in some cities is potable, virtually every person in the country, across age, education, and socioeconomic boundaries, drinks bottled water, and you should do the same—it is inexpensive and easy to find everywhere. At street stalls you may be wary of water served from pitchers, but look carefully and you'll

notice that it's been decanted from industrial-sized bottles of purified water. You may also be served water that is slightly tan or brown in color. The color comes from boiling the water with a few tea leaves, and it's fine to drink.

If you should come down with diarrhea, most cases are mild and only last for a day or two. Drink plenty of fluids and rest. More severe cases can be treated with a combination of antibiotics and antidiarrheal drugs. Before you depart, ask your doctor for a prescription of antibiotics to treat diarrhea, should it become necessary. Azithromycin and ciprofloxacin are currently recommended, but that may change; your doctor will know best and will also give you instructions on when you should take them. You can pick up antidiarrheal drugs, such as Imodium, in Thailand if necessary, but you might want to bring some from home if you want to make sure you have them should illness strike before you can pick some up.

If you have symptoms that last longer than a few days, or are accompanied by fever, chills, severe pain, and/or bloody stools, seek medical treatment.

CRIME

Thailand is generally a very safe country. Violent crimes are rare, and the type of gun violence seen in other parts of the world is virtually unheard-of. But while some make the mistake of painting the kingdom as an idyllic, peaceful place populated only by benevolent people, that's not entirely true either, and a scan of the local papers will reveal that crime occurs here too. As relates to travelers, there have been some notable crimes in recent years, including the rape and murder of a female tourist on Samui, shootings of tourists in Pai and Kanchanaburi, and continued violence in Pattaya. You must be mindful of your safety, even if the country feels idyllic and peaceful. If you are a woman traveling alone, always be aware of your surroundings. If you are involved in an argument or altercation with someone, particularly if alcohol consumption is involved, do everything you can to de-escalate the situation, including apologizing even if you do not think you are at fault. Bar fights involving travelers have occasionally turned fatal.

Petty Theft and Scams

Petty crimes and scams against foreigners are also common. Most of the people you meet and interact with will be kind and generous, but there are certainly taxi and *tuk tuk* drivers and others who will try to rip you off, more frequently in big cities and tourist areas. You can easily protect yourself from property crimes by leaving most of your valuables at home and safeguarding things such as digital cameras and computers. If your hotel room does not have a safe (or you don't feel confident in it), ask at the front desk whether they have a safe you can leave items in, and get a receipt for whatever you leave. If you're staying at a bungalow or inexpensive guesthouse and neither of those strategies is an option, do not flash money or valuables around, and do not leave them strewn about your room. Carry only as much cash as you need. There are ATMs all over the country (except in very off-the-beaten-path locations), and there is no need to have large sums of money with you.

Pickpocketing, especially in crowded markets, is not uncommon, but luckily it's easily avoidable if you follow the same common-sense guidelines you would in any other part of the world. Don't walk around with your bag open or wallet in a place it can easily be taken. If you are going to be in a crowded area, do not bring lots of bags with you. Walking around a market with a big backpack is asking for trouble. It is difficult to stay aware of your belongings when you have many of them.

The most common tourist scams are probably just inflated prices for transportation (and, unfortunately, Airports of Thailand sets the precedent for this from the moment you walk off the plane by trying to steer travelers toward their overpriced limo service instead of regular meter taxis). Unscrupulous taxi drivers will sometimes refuse to turn on the meter and try to negotiate inflated prices if they see that you are a foreigner. Your best defense is knowing how much things should cost. If a driver refuses to turn on the meter, just tell them you are getting out of the taxi and look for another one. Do not try to negotiate; an honest driver is bound to come along soon. Note that this rule doesn't apply if it's pouring rain or you're headed somewhere really out of the city.

Tuk tuk drivers in Bangkok sometimes engage in a scam where they offer you a very cheap price for a ride as long as you agree to a detour, usually a gem store where the driver will make a commission on anything you buy. Just politely decline the offer.

Rarely you will get a driver who will insist on taking you to the wrong place. Sometimes this is a mistake, but it may be because you've asked to go to a particular restaurant and the driver will get a commission if you go to another one. If a driver tells you that the place you want to go to is closed, the traffic is bad, or the place he's suggesting is better, just repeat your destination. If the driver insists, get out of the taxi.

Drugs

All illicit drugs are illegal in Thailand, although use of some drugs, especially marijuana, is not all that uncommon. You'll likely notice it on some islands and beach areas, being used as though it were totally legal. Locals may "know the ropes" and understand what they can get away with without raising the ire of the police, but those rules do not apply to foreign visitors. After all the movies and documentaries about foreigners getting arrested with drugs in Thailand, you'd have to be pretty stupid to have drugs in Thailand, as the consequences for being caught with large amounts of drugs, or even small amounts of hard drugs, are extreme. Drug dealers may face execution or life imprisonment, and your embassy won't be able to do much to help you.

Information and Services

MONEY
Currency

The Thai currency is the **baht,** and bills come in denominations of 1,000, 500, 100, 50, 20, and occasionally, an old 10B note, although these are no longer printed. Common coins are 10B, 5B, 2B, and 1B. Baht are broken up into satang; 100 satang equals one baht. There are no one-satang coins in circulation—in fact, the only ones you'll see are 25 satang and 50 satang. Most prices are expressed in baht, although in the supermarket you will come across items (for some reason often the ones on sale) with baht and satang pricing, and this is expressed as, for example, ฿25.50.

You must carry small bills with you in Thailand, so make sure to keep an ample supply of 20B and 100B bills (50s are harder to come by) in your wallet. Cab drivers will almost never have change for anything larger than a 100B bill, nor should they, considering that most only earn a few hundred baht per day. Two ways to make sure you have some smaller bills: When you withdraw money from an ATM, don't request amounts in even thousands. ATMS will dispense 100B bills, so if you take out 1,900B, you'll get at least four 100B notes. Also, 7-Elevens and other large convenience stores can always break a 1,000B note, so it might be worth it to buy that 15B bottle of water to keep some small bills in your pocket.

Exchange Rates

As of early 2011, the Thai baht was about 30 to the U.S. dollar and 43 to the euro. Most bank websites have currency conversion charts; if you can't find one, try www.oanda.com or www.xe.com. Note that these will give you interbank rates, not the amount you'll get as a regular banking consumer, which will most definitely be less favorable regardless of whether you are buying or selling. To make sure you get the best rate, do not bring dollars or traveler's checks to exchange when you arrive. Use your ATM card and withdraw in baht. Although

the Thai bank will charge you a fee and your bank may too, you will most likely get the best rate available.

ATMs

In Bangkok you will easily be able to find an ATM where you can withdraw from your home bank account if you're on the Cirrus, Plus, or Maestro network or have a debit card with a Visa logo on it. All major-bank ATMs will also prompt you to select English as the interface language, so you won't be guessing. One confusing thing for most travelers is that many Thai banks have cash-deposit machines and statement-update printers that look very much like ATMs. If you find yourself in front of one of these, look to your left or right; they are almost always next to normal ATMs. Also, the other machines will say "Deposit" or "Passbook Update" on them. When you're asked to select the account, remember that "current account" is the same as "checking account."

Most ATMs will dispense 10,000–20,000B maximum per transaction, depending on the limit you've set with your bank at home. Make sure you contact your bank and credit card companies before you travel to let them know you will be in Thailand, or else your transactions may be blocked to protect against potential fraud. If you try unsuccessfully to withdraw cash from the same bank three times (such as by choosing "savings account" when you want to withdraw from your checking account), the Thai ATM may confiscate your card. This can really be a drag, as bank policy generally requires that the card is sent back to your home bank, even if you're here. If you are having trouble withdrawing money, don't keep hitting buttons in hopes it will work. Figure out what's wrong and try again. Don't try a third time at the same bank; look for another bank's ATM.

Changing Money

Most money changers are run by major banks in Thailand, or else you can go into most large

Most ATMs have an English-language option.

branches to exchange money. Rates are posted, as are any fees or percentages that the bank will charge you. Some but not all banks will require a passport to change currency, so it's best to bring it with you.

Banks

All urban areas in Thailand have at least one bank, and in cities such as Bangkok or Phuket there are scores and scores, often in very convenient places such as inside malls, in standalone department stores, or next to any of the large hypermarkets such as Carrefour, Tesco, or Big C. Banking hours vary tremendously, with smaller banks in quieter areas open 9 A.M.–3:30 P.M. during the work week, and in big cities some stay open as late as 10 P.M. and over the weekend. Some of the larger banks, including **Kasikorn Bank** (www.kasikorn-bank.com), **Siam Commercial Bank** (www.scb.co.th), **Bank of Ayudhya** (www.krungsri.com), **Bangkok Bank** (www.bangkokbank.com), and **United Overseas Bank** (www.uob.co.th), have websites with English content

where you can find information about currency exchange and locations of branches.

Bank Transfers and Wiring Money

If you need cash in a pinch, there are numerous **Western Union** (www.westernunion.com) offices in Thailand; check the website for locations, but also check fees and exchange rates to understand the cost of the cash.

Traveler's Checks

You can exchange traveler's checks at major banks, foreign-exchange booths, and even some large hotels, although the fees you pay to both purchase them and change them can be significant when you add them up.

Credit Cards

Visa and MasterCard credit and debit cards are accepted in larger hotels and department stores; American Express less so. In general, cash is king in Thailand, and even at larger restaurants and some hotels you may be asked to pay with the real thing. If you're purchasing something expensive, such as jewelry, you may pay an additional 2–3 percent if you pay with plastic. Note that you'll probably also be charged a transaction fee by your credit card company at home (usually a percentage of the charge) if you buy anything in foreign currency. Some larger shops and duty-free stores will give you the option of charging your purchase in dollars or euros. Ask about the exchange rate, and if it's favorable, this may be the best option for you. If you don't often travel, remember that if you're using your credit card in a foreign country, you need to alert your credit card company beforehand. Otherwise you may risk having your card denied as the company tries to track you down.

VAT

The value-added tax, or VAT, is 7 percent in Thailand; everything you spend money on will be subject to it. All shops list prices for goods inclusive of the VAT, but restaurants and hotels generally add the VAT on afterward. Travelers are entitled to a refund when they leave the country by air, assuming each item purchased is more than 2,000B, total purchases exceed 5,000B, you buy them from a participating store (you'll see a sign in the window), fill out all the necessary paperwork when you make the purchase, and take the goods out of the country within 60 days. To claim your refund, you will need to take your paperwork, passport, and the goods you've purchased to one of the customs officers at the airport you are departing from. Do this before check-in, as you will need to show your purchases to the officer. Once you've gone through these steps, you can get a cash or credit card refund on the spot, minus a 100B fee. The Revenue Department has a Web page dedicated to understanding the VAT refund process (www.rd.go.th/vrt/eng-index.html); make sure to check it if you are making a large purchase.

Bargaining

While some people will tell you that bargaining is done everywhere in Thailand, that's not really the case. Bargaining is frequent in areas where many tourists shop, but it would be totally out of place to bargain for a bowl of noodles from a street vendor or a bag of fresh fruit at a neighborhood wet market. If you are shopping in a tourist market, be aware that you should bargain, because prices are sometimes inflated as much as double, particularly in markets or street-shopping areas in places such as Phat Phong in Bangkok, Patong Beach in Phuket, or the markets in Chiang Mai. Bargaining is an art and not a science, so there are no hard-and-fast rules. It's best to know how much you are willing to pay for something before you start the process, and be prepared to walk away politely if you can't agree on a price.

Tipping

Tipping practices are often confusing in Thailand for foreigners. If you're eating at a street stall or very casual restaurant, tipping is not expected. On the other end of the spectrum, nicer restaurants in large cities will often automatically add a 10 percent service charge to the bill, though it's not always clear that this actually gets to the server and isn't pocketed by management or the owners. When you get your bill, always ask if service is included, and then decide whether you want to leave an additional tip. Many people will just round off the bill to the nearest even number, and only in very touristy places will you be expected to tip.

COMMUNICATIONS AND MEDIA
Mail

Thailand Post (www.thailandpost.com) has locations across the country, although there are no guarantees you'll find someone who can speak English if you need to ask questions and cannot communicate in Thai. Stamps are difficult to find outside the post office, though your hotel or guesthouse can often sell you some. Mailboxes are painted red and usually have two slots, one for local mail and one for everything else. If you are sending something within Thailand, service is generally quick, inexpensive, and reliable. If you are sending heavy or bulky items from Thailand abroad, postage can be very expensive and take weeks to arrive. It's better to plan on bringing everything back with you. If you need to send something express, there are **FedEx** (www.fedex.com) and **DHL** offices in Bangkok that do express worldwide shipping.

Telephone

Mobile phones are so common in Thailand that it might be difficult to find a pay phone if you want to call home—or anywhere else, for that matter. If you do, note that long-distance pay phones are generally not coin-operated. You need to purchase a phone card first at a convenience store, but you'll need to know what type or color phone booth you need the phone card for, as there are a number of different companies. Yes, it's confusing. Look for phone booths near convenience stores; at least you can point to what you need.

Nearly all hotels have in-room phones, although most guesthouses don't, and many bungalows don't either. If you use one, your calls will be marked up sometimes double. If you really need to be in touch with people by telephone, the best bet is to pick up an inexpensive mobile phone and buy prepaid cards. Long-distance rates run as low as 6B per minute to the United States and Europe.

Thailand's country code is 66, and inside the country regional area codes are prefaced with a 0 and have one additional digit followed by a seven-digit number—0x/xxx-xxxx. Mobile phones begin with 08 followed by an eight-digit number. You always have to dial the area code, so if you're in Bangkok and you're calling another Bangkok telephone, you must dial 02 first. If you are calling Thailand from outside the country, dial the international access number used in the country you are in, plus the 66 country code, and then drop the leading 0, whether calling a fixed line or a mobile phone.

To make international calls from Thailand, you must dial 001, 006, 007, 008, or 009 first, then the country code and phone number. Why so many choices? 001 is the official

number, but the others offer cheaper rates. Just know that you'll almost always get routed over a VoIP line, and there may be a noticeable lag.

There are a number of venues throughout Thailand that have multiple phone numbers. These numbers are formatted differently throughout the book. For the example, if there are 10 different sequential phone numbers—02/222-2000, 02/222-2001, 02/222-2002, etc. through 02/222-2009—the phone number will be formatted as "tel. 02/222-2000 to 02/222-2009."

Mobile Phones

Calls from a mobile phone are cheap in Thailand and get even cheaper when the three largest providers, **AIS, DTAC,** and **True,** get into price wars, sometimes an annual occurrence. When that happens, calls can drop below 1B per minute. As in most parts of the world except the United States, you do not pay for incoming calls or text messages. If you have an unlocked tri-band or quad-band mobile phone and can remove your SIM card (ask your mobile service provider), bring it with you and buy a prepaid SIM when you arrive. This is the cheapest and easiest way to communicate when you are here. You can also pick up a new or used phone in Thailand, often for a lot cheaper than you'd find at home. All cities have mobile-phone stores that sell unlocked phones, and there are many secondhand phones available if you want to save some cash. Remember to have the seller test the phone for you so you know it works before you walk away with it. Renting a phone before you leave home or at the airport is generally far more expensive than buying a new phone of your own and should be considered only if you cannot go a few hours without mobile communication or do not have time to pick up a phone on your own.

SIM cards and the prepaid cards for the three largest mobile service providers can be found in any convenience store. Note that they sometimes sell their SIM cards under promotional names, such as Happy for DTAC or One Two Call for AIS. However, if you just ask for a SIM from one of the three, you should get what you want.

Internet Access

The Internet has penetrated even into the smallest urban areas in Thailand, though it has not yet reached rural areas. Any large city or touristy area will have plenty of Internet cafés where you can use the service by the hour or, if you have your laptop with you, many hotels and coffee shops also have wireless access.

Generally, Internet cafés in Thailand are either packed full of tourists on months-long sojourns or packed full of local teenagers playing computer games. Crime is pretty rare in either scenario, but keep an eye on your belongings anyway. It's easy to get distracted when you're writing home, and with all the commotion going on around you, you may just lose something valuable.

At least in Bangkok, Wi-Fi access is very common and continues to spread. Some places, including hotels and international coffee chains, still charge for the service, but in many places it's free, including any **Coffee World** coffee shop, nearly all of the English and Irish pubs in the city, and the **Bug & Bee**. Look for "Wi-Fi Hotspot" signs and ask the server if you need a password.

English-Language Press

In addition to wide availability of the *International Herald Tribune* in larger hotels, Thailand has two daily English-language newspapers, the *Bangkok Post* (www.bangkokpost. net) and the *Nation* (www.nationmultimedia. com). Although you won't find them in remote or rural areas, you will find them virtually everywhere else. You can also check them out online while you are visiting. If you're curious about what's making headlines in Thailand, check the website a few times before you visit.

In every place where large numbers of English speakers travel, there are small and not-so-small weekly and monthly publications catering to them or the advertisers who want their attention. At any hotel you'll find a stack of them, but you may not find them all that useful. Content is often dictated by the advertisers, so it's hard to trust the food and hotel reviews.

Websites

More and more content about Thailand is available on the Web every day, including tourist guides, expat forums where long-term foreign residents gripe about the difficulties of living in a foreign country, and personal travelogues. Spend some time surfing when you're planning your trip, and at the very least make sure to look at the **Tourism Authority of Thailand** website (www.tourismthailand.org) for specific information about the destinations you're planning to visit.

MAPS

While we've included as many helpful maps as possible in this edition, you'll still probably find yourself traveling into uncharted territory, especially if you are exploring some of the off-the-beaten-path recommendations. When you arrive at the airport, you'll be able to get reasonable tourist maps for free, or you can drop into one of the English-language bookstores in Bangkok to find more comprehensive road maps. **Google Maps** has just recently started using both Thai and English scripts in their Thailand maps, and is a great resource both for planning and once you are here. Spelling can be a little bit challenging, so you may have to try a few different variations of the location you're trying to map before you hit it. An excellent mapping resource available online is www.mapguidethailand.com. You can sort by province and search by any number of different things, including *wats,* beaches, and restaurants. The database does not cover everything but is surprisingly comprehensive, and the maps generated are very detailed.

WEIGHTS, MEASURES, ELECTRICITY, AND TIME ZONES

Thailand uses the metric system. See the conversion chart in the back of this book if you're on the U.S. or Imperial system, but remember a few easy rules—a meter is about the same as a yard, a kilogram is just over two pounds (2.2 to be more precise), and a kilometer is 0.6 miles. This is probably as much as you need to know while you're traveling here.

The current for household electricity is 220 volts. Plugs are either two-pronged flat or two-pronged round, like those in the United States and Japan. But just because the appliances you bring from home will plug into most sockets in Thailand without an adapter doesn't mean you should do it. If you are coming from North America, you're on a 110-volt system, and most appliances don't like change. Many an innocent hair dryer has melted, and more than a couple of small fires have been started by making this mistake. If you need to plug something in from home, you'll need a converter to drop the voltage down. Fortunately, most electronics with built-in batteries can take multiple voltages, so chances are you can easily charge your computer or phone. Check the charger or, if in doubt, the manufacturer's website. Note that all Mac laptops and virtually all other laptops are mutlivoltage, and many phones are too.

All of Thailand falls under one time zone, UTC+7. Thailand does not use daylight saving time and so, November–March, is 15 hours head of Pacific standard time, 12 hours ahead of Eastern standard time, and six hours ahead of Central European time.

RESOURCES

Glossary

cha yen iced tea

chedi pagoda

chofa spire-like ornamentations that adorn temple roofs

darma rule of Buddhism

gaeng or kaeng curry

gai chicken

gai yang grilled chicken with smoky, spicy sauce

guay teow traditional noodle soup

hat beach

khai eggs

khan toke the formal northern meal in which various dishes are shared and hands are used

khanom chin thin rice noodles with curry

khanom Thai coconut puddings scented with jasmine and other unexpected flavors

khao mountain

khao phad fried rice

khao soi soft noodles in sweet, savory rich yellow curry, covered with crispy fried noodles and usually served with chicken or beef

khlong canal

ko island

mahout elephant trainer

mai pen rai no worries

mai phet not spicy

mu or moo pork

muay Thai Thai boxing

naga sacred snake

nam phrik spicy dips served with a selection of fresh vegetables

nam tok marinated meat salad with sliced grilled beef or pork

pad thai stir-fried noodles with peanut sauce

ped duck

phra that relic of the Buddha

prang tower

prasat castle

Ramakien the Thai version of the *Ramayana*

roti pancake-like cooked dough, served with either sweet or savory fillings or dishes

sabai to be relaxed or comfortable

sala pavilion or sitting area

samlor rickshaw-like bicycles

satay grilled meat

soi side street

som tam shredded green papaya salad, with fresh long beans, tomatoes, dried shrimp, peanuts, lime juice, fish sauce, garlic, palm sugar, and chilies

song thaew pick-up trucks with benches in the back that essentially serve as a cross between a bus (they usually run on fixed routes) and a taxi (you hail one down and just climb in)

tambon community

tom yam kung spicy, aromatic soup with shrimp

tuk tuk three-wheeled motorcycle taxis

ubosot coronation hall

wai gesture of greeting and a sign of respect where people put their hands together in a prayerlike motion and bow their heads at each other

wat temple

wiharn Buddhist assembly hall

yam som o pomelo salad with shrimp

Thai Phrasebook

Unless you are staying exclusively in five-star resorts that cater to English-speaking foreigners, you'll notice pretty quickly that most people in Thailand speak little English. English-language studies are compulsory for all students, but even most college graduates do not speak English at any level of fluency. That fact, coupled with a different writing system, makes Thailand a bit of a challenge at best and frustrating at worst. Expect communication problems – after all, you are traveling in a foreign country. Of course, the language barrier is also a great opportunity. Although it's a travel cliché, it's still a sweet experience when little children come up to you to practice saying "hello," and students of all ages will usually be happy to try out a little English on willing foreigners, although they may be too shy to engage you first. If you are looking to spend an extended period of time here, there are plenty of places you can teach English, either on a volunteer or paid basis.

The Thai language, with its confusing tones and difficult-to-decipher writing system, is too difficult to master before taking a vacation. But learning a few words and phrases will make all the difference, especially words and phrases such as "hello" and "thank you." No one in Thailand will expect that you speak the language fluently as a vacationer, so a little bit of Thai will go a long way in terms of breaking the ice. You'll find that people across the country will react positively to any effort you make (even if that positive reaction involves a little bit of laughter).

The Thai alphabet has 44 consonants, more than 20 vowel forms, and four tone marks. The alphabet was invented by King Ramkhamhaeng in the 13th century and was undoubtedly influenced by the Khmer alphabet in use at the time. That may not help too much in understanding what the letters mean; many foreigners find the script difficult. If you're just here on vacation, you won't have the time to do much more than familiarize yourself with the way it looks, but if you want to learn the language, you'll need to master Thai script.

PRONUNCIATION AND TRANSLITERATION

Thai is a tonal language with five tones – low, high, mid, rising, and falling – and a the meaning of a word varies depending on how it is pronounced. Say the name *Bob* out loud as if you were yelling at your little brother, then as though you were picking up the phone and wondering if Bob was on the other line. To speakers of nontonal languages, Bob is Bob, although you've intonated the word differently in different contexts. To speakers of tonal languages, the first pronunciation and the second can mean completely different things. Tones are identified in Thai script through the use of different consonants, vowels, and tone marks, depending on the tone being expressed, but as Thai script can take months of study to master, your best bet is to memorize a few basic expressions and try them out when you arrive. Listen carefully to the way native speakers say common phrases (you'll hear plenty of hellos and thank yous) and do your best to imitate them.

A tonal language also presents another challenge for visitors, as tones are impossible to replicate with the paltry 26-letter Roman alphabet. The word *khao*, for example, means white, mountain, rice, news, he or she, knee, and to enter, depending on which tone you're using and whether the vowel is long or short. Using the Latin alphabet to transliterate Thai words is just a rough approximation, which is why Thai speakers will often misunderstand you or find your pronunciation of a word incomprehensible despite the fact that you are pronouncing it exactly the way it is spelled in Roman letters. This is also why you'll see Thai words spelled in English in so many different ways – *Petchaburi* and *Petburi* or *ko* and *koh* are just two common examples.

We've used the Thai Royal Institute system of transliteration in this book, as it is the official system and the one used to translate place names on road signs and other notices. This system isn't perfect – it ignores tones and vowel length completely – but it's the least complicated and doesn't require that you learn a new system of tone marks; it's an imperfect compromise but the best one for someone visiting Thailand for vacation.

In the case of proper names of sights, restaurants, shops, and lodging, we've used either whatever spelling is approved by the Tourism Authority, what is printed on commonly available maps, what the business goes by, or what is printed on Thai street signs, whether or not it is consistent with the Thai Royal Institute system.

MASCULINE AND FEMININE PARTICLES

Even if you can't make out many Thai words, you will notice that nearly everyone you speak with ends their sentences with either *ka* or *kap*. These are polite particles meant to convey respect, but in truth they are used nearly universally and regardless of whether you are speaking with your boss or the teenage cashier at 7-Eleven. Which one you use depends not on what you are saying or who you are speaking to, but your gender. Women always end their sentences with *ka*, men with *kap*, and you should be particularly careful about making sure you do too. You'll probably notice that the polite particles are also used on their own, meaning the equivalent in English of "OK," "go on," or "yes."

BASIC AND COURTEOUS EXPRESSIONS

Remember that everything you say should end with a polite particle. Here we've listed *sawadee* as hello, but you would almost never hear that phrase spoken without a *ka* or *kap* following it.

Hello/Goodbye *Sawadee*
How are you? *Sabai dee mai?*
I'm well. How are you? *Sabai dee. Sabai dee mai?*
OK; good. *Dee.*
Not OK; bad. *Mai sabai.*
Thank you. *Khopkhun.*
You're welcome/no worries. *Mai pen rai.*
yes *chai*
no (depending on context) *mai chai*
I don't know. *Mai ru.*
Just a moment. *Sak khru.*

Excuse me. *Khothot.*
Pleased to meet you. *Yindi thi dai ruchak.*
What is your name? *Chue arai?/Khun chue arai?*
Do you speak English? *Phut phasa Angkrit dai mai?*
I don't speak Thai. *Phut phasa Thai mai dai.*
I don't understand. *Mai khaochai.*
How do you say . . . in Thai? *Riak . . . wa arai nai phasa Thai?*
My name is . . . *Chan chue . . .* (female)/ *Phom chue . . .* (male)
Would you like . . . ? *Ao . . . mai?*
Let's go to . . . *Pai . . . kan thoe.*

TERMS OF ADDRESS

I (female) *chan*
I (female, very formal) *de chan*
I (male) *phom*
I (male, very formal) *kra phom*
you (formal) *khun*
you (very formal, to show high respect) *than*
you (familiar) *khun*
he/him *khao*
she/her *khao*
we/us *rao*
you (plural) *phuak khun*
they/them *phuak khao*
Mr./Sir *khun* or *khun phu chai* (very formal, used to address someone who has a higher position than you)
Mrs./Madam *khun* or *khun phu ying* (very formal, used to address someone who has a higher position than you)
Miss/young woman *khun* or *nong* (Nong translates as "younger brother" or "younger sister." It is used to address an unknown person who looks younger than you.)
wife *phan ra ra*
husband *sa mee*
friend *phuean*
sweetheart *wan jai*
boyfriend/girlfriend *fan*
son *luk chai*
daughter *luk sao*
older brother/sister *phee*
older brother *phee chai*

older sister *phee sao*
younger brother/sister *nong*
younger brother *nong chai*
younger sister *nong sao*
father *pho*
mother *mae*
grandfather (father's side) *khun pu or pu*
grandfather (mother's side) *khun ta or ta*
grandmother (father's side) *khun ya or ya*
grandmother (mother's side) *khun yai or yai*

TRANSPORTATION
Where is . . . ? *. . . yu thinai?*
How far is it to . . . ? *Pai . . . ik klai mai?*
from . . . to . . . *chak . . . pai . . .*
Where is the way to . . . ? *. . . pai thang nai?*
the bus station *sathani khonsong/khonsong*
the bus stop *pai rotme*
Where is this bus going? *Rotme khan ni pai nai?*
the taxi stand *pai taxi*
the train station *sathani rotfai*
the boat *ruea*
the airport *sanambin*
I'd like a ticket to . . . *Kho tua pai . . .*
first (second) class *chan nueng (song)*
round-trip *pai klap*
reservation *chong*
Stop here, please. *Yut thi ni.*
the entrance *thangkhao*
the exit *thang-ok*
the ticket office *thi khai tua*
near *klai* (rising tone)
very near *klai mak*
far *klai*
very far *klai mak*
to; toward *pai*
by; through (as in, I am going by/through Chiang Mai on my way to Pai) *pai thang*
from *chak*
turn right *liao khwa*
turn left *liao sai*
right side *dan khwa*
left side *dan sai*
straight ahead *trong pai*
in front *dan na/khang na*
beside *dan khang/khang*

behind *dan lang/lang*
the corner *hua mum*
the stoplight/traffic light *fai yut/sanyan fai charachon*
right here *thi ni*
somewhere *sak thi*
street; road *thanon*
highway *thangluang*
bridge *saphan*
toll way/toll charge *thangduan/kha phan thang*
address *thiyu*
north *nuea*
south *tai*
east *tawan-ok*
west *tawantok*

ACCOMMODATIONS
hotel *rongraem*
Is there a room available? *Mi hong wang mai?*
May I see it? *Kho du dai mai?*
What is the rate? *Rakha thaorai?*
Is there something cheaper? *Mi rakha thuk kwa ni mai?*
single room *hong diao*
double room *hong khu*
double bed *tiang diao* (king-size)
twin bed *tiang khu*
with private bath *mi hongnam suantua*
hot water *nam un*
shower *fakbua*
towels *phachettua*
soap *sabu*
toilet paper *thit chu*
blanket *pha hom*
sheets *pha pu tiang*
air-conditioned *ae* (air)
fan *phatlom*
key *kunchae*
manager *phuchatkan*

FOOD
I'm hungry. *Chan hio.* (female)/*Phom hio.* (male)
I'm thirsty. *Chan hio nam.* (female)/*Phom hio nam.* (male)
menu *menu*

to order food/order *sang ahan/raikan ahan*
glass *kaeo*
fork *som*
knife *mit*
spoon *chon*
napkin *pha chet pak*
soft drink *nam-atlom*
coffee/hot coffee/iced coffee *kafae/kafae ron/kafae yen*
tea/hot tea/iced tea *cha/cha ron/cha yen*
lime juice *nam manao*
bottled water *nam khuat*
beer *bia*
juice *nam phonlamai*
sugar *namtan*
snack *khanom*
breakfast *ahan chao*
lunch *ahan thiang*
dinner *ahan kham*
The check, please. *Chek bin* or *Kep ngoen duai.*
eggs *khai*
fruit *phonlamai*
pineapple *sapparot*
guava *farang*
watermelon *taeng mo*
rose apple *chomphu*
papaya *malako*
coconut *maphrao*
lime *manao*
durian *thurian*
jackfruit *khanun*
mango *mamuang*
fish *pla*
shrimp *kung*
chicken *gai*
beef *nuea*
pork *mu*
fried *thot*
grilled *ping/yang*
barbecue *babikhio*
not spicy *mai phet*
(prepared with) one chili *prik nung met*

SHOPPING
money *ngoen/tang*
bank *thanakhan*

Do you accept credit cards? *Rap bat khredit mai?*
How much does it cost? *Rakha thaorai?/ Ki baht?*
expensive *phaeng*
cheap *thuk*
more *mak kwa/mak khuen*
less *noi kwa/noi long*
a little *nitnoi*
too much *mak pai*

HEALTH
Help me, please. *Chuai duai.*
I am sick. *Mai sabai.*
Call a doctor. *Tho tam mo./Riak mo.*
Take me to . . . *Pha chan* (female)/*Pha phom* (male) *pai thi . . .*
hospital *rongphayaban*
drugstore/pharmacy *ran khai ya*
pain *puat*
fever *khai* (rising tone)
headache *puathua*
stomachache *puatthong*
burn *mai*
cramp *ta khrio*
nausea *khluen sai*
vomiting *achian/uak*
diarrhea *thongsia*
antibiotic *ya patichiwana*
pill; tablet *ya met*
acetaminophen/paracetamol *ya kae puat*
cream *ya tha*
birth-control pills *ya khumkamnoet*
condoms *thung yang anamai*
toothbrush *praengsifan*
toothpaste *yasifan*
dentist *mo fan*
toothache *puat fan*

POST OFFICE AND COMMUNICATIONS
long-distance telephone *thorasap thang klai*
I would like to call . . . *Chan/phom yak tho pai thi . . .*
collect/collect call *kep ngoen plaithang/ thorasap riak kep ngoen plaithang*

credit card *bat khredit*
post office *praisani*
by air mail *air mail/chotmai thang akat*
letter *chotmai*
stamp *sataem*
postcard *postcard/praisaniyabat*
registered/certified *longthabian*
money order *thananat*
box; package *khlong*
tape *tape*

AT THE BORDER

border *chaidaen*
customs *sunlakakon*
immigration *dan truat khon khao muang*
arrival card *bat khakhao*
inspection *kan truat/chut truat*
passport *passport/nangsuedoenthang*
profession *achip*
insurance *prakanphai*
driver's license *bai khapkhi*

AT THE GAS STATION

gas station *pam nam man*
gasoline *namman*
unleaded *rai san takua*
full *tem thueng*
tire *yang rotyon/yang*
air *air/khrueang prap-akat*
water *nam*
oil change *plian namman*
grease *charabi*
My ... doesn't work *...sia / ...mai thamngan*
battery *battery*
radiator *monam*
alternator *alternator/dai charge/dai panfai*
generator *generator/khrueang panfai*
tow truck *rot lak*
repair shop *ran som*

VERBS

to buy *sue*
to eat *kin*
to climb *pin*
to make *tham*
to go *pai*

to walk *doen*
to love *rak*
to work *thamngan*
to want *tongkan*
to need *tongkan/champen*
to read *an*
to write *khian*
to repair *som*
to stop *yut*
to get off (the bus) *long (rot me)*
to arrive *ma thueng*
to stay (remain) *yu (thi)*
to stay (sleep) *yu thi*
to leave *ok chak*
to look at *mong thi*
to look for *mong ha*
to give *hai*
to carry *thue/hio*
to have *mi*
to come *ma*

NUMBERS

zero *sun*
one *nueng*
two *song*
three *sam*
four *si*
five *ha*
six *hok*
seven *jed*
eight *paed*
nine *kao*
10 *sip*
11 *sip et*
12 *sip song*
13 *sip sam*
14 *sip si*
15 *sip ha*
16 *sip hok*
17 *sip jed*
18 *sip paed*
19 *sip kao*
20 *yisip*
21 *yisip et*
30 *samsip*
100 *nueng roi*
101 *nueng roi et*

200 *song roi*
1,000 *nueng phan*
10,000 *nueng muen*
100,000 *nueng saen*
1,000,000 *nueng lan*
one-half *khrueng*

TIME

What time is it? *Wela thaorai laeo?/Ki mong?*
It's one o'clock *Nueng nalika.*
It's four in the afternoon. *Sip hok nalika.*
It's midnight. *Thiang khuen.*
one minute *nueng nathi*
one hour *nueng chuamong*

DAYS, MONTHS, AND SEASONS

Monday *Wan Chan*
Tuesday *Wan Angkhan*
Wednesday *Wan Phut*
Thursday *Wan Pharuehatsabodi/Wan Pharue Hat*
Friday *Wan Suk*
Saturday *Wan Sao*
Sunday *Wan Athit*
January *Mokkarakhom*
February *Kumphaphan*
March *Minakhom*
April *Mesayon*
May *Phruetsaphakhom*
June *Mithunayon*
July *Karakadakhom*
August *Singhakhom*
September *Kanyayon*
October *Tulakhom*
November *Phruetsa Chi Ka Yon*
December *Thanwakhom*
today *wanni*
yesterday *muea wan*
tomorrow *phrungni*
a week *nueng sapda*
a month *nueng duean*
after *lang*
before *kon*
rainy season *ruedu fon*
cool season *ruedu nao*
hot/warm season *ruedu ron*

Suggested Reading

ART AND ARCHITECTURE

Gosling, Betty. *Origins of Thai Art.* Trumbull, CT: Weatherhill, 2004. An accessible early history of Thai art, Gosling's book is full of beautiful photographs of building details and sculptures to illustrate the history she lays out.

Kerlogue, Fiona. *Arts of Southeast Asia.* London: Thames & Hudson, 2004. This small, nicely illustrated, and easy-to-read book offers a basic overview of the history of art across the region. Although not specifically focused on Thailand, the information provided is essential to putting the art and artifacts in the country into a broader context.

Poshyananda, Apinan. *Modern Art in Thailand: Nineteenth and Twentieth Centuries.* Singapore: Oxford University Press, 1992. Although most books on art in Thailand focus on the distant past, Poshyananda explains the different influences on modern art in a comprehensive manner.

Ringis, Rita. *Thai Temples and Thai Murals.* Singapore: Oxford University Press, 1990. For those interested in more than a cursory tour of Thailand's scores of temples, this book offers an excellent overview of temple architecture and mural work. There are also in-depth descriptions of some of the most popular temples in the country.

Woodward, Hiram. *The Art and Architecture of Thailand: From Prehistoric Times through the Thirteenth Century.* Boston: Brill Academic Publishers, 2005. Woodward's book provides the first comprehensive survey of art in Thailand through the 13th century. The book is academic in nature and offers a sociohistorical view of art history. Those with an interest in archaeology will find it very useful.

HISTORY

Baker, Christopher, and Pasuk Phongpaichit. *A History of Thailand.* Cambridge, MA: Cambridge University Press, 2005. This is one of the few books that offers a modern history of the kingdom; it tracks the economic, political, and social changes in Thailand over the past 300 years.

Handley, Paul M. *The King Never Smiles.* New Haven, CT: Yale University Press, 2006. Banned in Thailand before it even hit the shelves, Handley's biography of King Bhumibol tells the story of how Thailand's current king came to power and how he has created an important role for the monarchy over the past 60 years. Handley, a former journalist based in Bangkok for over a decade, offers a well-researched though controversial look at the king's life and reign.

Higham, Charles. *The Archaeology of Mainland Southeast Asia: From 10,000 B.C. to the fall of Angkor.* Cambridge, MA: Cambridge University Press, 1989. Respected archaeologist Charles Higham takes readers through the region's early social history using archaeological evidence found in Southeast Asia. For those planning to visit any of the major Khmer archaeological sites, such as Phanom Rung or Phimai, this book offers in-depth (albeit dense and academic) information to complement a visit.

Somers Heidhues, Mary. *Southeast Asia: A Concise History.* London: Thames & Hudson, 2001. This is an easy and quick general overview of the history of the region for those looking for an understanding of Southeast Asia without devoting hours to study.

Tarling, Nicholas. *The Cambridge History of Southeast Asia, Vols. I and II.* Cambridge, MA: Cambridge University Press, 2000. These two volumes offer a comprehensive social and political history of the region as a whole, which is essential to adequately understand the history of Thailand.

Wyatt, David K. *Thailand: A Short History.* New Haven, CT: Yale University Press, 2003.

CULTURE
Cornwel-Smith, Philip, and John Goss. *Very Thai.* Bangkok: River Books Press, 2006.

Explains lots of seemingly quirky Thai cultural behaviors, including the obsession with tiny napkins.

Ziv, Daniel, Guy Sharett, and Sasa Kralj. *Bangkok Inside Out.* Jakarta: Equinox Publishing, 2004. This thoughtful, irreverent, and honest book explains all of the quirky, seemingly inconsistent pieces of the capital city without relying on clichés or judgmental descriptions. It's full of great photos too.

Internet Resources

There is tons of information about Thailand on the Internet, and no one should plan a trip here without taking advantage of some of the excellent resources available. The biggest annoyance is the many websites without original content whose sole purpose is to direct you to hotel or tour booking agencies. You'll know pretty quickly if you've stumbled onto one of these. Below is a list of reliable websites with informative, original content.

TRAVEL INFORMATION
Travel Authority of Thailand
www.tourismthailand.org
The Travel Authority of Thailand (TAT) may not offer the most objective view of the country's destinations, their destination guide covers every province in the country and has basic, reliable information. You may not want to plan your whole trip around what the tourism authority is saying, but this is a very good place to start your Internet research. The website also provides a calendar of events across the country and often highlights quirky or otherwise unknown destinations.

Bangkok Tourism Division
www.bangkoktourist.com
The Bangkok Tourism Division also has a website full of tourism information for visitors to the capital city. The site is not as slick as the TAT website, but the information is

generally accurate and the coverage of *wats* is extensive.

TRIP PRACTICALITIES
U.S. State Department
www.travel.state.gov/travel
Make sure to check the U.S. State Department's website for basic information about Thailand and any updates on safety, especially in the southernmost provinces.

Centers for Disease Control
www.cdc.gov/travel
Check out the Centers for Disease Control travel website for country-specific health information, including updates on recommended vaccinations and medications.

BLOGS
There are a handful of good blogs on travel and life in Thailand worth spending some time perusing. Since blog content changes so frequently and is often out of date within months, search for blogs on travel in Thailand when planning your trip to find travelogues of people who've recently been here.

Austin Bush Photography
www.austinbushphotography.com
Austin Bush's photography site has an excellent food blog with beautiful pictures of mostly casual restaurants, food stalls, and markets across

the country and is a must read for foodies visiting Thailand.

Bangkok Pundit
http://bangkokpundit.blogspot.com

This blog sometimes feels a little too insider-oriented for first-time visitors to Thailand, but it does offer a unique and sometimes funny perspective on current events and politics.

Promoting Thai Culture
www.richardbarrow.com

Resident expat Richard Barrow posts blog entries about travel around Bangkok, Thai culture, and a weekly piece about food in Thailand. His posts are usually in-depth and accompanied by great photos.

Index

List of Maps

Acknowledgments

This update could not have been completed without the help of Jodi Ettenberg, who updated the Chiang Mai and Northern Thailand chapters, and Deborah Nam-Krane, who revised and rewrote the History section.

I am grateful to nearly every shop keeper, hotel manager, travel agent and waitperson I have come across while traveling in Thailand. So many people across the country have offered advice, given me tours, shared family recipes and generally demonstrated sincere Thai hospitality. They are the reason Thailand is such a wonderful place to visit.

Contributing photographers include Thien Onn Ming of www.mingthein.com, who captured Thailand's beauty and vibrancy like no other, Linda True, who just so happened to have the perfect photos on her hard drive when I needed them most, Newley Purnell and John W. Brown, who not only researched and wrote the original Deep South chapter, but also took great pictures.

I am also grateful to all of my friends and colleagues who offered up excellent travel advice and shared their personal favorite places with me so that I could share them with you. And to the Bangkok travel group, who introduced me to the joys of travel in Thailand from that first trip to Samet when I'd been here only a few weeks. The group originally included David and Huyen, Koi and Joppe, Paul, Newley and Anasuya, Peter and Dung, Rob and Jean, Patrick and Linda, but in the six years I've been a part of it, has expanded to include new friends and lots of children, including my own. Here's to another generation of intrepid travelers with open hearts and minds!

www.moon.com

DESTINATIONS | ACTIVITIES | BLOGS | MAPS | BOOKS

MOON.COM is ready to help plan your next trip! Filled with fresh trip ideas and strategies, author interviews, informative travel blogs, a detailed map library, and descriptions of all the Moon guidebooks, Moon.com is all you need to get out and explore the world—or even places in your own backyard. While at Moon.com, sign up for our monthly e-newsletter for updates on new releases, travel tips, and expert advice from our on-the-go Moon authors. As always, when you travel with Moon, expect an experience that is uncommon and truly unique.

KEEP UP WITH MOON ON FACEBOOK AND TWITTER
JOIN THE MOON PHOTO GROUP ON FLICKR